W9-AAQ-817

CSET®

California Subject Examinations for Teachers

Fourth Edition

By C Roebuck Reed, Lee Wherry Brainerd, Rodney Lee, and the Staff of Kaplan, Inc.

PUBLISHING

New York

CSET® and California Subject Examinations for Teachers® are registered trademarks of the California Commission on Teacher Credentialing and National Evaluation Systems, Inc., which neither sponsor nor endorse this project.

This publication is designed to provide accurate and authoritative information in regard to the subject matter covered. It is sold with the understanding that the publisher is not engaged in rendering legal, accounting, or other professional service. If legal advice or other expert assistance is required, the services of a competent professional should be sought.

© 2010 by Kaplan, Inc.

Published by Kaplan Publishing, a division of Kaplan, Inc.
395 Hudson Street
New York, NY 10014

All rights reserved. The text of this publication, or any part thereof, may not be reproduced in any manner whatsoever without written permission from the publisher.

"Workers' Song," copyright © 1990 by Maya Angelou, from I SHALL NOT BE MOVED by Maya Angelou. Used by permission of Random House, Inc.

"Resistance," copyright © 1999 by Cindy Jackson. Used by permission of the sculptor.

Printed in the United States of America

10 9 8 7 6 5 4 3 2 1

ISBN-13: 978-1-4195-5029-4

Kaplan Publishing books are available at special quantity discounts to use for sales promotions, employee premiums, or educational purposes. For more information or to purchase books, please call the Simon & Schuster special sales department at 866-506-1949.

Table of Contents

Available Online

FOR ANY TEST CHANGES OR LATE-BREAKING DEVELOPMENTS

kaptest.com/publishing

The material in this book is up-to-date at the time of publication. However, the California Commission on Teacher Credentialing may have instituted changes in the test or test-registration process after this book was published. Be sure to carefully read the materials you receive when you register for the test.

If there are any important late-breaking developments—or any changes or corrections to the Kaplan test preparation materials in this book—we will post that information online at **kaptest.com/publishing**.

For customer service, please contact us at **booksupport@kaplan.com**

About the Authors

C Roebuck Reed is a freelance writer and documentary filmmaker. She has taught CSET prep courses in the Los Angeles area since the test's inception. She lives in Burbank, CA.

Lee Wherry Brainerd has been a teacher, editor, and textbook writer for over 34 years. She graduated with honors from Northern Illinois University with a B.A. in Education and French. Lee has taught English as a Foreign Language to K-12 students and was an adult educator with the National Education Center for 10 years. She has written or contributed to over 40 textbooks and test-prep books. Lee lives in Altadena, CA.

Rodney Lee has taught fourth and fifth grades at Ivanhoe Elementary (LA Unified School District) for the last seven years and has been an instructor for MSAT and CSET prep courses for the last three years. He attended Pasadena City College and then earned a B.A. in History and a Multiple Subject Teaching Credential from Occidental College. He lives in Los Angeles, CA.

The Staff of Kaplan, Inc. would like to acknowledge the contributions of Sandy Gade, Jung Lee, Steven Mercado, Meg Moyer, Ann Pizer, and Adam Reed to this project.

How to Use This Book

So, you've decided to become a credentialed teacher in the state of California. Among other requirements, in order to become an elementary school or special education teacher, you must pass the California Subject Examinations for Teachers (the CSET), a multiple-subject exam administered by National Evaluation Systems, Inc. (NES). (If you are seeking middle or high school certification in a specific subject, you need to take a single-subject test, not this exam. Visit www.cset.nesinc.com for more information.)

The good news about the CSET is that its questions clearly reflect the K−12 California Student Academic Content standards. The bad news is that those standards are extensive. Nevertheless, you are now in a good position to pass the exam because by purchasing this book you are taking the best possible path toward mastery of the standards. This guide will take you step-by-step through the process of preparing for the CSET.

In this section, you will learn about the structure of the CSET and how to study for it. You'll get a brief overview of each subject and some resources for further research. The remainder of the book delves into the content standards themselves and gives you the basics of all seven subjects covered on the exam. As always, it's up to you to learn the material, but we will tell you what kinds of questions are on the test and teach you strategies that will lead to success in answering those questions correctly.

As you work through the book, keep in mind that learning about these subjects isn't only about passing a standardized test; it's about making sure you are prepared to teach the children who will sit in your classroom, looking to you for information and guidance. Teaching is more than a career option; it's a calling, an honorable profession that requires you to give your best every day to those children. As you prepare for the CSET, you are preparing yourself to answer thousands of questions in the years after you pass the exam, to successfully resolve countless dilemmas in the classroom, and to serve as mentor to hundreds of eager young learners. It's an awesome challenge and responsibility, but one for which you have prepared and are still preparing. This is one step along the professional road you have chosen, the one with the fabulous view around every curve. Congratulations, and good luck!

INTRODUCTION

The CSET

The CSET consists of three subtests. Each subtest covers a group of related subjects. Subtest 1 tests your knowledge of language and literature; history and the social sciences; and the teaching of reading, writing, and spelling. Subtest 2 covers math and science, and Subtest 3 deals with physical education, human development, and the visual and performing arts.

Each subtest consists of multiple-choice questions and constructed-response questions. The multiple-choice questions test your knowledge of relevant facts, vocabulary, and information, as well as your ability to apply pedagogical techniques in classroom situations. Constructed-response questions test these things in addition to your ability to synthesize, condense, and convey knowledge. The readers who score your constructed responses are looking for clarity of thought and communication. Of course, the more you know about the subject of the constructed-response question, the better; but even if your knowledge of a particular question is rudimentary, a well-presented response, complete with examples and supporting arguments, can still earn a passing score.

Right now you may be thinking that one of the subtests will be harder for you than the others—you're probably right. As an elementary or special education teacher, you must have a broad knowledge base. Remember, learning how to use geometry to solve a problem, how to analyze a poem, and how to instruct a class in performing handstands will make you a better teacher. It's okay if you don't yet feel competent in all content areas—this book will provide the groundwork for success on the CSET. Learning is a lifetime proposition, especially for teachers. In fact, you can often be the most effective at teaching those subjects you have struggled with yourself.

How Do I Prepare for The CSET?

By reading this far, you have already taken a major step in preparing for the CSET. The next step is to set up your study plan. Use the book to assess what you know and what you need to learn, then pursue the knowledge you need to acquire, using the tips, techniques, and resources provided.

Look over the chapters, the content standards, and the questions for each subtest. Realistically decide how much time you need to devote to preparation. If you are a good test-taker, you have an advantage. But if you're like most people and standardized test-taking has never been your strong suit, allow yourself more time to absorb and practice applying the techniques that follow.

Make a study plan and stick to it. Schedule your study sessions, follow your schedule, and reward yourself for good behavior. Be realistic and stay focused on success. Self-discipline is crucial here: you are training for a triathlon! Once you know how much work you need to do, you'll know when you can successfully take the exam(s).

One, Two, or Three?

One of the best things about the CSET is that you can choose to take one subtest at a time. On the other hand, you may choose to take two on the same day, or you can take all three at once. No matter how many you choose to take on a given day, you will have five hours to finish everything. That's five hours to take one subtest, five hours to take two subtests, or five hours to take all three.

If you are a great test-taker with lots of self-confidence, and you only bought this book to brush up a bit, you may choose to take all three subtests in one sitting and get it over with. The rest of us, however, are well-advised to take no more than two subtests at once. In other words, it is mentally, physically, and emotionally grueling to take all three exams in a single five-hour marathon. Many examinees need five hours to give proper attention to just two subtests, and some say they use all five hours making sure they get the math right on Subtest 2.

Of course, if you're in a hurry to get your credential, you may need to take all three subtests at once. If that's the case, however, know that you must be extremely well-prepared. It won't do you any good to take all the tests on a single day if you don't pass all of them.

If you decide, for example, that you're pretty well prepared for Subtest 1 and Subtest 3, but Subtest 2 covers a lot of material you haven't thought about in years, you may want to sign up to take Subtests 1 and 3 on the same day, study for them, and get them out of the way. The CSET is offered about every other month throughout the school year, so that would give you two months to study for Subtest 2 in a focused way. Another advantage to taking the subtest(s) you feel most comfortable with first is that it gives you a greater degree of familiarity and comfort with the exam before you have to tackle your most difficult subtest.

You may be getting the sense that our bias is toward taking only one or two subtests in a single session. It is true that most examinees find it difficult to pass all three subtests at once. Some choose to use their first attempt as a way of finding out what they need to work on. A less expensive and less time-consuming method of self-discovery is to use this book to help you come up with a realistic plan.

Know Yourself

At the end of this book you'll find a full-length practice exam covering all three subtests. In addition, you will find practice sets at the end of each chapter which comprise another full-length exam. There is an online practice exam, as well, at the CSET website, cset.nesinc.com. Take one or more of these exams before deciding how many subtests to schedule on a single day. Whatever your decision, know that you are heading in the right direction by choosing to prepare wisely, and, subsequently, that your chances for success are therefore excellent.

How Do I Find the Time to Study?

Everyone's busy. We all have numerous commitments and responsibilities that make it difficult to set aside big chunks of time for studying. Try, instead, to carve out some small chunks of time for this purpose. One of the simplest and most important secrets of successful people is that they don't listen to their own excuses for not being able to do something.

Everybody has time to accomplish their goals. Here are some suggestions to help you maximize that time:

- **Make flashcards.** It takes about one minute to make a flashcard, and they are useful aids in studying for every subject on the CSET. Your success on both the multiple-choice and constructed-responses hinge on your knowledge of appropriate vocabulary. Use the glossaries in the review sections of this book as a starting point for your flashcards.

- **Find creative times to use your flashcards.** Brushing your teeth? Flashcards. Stirring the marinara sauce? Flashcards. Television commercial? Flashcards. There are enough spare moments in your day to make a real difference in your knowledge base, especially when you're motivated to find and use them.

- **Make a timeline.** For the history section, especially, this is a critical tool. The act of creating a timeline will teach you how one historical event leads to another. When creating your timeline, leave yourself lots of room to fill in information as your knowledge becomes more detailed. Feel free to draw pictures and to make comments.

- **Create outlines and mind maps.** At the end of each subject discussion, or following a particularly challenging section, create an outlined review for yourself. Take your new knowledge, add it to what you already knew, and create a shortened way for yourself to remember the information. Then see if you can condense it even further. Now expand it again. The process of doing this is remarkably similar to the process you need to go through in writing a constructed response.

- **Involve your friends and family.** One of the hardest things about studying for the CSET can be the feeling of isolation from your loved ones. But you don't always have to isolate yourself to study. Once you've made your flashcards, ask a friend or family member to quiz you. Chances are they'll be glad to help you. And it usually improves your memorization skills to have to perform for somebody else and recite study material aloud.

- **Have fun.** Maybe this doesn't fit into your current thinking about the CSET. You may be looking at this exam as just another hoop to jump through on your way to the classroom. However, if you can trade that perspective for one that regards this experience as an exciting challenge, then you can actually enjoy the process of learning and preparing for the test. You do enjoy learning, don't you? You've chosen to be a teacher, to share your joy of learning with children. This is an opportunity to prepare yourself for those tough questions children like to ask as well as to gain knowledge and skills you will use throughout your teaching career. So have fun!

THE KAPLAN METHOD

Multiple-Choice Questions

Step 1. Read the question carefully. As you read, underline or circle the key words and phrases that differentiate this particular question from all other possible questions.

Step 2. Rephrase the question to make sure you understand it. If possible, predict the correct answer.

Step 3. Read all the answer choices, eliminating (physically marking through) incorrect ones as you go.

Step 4. If two or more possible answer choices remain, go back to the question and search for matching/mirroring language or concepts that will point you toward the single correct answer.

Step 1: Read the question carefully.

The number one reason most test-takers miss questions is that they sometimes try to answer questions that were not asked. You may be thinking, *not me!* But are you sure? Our bodies, including our brains, are designed to speed up when we're under pressure. In many instances that's a good thing, a survival mechanism. Some standardized tests are designed to put time pressure on test-takers, meaning you have to work quickly. On the CSET, however, that kind of speed is unnecessary, and can be counterproductive. What *is* necessary is to be as meticulous and precise as you possibly can be. Often, on the questions that have you stumped, the right answer is indicated by the fit between the language of the question and that of the correct answer. This means you have to be aware of language, in both question and answer, in order to understand the clues offered by each question. A helpful technique, one that helps you focus on language and the meaning of the question, is to underline or circle the key words and phrases as you read. Important words and phrases differentiate each particular question from all other questions. They may direct you to look for a particular relationship (e.g., *which of the following best explains…* or *which is most likely to promote…*); or they may specify a qualifier, such as time or age range (e.g., *on the eve of the Civil War…* or *in a fourth grade class…*). As you take the practice tests in the book, practice this technique. Actually underline or circle the key language as you read each question so when test day comes, marking up your test booklet will be second nature for you.

If there is a short passage followed by a question, or questions, it is a good idea to read the question(s) before reading the passage itself. This gives you a sense of what kinds of things you are looking for in the passage. The question(s) may ask you about specific language (e.g., *in the following passage, what is meant by the term* powerful), or the question(s) may be more general in nature (e.g., *the excerpt above best illustrates which of the following principles*). In either case, reading the question(s) first prepares you to focus on the passage in a productive way, and use your time effectively.

Step 2: Rephrase the question.

It is a good idea to put each question into your own words to make sure you understand it. This technique takes some practice. For example, questions that begin *which of the following…* can be off-putting. If the question is, *which of the following is the most appropriate way to teach balance to a kindergarten class?*, you could rephrase it so that you say to yourself, *one of these (answers) is the best way to teach balance to kindergartners.* That helps fix in your mind that you are looking for the choice that describes the best way to teach balance to a kindergarten class. Once you understand the question, try to predict the correct answer, if you can, without looking at the answer choices first. That way, incorrect, but plausible, answers won't be so appealing.

Step 3: Read all the answer choices.

It can be tempting, especially when your brain is exam mode, to succumb to the first enticing answer so that you can move on. Resist temptation. Often there will be two similar answers, only one of which is actually correct. If you stop reading at choice **(B)**, you'll never see choice **(D)**, which may be the correct answer. As you read through the answers, eliminate *and physically mark through as you go* the choices you know to be incorrect. You make those marks so that you never have to deal with those incorrect answers again. Sometimes you can eliminate three wrong answers, leaving the fourth choice as the correct one by default. More often you will eliminate two answers and then wonder how on earth you're going to determine which of the remaining two is the right answer. That's where Step 4 comes in.

Step 4. Search for matching/mirroring language or concepts.

This can be a tricky technique to master, but it's worth its weight in extra points. What you want to do is go back to the question, look at the key words you've marked, search for any others you might have overlooked and mark those; then reread the two (or more) answers you have not yet eliminated for language that aligns with the language or concepts in the question. Here's an example:

> After World War II, women in the state of California and throughout the nation experienced a newfound political and economic power. Which of the following was the most important reason for their increased role outside the home?
>
> (A) The nineteenth amendment to the U.S. Constitution gave women the right to vote.
>
> (B) In the postwar economy it was necessary for families to have two incomes.
>
> (C) Feminist writers and activists urged women to liberate themselves from the yoke of oppression and work for social change.
>
> (D) Many women, urged to take jobs outside the home during the war, stayed in the workforce following the war and became increasingly independent and empowered.

On the first read-through, remember to circle or underline key words and phrases. *After World War II* is key, as it specifies the time period. *Women* is the next crucial bit of information. The only thing really important about the next phrase, *in California and throughout the nation,* is that this question will apply to women throughout the nation, so perhaps you'll want to underline *nation. Newfound* is an important concept; it implies a discontinuity with what came before. When you put it with the next phrase, *political and economic power,* you have the crux of the question. The actual question is asked in the next sentence. *Most important reason* is important, of course. *Increased sway* is a repetition of and reference to *newfound political and economic power. Outside the home* seems almost irrelevant at first glance, so we'll leave it aside for now, because the question has already been stated.

Rephrasing the question, you might say something like, *why did women in the United States become more powerful in politics and economics after World War II?* Now it's time to look at the answers. Choice **(A)** might be appealing because having suffrage—the right to vote—certainly would give a group increased political power. The nineteenth amendment, however, became law in 1920, more than 20 years before World War II began and therefore would have been unlikely to be the cause of increased power after that war. Mark through **(A)** so you don't have to look at that choice again.

Choice **(B)** is appealing at first glance. Certainly it has become harder and harder for families to make ends meet on a single income. But was that the case in the late 1940s and 1950s? Have you seen movies or television shows from that era? Few of the women in those shows worked outside the home. Did your mothers or grandmothers work during those years? For some of you, the answer is yes; but at that time, it was quite possible for a family to live comfortably on the earnings of a single worker. Note that the choice states *it was necessary for families to have two incomes.* Any time you see an absolute kind of word, such as *necessary,* make sure it is absolutely true before choosing the answer that contains it. Choice **(B)** is not true, so it is not the correct answer.

Choice **(C)** takes note of the feminist reform effort that took off in the 1960s and 1970s. Certainly, many women decided at that time to utilize the power of their votes. Feminists also urged women to become economically independent as a means of casting off the oppression of sexism. It *could* be the correct answer, but the time frame is off a bit. Feminism wasn't exactly rampant after the second World War. Still, the answer speaks to both political, and possibly economic power, and may be worth a second look; so we move on to **(D)**.

Choice **(D)** is true. During World War II, with so many men serving in the armed forces, there was a shortage of workers to fill positions in the defense industries as well as other businesses. The United States government launched a publicity campaign designed to entice women into the workforce to fill those jobs. Many women responded to the appeal to their patriotism and desire to serve the war effort. For the first time, many women did "men's work." And many of them liked it—so much so that, when the war ended and the men returned home, the women didn't want to leave their new jobs. This would certainly give women new economic power, but political power?

Now we have two choices, **(C)** and **(D)**, that could be correct. Going back to the question, which of the key words or phrases gives the clue to the right choice? It is the very first one, *after World War II.* Though each of the answers is factually correct on its own, only **(D)** speaks to the correct time period. The fact that many women stayed in the workforce after the war, earning their own paychecks, created the conditions that allowed feminism, with its exercise of political power, to bloom more than a decade later. To confirm **(D)** as the correct answer, look at the phrase *outside the home,* which we didn't underline the first time through. That phrase has come to be used by feminists and others who want to convey respect for women who work in the home (i.e., those who were formerly called *housewives*). Its use in the answer echoes its use in the question. The language of *outside the home* aligns with the phrase *political and economic power* to confirm the correct answer.

Constructed-Response Questions

Step 1. Read each question carefully. As you read, underline or circle the key words and phrases that differentiate this particular question from all other possible questions.

Step 2. Note how many parts the question has. Be sure to include subparts in your count. Write this number in your test booklet, so you will be sure to answer each part of the question.

Step 3. Before you start writing, brainstorm for vocabulary words and relevant concepts. Make your notes in the margins of your answer sheet, so you will be sure to include them in your answer. If you don't have a good command of details for a particular question, be sure to include in your answer the big picture concepts, such as the reason for studying/teaching the subject.

Step 4. Organize your thoughts. Remember, you are being tested on your ability to clearly convey information.

Step 1: Read each question carefully.

This is the same first step you go through when answering multiple-choice questions. Note the specific language used in the question. Often in constructed-response questions, there is an important piece of information that you can expand on in your answer. It may bring up associations in your mind, or it may simply direct you how to answer this particular question, as opposed to any other possible question on the topic. For example, if a constructed-response question in Visual Art shows you an art print and asks you to *discuss how the print is organized in terms of the principles of art*, that's a very different question from one that asks you to *discuss the artist's use of the elements of art.* If you aren't paying close attention, you might mistake one of those questions for the other; but in fact, they are not at all the same. (See Chapter 7 for the crucial difference between the principles and elements of art.)

Step 2: Note how many parts the question has.

The CSET test-makers are fond of writing constructed-response questions with multiple parts. If, for example, you have a question with two bullet points, you may be tempted to think of it as a question with two parts. However, often one of those bullet points, and sometimes both of them, contain two or more parts. History questions, for example, often ask for the *social, political, economic, and cultural effects* of something. If you see a question that contains that particular wording, you're looking at a four-part question; and you must answer each part or lose points for failing to do so. Count carefully, then write the number of parts to the question on your test booklet somewhere close to the question, so you can check back after you've finished planning your answer—but before you start writing—to make sure your response addresses all parts of the question.

Step 3: Brainstorm.

This is the most consistently short-changed portion of the constructed response process. People, responding to a surge of test-taking adrenaline, tend to get an idea for their answer and then just start writing. The problem comes when you get halfway through your answer and realize that you have two more, even better points to make and no room in which to write them. That's why you need to get all your thoughts to the surface before you start writing.

Although there's nothing to prevent your writing the constructed-response questions first, we recommend you save them for last in each section. That's because one or more of the multiple-choice questions might touch on points or spur thoughts that will be useful in writing the constructed responses. When you read the constructed-response question, take a few minutes (not seconds!) to think about the question. Try to remember everything you've ever read, heard, seen, or thought about that topic, including novels, movies, and television shows. If applicable, try to place yourself in the scenario, era, or situation mentioned in the question.

As a thought comes to mind, jot it down. One word is best, if it will serve to remind you of your thought. Jot down vocabulary you want to use in your answer, or dates and names, or formulas, if appropriate. It's okay to use the margins of your answer sheet for this jotting, but don't use the lined portion until you're ready to write. *Remember, you have no more than 20 lines on which to write your answer.*

Step 4: Organize.

Now that you have brought up all the stored information you have that could be useful in writing your answer, you are ready to organize that information. Why are you required to write constructed responses for the CSET? Probably because the credentialing commission wants to make sure you know how to organize and convey information. That's what teachers do—organize and convey information. If you can't organize your thoughts in writing, there will be a strong suspicion that you can't effectively convey information to your students. So take that extra few minutes to make sure your answer is well-organized before you start writing.

You don't need to write a masterful essay for each constructed-response question. In fact, for some questions, particularly in math and science, a bulleted list or diagram is sufficient. You do, however, need to write legibly and express your thoughts clearly. Make your main point first, give examples or arguments to support your point(s), and read over your answer as though you've never seen it before to verify that it says what you mean to say. Last, but certainly not least, confirm that your handwriting is legible; you'll get no credit for an answer that can't be deciphered.

SUBTEST 1 DEMYSTIFIED

Subtest 1 contains 52 multiple-choice questions, 26 each on the two main subject areas: reading, language, and literature; and history. There are also four constructed-response questions, two in each of the areas. Each of these two areas, however, consists of several subareas you need to know about.

Reading, Language, and Literature

Language and Linguistics

The CSET tests for knowledge of strategies for teaching language-related subjects such as reading, writing, and spelling. Included in this topic are theories of language development and acquisition of both first and second languages, as well as appropriate assessment techniques. Teachers who teach reading have to know the basic components and structures of language, using concepts from linguistics, such as phonemic awareness and morphology.

Non-written and Written Communication

There are differences between the language we speak and the language we are expected to write. Teachers must be aware of these differences and must be able to clearly communicate them to their students, including the conventions of standard written English (structure, spelling, etc.). The CSET also contains questions about the writing process itself, from inception through publication.

Texts

Teachers are expected to be able to interpret texts and to support their interpretations using textual materials. They must understand various genres, focusing on children's literature, and the conventions of those genres.

Resources

Chapter 1 contains a solid introduction to reading, language, and literature topics. If you feel you need more information, however, here are some excellent resources that can be accessed online:

URL	Description
cal.org/resources	The Center for Applied Linguistics has information for educators as well as useful links (click *Resources*).
ed.gov/about/pubs/intro/pubdb. html	ERIC Digest (funded by the Office of Educational Research and Improvement of the U.S. Department of Education) contains a wealth of short reports (1,000– 1,500 words) on topics of current interest in education. Search by topic.
www.riggsinst.org/literacy.aspx	This site is devoted to resources for phonetics and reading instruction.

History and Social Science

World History

Teachers need to understand the sweep of human history. Teaching isolated facts, devoid of context, leads children to think of history as boring and irrelevant to their lives. You may have been taught this way yourself, but it's never too late to be inspired by history. The more you learn, the more you want to know about the development of human cultures, how they survived and thrived, what caused their downfalls, and how we came to this precise moment in history.

The CSET asks about ancient civilizations around the world, and particularly how they were influenced by geography. It tests your knowledge of medieval times, both in Europe and in Asia; and it expects you to know about the development of our modern religious, political, and economic systems.

U.S. History

There are four eras of American history covered by the CSET: the Colonial Era to Independence, Constitutional Development and Early Republic, Civil War and Reconstruction, and Industrial America.

The Colonial Era starts with European exploration, includes colonial relations with Native Americans and European rulers, and concludes with the Revolutionary War. As always in the social science section, it focuses on various causes and effects of each topic. Constitutional Development and the Early Republic covers the discussions and events that led to the creation of our Constitution, as well as the form and structure of government set forth by the Constitution. It continues with the westward movement and its effects on Native Americans and foreign governments. As the U.S. expanded, the issue of slavery grew more and more controversial. The CSET tests your knowledge of the events and debates surrounding slavery that lead up to the Civil War, as well as the course of the war, and its aftermath, Reconstruction. The final section covered is the growth of urban America as a result of increasing industrialization. The CSET stops short of the twentieth century in U.S. History.

California History

California history can be broken into two parts: pre-Gold Rush and post-Gold Rush. You will need to know what the state was like before the Gold Rush, who lived here in pre-Columbian times and what their lives were like, as well as the stories of Spanish settlement, Mexican rule, and the Mexican American War. You will also be tested on your knowledge of the Gold Rush itself, and its impact on the land, the people, and statehood. You need to know about subsequent waves of immigration into the state and how those immigrants influenced the economics and politics of the region. As with world and U.S. history, you will be tested on your knowledge of geography and its influence on the people who live there.

Resources

Chapter 2 presents the basic outline of history in the three target areas, introducing you to the important topics and questions in the social science arena and providing you with powerful tools for approaching your study of history. If you feel you need more information, however, here are some resources that can be accessed online:

Topic/URL	Description
World History	
unc.edu/awmc/mapsforstudents.html	The University of North Carolina Chapel Hill maintains a site with downloadable maps of the ancient world.
eawc.evansville.edu/eawcindex.htm	Many links and resources for the study of ancient and medieval times are on this website, sponsored by the University of Evansville.
campus.northpark.edu/history/	Timelines, chronologies, and more can be found at this North Park University-sponsored site.

Topic/URL	Description
ancientmexico.com/	What this site lacks in detail, it makes up for in colorful maps, timelines, flash movies, and more about pre-Columbian Mesoamerica.
U.S. History	
xroads.virginia.edu	There are many American history documents, maps, and links at this University of Virginia site.
lib.utexas.edu/maps/histus.html	This University of Texas site has an extensive American map collection.
pitt.edu/~poole/eledHistUS.html	This site presents several topics of interest to teachers of U.S. history, including links and a timeline, from the University of Pittsburgh.
California History	
cogweb.ucla.edu/Chumash/	This site offers an excellent summation of early Southern California history, as well as links to other resources, including a timeline.
memory.loc.gov/ammem/cbhtml/ cbgeog.html	A good summation of California history can be found at this Library of Congress site.
infoplease.com/ce6/us/ A0857126.html	Historical information about California's economic development is on this site.
californiamapsociety.org	The California Map Society offers this site, which has a good section on understanding maps and stories behind California maps.

SUBTEST 2 DEMYSTIFIED

Subtest 2 contains 52 multiple-choice questions, 26 each on the two main subject areas: science and math. There are also four constructed-response questions, two in each of the areas. Each of these two areas, however, consists of several subareas you need to know about.

Science

There are three subject areas within the field of science covered on the CSET. They are: physical science, life science, and earth and space science. Each one has a rather extensive knowledge base, on which you will be tested. You may also encounter a question or two on scientific tools and methods.

Physical Science

In order to understand physical science, you must first understand the structural and physical properties of matter. Structure of matter covers topics ranging from atomic structure through molecular structure and on to compounds, solutions, and mixtures. You will be asked to compare and contrast physical and chemical changes of matter and to be familiar, in a basic way, with the Periodic Table of Elements.

The CSET also asks about the principles of motion and energy. You must know what forces act upon objects and how to use simple machines to amplify force. You will need to identify various forms of energy, understand the relationship of heat and temperature, and know the sources and properties of light and other waves. You must be able to apply your knowledge of energy to questions about renewable and nonrenewable resources.

The review of chemistry and physics basics in Chapter 3 will get you on the right track.

Life Science

Living organisms, both plant and animal, are the subject of life science questions on the CSET. Questions range from the structures and organization of systems, such as organ systems, to the functions and operations of those systems, to the underlying principles of chemistry that allow biological systems to exist.

There are always questions on the CSET about ecosystems. You need to understand the characteristics of ecosystems, the kinds of environmental resources that must exist in an ecosystem, and the flow of energy and matter through an ecosystem in terms of its inhabitants.

Immediate life cycles, involving reproduction, as well as the longer process of evolution, are also covered by the CSET. You must be able to distinguish sexual from asexual reproduction; understand types of cells and their functions, including cell division; and be able to diagram life cycles of familiar animals. You also need to understand the evidence supporting Darwin's theory of evolution and the principle of natural selection.

Earth and Space Science

Earth science focuses on the structure and composition of the Earth. You need to understand the formation and composition of different kinds of rocks and minerals. You need to know the characteristics of landforms as well as their processes of creation and change. You must understand the theory of plate tectonics and its implications regarding the mechanisms of both short- and long-term change on the Earth's surface.

You must also understand the Earth's atmosphere and its bodies of water, particularly as they are united in the water cycle. You may also be asked about the mechanisms affecting the atmosphere and water, such as climate, tides, and topography.

The knowledge of space science required for the CSET includes an understanding of the relationships in space of the Earth, Sun, and moon and how those relationships explain the observed positions of the sun and moon throughout daily, monthly, and yearly cycles as well as how they relate to our concepts of time and time zones. You must also identify and describe the planets and other objects in the solar system as well as other bodies and systems in the universe.

KAPLAN

Resources

This book introduces all the science topics you will find on the CSET. If you feel you need more information in a particular area, however, here are some resources that can be accessed online:

URL	Description
homeworkspot.com/elementary/science/	This website has many links to science topics covered by the CSET, as well as ideas for the classroom.
teach-nology.com/teachers/subject_matter/science/	The subjects of interest on this website include physics and earth science with many links.
specialedprep.net	More science links can be found here.
howstuffworks.com	This fascinating website covers numerous topics in science and features photos, video, and text.

Math

CSET math can be classified into four subject areas: number sense; algebra and functions; measurement and geometry; and statistics, data analysis, and probability. Each of these areas consists of two or more sub-areas.

Number Sense

The CSET tests your understanding of numbers; number systems, including whole, integer, and rational number systems; and the relationships among numbers. You must be able to represent numbers in exponential and scientific notation and capable of describing the relationships among the algorithms for addition, subtraction, multiplication, and division. The test will require you to work with fractions and positive, negative, and fractional exponents.

Also on the CSET, you will be required to apply standard algorithms to computations and demonstrate an understanding of order of operations. You must round numbers, estimate, and place numbers on a number line.

Algebra and Functions

Tables, graphs, verbal rules, and symbolic rules are all ways of representing patterns. Ratios and fractions are both ways of representing proportions. You must grasp the equivalences among these differing ways of representation and be capable of translating among them.

You will be asked to express equalities and inequalities in different ways, to recognize equivalent algebraic expressions when you see them, and to represent geometric problems algebraically. You will also need to understand linear equations and quadratic equations and be able to graph and solve them.

Measurement and Geometry

The CSET requires you to understand the characteristics of two- and three-dimensional figures and to compare them for similarity, congruence, or lack thereof. You must have a thorough comprehension of the Pythagorean theorem and its converse.

You will need to construct and work with representations of geometric objects. You need to be able to combine and dissect two- and three-dimensional figures into other familiar shapes.

On Subtest 2 of the CSET, it will be necessary for you to estimate and measure length, angles, area, perimeter, volume, weight/mass, and temperature. You must be able to estimate equivalent measures using the metric system as well as the customary systems of measurement. Additionally, you must solve problems using time and miles per hour variables.

Statistics, Data Analysis, and Probability

On the CSET you have to understand data collection and use. You must be able to determine mean, median, mode, and range of a collection of data and to represent data through graphs, tables, and charts. You must also be familiar with basic survey design.

You are required to interpret tables, graphs, and charts representing data sets. You must understand how to use a random sample to draw conclusions about a population and know how to identify possible sources and effects of bias in data collection.

You need to understand the concepts of chance and probability and must also be able to express these concepts in a variety of ways, including as ratios, decimals, percents, and proportions.

Resources

If you're not comfortable with all these math concepts, relax. Remember that math is about vocabulary as much as concepts, and know that all the math you've taken will come back to you as you work through this book. If you feel you need more information in a particular area, however, here are some resources that can be accessed online:

URL	Description
learner.org	This across-curriculum website offers K–12 teacher resources, interactives, and videos in math and science.
mathforum.org/math.topics.html	Drexel University sponsors this site with links to resources for K–12 math as well as more advanced problems.
math.utah.edu/~alfeld/math.html	These thoughts, both practical and philosophical, on understanding math are shared by Peter Alfeld, from the University of Utah.
mathnerds.com	Mathematicians answer your questions

SUBTEST 3 DEMYSTIFIED

Subtest 3 contains 39 multiple-choice questions, 13 each on the three main subject areas: physical education, human development, and the visual and performing arts. There are also three constructed-response questions, one in each of the areas. Each of these three areas consists of several subareas you need to know about.

Physical Education

Sound physical education consists of movement skills and movement knowledge. It also consists, however, of the development of healthy habits and self image, and social and cultural development. Your knowledge of all these topics and how to apply that knowledge are tested on the CSET.

Movement Skills and Knowledge

The basic vocabulary of physical education is used to express concepts related to awareness of body and space, locomotor and nonlocomotor skills, and object manipulation. These skills, and others, such as knowledge of biomechanics, are taught within a framework of developmental appropriateness, which teachers must be familiar with.

In addition to teaching movement skills and principles related to movement skills, teachers must also instruct students in exercise physiology and the health benefits of physical fitness. The CSET tests your comprehension of fitness components, such as flexibility and endurance, and your awareness of the elements of appropriate fitness practices.

As a teacher, you will be expected to be able to select from a large repertoire of games, sports, and activities, such as dance, in planning age-appropriate physical education lessons. This means knowing the rules of common games and sports and the steps of dances, particularly those from other times and places. It is also important to be able to integrate physical education with academic content areas.

Physical Growth, Personal Development and Self Image

There are questions on the CSET about physical growth and development in kindergartners through eighth graders. Specifically, you must understand the progressive acquisition of gross and fine motor skills, the influence on and timing of growth spurts in relation to physical performance, and the impact of both positive and negative factors on physical health and general well-being.

You are also expected to understand the role physical activity plays in promoting positive self image. In particular, you need to know how to promote individual goal-setting as a means of encouraging lifelong participation in physical activity.

Social Development

Historically, one of the reasons children have failed to maintain physical activity beyond physical education classes is that less gifted athletes have shunned the competitive atmosphere that has too often dominated these classes. Teachers, especially at the elementary level, must be aware of ways to promote enjoyment of physical activity by all students.

To enhance inclusiveness, and so enjoyment by all, you must encourage cooperation above competition. You should also practice cultural inclusiveness by teaching the cultural and historical aspects of a variety of movement forms.

Resources

If physical education is not a strong area for you, you may want to get more specific information about games, sports, and dances. Here are some resources that can be accessed online:

URL	Description
homeworkspot.com/ elementary/health/	This website contains links to a variety of health and fitness resources.
pecentral.org/	This is another site with links to physical education resources.
basketball.com/nba/rules/ index.shtml volleyball.org/rules drblank.com/slaws.htm (soccer)	You can usually find out the rules and/or strategies for individual sports by using the sport's name, plus the word *rules* to search. Here are websites with rules for some common sports.
ehow.com/video_2346637_ gymnastics-positions- beginners.html	This website presents some basic gymnastics moves via videos, as you might be asked to describe them.

Human Development

Human development testing on the CSET most often takes the form of situational questions. You may be asked what kind of activity would be most effective at getting third graders to cooperate with each other or which of several skills kindergartners would find most difficult. Questions focus on cognitive, social, and physical development as well as influences on development from birth through adolescence.

Cognitive Development

Although the CSET has not in the past asked questions about specific theorists, you are expected to know and be able to apply accepted ideas about cognitive, lingustic, and moral development from birth through adolescence. In particular, you may be asked about the characteristics and impact of creative play on cognitive development and concepts regarding and implications of the idea of multiple intelligences.

Social and Physical Development

Without necessarily needing to quote specific theorists, you will need to understand current concepts related to the development of temperament and personality, such as attachment and identity. You must comprehend the impact of play and prosocial behavior on social and physical development. In particular, you must be knowledgeable about the implications of developmental differences, including those of children with special needs.

Influences on Development

For the CSET you need to be aware of the impact of various influences on development from birth through adolescence. These include genetic influences and environmental influences, such as cultural, economic, and gender differences. You must also be able to identify possible sources and impacts on development of neglect and abuse.

Resources

If you have not taken human development courses, you may want to do additional research to learn more about theories and applications of current thought. Here are some resources that can be accessed online:

URL	Description
wikipedia.org/wiki/developmental_psychology	This site presents an excellent overview of the main currents of thought in human development and offers many links.
chiron.valdosta.edu/whuitt/col/cogsys/piaget.html	This site, focused on the work of Jean Piaget, contains links to information about other theorists as well links.
vtaide.com/png/ERIK1-4.htm	This is a concise presentation of Erik Erikson's stages of human development.
psychology.about.com/od/developmentalpsychology/a/kohlberg.htm	This site contains a summary of Lawrence Kohlberg's stages of moral development.
ship.edu/%7Ecgboeree/maslow.html	This website presents Abraham Maslow's Hierarchy of Needs.
tip.psychology.org/vygotsky.html	Information and links about Lev Vygotsky are found on this website.

Visual and Performing Arts

The four arts areas covered on the CSET are: dance, music, theater, and visual art. For each one of these areas, you must learn relevant vocabulary and familiarize yourself with historical and cultural traditions. You will also be required to understand the bases for critical analyses of each art and to articulate the value of arts education.

Dance

In order to teach dance, you must understand the elements of dance, such as time, space, force, and energy. You must also be familiar with techniques for teaching dance to children, as well as knowing some dances to teach. These dances should be drawn from various cultural traditions and should be taught in age appropriate sequences. You must also be able to teach children how to make critical judgments based on the elements of dance.

Music

Music education includes teaching the elements of music, such as pitch, rhythm, and timbre. It also includes musical concepts such as musical notation and a knowledge of what constitutes appropriate vocal and instrumental music for children. You must be familiar with musical traditions from different cultures as well as be able to articulate the criteria for making judgments based on the concepts and elements of music.

Theater

As a teacher, you must be able to apply the elements and principles of theater to the creation of dramatic activities. You need to understand personnel roles in theater, such as director, producer, actor, and designer; you are also expected to know techniques for preliminary activities such as improvisation and character development. Additionally, you must be aware of the history of theater in different geographical areas and cultural traditions.

Visual Art

For the CSET, you must master the elements of art, such as line, form, color, shape, and texture, and the principles of art, such as balance, contrast, and unity. Visual art has an extensive vocabulary and an expansive range of techniques, which you must be familiar with. You must be able to choose appropriate activities for various developmental levels. You also need to be able to identify and discuss various styles of visual art from other times, places, and cultures.

Resources

The arts are a vitally important means of reaching children and engaging them in the educational process. The knowledge base required is vast but rewarding, both professionally and personally. Here are some resources that can be accessed online:

URL	Description
pitt.edu/~poole/eledMusicArt.html	This website contains links to numerous resources for teaching arts in elementary school.
artswork.asu.edu/arts/teachers/lesson/dance/	This site contains links to lesson plans in the arts for elementary school teachers.
pitt.edu/~poole/eledArt.html	The links on this site point to visual arts sites.
witcombe.sbc.edu/ARTHLinks.html	This site thoroughly covers art from various cultural traditions.

SCORING THE CSET

To pass the CSET, an individual must obtain a minimum scaled score of 220 in each of the three subtests. To ensure fairness, a raw score (the number of questions you answered correctly) is converted to a scaled score that reflects the difficulty of a particular version of the exam.

On the CSET, there is no penalty for guessing, so it is important to make your best effort to answer each question, using the answering strategies in this book. The readers who score your constructed responses use a focused holistic scoring methodology. That is, they decide on the overall effectiveness of your response, while also keeping in mind a pre-determined set of performance characteristics they are looking for.

Your scaled score for each subtest is a combination of your machine-scored multiple-choice answers and your reader-scored constructed responses. If you passed a particular subtest of the CSET, the score report will simply say that you passed. If you did not pass, your score will be shown as a scaled score below 220. In either case, the score report will also provide information about your performance on the various domains of each subtest, so that you can see which areas are strengths and which areas need improvement.

It takes approximately one month for a CSET exam to be scored and mailed or posted on the Internet. You can learn how to check the Internet for your scores, when they become available, at cset.nesinc.com. This website also has information about securing additional copies of your score report(s), and about canceling or verifying a score, as well as other score-related questions you may have.

CSET REGISTRATION

The CSET is administered six times during the academic year. The deadline for regular registration is approximately one month before the exam, although for additional fees you can register closer to the test date. Each subtest costs $70.00, plus any additional fees for late registration.

There are three ways to register for the exam: by mail, by telephone, or online. Telephone registration is available only for late and emergency registrations, and you can't register by mail on an emergency basis; but you can register online at any time up to the final deadline.

If you need special arrangements for religious reasons or due to physical, cognitive, or emotional disabilities, you must notify the test administrators. Details are in the registration bulletin for Single Subject Examinations for Teachers at cset.nesinc.com.

If you do not pass one or more subtests, you may retake the subtests that you have not passed. There is no limit to the number of times you may take any subtest that you have not passed. Each time you do, however, you need to reregister.

Make sure to check the CSET Registration Bulletin for additional test date information. Remember that it is possible to register until approximately four days before the exam date (additional fees will apply). When you pick your test date(s), be sure you're leaving yourself enough time to prepare for the exam(s).

In addition to the practice sets and subtests in this book, you may want to explore the computer-administered practice test (which you can print out too) on the CSET website. Finally, any further questions you have about registration, administration, or scoring may be resolved at the CSET FAQs page at csetnesinc.com/CS15_faq.asp. Now, you're on your way!

KAPLAN

| PART ONE |

Subtest 1

ABOUT SUBTEST 1

Subtest 1 of the CSET Multiple Subjects Exam covers the areas of Reading, Language, and Literature (covered in Chapter 1) and World, American, and California History (Chapter 2). There are 52 multiple-choice questions on Subtest 1, 26 in each of the two general areas. There are four constructed-response questions, two of them in the language arts and two in history. In history you can count on having eight or nine questions in each of the three historical areas, while the language arts questions are difficult to pigeonhole into categories.

In both subjects, you are likely to be asked to apply underlying principles to specific questions. For example, in language arts you may be asked to write a constructed response in which you must use your knowledge of the stages of spelling development to analyze a particular student's spelling development. In the history questions, you may be shown excerpts of original documents and asked what the authors were trying to accomplish through their writing.

The good news is that in language arts you are dealing with the very core of your competencies as a K–12 or special education teacher. You already know the basic principles, and this book will be a good refresher to help you understand the types of questions you will encounter on the exam. CSET history questions do not require you to memorize lists of names and dates. The state of California is much more interested in your understanding of the course of history and the principles of the social sciences and responsible citizenship.

This book will point out for you when a subject is of particular importance. As always, if you are not at all knowledgeable about the subject, it is crucial that you seek out more information to gain a deeper understanding than can be obtained from a short review. You can often use italicized words from the chapters to guide you in your search. Both of these subjects are rewarding on their own terms. The CSET is a good motivator for you to learn more about these topics; fortunately, that knowledge will stand you in good stead in the classroom as well.

Chapter 1: **Reading, Language, and Literature**

THE BIG PICTURE

Perhaps the most important task of an elementary school teacher is language instruction. However, that straightforward-sounding pronouncement is loaded with hidden complications—minefields of disagreement that make it difficult for a teacher to execute this basic task with confidence. How do you know which of the competing methods is best for teaching language skills? And even if you believe your pedagogy is sound, how can you be sure that the CSET exam makers and readers agree with you?

Relax. The CSET is focused on the revelations of current, uncontroversial research in the field of language instruction. If you are well-informed in that area, you have nothing to worry about; and if not, well, that's why you are preparing for the exam. Anything you learn along the way not only prepares you for the test, it also prepares you for your work in the classroom.

This chapter introduces you to mainstream academic ideas about language instruction. You may want to pursue further knowledge on your own, to ensure complete confidence on the exam. The Internet resources listed in the Subtest 1 section of the Introduction are good taking-off points for further research. These resources link you to online research papers and additional resources in areas of particular interest to you.

For purposes of the CSET, the subjects of reading, language, and literature are divided into three main areas: language and linguistics, written and non-written communication, and texts. This chapter discusses each one in turn, giving you necessary vocabulary and introducing the main currents of thought in each field. At the end of the chapter you'll find vocabulary words and definitions you should be familiar with from the text.

THE KAPLAN METHOD

Multiple-Choice Questions

Step 1. Read the question carefully. As you read, underline or circle the key words and phrases that differentiate this particular question from all other possible questions.

Step 2. Rephrase the question to make sure you understand it. If possible, predict the correct answer.

Step 3. Read all the answer choices, eliminating (physically marking through) incorrect ones as you go.

Step 4. If two or more possible answer choices remain, go back to the question and search for matching/mirroring language or concepts that will point you toward the single correct answer.

Constructed-Response Questions

Step 1. Read each question carefully. As you read, underline or circle the key words and phrases that differentiate this particular question from all other possible questions.

Step 2. Note how many parts the question has. Be sure to include subparts in your count. Write this number in your test booklet, so you will be sure to answer each part of the question.

Step 3. Before you start writing, brainstorm for vocabulary words and relevant concepts. Make your notes in the margins of your answer sheet, so you will be sure to include them in your answer. If you don't have a good command of details for a particular question, be sure to include in your answer the big picture concepts, such as the reason for studying/teaching the subject.

Step 4. Organize your thoughts! Remember, you are being tested on your ability to clearly convey information.

LANGUAGE AND LINGUISTICS

There are many interesting branches on the tree of linguistics, but the one that primarily concerns teachers is the theoretical and practical branch of educational linguistics. This branch includes the linguistic principles teachers need to be aware of and use in language instruction, including structural linguistics, generative/transformational approaches, and prescriptive (traditional) grammar. Additionally, teachers must incorporate an understanding of sociolinguistics into their classroom approaches. The theoretical aspects of linguistics are more important as background for the CSET than as individual theories *per se*. The language portion of Subtest 1 focuses primarily on the practical application of linguistic theory in the classroom.

While it is important to understand the basics of educational linguistics, it is even more important to have a firm grasp of literacy development, both spoken and written. There are milestones that can be understood and assessed for literacy development. For the purposes of the CSET, literacy is interpreted in broad terms; the concept encompasses listening, speaking, reading, writing, and spelling. How do you know whether a child is meeting standards? What assessments can reveal progress, or lack thereof? These are questions you must know the answers to; but first, you need to know the building blocks of communication through language: phonemes, morphemes, syntax, and semantics.

Test Yourself

Utilizing the principles of morphology, the definition of *primogenitor* can be determined to be

(A) the best choice of words

(B) the top floor of a building

(C) a lovely photograph

(D) an ancestor

The correct answer is **(D)**, an ancestor. This is not a typical CSET question—the exam is not a vocabulary test. Rather, it is an opportunity to practice *morphology,* the study of word structure. *Primo* is derived from the same root as *prime,* meaning *first. Genitor* is related to the words *genesis, generation, generate,* and *genetic,* among others. What do all these words have in common? They all relate to *origins.* When you put these word roots together (*first + origins*), you can correctly guess the meaning of this uncommon word.

Structural Linguistics

The most basic linguistic information consists of the knowledge that language can be broken down into units. The smallest sound units of spoken language are called *phonemes.* Phonemes are sounds that signal differences in meaning. For example, the words *bat* and *rat* differ in meaning because of the phonemes *b* and *r.* Those two words also share two phonemes: the phonemes represented by the letters *a* and *t,* respectively.

Morphemes are the next building block of language. Morphemes are the sound sequences (sequences of phonemes) that convey meaning. *Bat* and *rat* are both morphemes, conveying quite different meanings, despite differing by only a single phoneme. If you add the letter *s* to either of those morphemes, you have a different morpheme. *Bat* and *bats* differ in meaning. In English, the letter *s* is both a phoneme and a morpheme; that is, it is a single sound (phoneme) that also conveys meaning (morpheme).

It is important to keep in mind that in English and in all languages, these phonemes and morphemes are completely arbitrary. There is no inherent reason that the sound represented by the letter *s* should signify the idea *more than one.* Other languages may employ a different approach to signifying the plural. In teaching, understanding the arbitrariness of English (and all other) language units is crucial because that awareness helps you understand the reasons for student errors in language use.

Phonology is the study of the way sounds function in a language. If you listen to someone speaking Chinese (or Armenian, or Spanish, or Swahili), you immediately recognize that the sound system is different from that of English. Some of the phonemes are different from those of English; some are the same but function differently (have different meanings); some are the same and have similar functions (e.g., the plural *s* in Spanish).

Even within the English language, the same letter can have different sounds. The letter *c* has both a soft sound, like the letter *s,* and a hard sound, like the letter *k.* It can also be combined with other letters to form other phonemes, for example with the letter *h* to make the phoneme *ch,* as in *child.*

The significance of phonology for teachers is that it engenders *phonological awareness*. Phonological awareness, also known as *phonemic awareness,* is an understanding of the fact that words are composed of sounds called phonemes. This awareness is the essential foundation for learning to read and write. Research shows that phonological awareness is both a precondition for learning to read and a consequence of reading. Children who do not have this awareness do not learn to read. Reading, essentially, is the linking of sounds (phonemes) to the letters and letter combinations that signify those sounds. Children who learn conscious strategies for linking phonemes to their graphic representations become both better readers and better spellers. The state of California wants you to know this fact and to be prepared to help children develop phonemic awareness. Only after children develop phonemic awareness (*bat* starts with the sound *b*) are they ready to use phonics to develop word attack strategies and learn to read.

Structural linguists also examine the ways sounds and letters are combined to form words. This study of word structure is called *morphology*. Think of the structure of the word *morphology*. *Morph-* refers to form or structure; think of other words you've heard that root in. The suffix *-ology* refers to study or knowledge of; think of other words that end in *-ology*. For example, *psychology* is the study of the human *psyche,* from the Greek word that refers to behavior, thought, and emotion.

Prescriptive Linguistics

When words are combined into sentences, they can be linguistically analyzed in terms of their *syntax*. Syntax is sentence structure. Traditional, prescriptive linguistics teaches us how to break down sentences into their component parts (the nouns, verb, adjectives and so forth) that are governed by grammatical rules as they are combined into sentences.

The CSET requires teachers to have a good working knowledge of syntax. You may be asked to choose the best correction for a faulty sentence or identify the essential missing component of a complete sentence (most often, the verb). You may have to identify a prepositional phrase or relative clause, so if you're not sure what those are, you may want to look them up in a grammar book or type those words into an Internet search engine. Knowledge of syntax and traditional grammar will make you a more effective teacher of both reading and writing.

Generative/Transformational Linguistics

A step beyond syntax is *semantics*. Semantics is the study of the ways in which sounds, words, sentences, etc., are used to convey meaning in language, including the effect of context on meaning. The best-known thinker about semantics is Noam Chomsky. He developed the generative/transformational approach to linguistics, which has become influential over the past fifty years.

Chomsky became interested in how it is that people acquire language skills in the absence of formal instruction. Why, he wondered, do English children become fluent in English in their first few years of life, while Russian children become fluent Russian speakers and Japanese children master Japanese? He decided that human brains are somehow structured to make sense of language, to acquire the specific sets of phonemes, morphemes, and syntactical structures that belong to specific languages. He called this structural predisposition a *Language Acquisition*

Device (LAD). In other words, the variations in languages are superficial, surface differences; the LAD is universal, ensuring that all human languages share the same logical syntax, or underlying, deep structure.

Chomsky's thinking led to his idea of a *Universal Grammar* underlying all the apparent differences of the world's languages. It also led to a revolution in the field of educational psychology, which moved away from the behavioralists' conviction that children acquire language primarily through imitation and reinforcement and toward the ideas of cognitive psychology, that children actively participate in (generate) their own language acquisition, using their LADs to make sense of (transform into meaning) the language that swirls around them from birth.

Sociolinguistics

Despite the deep structure presumed to underlie the superficial manifestations of languages, there are real and important differences in the ways languages are used in the human world. Before infants can speak, they generate hypotheses about the language they hear; and those hypotheses are always anchored in social contexts. Language is used within particular contexts. Different contexts call for different uses of language. The social, physical, and cultural contexts of language use are topics of study within the field of *pragmatics*. Because language usage cannot be separated from the social and cultural context within which it occurs, teachers must be aware of the varying backgrounds of their students so that they can be sensitive to the ways the students' backgrounds affect their language use.

For example, different cultural communities have different ways of approaching storytelling. Not all cultural traditions have the "happily ever after" structure as a feature of their stories. Another example of cultural difference is that some cultures prize accommodation over our ideal of truth-telling. A student (or parent) may tell you what she thinks you want to hear, as a means of keeping social relations smooth, rather than disagree with you or disappoint you. These kinds of cultural differences fall within the scope of sociolinguistic studies, as they are language-related aspects of communication.

Language Development and Acquisition

Milestones of Language Acquisition

Teachers must know what milestones in the acquisition of language are normal for children. Though different schools of thought classify developmental milestones differently, observers agree that there are predictable, definable stages of language acquisition. Briefly, the stages of language development are:

- Birth to one year: cooing, then babbling
- One to two years: holophrastic speech (one-word utterances)
- Eighteen months to thirty months: telegraphic speech, mostly content words without affixes or function words
- Two to five years: emergent speech/grammar explosion
- Five to seven years: intermediate language fluency
- Seven years to adulthood: increasing fluency

The exact timetable of these stages depends on the individual. For example, many five-year-olds entering kindergarten will still be mastering morphological rules, a typical feature of emergent speech. They will say, "I goed to my friend's house yesterday." This grammatically incorrect utterance actually employs a sophisticated, though unconscious, understanding of grammar. The child knows that the way to form the past tense of most English verbs is to add the *-ed* suffix. This is an application of what Chomsky calls Universal Grammar, enabled by the Language Acquisition Device. The child has observed, verified, and used a rule of English grammar, which is incorrect in this case not because the child failed to observe the rule, but because the verb fails to follow the rule.

The elementary teacher needs to know that children of school age are acquiring vocabulary at a rate of up to twelve new words a day. This is accompanied by an increasing understanding of grammatical and morphological rules. To the extent that a child understands language as an object, as something that can be mastered, the child has developed *metalinguistic* awareness. The teacher can help the child develop metalinguistic awareness as part of a general *metacognitive* approach to learning. In these examples, the morpheme *meta-* means *transcending* or *beyond.* Someone who has a metacognitive approach to learning knows there are skills that can increase learning efficiency and effectiveness; this is someone who has learned how to learn. Increasing metacognitive skills is a primary objective of the educational process.

Lev Vygotsky and the Zone of Proximal Development

While Chomsky's theories focus on biological aspects of language acquisition, Lev Vygotsky's theories concern the influence of the social environment on language development. Vygotsky started from the conviction that our experience of the world is largely determined by language. By the time we are seven years old and fluent in our native tongue, language has become internalized; our thoughts are no longer blurted out for all to hear. At the same time, it has become virtually impossible for us to think without using the conceptual categories provided for us by our acquired language. (Try thinking about something without using words.) Language largely determines the nature of our thoughts, our personalities, and our social interactions. Thus we come full circle: our social environment determines the language we acquire, which in turn creates (in interaction with others) our social environment.

In his thoughts about language acquisition and use, Vygotsky came to the conclusion that the best way for children to acquire new language skills is to be taught within their *Zone of Proximal Development (ZPD).* The ZPD is the area that lies just beyond the child's capacity to solve problems on his own. Within the ZPD, the child is capable of solving problems (concerning, in this instance, language acquisition) with assistance. Beyond the ZPD, the child will not be able to understand the solutions to problems, even with assistance. This concept requires teachers to understand where the ZPD is for each child in the classroom.

One way to determine a child's ZPD and how to operate within it is to observe the child in creative play. Children naturally operate at the boundaries of their capacities while engaged in unstructured play. The teacher can then use the observed boundaries to determine the child's ZPD and create a *scaffolding* for the next steps in learning. The scaffold is the support the teacher gives that enables the child to extend his knowledge. When new knowledge is mastered, the teacher uses that as a scaffold to enable the child to go one step further, and so on.

Stephen Krashen and Second Language Acquisition

Probably the most influential theorist in second language acquisition is Stephen Krashen. Building on Vygotsky's Zone of Proximal Development, Krashen stresses the difference between *traditional language learning,* with its emphasis on studying rules of grammar and building vocabulary, and *natural language acquisition,* modeled on the way young children absorb a native tongue. Language acquisition is largely unconscious and is dependent on comprehensible input, that is, the input appropriate to the ZPD.

The implications for teachers of Krashen's Learning/Acquisition Theories are that children are naturally (Chomsky and LAD) equipped to acquire language in an unconscious way if exposed to comprehensible input (Vygotsky and ZPD). Comprehensible input must be scaffolded within the ZPD so that the language learner can understand it. As the learner understands meaning, she uses her LAD to create structure. This minimizes the need for formal language instruction. In fact, because it is a daunting task to learn another language, over-correction and bombardment with grammatical rules can lead the language learner to construct an affective filter of anxiety and low self-confidence that blocks language acquisition. Teachers should allow beginning English speakers to make mistakes, as they would a toddler, and save more formal instruction for when language learners have reached the stage of writing the language with some fluency.

Literacy and Literacy Assessment

The concept of literacy is a broad one, which encompasses a continuum of skills, attitudes, and perceptions. At its most basic level, literacy involves the decoding and generation of written words, using proper spelling. Literacy doesn't stop there, however. In its broadest sense, literacy is the ability to send and receive communication. It involves listening and speaking, reading and writing, and the capacity to seek out and retrieve information.

Literacy assessment is a crucial aspect of effective teaching. There are many kinds of assessment tools, and each has its place in the teacher's repertoire. Assessment can be formal or informal, but it should be ongoing. The basis for effective assessment is a sound knowledge of normal literacy development with respect to speaking, listening, reading, and spelling.

Speaking and Listening

As was discussed in the section on language development, linguistic development is ongoing in elementary-school children. From a knowledge base of about 5,000 words upon entering school, a child's vocabulary grows by several thousand words each year. A child's speaking vocabulary is an important factor in learning to read because, no matter how well a child sounds out words, she is unable to comprehend a written word that is not in her speaking/listening vocabulary. It is not enough for students to passively receive new words; they must actively use the words in order to truly master them. As students progress in school, they also must master academic language, which is the language of literacy.

There are numerous ways for a teacher to enhance children's vocabularies. One of the best ways is by reading aloud from appropriate literature, which is a good way to utilize the Whole Language approach to reading. Teachers can also model good speaking vocabularies, making sure to contextually convey the meanings of words that might be unfamiliar. You can also use more formal strategies, such as assigning vocabulary words to be learned and used in sentences. The best way for students to enhance their vocabularies, however, is through independent reading.

Reading

The basis of becoming a reader is phonological, or phonemic, awareness. This is an awareness that there are certain repeated sounds that form the basis of the English language. A child who does not have this awareness cannot learn to read. There are many strategies for building phonemic awareness, one of the earliest of which is rhyming activities. Once children can hear and say rhyming patterns, they are ready to distinguish different ending sounds in words, such as *can* and *cat,* or *hat* and *ham*. Then they are ready to start segmenting words into their component phonemes. One way to teach this is to lead the class in stretching out the sounds in words, which can be made into a wonderfully silly game. Once they can segment words into phonemes, children are ready to develop the ability to combine phonemes into words. All of these activities can be done orally, before children actually begin learning to read.

An additional concept—one that often precedes school attendance—is the *alphabetic principle,* the idea that written language represents the sounds of spoken language by means of the alphabet. While many children grasp this principle before starting school, they are usually at the level of invented writing and spelling rather than actual representation. They also need phonemic and phonics instruction before they can begin reading and writing.

To enhance your own phonological knowledge, review the phonetic alphabet. (Look for it in the opening pages of most dictionaries.) Think about the way sounds are represented by letters and letter combinations. The CSET has asked questions about the pronunciation of vowel combinations, so it is a good idea to think about the topic before you get into the exam room. If you have the opportunity, watch the episode of *I Love Lucy* that features Ricky trying to read words made with the letter combination *ough;* it will help raise your awareness. The words *through, though, bough,* and *rough* are all pronounced quite differently. How would you explain that to your students?

Once a child masters the phonemes represented by letters and letter combinations, he learns to *decode* words (identify using word attack strategies); and he practices reading with texts of ascending difficulty, working at each level until he becomes a fluent reader. *Fluency* is defined as the ability to read with appropriate speed and intonation. A fluent reader recognizes most words on sight and is able to read in phrases. A child who struggles over many words is not reading fluently. If he has to expend his mental energy on decoding words, he is unlikely to be grasping the full meaning of what he is reading. There are about 100 words that make up almost half of the commonly encountered words in beginning texts. Many of these are difficult to decode (*the, our, an,* etc.), so they must be explicitly taught and practiced until they can be read automatically.

A skill that develops later in the process of learning to read is the use of contextual clues to check comprehension. Along with context, a more advanced reader uses her knowledge of morphological and spelling patterns to decode new words. As children master phonics, they can begin to break words into their morphological components, rather than just thinking of them as long words. In this way, students acquire the ability to independently acquire new vocabulary as their reading horizons expand. Keep in mind that decoding is not the goal of reading, but rather a means toward the goal, which is comprehension. Comprehension is an active process of constructing meaning from, and along with, a written text. Strategies for enhancing comprehension include having the students make predictions, retell narratives, and determine main ideas.

No matter how skillful a teacher is at explicit instruction, all efforts will fall short unless the students come to associate reading with pleasure. A teacher's ultimate job is to model enthusiasm for reading so that students will be motivated to construct lives in which reading matters. Providing a stimulating learning environment replete with appropriate reading materials helps motivate students to become avid readers.

Reading Difficulties

Research has shown that most children of normal intelligence who lag behind in learning to read exhibit abnormal patterns in the areas of the brain that process phonemes. When the children try to read, those brain areas behave differently from the brains of normal readers. These children are said to have difficulty with phonological processing, which leads to their difficulty in decoding words. Phonological core deficits and low phonemic awareness are prevalent in children with dyslexia. These children have trouble with both segmenting and blending speech sounds. They may actually store faulty representations of phonological information that are then inaccurately applied during reading tasks.

Children with phonological processing deficits need more explicit instruction in segmenting and blending sounds as well as additional metacognitive strategies for distinguishing and differentiating speech sounds and visual representations. They also may be encouraged to develop a larger sight vocabulary of core words that can be automatically identified. Other interventions include reading along while listening to words being read aloud and repeating what has just been read. These children may also derive increased benefits from learning to correctly spell the words they are learning to read.

Another reason for delayed reading levels is a literature-poor home. Children who are neither exposed to reading in the home nor motivated by parents who read frequently need more explicit instruction than those from more advantaged backgrounds. They also need more exposure to interesting literature. Research shows that teachers who pursue a teaching strategy that features generous amounts of whole language exposure coupled with explicit phonological instruction have the best classroom results.

Spelling

In the past, the CSET has asked both multiple-choice and constructed-response questions on spelling development. Spelling has traditionally been taught by rote memorization; but research has shown that phonemic-awareness is closely related to improvements in spelling and has revealed five stages of spelling development.

In the *pre-communicative* stage, a child is aware that letters represent sounds, but is unclear about actual correspondences. The child uses invented spellings, may know only a few letters of the alphabet, and tends to favor capital letters over lower-case ones.

As the child receives initial instruction, he reaches the *semiphonetic* stage. At this stage, the child understands letter-sound correspondence as a principle, though his grasp is far from thorough. He will often, for example, use a single letter to represent a word or syllable (e.g., *u* instead of *you*).

At the *phonetic* stage of spelling development, children begin to systematically represent speech sounds with letters or groups of letters in a logical way. For example, a child may write *kom* instead of *come* or *dun* instead of *done*.

In the *transitional* stage, the speller moves from a dependence on sound and phonology to the use of visual memory and an understanding of word structure. She may, for example, write *highed* instead of *hide* or *egul* instead of *eagle*.

A speller in the *correct* stage knows the correct spellings of many words by memory. He also has learned the basic rules of English orthography (correct spelling), including those involving silent consonants, affixes, and irregular spellings. He can usually identify incorrectly spelled words.

Spelling and writing are best taught in conjunction with each other. Teachers can instruct in meta-cognitive techniques for spelling, such as word structure, word families, and spelling patterns; but it is best to avoid early emphasis on the mechanical aspects of spelling. Purposeful writing is the best tool to enhance spelling development. When formal instruction is appropriate, teachers should use words from the students' own writing, together with high frequency words that are frequently misspelled. For further information on spelling development correlated to grade level, see the English-Language Arts Content Standards for California Public Schools at cde.ca.gov/be/st/ss/engmain.asp.

Assessment

Development in all literacy areas must be continuously monitored and evaluated. There are many tools that may be used to assess language and literacy skills. These assessment tools may be formal, or they may be informal.

Formal assessments are generally *summative* in nature. That is, they take place after a period of learning and are designed to evaluate how well the learning has taken place. Standardized tests are the ultimate summative assessment tools. They are more useful for evaluating groups of students, and thus effectiveness of instruction, than for individual evaluation.

Informal assessments are formative in nature. They are ongoing, classroom-based, and oriented toward individual achievements. Assessment may be performed by the teacher, by peers, or by students themselves. Because they are ongoing, informal assessments provide immediate, useful information. Examples of informal assessments are: portfolios, observations, reading or spelling inventories, student discussions, and running records. Research has shown that student self-assessment is particularly effective in enhancing student achievement by enhancing motivation.

NON-WRITTEN AND WRITTEN COMMUNICATION

Written communication differs from non-written (spoken) communication in many ways. Most notably, written communication is more formal and more standardized than spoken communication, which tends to vary greatly, depending on the speaker and the audience. Children bring to the classroom varying perceptions about language, formed by their experiences within a particular subset of language users (see earlier section on Vygotsky).

Some children will have formed their ideas about language within a community that primarily uses a language other than English. For these children, the teacher will need to provide a comfortable environment in which to acquire basic English skills (see earlier section on Krashen). It is important for teachers to understand areas of overlap and of difference between the child's native language and English. A child whose native language is historically related to English—such as German, Greek, and the Romance languages (derived from Latin), which are French, Spanish, Italian, Portuguese, and Romanian—will have areas of similarity (e.g., common root words) she can build on; but every language shares, at a minimum, the common structure of subject and predicate.

Some native English speakers will start school having learned a dialect of English that varies considerably from the standard English norm. These children will have to learn standard English in order to achieve academic success. Even children who have grown up in environments where standard English is the dominant language form often have difficulty learning the requirements of written English.

Test Yourself

Research has shown that the common denominator of those successful in any field is

(A   talent

(B) effort

(C) motivation

(D) good fortune

The correct answer is **(B)**. Studies show that there is an extremely high correlation between the amount of effort expended and the degree of success. Naturally, there must be motivation in order to expend the effort required to succeed, but motivation, in itself, is not sufficient. Both talent and luck play a role, as well, but effort is the deciding factor in almost every case. Fortunately, effort is the one element most within the individual's control. Teachers can explicitly teach this fact and can also encourage the exertion of effort by setting high standards, which conveys respect for the students' abilities.

Conventions of Standard Written English

Standard written English has conventions of structure, spelling, capitalization, and punctuation. Teachers must be conversant with correct forms of all of these. In the past, CSET questions have focused on structure at the level of the sentence and the paragraph.

The Sentence

You may be asked questions about sentence revision. Look for a revision that will best improve the clarity of the sentence. A good sentence makes sense, without being needlessly wordy or complicated. If you feel you need to brush up on your sentence structure or grammar skills, find a website that teaches what you need to know. Try search terms such as *grammar, sentence structure,* or whatever particular topic you're interested in.

The Paragraph

A paragraph is a group of sentences on a single topic. There are three types of sentences a paragraph may contain: the topic sentence, the body sentences, and the concluding sentence. The topic sentence is often the first sentence of the paragraph, but it doesn't have to be. It is almost always the most general sentence of the paragraph; it conveys the paragraph's subject. Body sentences contain supporting details, analysis, and evidence that expand on the topic sentence. The concluding sentence is often the last or next to last sentence and of the three types is the least essential to the paragraph.

If you are asked to revise or evaluate a paragraph, first determine the topic by reading the paragraph, then look for the sentence that best describes the topic in general, inclusive terms. That will be the topic sentence (it is usually the first or second sentence). Then pay attention to the logic of each supporting sentence. An argument (the type of paragraph you're likely to see on the CSET) must be clearly and logically presented. It may help to put each sentence into your own words so that you are not distracted by difficult or unusual language. If one sentence/thought does not logically follow another, that sentence may be misplaced, and is likely to be the subject of a revision question. Pay particular attention to language that is intended to persuade you of the author's point of view. If a persuasive point is made, ask yourself what information you might need to objectively evaluate the argument.

The Writing Process

Teaching the conventions of good writing is important, but an early focus on conventions often leaves students feeling insecure and suffering from writer's block (the *affective filter*). A better primary focus of instruction is on the stages of writing, the process by which an idea becomes a finished product.

The first stage is *prewriting*. Prewriting includes a variety of techniques designed to help the writer develop and organize her thoughts. One of the most basic techniques is *brainstorming*. In this technique, the writer enjoys her creative process without evaluation or criticism. She writes down as many ideas as she can come up with, letting her mind range as widely as possible. After the brainstorming process is complete, she will come back and think about the practicality and usefulness of her ideas, but not during the process itself. Another way to approach this non-critical idea generation phase is to engage in *freewriting*. Again, the object is to write down the ideas as they come, without regard to structure, grammar, spelling, or even logic; to turn off the inner critic. Once ideas have been generated and evaluated, the writer must *organize* her thoughts. There are many organizational tools, from the traditional outline to the current favorite: *mind mapping*. A mind map starts with the central topic written in the center of a piece of paper. Subtopics branch out from the center, with their individual components clustered around them. Use simple words or phrases, even images, to represent the ideas. Use color; make it fun. Don't worry about the structure; it will evolve on its own.

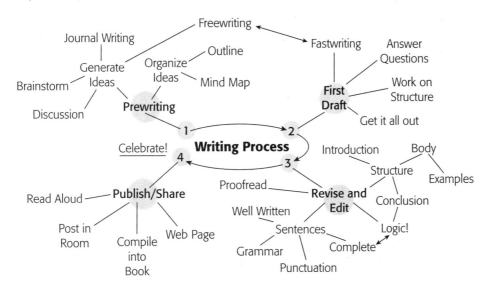

Once the general ideas and structures are in place, it's time to generate a *first draft*. The goal of the first draft is to get everything down on paper. The inner critic should not be too active yet, lest it interfere with momentum; but it should be alert to gaps in logic or structural problems (organization and focus). Save questions of grammar, spelling, and punctuation for later, though.

The most time-consuming phase of the writing process is usually the *revision and editing* phase. This is the time to get everything right. First, logic and structure should be double-checked. The most important question for the writer to ask himself is, "Does this make sense?" The work should have an introduction, a body with examples and details, and a conclusion. Each sentence must be checked for its completeness, grammatical correctness, and punctuation. There must be at least one more draft, which reflects the revisions (and there are always revisions). Current educational theory emphasizes the importance of teaching students to be the primary critics and correctors of their own, and their peers', work, rather than relying on correction by the teacher in every instance. The teacher's role is primarily to ask questions and make suggestions. When revisions satisfy the writer, he proofreads one more time, and then the work is ready for the final step.

The last step in the writing process—not under any circumstances to be overlooked—is publication. This step is primarily the teacher's responsibility and can range from reading the final work aloud, to posting it on a bulletin board, to putting it up on the class web page. Good writing is an achievement to be shared and celebrated.

KAPLAN

Genres of Writing

The two basic kinds of writing are *fiction* and *nonfiction*. All prose (non-poetry) writing falls into one of these two categories. If it's primarily made up, a story invented by the writer, it's fiction. Otherwise, it's nonfiction. Each of these two categories contains several genres, or forms, of writing. In the fictional realm, there are the short story, the novel, the play, the screenplay, and numerous experimental forms. The nonfiction category contains essays, textbooks, research papers, journalism, and more. This book will discuss fiction writing in more detail shortly; first it will deal with nonfiction.

Two means of determining genre in nonfiction are: length and purpose. For example, the difference between an essay and a book is, essentially, length. Purpose is a somewhat more nuanced determinant of genre. If a book-length work is meant to instruct, it's probably a textbook (or a test prep guide). If it is meant to inform, more than to instruct, it's journalism. If it's meant to persuade, it's a polemic. There is a continuum from objective instruction or information to polemic persuasion, and it's not always easy to define exactly where on the continuum a particular work falls.

Persuasion

In today's media-dominated society, it has become increasingly crucial that people understand and analyze the messages they receive. It's easier to do than you may think, but it does require both instruction and practice. The state of California and the makers of the CSET believe that potential teachers should learn these techniques for analyzing persuasive messages and teach them to their students.

Persuasive writing and speech can be identified by its agenda, its purpose. It is designed to get us to think or feel a certain way. Persuasive writing and speech may use logical argument, as, for example, on the newspaper's editorial pages; or it may appeal primarily to emotion, as advertising often does. The job of the critical reader/listener is to ask questions such as:

What does the writer/speaker want me to think/feel?

How do I know what the writer/speaker wants?

What specific language and/or images are used to appeal to my logic or emotions?

Are there any flaws in the logic, any gaps or illogical leaps?

Here is an example of persuasive writing that appeals to the emotions: "Fluffy was born to a mother who desperately loved her, but when Fluffy was six weeks old, she was killed; because no one else wanted her. Every year one million babies are killed because animals can't practice birth control." By evoking the image of mother and baby, using the phrases *desperately loved,* and *one million babies are killed,* and personifying the animal with the name *Fluffy,* the author hopes to get us to identify with the plight of unwanted pets. What action does the author hope will result from this? (Spay and neuter your pets.)

To identify emotional appeals, look at the language used. Examine each word and every phrase, and pay attention to how they make you feel. If you react emotionally to a word (*desperately loved, killed*), chances are that is because the author wants you to react that way; she is trying to persuade you by appealing to your emotions. Persuasive appeals to logic employ slightly different language, but often the language is just as laden with connotations. Look for phrases like *bitter irony* or *unfair advantage;* check for loaded language that will lead you to make judgments, such as *virile* or *vacillating, sublime* or *ridiculous*. Finally, think about what is implied, or *implicit*, as well as what is *explicit* in the piece. Persuasive writing or speaking is a legitimate endeavor, but it is our responsibility as readers/listeners to keep from being manipulated by the writers/speakers; and it's your responsibility as a teacher to help students learn to protect themselves as well. You can practice your analysis of persuasive messages every day by asking yourself questions about what you see and hear. If a message is aimed at persuading you of something, try looking for omitted facts or counter-arguments, even if you agree with the message. As you practice, you'll realize you're getting better in your analyses; and that will make you a better teacher, as well as a better CSET-taker.

Faulty Logic

Not all persuasive messages appeal strictly to the emotions. In fact, there are many logical tricks that can be played by a skillful writer. One of the more common is to offer an opinion disguised as fact. For example, *If Martin Luther King, Jr. had not been killed, Civil Rights struggles would have advanced much further than is now the case*. This is an opinion. You may agree with this opinion, but the crucial test for fact vs. opinion is: can it be verified? In this case, there is no way to verify the statement; therefore it is an opinion.

These are some frequently encountered logical fallacies:

Ad hominem is an attack launched against a person and then, by implication, the person's position. Think of this as the contamination effect. *The candidate is a cowardly man, who will cave in to special interests*. In this case, no evidence is offered; there's merely an assertion (in this case, unsupported) of cowardice, as though that proves the candidate will bow to special interests.

False causality involves treating two or more coincidental conditions as though one causes the other. This logical lapse is featured in the joke about the man who digs a trench all the way around his house. When his neighbor asks why the trench, the man says it's to keep the tigers away. The neighbor points out that there are no tigers within a hundred miles; whereupon the man says, "See how well it works?"

The red herring is an irrelevant point, one designed to distract attention from the argument at hand. For example, in a discussion of underfunded schools, an opponent of a school bond might argue that last year two of the district's teachers were convicted of felonies, a statement both irrelevant to whether or not the bond should pass and obviously designed to turn voters against the schools.

Overgeneralization often features stereotyping. *Never trust anyone over thirty* was a common overgeneralization of the 1960s. If the statement features a word such as *almost, usually,* or *perhaps*, it's not technically an overgeneralization. Look for *never, always, inevitable,* or similarly absolute words.

The bandwagon effect counts on your being convinced by a position's popularity. The classic example is probably, *But mom, everybody else's mom lets them do it!*

Begging the question involves including an assumption within the argument, as though the assumption had already been proven. This is sometimes called *circular reasoning*. An example is, *Because I always tell the truth, I am not lying to you now.*

Research Writing

Another genre of nonfiction that merits the attention of elementary teachers is the academic research paper. Academic research covers a broad range of works, from the second grader's one page report to the Ph.D. dissertation. Teachers must be knowledgeable about both library resources, such as the Reader's Guide to Periodicals, and Internet resources, such as search engines. If it's been a while since you checked out all the reference resources in the library and refreshed your memory of the Dewey Decimal System, now would be a good time to brush up on your skills. If Internet research has intimidated you, just take the plunge. Don't have access? Almost all libraries now have Internet-connected computers for you to use. You can even ask the librarian for help getting started.

Accessing resources is the first step in writing a good research paper. The last step is compiling a bibliography, but it's a step you must be preparing for from the beginning by keeping accurate notes on your sources. There are several standard formats for bibliographies, but the most commonly accepted is the Modern Language Association (MLA) style. If you are not familiar with this, you should look it up, either online or at the library (or online at the library) and familiarize yourself. The CSET may well contain a question on writing bibliographies.

Non-written Communication

Surveys reveal that Americans are more afraid of public speaking than of dying. Perhaps that's because most of them simply haven't had enough practice. Speaking before a group is essentially the same kind of communication that speaking to one other person is. In both public and private speech situations, however, there are stylistic differences between formal speech and informal speech. At one extreme, two high school friends employ elliptical speech, full of slang: "Remember that time…with that dude, and that 'shake? Dude, that was whack!" The same speaker, in a more formal situation, might say, "Do you remember the time we watched a boy spill his milkshake and then try to clean it up? That must have been embarrassing!"

A primary difference between oral communication and written communication is the presence of contextual clues. A speaker can point, shrug, nod, wink, or employ any number of other gestures to convey meaning. She can, in most cases, observe the reactions of her audience and gauge their comprehension and degree of agreement. A speaker also enjoys a flexibility that a writer does not; once the writing is published, it is difficult to retract or revise, but a speaker can add or delete or revamp as necessary in the moment. Finally, a speaker is almost always speaking to a particular, known audience and so may choose to employ a dialect or jargon or slang that will be understood by that audience; whereas a writer usually chooses to write for as broad an audience as possible, and so uses the conventions of standard English. A speaker who does not know her audience may choose to use those conventions as well, as for example, a television news anchor or commentator.

A teacher must be aware of what makes an effective speaker. For one thing, you'll be doing a lot of public speaking. It is important to know how to hold the attention of an audience. Use your body as well as your voice to keep the class from being lulled to sleep. Vary your rate of speech and the volume of your speech. It can be tempting to just pick up the pace and the volume if you perceive you're losing your audience. That can result in your speaking faster and faster, louder and louder, as your class collectively tunes out. Try, instead, lowering your voice in order to get their attention. Make sure that you're not always speaking either rapidly or slowly. Perhaps most importantly, move a lot. Make lots of gestures, employ animated facial expressions, and walk around the room. Stand near a student who's not paying attention; go to the back of the room to talk for a few minutes; prowl the aisles. Not knowing where you're going next is a strong motivator for students to pay attention.

TEXTS

The CSET provides many opportunities to analyze texts. Teachers are expected to be able to read texts for both explicit and implicit messages and to use evidence from the texts to support their interpretations. They must be able to identify genres and subgenres and to discuss texts in terms of literary devices and traditions.

Test Yourself

From the following list of words used in a poem, determine the tone the poet establishes in the poem: *long, silent, blind, blackness, stumble, fall, silent, dry, run, runs, turn, nobody, dark, doorless, turning, turning, forever, nobody, waits, follows, pursue, stumbles, rises, nobody.*

(A) anxious

(B) ordinary

(C) passive

(D) angry

The correct answer is **(A)**. These words are from the poem *The Street* by Octavio Paz, which is reproduced on the CSET website: cset.nesinc.com. When you read a poem or other text, underline words that evoke feelings, images, and associations. These are the words that will point you toward the author's meaning and intentions, which are often conveyed as much by tone as by literal word meanings. On the CSET, you are more likely to see an entire poem than a list of words like this, so it will be up to you to compile your own list as you read the text.

Genres and Subgenres

All written work is either *poetry* or *prose*. There are three kinds of poetry, which will be discussed later in the chapter in the section on poetry. Prose can be classified into *fiction* or *nonfiction*. The previous section on writing dealt with nonfiction and its genres; this section will discuss the genres and conventions of fiction. The three main genres of fiction are *short stories, novels,* and *plays* (including *screenplays*). The short story was classically defined by Edgar Allan Poe, who was the first to identify the genre. Most salient to the definition is the requirement that a short story be short enough to be read in a single sitting. Anything longer than that is a novel, or the shorter *novella.* The play is meant to be performed, and it is discussed in Chapter 7 of this book. Any one of these genres may employ a subgenre, such as *satire, parody,* or *allegory*.

KAPLAN

Satire

Satire exposes, often humorously, the follies, foibles, and vices of a group or system (e.g., institutions, ideas, or societies). It often employs elevated, formal language to skewer the pretensions of the powerful. Criticism is always present, but often implied rather than explicit. *Gulliver's Travels* is the prototypical satire, often read by upper elementary children as an adventure, but properly appreciated as a humorous criticism of the foibles of author Jonathan Swift's time.

Satires often use *irony* to make a point. Irony is one of the more often misused terms in literary analysis. Irony is the tension, or difference, between what is expected (or what appears to be) and what actually is the case. For example, it would be ironic if the firehouse burned down, as that's not what common perceptions about fire departments lead you to expect. It is not ironic for it to rain on your wedding day or to encounter a traffic jam when you're running late.

Parody

Parody is a humorous form that uses as a point of departure another, well-known work. It mimics the style and conventions of the other, serious work. Mark Twain's *A Connecticut Yankee in King Arthur's Court* is a parody of more serious Arthurian writings, such as Sir Thomas Mallory's *Le Morte D'Arthur*. Better known examples of contemporary parody are song parodies, which adopt the melody of a hit song and rewrite the lyrics for humorous effect.

Allegory

An *allegory* is an extended *metaphor*. Metaphor is a comparison between two unlike things as though they were the same. (*Life is a bowl of cherries*.) When the metaphor is carried throughout an entire narrative, it becomes allegory. An allegory has one surface meaning and another underlying meaning. Allegory is one of the primary tools authors can use to draw parallels between specific events, as portrayed in the story, and more general, abstract ideas.

The medieval morality play *Everyman* (Anon.) is a drama in which the character Everyman asks various other characters to accompany him to his death, but the only one who will stick around to the end is Good Deeds. The play is an allegory of life and death, and the characters are personifications of abstract qualities. (*Personification* attributes human qualities to non-human animals or objects.) *Animal Farm*, by George Orwell, is a twentieth-century example of an allegory which personifies animals. Personification and allegory are not necessarily linked, however.

Children's Literature

Much children's literature, both traditional and contemporary, takes the form of *fantasy*. Fantasy subgenres include fairy tales, folktales, and mythology (subgenres not created specifically for children, as there was no children's literature *per se* before the late 1700s); books such as *Alice in Wonderland*, *The Wizard of Oz,* the works of Dr. Seuss; and the subgenre of science fiction. Fantasy often employs *archetypes*, which are models or patterns instantly recognizable for their universal characteristics (e.g., the wicked stepmother, the wise king, the foolish boy), to anchor the fantastical story in psychological reality.

Traditional tales, such as folk tales and fables, originated and developed over time through oral traditions. They were not written down until they had already been repeated for many generations. As a story was repeated, it was polished and simplified until only the simple, beautiful bones of the story remained constant. Likewise, language that had been used by gifted storytellers was repeated by subsequent retellers until the story was finally written down. As a result, these tales come to us characterized by simple narrative structures and language that often repeats key words and phrases. Many of these stories convey some understanding of the world.

The word *mythology* comes from the Greek word *mythos,* meaning *story*. It has come to be used for the stories every culture creates in order to make sense of the world. It is natural and very common for people to wonder where they came from, what their purpose is, and what the meaning of life could be. Mythologies are culturally approved answers to these questions and lessons to live by. Every culture has mythological stories, always including a creation story that details the origin of the people, often from underground or from beyond the sky. Mythological cycles also recount tales of gods, humans, and often animals in a distant time, very like, and yet unlike, our own.

More modern children's fiction is often more realistic. Authors such as Judy Bloom and Beverly Cleary write stories about recognizable characters in plausible situations. They build on traditions passed down from such authors as Louisa May Alcott (*Little Women*) and Mark Twain (*The Adventures of Huckleberry Finn*).

ANALYSIS OF TEXTS

In order to effectively analyze texts, it is necessary to understand some of the writer's options. The first choice a writer makes is between poetry and prose. If she chooses prose, she must then decide between fiction and nonfiction. If she chooses to write fiction, she then has at her disposal a number of conventions commonly used in fiction writing.

The Four Rhetorical Strategies

Rhetoric is the term for a collection of strategies and language choices writers use to achieve their goals. Even writers who seem to have no overt agenda make rhetorical choices designed to convey their perspectives. In the case of fiction writers, the choices are meant to create a world that will seem real, or at least plausible. There are four basic rhetorical approaches, which most writers employ in a mix-and-match fashion. They are:

- *Narrative* writing tells a story. It describes events and actions sequentially, though not necessarily chronologically.
- *Expository* writing presents information. In the case of fiction, this is background information necessary to understanding the story. Good fiction writers minimize exposition and try to surround it with action whenever possible, as exposition is usually not as compelling as narration.
- *Persuasive* writing is designed to convince the reader of the author's point of view. You read a discussion of this rhetorical strategy in the previous section on written communication.
- *Descriptive* writing paints a picture of the fictional world. It includes appeals to all the senses. Good writers are usually skilled at conveying sensory detail.

KAPLAN

The Elements of Fiction

In order to talk about fiction, it is necessary to know the elements that comprise it. Though much contemporary fiction experiments with standard structures, the CSET focuses on traditional forms. Traditional fiction writing includes, at a minimum, certain elements like plot, characterization, setting, theme, and point of view.

Plot

Plot is what happens in a story. It is the narrative structure of the fictional work. A typical narrative structure starts with (usually minimal) exposition, which introduces the characters (or at least the main character), the setting, and any necessary prelude to the story. Soon the main character encounters an obstacle or complication which requires him to act. This starts the *rising action,* which is then fueled by further complications, which are met by more action from the characters. This continues until the *climax,* which is the high point of the story, the most exciting moment. Usually, then, the author wraps up the story as quickly as possible. This wrapping-up is called the *denouement,* a French word meaning *unknotting* or *untwisting.*

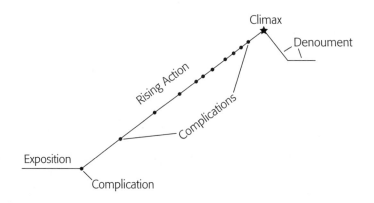

Characterization

Characterization is the creation of characters that populate the story. Characters may be nonhuman, as in *Charlotte's Web,* but successful characterization involves presenting the characters' human traits in order to evoke emotional responses from the reader. The main character in a work of fiction is usually meant to be sympathetic and is often known as the *hero* or the *protagonist.* The character who opposes the protagonist is called the *antagonist* or sometimes the *nemesis.* Both *dialogue,* the conversation between two or more characters, and *interior monologue,* a character's thoughts and feelings, are important means of establishing character.

Setting

Setting is the environment in which the story takes place. It includes all aspects of the physical surroundings as well as the time period and social environment in which the action occurs. Setting is often an important clue to the author's purpose in writing the story (the theme).

Theme

Theme is the central or unifying concept of the story. It is what the author hopes to convey with his writing, the perception, feeling, or idea that he wants to communicate. *Love conquers all* is an example of a theme (most romances), as is *goodness is rewarded* (*Cinderella*), and *careful what you wish for* (*The Three Wishes*). In determining theme, it is important to take into account the author's time period and social/cultural context, if those are known.

Point of View

Point of view is the perspective from which the story is told. If the storyteller, or *narrator,* is saying *I (did this* or *said that),* the point of view is *first person*. This limits the information that can go into the story, because the author can present only what the narrator knows, and any one person's perspective is naturally limited. If the author's is clearly the voice being heard, the point of view is *third person*. *Third person omniscient* may include information about what any and all characters are thinking and feeling, as well as any other information or perspectives the author wishes to present. This point of view is the least restrictive for the writer. *Third person limited* point of view, as its name implies, is restricted to the experiences, thoughts, and feelings of a single person other than the narrator.

Language Tools

When it comes to interpreting passages for the CSET, you will be most interested in analyzing the work at the level of the sentence and the individual word. The choices authors make in word use reveal much about their intentions. Therefore, it really pays off to look at each word carefully. Some types of words, particularly adjectives and verbs, will usually be more revealing than others, but develop the habit of examining each word in a passage for all its implicit meanings (connotations) as well as its explicit meanings (denotations).

Style and Tone

Style, or word choice, is a major contributor to the meaning of a literary work. At the level of the sentence and the individual word, authors make stylistic choices that set the *tone*, or attitude, of their work. Examination of the writer's choice of adjectives can be an especially useful strategy in assessing tone. For example, a good student could be described as *scholarly* or as *bookish*. These two words both mean (denote) *studious,* but they have very different connotations, or associations. *Scholarly* brings with it associations of respect and status, while *bookish* has insulting connotations, implying a person who is not well-rounded by virtue of spending so much time with books. Which one of these words an author chooses to use in describing a studious person will reveal her attitude toward that character. Tone, however, is a term usually applied to the work as a whole, or at least to a section of a work.

Figures of Speech

Another means of deducing tone is to look at the author's use of figurative language, such as *figures of speech*. Figures of speech, also called rhetorical *tropes,* are uses of language that are not meant to be taken literally, or at least not *only* literally. For example, in the sentence, *The forces of change were already closing in on our little farm like a speeding freight train,* it is understood that the forces of change are not a literal freight train. However, we are meant to interpret the author's meaning by using connotations for the object *freight train*. What is the author's attitude toward *forces of change?* Anything hit by a freight train is pretty much obliterated, so we could say from this one sentence that the tone is related to tragedy. Depending on the context surrounding this sentence, the tone could be resigned, determined, frightened, or something else. Again, it takes more than one sentence to set tone.

In the example just cited, *freight train* is a *symbol*. That is, it signifies, or stands for, something else. Writers often use symbols, again because of their connotations. If you see a reference to a lion, ask yourself if it's really just a lion or meant to evoke connotations of bravery, dominance, ferocity. If the writer mentions a lamb, is it really just a lamb, or are you meant to think of gentle meekness? Language is full of symbols, so when you have to interpret a passage for the CSET, look closely at the language and ask yourself if the author is using *rose* literally (only), or if he wants you to also think of the rose's thorns.

Poetry

Maybe you're one of the many literate people who cringe at the mention of poetry. You've never understood the stuff, and your English teacher always told you that your interpretations were wrong. If so, then shame on your English teacher. Poetry is the most subjective form of writing, the form most open to a variety of interpretations. The key to understanding poetry—especially the kind of poetry presented on the CSET—is to trust yourself. Trust your emotional reactions to the language the poet uses. Read the poem, and hear it in your mind. Poetry is like music, employing language instead of notes; it has rhythms (meter), which are created by the naturally emphasized syllables of the words.

Poetry appeals to your senses. Look for words that evoke smell, taste, sound, sight, and touch. The first time you read a poem, instead of trying to understand it logically, just relax and let the language soak in. The second time you read it, underline sensory language and words that could be symbols. Look for such figures of speech as metaphors (previously defined, remember?) and *similes,* which are comparisons of two dissimilar things using *like* or *as.* (For example, *He was strong as an ox* is a simile.) Identify personification (e.g., *the sky is crying*). Find *parallelism,* a structural device in which words, phrases, or ideas are repeated, once or several times. Notice the poet's choice of adjectives, her choice of verbs. Don't even worry about what the poem means until you've read it through two or three times, heard it, felt it, and identified the poetic uses of language. If you let yourself feel the poem, you'll understand what it means. If you're anxious about understanding it, you won't be able to feel it.

The CSET, in the past, has used poems that do not have difficult language, or even difficult syntax (unlike some poems you may have read in school). The questions that have been asked relate to the poet's meaning, as revealed through the use of language. Take a deep breath: if you can relax and trust yourself, you can answer the questions, and maybe even appreciate the poems.

Glossary

Allegory: an extended metaphor, with one surface meaning and another underlying meaning

Antagonist: the character who opposes the main character in a work of fiction

Archetypes: models or patterns instantly recognizable for their universal characteristics

Characterization: the creation of characters to populate a story

Climax: the high point of a narrative

Connotation: the set of associations a word conveys, as opposed to its strict definition

Denotation: the definition of a word

Denouement: the wrap-up of a story, after the climax

Descriptive writing: writing that paints a picture of a fictional world

Dialogue: conversation between two or more characters in fiction

Expository writing: writing that presents information critical for understanding of a whole piece

Figures of speech (such as metaphor, simile, and symbol): uses of language that are not meant to be taken literally

Formative assessments: informal assessments that are ongoing, classroom-based, and oriented toward individual achievements

Interior monologue: (in fiction) reveals a character's thoughts and feelings

Irony: the tension, or difference, between what is expected (or what appears to be) and what is actually the case

Language Acquisition Device (LAD): the innate structural predisposition of the human brain to make sense of language (to acquire the specific sets of phonemes, morphemes, and syntactical structures that belong to any specific language system)

Metacognition: the awareness that there are skills that can increase learning efficiency and effectiveness; learning how to learn

Metaphor: a comparison between two unlike things as though they were the same

Meter: the rhythm of a poem. It may be regular or irregular

Morphemes: the sound sequences (sequences of phonemes) that convey meaning

Morphology: the study of word structure

Narrative writing: writing that tells a story

Natural language acquisition: a type of learning modeled on the way young children absorb a native tongue (as opposed to traditional language learning, with its rule-oriented teaching)

Parallelism: a structural device in which words, phrases, or ideas are repeated, once or several times

Parody: a humorous subgenre of fiction that mimics the style and conventions of another, serious work

Personification: the attribution of human qualities to non-human animals or objects

Persuasive writing: writing designed to convince the reader of the author's point of view

Phonemes: sounds that signal differences in meaning

Phonological awareness (phonemic awareness): the understanding that words are composed of sounds called phonemes

Phonology: the study of the way sounds function in language

Plot: what happens in a story

Point of view: the perspective from which a story is told

Pragmatics: the study of the social, physical, and cultural contexts of language use

Protagonist: the main character in a work of fiction

Rhetoric: the term for a collection of strategies and language choices writers use to achieve their goals

Satire: exposes, often humorously, the follies, foibles, and vices of a group or system (e.g., institutions, ideas, or societies)

Scaffolding: the support a teacher provides to enable a student to extend his knowledge

Semantics: the study of the ways in which sounds, words, sentences, etc., are used to convey meaning in language, including the effect of context on meaning

Setting: the environment in which a story takes place

Simile: a comparison of two dissimilar things using *like* or *as*

Summative assessments (e.g., standardized tests): take place after a period of learning and are designed to evaluate how well the learning has taken place

Symbol: a use of figurative language in which a word or phrase signifies, or stands for, something else, in addition to itself

Syntax: the grammatical structure of sentences

Theme: the central or unifying concept of a work of art

Tone: a term for the attitude of an artistic work

Universal Grammar: the general properties that underlie and govern the development of all human languages

Zone of Proximal Development (ZPD): the difference between a child's capacity to solve a problem on his own and his ability to solve the problem with assistance

PRACTICE SET

1. Which of the following phonological awareness skills is considered easiest for young students to acquire?

   (A) blending sounds together to form a spoken word (e.g., *b* + *u* + *g* = *bug*)

   (B) identifying the initial sound in a word (e.g., *k* in *kitty*)

   (C) recognizing that two words contain the same phoneme (e.g., *cheese* and *lunch*)

   (D) identifying a word that does not belong in a group of spoken words (e.g., *cake, cane, man*)

2. The study of how sounds, words, phrases, and sentences combine to convey meaning and context is

   (A) syntax

   (B) morphology

   (C) semantics

   (D) phonology

3. Which of the following represents the morphology of the word *astronomy*?

   (A) as-tron-o-my

   (B) *astronomy* comes from the Greek language

   (C) *astron* = star(s) + *nomos* = law; therefore, *astronomy* = the law of the stars

   (D) a science involving the observation and explanation of events occurring outside Earth and its atmosphere

4. Which of the following statements is *not* a good pedagogical reason for a teacher to dictate *grill* and *girl* to her third-grade students?

   (A) Students will need to listen for subtle differences in sound.

   (B) The dictation will encourage phonological awareness.

   (C) Students will begin to understand the influence of vowel-like consonants—in this case *r*—on a vowel—in this case *i*.

   (D) Students will better understand prescriptive grammar.

5. Some common vowel patterns are associated with more than one pronunciation (e.g., the *oo* in *wood* and *moon*). Which of the following nonsense words illustrates a vowel pattern that is highly consistent in its pronunciation?

   (A) strow

   (B) klead

   (C) wough

   (D) nain

KAPLAN

6. The languages of the world are similar to each other in all of the following ways *except*

   (A) the rules of morphology (e.g., adding *s* to a singular noun to make it plural)

   (B) the basic principles of phrase structure (e.g., subject-predicate order in a sentence)

   (C) the fact that the phonemes and morphemes of a language are arbitrary

   (D) a logical syntax

7. In which of the following sentences is the italicized word used correctly?

   (A) Do you often *complement* your students?

   (B) These shoes will certainly *complement* your new dress.

   (C) Fortunately, the newborn had the entire *compliment* of fingers and toes.

   (D) Stan is shy and Maria is outgoing; they *compliment* each other nicely.

8. What kind of verbal is the word *cooking* in the sentence "I think cooking should be taught in elementary school"?

   (A) a gerund

   (B) an infinitive

   (C) an adverbial

   (D) a participle

9. Which of the following word identification strategies is typically easiest for young children to practice while reading?

   (A) sounding out, by applying phonics knowledge

   (B) using context clues of surrounding words

   (C) recognizing sight words

   (D) analyzing word structure

10. Which of the following sentences contains a relative clause?

    (A) Chloe is a capable swimmer, but she couldn't beat her best friend Sally in the relay.

    (B) The book that fell open was leather bound.

    (C) When I move from Sacramento, will you write me?

    (D) After studying all night, Tim overslept and he missed his exam.

11. The field of pragmatics considers the social, physical, and cultural contexts of languages. Which of the following is *not* an example of a pragmatic element of a culture?

    (A) Italian speakers use expressive hand movements when talking.

    (B) Japanese speakers employ neutral or respect forms of their language when addressing strangers and elders.

    (C) Senegalese *griots* (oral historians) sing about a lineage of ancestors and their deeds.

    (D) English speakers can pronounce "read" as either [reed] or [red].

12. Which of the following is the best example of Noam Chomsky's theory of Universal Grammar, as reflected in a child's linguistic error?

    (A) "Tommy ain't sharing!"

    (B) "Me want the puzzle!"

    (C) "My kitty is not never coming back."

    (D) "I see three mans."

13. Prewriting strategies include all but which of the following:

    (A) outlining

    (B) webbing

    (C) editing

    (D) note-taking

Use the excerpt below to answer the question that follows.

[1]Our belief in the inherent worth and dignity of every person, the democratic process, a world community in peace, and respect for the interconnected web of life on this earth inspires us all to social action. [2]As youth, we must be on the forefront of all movements for peace and justice. [3]We are not just the future; we are the present! [4]These are our lives, right now, that are affected by every policy and practice in this world. [5]Therefore, we need to use our energy and power to change systems of oppression and injustice.

14. Which of the following is the topic sentence of the above paragraph?

    (A) Sentence 1

    (B) Sentence 2

    (C) Sentence 3

    (D) Sentence 4

KAPLAN

15. Which of the following presentation components would be most important to a poetry recitation?

    (A) organization and volume

    (B) pace and organization

    (C) gesture and volume

    (D) pace and enunciation

Read the passage below; then answer the two questions that follow.

[1]Schoolwork may be associated with non-school environments. [2]What about the kitchen? [3]The den? [4]In fact, any room in which a student habitually studies becomes a learning space or a place associated with thinking. [5]Some students need to engage in sports or other physical activity before they can work successfully; being sedentary seems to inspire others. [6]Some need a less flexible schedule than others, while it is understood that a very few can sit and not rise until their task is completed. [7]Some students work quickly and efficiently, while others cannot produce anything without much dust and heat. [8]If asked what space is reserved for learning, many students would suggest the classroom, the lab, or the library.

[passage adapted from uottawa.ca/academic/arts/writcent/hypergrammar/grammar.html]

16. Which of the following changes listed below could best improve the logical organization of the above passage?

    (A) Move Sentence 2 so that it follows Sentence 4.

    (B) Move Sentence 5 so that it follows Sentence 1.

    (C) Move Sentence 7 so that it follows Sentence 8.

    (D) Move Sentence 8 so that it follows Sentence 1.

17. Which of the following revisions of Sentence 6 would improve the style of the passage?

    (A) Some need a less flexible schedule than others, while a very few can sit and not rise until their task is completed.

    (B) Some need a less flexible schedule than others; nevertheless, a very few can sit and not rise until their task is completed.

    (C) Some students have need of a less flexible schedule than others, while a very few have need of sitting and not rising until their task is completed.

    (D) Some need a less flexible schedule than others need, and a very few can sit and not rise until their task is completed.

18. According to Krashen's Natural Language Approach, learning a second language should include which of the following?

    (A) a traditional, formal approach to the language

    (B) attention to grammatical mistakes made by the student

    (C) knowing all the grammar and syntax rules

    (D) care not to overcorrect the student

19. Which one of the following sentences is *not* correctly punctuated?

    (A) Fight road grime by washing your car frequently, however, don't scrub off the protective wax.

    (B) Fight road grime by washing your car frequently, but don't scrub off the protective wax.

    (C) Fight road grime by washing your car frequently. However, don't scrub off the protective wax.

    (D) Fight road grime by washing your car frequently; however, don't scrub off the protective wax.

20. A teacher has many and varied objectives in the teaching of literacy to his students. Considering this, which of the following is *least* likely to be an objective?

    (A) the decoding of written words by reading

    (B) developing appropriate assessment tools

    (C) generating words using proper grammar and spelling

    (D) learning to seek out and retrieve information

    Use the following speech excerpt to answer the two questions that follow.

    [1]The Arctic National Wildlife Refuge is home to caribou, moose, musk oxen, wolves, foxes, grizzlies, polar bears, and migratory birds. [2]Leaders in the oil industry believe the refuge is the perfect site for the "environmentally sensitive exploration" of oil, in other words, drilling. [3]Environmentalists are wondering, "What will become of the wildlife?" [4]I believe the cost to our environment of such destructive drilling is too high.

21. Which of the following sentences most strongly suggests that the above speech excerpt is persuasive in its intent?

    (A) Sentence 1

    (B) Sentence 2

    (C) Sentence 3

    (D) Sentence 4

22. Which of the following research questions provides the most appropriate starting point for an objective investigation into the issues raised in this excerpt?

    (A) Are there other endangered refuges in the Unites States?

    (B) How do the opponents of oil exploration plan to organize protest?

    (C) How do the proponents of drilling propose to be environmentally sensitive in their exploration for oil?

    (D) Why are environmental issues the business of oil lobbies?

23. What subject matter is most likely to be found in a parable?

    (A) the origins of the earth and human beings

    (B) a moral tale involving animals as characters

    (C) the history of a culture

    (D) the importance of love

Read the excerpt below from Carl Sandburg's poem "Chicago"; then answer the two questions that follow.

Chicago

Hog Butcher for the World,

Tool Maker, Stacker of Wheat,

Player with Railroads and the Nation's Freight Handler;

Stormy, husky, brawling,

City of the Big Shoulders.

24. In this poem, Sandburg suggests that the source of Chicago's raw energy and optimism is

    (A) its vigorous laboring class

    (B) a muscular, male pair of shoulders

    (C) the nation's railroad system that connects it with other urban centers

    (D) the production of meat

25. What literary device is Sandburg using when addressing the city of Chicago as an individual?

    (A) allusion

    (B) simile

    (C) alliteration

    (D) personification

26. The Muppets' "Monsterpiece Theater" mimics the PBS show "Masterpiece Theater." This type of work is called a(n)

    (A) fantasy

    (B) parody

    (C) novella

    (D) allegory

Constructed-Response Question 1

Read the poem below, "Workers Song," by Maya Angelou; then complete the exercise that follows.

Workers Song

Big ships shudder down to the sea

Because of me

Railroads run on the twinness track

'Cause of my back

Whoppa, Whoppa

Whoppa, Whoppa

Cars stretch to a super length

'Cause of my strength

Planes fly high over seas and lands

'Cause of my hands

Whoppa, Whoppa

Whoppa, Whoppa

I wake

Starts the factory humming

I work late

Keep the whole world running

And I got something...something coming...coming

Whoppa, Whoppa

Whoppa

Describe the use of sound devices—such as alliteration, onomatopoeia, and rhyme scheme—in Angelou's poem. Be sure to cite specific evidence from the text.

_____

_____

_____

_____

_____

Constructed-Response Question 2

Complete the exercise that follows.

Identify two influences that would facilitate language acquisition during early to middle childhood, citing examples of each.

_____

_____

_____

_____

_____

_____

_____

_____

_____

_____

_____

_____

_____

_____

_____

_____

_____

_____

_____

_____

_____

_____

_____

_____

_____

_____

KAPLAN

ANSWER KEY

1. B	8. A	15. D	22. C
2. C	9. A	16. D	23. B
3. C	10. B	17. A	24. A
4. D	11. D	18. D	25. D
5. D	12. D	19. A	26. B
6. A	13. C	20. B	
7. B	14. B	21. D	

ANSWERS AND EXPLANATIONS

1. B

The most basic skill in phonological awareness begins with children identifying simple phonemes, the easiest being initial hard consonants, such as *b* in *boy*. The other three choices, (A), (C), and (D), are more advanced skills.

2. C

Semantics is the study of how sounds, words, phrases, and sentences combine to convey meaning and context. Syntax (A) is sentence structure. Morphology (B) is the study of word structure, of how sounds and syllables combine to produce meaning. Phonology (D) is the study of the way sounds function in a particular language.

3. C

Morphology is the study of word structure (how word parts combine to form words) as in (C). Choice (A) refers to syllabification—how the word *astronomy* is divided into syllables. Choice (B) concerns the word's derivation: *astronomy* comes from the Greek language. Choice (D) cites the definition of *astronomy*.

4. D

Choices (A), (B), and (C), are all appropriate pedagogical reasons to dictate close-sounding words. Choice (D) is correct because this particular dictation would reflect issues of structural linguistics, not prescriptive (or traditional) grammar.

5. D

The *ai* vowel pattern is associated with the "long *a*" sound in words such as *rain, maid,* and *praise*. Studies of sound-symbol correspondences in English have found very few exceptions to this rule (one being *said*). Choices (A), (B), and (C) are associated with multiple pronunciations: the *ow* in *strow* is found in *cow* and *slow*; the *ea* in *klead* is found in *bread* and *team*; the *ou* in *wough* is found in *ought, rough, doubt,* and *although*.

6. A

The rules of morphology change from language to language; for example, adding *s* to a singular noun to make it plural applies (as a general rule) to English, Spanish, and French, but not to German, Wolof, or Japanese. The remaining three choices, (B), (C), and (D), reflect truths for all languages.

7. B

The homonyms *complement* and *compliment* are often confused. Choice (A) should read *Do you often compliment your students?* Choice (B) uses *complement* correctly, with its meaning "to make something complete or perfect." Choice (C) should read *Fortunately, the newborn had the entire complement of fingers and toes,* the word *complement* meaning "an entirety of something." Choice (D) should read *Stan is shy and Maria is outgoing; they complement each other nicely.*

8. A

A gerund is the *–ing* form of a verb when it is used as a noun, as it is in this question. An infinitive **(B)** is the "to" form of a verb that can be used as a noun, as in *Sheila loves to cook.* As for **(C)**, *cooking* cannot be an adverbial. A participle **(D)** can be part of a verb, as in *Tina was cooking a meal* or an adjective, as in *He forgot his cooking apron.*

9. A

"Sounding out" typically comes before understanding context **(B)**, recognizing sight words **(C)** or the most complex skill, analyzing word structure **(D)**. A young reader experiments with the phonics rules of his language (e.g., "bath" may at first be read as "buh-aah-tuh-huh"—*b* as in *boy*; and *at* looks like *at* as in *cat*, until the reader recognizes— or is shown—that *t + h* goes together in our phonics system, as a blend that is similar to *th* in *the* or even closer to *th* in *tooth*).

10. B

A *clause* is a group of words consisting of a subject and a predicate, the two main types being *independent* and *dependent*. An independent clause can stand alone as a viable simple sentence. A dependant clause cannot stand alone as a sentence—it "depends" on an independent clause. In the correct choice **(B)**, "The book that fell open was leather bound," *that fell open* is a relative clause serving as a modifying clause or an adjective clause to *book*. The remaining choices contain no relative clauses. Choice **(A)** is a compound sentence; **(C)** is a complex interrogatory; and **(D)** is a compound-complex sentence.

11. D

Pragmatics is a systematic way of explaining language use in context. It seeks to explain aspects of meaning that cannot be found in the plain sense of words or structures, as explained by semantics. Choices **(A)**, **(B)**, and **(C)** present social, physical, or cultural contexts for communication: Italian speakers use expressive hand movements when talking; Japanese speakers employ neutral or respect forms of their language when addressing strangers and elders; and Senegalese *griots* (oral historians) sing about a lineage of ancestors and their deeds. Choice **(D)** describes merely a pronunciation issue that is not related to a cultural difference or language in a special context.

12. D

Universal Grammar is a theory of linguistics proposing the existence of underlying principles of grammar shared by all languages. These underlying principles are said to be innate to all human beings. This theory does not attempt to claim that all human languages have the same grammar; rather, it proposes that there exists an underlying set of rules that helps children to acquire their particular language. In this question, the best example of a child's error using Universal Grammar is **(D)**. The young speaker says *mans* instead of *men* because he or she has already (innately) absorbed and understood that, in English, plurals are *usually* formed by adding "s" (or the "s" sound, as in "buses"). The speaker has not yet learned that the plural of *man* is *men*—an exception to the rule. The remaining three choices are grammatical mistakes, but they are not based on a universal rule. In **(A)**, the speaker uses the colloquial or slang word "ain't." In **(B)**, the speaker uses the objective pronoun *me* in lieu of the correct nominative pronoun *I*. In **(C)**, the speaker uses a double negative.

13. C

Editing is not a prewriting strategy—it follows drafting or writing and includes proofreading and revising. Prewriting is the initial creative stage of writing and may include techniques such as outlining **(A)**, webbing **(B)**, and note-taking **(D)**.

14. B

In this passage, the second sentence, *As youth, we must be on the forefront of all movements for peace and justice*, is the topic sentence because it expresses the main thought from which all the other sentences in the paragraph emanate. The other three choices **(A)**, **(C)**, and **(D)** are sentences that elaborate on the topic sentence.

15. D

Organization (in **(A)** and **(B)**) is not a presentation component, and, in any case, would not be an issue in a poetry recitation. Gesture and volume **(C)**, while necessary to consider, would not be the *most* important elements of a poetry recitation. Since poetry often engages wordplay, rhythm, meter, and/or rhyme for impact, pace and enunciation **(D)** are especially crucial for a dramatic, clear, and effective poetry reading.

16. D

The final sentence **(D)** needs to be moved to right before "What about the kitchen? The den?" because those questions are countering the statement that *many students would suggest the classroom, the lab, or the library* are the only spaces for learning. The other three choices would not make sense if they were moved according to the suggestions in **(A)**, **(B)**, or **(C)**.

17. A

The sentence as it stands in the passage, *Some need a more flexible schedule than others, while it is understood that a very few can sit and not rise until their task is completed* contains the awkward and wordy clause *while it is understood that.* Replacing that with the simple and elegant *while* **(A)** works well with the directness and rhythm of the passage. In **(B)**, *nevertheless* doesn't make sense as a transition. Like the original, both **(C)** and **(D)** are awkward and wordy, adding unnecessary verbiage to the sentence.

18. D

According to Krashen, teaching too many formal rules before students have acquired enough of the language leads to hesitancy, insecurity, and resistance. The time to correct student mistakes is on a written assignment, or in a formal speaking situation, and only after the student has acquired basic fluency in the language. Choice **(D)**, not overcorrecting, supports Krashen's theory. The other choices include techniques contrary to the theory and are therefore incorrect.

19. A

Choice **(A)** is called a run-on (or sometimes a comma splice) because it contains two independent clauses connected by only a comma (a run-on may also have no punctuation at all between the two or more independents). Choice **(B)** is punctuated correctly because the independent clauses are held together by a comma and the coordinating conjunction *but*. Choice **(C)** correctly offers the two independent clauses as separate sentences using periods. Choice **(D)** injects a semi-colon and the transition word *however* (a conjunctive adverb) with its attending comma. Remember when using semicolons that the two independent clauses must share a related or common idea.

20. B

All three of the statements in **(A)**, **(C)**, and **(D)** correctly concern objectives the teacher of literacy has for his or her students. In the broadest sense, literacy encompasses listening, speaking, reading, and writing skills. Moreover, **(B)** is the only statement that concerns developing assessment tools *by* the teacher, *for* the teacher (a very crucial aspect of effective teaching).

21. D

Most of the excerpt adopts an expository, neutral tone that might be found in a purely informational speech. However, Sentence 4, **(D)**, *I believe the cost to our environment of such destructive drilling is too high,* reveals that the author has a strong opinion and is trying to persuade the listener to adopt that opinion. The clause *I believe* signals an opinion. The meaning of the sentence plus the choice of the word *destructive* are also indicators of persuasive writing. The other choices, **(A)**, **(B)**, and **(C)**, do not reflect a persuasive tone.

22. C

In the passage, the author says that the cost to our environment of such destructive drilling is too high. Presumably, the author will detail his or her objections to the exploration for oil and the environmental damage it may cause. A researcher who wants to conduct an objective investigation of this issue should also seek out and evaluate the arguments raised by those holding the *opposite* view—in this case, the oil industry. Choice **(C)** asks how the oil industry plans to explore for oil while remaining sensitive to the refuge's ecosystem, making it the correct choice. Choices **(A)**, **(B)**, and **(D)** are interesting research questions, but they are outside the scope of the topic set down in the passage.

23. B

Parables, fables, and allegories are all storytelling venues that present a moral tale, very often one involving animals as characters **(B)**. The origins of the earth and human beings **(A)** are usually explored in the mythology of an ancient culture. The history of a culture **(C)** does not imply a moral lesson, as with a parable, fable, or allegory. The importance of love **(D)** may be one lesson learned from a particular parable, but it is not the subject matter most likely to be found in a parable.

24. A

The excerpt opens Sandburg's poem "Chicago," which is a lively portrait of a flourishing urban center. The poem begins with (and maintains) a lot of energy, its initial images being of a butcher, tool maker, harvester, and freight handler—the laboring class **(A)**. "Player with Railroads" and "Stormy, husky, brawling," suggest giants full of energy and optimism. Choice **(B)** is wrong because Sandburg is not being literal with the image of "Big Shoulders"; but, rather, they serve as a metaphor for Chicago's strength and its national status as freight capital. Railroads **(C)** and meat production **(D)** are just two of the several types of hard labor Sandburg cites.

25. D

Recall that *personification* attributes human qualities to non-human animals or objects. Even in this brief excerpt, Sandburg personifies Chicago by calling it Butcher, Maker, Stacker, Player, and Handler and by using human characteristics such as *husky*, *brawling*, and *big shoulders.* Choice **(A)** is incorrect because allusion is an indirect device; and Sandburg's images are very direct. A simile **(B)** is a figure of speech that expresses a resemblance between things of different kinds using *like* or *as*—words not found in the excerpt. Alliteration **(C)** is the repetition of the same sound and has nothing to do with addressing Chicago as an individual.

26. B

The correct choice, parody, is a humorous form that imitates the style and conventions of a serious work. The giveaway, even if you don't know the Muppets, is the title: *Monsterpiece Theater*, a direct mimicry of the PBS title *Masterpiece Theater*. A fantasy **(A)** is a genre that emphasizes fantastical events and often has archetypes for characters. A novella **(C)** is a short novel. An allegory **(D)** is a story based on an extended metaphor. Neither fantasy, allegory, nor novellas employ mimicry as a rule, so therefore are incorrect choices.

Constructed-Response Sample Essay 1

Angelou's evocative poem is meant to be read aloud, to fully emphasize its rhythms and sound devices. This is a characteristic of her poems: they are very rhythmic and deceptively simple sounding. Angelou is playful with words, such as "twinness." "Workers Song" contains many examples of alliteration or repetition of sounds, such as "ships shudder," "railroads run," "twinness track". The second stanza has numerous hard "c" and "s" sounds: cars, stretch, super, 'cause, strength, planes, seas, lands, 'cause, hands." The third stanza repeats droning "m" and "n" sounds, like an engine or a motor: humming, running, something, coming.

"Whoppa" is onomatopoetic because it sounds like a mechanical factory noise, one that is repeating, dull, infinite. The repetition of the chorus, Whoppa, Whoppa, Whoppa, Whoppa, is rhythmic and monotonous, connoting a machine—in this case, a person being described (treated?) as a machine or a cog in the wheel of industry. A slave maybe, a factory worker, a fruit picker? Interestingly, at the end of the poem, the Whoppa chorus is cut short—was the eternally laboring worker's life cut short?

As for rhyme scheme, this poem is AABB in the stanzas. The second and fourth lines in the first two stanzas are short and sound similar: Because of me, 'Cause of my back, 'Cause of my strength, 'Cause of my hands. The last stanza has very short first and third lines: I wake, I work late (repeating I, w, k, and long a sounds). All of these sound devices are as essential to the power of the poem as the simple, direct vocabulary.

Constructed-Response Sample Essay 2

Two influences that would facilitate language acquisition during early to middle childhood are playmates and creative learning methods.

As children grow from early childhood to middle childhood, as playmates they have increasing influence upon each other. Maturing children become less egocentric and more curious about how others speak and behave. Their language base expands as they become better listeners and mimics. They also grow emotionally, wanting to express their feelings and ideas more and more precisely to each other and to their mentors. Playmates learn to exchange ideas, negotiate, and interact—with the more advanced communicators serving as models for the less advanced. Teachers may encourage playmates' reading together and playing word games.

Influenced by teachers and parents, children acquire, adapt, and expand various learning techniques that are age-appropriate. This is due to growing mental capacity as well as expanded experience. For instance, children are better able to retain information ("plurals are formed by adding -s"), remember patterns ("I am, you are, he is"), use mnemonics ("i before e"), and understand exceptions to the rule ("except after c"). In particular, they can learn to be conscious of the ways they learn best; that is, they can learn metacognition.

Chapter 2: **History and Social Science**

THE BIG PICTURE

The CSET covers three overlapping fields of historical study: world history, United States history, and California history. The test-makers, and the State of California, are much less interested in quizzing you on specific dates in history than in evaluating your understanding of cause and effect throughout the sweep of history. For those of you who have never liked history or who have trouble remembering dates, that is good news. It is appropriate that the word *history* contains the word *story*. We all like good stories, so the challenge for the teacher of history is to tell compelling stories that students will absorb the way they absorb the stories in books and movies—in other words, effortlessly.

One very important thing to remember about history is that it is not objective truth. Where human affairs are concerned, there's no such thing as objective truth; at best, any given version of history is subjective truth. It is told from someone's perspective, and that someone is almost always representative of the winner(s) in the struggles of history. That is why, if you look at a U.S. history textbook written in the 1950s, say, you will read about the gloriously successful Indian Wars against the bloodthirsty savages. As historians have come to examine their cultural biases, however, accounts of the Indian Wars have more often tried to present both the white settlers' perspectives on the Indians (Amerindians) and the Native Americans' perspectives on the usurpers of their lands. There is a value system embedded in current educational takes on history: the assumption is that *might* does not necessarily make *right;* that the powerful have a responsibility to not abuse the rights of the less powerful, despite sometimes conflicting economic (and other) interests. Employing this line of reasoning leads to the logical conclusions that history is full of injustice and that even the United States has not always conducted itself admirably when engaged in conflict. That is a fairly recent understanding on the part of mainstream historians, and it underlies many of the history questions on the CSET.

Also incorporated into the history questions are other fields of social science, such as economics, anthropology, sociology, political science, and archeology. Teachers are expected to be familiar with the basic questions and tenets of each of these fields, and to be able to incorporate their understandings into analyses of historical events.

Eager to correct a longstanding deficiency in the American educational system, makers of the CSET also insist that you be conversant with geography. That means you must understand the effects of Earth's geographical features on human societies, in general and in particular instances, as well as human effects on the environment. It also means you must be able to identify regions of the world when presented with unlabeled maps. For those of you educated under the afore-mentioned geography-deficient system, there may be some catching up to do! Don't be daunted by this challenge, however: the study of geography can be fascinating and rewarding. It is, after all, the study of the world we live in. To overcome your unfamiliarity with geography, do a little redecorating, at least while you're studying for the CSET. Purchase some maps, or download them from the Internet. Look particularly for topographical maps (which show geological features) and historical maps, which show the evolution, over time, of human settlements (migrations) and systems (political, religious, etc.). Once you have your maps, put them up where you'll see them, and then spend time looking at them and thinking about them. Learn to recognize the patterns that are unique to each place and era. There will be map work on the CSET.

The goals of social science education are to increase students' knowledge and understanding of cultures and institutions. Understanding requires critical thinking skills, which are tested on the CSET. That's one reason the exam is not a test of simple facts. When you teach social science to your students, you are expected to convey an understanding of democratic principles and civic values, which will lead to increased civic and social participation as the students grow into think-ing members of our democratic society. Our innovative system of ideals cannot survive without the informed use of critical thinking skills by its participants. History is important, in large part, for the light it shines on current events. Understanding the lessons of history spares us from repeating past mistakes.

THE KAPLAN METHOD

Multiple-Choice Questions

Step 1. Read the question carefully. As you read, underline or circle the key words and phrases that differentiate this particular question from all other possible questions.

Step 2. Rephrase the question to make sure you understand it. If possible, predict the correct answer.

Step 3. Read all the answer choices, eliminating (physically marking through) incorrect ones as you go.

Step 4. If two or more possible answer choices remain, go back to the question and search for matching/mirroring language or concepts that will point you toward the single correct answer.

Constructed-Response Questions

Step 1. Read each question carefully. As you read, underline or circle the key words and phrases that differentiate this particular question from all other possible questions.

Step 2. Note how many parts the question has. Be sure to include subparts in your count. Write this number in your test booklet, so you will be sure to answer each part of the question.

Step 3. Before you start writing, brainstorm for vocabulary words and relevant concepts. Make your notes in the margins of your answer sheet, so you will be sure to include them in your answer. If you don't have a good command of details for a particular question, be sure to include in your answer the big picture concepts, such as the reason for studying/teaching the subject.

Step 4. Organize your thoughts! Remember, you are being tested on your ability to clearly convey information.

WORLD HISTORY

World History is a rather extensive subject, about which innumerable volumes have been written. Please do not think that because you have read and absorbed the general background in this section of this chapter, you know all you need to know about the histories of the world's civilizations. What you should feel confident of after reading this chapter is that you have an understanding of the sweep of history, of the ways civilizations have developed in interaction with each other and their individual environments to produce this historical moment we are living in. There are patterns to history, patterns all the social sciences endeavor to uncover; and if you understand and can identify these patterns, you are well on your way to understanding the course of history. Drawing timelines is a very helpful visual tool for both yourself and your students.

If you want to be sure you know about all the World History that might be covered on the CSET, use the content standards developed by the State of California to guide further study. You will find them online at cde.ca.gov/be/st/ss/.

Test Yourself

It used to be said that, "The sun never sets on the British Empire." The most accurate interpretation of this saying is:

(A) The British military never sleeps.

(B) The Greenwich Meridian is central to the world's time-keeping system.

(C) British rule will never end.

(D) Britain rules lands all around the globe.

The correct answer is **(D)**. From the beginning of the Age of Exploration until the mid-twentieth century, Great Britain established and maintained an empire that had outposts in many areas of the world. If it was nighttime in England, it was daytime in Australia. If Canada was dark, Rhodesia (now Zimbabwe) was light. One way to examine history is to look at the succession of empires in various parts of the world. The rise, expansion, and fall of empires both gives a good sense of the course of history and provides lessons that can productively be applied to contemporary studies. As cultural critic George Santayana famously said, "Those who do not remember history are doomed to repeat it."

Ancient Civilizations

The Evolution of Culture

Paleontologists have found evidence suggesting that humans evolved in Africa over the past few million years. There is discussion about exactly which fossils to identify as humans, or as human ancestors; and the discussion itself continues to evolve as DNA technology is put to use and as additional fossils are found all over the world. Scientists agree that early humans lived in small, mobile bands of relatives without permanent shelter and were primarily vegetarians who scavenged for fruits, roots, and other edible plant substances. At some point, increases in brain size and other genetic changes led to our ancestors' control over fire, tool use, tool making, and language; and human life began to evolve into a form of interdependent group life we would recognize. An early innovation was the ability to hunt, enabled by tool (weapon) making and the ability to cooperate with fellow hunters through the use of language. As early man began to hunt, early woman continued to gather more readily available foods. In *hunter/gatherer societies*, as they are known, the gatherers usually contribute more calories to fill daily needs than do the hunters, though the hunters' contributions are more often celebrated, as an occasion for a feast.

Psychologist and sociologist Abraham Maslow points out in his Hierarchy of Needs that before individual humans can turn their attention to the finer things in life, they must have certain basic needs met. The first level is physiological needs, i.e., people must know they have enough to eat and drink and a warm place to sleep. Any group of people that spends its days wandering around, looking for food, then deciding where to spend the night and hoping it will be safe, has little time or psychic energy to develop civilization. The hunter gatherer lifestyle, prevalent worldwide until a few thousand years ago, is not conducive to sophisticated culture. The development of culture requires time to ponder—it requires leisure time.

The first big turning point in human civilization came about 12,000 years ago when certain geographically-advantaged groups began to practice the intentional sowing and harvesting of plants. This practice required them to remain in one place throughout the crop cycle, and so more permanent dwellings were constructed out of easily available materials. In order to pursue agriculture, the groups needed fertile soil, a sufficiently long growing season, and a good supply of water. These conditions were met in the river valleys of the Tigris and Euphrates rivers (the Fertile Crescent) in the Middle East and the Nile in Egypt, and there is where the earliest civilizations evolved.

The second level of Maslow's hierarchy is security and safety. River settlements were relatively easy to defend, as the inhabitants needed to protect only three sides (before the development of technology for floating on water), or fewer than three sides in the crook of a river bend. As Maslow's thinking predicts, once there was a dependable supply of food and relative security, the populace began to produce the artifacts of civilization—writing, mathematics, science, philosophy, and art. All human cultures share, at a minimum, four characteristics: the creation of tools or technology, the development of language, the existence of belief systems to explain life's questions, and long-lasting institutions or ways of doing things. By examining these four characteristics, it is possible to describe the evolution of a particular civilization.

For people to gather and settle in large groups, there must be a dependable food supply. The Sumerians of the Middle East learned to irrigate their crops and plant and harvest in certain seasons, they were therefore able to feed many people. Their cities grew and thrived. Soon afterward, people along the Ganges River in India and the Yellow River in China also learned how to provide food for urban centers; and Indian and Chinese civilizations flourished. Notice that these early civilizations shared the geographic characteristic of being located along major rivers.

The innovations of planting, watering, harvesting, preserving, and storing spread throughout the Middle East. By c. 2000 B.C.E. (also known as B.C.), major civilizations flourished in the areas of Mesopotamia (present-day Iraq), Northern Africa, and Asia Minor. Their domination was brought to an end by an invasion of nomads from the North, who had learned to fashion weapons from iron. These warriors soon overcame the Assyrians, Babylonians, and Egyptians, who could not effectively defend themselves using their weapons made with Bronze-Age technology. This was the beginning of the Iron Age.

The civilizations you should be familiar with from this era and part of the world are *Sumeria, Babylonia, Assyria* (Mesopotamian civilizations), *Egypt* and *Kush* (African civilizations). In particular, you should be familiar with the Babylonian legal code known as Hammurabi's Code. This is significant as the first known example of a written system of law, to be applied equally to all subjects; and is therefore the antecedent of modern legal systems.

As the Iron Age dawned, the disruptions to established civilizations left openings for other civilizations to emerge. Kush took advantage of this opportunity to shake off Egyptian domination. Similarly, the seafaring Phoenicians sailed to prominence around the Mediterranean; and around 1000 B.C.E., a small group of tribes in Palestine, who had migrated from Egypt a few centuries earlier, united to form a kingdom based on their (at the time unique) practice of *monotheism* (the worship of only one god). These people, the Hebrews, developed the religious philosophy that became the basis for the Judeo-Christian culture we have inherited.

Thinking About Civilizations

It is important for you to familiarize yourself with the ancient civilizations mentioned here, as well as all the other historical topics discussed in this chapter, in more detail. The Internet has many resources—remember, the more terms you type in, the more specific your results will be.

While researching, look for information about the geography of the civilization you're investigating. Think about how natural features such as rivers, mountains, oceans, and deserts influenced the choices people made about how to live. Investigate the economy of the civilization. Geography often influences economy; for example, it's difficult to establish a trading economy if you're located in an inaccessible mountain region. Learn how most people earn their livings in the society. Consider the social structures of the society. Answer questions about how people live with one another: how large are the groups they live in? What are the family structures? Who is important to the society, and who is considered less so? Find out about the religious and political life of the civilization. In ancient civilizations, religion and political power are often closely related; power is considered to flow from the gods through the political leaders, who are often priests themselves. Find out something about the religious beliefs of each society you learn about.

The Rest of the World

For too long, the American educational system had a Eurocentric view of history. The philosophy seemed to be that if it didn't happen within the Judeo-Christian tradition, it wasn't important. The state of California is working to correct that view, but it may mean there will be historical material on the CSET that you never learned in school. In terms of the Ancient World, there are questions on African cultures (Kush), Asian cultures (India, China), and American cultures (Maya, Inca, Aztec). Be sure you know what contributions each of these cultures made in terms of knowledge, technological innovation, and religious/philosophical thought. Be sure you can locate each one on a map and that you know how the region's geography influenced the culture's development. For example, you may be shown a map of the west (Pacific) coast of South America and asked to identify the pre-Columbian civilization that flourished there, creating terraced mountain farms and an extensive network of roads (Inca).

Try not to think of investigating these ancient cultures as an onerous task. You will learn things that will amaze you. Did you know that the Maya used three separate calendars, and that their calendars were more accurate than ours today? Did you know that there are more than a dozen major languages spoken in India, and that most of them are classified as Indo-European (related to European languages)? Are you aware that the Chinese were the first to make paper and gunpowder and to use a compass? The more you learn about these early civilizations, the more you'll want to learn.

China

History questions on the CSET have often focused on Asian religious and philosophical traditions. When you're thinking about the development of a culture, look first to the society's great thinkers: they have influenced every aspect of the culture, from family structures to politics and from art to economics. Two Chinese philosophers have had an enormous impact on Chinese life, in both the public and the private realm. Interestingly, these two men may very well have been contemporaries over 2,500 years ago. Their names are Confucius and Lao-tzu.

Confucius was born around 500 B.C.E. At that time China already had a long sense of itself as a people and a nation. Confucius incorporated into his thinking many of the principles and elements of older Chinese traditions. Central to *Confucianism* is the concept of respect. One must respect one's parents and family, one's government and rulers, and must live an upright life as a sign of self-respect. Over time, Chinese rulers found this approach to be appealing, as it supported the people's tendency to respect authority.

Lao-tzu built on the existing Chinese concepts of *yin* and *yang*, the complementary polarities of all existence, in formulating his mystical philosophy of *Taoism*. The essence of the Tao is balance: one must strive to be aware of the order and harmony of all existence and to live in accordance with it. Only in balance and harmony can one live a successful life.

India

Around the same time that Confucius and Lao-tzu were making their mark on China, a prince was born in India. When he was in his twenties, this prince rejected his destiny and embarked on a mission to discover the sources of human suffering. He came to be called Gautama Buddha, or

[handwritten notes in top margin: Confucious-practical / Tao-wordly "myshcal"]

the Buddha. The Buddha taught that the primary source of suffering is failure to control one's desires. The Buddha's pupils (and their pupils, and so on) elaborated on his teachings over the years, changing and adding in various ways.

Buddhism spread all over Asia, and incorporated elements from other religions. For example, with Hinduism it shares a belief in *karma,* or a fate that is earned, and in *reincarnation,* or rebirth after death, as well as the possibility of attaining spiritual Enlightenment and being freed from the karmic cycle of birth, death, and rebirth.

Hinduism was the predominant religion of India since before historic times. In the Hindu world-view that evolved in the last few centuries B.C.E., an individual's karma caused him or her to be born into a particular social status. The Hindus identified four social groups, or *castes,* from the highest, the *Brahmins,* to the lowest, called the *Untouchables.* After Gandhi led a popular movement to free India from British colonial domination in the twentieth century, the modern Indian government officially outlawed the caste system; although legislation, of course, often takes quite some time to effect actual change in the way people live.

The Greeks

One of the most interesting paths into the study of ancient Greek civilization is through its religious stories, which we call *mythology.* The Greeks had many gods and goddesses in their pantheon, led by Zeus. Greek mythology consists of stories about the gods, who had human-style weaknesses and disagreements. Another series of Greek stories comes from *The Illiad* and *The Odyssey* by Homer.

We owe much of our literary heritage to the Greeks (our theater traditions), and the same is true of our scientific approach to medicine, our philosophy (the educational philosophy of Aristotle and Socrates), our mathematics (geometry), and in particular, our democratic approach to governance. From before 3000 B.C.E. through the conquest of the known world by Alexander the Great in the fourth century B.C.E., until they were conquered by the Romans around 200 B.C.E., the Greeks developed their culture, while living in separate *city states,* which sometimes cooperated and sometimes fought each other. The best known city states were Athens, renowned for its philosophers and artists, and Sparta, the preeminent military and athletic center.

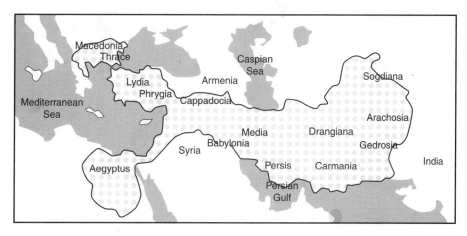

The Empire of Alexander the Great, approximately 320 B.C.E.

The Romans

When the Romans conquered Greece, about 500 years after the founding of Rome, they incorporated much of Greek culture into their traditions. Roman greatness stemmed mainly from their military prowess but also from their ability to learn from those whom they conquered. Though, as in Greece, only those who met certain criteria (non-slave, property owners) could cast votes, the Romans did practice a form of democracy throughout much of the duration of their empire. One of the highest expressions of Roman political development was the creation of the Emperor Justinian's Code in 529 C.E. (also known as A.D.) The *Justinian Code* is considered to be the basis for justice systems in use throughout much of the western world, including the United States. The first known written legal code, however, *the Code of Hammurabi,* in ancient Babylon, predated the Justinian Code by about 2,000 years. As the Romans expanded their empire, they enjoyed a standard of living unequalled in the world. They engaged in massive public works projects, building roads and bridges, even delivering water to the houses of Rome through an aqueduct system. The arts flourished, particularly architecture. In the fourth century C.E., the empire had grown large and begun to experience disorder, fear, and chaos. The emperors adopted the relatively new religion of Christianity in an attempt to unite the people, but in addition to internal unrest, the heart of the empire was under attack by Germanic warriors from northern Europe. In the fifth century, Rome fell to the invaders. The eastern half of the empire survived for nearly a thousand years as the Byzantine Empire ruled from what is now Turkey.

Be sure that you can locate ancient Rome on a map. Rome is in modern Italy, which looks like a high boot jutting from Southern Europe down into the Mediterranean Sea. At its height, the Roman Empire took up much of Europe, the Middle East, and northern Africa.

Incorporate Greek customs/ideas

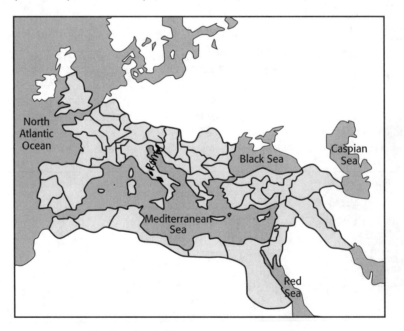

The height of the Roman Empire, 116 C.E.

The Middle Ages

During the upheaval that followed the fall of the Roman Empire, Europe lacked a strong political and economic center to provide direction. Under Roman rule, the various tribes of Europe had been Christianized. Christianity spread the way religious movements usually do—through military conquest coupled with economic domination. In other words, the priests followed the soldiers and became important representatives of the rulers in Rome. When the soldiers left after the fall of Rome, the missionaries stayed and worked with the political powers that emerged. A social, political, and economic system called *feudalism* evolved in Europe. This was the dominant system in what we now call the *Medieval* period, or the *Middle Ages*.

Feudalism is a social, economic, and political system in which power is decentralized, and a varying number of lords hold land, or *fiefs,* on which they allow others to live and work in return for loyalty and service. The service may be military or economic, in the form of farmwork. Besides the lords (including the king or other ruler), there are *vassals,* sometimes called knights. They are more privileged than the *serfs,* or peasants, who work the land in return for protection. The king is not all-powerful; most power (economic and military) is held on the local level.

[handwritten margin notes: fief-landowner / lords / vassals-knights / serfs-work for fief]

During the Medieval period in Europe, from the fall of the Roman Empire until the Renaissance, the Roman Catholic Church was also extremely wealthy and powerful, more so than any lord or king. The most glorious remnants of the Medieval period in Europe are the many magnificent cathedrals, which often took more than a hundred years to complete. Commonly, Church officials were the only educated people in a rural area, and few lords were brave enough, or foolish enough, to challenge Church authority. The only way to reproduce books was to laboriously copy them by hand, a task that fell largely to the monks. The Bible and other religious writings were the most often reproduced, and few outside the Church could read them. The population depended on Church authorities to tell them what God wanted from them; and if a lord or wealthy vassal wanted his son educated, the boy was sent to a monastery to study, and usually to become a monk or priest.

The Crusades

One thing the Church wanted was to recapture the holy land. During the Medieval period, Islam had been founded by Muhammad, the Prophet (born 570 C.E. in Mecca, Saudi Arabia). Muhammad wrote his revelations in the Muslim holy book, the Koran (Qu'ran). This monotheistic religion, which accepts both Christian and Jewish texts as part of its tradition, spread rapidly throughout the Middle East, Africa, even parts of southern Europe, most notably Spain and the Balkans. As with Christianity, the spread was accomplished through a mixture of military prowess and economic incentive. What has been referred to as the "Dark Ages" for Christian Europeans was a golden age for Islam.

By 1100, Muslims controlled Palestine, including the Christian (and Muslim, and Jewish) holy city of Jerusalem. The head of the Church, the Pope, issued a call for holy warriors to liberate the holy land from the infidels. For almost two hundred years, waves of Christian soldiers invaded Muslim territories in futile attempts to regain control of these lands. Many thousands on both sides died; and despite some temporary Christian victories, the Muslims remained in control of the Middle East. This series of invasions by Europeans is known collectively as the *Crusades.*

Feudal Japan

A feudal structure also existed in Japan from the twelfth century C.E. to the fifteenth century. There are many parallels between Japanese feudalism and European feudal life. The *daimyo* was the feudal lord, the *shogun* was the equivalent of a medieval European king, and the well-known *samurai* warrior served his *daimyo* or *shogun* as the vassal (knight) served his lord or king. The peasants (serfs) were guided by their religious leaders (who were Buddhist and Shinto, not Christian); and art and architecture served both religion and powerful earthly leaders. The code of the knights in Europe was chivalry, and in Japan the code was called *bushido*.

The Magna Carta

One of the most important legal developments of European history was the signing of the *Magna Carta* in 1215 by King John of England. While the feudal lords controlled much of the land and resources of feudal England, the King (by "divine right") was still able to exercise considerable power. The major significance of the Magna Carta is that, for the first time, the king consented to be restrained by rule of law. This document is considered the foundation of the English Common Law system that followed it, and also for the American Constitution (particularly the fifth and sixth amendments), which derived much from the English system.

The Renaissance

Renaissance is a French word meaning *rebirth*. The Renaissance is the name given to the flowering of European culture at the end of the Medieval period. The movement started in Italy in the fourteenth century, and over the next two hundred years or so, spread throughout Europe. It was a movement of awareness, of interest in the arts and revived interest in the intellectual traditions of the Greeks and Romans (humanism), among others. Renaissance artists, such as Leonardo da Vinci, explored techniques and subjects outside the rigid religious parameters that had been customary during the Medieval period. Renaissance thinkers, such as Copernicus and Galileo, challenged Church orthodoxy when they suggested that the Earth and its creatures were not at the center of divine creation. The importance of Copernicus' discovery that the Earth revolved around the Sun, not vice versa, paved the way for the scientific discoveries that continue to reveal the nature of the universe.

One of the most important inventions during the Renaissance, and arguably one of the most important human discoveries of all time, was the printing press. When you think about the course of history, it is instructive to consider the impact of inventions and discoveries. The printing press set the stage for our educational system. Once books could be printed and made available—and the first book printed, around 1450, was the Gutenberg Bible—there was incentive for people to learn to read. As more people learned to read, a culture of learning emerged and grew into the so-called Age of Enlightenment. Now we have mass communication, including the Internet, that reaches much of the world and leads some to dub today's era the Information Age. On a more immediate scale, the printing press made it possible for a disenchanted former priest named *Martin Luther* to widely distribute his protests against the Church and its practices in 1517. Luther's protests led to the formation of alternative, *Protestant* Christian churches, subsequent religious wars and persecutions in Europe, and the eventual emigration of many Protestant sects to the New World.

Looking at History

There are several lenses through which it is useful to look at history. One such lens is discovery or invention, as was discussed in the previous section. When people learned to harness fire, it enabled them to live in cooler climates, cook their food, and see inside caves as they created art on the walls. The invention of the wheel enabled overland trade to flourish and encouraged migration. Writing promoted the continuity of knowledge, beyond what could be remembered from one generation to the next; it enabled Isaac Newton to speak of "standing on the shoulders of giants," in achieving his scientific discoveries. There are many other discoveries and inventions that are important enough to have revolutionized the way people live.

A second way to examine history is in terms of wars and powerful people. This is a traditional lens, one that many generations of school children have used. The CSET focuses less on wars in world history than you might expect; still it is a good idea to learn about major conflicts from the Greek Peloponnesian War of the fifth century B.C.E. through the two World Wars of the last century. As always, look at causes and effects.

Human migration is another important way to learn to look at history. If scientists are correct to believe that humans originated in Africa, the implication is that human settlements in all other parts of the world were a result of migration. We know that all people are closely related genetically, so theories about dispersal of populations are supported by evidence. We have much more detailed information about more recent human migrations. For example, most of the population of the United States has ancestors who arrived here within the past four hundred years, and often much more recently. Historians, including those who write this section of the CSET, see migratory movements as important causes and results of natural events (e.g., droughts, ice ages, destruction of habitats) and human events (e.g., wars, persecutions, perceived opportunity). The makers of the exam are particularly interested in the consequences of human migrations on any inhabitants whose lives were altered by foreign conquerors.

The Age of Exploration

During the Renaissance, and continuing through the Enlightenment, European countries focused their attention outward. Due to having the world's most advanced sailing vessels, Europeans explored and settled the "new" world—the Americas. They conquered existing civilizations, using their superior military technology. In so doing, they spread European culture around the globe, from Africa to America, from Australia to India.

In the beginning, the European explorers were looking for new routes to Asia. During the Crusades, Europeans had been introduced to trade with Asia and had developed a taste for the spices and other goods from that part of the world. Overland routes to Asia, however, were long and thus expensive. Europeans had a pretty good idea that the world was round, but they had no idea that the Atlantic and Pacific were two different oceans separated by two new continents. They thought they would be able to find new trade routes that would enable them to sail from Europe to India (with which much of the trade occurred) and other parts of Asia.

The Spanish focused their explorations on what is now Florida and the area south, from present-day Mexico down through South America. Encountering so much land, the Spanish explorers struck out on foot towards the west. The English explored much of North America's east coast, looking for river routes (or a Northwest Passage) to take them through the land mass. The French and Dutch also made voyages of discovery to North America and set up profitable trading outposts from what is now New York (previously New Amsterdam) north to Canada. The Portuguese were particularly proficient sailors, but they did not manage to convert their discovery to much of a gain in either trade or land, as the water routes to Asia were not really an improvement on land routes.

Once it was realized that the Americas were huge land masses, there was fierce competition for the new territory. The Spanish took an early lead, starting with Columbus' voyages of exploration; and they were the first to actively conquer, kill, and/or subjugate the native peoples of the Americas. This topic will be discussed further in the American history section.

The Enlightenment

Following the invention of the printing press, the increase in literacy among European people led to an explosion of activity in the areas of science and philosophy, focusing on the physical world and our place in it. As a result, the seventeenth through nineteenth centuries are often referred to as the Enlightenment. Isaac Newton, born at the beginning of this era, used what he learned from classic books and his original insights into developing the laws of universal gravitation to revolutionize physics. Some major writers/philosophers of this era were Descartes, Voltaire, and Rousseau in France, and John Locke and David Hume in the British Isles.

One important development that resulted from Enlightenment thinking was the political philosophy that led to the creation of the United States—and in the following decade, the French Revolution. Enlightenment thinkers emphasized the use of reason, and focused on experience and the observable, rather than on principles and speculation; and they strongly believed in the ability of reasonable people to achieve progress, even perfectibility, in human institutions. They realized that the workings of nature could be discovered, using the scientific method, and that blind submission to authority—especially that associated with nationalism—was not in the people's best interest.

The Modern Era

Enlightenment thinking still exerts a profound influence in today's world. Those of us who practice democracy, in particular, maintain a belief in the power of rational thought and the perfectibility of world systems. In fact, many of the world's nations have moved toward democratic systems of government. The colonial powers, as exemplified by Great Britain, have relinquished most of their foreign holdings (often after costly wars of independence); and most of the resulting new nations have at least made attempts at Enlightenment-style governments, though many of those have been hijacked by powerful "lords" of various descriptions.

Another major development of the modern era, perhaps its defining development, was the advent of the Industrial Age. Prior to the invention of the steam engine, there was no efficient way to run industrial machinery; nor was there a means of powering the overland transportation necessary to effectively distribute goods on a large scale. Subsequent advances in energy production have fueled (so to speak) continuing advances in both mass production and mass distribution. Our primary energy sources now are fossil fuels, which have the double disadvantage of being non-renewable, and thus finite in supply, as well as being harmful to the atmosphere when burned. Nevertheless, the last couple of centuries have seen vast amounts of wealth creation, greatly raising the standard of living in industrialized countries.

Economics

As always, economics has been a mighty force in the development of history. *Economics,* as a social science, deals with the production, distribution, and consumption of goods and services. The economic policies of governments affect the lives of their citizens in ways large and small. Economic considerations usually underlie wars and other foreign policies of nations, though often the economic considerations must be inferred from the causes and effects of the policies. When you are asked a constructed-response question on this section of the CSET, remember to always consider the economic aspects of the question and address them in your answer.

At the same time that European nations were growing their colonial empires, they were practicing an economic policy of *mercantilism.* Mercantilism (from the same root as *merchant*) is, in this context, the practice of state regulation and control of the economy in an attempt to insure and increase prosperity. Each state approached this differently, but over several hundred years—from about 1600 to 1900—mercantilism evolved into the economic system called *capitalism.* Capitalism, while still regulated by the state, encourages the accumulation of wealth and property by individuals. Individuals, not the state, control the *means of production* (e.g., factories); and the workers who provide the labor receive a wage for their work. The philosopher Karl Marx argued that this kind of labor is equivalent to feudal serfdom. Marx believed that workers should control the means of production and share in the profits of their labor. This philosophy of *socialism* evolved in the twentieth century into *communism,* in which the state controls the means of production and distributes the profits, ostensibly for the benefit of the people. In addition to operating in a socialist manner economically, communist governments extend state control into social and political realms as well. Among large nations, only Russia (later the Soviet Union) and China experimented with communism; and both experiments were failures. China, while nominally still a communist country, has moved increasingly toward capitalism in the economic realm over the past twenty or so years.

Both socialism and capitalism have upsides and downsides as economic systems. In simplified form, the arguments against each system are that capitalism favors the powerful (wealthy) at the expense of those who produce the wealth (the workers); but socialism, by taking a large share of owner profits for redistribution to the workers, provides insufficient reward to entrepreneurs; so that it stifles innovation, and society does not move forward. Communism, in particular, has failed to benefit those not in power.

It is important to think about the effects of different economic systems on the people who participate in them. The CSET will expect you to think of economic issues in terms of a *cost-benefit* analysis: what is gained, by whom; and what is lost or sacrificed, and by whom. Economic choices are created by the existence (or the perception) of *scarcity.* The most commonly cited concept of economics is the *law of supply and demand.* If supply is greater than demand, the value of a product is lower; if demand is greater than supply, the value is higher. Ask yourself what is produced in a given economic system. How is it produced, and who profits from production? Are the interests of the less powerful protected from exploitation by the powerful? Who is better off under a given system than under another, and why? What are society's most compelling interests and what is the most effective way to realize them? The answers to these questions—and even the act of asking the questions—will affect both your score on the CSET and how you think about the future of the society you live in.

UNITED STATES HISTORY

The Grand Experiment

The history of the United States is unique for at least two reasons. First, for the only time since history began to be recorded, there was a mass migration in which one group of people overwhelmed and virtually extinguished another. Prior to the arrival of the Europeans, North America had a thriving population of native peoples who, within a few hundred years, were driven from their land and to the brink of physical and cultural extinction. Second, for the first time, a nation was founded on democratic principles, as a conscious attempt to put idealistic notions of government into practice. The tension between these two sets of circumstances continues to influence events in this country to this day.

In addition to the unique aspects of U.S. history, there are also the usual historical considerations mentioned in the last section: economic forces, discoveries and inventions, and other social, political, and cultural developments and influences shaping the country. This discussion of American history will focus on several recurring themes and will use them as lenses through which to view each period of the country's development. The themes are: migration/immigration, expanding democracy vs. contracting democracy, states rights vs. federalism, isolationism vs. engagement, and civil rights/labor rights. Because the CSET limits its questions on U.S. history to pre-twentieth century events, this discussion will stop there.

Test Yourself

The first ten amendments to the Constitution of the United States are often referred to as the Bill of Rights. This is because:

(A) They are focused on individual rights.

(B) They set forth the laws of the country.

(C) They list the rights and responsibilities of citizenship.

(D) They are more right than the rest of the Constitution is.

The correct choice is **(A)**. The first ten amendments were drafted by James Madison in response to anti-federalist complaints that the Constitution did not protect individuals and states from abuses of the federal government. The Federalists had written a Constitution that created a strong federal government, reacting to the weak Articles of Confederation that had failed to guide the country. The Anti-Federalists became alarmed that individual rights were in danger and demanded provisions that would protect important individual rights, such as the right to free speech and free assembly, and the protection against unreasonable search and seizure.

Exploration

Toward the end of the fifteenth century, Columbus sailed west from Spain and landed on what he thought was an island outpost of India. He had, in fact, landed on an island in the Caribbean. Following this confirmation of land across the Atlantic Ocean, European countries and their large trading companies began searching in earnest for a water route to Asia in order to maximize their trade advantage.

Ferdinand Magellan, a Portuguese sailing for Spain, was the first to *circumnavigate* the globe (at least his ship was—Magellan died on the journey). Sir Francis Drake, sailing for England, was the second. The only way to get from Europe to Asia by sailing west was to go around the southern-most tip of South America; but the Europeans didn't know that. They thought there might be a shorter route, so they continued to mount expeditions.

The French sent Jacques Cartier on a more northerly course, into present day Canada, looking for a Northwest Passage. Cartier sailed up the St. Lawrence River, hoping it would be his passage to India. Of course, he failed to find such a passage; but he did establish mostly friendly relations with the Amerindians, a precedent that would become important two hundred years later. The French continued to search for the Northwest Passage, carving out their northern niche in the New World. Among the more prominent French explorers was Samuel de Champlain, who mapped the coastline from Cape Cod to Nova Scotia, explored the Great Lakes, and founded Montreal. Lake Champlain, situated on the border between New York and Vermont, is named for him. He also was instrumental in establishing the fur trade, which dominated French economic enterprises in the New World for many years.

The Dutch East (later West) India Company sent the Englishman Henry Hudson in search of the Northwest Passage. Instead, he found the mouth of the Hudson River and what is now New York harbor. The Dutch company subsequently established the settlement of New Amsterdam on the site and began trading in furs. Eventually the English took over the settlement and renamed it New York.

The English, meanwhile, were exploring the Atlantic coastline of what is now the United States, and claimed most of it (Florida being the exception). The first permanent English settlement was established at Jamestown, Virginia, in 1607. Thirteen years later, the Pilgrims landed at Plymouth Rock, Massachusetts. They were not official representatives of England and were, in fact, fleeing religious persecution by the English.

The *Conquistadores*

Throughout the sixteenth century, the Spanish actively explored Central and South America, by ship and overland, establishing colonies and looking for riches. They are known collectively as *conquistadors,* those who conquer. After Columbus, one of the first of the Spanish explorers was Balboa. He had settled on a Caribbean island but found himself in debt and went to the main-land, relocating on the east coast of what is now Panama. (Panama is the narrowest point in the Americas, which is why the Panama Canal was built there by the U.S. in the early twentieth century to provide a throughway from the Atlantic to the Pacific without going around South America.) Going on an overland expedition across the Isthmus of Panama, Balboa spied the Pacific Ocean in 1513.

The Aztec Empire

Hernando Cortes (or Cortez) was the first real *conquistador*; he conquered the Aztecs around 1521. The Aztecs had established an empire in central Mexico, which they ruled from their capital city of Tenochtitlán. Aztec culture was complex, with multiple calendars, a system of writing, and an economy that was heavily dependent on tribute from the neighboring subject peoples. Their worship of a supreme sun god was intimately connected with human sacrifice. Tenochtitlán was ideally situated in the middle of a lake, making it almost invulnerable to conquest; however, the Aztec ruler Mocteuzma saw the arrival of Cortes as a divine occurrence (perhaps his plumed helmet made him look like the feathered serpent-god) and so made the mistake of allowing the Spanish into the city.

The Inca Empire

Francisco Pizarro, born in Spain, settled in Panama around 1520. After several shorter expeditions of exploration, he managed to get himself appointed Governor of Peru by the Spanish crown, despite the fact that Spain did not control Peru, on the west coast of South America. Peru was actually controlled by the Inca, one of the great Amerindian civilizations of pre-Columbian America. The Incan empire extended from the equator to Chile, between the Andes Mountains and the Pacific Ocean. Beginning around 1200 C.E., the Inca had conquered all the peoples of this area, introduced the practice of terracing and irrigating the steep mountainsides, and built a system of roads that enabled trade along the coast. Their empire was centered in Peru. When Pizarro and his men arrived, the Inca were in the grips of a smallpox epidemic (the Amerindians had no resistance to smallpox, which they had not encountered before); they were also experiencing a civil war. With the help of tribes who had been under the domination of the Inca, Pizarro and fewer than 200 men were able to defeat the Incan army of 40,000 within five years and take possession of their treasures as spoils of war.

The Maya Empire

The third major native Amerindian empire, the Maya, was more widely dispersed, and the enormous empire seems to have already splintered prior to the arrival of the conquistadors. Like the Aztecs, the Maya built stepped pyramids, utilized multiple calendars, and possessed extensive astronomical knowledge. They had understood the concept of zero before the Europeans had. Their civilization had peaked, however, several hundred years before the arrival of the Spanish. No one is certain why the Mayan civilization declined, because archeologists are still deciphering their complex hieroglyphic system of writing; though war among local groups seems to have been a major factor. There is speculation that the wars were economic in nature, because of food scarcity brought on by overfarming the land. Due to their geographical range—from the jungles of the Yucatan Peninsula in Mexico to the highlands of Guatemala—they could not all be conquered at once. After several failed Spanish attempts at conquest, Francisco Montejo managed to take the Mayan city that is now Merida in the Yucatan. The last of the Maya remained fiercely independent well into the nineteenth century.

Early Settlements

The Colonial Era in North America lasted from approximately 1500 until the American War of Independence (Revolutionary War) beginning in 1775. Despite the fact that Spain controlled Florida, and the Dutch initially settled in New York and Pennsylvania (along with the Swedes and Germans), the Colonial Era in what is now the United States was primarily a period of English settlement.

The primary reasons for immigration were the search for economic opportunity, freedom of religious expression, and adventure. Generally, those seeking religious freedom settled primarily in the northern colonies; those seeking economic gain settled farther south. That may be one reason that slavery became more well-established in the south, despite being legal in all the colonies (except in Georgia, initially).

The South

The first permanent English settlement in America was Jamestown, Virginia, settled in 1607. Soon the colonial settlers had introduced the native crop tobacco to the English, and a trading relationship was established. Despite its geographical location as one of the northernmost of the southern states, Virginia was the cultural epicenter of the South until well after American independence. In 1634 the English king granted the land that is now Maryland to the Calvert family. A colony was to be established for Catholics, so that they could escape the religious persecution they had endured in England since the Reformation. Lord Baltimore later opened the colony to all, and the Maryland Toleration Act of 1649 reduced instances of religious discrimination. North Carolina was not established as a colony until 1663, despite two attempts at settlement that had failed prior to the establishment of Jamestown. South Carolina was part of the 1663 charter granted to North Carolina, and the two were not separated until 1729. Georgia was founded in 1733 as a buffer against the Spanish in Florida. It was the last of the original thirteen colonies to be established. James Oglethorpe brought unfortunates from England's overflowing debtors' prisons to Georgia and was appointed to the post of governor.

The farms in the South were the largest and most prosperous in the colonies. Many fortunes were made on the backs of white indentured servants and African slaves, who were first brought to Virginia in 1619 to work on the tobacco plantations when the settlers' attempt to use the Amerindians as slaves was unsuccessful. Remember that in economic systems, including the southern plantation economy, there are benefits and there are costs. For almost 250 years, southern Americans didn't see the costs of their "peculiar institution" of chattel slavery, in which people are treated as personal property. The costs were all too obvious in Africa, where informal intertribal warfare soon evolved into a system of organized raiding that kept the slave trading ships supplied with human cargo. By the eighteenth century, European countries had colonized Africa; and the enmities engendered by the slave trade weaken Africa to this day. Over time, the practice of slavery would weaken the United States as well; but in the colonial period, it seemed an attractive way to maximize profits.

The North

The first settlers to arrive in Massachusetts were the Pilgrims, who were destined for northern Virginia and supposedly opted to settle in the Plymouth area because it was not under Virginia's jurisdiction. A religious group who had broken away from the Church of England, they had first moved to Holland to escape English persecution. Failing to thrive there, a group of them set sail in the fall of 1620. They arrived at the beginning of winter, not well equipped for survival. Thanks to the native people, they made it through the severe winter; and relations between the two groups remained friendly for some time. William Bradford was prominent among the group, served thirty years as its governor, and first used the term *pilgrims* to define it. Their document, the Mayflower Compact, was the first declaration of self-government in the New World. But the establishment of the government and social structure of the New England region was most influenced by the Puritans. They arrived in Massachusetts Bay in 1629 and founded the largest colony of Puritans, eventually absorbing the tiny Plymouth Colony. Their governor, John Winthrop, wrote that the Puritans had a covenant with God to create the perfect society—a "city on a hill" (*Massachusetts* is said to mean this in a native language).

Not everyone found religious freedom in the Massachusetts Bay Colony. In 1636 Roger Williams and a small band of followers, having been exiled from Massachusetts for independent religious thought, made their way to Rhode Island. There they established a colony that accepted all who sought religious freedom, not only those who believed as they did. Theirs was the first government in America to recognize the separation of church and state.

Another group that disagreed with the religious intolerance of the Puritans in Massachusetts settled in New Hampshire in 1638. Their Exeter Compact was modeled after the Mayflower Compact.

Over time, other settlers made their way inland from the Massachusetts Bay Colony to the Connecticut Valley, and in 1639 a group of farmers (planters) drew up a constitution—the Fundamental Orders—for a Connecticut Commonwealth. It is said to be the first constitution that recognized no authority other than its own, and it governed the commonwealth for over one hundred years.

Mid-Atlantic Colonies

Not all settlers in America were English, however. In 1638 a delegation from Sweden landed at Delaware Bay, the site of present day Wilmington, and established a Swedish colony. Soon more ships arrived from Sweden, and farms sprang up nearby. Swedish rule lasted less than twenty years, and after a brief time of being rather leniently governed by the Dutch, Delaware became part of the land granted to William Penn in 1681.

William Penn was a different kind of English religious dissenter, a Quaker. His father, a naval admiral, had won the favor of the king; and so Penn was granted substantial land in America. Upon his arrival, Penn first negotiated treaties with the native peoples (and the Quakers remained at peace with them). He also set up a constitution that guaranteed rights and freedoms to all religions and to women. Pennsylvania, as the colony came to be called, was perhaps the first true Enlightenment-inspired governmental entity, and was the first state to abolish slavery—albeit gradually—beginning in 1780.

13 Colonies, approximately 1775

The French and Indian War

In 1756 tensions that had been simmering between the French and the British in America (an extension of the squabbles and wars ongoing since at least 1066) rose to the boiling point and war was declared. At stake were the New World property claims of both sides. This conflict is sometimes called the French and Indian War (after the Amerindian allies who fought the British and their colonists), and sometimes called the Seven Years' War.

George Washington made a name for himself in this war, which ended in 1760 with the defeat of the French and their Indian allies (remember that the French had always treated the native peoples with more respect than the British did). The Treaty of Paris in 1763 ordered that the French be completely *removed* from North America. The Spanish, for their part, relinquished control of Florida in return for New Orleans and all lands west of the Mississippi River. The British now were in control of all land east of the Mississippi, but only for a few more years.

Growing Discontent

In the first part of the eighteenth century, the colonies were undergoing a religious revival called the *Great Awakening*. There were several preachers, in various regions, who started to speak of Christian salvation as something under the control of the individual. Prior to this, to many colonists, the prevailing interpretation of religion in New England had been that God decided who would be saved; and nothing one could do would change this *election* or non-election to heaven. The Great

Awakening changed the prevailing conception of Christianity to one of individual salvation. This weakened the bonds of authority previously enjoyed by the clergy and gave the colonists the will to challenge political authority, which had drastic consequences.

The Proclamation of 1763, issued by the king of England, forbade colonists to move west of the Appalachian Mountains. Ten thousand troops were stationed in the colonies to make sure the proclamation was obeyed. To pay for the troops, as well as the long and expensive war, the British crown saw a need to raise taxes in the colonies. In 1764 a tax called the Sugar Act combined new taxes on many imports (e.g., sugar) with greater enforcement of previous tax laws. Adding insult to injury, the colonists were then forced to provide housing for the British soldiers (the Quartering Act). They protested in pamphlets and newspapers, and subsequently the Stamp Tax of 1765 taxed all legal documents, including, of course, newspapers. The Stamp Act was perhaps the most important event of the revolutionary era. The Stamp Act Congress of 1765 was the first assembly of colonists created to oppose British regulation. In fact, the Congress' success in organizing a colonial boycott of British goods resulted in Parliament's rescinding of the Stamp Act the following year. The Townshend Acts of 1767 further tightened the taxation and regulatory noose.

After this long string of new taxes, and with no voice in English Parliament, the colonists were fed up. They boycotted British products, protested in writing, and sent emissaries to the king, all to no avail. In 1773, realizing that the Townshend Acts' taxation of tea (among other things) was not bringing in the anticipated revenues, the British passed the Tea Act. This prompted the guerilla theater response of the Boston Tea Party, where colonists dressed up like Indians and dumped tea from aboard British ships into Boston Harbor. Not amused, the British responded harshly with more restrictions on colonial town meetings and other penalties, the *Intolerable Acts* (or Coercive Acts). In 1774 the First Continental Congress met in Philadelphia to plan steps for resistance to British authority. Not intimidated, the British general in the colonies issued orders in 1775 for the colonists' growing stockpiles of arms and ammunition to be destroyed. Colonists in Lexington and Concord (Connecticut), warned by William Dawes and Paul Revere of the coming troops, defended their supplies; and the War of Independence had begun.

If you are unfamiliar with these events, there are many excellent resources that will fill in the details for you. You can search online, using any of the terms mentioned, or consult a book, textbook or otherwise. The Revolutionary War of the United States was unique, in that it was not fought by an underclass against an aristocracy. The leaders of the Revolution were not disadvantaged people; most simply objected to disrespectful treatment and "taxation without representation." Some of the more radical of the leaders, however, saw this as an opportunity to found a nation, for the first time ever, on the Enlightenment principles of equality and justice for all.

The Revolutionary War

More than a year after the "shots heard 'round the world" were fired at Lexington and Concord, representatives of the thirteen colonies met for the Second Continental Congress and signed the Declaration of Independence, authored by Virginia plantation owner Thomas Jefferson. There was quite a bit of gallows humor among them, for they knew they would be hanged if the revolution failed. It was an act of courage to sign the Declaration; but it was important to them to state their principles, especially since they sought foreign aid from the French in their struggle with Britain.

One principle was that men were justified in overthrowing an unjust government. Another was that all are equal in their right to "life, liberty, and the pursuit of happiness."

By the fall of 1776, it seemed likely that the Declaration signers would soon be hanging, for the war effort was going badly. The volunteer army was hungry and inadequately supplied. They were camped on the southern banks of the Delaware River, across from the stronger British army. On Christmas Eve, however, General George Washington loaded the troops in boats, crossed the river, and surprised and defeated the British at Trenton, New Jersey.

At first the British strategy had been to contain the revolution within New England. After the defeat at Trenton, however, they ramped up their efforts. They sent one army down from Canada, and another up from New York, with the aim of crushing Massachusetts between the two. Instead, the patriot army made a stand at Saratoga, New York, and soundly defeated the British. This major victory had the effect of persuading France (no friend of England, remember) to join the Revolutionary cause in 1778. The addition, in particular, of French naval power was instrumental in the patriots' success. In the following two years, first Spain, then the Netherlands joined with the rebels, forcing England to divert some of its focus from the ongoing revolution.

Notwithstanding the addition of allies, the Continental army was struggling in 1780. The war had been raging in their homeland for almost five years, their troops were stretched thin, and the fighting had shifted to the south. Desperate, the revolutionaries managed a couple of victories in fall of 1780 and spring of 1781 in South Carolina, forcing the British to retreat to a position at Yorktown, near the mouth of Chesapeake Bay in Virginia. With the help of the French, Washington's troops surrounded the troops of British general Lord Cornwallis. Finally, in October of 1781, the British surrendered.

The Hard Part: Governing

While the war for independence was being waged, the founders were already thinking about how best to govern the new country. Although a committee began working on Articles of Confederation before the Declaration of Independence was signed in 1776, it was 1781 before the finished Articles were adopted. Almost as soon as they were in place, it became apparent that, in their zeal to do away with the tyranny of excessive government, the founders had set up a government that could not effectively function. In particular, Congress could not raise money from the states, so it had no budget; nor could it regulate trade or conduct foreign policy without obtaining consent from the states on each matter.

The Constitution of the United States

In 1787 a Constitutional Convention was called to revise the Articles of Confederation. The Convention ended up with a completely new document, the Constitution of the United States, which gave the federal government much more power. After it was adopted, it had to be ratified by at least nine of the states (today, the process for changes to the Constitution requires the ratification of 2/3 of Congress and 38 of 50 states), but ratification took place only after long and heated debate about the proper role of the federal (central) government.

On one side of the debate were James Madison, Alexander Hamilton, and John Jay, who had expressed their position in the *Federalist Papers*. They were in favor of a strong federal government because they felt that it could be trusted to do the right thing more of the time than the states could. On the other side of the debate, the anti-federalists were strong believers in the inherent capacity of humanity to do the right thing; and they favored more individual rights and more power resting at the state level, rather than with the federal government.

The Constitution that came out of this debate strove to correct the deficiencies of the Articles of Confederation. Anti-federalists however, were concerned that individual rights were endangered; their arguments threatened to prevent the ratification of the Constitution in several states. In response, Federalists agreed in principle to draft a bill of rights to ensure that individuals and states would not suffer from excessive and arbitrary federal power. James Madison wrote the first ten amendments to the Constitution; they were ratified in 1791—four years after his initial draft. These ten amendments are known collectively as the Bill of Rights, and they remain the cornerstone of our individual civil rights.

The most pressing issue early on in the Convention was the issue of representation. Large states, such as Virginia, believed that representation in Congress should be based on population. Small states, like New Jersey, believed such a plan would leave states with smaller populations at a distinct disadvantage. The issue of representation threatened to break up the convention itself. Such an event would have placed the future of the new country in jeopardy. However, this impasse was settled by the *Great Compromise* whereby the Congress would be divided into two houses: the House of Representatives would be based on the population while the Senate would have equal representation—two senators from each state. Both the large and small states were satisfied with the arrangement. But the southern, slave-holding states favored a strong role for the states. Their economic systems depended on slave labor, and they saw that the northern states viewed slavery as incompatible with notions of equality and justice; therefore they made sure that the Constitution implicitly allowed slavery, by the inclusion of such provisions as the *Three-Fifths Compromise* (in counting population for representation, each slave would count for three-fifths of a free person). In addition to initially failing to free the slaves, the Constitution also did not give equal rights to women, who were, for example, denied the right to vote. However, it was a giant leap forward for human government. For one thing, it created a democratic form of government that depends for its very existence on the consent of the governed. It also established a flexible and resilient government that has survived several constitutional crises by balancing power (e.g., among the three branches of government) and interests (e.g., of small states and large states via the Electoral College and the two houses of Congress) and by containing a provision for change through the process of constitutional amendment. To create this document, the founders drew on several precedents: the Magna Carta, the English Bill of Rights of 1689, the Mayflower Compact, the Virginia House of Burgesses, and the institution of the New England town meeting.

To satisfy both the Federalists and the anti-federalists, the Constitution spells out certain roles for the federal government and other roles for the states. This system of division of power is called *federalism*. Still other functions, such as taxation and court systems, are concurrent (shared). This federalist versus states rights debate has continued throughout the history of the republic, with the U.S. Supreme Court often called upon to determine the intention of the Constitution's framers.

Federalism in the Constitution	
Rights Reserved for the Federal Government	**Rights Reserved for the States**
Print money	Conduct elections
Regulate interstate and international trade	Ratify amendments to the Constitution
Make treaties and conduct foreign policy	Issue licenses
Declare war and field armed forces	Regulate intrastate (within the state) to business
Establish post offices	Establish local governments
Make the laws necessary to execute these powers	Take measures for public health and safety
	Any other powers the Constitution does not reserve for the national government or prohibit the states from using

Separation of Powers

One of the cornerstones of our republic is the system of *checks and balances* written into the Constitution. This system is based on the concept of a government with three separate branches, the *legislative,* the *executive,* and the *judicial.* The legislative branch (Congress) makes the laws; the executive branch (President and administrative departments) sees that the laws are executed; and the judicial branch (federal court system, including the Supreme Court) interprets the laws that Congress makes.

Political Parties

Most of the founders were opposed to the establishment of political parties, and they are not among the requirements of the Constitution, but political parties developed naturally out of the differing philosophies at play in the early days of the republic. The first two parties, not surprisingly, were the *Federalist* and the *Democratic-Republican* parties.

The Federalists, led by Alexander Hamilton, John Adams, and John Jay, believed in a strong central government and were the driving force behind the Constitution's ratification. They believed in "loose construction," or the view of interpreting the Constitution broadly for the benefit of the nation. They wanted to create a national bank and to use government funds to support industrialization by such means as government road and canal building.

The Democratic-Republicans led by Thomas Jefferson and James Madison, were strongly in favor of individual rights. They opposed the "loose construction" ideas of the Federalists and instead advocated "strict construction"—a view that held that only those powers explicitly mentioned in the Constitution were federal powers. All others belonged to the states because a strong federal government was potentially capable of oppressing the individual. They also opposed industrialization, preferring that the U.S. retain an agricultural economy; and so they opposed government

[handwritten margin note: France's CLAIM to the land (which France bought from Spain)]

[handwritten margin note: Incorrect. The land is Native American; Jefferson buys]

funding of roads and other programs to aid industrial development. They did not think a national bank was a good idea as no mention of it existed in the Constitution.

Each of the two groups tried to persuade people to back their agendas. After 1800, the Democratic-Republicans were successful in their "no to big government" message; and by the election of 1816, the Federalist Party was basically defunct.

The Democratic-Republicans (more popularly known as "Republicans") later evolved into the Democratic Party of Andrew Jackson, and today's Democrats are the world's oldest existing political party. Their natural supporters were those who favored states' rights over federal power and those without the power or influence to determine policy, and so the Democratic party organized around the concept of defending the powerless against the wealthy and powerful. By 1836 those who supported the Federalist position had reorganized into the Whig party. The Whigs supported many of the old Federalist goals, and ultimately they became the nucleus of the modern Republican party, formed in 1854.

In the early 1850s the Republican Party was organized by a group of former Whigs and *free-soilers*, essentially those opposed to the expansion of slavery into the new western territories. By championing such a popular cause, the Republicans did well in the 1856 election (their first); and in 1860 their nominee, Abraham Lincoln, was elected president.

Westward Expansion

Remember that after the French and Indian War, the unpopular Proclamation of 1763 forbade the colonists to move west of the Appalachian Mountains. Colonists were disobeying this proclamation even before the Revolutionary War began; and as soon as American independence was declared, they started moving in earnest onto the open land (save for the Amerindians) to the west. Naturally, the tribes who lived on this land were not enthusiastic about this move to usurp their land; and hostilities were an ongoing factor of frontier life.

The people of the United States seem to have implicitly always seen themselves as destined to span the continent, but it wasn't until 1845 that a newspaper editor coined the phrase *manifest destiny*. Those two words encapsulated the American people's vision of themselves as destined to spread their political philosophy throughout the hemisphere. In fact, many at that time saw America's rightful role in the world at large as the disseminator of democracy; and some even believed in enforcing democracy with military might, if need be.

America's quest for land began with a purchase: in 1803 President Thomas Jefferson bought a large tract of land from France. Known as the *Louisiana Purchase*, this acquisition included much territory to the west of the existing United States and basically doubled the country's territory. That same year, President Jefferson commissioned explorers Lewis and Clark to find a route to the Pacific Ocean. In 1819, following the movement into Florida by many settlers, President James Monroe acquired that territory from Spain. The Oregon Territory (below the 49th parallel; today's modern U.S.-Canadian border) was obtained from Great Britain in 1846, and that same year President James K. Polk went to war with Mexico to gain even more territory in the southwest. The dispute with Mexico was originally about the U.S. annexation of Texas in 1845, but with the Treaty of Guadalupe Hidalgo in 1848, which ended the Mexican-American War, the United States added territory that included California, and the modern-day states of Arizona, New Mexico, Nevada, Utah, and parts of Colorado and Wyoming. America's sea-to-shining-sea expansion had reached its conclusion, but the westward migration of the population continues to this day.

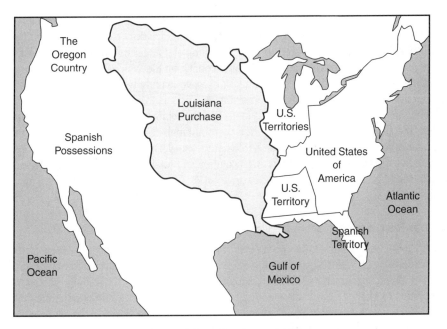

The Louisiana Purchase, 1803

Two Americas

In the early days of the Republic there were a number of axes along which the people's interests divided. The founders tried to compromise between interest groups, between large states and small, between wealthy interest groups and the common citizen, and between those who wanted a strong federal government and those who did not.

One of the deepest divisions, however, was between the southern states and the northern states. The reason for the split was the existence of slavery. Southern states depended for their livelihood on the institution of slave labor (although most white southerners were small farmers, who did not own slaves). Northern states, not depending on slaves economically, increasingly saw slave-owning as incompatible with the ideals of this bold Enlightenment-inspired country.

As tensions mounted, legislators tried to extend the compromises that were the cornerstone of the Constitution. In particular, the *Missouri Compromise* of 1820 tried to resolve the conflicts raised by the addition of new territories as either slave or non-slave owning areas. Southern legislators were trying to preserve the power of slave-owning states, while northern legislators preferred to limit slavery to existing slave states. As early as the 1820s, southerners argued that the concept of *nullification* allowed southern states to refuse to obey laws they did not agree with. For example, a civil war loomed in 1832 when South Carolina nullified a new tariff and President Andrew Jackson threatened to send the federal army into that state to enforce federal law. Yet, cooler head prevailed as both sides agreed to a compromise and the tariff was eventually reduced. In 1850, some southerners again threatened to secede if California was admitted into the Union as a free state. Southerners feared that California would tip the sectional balance in favor of the North. The Compromise of 1850 temporarily resolved the issue by granting southerners a stronger fugitive slave law and popular sovereignty in the newly conquered territory from

Mexico in exchange for California's statehood. (Popular sovereignty provided territories the right to decide for themselves whether or not they wanted to officially adopt slavery within their borders.) While many Northern legislators tried to avoid a confrontation over the slavery issue, the *Kansas-Nebraska Act* of 1854 brought it to national attention. Using the concept of *popular sovereignty*, this act finally got the attention of the Northern public, which had been sensitized to the slavery issue by, among other things, Harriet Beecher Stowe's popular book, *Uncle Tom's Cabin.* When the otherwise moderate (but anti-Kansas-Nebraska Act) Abraham Lincoln was elected President in 1860, the stage was set for open rebellion by southern states. Led by South Carolina, the seven states from the lower South exercised what they saw as their right of *secession,* that is, the right to leave the Union if they wanted to. Lincoln refused to allow dissolution of the Union, and the Civil War began.

The War Between the States

Although there were statesmen on both sides trying to prevent a civil war, there were also many southern "Fire-Eaters" refusing to compromise. In April 1861, secessionists fired on the last remaining Union stronghold in the South, Fort Sumter in South Carolina, starting the Civil War. Within weeks, a total of eleven states had seceded. Twenty-one states remained in the Union.

In addition to having more than twice the population of the newly-formed Confederacy, the Union had several other advantages. The Confederacy had no navy, no banking system, and no factories to speak of. Their economy depended on trading cotton grown on the plantations with European countries for all non-farm-generated necessities of life. The Union was already industrialized to a great extent; Union factories produced munitions and other goods for Union soldiers. The railroad system, banking system, and other aspects of the economy were in place and thus the suffering of the Union populace during the war was minimized.

Advantages of the Confederacy were that many of their officers were outstanding West Point graduates, and their soldiers were accustomed to handling firearms because of their rural culture. Additionally, most of the war was fought in the South; and people who are defending their homeland are notoriously reluctant to give up even a hopeless cause.

The Union quickly took advantage of its navy to institute a blockade of Southern ports; nothing could go in or out. This was a brilliant tactic, as Confederate cotton rotted on the docks, and the economy slowly starved throughout the four-year war. With few factories, the Confederacy ran out of ammunition and other supplies. The South ran up an early string of military victories; but in 1863 the tide turned at the Battle of Gettysburg, in which over 50,000 Americans from both sides died in three days. Following the Union victory at Gettysburg, President Lincoln delivered his famous Gettysburg Address and the Confederacy never recovered from the defeat.

Although he initially resisted freeing the slaves (he considering reuniting the country to be his most important task), President Lincoln yielded to pressure and on January 1, 1863, the *Emancipation Proclamation* took effect, freeing all slaves in regions still fighting against the Union. Later that year, Lincoln promised amnesty to all Confederates who would take an oath of allegiance to the Union and agree to accept emancipation. It was not until spring of 1865 that General Robert E. Lee surrendered for the Confederacy on the steps of the Appomattox courthouse. In December of that year, Congress passed the Thirteenth Amendment, abolishing slavery throughout the United States.

The tensions that led up to the Civil War, the attempts at compromise, and the battles of the war itself are all part of the most dramatic chapter in American history. If you are unfamiliar with these events, please seek out the necessary resources to learn more about this period, one that reverberates through American politics and policies to this day.

Reconstruction

President Lincoln's first priority, throughout the war and after its end, was the reunification and *reconstruction* of the states. However, he did not get to carry out his plans to heal the wounds inflicted by war. Five days after Lee's surrender, Lincoln was assassinated. Andrew Johnson, Lincoln's vice president, became president. He intended to carry out Lincoln's plan for reconciliation. This *Ten Percent Plan* (so-named because under the plan a state could be readmitted to the Union if ten percent of the former Confederates in the state who had voted in the 1860 elections vowed loyalty to the Union) included returning confiscated property to its former owners; but the plan was opposed by members of Johnson's own Republican Party. The *Radical Republicans* were outraged by the former Confederate officials who were being elected to Congress, and they refused to seat those representatives. Nor could they accept the so-called *black codes* passed by the Southern states. These codes were designed to restrict the rights and freedoms of former slaves.

Republicans passed a series of acts to remedy the situation, but Johnson vetoed them. Matters came to a head with impeachment proceedings against President Johnson. He survived the attempt to remove him from office; but the Radical Republicans were able to get the Thirteenth, Fourteenth, and Fifteenth Amendments to the Constitution passed, abolishing slavery, providing for equal protection and due process for all citizens, and giving freed slave men the right to vote. Once-freed slaves could no longer be denied the vote, Republicans began to be elected to many offices in the South.

The plantation/slave economy of the South lay in ruins. The Southern states were full of Union soldiers, and reconciliation had failed. The Ku Klux Klan had been formed to resist Northern attempts to enforce civil rights for the freed slaves, but the soldiers were managing to foil most of the Klan's efforts. Then, in 1877, Reconstruction abruptly ended.

In 1876, Republican Rutherford B. Hayes and Democrat Samuel Tilden ran against each other for President. Tilden won the popular vote, but Hayes managed to take the electoral vote by promising to end Reconstruction if Southerners voted for him. Hayes took office, and Reconstruction ended. Southern states promptly reinstated the old black codes, now called "Jim Crow" laws. Segregation and the philosophy of *separate but equal* (which in reality was separate but not equal), along with election rules designed to deny blacks the vote, were practiced in the South until the civil rights movement of the 1960s defeated them.

The Industrial Era

Although the northeastern section of the United States had begun to industrialize before the Civil War, after the war, the pace accelerated. Industrialization was fueled by the availability of a cheap labor pool in the form of recent immigrants, and newly built factories attracted even more immigrants to the states.

Germans constituted the largest number of immigrants to the U.S. between 1850 and 1900, successfully developing farms in the Midwest and skilled trades in larger cities. Another major wave of immigration came from Ireland beginning in the late 1840s. The Irish were starving because their staple food, the potato, had been decimated by a potato blight. When they arrived in the northeast, they were not welcomed. There were even riots by native Protestant Americans to protest the Irish taking of jobs away from the natives. Many Irish moved westward; some to the California Gold Rush of 1849; many to work on building the railroads that linked the northeast with the west and made commerce feasible between the two regions. A large percentage of Irish immigrants, however, lived in the nations largest cities such as New York, Boston, and Philadelphia.

Joining the Irish in the Gold Rush, and later on railroad construction, were Chinese immigrants. The Chinese also were the targets of discrimination and exclusion. Many of them successfully set up small businesses and inspired envy that resulted in discriminatory laws, culminating in the Chinese Exclusion Act of 1882, which prohibited Chinese immigration. That law was not repealed until World War II.

In the last decade of the nineteenth century, southern and eastern Europeans, the so-called "New Immigrants," swelled the populations of the eastern and Midwestern cities. Due to their large numbers and cultural differences from their English-speaking Protestant neighbors, Italians and Poles and others tended to settle in separate neighborhoods, or ghettos. By the second and third generations of immigrant families, however, cultural differences were minimized and they were assimilated into the *melting pot* of American society.

The Gilded Age

As railroads were built across America, they became central to American commerce; and those who owned the railroads began to exert enormous political and economic influence. The same was true for the industrialists who controlled industries such as steel, and for those who owned the big oil companies. In the decades following the Civil War, these men became so powerful that some historians have termed them (and their successors) the *Captains of Industry,* while others call them *Robber Barons.* It is undoubtedly true that the federal government was to a large extent controlled by these wealthy, powerful industrialists; and the presidency of Ulysses S. Grant (the commander of the Union Army during the Civil War) is sometimes called the most corrupt in U.S. history because of his indebtedness to these special interests.

While, on the one hand, this era suffered much corruption, on the other hand, it transformed American society. While some people were leaving cities and going to homestead land in the west (after passage of the Homestead Act promoted settlement on the prairies), others were giving up farm life to come work in city factories. Unmarried young women, even children, were often employed, as they were an excellent source of cheap labor. In response to exploitative practices, the American labor movement was born in the 1880s. Several influential unions were founded, and the last decade of the century saw frequent battles to define the respective rights of corporations and workers. The *Sherman Antitrust Act,* passed in 1890, placed limits on the extent to which a combination of firms or corporations could consolidate for the purpose of reducing competition and controlling prices throughout a business or an industry. However, the act had no real enforcement mechanisms and big business continued to circumvent the law until the Progressive era of the early twentieth century.

Themes of American History

When you think about American History (and you will need to think about it to pass Subtest 1), keep in mind the big themes that resonate throughout this country's story. They are:

1. Immigration and migration: who moved where, and why? Who was here already, and what happened to them? Who was left behind, and what happened to them? How did large-scale population shifts affect the demographic makeup of the whole country? How was the economy affected? How about the culture? Both local and national politics?

2. Federalist vs. States Rights: At any given moment in U.S. history, one group is usually arguing for a stronger federal government, while another group is arguing just as strenuously against it. Who is taking which side and why? What are the arguments on both sides (they change from era to era)? What might have happened if the group that lost a particular round of the argument had, instead, won it? What is your position in the current round of discussion? Why?

3. Isolationism vs. Engagement: Another continuing argument concerns the U.S. right/ responsibility to intervene in the affairs of foreign nations. In each era, who was arguing which side, and why? How has the discussion changed over time, and for what reasons? What do you think about U.S. involvement in foreign affairs? Should this country involve itself in matters that don't involve U.S. self-interest? If not, how narrowly or broadly do you define self-interest?

4. Expanding Democracy vs. Contracting Democracy: Remember that the United States is a republic, not a direct democracy; the will of the people is expressed through elected representatives, not directly by the people. Elected officials have interpreted "will of the people" in different ways. Think of the eras in which the people have influenced government to emphasize the Bill of Rights as opposed to eras in which people have allowed their representatives to enact legislation and pursue policies that concentrate power in the hands of the few. The former will be eras of expanding democracy; the latter, times of contracting democracy. Remember that the people always have the ultimate power; though sometimes they choose not to use it by, for example, not voting.

5. Perhaps the most crucial, most divisive, most unique challenge that has perplexed the U.S. throughout its history is the question of individual rights. How far can/should "We the government" go in protecting the rights of individuals (minorities, women, workers, homosexuals)? When do the interests of society as a whole, or the most powerful members of society, outweigh the "inalienable rights" of some of its members? Is there a guiding principle, or must decisions be made on a case-by-case basis? There have been demonstrations, riots, even a civil war, over this issue. It doesn't promise to go away any time soon. How can we discuss the continuing questions in a way that won't lead to more violence? How can we teach children about individual rights in a way that will help them make responsible, informed decisions when they too become voting citizens of the United States of America?

KAPLAN

CALIFORNIA HISTORY

Immigration is the key to the California History section of the CSET. Each wave of immigrants that has arrived in the Golden State has influenced the culture and the social, political, and economic landscape. The story starts with the first inhabitants, the Amerindians, and continues today, with immigrants arriving from other states and other nations. Once again, timelines may help here.

Another topic certain to be on the CSET is California geography. California has several distinct geographical and climatic regions, with associated natural resources and types of industry. From the coastal regions, to the mountain ranges, to the deserts, California's past and present are intimately tied to its geography.

Test Yourself

The natural substance used by native California tribes to waterproof their canoes and baskets was

(A) plastic

(B) asphalt

(C) gum

(D) acorn paste

The correct answer is **(B)**. Asphalt is a naturally-occurring tar-like substance that seeps to the surface in many California locations. One of the most famous of these locations is the La Brea Tar Pits in Los Angeles, where scientists still excavate fossils of Stone Age animals that got trapped in the sticky asphalt. Asphalt is quite pliable when warm, but hardens to an impermeable substance when cooled. That makes it an excellent waterproofing substance, a purpose for which it is still used in road building. Native Californians did make and use acorn paste, but for food, not for waterproofing.

A Rich Land

Geographically, California is the third largest state in the United States. It has both the highest point in the forty-eight contiguous states, Mount Whitney, and the lowest point in the U.S., in Death Valley. It has about 850 miles of coastline, a major mountain range (Sierra Nevada), several other ranges (coastal ranges, Cascade range), two major deserts (Mojave and Colorado), and the most productive farmland west of the Rocky Mountains (Central Valley).

With such incredible diversity of geography, it is little wonder that California is also economically, politically, and culturally diverse. Geography is intimately connected with how people lead their lives and therefore with the course of history. Illustrative of this fact is the diversity of the Amerindian cultures in California prior to contact with Europeans.

The First Wave

We don't know when the Amerindians arrived in America. It was long thought that human occupation of the Americas went back less than 10,000 years, but archeologists are now discovering sites that were inhabited possibly as much as 40,000 years ago. One line of speculation has these first immigrants taking a northern route from Asia via a land bridge that crossed the Bering Strait. Another group of scientists believes they arrived on South American shores in boats. It's possible that they came from both directions, in successive waves that spread until they covered both North and South America. Whether the ancestors of California's first people came from the north or the south, it required quite a trek to reach California. When the first European explorers sailed along the California coastline in the sixteenth and seventeenth centuries, there were probably several hundred different tribes living in six distinct geographical areas.

In the northern part of the state, there were two groups: From the coast to the area around Mt. Shasta lived the Yurok, the Hupa, and the Shasta, among others. They lived in a lush, temperate climate, with abundant fish and game. The presence of plenty gave them much time to develop rich religious and cultural traditions. The Modoc and Achumawi lived east of Mt. Shasta, one of the Cascade Range of mountains. They shared many cultural traits with their coastal neighbors, though their climate was somewhat more harsh. The tribes in both these groups constructed homes from the plentiful trees in their environment.

In the central part of the state, from the coast almost to the eastern border, lived the most populous related group, the Pomo, Miwok, Maidu, and Yokuts. Their homes were often constructed of *tule* (reeds). They fished the ocean and rivers, and salmon was a substantial part of their diet. In the winter they lived in the lowlands; but as the snows melted, they spent a great part of the warmer months in the mountains.

The easternmost part of the state, all along the current state border, was inhabited by the Shoshone, Paiute, and Washo. Culturally, they were close to their Great Basin neighbors in present day Nevada and Arizona. Theirs was a drier climate, without the big trees of the northern tribes. Pinon nuts were a staple of their diet, but they also hunted and fished the streams. Like the other California tribes, they engaged in lively trade with their neighbors all around them. Tightly woven water-carrying baskets were one of their specialties.

Most of the south, from present-day Santa Barbara to San Diego, was the land of the Chumash, Tongva (Gabrielino), Salinan, and Cahuilla. The coastal tribes made large, light plank canoes, called *tomols,* which could easily take to the ocean. They also hunted and fished. Acorns were a major food staple for these groups (as for most California Indians); and they prepared them in numerous ways. After leaching toxins from the pounded acorns, they made many dishes out of acorn flour, from acorn soup to flat cakes. Like the other tribes, they were accomplished basket weavers; and they also crafted bowls and sculptures from soapstone. These were major trade items for them. Their conical houses were constructed of poles, touching and tied in the center, and covered with woven mats.

In the southeastern corner lived the Quechan (Yuma) and Mohave tribes. They shared cultural ties, including language, with the Great Basin tribes to the north. Their environment was the arid desert, but they had mastered the art of desert living. They knew where the oases were, and the Colorado River was an ever-flowing source of life-giving water.

Due to their relative geographic isolation from each other, the California Indians tended to live in small groups, made up of large families, or clans, with very loose political structures. They both traded with and warred with each other, as people will do, but more often they lived relatively easy lives of balance on the land. It provided them with everything they needed, and they did not take more than they required. As you might expect from a people who did not have to work too hard for their existence, the California Indians had lives rich in religious, ceremonial, and artistic expression. Life changed, however, with the arrival of Spanish missionaries and soldiers, and then settlers, who came first from the south.

The Explorers

In 1542 Spanish explorer Juan Cabrillo sailed up the Pacific coast in search of the fabled Northwest Passage. He got as far as the San Francisco Bay area, claiming the land as part of the Spanish territory of *Alta California* (north of Baja California), before turning back. Over 35 years later, Sir Francis Drake, the English sailor who raided Spanish ships on behalf of Queen Elizabeth, sailed up the California coast and on to the Pacific Northwest. Sebastian Cermeno was sent by the viceroy of New Spain (much of present-day Mexico and Central America) to find safe harbors in Alta California. He found Monterey Bay, but lost his galleon (ship) in a storm. Sebastian Vizcaino explored the coast in more detail for Spain in 1602. He named many of the coastal areas, such as San Diego, Santa Barbara, and Monterey; and he made the first useful maps of the area. After Vizcaino's expedition, however, Spain's interest in California was shelved for more than 150 years.

All of these explorers were received courteously by the native peoples. After Cermeno's shipwreck, the Miwok shared their acorns with the Spanish, likely saving their lives. The Spanish, for their part, had no second thoughts about claiming the Amerindians' land for Spain, as though the natives had no valid claim to the land they lived on.

The Missionaries

In 1763 the French and Indian War (Seven Years' War) between France and England ended. Spain relinquished all North American claims east of the Mississippi River (most of their holdings were in the west anyway). In 1768, Jose de Galvez was the Visor General of New Spain. He also was an ambitious man, who convinced the king that it was urgent to settle California before the English or the Russians (who had sailed down the Northwest Pacific Coast from the north). He proposed a group of four expeditions to establish bases in the region. Two of the expeditions went by sea and two by land. They reconvened in July of 1769 in San Diego. The group included Gaspar de Portola, who would later establish Mission Dolores, the northernmost of *California's Mission System*, in present day San Francisco.

Also a member of this so-called *"sacred expedition"* was Father Junipero Serra, who promptly founded, near present day San Diego, the first of the original twenty-one Spanish Catholic missions in California. He then continued up the coast, personally establishing seven of the missions, which were spaced to be a single day's travel apart (on *El Camino Real,* the Royal Road). After Serra's death in 1784, Father Fermin Lasuen established nine more of the twenty-one missions.

From the very beginning, life was hard on the missions. The overland expeditions to San Diego had lost many of their men (mostly Indians from Baja California) on the journey. The Spanish needed to establish agricultural fields in order to survive, and they needed to do it quickly. For that purpose, they pressed native people into service. Over time, most of the coastal Indians became farm workers on and around the missions. The Spanish taught the Indians Christianity and agriculture. Unfortunately, they also spread diseases against which the natives had no immunity. Nor did many of the Indians like the nature of farmwork; but because the missions depended on their labor, the natives were forbidden to leave the missions. Father Serra persuaded the Viceroy in New Spain to issue a series of regulations that mandated humane treatment of the missions' labor force, but it was not possible to enforce the regulations, and abuses of the Indians continued. One practice, which we would consider an abuse now, but which the missionaries believed necessary, was the imposition of European culture beyond the practice of Christianity. Native culture was considered inferior and counter to Christian practices. The Spanish also wanted to acculturate the Indians so that they could take the place of Spanish settlers in claiming the land. Between the suppression of culture and the decimation of the population due to illness, Amerindian cultures in California were severely damaged during this period.

The mission fields introduced many new plants to California. The missionaries brought olive trees and orange trees. They introduced wheat and barley. They also brought farm animals, and thus the agricultural sector of California's economy was born.

The Presidios and Pueblos

It was always the intention of the emissaries from New Spain to fortify the California coast against possible attack by other European powers. The missions themselves were initially quasi-fortified. The anticipated attacks by Europeans never materialized; however, there were soon Indian revolts to deal with. When they realized their predicament, the native workers rebelled. Violent suppression of the revolts led to still more revolts, and the Spanish response was to build real forts, called *presidios,* to which the missionaries and settlers could retreat when under attack by angry workers.

Over time, towns began to grow around the missions and presidios, as settlers moved up from what is now Mexico. These towns were called *pueblos.* They were built around a church and a town square. The missions, pueblos, and presidios depended on each other for survival, and all three were crucial means of imparting Spanish culture, values, and social order to California inhabitants in the eighteenth century.

Mexican Independence

Growth was slow in California under Spanish rule. In 1810 Mexico began a war with Spain for its independence. The war lasted until 1821, when Mexico became an independent country. At that time, Mexico included much of what is now the southwestern United States, including California.

The new Mexican government had little interest in the mission system. It felt the missions were too powerful and that they were not just in their treatment of the Indians; officials pointed to the frequent native rebellions to support their position. In 1833 the governor of California, Jose Figueroa, closed the missions (except for the churches). He wanted the Native Americans to share in land ownership with Mexican settlers; however, few Indians ever received land, and their old way of life was no longer possible. Land was granted primarily to those who were already wealthy; and the result was a *rancho system*, with a few large landowners, and many landless workers. Residents of the region called themselves *Californios,* to distinguish themselves from other Mexicans. They identified as Californios, although they were also Mexican citizens. Mexico ruled California until 1848, and its stamp on the state's culture is strong.

The Mexican-American War

During the early 1800s, sailing vessels from the United States regularly stopped at California ports. Sometimes there was trade, and sometimes sailors and passengers got off and stayed. As the western half of the continent was explored, settlers from the eastern half often made their way to California in wagon trains, through the dangerous mountain passes and the more danger-ous deserts. The Mexican government did not discourage settlers, and so there were many U.S. citizens living in California by mid-century; though the region was still sparsely populated.

In 1845, Congress and U.S. President John Tyler decided to annex Texas, which had earlier bro-ken away from Mexico in 1836, though Mexico did not regard it as independent. When no agree-ment could be reached with Mexico, Polk sent U.S. troops to establish the boundary line. War broke out in 1846, and the United States' goals openly included acquiring Mexican territory west to the Pacific. California was part of the territory now being fought over.

Despite a brief attempt at the beginning of the war to establish an independent California repub-lic (the *Bear Flag Revolt*), California was soon under U.S. control. In 1848, the war ended with signing of the Treaty of Guadalupe Hidalgo. The United States had achieved its Manifest Destiny, to stretch from "sea to shining sea." As part of the treaty's settlement, the Californios were to keep their lands and positions. That promise proved difficult to keep, however. For one thing, California was about to experience an inundation of new settlers.

Gold!

In 1847, while building a sawmill in the Sierra Nevada foothills, workers for Johann Sutter discov-ered gold. Some say it was the foreman, James Marshall, who found the gold; some believe it was one of the Maidu workers. In any case, both Marshall and Sutter agreed to keep the discov-ery a secret. Gold can be a hard secret to keep, though.

A merchant named Sam Brannon decided to publicize the gold find. He wanted to get rich, but his plan didn't involve digging—at least not on his part. Before he ran through the streets of San Francisco with a bottle of gold dust, Brannon bought every shovel, pick axe, and pan in the region.

Word of the discovery filtered back east, and President Polk decided a gold rush was just what was needed to fill the newly acquired land with settlers. He promoted the find, and in 1849 all routes to California—over the mountains, across the ocean, and through the desert—were jammed with the *forty-niners,* all looking to strike gold, and all in need of shovels, pick axes, and pans. Sam Brannon became the richest of them all by *buying low* (e.g., a shovel for fifteen cents) and *selling high* (e.g., a shovel for twenty dollars). He could do this because he controlled the supply, and there was a great demand for the product (remember the economic law of supply and demand).

The first miners to arrive were native Californios and Amerindians. Soon, they were joined by thousands from Mexico, Oregon, Hawaii, and South America. At the end of 1848 there were 6,000 miners, some of whom struck it rich.

The forty-niners were not so lucky. The overland route from the east coast took three to four months and was difficult and dangerous, but that was the route most of the forty-niners took. Some of them traveled by sea, primarily around the tip of South America. That route was expensive, took five to eight months, and the storms in the southern Atlantic sank many ships. Another sea route from the east coast involved sailing to Central America, crossing the Isthmus of Panama, and boarding another ship to sail to California. Many Chinese and other Asians had also heard about the gold and boarded ships for California.

By the end of 1849, there were over 40,000 miners in the central Sierra Nevada foothills. It was a recipe for disaster. There were few shops, even fewer women, and practically no law enforcement. The early miners (Californios and Amerindians) were forced off the land. Then laws were passed to tax Asian and Mexican miners at disproportionate rates. Such institutions as police and other government functions had not yet caught up with the dramatic increase in population. Lawlessness and exploitation were rampant, and the ones who really got rich were the merchants who supplied the miners.

In 1853 the process of *hydraulic mining* was discovered. The miners used powerful hoses to shoot water at the hillsides in an attempt to wash away the soil and uncover gold. This process had two disadvantages: it damaged the environment, washing away hillsides into the streams and killing fish; and it forced individual miners to work for large companies that could afford equipment, instead of mining for themselves. The Gold Rush was over, but California had been populated.

Statehood

California and the United States wasted no time in putting the territory on the road to statehood. In June of 1849, less than a year and a half after the end of the Mexican-American War, and in the midst of the Gold Rush, the military governor announced that a state government was to be formed. In September, a constitutional convention met; and in November of 1849, the people of California approved their first constitution. Notably, the constitution did not allow slavery, a contentious topic in the United States at the time. In 1850 California became the thirty-first state.

During the first few years of statehood, many Californios lost their land to *squatters,* who felt that "Mexicans" shouldn't occupy the ranchos. The *Land Commission* was established to settle the Californios' claims. Only the rancheros who could afford the time and money to pursue their claims for as long as seventeen years got to keep their land; many of them lost it.

The Californios weren't the only ones to lose their land. The Native Americans who still lived on attractive areas of land were pushed off by settlers. The U.S. signed eighteen treaties with the Indians in 1851 and 1852, promising them large reservations, but those reservations never materialized. Soldiers sometimes cleared people off their land to make room for the settlers. In 1872 the Modoc tried to retake their land in northern California by force. The *Modoc War* was short, and the Modoc were forced back to a reservation in Oregon; their leader was hanged.

Transportation and Growth

Even after the Gold Rush ended, people wanted to come to California. In 1858, stagecoaches began bringing settlers and mail. The three-week trip was bumpy and crowded, but it was a definite improvement over the wagon train. In 1860, Pony Express riders began carrying mail in the lightning time of ten days from Missouri to California. They were put out of business in 1861 when the first telegraph line was completed, enabling, for the first time, almost instantaneous communication between the coasts.

Although the steam engine had been powering trains on the east coast since about 1830, it seemed highly impractical to build a railroad all the way across the continent. Still, a man named Theodore Judah organized a group of investors to help make that impractical feat possible. The so-called Big Four lobbied Congress for assistance; and within a year, President Lincoln signed the Pacific Railroad Act of 1862. The Act provided loans to the *Central Pacific Railroad,* owned by the Big Four (including future senator Leland Stanford), and another company, the *Union Pacific,* so that they could build a transcontinental railroad. When the companies experienced difficulties, partially due to the ongoing war, another Railroad Act in 1864 provided more funds and also gave the railroads ten square miles of land adjacent to the tracks for every mile of track laid. Construction began in 1863, and the line was finished in 1869. The work was done primarily by Chinese and Irish immigrants, who had trouble getting work that was less dangerous and better-paying. Many of the workers died in accidents. The Big Four became the richest men in California.

The Central Pacific Railroad was renamed the Southern Pacific Company. It soon controlled all the railroads in California—they had a monopoly on rail transport—as well as other transportation facilities, such as San Francisco Harbor. Business was booming. Interstate commerce was fueled by the new mode of transportation (and, later, the invention of the refrigerated train car), and the Southern Pacific Company could set its fees as high as it wanted. Representatives of the company met with government officials to determine the regulation of their industry. They paid large sums of money to legislators, who then passed laws favorable to the company. The president of Southern Pacific, Leland Stanford—a California governor and then a U.S. senator from the state—used his position to advance his company's position. The people began to resent this huge monopoly they called the "octopus" after a book of the same name that criticized the industry for having an arm in practically every sector of state commerce.

All around the United States, people were starting to feel that huge corporations were exercising too much power, even to the extent of controlling the government. Californians joined the burgeoning reform movement. In 1910, Hiram Johnson, the Republican candidate for governor, vowed to break the Southern Pacific's grip on the state. He was elected, and adopted the progressive goals that had been formulated by reformers. The Progressives (who briefly had their own national political party) favored workers' rights and the people over the big corporations. They believed in direct democracy, or *popular sovereignty;* and they were successful at improving the lives of many Californians. Nationally, Progressives passed many reforms; and California was the sixth state to grant women the vote (before the U.S. ratified the 19th Amendment, giving women suffrage, in 1920). Most notably, they also got a new state constitution written and passed.

The California Constitution

The state of California has a constitution that is designed to give power more directly to the people than is the case in the national government, or in most other states. It has three mechanisms for accomplishing this feat: the initiative, the referendum, and the recall. These mechanisms reflect the concept of popular sovereignty. One criticism of the concept of popular sovereignty—too often valid—is that it requires a well-informed electorate in order to succeed. A level of mere casual interest in the electoral process can produce undesirable results.

The *initiative* process gives individual citizens, or groups of citizens, the power to place a proposed law on the ballot. The people then vote for or against each initiative. In order for the proposed law or amendment to qualify for the ballot, its supporters must collect signatures equal to a small percentage of the electorate that voted in the most recent gubernatorial election. The initiative process truly does give citizens the initiative, but it has also often been abused by special interest groups who hide their agendas through misleading campaigns, long on emotion-laden advertising and short on information. Many initiatives have also turned out to be in conflict with the state constitution and have been declared void by the courts. One initiative, Proposition 13, passed in the 1970s, restricts property tax hikes and is favored by much of the population; but property taxes that don't rise with inflation have resulted in a drastic reduction over the years in funding for public education.

A *referendum* involves a statute or amendment that has passed the state legislature, which has then placed the proposed law on the ballot for approval by the electorate. A *recall* is a mechanism for ending an elected official's tenure in office before it is scheduled for completion. Again, it is initiated by any citizen and requires the signatures of a percentage of the number voting in the last gubernatorial election. The recall process in California was dramatically demonstrated in 2003, when Democratic Governor Gray Davis was removed from office by a majority of California voters and replaced with movie star Republican Arnold Schwarzenegger.

Immigration Matters

Chinese Immigration

Many of the Chinese laborers who worked to build the railroads later settled in San Francisco. Joining them was a steadily increasing flow of Chinese immigrants. Angel Island was the point of entry for these immigrants, as Ellis Island was for Europeans coming to New York City. The immigrants took low wage jobs at first, but many were able to become small business entrepreneurs and live the American dream.

It wasn't long before non-Chinese Americans began to resent Chinese immigrants. The Depression of the 1870s made matters worse, as the Chinese were blamed for the lack of jobs and thus suffered violence and damage to property. Racial epithets abounded, and a movement began to bar further immigration from China. Many local and state laws were passed to this effect, but the Chinese hired lawyers to fight back, and most of the laws were struck down as unconstitutional.

KAPLAN

In 1882, however, the Chinese Exclusion Act was passed with overwhelming support in the U.S. Congress. It barred immigration of Chinese laborers and gave immigration officials broad latitude to interpret the term *laborer*. Even wives of those already in the states were forbidden to join them. Furthermore, all Chinese already in the U.S. were made ineligible for citizenship.

Japanese Immigration

Other Asians were also discriminated against. When Hawaii became a U.S. territory at the turn of the century, many Japanese who had been living there moved north to the contiguous states. This prompted widespread racist fears and led to the 1907 *Gentleman's Agreement,* a treaty with Japan that allowed wives to join their husbands in the U.S. on the condition that the Japanese government deny exit visas to any men wishing to emigrate to the states. This treaty resulted in a wave of so-called *picture brides,* who were married by proxy in Japan to men they had never met.

Mexican Immigration

During this time—as well as before and since—California's border with Mexico proved difficult to seal. Immigrants from Mexico, Central and South America, and Asia continued to cross the border with great regularity. Ever since the great influx of European descendants arrived during the Gold Rush, the percentage of Latinos of Mexican descent in the California population has steadily risen. Immigration from Mexico remains a contentious topic. Despite many heated debates and occasional efforts to increase security, California's border with Mexico has been and continues to be easily crossed, though fraught with all-too-frequent loss of life and cases of exploitation of those who want the better life they feel the U.S. offers.

Continuing Discrimination Against Asians

In 1913, 1917, 1920, 1923, 1924, and 1934 the U.S. Congress passed laws aimed either at broadening the categories of Asians to be excluded from the United States (Indians, Filipinos) or at preventing them from owning property. It was not until the Magnuson Act of 1943 that the trend of discrimination started to reverse itself.

Unfortunately, at that time the United States was at war with Japan; and in 1942 the government rounded up all people of Japanese descent living on the west coast and sent them to *relocation camps* for internment throughout the war. All of their property, except what they could carry or sell, was confiscated and warehoused. Many families lost most if not all of their property as a result. At the same time that their families were confined, many young men of Japanese ancestry fought in the U.S. armed forces and died for their country. Finally, in 1988, President Reagan issued a formal apology and minimal, symbolic financial restitution was made to the internees.

The Tide Turns

Though there had been partial immigration reform throughout the 1940s and 1950s, it wasn't until President Johnson signed the Immigration Act of 1965 that U.S. immigration law became as equitable as one might expect from a country with such high ideals. This Act, intended to dovetail with the civil rights acts of the same period, established immigration quotas by eastern and western hemispheres, rather than by country. Immigrants were evaluated for admittance based on their skills, their need for family reunification, or their status as political or economic refugees.

The result was a flood of immigrants from Asia, many of whom came to California. The act also made possible the immigration of a large number of refugees from the political turmoil in Central America that was especially pronounced in the 1980s.

Immigration issues remain a controversial topic in California in particular and the U.S. in general. Many continue to blame immigrants for taking jobs away from existing residents, for overpopulation and resulting environmental degradation, and for requiring expensive public services (including education and health care). They are particularly concerned about the illegal immigrants who enter from the state's border with Mexico. Others believe that immigrants are hard-working, take low-paying jobs citizens don't want to perform, and pay taxes just like other workers. Meanwhile, California's population growth continues to outpace that of the United States at large (by 2000 the state accounted for about 13% of the nation's total population).

California's Economy

Agriculture and the Migrant Worker

One group of immigrants to California not discussed in the previous section were the Great Depression era refugees from the Great Plains states. During the Great Depression, many people lost their jobs; but the Great Plains were especially hard hit due to a severe drought that turned the entire region into a "Dust Bowl." In the 1930s more than 350,000 people left failed farms and lost jobs to come to California.

Despite the fact that the groups of California residents at the state line were not welcome-wagoners, but rather aimed to keep the so-called *Okies* out, the influx of would-be workers continued. Many of these immigrants found jobs as farm laborers. Along with Mexican immigrants, they were migrant workers, following the crops from farm to farm. The Okies joined with the Mexican migrant workers to strike and rally for better working conditions, but few advances were made until *Caesar Chavez* and *Dolores Huerta* founded the United Farm Workers Union in 1962.

Agriculture continues to be a vital part of California's economy, accounting for ten percent of all the jobs in the state. California is the largest agricultural growing and processing state in the nation, and the state's Central Valley is its largest agricultural area. Over half of all the fruits, nuts, and vegetables in the country come from California. The number one crop is cotton; dairy products are also important to the agricultural industry.

Manufacturing

The state's top manufactured product is electrical equipment. The *Silicon Valley* around Santa Clara is the largest producer of electronics, such as computers; though Los Angeles and Sacramento also boast large production facilities.

The aerospace industry got its start in California during World War II, when large military contracts were awarded to local companies to build aircraft for the war effort. The primary locations in the state for this industry are near Los Angeles, including Long Beach.

The apparel industry is also a major contributor to the California economy. Many clothing designers and manufacturers are located in the Southern California area. As might be expected from the state's climate, much of the apparel industry focuses on casual, warm weather clothing.

Other Industry

Tourism accounts for thirteen percent of the state's gross domestic product. Tourists visit to enjoy the state's theme parks and urban centers, as well as its many natural wonders, including nine national parks. Many state residents work in service industry jobs that support tourism.

California's entertainment industry is both a tourist draw and an economic force on its own. It employs more than 500,000 people and contributes over thirty billion dollars annually to the state's economy.

Other industries that are economic forces in California are trade (particularly with Pacific Rim countries) and transportation (including large ports), mining and natural resources, construction, and financial services. California has a diversified economy that ranks above those of most nations in terms of generated wealth. Some estimates show that California's economy in and of itself ranks as the sixth largest economy in the world!

Water

If California's economy has an Achilles heel, it just might turn out to be water. For more than one hundred years, the state's growing coastal cities have needed to import water from other parts of the state. Water is generally considered a renewable resource, but we have yet to learn how to quickly and effectively recycle water that has been polluted by the chemicals we use in manufacturing, agriculture, and everyday life. Instead, much contaminated water flows back into the earth's water supply, contaminating still more water in the process.

San Francisco's Water

In the early 1900s San Francisco's government officials decided that the growing city would soon need more water. They started trying to build a dam across the Tuolumne River that would flood Yosemite's Hetch Hetchy Valley. Many people thought flooding this beautiful area was too high a price to pay for San Francisco's growth; one of the most vocal opponents to the dam was naturalist John Muir.

Despite the fierce opposition, the U.S. Congress approved the Hetch Hetchy Dam in 1913. It took nine years to build the dam. Then an *aqueduct* had to be constructed to carry the water from the reservoir to the city. San Francisco did not start getting water from the reservoir until 1934. The Hetch Hetchy Aqueduct remains the main water source today for the people of San Francisco.

The Salton Sea

In 1900 an engineer named George Chaffey came up with the idea of building a 70-mile-long canal from the Colorado River to the Colorado Desert. The company he worked for owned land there, and it planned to irrigate the desert and sell it at a profit for farming.

The project was successful, and by 1902 over 2,000 people were living in the newly renamed Imperial Valley. After Chaffey's company sold its interest in the area, the canal's owner tried to bring even more water to the valley, causing a huge flood. That flood created the Salton Sea, which then became closed off to fresh water. The Imperial Valley now gets its water from other canals, and it is still a farming center.

The Central Valley

Another major farming area that receives water from far away is the Central Valley, named for its location in the center of the state. The Central Valley is 450 miles long; and the Sacramento and San Joaquin Rivers are in the north valley, while most of the agricultural activity is in the south. During the Great Depression, the *Central Valley Project* (CVP) was authorized to bring water from the north to meet farming needs in the south. One of the first steps was to construct the massive Shasta Dam, which is the second largest dam in the country.

The Central Valley Project was never completed as originally envisioned, though it is still an extensive project. One consequence of the project was the draining of extensive marshlands, including wildlife habitat, in the north. In the 1960s and 1970s environmental activists were able to block one of the biggest elements of the project, the damming of the American River; but the Central Valley Project is still one of the largest reclamation projects ever undertaken.

Los Angeles' Water

In 1900 the population of Los Angeles was over 100,000 and growing. The Los Angeles River supplied all the city's water, but the river could be affected by drought conditions. The men who ran the water department realized that they needed to locate another water source. William Mulholland, head of the department, had been told about the Owens River, 100 miles north of Los Angeles, along a steady rise in elevation. The river supplied a rich farming valley with plenty of water.

Mulholland and his partner secured the water rights without valley residents knowing what they were up to. Then they built an aqueduct that would bring the Owens River water to Los Angeles. In 1913 the aqueduct became operational, and it has supplied much of the water for Los Angeles ever since. The Owens Valley, meanwhile, has become dry and useless land.

By the beginning of World War II, Los Angeles' population was well over 1.5 million and still growing. The city needed more water, so it extended the aqueduct to Mono Lake and began draining water from the creeks that feed the lake. In 1970 the city completed a second aqueduct and prepared to drain Owens Valley groundwater. At that point, the Owens Valley government filed lawsuits to force the city to evaluate the environmental impact of its water consumption; and the groundwater plan was put on hold. In the late seventies and early eighties, citizens concerned about the failing health of Mono Lake filed suit to stop a planned increase in water drainage from the lake. The city was forced to moderate its consumption of water from the lake, which has now recovered to some extent.

The water supply for Los Angeles remains a thorny issue. There is not enough water locally to support a population that now exceeds three and a half million, the second largest in the United States. Many cities in the state face similar problems. Additionally, chemicals used by agricultural

KAPLAN

producers continue to pollute a diminishing clean water supply. Citizens remain resistant to enforced water conservation measures, and every year more people settle in the state. Scientists are trying to come up with additional sources of water (such as desalinization), and environmental activists are encouraging innovative conservation measures, but California's water supply seems destined to remain a source of concern for the foreseeable future.

Glossary

Aqueduct: a man-made channel constructed to convey water from one location to another

Bear Flag Revolt: a brief attempt at the beginning of the Mexican-American War to establish an independent California republic

Bushido: the code of knights in feudal Japan, the equivalent of chivalry in Europe

California's Mission System: a *"sacred expedition"* in which twenty-one Spanish Catholic missions were established, spaced to be a single day's travel apart on *El Camino Real* (the Royal Road)

Californios: residents of the rancho system in California just before the Mexican-American War, mainly composed of Mexican citizens who identified more as Californios than as Mexicans

Capitalism: an economic system regulated by the state that encourages the accumulation of wealth and property by individuals

Caste: a division of society based on differences of wealth, inherited rank or privilege, profession, or occupation

Central Valley Project (CVP): a federal water project undertaken by the Bureau of Reclamation in 1935 as a long-term plan to effectively use water in California's Central Valley

Checks and balances: written into the Constitution, this concept is one of the cornerstones of our republic, encompassing three branches of government and a system for them to act as watchdogs for the others

Circumnavigate: to sail completely around the Earth

Code of Hammurabi: the first known written legal code, developed in ancient Babylon, predated the Justinian Code by about 2,000 years

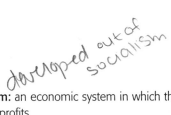
developed out of socialism

Communism: an economic system in which the state controls the means of production and distributes the profits

Conquistadores: Spanish explorers that sought riches in Central and South America, establishing colonies along the way

Daimyo: Japanese feudal lord

Democratic-Republican party: one of the first two political parties in the United States, led by Thomas Jefferson and James Madison; opposed the Federalist party and was strongly in favor or individual rights

Economics: a social science dealing with the production, distribution, and consumption of goods and services

Emancipation Proclamation: a proclamation made by President Lincoln in 1863 freeing all slaves in regions still fighting against the Union

Executive branch: a branch of the system of checks and balances that sees that the country's laws are executed

Federalism: a system of government consisting of a number of self-governing regions (states) united by a central (federal) government

Federalist Papers: a series of articles written in 1787 by Alexander Hamilton, James Madison, and John Jay to gain popular support for the then-proposed Constitution

Feudalism: a social, economic, and political system in which power is decentralized, and a varying number of lords hold land on which they allow others to live and work in return for loyalty and service

Fief: land held by lords under the feudal system

Forty-niners: nickname for the influx of people that arrived in California, starting in 1849, in search of gold

Free-soilers: a minor but influential political party in the pre-Civil War period that opposed the extension of slavery into the western territories

Gentleman's Agreement: a 1907 treaty with Japan that allowed wives to join their husbands in the U.S. on the condition that the Japanese government deny exit visas to any men wishing to emigrate to the states

Great Awakening: a religious revival in the colonies during the first part of the eighteenth century

Great Compromise: a decision made by the Constitutional Congress splitting Congress into two houses, one based on population (House of Representatives), and one based on equal representation (the Senate)

Hunter/gatherer societies: an early society in which men hunted for meat and women gathered more readily available food

Initiative: a process that gives individual citizens, or groups of citizens, the power to place a proposed law on a ballot

Intolerable Acts (or Coercive Acts): British reaction to the Boston Tea Party, including more rigid restrictions on colonial town meetings and other harsh penalties

Judicial branch: a branch of the system of checks and balances that interprets Congressional laws

Justinian Code: considered to be the basis for the justice systems in use throughout much of the western world, including the United States

Land Commission: established to settle the Californios' land claims during the first few years of California's statehood

Law of supply and demand: a basic economic principle stating that if supply is greater than demand, the value of a product is lower; if demand is greater than supply, the value is higher

Legislative branch: a branch of the system of checks and balances that makes Congressional laws

Louisiana Purchase: 1803 purchase made by President Thomas Jefferson that essentially doubled the United States' territory

Manifest destiny: an 1845 phrase encapsulating the American vision of western expansion

Mercantilism: the practice of state regulation and control of an economy

Missouri Compromise: 1820 legislation that tried to resolve the conflicts raised by the addition of new territories as either slave or non-slave owning areas

Monotheism: the worship of only one god

Nullification: a concept espoused by southerners following the Missouri Compromise that would have given southern states the right to refuse to obey laws they did not agree with

"Octopus": a term used to describe the Central Pacific Railroad's monopoly for having an arm in practically every sector of California's commerce

Pilgrims: a religious group who had broken away from the Church of England, first relocating to Holland to escape persecution, then setting sail in the fall of 1620 to become the first settlers to arrive in Massachusetts

Popular sovereignty: a direct democracy

Presidio: forts built by the Spanish to offer protection to California's missionaries and settlers during periods of violent revolt by native workers

Pueblos: towns based around California's missions and presidios, built around a church and a town square

Rancho system: a land allotment system defined by a few large landowners and many landless workers

Recall: a mechanism for ending an elected official's tenure before its scheduled completion

Reconstruction: President Lincoln's first priority after the Civil War to reconcile the warring sides and rebuild areas affected by war

Referendum: a statute or amendment that has passed the state legislature, which is then placed on a ballot for approval by the electorate

Reincarnation: a religious belief in which, after physical death, a rebirth in another body occurs; a central tenet of Hinduism, among other religions

Relocation camps: internment camps that held people of Japanese descent during World War II

Renaissance: a French word meaning *rebirth*; the name given to the flowering of European culture at the end of the Medieval period

Secession: the self-given right of the seven states of the lower South to leave the Union if they so desired

Separate but equal: a philosophy, along with election rules, that was designed to deny blacks the right to vote after reconstruction ended

Serf: peasants who work on land in a feudal system

Shogun: in feudal Japan, the equivalent of a medieval European king

Silicon Valley: a nickname for the southern part of the San Francisco Bay Area in northern California, originally referring to the concentration of silicon chip innovators and manufacturers, but eventually referring to the entire concentration of all types of high-tech businesses

Socialism: an economic system in which workers control the means of production and share in the profits of their labor

Ten Percent Plan: a plan created by President Lincoln before his assassination, and carried out by his successor, Andrew Johnson, stating that a state could be readmitted to the Union if ten percent of the former Confederates in the state who had voted in the 1860 election vowed loyalty to the Union

Three-Fifths Compromise: an initial rule in the Constitution stating that in state population counts, each slave would count for three-fifths of a free person

Vassal: the equivalent of a knight in the feudal system

PRACTICE SET

1. Which of the following describes the geographical setting in which early civilization was most likely to emerge?

    (A) An open, grassy plain with plenty of room and food for livestock

    (B) Rolling hills that provided vantage points from which to scout for enemy invasions

    (C) A temperate river delta that flooded regularly, resulting in fertile soil for crops

    (D) Dense jungle with edible plants and game enough for hunting and gathering

2. Which of the following groups of Middle Eastern tribes are credited with bringing the concept of monotheism to the world?

    (A) Hebrews

    (B) Egyptians

    (C) Kush

    (D) Persians

Use the list below to answer the question that follows.

> I. belief in reincarnation (rebirth after death)
>
> II. practice a caste system, with four social groups, membership in which is determined by birth
>
> III. drive to attain enlightenment, which brings freedom from rebirth
>
> IV. belief in the concept of karma, that one's fate is earned by one's past deeds

3. The tenets listed above are most accurately attributed to which of the following religious belief systems?

    (A) Buddhism

    (B) Islam

    (C) Confucianism

    (D) Hinduism

4. Which of the following modern disciplines was NOT influenced by the civilization of ancient Greece?

    (A) philosophy

    (B) anthropology

    (C) theater

    (D) mathematics

5. Which of the following empires splintered from the Egyptian empire and established a vigorous trade in precious metals, while retaining many characteristics of Egyptian civilization?

   (A) Phoenician

   (B) Mayan

   (C) Babylonian

   (D) Kush

6. Which of the following was a contributing factor to the decline of the Roman Empire?

   (A) the size of the empire forced the hiring of mercenaries for its defense forces

   (B) the empire's public education system failed for lack of tax revenues

   (C) corruption invalidated the results of Roman elections

   (D) widespread starvation made the people receptive to new leadership

7. Which line in the table below correctly places terminology from both Japanese feudalism and European feudalism?

Line	Japanese Feudalism	European Feudalism
1	peasants	serfs
2	daimyo	shogun
3	samurai	vassals
4	chivalry	bushido

   (A) Line 1

   (B) Line 2

   (C) Line 3

   (D) Line 4

8. Which of the following was the most powerful and wealthy force in medieval Europe?

   (A) king

   (B) lord

   (C) church

   (D) state

KAPLAN

9. Which of the following was primarily responsible for the introduction of spices and other Asian goods to medieval Europe?

   (A) the Crusades
   (B) Christopher Columbus
   (C) the Phoenicians
   (D) the Vikings

10. Which of the following geographical features were the French searching for in their early explorations of North America?

    (A) The St. Lawrence River
    (B) The Great Lakes
    (C) The Northwest Passage
    (D) The Pacific Ocean

11. Which of the following Native American empires covered a land area characterized by diverse geographical features, from jungle coastline to highlands, with widespread and often competing power centers?

    (A) Aztec
    (B) Maya
    (C) Inca
    (D) Iroquois

12. Which of the following best expresses one reason slavery became entrenched in the southern colonies prior to the Revolutionary War but never took hold in the northern colonies?

    (A) The southern colonies were settled primarily by Spain, which had no moral qualms about slavery; but the English, who abhorred slavery, settled in the north.
    (B) The southern colonies were settled primarily as penal colonies, with an anything-goes attitude; but the northern colonies were more strictly governed by England.
    (C) Geographically speaking, the southern colonies were closer to the route the slave traders took from Africa; so southern slavery was more economically feasible.
    (D) The geography of the northern colonies was less conducive to highly labor-intensive cash crop agriculture than were the southern colonies.

13. Which of the following pairs of colonies BEST reflect truly tolerant havens for religious freedom, rather than being devoted to the practice of only one brand of religion?

    (A) Rhode Island and Pennsylvania
    (B) Massachusetts and New York
    (C) Connecticut and New Hampshire
    (D) Maryland and Virginia

14. The Proclamation of 1763 was an unpopular edict that led to further unrest in the British colonies. Which of the following best represents the content of this proclamation?

    (A) Colonists were forbidden to move west of the Appalachian Mountains.
    (B) Colonists were required to pay for the housing of British troops.
    (C) Colonists were required to pay taxes on many imported goods.
    (D) Colonists were required to sign oaths of loyalty to the English king.

15. Which line in the table below best matches the name of an event in the Revolutionary War to an accurate description of the event's effect?

Line	Event	Effect
1	Battle of Concord	Caused massive defection of British troops
2	Battle of Saratoga	Persuaded France to ally with the revolutionaries
3	Crossing the Delaware	Captured badly needed food supplies for starving revolutionary army
4	Battle of Yorktown	Decimated revolutionary troops and prolonged the war

    (A) Line 1
    (B) Line 2
    (C) Line 3
    (D) Line 4

16. Which of the following sums up the reasons the Articles of Confederation proved inadequate governing documents for the newly formed United States?

    (A) They concentrated too much power in the hands of too few.
    (B) They did not adequately protect the interests of minorities.
    (C) They gave the federal government too few powers.
    (D) They did not give women the right to vote.

17. The concept of Manifest Destiny, which was popular in the nineteenth century, is best exemplified by which of the following U.S. actions?

    (A) the Louisiana Purchase
    (B) the impeachment of President Andrew Johnson
    (C) the Civil War
    (D) the Mexican-American War

18. After President Lincoln's assassination, his vice president, Andrew Johnson, became president. His plans for reconstruction of the Confederate states failed for which of the following reasons?

    (A) Congress thought Johnson's reconstruction plan too lenient on the south.
    (B) The Confederate states refused to grant full rights to the freed slaves.
    (C) The Ku Klux Klan organized effective resistance to reconstruction efforts.
    (D) Lincoln's supporters in Congress blocked efforts to bring the Confederate states back into the Union.

19. Which of the following was a staple of the diet of the majority of California's Indians?

    (A) beef
    (B) acorns
    (C) mutton
    (D) beets

20. Which of the following was the primary reason Spain decided in 1768 to establish missions in California?

    (A) Father Serra persuaded the king to help him save the natives' souls.
    (B) Juan Cabrillo had found evidence of gold deposits near the coast.
    (C) Jose de Galvez convinced the king it was urgent to establish settlements before the English did.
    (D) The Spanish king wanted to expand the territories he would leave to his sons.

21. Which of the following activities was introduced by the Spanish missionaries and later became a major economic force in California?

    (A) tourism
    (B) fishing
    (C) agriculture
    (D) gold mining

22. California's native peoples began, after a time, to rebel against the conditions of their labor on the mission farms. Which of the following was the Spanish response to their revolts?

    (A) build pueblos
    (B) build more missions
    (C) build prisons
    (D) build presidios

23. Which of the following accurately describes a result of the Treaty of Guadalupe Hidalgo?

    (A) the freedom of Mexico from Spanish rule

    (B) the U.S. acquisition of land from Mexico

    (C) the establishment of an independent California

    (D) the end of the Bear Flag Rebellion

24. Which of the following groups became most wealthy as a result of the Gold Rush?

    (A) early miners

    (B) later miners

    (C) law enforcement officials

    (D) merchants

25. Which of the following best states the purpose of the Land Commission in the years following California statehood?

    (A) to adjudicate the conflicts between Californios and U.S. settlers who took their ranchos

    (B) to settle disputes between California Indians and miners who had settled on their claims

    (C) to help settlers establish homesteads on vacant California land

    (D) to resolve discrepancies in court records from the days of Mexican rule

26. Which of the following was the monopolistic industry that became known as "the octopus" at the end of the nineteenth century?

    (A) agriculture

    (B) mining

    (C) steel

    (D) the railroad

KAPLAN

Constructed-Response Question 1

Complete the exercise that follows.

The Constitution of the United States drew many of its legal concepts from centuries of precedent in the western world.

Name three influences on the development of western legal thought.

Discuss how each influence was important in the development of legal tradition.

Magna Carta

enlightenment thinking - John Locke

Hammarabi's code?

Justinian code?

Leviathan - thomas Hobbes

Constructed-Response Question 1

Complete the exercise that follows.

The Constitution of the United States drew many of its legal concepts from centuries of precedent in the western world.

Name three influences on the development of western legal thought.

Discuss how each influence was important in the development of legal tradition.

Magna Carta

enlightenment thinking -John Locke

Hammarabi's code?

Justinian code?

Leviathan-Thomas Hobbes

Constructed-Response Question 2

Complete the exercise that follows.

The Immigration Act of 1965 was a sweeping reform of United States immigration policy.

Discuss this act in comparison to U.S. immigration policies prior to 1965.

Describe the impact of this act on California's population.

_____

_____

_____

_____

_____

_____

_____

_____

_____

_____

_____

_____

_____

_____

_____

_____

_____

_____

_____

_____

_____

_____

ANSWER KEY

1.	C	8.	C	15.	B	22.	D
2.	A	9.	A	16.	C	23.	B
3.	D	10.	C	17.	D	24.	D
4.	B	11.	B	18.	A	25.	A
5.	D	12.	D	19.	B	26.	D
6.	A	13.	A	20.	C		
7.	C	14.	A	21.	C		

ANSWERS AND EXPLANATIONS

1.   C

The earliest civilizations were in the so-called Fertile Crescent in the Middle East, along the Tigris and Euphrates rivers. These rivers provided ideal conditions for agriculture to emerge, and regular crops provided enough respite from the grind of daily hunting and gathering that people could devote time and attention to the pursuits of civilization—art, religion, learning —that require leisure time. The locations described in the other answers are all viable habitats for humans, but agriculture is considered a prerequisite for the development of civilization.

2.   A

Today's Jews worship the one God their Hebrew ancestors worshipped 3,000 years ago. At that time, their neighbors and other groups still practiced polytheism, the worship of more than one god. Christians and Muslims derived their monotheistic concepts from the Jewish, or Hebrew, philosophy of one God. The other groups mentioned all worshiped multiple gods when the Hebrews developed monotheism.

3.   D

While Hinduism **(D)** shares with Buddhism **(A)** a belief in karma and in the possibility of enlightenment, which brings relief from the burden of reincarnation, (Statement I), Buddhists do not practice the caste system (Statement II). Confucianism **(C)** is a philosophical system practiced in China that emphasizes respect for others, especially authority. Islam **(B)** does not share any tenets listed in the question with Hinduism.

4.   B

Anthropology—the study of peoples—was not founded as a discipline until the twentieth century. Today's philosophy (Aristotle, Socrates, Plato), theater (Sophocles, Aristophanes, tragedy as a form), and mathematics (particularly geometry) were all greatly influenced by the ancient Greeks, as were art, architecture, medicine, and many other disciplines. The Greeks were also our predecessors in practicing an early form of democracy.

5.   D

Originally dominated for centuries—both politically and culturally—by the Egyptians, the people of Kush (also known as Nubia), in what is now Sudan, became a powerful force in about 750 B.C.E. They were advantageously located on trade routes in northern Africa and benefited from rich gold and emerald mines in their land. The land also yielded iron ore and the timber required to fuel the processing of ore into usable iron, so they also had a thriving iron industry. The Babylonian civilization **(C)** preceded the Kush and could not be considered a splinter kingdom of Egypt, nor could the Phoenician **(A)** or the Mayan **(B)**.

6.   A

Rome overextended its empire, necessitating the use of mercenaries, whose loyalties tend not to run past the last paycheck. In addition, it suffered from political instability (in its last stage, the Empire split into two parts) and from an economy that depended on tribute from its conquered peoples. Any of the other factors could lead to the downfall of an empire, but the Roman Empire had no public school system **(B)**; its elections were limited to the wealthy few **(C)**; and starvation was not a wildespread problem **(D)**.

KAPLAN

7. C

There are many parallels between Japanese Feudalism and European Feudalism, but the terminology used to describe them differs. Each had a decentralized power structure, with the King (Shogun) being just slightly higher status than a powerful Lord (Daimyo). The Lords/Daimyos were served by Vassals or Knights (Samurai), who lived by a code of honor called chivalry (bushido). At the bottom of the social heap were the serfs or peasants, who worked in return for protection.

8. C

The Roman Catholic church was much more wealthy and powerful than any individual lord, or even king, in medieval Europe. The feudal system that characterized medieval times had a decentralized power structure, in which each individual lord **(B)** controlled his own fiefdom and owed only loose allegiance to a king **(A)**, who might not have as many resources (state, **D**) at his disposal as a wealthy lord did. The Church, on the other hand, was united (under the Pope), wealthy, and the powerful sole source of access to heaven as well as to books and education.

9. A

For almost two hundred years, starting around 1100 C.E., wave after wave of Crusaders **(A)** left Europe for the Middle East, in an attempt to free Jerusalem from the Muslims. While they were on their journeys, they learned about the spices from India that so deliciously masked the flavors and aromas of spoiled meat, which was common prior to the discovery of year-round refrigeration techniques. Both the Vikings **(D)** and the Phoenicians **(C)** were early seafarers, who sailed to much of the world prior to Columbus' voyages **(B),** but neither group was responsible for the popularization of spices and other Asian goods.

10. C

Jacques Cartier was the first French explorer to search for the fabled Northwest Passage to India. In the course of his voyages, he sailed up the St. Lawrence River **(A)**, laying claim to the land on behalf of France. The French did locate some of the Great Lakes **(B)**, but that is not what they were searching for. They did not know about the Pacific Ocean **(D)** but, rather, thought there would be a passage, such as a river, that would provide a shortcut to India.

11. B

The Maya controlled a far-flung empire that ranged from the jungles of the Yucatan to the mountains of Guatemala. Though there probably had been more cooperation in the past, by the time the Spanish arrived there was intense competition and warfare among the various power centers, each with its own ruler. The Aztec **(A)** operated within a more restricted area in central Mexico. Their capital, Tenochtitlán, was uniquely situated in the middle of a lake. The Inca **(C)** controlled much of the west coast of South America, operating in a long, narrow strip of land between the Pacific Ocean and the Andes Mountains. This unique geography led them to construct a highway system for faster transportation/communication with the far reaches of the empire as well as a sophisticated system of irrigated terraces on the slopes of the mountains. The Iroquois **(D)** occupied the northeastern part of what is now the United States, and their geography ran more to hilly woodlands.

12. D

Those who settled in the New England and Mid-Atlantic colonies did not see slavery as a righteous institution. Those who settled the southern colonies tended to be more interested in furthering their economic status than in religious freedom. Also, the southern climate was more conducive to the large plantations that made slavery economically feasible. Choice **(C)** is partially correct, in that the south is closer to Africa, but the statements in **(A)** and **(B)** are incorrect.

13. A

Roger Williams was expelled from Massachusetts for disagreeing with its religious leaders. He made his way to Rhode Island and established that colony as the first to recognize the separation of church and state. William Penn, a Quaker, established Pennsylvania as a haven of tolerance for the religious beliefs of even non-Quakers and enshrined those principles in the colony's constitution. None of the other answer choices is correct. The states mentioned in **(B)**, **(C)**, and **(D)** were not established as havens for religious freedom-seekers.

KAPLAN

14. A

After the end of the French and Indian War, England wanted to avoid angering the Native Americans in the newly acquired Ohio Valley and to keep the colonists where they could be controlled more easily. The Proclamation of 1763 forbade them to move west, thereby angering the colonists. This proclamation was the first in a string of edicts that inflamed rebellion, including those described in **(B)** and **(C)**. Choice **(D)** does not describe an actual edict.

15. B

The Battle of Saratoga was a decisive victory for the revolutionaries and was all the impetus the French needed to join cause with the rebels against the British. This alliance proved to be a major turning point in the war. The Battle of Concord **(A)** usually linked with Lexington, was the first skirmish in the war. The crossing of the Delaware **(C)** led to much-needed victory but was not carried out to obtain food. The Battle of Yorktown **(D)** was a huge victory against the British, one that hastened the end of the war, not prolonged the war as stated in the answer choice.

16. C

Among the powers not granted to the federal government in the Articles of Confederation were the ability to raise money from the states (hence, no money to spend), the ability to regulate interstate trade, and the ability to conduct national foreign policy. Although thought by some to be true, none of the other issues stated in the answer choices (the concentration of power in the hands of few **(A)**, the inadequate protection of minority groups' interests **(B)**, and the exclusion of women from voting **(D)**) was crucial to the debate over the governing documents.

17. D

In 1845 a newspaper editor coined the phrase Manifest Destiny. Those two words described the American people's vision of themselves as destined to spread their political philosophy throughout the hemisphere. In particular, they saw the United States as stretching from "sea to shining sea." The Louisiana Purchase in 1803 **(A)** greatly expanded United States territory, but prior to the coining of the term. Choices **(B)** and **(C)** do not relate to Manifest Destiny, but the Mexican-American War was a thinly-disguised land grab that helped fulfill that destiny.

18. A

Johnson proposed a Ten Percent Plan, under which a state could be readmitted to the Union if ten percent of the former rebels in the state vowed loyalty to the Union, but the so-called Radical Republicans blocked his plans, and then impeached him. The other choices do not describe Johnson's problems accurately. The former Confederate states took every opportunity for the next hundred years to deny full rights to blacks **(B)**, but that was not the core of Johnson's problems; instead it was a major reason why the Republicans in Congress demanded that southern states ratify the 14th Amendment *before* they would be allowed back into the Union. The Ku Klux Klan was a force of resistance **(C)**, but not the cause of Johnson's failure. Lincoln's supporters mostly backed efforts to reunite the Union **(D)**, as that had been Lincoln's main concern, unlike the Radical Republicans, who wanted to punish the former Confederates.

19. B

California's Indian tribes lived in a diverse array of habitats. They were hunters and gatherers, most of whom did not practice agriculture. Their various environments featured plentiful fish and game as well as numerous plant foods that provided daily sustenance. One of the important staples for most of the native peoples was acorns **(B)**. California has several varieties of native oak trees; and acorns can be prepared by cracking them open, leaching the bitter taste from the pounded pulp, and then using the resulting flour in a number of dishes, from soup to bread. Beef **(A)**, mutton **(C)**, and beets **(D)** were not staples of the tribes' diets.

20. C

Jose de Galvez was the Visor General of New Spain. Although England had shown little interest in the land the Spanish called Alta California, he persuaded the king that Spain needed to settle the land in order to prevent the English (and the Russians) from trying to claim the territory **(C)**. Father Serra **(A)** was a member of the first settlement expedition, but not its instigator. Cabrillo **(B)** was the first explorer of California, in 1542 and was not involved with the establishment of California's missions. Choice **(D)**, the Spanish king wanting to leave land to his sons, although true, was not a prime reason for the establishment of the missions.

21. C

The missionaries brought olive trees and orange trees with them when they came up from what is now Mexico. They also introduced wheat and barley to the area. Prior to their arrival, the California Indians did not practice extensive agriculture. In addition, the missionaries brought the first livestock to California. Tourism **(A)** was not a concern for the missionaries. Fishing **(B)** was practiced extensively by the native peoples before the missionaries arrived. Gold mining **(D)** was not introduced by the missionaries.

22. D

A presidio is a fort. As the Amerindian revolts grew in frequency and intensity, the Spanish inhabitants of the missions and the nearby pueblos (towns) began to retreat to the newly-constructed presidios for protection whenever rebellion threatened. Missions **(B)**, pueblos **(A)**, and presidios **(D)** played important roles in the establishment of Spanish culture in California, but missions and pueblos were not established to counter the Amerindian revolts.

23. B

The Treaty of Guadalupe Hidalgo marked the end of the Mexican-American War in 1848. Under the terms of the treaty, the United States acquired much land that had previously belonged to Mexico, including California. Mexico gained independence from Spain **(A)** in 1821. The Bear Flag Rebellion **(D)** was an extremely short-lived attempt to establish an independent California state **(C)**. It was ended by the arrival of U.S. troops in the area.

24. D

From the merchant who bought up all the digging supplies prior to publicizing the gold discovery, to Levi Strauss, who made his first denim pants for the miners, the ones who really made money from the gold rush were the merchants. The early miners **(A)** made more than the later miners **(B)**, but striking it rich was strictly a hit-or-miss proposition even for those that arrived earliest. Law enforcement officials **(C)** were in short supply, though probably some took the opportunity to profit from their positions.

25. A

Following statehood in 1850, many of the wealthy Californios who had been granted large ranchos by the Mexican government lost their land to squatters who felt that they had the right to take land belonging to "Mexicans." The Californios had been promised they could remain on their land when it became part of the United States. The Land Commission was established to settle the Californios' claims, but it took years and much money for the Californios to defend their property rights. Many of them lost their land. The California Indians **(B)** were even less fortunate—every one of the dozens of treaties with the government that guaranteed them land was broken, and their cultural heritage was all but destroyed. Choices **(C)** and **(D)** do not describe the purpose of the Land Commission.

26. D

When the company that would become the Southern Pacific Railroad persuaded Congress to provide assistance in building the transcontinental railroad, they took a huge risk. Congress rewarded the company, and its east coast counterpart, vast quantities of land along the rail right-of-way. This, coupled with the monopoly the company enjoyed on all California rail (and most other) transport, gave Southern Pacific enormous wealth and power and the nickname "the octopus." Californians came to resent the company's unrestricted ability to set prices and exercise other controls, and that resentment led California to adopt a new progressive constitution meant to give power directly to the people.

KAPLAN

Constructed-Response Sample Essay 1

1. The first written legal code was the Code of Hammurabi in ancient Babylonia, around 1500 B.C.E. It was a long list of rules meant primarily to govern commerce. The reason it was important in the development of legal tradition is that it set a precedent for writing down laws, instead of depending on the whims of an individual ruler for justice. That meant everyone had to follow the same rules; that wealthy or influential people would not receive preferential treatment.

2. The Justinian Code was adopted by the Emperor Justinian around 500 C.E. in the eastern Roman Empire. There were many different laws that had been commonly used in the Roman Empire, but they had never been gathered together into one document (actually four large books). One of the books contained proposed improvements to the set of laws. The other books contained cases in which the laws had been applied. That is the basis for our system of case law, where interpretations of the law are often based on interpretations of law in past cases. Other countries (most of Europe) use this Roman Law as the basis for their legal systems, while England and the U.S. use only certain aspects of it.

3. The Magna Carta was signed, under duress, by King John of England in 1215. It was the first time that a king had consented to be restrained by the same rule of law that applied to his subjects. Together with the Justinian Code, the Magna Carta is a foundation of the English Common Law system. The U.S. Constitution draws much of its inspiration from the Common Law system, and so we are indebted to the Magna Carta as well.

Constructed-Response Sample Essay 2

The Immigration Act of 1965 revised what had been a country-by-country piecemeal approach to immigration regulation. It established immigration quotas by hemisphere, rather than by country. It did away with many older laws that were discriminatory in intent and effect.

Prior to 1965, Asian immigrants had been subject to restrictive laws that forbade entry to the United States. The Chinese Exclusion Act of 1882, for example, barred immigration of Chinese laborers and made Chinese immigrants already here ineligible for citizenship. The Gentleman's Agreement of 1907 was aimed at keeping Japanese men out of the country, and other laws were aimed at excluding immigrants from other Asian countries.

When the restrictions on Asian immigration were lifted, there was an influx of Asians into the U.S. In particular, after the Vietnam War, many southeast Asian refugees came to the west coast, including California. The 1965 act also established conditions under which immigrants could enter, and special consideration was given to political refugees. During the 1980s period of unrest in Central America, many refugees from El Salvador and Nicaragua settled in California. California's population has increased greatly since 1965, and this act is one of the primary reasons for the increase.

KAPLAN

| PART TWO |

Subtest 2

ABOUT SUBTEST 2

Subtest 2 of the CSET Multiple Subjects Exam covers the areas of Science (covered in Chapter 3) and Mathematics (covered in Chapter 4). There are 52 multiple-choice questions on Subtest 2, 26 in each of the two general areas. There are four constructed-response questions, two of them in science and two in math. In science, you are likely to encounter mostly biology questions, whereas the math section focuses mostly on algebra and geometry.

In both subjects, you are likely to be asked to apply underlying principles to specific questions. For example, in the science section, you may be asked to write a constructed response in which you must use your knowledge of the process of natural selection to analyze the patterns of a given community. In the math questions, you may be asked to order a set of data from least to greatest, in which you must use your knowledge of reducing fractions and other mathematical processes.

The science and math sections of the CSET may seem broad, but it is essentially a review of the topics you studied in high school. Be sure to seek out additional information on any topic you find difficult. Most test-takers feel that the CSET science and math questions are elementary, rather than advanced, so if you study these next chapters closely, you will be way ahead of the game.

Chapter 3: **Science**

THE BIG PICTURE

CSET Science will test your basic knowledge of physical science, life science, earth and space science, and scientific tools and methods. In this chapter, you will find a comprehensive review of these topics as well as a practice set of questions with answers and explanations.

THE KAPLAN METHOD

Multiple-choice Questions

Step 1. Read the question carefully. As you read, underline or circle the key words and phrases that differentiate this particular question from all other possible questions.

Step 2. Rephrase the question to make sure you understand it. If possible, predict the correct answer.

Step 3. Read all the answer choices, eliminating (physically marking through) incorrect ones as you go.

Step 4. If two or more possible answer choices remain, go back to the question and search for matching/mirroring language or concepts that will point you toward the single correct answer.

Constructed-response Questions

Step 1. Read each question carefully. As you read, underline or circle the key words and phrases that differentiate this particular question from all other possible questions.

Step 2. Note how many parts the question has. Be sure to include sub-parts in your count. Write this number in your test booklet, so you will be sure to answer each part of the question.

Step 3. Before you start writing, brainstorm for vocabulary words and relevant concepts. Make your notes in the margins of your answer sheet, so you will be sure to include them in your answer. If you don't have a good command of details for a particular question, be sure to include in your answer the big picture concepts, such as the reason for studying/teaching the subject.

Step 4. Organize your thoughts! Remember, you are being tested on your ability to clearly convey information.

PHYSICAL SCIENCE

Physical Science includes the fields of chemistry and physics. Although the information here is a good review of the science you may remember from high school and college, remember to seek out more information about concepts that interest you or that you do not understand. Let's start with some general chemistry concepts.

Test Yourself

The order of elements in the Periodic Table is based on

(A) the number of neutrons
(B) the radius of the atom
(C) the atomic number
(D) the atomic weight

The correct choice is **(C)**. The Periodic Table arranges the elements in increasing atomic numbers.

Atomic Structure

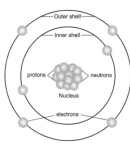

The atom is the basic building block of matter, representing the smallest unit of a chemical element. In 1911, Ernest Rutherford provided experimental evidence that an atom has a dense, positively charged nucleus that accounts for only a small portion of the volume of the atom. The nucleus, which is the core of the atom, is formed by two subatomic particles, called protons and neutrons. A third form of subatomic particle known as electrons exist outside the nucleus in characteristic regions of space called orbitals. All atoms of an element show similar chemical properties and cannot be further broken down by chemical means.

Subatomic Particles

Protons

Protons carry a single positive charge and have a mass of approximately one atomic mass unit (abbreviated as amu). The atomic number Z of an element is equal to the number of protons found in an atom of that element. All atoms of a given element have the same atomic number; in other words, the number of protons an atom has defines the element. The atomic number of an element can be found in the periodic table (see the section about the periodic table that is found later in the lesson) as an integer above the symbol for the element.

Neutrons

Neutrons carry no charge and have a mass only slightly heavier than that of protons. The total number of neutrons and protons in an atom, known as the mass number, determines its mass.

Electrons

Electrons carry a charge equal in magnitude but opposite in charge to that of protons. An electron has a very small mass, approximately 1/1,837 the mass of a proton or neutron, which is negligible for most purposes. The electrons farthest from the nucleus are known as valence electrons. The further the valence electrons are from the nucleus, the weaker the attractive force of the positively charged nucleus and the more likely the valence electrons are to be influenced by other atoms. Generally, valence electrons and their activity determine the reactivity of an atom. In a neutral atom, the number of electrons is equal to the number of protons. A positive or negative charge on an atom is due to a loss or gain of electrons; the result is called an ion. A positively charged ion (one that has lost electrons) is known as a cation; a negatively charged ion (one that has gained electrons) is known as an anion.

Subatomic Particle	Relative Mass	Charge	Location
Proton	1	+1	Nucleus
Neutron	1	0	Nucleus
Electron	0	−1	Electron orbitals

Atomic Weight and Isotopes

To report the mass of something, a number is generally presented with a unit of measurement, such as pounds (lbs), kilograms (kg), grams (g), etc. Because the mass of an atom is so small, these units are not very convenient, and new ways have been devised to describe how much an atom weighs. A unit that can be used to report the mass of an atom is the atomic mass unit (amu). One amu is approximately the same as 1.66×10^{-24} g. How is this particular value chosen? The answer is that it is chosen so that a carbon-12 atom, with 6 protons and 6 neutrons, will have a mass of 12 amu. In other words, the amu is defined as one-twelfth the mass of the carbon-12 atom. It does not convert nicely to grams because the mass of a carbon-12 atom in grams is not a round number. In addition, since the mass of an electron is negligible, the mass of the carbon-12 atom is considered to come from protons and neutrons.

Since the mass of a proton is about the same as that of a neutron, and there are six of each in the carbon-12 atom, protons and neutrons are considered to have a mass of $\frac{1}{12} \times 12$ amu $= 1$ amu each.

While it is necessary to have a way of describing the weight of an individual atom, in real life one generally works with a huge number of them at a time. Atomic weight is the mass, in grams, of one mole (mol) of atoms. Just like a pair corresponds to two, and a dozen corresponds to twelve, a mole corresponds to about 6.022×10^{23}. The atomic weight of an element, expressed in terms of g/mol, therefore, is the mass in grams of 6.022×10^{23} atoms of that element. The product of the equation (presented using scientific notation) that corresponds to a mole is known as Avogadro's number. Why is this particular value not something like 1×10^{24}, for example? Once again, the answer lies in the carbon-12 atom. A mole of carbon-12 atoms weigh exactly 12 g. In other words, a mole is defined as the number of atoms in 12 g of carbon-12. If an element were made of a mole of atoms heavier than carbon-12 (such as oxygen), it would have an atomic weight greater than 12 g/mol. If, on the other hand, an element were composed of a mole of atoms lighter than carbon-12 (such as helium), it would have an atomic weight less than 12 g/mol.

The atomic weight of an element is also found in the periodic table—it is the number that appears below an element's symbol. Notice, however, that these numbers are not whole numbers, which is odd considering that a proton and a neutron each have a mass of 1 amu and an atom can only have a whole number of these. Furthermore, even carbon, the element with which we have set the standards, does not have an exact mass of 12. This is due to the presence of isotopes, as mentioned above. The masses listed in the periodic table are weighted averages that account for the relative abundance of various isotopes. The word weighted is important: it is not simply the average of the masses of individual isotopes; it also takes into account how frequently one encounters a particular form of isotope in a sample of an element. There are, for example, three isotopes of hydrogen, with zero, one, and two neutrons respectively. Together with the one proton that makes it hydrogen in the first place, the mass numbers for these isotopes are 1, 2, and 3. The atomic weight of hydrogen, however, is not simply 2 (the average of 1, 2 and 3) but about 1.008, that is, much closer to 1. This is because the isotope with no neutrons is so much more abundant that we count it much more heavily in calculating the average.

Nuclear Chemistry

Now that you understand atomic structure, it's time to review nuclear chemistry.

The Nucleus

At the center of an atom lies its nucleus, consisting of one or more nucleons (protons or neutrons) held together with considerably more energy than what is needed to hold electrons in orbit around the nucleus. The radius of a nucleus is about 100,000 times smaller than the radius of an atom. Before we go on, let's review some concepts we've just read about.

Atomic Number Z

An element's atomic number is defined by the number of protons in its nucleus; the name atomic number Z is used to represent this number. The letter Z represents an integer that is equal to the number of protons in a nucleus. The number of protons is what defines an element: an atom, ion, or nucleus is identified as carbon, for example, only if it has six protons. Each element has a unique number of protons. The letter Z is used as a presubscript to the chemical symbol in isotopic notation, that is, it appears as a subscript before the chemical symbol. The chemical symbols and the atomic numbers of all the elements are given in the periodic table. You will find more information about the periodic table later in the lesson.

Mass Number A

When calculating mass number, A is an integer equal to the total number of nucleons (neutrons and protons) in a nucleus. Let N represent the number of neutrons in a nucleus. The equation relating A, N, and Z is simply:

$$A = N + Z$$

Isotopes

Different nuclei of the same element will by definition all have the same number of protons. The number of neutrons, however, can be different. Nuclei of the same element can therefore have different mass numbers. For a nucleus of a given element with a particular number of protons (atomic number Z), the various nuclei with different numbers of neutrons are called isotopes of that element.

Example: The three isotopes of hydrogen are:

$^1_1$H: A single proton; the nucleus of ordinary hydrogen.

$^2_1$H: A proton and a neutron together; the nucleus of one type of heavy hydrogen called deuterium.

$^3_1$H: A proton and two neutrons together; the nucleus of a heavier type of heavy hydrogen called tritium.

Note that despite the existence of names like deuterium and tritium, they are all considered hydrogen because they have the same number of protons (one). The example shown here is a little bit of an anomaly because in general isotopes do not have specific names of their own.

Atomic Mass And Atomic Mass Unit

Atomic mass is most commonly measured in atomic mass units (abbreviated amu). By definition, 1 amu is exactly one-twelfth the mass of the neutral carbon-12 atom. In terms of more familiar mass units:

$$1 \text{ amu} = 1.66 \times 10^{-27} \text{ kg} = 1.66 \times 10^{-24} \text{ g}$$

Atomic Weight

Elements have different masses because of isotopes. Atomic weight refers to a weighted average of the masses of an element. The average is weighted according to the natural abundances of the various isotopic species of an element. The atomic weight can be measured in amu.

Nuclear Reactions

Nuclear reactions such as fusion, fission, and radioactive decay involve either combining or splitting the nuclei of atoms. Since the binding energy per nucleon is greatest for intermediate-sized atoms, when small atoms combine or large atoms split a great amount of energy is released.

Fusion

Fusion occurs when small nuclei combine into a larger nucleus. As an example, many stars—including the sun—power themselves by fusing four hydrogen nuclei to make one helium nucleus. Through this method, the sun produces 4×10^{26} joules (J) every second. Here on earth, researchers are trying to find ways to use fusion as an alternative energy source.

KAPLAN

Fission

Fission is a process in which a large nucleus splits into smaller nuclei. Spontaneous fission rarely occurs. However, by the absorption of a low-energy neutron, fission can be induced in certain nuclei. Of special interest are those fission reactions that release more neutrons, since these other neutrons will cause other atoms to undergo fission. This, in turn, releases more neutrons, creating a chain reaction. Such induced fission reactions power commercial electricity-generating nuclear plants.

The Periodic Table

Periodic Table of the Elements

Group

Period

1 IA 1A																	18 vIIIA 8A
1 H 1.008	2 IIA 2A											13 IIIA 3A	14 IVA 4A	15 VA 5A	16 VIA 6A	17 VIIA 7A	2 He 4.003
3 Li 6.941	4 Be 9.012											5 B 10.81	6 C 12.01	7 N 14.01	8 O 16.00	9 F 19.00	10 Ne 20.18
11 Na 22.99	12 Mg 24.31	3 IIIB 3B	4 IVB 4B	5 VB 5B	6 VIB 6B	7 VIIB 7B	8 ------- VIII ------ 8B	9	10	11 IB 1B	12 IIB 2B	13 Al 26.98	14 Si 28.09	15 P 30.97	16 S 32.07	17 Cl 35.45	18 Ar 39.95
19 K 39.10	20 Ca 40.08	21 Sc 44.96	22 Ti 47.88	23 V 50.94	24 Cr 52.00	25 Mn 54.94	26 Fe 55.85	27 Co 58.47	28 Ni 58.69	29 Cu 63.55	30 Zn 65.39	31 Ga 69.72	32 Ge 72.59	33 As 74.92	34 Se 78.96	35 Br 79.90	36 Kr 83.80
37 Rb 85.47	38 Sr 87.62	39 Y 88.91	40 Zr 91.22	41 Nb 92.91	42 Mo 95.94	43 Tc (98)	44 Ru 101.1	45 Rh 102.9	46 Pd 106.4	47 Ag 107.9	48 Cd 112.4	49 In 114.8	50 Sn 118.7	51 Sb 121.8	52 Te 127.6	53 I 126.9	54 Xe 131.3
55 Cs 132.9	56 Ba 137.3	57 La* 138.9	72 Hf 178.5	73 Ta 180.9	74 W 183.9	75 Re 186.2	76 Os 190.2	77 Ir 190.2	78 Pt 195.1	79 Au 197.0	80 Hg 200.5	81 Tl 204.4	82 Pb 207.2	83 Bi 209.0	84 Po (210)	85 At (210)	86 Rn (222)
87 Fr (223)	88 Ra (226)	89 Ac~ (227)	104 Rf (257)	105 Db (260)	106 Sg (263)	107 Bh (262)	108 Hs (265)	109 Mt (266)	110 --- ()	111 --- ()	112 --- ()	114 --- ()		116 --- ()			118 --- ()

Lanthanide Series*	58 Ce 140.1	59 Pr 140.9	60 Nd 144.2	61 Pm (147)	62 Sm 150.4	63 Eu 152.0	64 Gd 157.3	65 Tb 158.9	66 Dy 162.5	67 Ho 164.9	68 Er 167.3	69 Tm 168.9	70 Yb 173.0	71 Lu 175.0
Actinide Series~	90 Th 232.0	91 Pa (231)	92 U (238)	93 Np (237)	94 Pu (242)	95 Am (243)	96 Cm (247)	97 Bk (247)	98 Cf (249)	99 Es (254)	100 Fm (253)	101 Md (256)	102 No (254)	103 Lr (257)

The periodic table arranges elements in increasing atomic numbers. Its spatial layout is such that a lot of information about an element's properties can be deduced simply by examining its position. The vertical columns are called *groups*, while the horizontal rows are called *periods*. There are seven periods, representing the principal quantum numbers $n = 1$ to $n = 7$, and each period is filled more or less sequentially. The period an element is in tells us the highest shell that is occupied, or the highest principal quantum number. Elements in the same group (same column) have the same electronic configuration in their valence, or outermost shell. For example, both magnesium (Mg) and calcium (Ca) are in the second column; they both have two electrons in the outermost s subshell, the only difference being that the principal quantum number is different for Ca ($n = 4$) than for Mg ($n = 3$). Because these outermost electrons, or valence electrons, are involved in chemical bonding, they determine the chemical reactivity and properties of the element. In short, elements in the same group will tend to have similar levels of chemical reactiveness.

Valence Electrons and the Periodic Table

The valence electrons of an atom are those electrons in its outer energy shell. The visual layout of the periodic table is convenient for determining the electron configuration of an atom (especially the valence electron configuration).

Periodic Trends of the Elements

The properties of elements exhibit certain trends, which can be explained in terms of the element's position the periodic table or its electron configuration. In general, elements seek to gain or lose valence electrons so as to achieve the stable octet formation possessed by the inert or noble gases of Group VIII (last column of the periodic table). Two other important general trends exist. First, as one goes from left to right across a period, it becomes clear that the number of electrons for each element increases one at a time; the electrons of the outermost shell experience an increasing amount of nuclear attraction, becoming closer and more tightly bound to the nucleus. Second, scanning a given column for a group element from top to bottom shows that with each element the outermost electrons become less tightly bound to the nucleus. This is because the number of filled principal energy levels (which shield the outermost electrons from attraction by the nucleus) increases downward within each group. These trends help explain elemental properties such as atomic radius, ionization potential, electron affinity, and electronegativity.

Atomic Radius

The atomic radius is an indication of the size of an atom. In general, with each element in a period the atomic radius decreases across a period (from left to right on the table). Within each group, the atomic radius increases (from top to bottom on the table). The atoms with the largest atomic radii are found in the last period (bottom line) of Group I (farthest to the left).

As one moves from left to right across a period, the number of electrons in the outer shell increases one at a time. Electrons in the same shell cannot shield one another from the attractive pull of protons very efficiently. As the number of protons increases, a greater positive charge is produced and the effective nuclear charge increases steadily across a period. This means the valence electrons feel an increasingly strong attraction towards the nucleus, which causes the atomic radius to decrease.

As one moves down a group of the periodic table, the number of electrons and filled electron shells will increase, but the number of valence electrons will remain the same. Thus, the outermost electrons in a given group will feel the same amount of effective nuclear charge, but electrons will be found further from the nucleus as the number of filled energy shells increases. Thus, the atomic radius increases.

Ionization Energy

The *ionization energy* (IE), or *ionization potential*, is the energy required to completely remove an electron from an atom or ion. Removing an electron from an atom always requires an input of energy, since it is attracted to the positively charged nucleus. The closer and more tightly bound an electron is to the nucleus, the more difficult it is to remove, and the higher its level of ionization energy. Ionization energies grow successively. The *first ionization energy* is the energy required to remove one valence electron from a parent atom; the *second ionization energy* is the energy needed to remove a second valence electron from an ion with a +1 charge to form an ion with a +2 charge, and so on.

Ionization energy increases from left to right across a period as the atomic radius decreases. Moving down a group, ionization energy decreases as the atomic radius increases. Group I elements have low ionization energies because the loss of an electron results in the formation of a stable octet.

Electron Affinity

Electron affinity is the energy released when an electron is added to a gaseous atom. It represents the ease with which an atom can accept an electron. The stronger the attractive pull of the nucleus for electrons, the greater the electron affinity will be. A positive electron affinity value represents energy release when an electron is added to an atom.

A crude way of describing the difference between ionization energy and electron affinity is that the former tells us how attached the atom is to the electrons it already has, while the latter tells us how the atom feels about gaining another electron.

Electronegativity

Electronegativity is a measure of the attraction an atom has for electrons in a chemical bond. The greater the electronegativity of an atom, the greater its attraction for bonding electrons. This concept is related to ionization energy and electron affinity: Elements with low ionization energies and low electron affinities will have low levels of electronegativity because their nuclei do not attract electrons strongly, while elements with high ionization energies and high electron affinities will have higher levels of electronegativity because of the strong pull the nucleus has on electrons. Therefore, electronegativity increases from left to right across periods. In any group, electronegativity decreases as the atomic number increases, as a result of the increased distance between the valence electrons and the nucleus—that is, greater atomic radius.

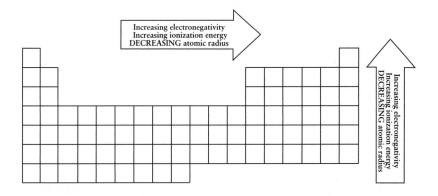

Types of Elements

The elements of the periodic table may be classified into three categories: metals, located on the left side and the middle of the periodic table; nonmetals, located on the right side of the table; and metalloids (semimetals), found along a diagonal line between the other two.

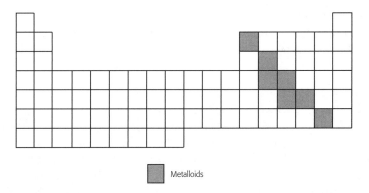

Metalloids

Metals

Metals are shiny solids at room temperature (except for mercury, which is a liquid), and generally have high melting points and densities. Metals have the characteristic ability to be deformed without breaking. Metal's ability to be hammered into shapes is called *malleability;* its ability to be drawn into wires is called *ductility*. Many of the characteristic properties of metals, such as large atomic radius, low ionization energy, and low electronegativity, are due to the fact that the few electrons in the valence shell of a metal atom can easily be removed. Because valence electrons can move freely, metals are good conductors of heat and electricity. Group IA and IIA represent the most reactive metals. The transition elements are metals that have partially filled *d orbitals*.

Nonmetals

Nonmetals are generally brittle in a solid state and show little or no metallic luster. They have high ionization energies and electronegativities, and are usually poor conductors of both heat and electricity. Most nonmetals share the ability to gain electrons easily (i.e., they tend to form negative ions), but otherwise they display a wide range of chemical behaviors and reactiveness. Nonmetals are located on the upper right side of the periodic table; they are separated from the metals by a line cutting diagonally through the region of the periodic table containing elements with partially filled *p orbitals*.

Metalloids

In the periodic table, the metalloids, or semimetals, are found along the line between the metals and nonmetals. The properties of metalloids vary considerably; their densities, boiling points, and melting points fluctuate widely. Their ionization energies and electronegativities lie between those of metals and nonmetals; therefore, these elements possess characteristics of both those classes. For example, silicon has a metallic luster, yet it is brittle and not an efficient conductor. The reactivity of metalloids is dependent upon the element with which they are reacting. For example, boron (B) behaves as a nonmetal when reacting with sodium (Na) and as a metal when reacting with fluorine (F). The elements classified as metalloids are boron, silicon (Si), germanium (Ge), arsenic (As), antimony (Sb), polonium (Po), and tellurium (Te).

The Chemistry of Groups

Elements in the same group have the same number of valence electrons, and hence tend to have very similar chemical properties.

Alkali Metals

The alkali metals are the elements of Group IA. They possess most of the physical properties common to metals, yet their densities are lower than those of other metals. The alkali metals have only one loosely bound electron in their outermost shell, giving them the largest atomic radii of all the elements in their respective periods. Their metallic properties and high levels of reactivity are determined by the fact that they have low ionization energies; thus, they easily lose their valence electron to form univalent *cations* (cations with a +1 charge). Alkali metals have low levels of electronegativity and react very readily with nonmetals, especially halogens.

Alkaline Earth Metals

The alkaline earth metals are the elements of Group IIA. They also possess many characteristically metallic properties. Like the alkali metals, these properties are dependent upon the ease with which they lose electrons. The alkaline earth metals have two electrons in their outer shell and thus have smaller atomic radii than the alkali metals. Alkaline earths have low electronegativities and low electron affinities.

Halogens

The halogens, Group VIIA (second to last column of the periodic table), are highly reactive non-metals. They have seven valence electrons, one short of the favored octet configuration. Halogens are highly variable in their physical properties. For instance, at room temperature, the halogens range from gaseous (F_2 and Cl_2) to liquid (Br_2) to solid (I_2). Their chemical properties are more uniform: The electronegativities of halogens are very high, and they are particularly reactive toward alkali metals and alkaline earth metals, which *want* to donate electrons to the halogens to form stable ionic crystals.

Noble Gases

The noble gases, also called inert gases, are found in Group VIII. They are fairly nonreactive because they have a complete valence shell, which is an energetically favored arrangement. As a result, they have high ionization energies. They possess low boiling points and are all gases at room temperature.

Transition Elements

The transition elements are those that are found between the alkaline earth metals and those with valence *p electrons* (the last six columns of the periodic table). The numbering of the groups can get rather confusing because of the existence of two conventions, but you needn't be too concerned with this. These elements are metals known as transition metals. They are very hard and have both high melting and boiling points. As one moves across a period, the five *d orbitals* become progressively more filled. The *d electrons* are held only loosely by the nucleus and are relatively mobile, contributing to the malleability and high electrical conductivity of these elements. Chemically, transition elements have low ionization energies and may exist in a variety of positively charged forms or oxidation states.

Chemical Bonding

The atoms of many elements can combine to form molecules. The atoms in most molecules are held together by strong attractive forces called chemical bonds. These bonds are formed via the interaction of the valence electrons of combining atoms. The chemical and physical properties of the resulting molecules are often very different from those of their constituent elements. In addition to the very strong forces within a molecule, there are weaker intermolecular forces between molecules. These intermolecular forces, although weaker than the intramolecular chemical bonds, are of considerable importance for understanding the physical properties of many substances.

Processes that involve the breaking and forming of chemical bonds are generally considered chemical processes, while those that only involve interactions between molecules are generally considered physical processes.

In the formation of chemical bonds, many molecules contain atoms bonded according to the octet rule, which states that an atom tends to bond with other atoms until it has eight electrons in its outermost shell. These chemical bonds form a stable electron configuration similar to that of noble gas elements. Exceptions to this rule are as follows: hydrogen, which can have only two valence electrons (the configuration of He); lithium and beryllium, which bond to attain two and four valence electrons, respectively; boron, which bonds to attain six; and elements beyond the second row, such as phosphorus and sulfur, which can expand their octets to include more than eight electrons by incorporating *d* orbitals.

When classifying chemical bonds, it is helpful to introduce two distinct types: *ionic bonds* and *covalent bonds*. During ionic bonding, one or more electrons from an atom with a lower level of ionization energy are transferred to an atom with great electron affinity; the resulting ions are held together by electrostatic forces. During covalent bonding, an electron pair is shared between two atoms. In many cases, the bond is partially covalent and partially ionic; such bonds are called polar covalent bonds.

Ionic Bonds and Compounds

When two atoms with large differences in electronegativity react, the atom that is less electronegative completely transfers its electrons to the atom that is more electronegative. The elements with higher degrees of electronegativity remove electrons from less electronegative elements. The atom that loses electrons becomes a positively charged ion, or *cation*, and the atom that gains electrons becomes a negatively charged ion, or *anion*. In general, the elements of Groups I and II (low electronegativities) bond ionically to elements of Group VII (high electronegativities).

Ionic compounds have characteristic physical properties. They have high melting and boiling points due to the strong electrostatic forces between ions. They can conduct electricity in liquid and aqueous states, though not in solid states. Ionic solids form crystal lattices consisting of infinite arrays of positive and negative ions. In this arrangement, the attractive forces between ions of opposite charge are maximized, while the repulsive forces between ions of like charge are minimized.

Covalent Bonds

When two or more atoms with similar electronegativities interact, they often achieve a noble gas electron configuration by sharing electrons in what is known as a covalent bond. However, noble gas configuration is not always attained; there are exceptions to this rule. The binding force between two atoms results from the attraction that each electron of the shared pair has for the two positive nuclei. A covalent bond can be characterized by two features: bond length and bond energy. Bond length is the average distance between the two nuclei of atoms involved in forming the bond; bond energy is the energy required to separate two bonded atoms. As bond length decreases, bond strength increases.

Types of Covalent Bonding

The nature of a covalent bond depends on the relative electronegativities of the atoms sharing the electron pairs. Whether covalent bonds are considered polar or nonpolar depends on the difference in electronegativities between the atoms. Polar covalent bonding occurs between atoms with small differences in electronegativity. Nonpolar covalent bonding occurs between atoms that have the same electronegativities. This occurs between all of the diatomic elements, such as oxygen, nitrogen, etc.

Chemical Reactions

In the last section, we discussed how atoms combine and are held together by bonds that can be either ionic or covalent. When atoms combine, that process may result in the loss of some individual properties, while new characteristics may be gained. Water, for example, is formed from two hydrogen atoms and an oxygen atom, but it does not really behave like the elements hydrogen or oxygen.

A compound is a pure substance that is composed of two or more elements in fixed proportion. Compounds can be broken down chemically to produce their constituent elements or other compounds. All elements, except for some of the noble gases, can form new compounds by reacting with other elements or compounds. These new compounds can also react with elements or compounds to form yet more compounds.

Molecules

A molecule is a combination of two or more atoms held together by covalent bonds. It is the smallest unit of a compound that displays the properties of that compound. Molecules may contain two atoms of the same element, as in N_2 and O_2, or may be composed of two or more different elements, as in CO_2 and $SOCl_2$.

Earlier, we discussed the concept of atomic weight. Like atoms, molecules can also be characterized by their weight. Molecular weight is simply the sum of the weights of the atoms that make up a molecule.

Types of Chemical Reactions

There are many ways in which elements and compounds can react to form other species; memorizing every reaction would be impossible, as well as unnecessary. However, nearly every inorganic reaction can be classified into at least one of four general categories.

Combination reactions are those in which two or more reactants form one product. The formation of sulfur dioxide by burning sulfur in air is an example of a combination reaction.

A *decomposition reaction* is defined as one in which a compound breaks down into two or more substances, usually as a result of heating. An example of a decomposition reaction is the breakdown of mercury (II) oxide. Energy is released in these types of reactions typically; they are exothermic.

Single displacement reactions occur when an atom (or ion) of one compound is replaced by an atom of another element. For example, zinc metal will displace copper ions in a copper sulfate solution to form zinc sulfate.

In *double displacement reactions*, also called metathesis reactions, elements from two different compounds displace each other to form two new compounds. For example, when solutions of calcium chloride and silver nitrate are combined, insoluble silver chloride forms in a solution of calcium nitrate.

Neutralization reactions are a specific type of double displacement that occurs when an acid reacts with a base to produce a solution of a salt and water. For example, hydrochloric acid and sodium hydroxide react to form sodium chloride and water.

Balanced Equations

Chemical equations express how much and what type of reactants must be used to obtain a given quantity of product. From the law of conservation of mass, during reactions the mass of the reactants must be equal to the mass of the products. More specifically, chemical equations must be balanced so that the product contains the same number of atoms as the reactants.

The Gas Phase

Among the different phases of matter, the gaseous phase is the simplest to understand and model, since all gases, to a first approximation, display similar behavior and follow similar laws, regardless of their identity. The atoms or molecules in a gaseous sample move rapidly and are far apart. In addition, intermolecular forces between gas particles tend to be weak; this results in certain characteristic physical properties, such as the ability to expand in order to fill any volume and to take on the shape of a container. Furthermore, gases are easily, though not infinitely, compressible.

Descriptive Chemistry of Some Common Gases

There are certain miscellaneous facts about the properties of some common gases one should be aware of. These properties are exploited in qualitative tests designed to detect their presence.

- **Oxygen:** Molecular oxygen, O_2, is a reactant in combustion reactions. If a glowing splint is lowered into a test tube containing oxygen, it will reignite.
- **Hydrogen:** When ignited in air, H_2 burns with a blue flame.
- **Nitrogen:** N_2, the largest component of air (a little less than 80% by volume), is relatively inert.
- **Carbon dioxide:** CO_2 produces a moderately acidic solution when dissolved in water. When carbon dioxide is passed through limewater, the solution turns cloudy from the formation of insoluble calcium carbonate. The precipitation of calcium carbonate, however, does not go on indefinitely. As just mentioned, water containing CO_2 is slightly acidic, and this causes calcium carbonate to dissolve.

Kinetic Molecular Theory of Gases

All gases show similar physical characteristics and behavior. A theoretical model to explain why gases behave the way they do was developed during the second half of the nineteenth century. The combined efforts of Ludwig Boltzmann, James Clerk Maxwell, and others led to the *kinetic molecular theory of gases*, which gives us an understanding of gaseous behavior on a microscopic, molecular level. Like the gas laws, this theory was developed in reference to ideal gases, although it can be applied with reasonable accuracy to real gases as well. The assumptions of the kinetic molecular theory of gases are as follows:

1. Gases are made up of particles whose volumes are negligible compared to the container volume.
2. Gas atoms or molecules exhibit no intermolecular attractions or repulsions.
3. Gas particles are in continuous, random motion, undergoing collisions with other particles and with the container walls.

4. Collisions between any two gas particles are elastic, meaning that no energy is dissipated or, equivalently, that kinetic energy is conserved.

5. The average kinetic energy of gas particles is proportional to the absolute temperature of the gas, and is the same for all gases at a given temperature.

Condensed Phase and Phase Changes

When the attractive forces between molecules overcome the random thermal kinetic energy that keeps molecules apart during the gas phase, molecules cluster together, unable to move about freely and then enter the liquid or solid phase. Because of their smaller volume relative to gases, liquids and solids are often referred to as the condensed phases.

General Properties of Liquids

In a liquid, atoms or molecules are held close together with little space between them. As a result, liquids, unlike gases, have definite volumes and cannot be expanded or compressed easily. However, molecules can still move around and are in a state of relative disorder. Consequently, a liquid can change shape to fit its container, and its molecules are able to diffuse and evaporate.

One of the most important properties of liquids is their ability to mix, both with each other and other phases, which forms solutions. The degree to which two liquids can mix is called their miscibility. Oil and water are almost completely immiscible because of their difference in polarity. When oil and water are mixed, they normally form separate layers, with oil on top because it is less dense. Under extreme conditions, such as violent shaking, two immiscible liquids can form a fairly homogeneous mixture called an emulsion. Although they look like solutions, emulsions are actually mixtures of discrete particles too small to be seen distinctly.

General Properties of Solids

In a solid, the attractive forces between atoms, ions, or molecules are strong enough to hold them together rigidly; thus, the particles' only motion is vibration about fixed positions, and the kinetic energy of solids is predominantly vibrational energy. As a result, solids have definite shapes and volumes.

Phase Equilibria and Phase Changes

The different phases of matter interchange upon the absorption or release of energy, and more than one of them may exist in equilibrium under certain conditions. *Dynamic equilibrium* is a condition that permits two opposing processes to occur in a manner that the outcome's net change is zero.

Gas-Liquid Equilibrium

The temperature of a liquid is related to the average kinetic energy of the liquid molecules; however, the kinetic energy of the individual molecules will vary (just as there is a distribution of molecular speeds in a gas). A few molecules near the surface of the liquid may have enough energy to leave the liquid phase and escape into the gaseous phase. This process is known as *evaporation* (or *vaporization*). Each time liquid loses a high-energy particle, the average kinetic energy of the remaining molecules decreases, which means that the temperature of the liquid decreases. Evaporation is thus a cooling process. Given enough kinetic energy, the liquid will completely evaporate.

If a cover is placed on a beaker of liquid, the escaping molecules are trapped above the solution. These molecules exert a countering pressure, which forces some of the gas back into the liquid phase; this process is called *condensation*.

Atmospheric pressure acts on a liquid in a similar fashion as a solid lid. As evaporation and condensation proceed, a state of equilibrium is reached in which the rates of the two processes become equal; that is, the liquid and vapor are in dynamic equilibrium. The pressure the gas exerts when the two phases are at equilibrium is called the *vapor pressure*. Vapor pressure increases as temperature increases because more molecules will have sufficient kinetic energy to escape into the gas phase. The temperature at which the vapor pressure of the liquid equals the external (most often atmospheric) pressure is called the boiling point. In general, then, the temperature at which a liquid boils is dependent on the pressure surrounding it. We know water boils at 100°C because at this temperature its vapor pressure (or the pressure exerted by the gas phase H_2O molecules) is equal to one atmosphere. At places of high elevation, the surrounding pressure is lower than 1 standard atmospheric pressure (atm), so water boils at a lower temperature. By controlling the ambient pressure, we can change the temperature at which water boils. This is the principle behind pressure cookers. By maintaining high pressure, water can reach a temperature higher than 100°C before it vaporizes, thus making it more effective at heating things.

Liquid-Solid Equilibrium

The liquid and solid phases can also coexist in equilibrium. Even though the atoms or molecules of a solid are confined to definite locations, each atom or molecule can undergo motions about some equilibrium position. These motions (vibrations) increase when energy (most commonly in the form of heat) is supplied. If atoms or molecules in the solid phase absorb enough energy in this fashion, the solid's three-dimensional structure breaks down and the liquid phase begins. The transition from solid to liquid is called *fusion* or *melting*. The reverse process, from liquid to solid, is called *solidification*, *crystallization*, or *freezing*. The temperature at which these processes occur is called the *melting point* or *freezing point*, depending on the direction of the transition.

Whereas pure crystals have very distinct, sharp melting points, amorphous solids such as glass tend to melt over a larger range of temperatures, due to their less-ordered molecular distribution.

Gas-Solid Equilibrium

A third type of phase equilibrium exists between gases and solids. When a solid goes directly into the gas phase, the process is called *sublimation*. Dry ice (solid CO_2) sublimes under atmospheric pressure; the absence of a liquid phase makes it a convenient refrigerant. The reverse transition, from a gaseous to solid phase, is called *deposition*.

Solution Chemistry

Solutions are homogeneous mixtures of substances that combine to form a single phase, generally the liquid phase. Many important chemical reactions, both in the laboratory and in nature, take place in solution (including almost all reactions in living organisms). A solution consists of a *solute* dissolved in a *solvent*. The solvent is the component of the solution whose phase remains the same after mixing. For example, a solid cube of sugar dissolved in water yields a liquid mixture of water and sugar. In this example, water is the solvent and sugar the solute.

If the two substances are already in the same phase, the solvent is generally taken to be the component present in greater quantity. Solute molecules move about freely in solvent and can interact with other molecules or ions; consequently, chemical reactions occur easily in solution.

Acids and Bases

Many important reactions in chemical and biological systems involve two classes of compounds—acids and bases. The presence of acids and bases can often be easily detected because they lead to color changes in certain compounds called indicators, which may be in solution or on paper. A particular common indicator is litmus paper, which turns red in acidic solution and blue in basic solution. A more extensive discussion of the chemical properties of acids and bases is outlined below.

Definitions of Acids and Bases

The first definitions of acids and bases were formulated by Svante Arrhenius toward the end of the nineteenth century. Arrhenius defined an acid as a species that produces H+ (protons) in an aqueous solution, and a base as a species that produces OH– (hydroxide ions) in an aqueous solution.

A more general definition of acids and bases was proposed independently by Johannes Brønsted and Thomas Lowry in 1923. A Brønsted-Lowry acid is a species that donates protons, while a Brønsted-Lowry base is a species that accepts protons. At approximately the same time as Brønsted and Lowry, Gilbert Lewis also proposed definitions for acids and bases. Lewis defined an acid as an electron-pair acceptor, and a base as an electron-pair donor. Lewis's are the most inclusive definitions; however, we will focus our attention on Brønsted-Lowry acids and bases.

Properties of Acids and Bases

The behavior of acids and bases in solution is governed by equilibrium considerations. It's important to know that pH (proton concentration) and pOH (Hydrogen ion concentration) are not totally independent of each other: Knowing the value of one allows us to calculate the other.

For example, in pure water (H_2O), pH and pOH would be equal as they both have a value of 7. A solution with equal concentrations of H+ and OH– is neutral. A pH below 7 indicates a relative excess of H+ ions, and therefore an acidic solution; a pH above 7 indicates a relative excess of OH– ions, and therefore a basic solution.

Radioactive Decay

Radioactive decay is naturally occurring and spontaneous. It is characterized by the decay of certain nuclei and the emission of specific particles. It could be classified as a certain type of fission. The *reactant* in radioactive decay is known as the *parent isotope* while the product is the daughter isotope.

Alpha Decay

Alpha decay is the emission of an α particle, which is a ^{4}He nucleus that consists of two protons and two neutrons. The alpha particle is very massive (compared to a beta particle, see below) and doubly charged. Alpha particles interact with matter very easily; hence they do not penetrate shielding (such as lead sheets) very far.

Beta Decay

Beta decay is the emission of a beta particle (β). Despite the equivalence between electrons and beta particles, it is important to realize that these particles are not electrons that would normally be found around the nucleus in a neutral atom. Rather, they are products of decay emitted by the nucleus. This is particularly true when a neutron in the nucleus decays into a proton and an electron. Since an electron is singly charged, and about 1,836 times lighter than a proton, the beta radiation from radioactive decay is more penetrating than alpha radiation.

Gamma Decay

Gamma decay is the emission of gamma rays (γ), which are high-energy photons. They carry no charge and simply lower the energy of the emitting (parent) nucleus without changing the mass number or the atomic number. In other words, the daughter's **A** is the same as the parent's, and the daughter's **Z** is the same as the parent's.

Radioactive Decay Half-Life ($t_{1/2}$)

In a collection of a great many identical radioactive isotopes, the half-life of a sample is the time it takes for half of the sample to decay. For example: If the half-life of a certain isotope is four years, what fraction of a sample of that isotope will remain after 12 years?

Solution: If four years is one half-life, then 12 years is three half-lives. During the first half-life—the first four years—half of the sample will have decayed. During the second half-life (years five to eight), the remaining half will decay, leaving one-fourth of the original. During the third and final period (years nine to 12), half of the remaining fourth will decay, leaving one-eighth of the original sample. Thus the fraction remaining after three half-lives is one-half or one-eighth.

The fact that different radioactive species have different characteristic half-lives is what enables scientists to determine the age of organic materials. The long-lived radioactive carbon isotope ^{14}C, for example, is generated from nuclear reactions induced by high-energy cosmic rays from outer space. There is always a certain fraction of this isotope in the carbon found on Earth. Living things, like trees and animals, are constantly exchanging carbon with the environment, and thus will have the same ratio of carbon-14 to carbon-12 within them as is present in the atmosphere.

Once they die, however, they stop incorporating carbon from the environment, and start to lose carbon-14 because of its radioactivity. The longer the species has been dead, the less carbon-14 it will still have. For example, if a sample is taken from an item or the body and the ratio of ^{14}C to ^{12}C is half of that present in the atmosphere, we would conclude that the species existed about one half-life of ^{14}C ago.

Organic Chemistry

Organic chemistry is the study of compounds containing the element carbon. This covers a wide range of compounds, including proteins, alcohols, steroids, sugars, and compounds found in petroleum, just to name a few. The reason we can study them as facets of one subject is because of the unifying bonding properties of carbon.

Hydrocarbons

Hydrocarbons are compounds that contain only carbon and hydrogen atoms. Depending on the kinds of bonds found between carbon atoms (only single bonds can exist between carbon and hydrogen), hydrocarbons can be classified into one of four classes: alkanes, alkenes, alkynes, and aromatics.

Alkanes, Alkenes, and Alkynes

Alkanes are hydrocarbons that contain only single bonds. They are all named by attaching the suffix -ane to a prefix that indicates the number of carbon atoms. These prefixes will be used again in the naming of other hydrocarbons and it is therefore worth knowing at least a few.

# of C Atoms	Prefix	Name of Alkane	Molecular Formula
1	meth-	methane	CH_4
2	eth-	ethane	C_2H_6
3	prop-	propane	C_3H_8
4	but-	butane	C_4H_{10}
5	pent-	pentane	C_5H_{12}
6	hex-	hexane	C_6H_{14}

Alkenes are hydrocarbons involving carbon-carbon double bonds. They are named using the same scheme as alkanes, except that their suffix is -ene.

Alkynes are hydrocarbons involving carbon-carbon triple bonds. They follow the same naming scheme as alkanes and alkenes, but use the suffix -yne.

KAPLAN

Aromatics

Certain unsaturated cyclic hydrocarbons are known as aromatics. We need not concern ourselves with exactly what makes a compound aromatic, but all such compounds have a cyclic, planar structure in common and possess a higher degree of stability than expected.

Oxygen-Containing Compounds

Organic compounds that include oxygen in addition to carbon and hydrogen include alcohols, ethers, carbohydrates, and carbonyl compounds such as aldehydes, ketones, esters, and carboxylic acids.

Nitrogen-Containing Compounds

Nitrogen-containing compounds are another large class of organic compounds. The most important nitrogen-containing functional group is the amine group, $-NH_2$, which is found in amino acids, the basic building blocks of proteins.

Now that you have reviewed the basics of chemistry, you can start to review the basics of physics.

Kinematics

Kinematics is the branch of mechanics dealing with motion. It is the study of how things move: how far things move, how fast they move, and how long it takes them to move. While *distance* is the total amount of space moved, without a particular direction, displacement is very different. *Displacement* is a vector quantity that describes a change in position, and it has both direction and magnitude. To calculate the average speed of an object, take the total distance covered, and divide it by the total time it took to cover the distance:

$$\text{Average speed} = \frac{\text{Total distance}}{\text{Total time}}$$

$$V = \frac{D}{T}$$

In the equation above, v stands for speed, d is for distance, and t is time.

Average velocity is the ratio of the displacement vector over the change in time, and is a vector quantity. *Acceleration* (a) is the rate of change of an object's velocity. To calculate acceleration, divide an object's *velocity* (v) or *change in velocity* (v) by the change in *time* (t). The equation is as follows:

$$\text{Acceleration} = \frac{\text{Change in velocity}}{\text{Change in time}}$$

Newtonian Mechanics

Dynamics is the study of what causes motion; that is, the *forces* that lead to motion, such as pulling or pushing. Dynamics is often referred to as Newtonian mechanics or Newton's laws of motion, after Isaac Newton, who published his groundbreaking three laws of motion in 1687.

Force is a vector quantity. Forces are observed as the push or pull on an object. Forces can either be exerted between bodies in contact (such as the force a person exerts to push a box across the floor), or between bodies not in contact (such as the force of gravity holding the Earth in its orbit). The unit for force, in SI, is the Newton (N).

Newton's First Law of Motion

A body either at rest or in motion with constant velocity will remain that way unless a *net force* acts upon it. This law is often known as the law of intertia.

Newton's Second Law of Motion

A net force applied to a body of a mass will result in that body undergoing acceleration in the same direction as the net force. The magnitude of the body's acceleration is directly proportional to the magnitude of the net force and inversely proportional to the body's mass. This can be expressed as:

$$F_{net} = \Sigma F = ma$$

Newton's Third Law of Motion

If body (A) exerts a force (F) on body (B), then body (B) exerts a force (-F), that is equal in magnitude and opposite in direction, back on (A). In Newtown's own words, "to every action there is always an opposed but equal reaction." The concept can be expressed as:

$$F_B = -F_A$$

Gravity

Gravity is an attractive force felt by all forms of matter. The magnitude of the *gravitational force* (F) is given as:

$$F = \frac{Gm^1m^2}{r^2}$$

In this approach, (G) is the gravitational constant (6.67×10^{-11} N • m^2/kg^2), m^1 and m^2 are the masses of the two objects, and (r) is the distance between their centers.

Friction

Whenever two objects are in contact, their surfaces rub together creating a friction force. *Static friction* (f_s) is the force that must be overcome to set an object in motion. For example, to make

KAPLAN

a book that is at rest start to slide across a table, a force greater than the maximum static force is required. However, once the book starts to slide, the friction force is not as strong. This new friction force is called *kinetic friction*.

Work And Energy

There are many words in physics that may be used quite differently outside the context of a physics course—work and energy are two such words.

Work

Essentially, you can think of work as responsible for changing the energy of an object. Work is defined as the scalar product of force (F) and displacement (d):

$$W = Fd$$

Work is expressed in *joules* (J) as it is the product of force and displacement. A joule is a unit of work or energy equal to the work done by applying a force of one newton through a displacement of one meter. Work can be written out in the following equation:

$$W = Fd \cos \theta$$

In this approach, θ is the angle between the applied force and the displacement.

Energy

A body in motion possesses energy called *kinetic energy*. A body can also possess *potential energy*, which depends on a body's position rather than motion. An example of potential energy is the gravitational potential energy an object has when it is raised to a particular height. Objects on Earth have greater potential energy the further they are from the surface.

Conservation of Energy

When the work done by nonconservative forces is equal to zero or there are no nonconservative forces (such as an object falling without air resistance), the total amount of energy, also known as the total mechanical energy, remains constant. In such a situation, there is a conservation of energy.

Power

The amount of work required to perform an operation is less important than the amount of time required to do the work. *Power* is the rate at which work is done and the equation to calculate it is:

$$P = \frac{\text{Work}}{\text{Time}}$$

Waves

Waves contain individual particles that move back and forth with simple harmonic motion. In *transverse waves* the particles oscillate perpendicular to the direction of the wave motion. String elements move at right angles to the direction of travel of a wave. In the case of *longitudinal waves*, particles oscillate along the direction of the wave motion.

Traveling waves are best described by example: If a string that is fixed at one end is moved from side to side, a wave travels down the string. When the wave reaches a fixed boundary, it is reflected and inverted. If the free end of the string is continuously moved from side to side, two waves are created—the original wave moving down the string, and a reflected wave moving the other way. These waves interfere with each other.

If a string is fixed on both ends, and waves are created, certain wave frequencies can result in a waveform remaining in a stationary position—known as *standing waves*.

Sound Waves

Sound is transmitted by the movement of particles along the direction of motion of the sound wave. As such, sound is a longitudinal wave. More generally, sound is a mechanical disturbance that is dependent upon a medium for travel. It can be transmitted through solids, liquids, and gases; it cannot be transmitted through vacuum. The speed of sound in a medium is determined by the spacing of particles. The smaller the spacing between particles, the faster sound will travel in that medium. For this reason, sound travels faster in a solid than in a liquid, and faster in a liquid than in a gas.

For sound to be produced, there must be a longitudinal movement of air molecules—produced by the vibration of a solid object that sets adjacent molecules into motion, or by means of an acoustic vibration in an enclosed space. Sound produced by string and percussion instruments, such as the guitar, violin, and piano, comes from solid objects. Using these instruments as an example, a string or several strings are set into motion and vibrate at their normal mode frequencies. Since the strings are very thin, they are ineffective in transmitting their vibration to the surrounding air. A solid body is employed to provide a better coupling to the air. In the case of a guitar, the vibration is transmitted through the bridge to the body of the instrument, which vibrates at the same frequency as the string.

Sound created by acoustic vibration includes sound from instruments such as organ pipes, the flute, and the recorder. There are no moving parts—sound is produced by a vibrating motion of air within the instrument. In the case of an organ pipe, pitch is determined by the length of the pipe. However, instruments such as the recorder and the flute are able to generate more than one pitch by the opening and closing of holes. The sound of the human voice is created by air passing between vocal cords. Pitch is controlled by varying tension of the cords.

Electric Charge

Charge may be either positive or negative. A positive charge and a negative charge attract one another; positive repels positive; and negative repels negative. These fundamental concepts are the foundation of Coulomb's law, which is essential to understanding all electrical phenomena. The SI unit of charge is the *Coulomb* (C).

KAPLAN

Current, Voltage, and Resistance

The flow of a charge is called an *electric current*. There are two types of basic currents: *direct* and *alternating*. The charge of a direct current flows in one direction only; the flow of an alternating current changes periodically. When two points at different electric potentials are connected by a conductor (such as a metal wire), charge flows between the two points. In a conductor, only negatively charged electrons are free to move. These act as charge carriers, and move from low to high potentials. The direction of the current is taken as the direction in which positive charge would flow, from high to low. Thus the direction of current is opposite to the direction of electron flow.

Resistance is the opposition within a conductor to the flow of an electric current. The opposition takes the form of an energy loss or drop in potential. *Ohm's law* states the voltage drop across a resistor is proportional to the current it carries. Current is unchanged as it passes through a resistor. This is because no charge is lost inside a resistor. The SI derived unit of electrical resistance is the *Ohm* (Ω).

LIFE SCIENCE

One way to solve a puzzle is to put together the pieces in larger and larger assemblies until the entire puzzle is complete. Biologists try to gain understanding about living systems in a similar way, by studying life at many levels and then putting all of the pieces together in one complete picture. Looking at biology from this perspective, the behavior of molecules is observed to explain the workings of cells, which in turn explain the function of tissues, organs and organisms. From there, we can explain populations and ecosystems, and the changes in life through time called evolution that have created the great diversity of life on earth today.

Test Yourself

Which of the following is NOT a member of the Mollusca Phylum?

(A) abalone

(B) sea snail

(C) sea urchin

(D) oyster

The sea urchin **(C)**, is the only animal listed that is not a mollusk; it is an echinoderm, characterized by living only in the sea (never in freshwater), the ability to regenerate, and tube feet.

Biological Chemistry

Life is, at one level, an extremely sophisticated form of chemistry. Living organisms, whether they are rose plants or goldfish, are composed primarily of a few common types of molecules. The tissues within organisms play many different roles, but contain the same chemical building blocks throughout.

At the elemental level, all life is composed primarily of carbon, hydrogen, oxygen, nitrogen, phosphorous and sulfur, with traces of other elements—like iron, iodine, magnesium, and calcium—that are also essential for life. Salts like sodium chloride are also essential components of life, but since they do not contain carbon they are known as *inorganic compounds.* Chemicals that contain carbon are called *organic compounds*, and include the major types of biological molecules found in all organisms, including proteins, lipids, carbohydrates, and nucleic acids. Before we explore these molecules, let's look at a vastly important and seldom appreciated inorganic molecule of life: water.

Water and Its Properties

Water is the only compound that exists in the Earth's natural environment as a solid, a liquid, and a gas. Life is not possible without water. The presence of liquid water allowed life to evolve and to persist on earth. The unique properties of water that allow it to play this role are based on the way the water molecule is put together.

The strong hydrogen bonds between water molecules give water its many special properties. These bonds between water molecules that hold the molecules together give water structure and take a lot of energy to break. Hydrogen bonds give water a great deal of cohesion and surface tension compared to other liquids, allowing trees to transport water from their roots all the way to their leaves in a single long column of water. Bonds between water molecules also mean that it takes a great deal of energy to heat water and to make it boil compared to other liquids. Remember, heat in a liquid or gas is carried in the movement of the molecules: more heat means more rapid movement of molecules. When you add heat energy to water, the energy must break bonds between molecules before it can increase their movement to increase the temperature of the water. Liquid hydrocarbons, like octane, in contrast, have very low boiling points because the molecules in the liquid are held together very weakly and when heat is added the molecules easily move about rapidly (heat) and leave the liquid (boil). The great deal of energy that water requires to heat or boil means that our body temperature is stable and we can cool ourselves through evaporation using sweat. Water's ability to absorb heat also means that water remains liquid over a range of temperatures common on our planet.

Another handy feature of water is that the solid form of water, ice, is less dense than its liquid form. The water molecules in ice are held apart from each other in a crystalline lattice of hydrogen bonds, while in water they move about more loosely and pack together more closely. As a result, ice floats on top of water. One of the many benefits derived from this property is that in winter, water freezes on top of lakes first and insulates the layers below from further cooling and freezing, allowing life to prosper in the water beneath the ice. If ice were denser than liquid water, then lakes would freeze from the bottom up and freeze solid.

One more feature of water that is important to life is its ability to dissolve many different things. Life involves chemistry between molecules dissolved in water, so the ability of water to dissolve things is essential to life.

KAPLAN

Solutions in Water

Life involves molecules in solution, but what does it mean if we say something is in solution? When we dissolve sugar in water, and the crystals disappear, what happens to the molecules in the crystals? Solids in crystals contain organic or inorganic molecules packed together and interacting together with one or more type of bond. If the molecules are polar, then they interact with each other in the crystal through polar covalent bonds. Water can also form dipole-dipole interactions with these molecules, displacing their interactions with each other and allowing the molecules to leave the crystal to float surrounded by water molecules. As more and more molecules of sugar leave the crystal in this way, the crystal disappears, with the sugar molecules dissolved in water to form a solution. In a solution, the substance that does the dissolving is called the *solvent*, and the molecules that are dissolved are called the *solute*.

Acids and Bases

Acids and *bases* are particularly important types of solutes in biology. There are a few different ways that people define acids and bases. For our purposes, an acid is defined as a proton donor and a base is a proton acceptor. A proton (H^+) is a hydrogen atom stripped of its single electron leaving a positively charged proton. One famous example of a strong acid is hydrochloric acid: HCl. Chlorine atoms have a relatively weak affinity for hydrogen atoms, and in HCl they are held together not covalently but by ionic bonds. Water can easily dissolve HCl, to form H^+ and Cl^-. In this case, since HCl donates its proton, it is an acid. In the reverse reaction, Cl^- would accept a proton to form HCl again, making Cl^- a base in this reverse reaction. However, Cl^- has very little affinity for H^+ ions, making it a weak base, and meaning that the reverse reaction is not favored.

Another example of an acid is water itself. H_2O can dissociate to donate a proton, forming H^+ and OH^-. Not only can water be an acid, but water can also be a base, acting as a proton acceptor. The H^+ donated by one water molecule can be accepted by another one to form H_3O^+.

A substance that reduces the hydrogen ion concentration in a solution is known as a base. An example of this is NaOH, a strong base that favors dissociation into sodium and hydroxide ions. The hydroxide ions in solution react with protons to reduce the acidity of the solution. Ammonia is an example of a base that will bind a hydrogen ion from the solution.

pH Scale

The pH for acidic solutions is less than 7 and the pH of basic solutions is greater than 7. In the human body, the pH in the blood and tissues is about 7.4. This pH is carefully maintained and controlled since large changes in pH can harm cells and tissues. pH can also affect the environment. Acid rain forms when industrial wastes lower the pH of rain water. It has a pH that is twenty five times more acidic than normal rain. Acid rain causes considerable damage to the environment.

Biological Molecules

Carbohydrates

One of the main classes of biological molecules is *carbohydrates*, or sugars. The functions of carbohydrates include important roles in energy metabolism and storage, and structure of the cell and organisms. One carbohydrate, *cellulose*, provides the cell wall of plants, and is the singularly most abundant biological molecule on earth. Carbohydrates are built from simple building blocks, starting with simple sugars that have only a single sugar monomer. All carbohydrates are composed of carbon, hydrogen and oxygen.

Lipids

Lipids play important roles in energy metabolism and in cellular membranes. Like carbohydrates, lipids are composed of carbon, hydrogen, and oxygen, but lipids are very distinct from carbohydrates in their structure and function. Lipids have much lower oxygen content than carbohydrates and are less oxidized, storing more energy than carbohydrates.

Lipids are the chief means of long-term energy storage in animals, since lipids store and release more energy for their weight than any other class of biological compounds. A key trait for most animals is motility, which requires efficient energy storage. A potato can afford to store its energy as starch, since it does not move around too much, but if a deer stored all of its energy as carbohydrates rather than fat it would be a slow-moving snack for any predator. The lipids used by animals to store energy are *triglycerides.*

Proteins

The basic structure of proteins is simple. *Proteins* are polymers formed by joining simple building blocks called *amino acids* together in a process called *translation*. Proteins provide cells with the ability to carry out a broad range of functions, including the following:

Type of Protein	Function	Examples
Hormonal	Chemical messengers	Insulin, glucagon
Transport	Transport of other substances	Hemoglobin, carrier proteins
Structural	Physical support	Collagen
Contractile	Movement	Actin/myosin
Antibodies	Immune defense	Immunoglobulins
Enzymes	Biological catalysts	Amylase, lipase, ATPase

Enzymes

Enzymes act as biological catalysts to speed up chemical reactions and make them useful for living organisms. Almost all enzymes are proteins. Proteins make versatile enzymes due to the great variety of amino acids that can be employed. Any biological molecule that can catalyze a reaction would be an enzyme, however.

KAPLAN

The nature of an enzyme's environment affects its activity. Important factors in the environment affecting enzymes include the temperature, the presence of coenzymes, the location of an enzyme in the cell, the pH of the surrounding solution, other factors that affect enzyme folding, and the presence of molecules that inhibit or activate enzyme activity.

Nucleic Acids

Nucleic acids are another class of the essential biological molecules found in all living organisms, acting as informational molecules, including DNA and RNA. All organisms (except for some viruses, which most people do not classify as truly living) use DNA as their genome. Nucleic acids are polymers formed by joining together specific monomers called nucleotides. An example of a nucleotide is ATP, which is created when an organism eats carbohydrates and fats that contain chemical energy and digests these molecules to trap their chemical energy. ATP is then used in cells to do most activities that require energy input.

Photosynthesis

To survive, all organisms need energy. Herbivores get energy by eating plants and carnivores by eating herbivores. The foundation of all ecosystems and the source of the energy in these eco-systems and on planet earth as a whole is *photosynthesis*. Plants are self-feeders that generate their own chemical energy from the energy of the sun through photosynthesis. There are also many photosynthetic organisms such as blue-green algae that contribute significantly to global productivity. The chemical energy that plants get from the sun is used to produce glucose that can be burned in mitochondria to make ATP, which is then used to drive all of the energy-requir-ing processes in the plant, including the production of proteins, lipids, carbohydrates, and nucleic acids. Animals eat plants to extract this energy for their own metabolic needs. In this way, photo-synthesis supports almost all living systems.

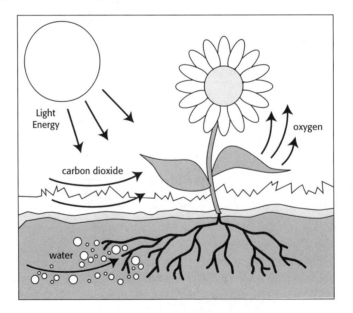

Photosynthesis

Photosynthesis occurs in plants in the *chloroplast*, an organelle that is specific to plants. Chloroplasts are found mainly in the cells of the *mesophyl*, the green tissue in the interior of the leaf. The leaf contains pores in its surface called *stomata* that allow carbon dioxide in and oxygen out to facilitate photosynthesis in the leaf. The chloroplast has an inner and outer membrane and within the inner membrane a fluid called the *stroma*. In addition, the interior of the chloroplast contains a series of membranes called the *thylakoid membranes* that form stacks called *grana*.

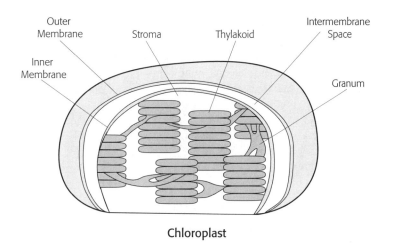

Chloroplast

The Genome and Gene Expression

Plants, animals, and bacteria may differ in their form, biochemistry, and lifestyle, but they all share a common molecular biology that underlies the inheritance and expression of traits. All living organisms inherit traits from their parents and these traits are encoded by the molecule called DNA.

By comparing the features of parents with their children, people have long known intuitively that animals transfer genetic traits from one generation to another. Many years ago Mendel pioneered studies of the genetic behavior of traits passed between generations of pea plants. The discovery of the identity of the molecules that store and transfer genetic information is relatively recent, however. *Genes* encode these physical traits, and many scientists once believed that proteins had to be the genetic material, since nucleic acids such as DNA had such simple components it was difficult to see how DNA could carry such complex information. Through many elegant experiments, however, it was proven that DNA is the genetic material except in certain viruses, and with the elucidation of the structure of DNA by Watson and Crick in 1953, it became clear how DNA could play this role.

The basic outline of information flow in living organisms includes the following concepts that are the foundation of modern molecular biology:

1. DNA is the genetic material, containing the genes that are responsible for the physical traits (phenotype) observed in all living organisms.

2. DNA is replicated from existing DNA to produce new genomes.

3. RNA is produced by reading DNA in a process called *transcription*.

4. This RNA serves as the message used to decode and transmit the genetic information and synthesize proteins according to the encoded information. This process of protein synthesis is called *translation*.

DNA Structure

DNA is built from simple building blocks called *nucleotides* of which DNA contains four types: *adenine* (**A**), *guanine* (**G**), *thymine* (**T**), and *cytosine* (**C**). Each nucleotide contains three parts: a five-carbon sugar (deoxyribose), a phosphate group, and a nitrogenous base that distinguishes each of the four nucleotides (**A**, **G**, **T** or **C**).

To make DNA, nucleotides joined together in long regular strands of nucleotide building blocks. The phosphate group on one nucleotide forms a covalent bond to the sugar group on the next nucleotide to make a phosphate-sugar backbone in the polymer with the nitrogeneous base groups projecting to one side, exposed. One polymer strand alone forms half of a DNA double helix—the other half is another strand oriented in the opposite direction. The two strands bind together to form the familiar DNA *double helix* with two strands wrapped around each other.

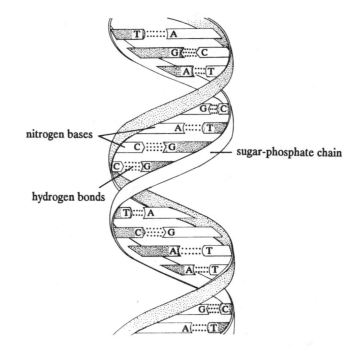

DNA Molecule

DNA Replication

When Watson and Crick built their model for DNA, they felt it must be correct because of the elegance of its design and the solution for DNA replication that the structure immediately suggested. The precise base-pairing of the DNA double helix means that each of the two strands contains a complete and complementary copy of the encoded information found on the other strand. **A** on one strand means that the opposite strand must contain **T** in the same position, and so on, throughout the length of each chromosome in the genome. If the two strands are separated, breaking apart the hydrogen bonds between bases that hold the strands together, then a single strand has all of the information needed to synthesize a new matching strand. As the new strand of DNA is made, all that must be done is to match up the correct bases on the new strand to have the same base-pairing as the old strand and then link the new nucleotides together. The existing DNA strand that is read to make a new complementary copy is called the *template*.

DNA Repair

The DNA in the genome encodes all of the information cells and organisms need to function. Every enzyme in the cell is encoded in the genome, each with its own coding gene. If there are mistakes in the genome, then defective enzymes will be made and the cell or organism may not be able to function normally. DNA replication would introduce errors in the genome if the process were not tremendously accurate. Exposure to certain chemicals, UV light, and radiation can also alter DNA and introduce these harmful mistakes into the genome. During the growth and life of an organism, cells will go through many rounds of cell division, making it all the more important that mistakes are not created in the genome during DNA replication.

The structure of DNA provides a way to keep the genome free of mistakes during DNA replication. If a mistake is made, base pairs will not fit properly into the normal double helical structure of DNA. DNA polymerase detects and fixes these mistakes, proofreading DNA as it replicates and correcting the mistakes to form the correct base pairing once again. Various mechanisms also repair DNA damage caused by chemicals and radiation, but occasional mistakes occur still, resulting in changes in the genome called mutations.

The sequence of nucleotides in a gene determines the sequence of amino acids in the resulting protein. Since the function of a protein depends on the sequence of its amino acids, a change in the sequence can change or harm a protein's function. In a *mutation*, nucleotides are added, deleted, or substituted to change the sequence of a gene. In some cases, inappropriate amino acids are created in a polypeptide chain, and a mutated protein is produced. Genetic diseases are caused by harmful mutations in genes.

Recombinant DNA Technology

Recently, scientists found tools to manipulate DNA to change genes and organisms in highly specific ways. Not only has this helped scientists to understand life, it has led to a greatly improved understanding of disease and to medicines derived from genes and the proteins they encode.

One thing scientists do to DNA is to take segments containing genes and move them from one piece of DNA to another. To move genes, scientists must have a way to cut out a specific section of DNA that has a gene or a piece of a gene in it.

Sequencing DNA allows the entire nucleotide sequence of genes to be known and studied. Today, the genomes of entire organisms are being sequenced. The sequencing of the human genome in the Human Genome Project was completed in 2003. The information from the Genome Project is likely to have profound consequences in the future for medical research.

RNA

RNA is produced by reading genes from DNA. Like DNA, RNA is a polymer of nucleotides. Both DNA and RNA are nucleic acids and the structure of RNA is very similar to single-stranded DNA. During RNA synthesis, the nucleotides in RNA are temporarily matched to base pair with the DNA template similar to the base-pairing of DNA with DNA during DNA replication. There are, however, a number of important differences.

KAPLAN

DNA-Unique Features	RNA-Unique Features
Double-stranded except when replicating	Nearly always single-stranded
Deoxyribose sugar in the nucleotides	Ribose sugar in nucleotides
Thymine base forms a thymine-adenine base pair (T-A)	Uracil base instead of thymine. The base pair is uracil-adenine (U-A)
Replicates DNA → DNA	Does not normally replicate (except in the case of some viruses)
Only one type of DNA per organism. This DNA acts as the original source of information, acting like a master record. Its information is copied onto RNA molecules.	Three types of RNA (mRNA, tRNA, rRNA)

There are three types of RNA with distinct functions: *messenger* RNA (mRNA), *ribosomal* RNA (rRNA) and *transfer* RNA (tRNA). mRNA encodes gene messages that are to be decoded in protein synthesis to form proteins. rRNA is a part of the structure of ribosomes and is involved in translation (protein synthesis). tRNAs also play a role in protein synthesis, as it contributes appropriate amino acids to the translation process. The central role of RNAs in key cellular processes is believed by some to support the idea that life originated as an RNA-centered form that later evolved to use protein enzymes and DNA genomes.

Cell Structure and Organization

The role of the cell in modern biology is so inherent in the way we view life that is easy to overlook its importance. Cells were unknown until the development of the microscope in the seventeenth century allowed scientists to see cells for the first time. Matthias Schleiden and Theodor Schwann proposed that all life was composed of cells in 1838, while Rudolph Virchow proposed in 1855 that cells arise only from other cells. The *cell theory* based on these ideas unifies all biology at the cellular level and may be summarized as follows:

- All living things are composed of cells.
- All chemical reactions of life occur in cells or in association with cells.
- Cells arise only from preexisting cells.
- Cells carry genetic information in the form of DNA. This genetic material is passed from parent cell to daughter cell.

Prokaryotic Cells

Prokaryotes include bacteria and cyanobacteria (blue-green algae), unicellular organisms with a simple cell structure. These organisms have an outer lipid bilayer cell membrane, but do not contain any membrane-bound organelles, unlike their cousins the eukaryotes. Prokaryotes have no true nucleus and their genetic material consists of a single circular molecule of DNA concentrated in an area of the cell called the nucleoid region.

Prokaryotes may also contain plasmids, small circular extrachromasomal DNAs containing few genes. Plasmids replicate independently from the rest of the genome and often incorporate genes that allow the prokaryotes to survive adverse conditions. Bacteria also have a cell wall, cell membrane, cytoplasm, ribosomes, and, sometimes, flagella that are used for locomotion. Respiration in prokaryotes occurs at the cell membrane, since there are no other membranes present at which a proton gradient could be created for ATP synthesis to take place.

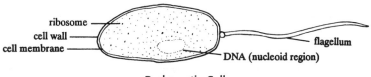

Prokaryotic Cell

Eukaryotic Cells

All multicellular organisms (you, a tree, or a mushroom) and all unicellular protists (amoeba or paramecia) are composed of *eukaryotic cells*. A eukaryotic cell is enclosed within a lipid bilayer cell membrane, as are prokaryotic cells. Unlike prokaryotes, however, eukaryotic cells contain organelles, membrane-bound structures within the cell with specific functions isolated in separate compartments. The separation of the organelle membrane and interior from the rest of the cell allows organelles to perform distinct functions isolated from other activities, which is not possible in prokaryotes. This prevents incompatible processes from mixing together, allows step-wise processes to be more strictly regulated, and can make processes more efficient by making them happen in a single constrained place. The *cytoplasm* is the liquid inside the cell surrounding organelles.

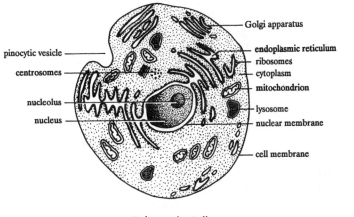

Eukaryotic Cell

Although both animal and plant cells are eukaryotic, they differ in a number of ways. For example, plant cells have a cell wall and chloroplasts, while animal cells do not. Centrioles, located in the centrosome area, are found in animal cells but not in plant cells.

Summary of Cell Properties				
Structure	Nucleus?	Genetic Material?	Cell Wall?	Cell Membrane?
Eukaryote	Yes	DNA	Yes/No	Yes
Prokaryote	No	DNA	Yes	Yes
Structure	Membrane Organelles?		Ribosomes?	
Eukaryote	Yes		Yes	
Prokaryote	No		Yes*	

*Ribosomes in prokaryotes are smaller and have a different subunit composition than those in eukaryotes.

Plasma Membrane

The *plasma membrane* is not an organelle but is an important component of cellular structure. To carry out the biochemical activities of life, life must retain some molecules inside the cell and keep other material out of the cell. The plasma membrane (also called the *cell membrane*) encloses the cell and exhibits *selective permeability*; it regulates the passage of materials into and out of the cell.

Organelles

Eukaryotic cells have specialized membrane-bound structures called *organelles* that carry out particular functions for the cell. Organelles include the nucleus, endoplasmic reticulum, Golgi apparatus, lysosomes, microbodies, vacuoles, mitochondria, and chloroplasts. The lipid bilayer membranes that surround organelles also regulate and partition the flow of material into and out of these compartments, just as the plasma membrane does for the cell with its exterior environment.

Nucleus

One of the largest organelles of the cell is the *nucleus*. The nucleus is the site in which genes in DNA are read to produce messenger RNA (transcription), mRNA is spliced, and the DNA genome is replicated when the cell divides. Other activities like glycolysis and protein synthesis are excluded from the nucleus. The nucleus is surrounded by a two-layer *nuclear membrane* that maintains a nuclear environment distinct from that of the cytoplasm. Nuclear pores in this membrane allow selective two-way exchange of materials between the nucleus and cytoplasm, importing some proteins into the nucleus that are involved in transcription, mRNA splicing, and DNA replication, and keeping out other factors like those involved in glycolysis and translation. The nucleus contains the DNA genome complexed with proteins called *histones* involved in packaging DNA and regulating access to genes. A dense structure within the nucleus in which ribosomal RNA (rRNA) synthesis occurs is known as the *nucleolus*.

Ribosomes

Ribosomes are not membrane-bound organelles but are relatively large complex structures that are the sites of protein production and are synthesized by the nucleolus. They consist of two subunits, one large and one small; each subunit is composed of rRNA and many proteins. Free ribosomes are found in the cytoplasm, while bound ribosomes line the outer membrane of the endoplasmic reticulum. Prokaryotes have ribosomes that are similar in function to eukaryotic ribosomes, although they are smaller.

Endoplasmic Reticulum

The *endoplasmic reticulum* (ER) is a network of membrane-enclosed spaces connected at points with the nuclear membrane. The network extends in sheets and tubes through the cytoplasm. If this network has ribosomes lining its outer surface, it is termed *rough endoplasmic reticulum* (RER); without ribosomes, it is known as *smooth endoplasmic reticulum* (SER). The ER is involved in the transport of proteins in cells, especially proteins destined to be secreted from the cell. SER is involved in lipid synthesis and the detoxification of drugs and poisons, while RER is involved in protein synthesis.

Golgi Apparatus

The *Golgi* is a stack of membrane-enclosed sacs. It receives vesicles and their contents from the ER and modifies proteins. Next, it repackages them into vesicles and ships the vesicles to their next stop, such as lysosomes, or the plasma membrane. In cells that are very active in the secretion of proteins, the Golgi is particularly active in the distribution of newly synthesized material to the cell surface.

Lysosomes

Lysosomes contain hydrolytic enzymes involved in intracellular digestion, degrading proteins and structures that are worn out or not in use. Maximally effective at a pH of 5, these enzymes are enclosed within the lysosome, which has an acidic environment distinct from the neutral pH of the cytosol (the fluid portion of the cytoplasm). Lysosomes fuse with endocytic vacuoles, breaking down material ingested by the cells. They also aid in renewing a cell's own components by breaking them down and releasing their molecular building blocks into the cytosol for reuse.

Microbodies

Microbodies can be characterized as specialized containers for metabolic reactions. The two most common types of microbodies are *peroxisomes* and *glyoxysomes*. Peroxisomes contain oxidative enzymes that catalyze a class of reactions in which hydrogen peroxide is produced through the transfer of hydrogen from a substrate to oxygen. These microbodies break fats down into small molecules that can be used for fuel; they are also used in the liver to detoxify compounds, such as alcohol, that may be harmful to the body. Glyoxysomes, on the other hand, are usually found in the fat tissue of germinating seedlings. They are used by the seedling to convert fats into sugars until the seedling is mature enough to produce its own supply of sugars through photosynthesis.

Vacuoles

Vacuoles are membrane-enclosed sacs within the cell. They are formed after endocytosis and can fuse with a lysosome to digest their contents. Contractile vacuoles in freshwater protists pump excess water out of the cell. Plant cells have a large central vacuole called the tonoplast that is part of their endomembrane system. In plants, the tonoplast functions as a place to store organic compounds, such as proteins, and inorganic ions, such as potassium and chloride. Wastes can be stored here as well.

Mitochondria

Mitochondria are sites of aerobic respiration within the cell and are important suppliers of energy. Each mitochondrion has an outer and inner membrane. The outer membrane has many pores and acts as a sieve, allowing molecules through on the basis of their size. The inner membrane has many convolutions called *cristae*, as well as a high protein content that includes the proteins of the electron transport chain. The area bounded by the inner membrane is known as the *mitochondrial matrix*, and is the site of many of the reactions in cell respiration. Mitochondria are somewhat unusual in that they contain their own circular DNA and ribosomes which enable them to produce some of their own proteins and to self-replicate through binary fission.

Chloroplasts

Chloroplasts are found only in algal and plant cells. With the help of one of their primary components, chlorophyll, they function as the site of photosynthesis. They contain their own DNA and ribosomes exhibit the same semiautonomy as mitochondria.

Cytoskeleton

The cell gains mechanical support, maintains its shape, and carries out cell motility functions with the help of the *cytoskeleton*, composed of *microtubules*, *microfilaments*, *intermediate fibers*, and chains and rods of proteins each with distinct functions and activities.

Microtubules. *Microtubules* are hollow rods made of proteins. When polymerized, microtubules radiate throughout the cells and provide it with support and a framework for organelle movement within the cell. *Centrioles* and the *mitotic spindle,* which direct the separation of chromosomes during cell division, are composed of microtubules.

Cilia and Flagella. *Cilia* and *flagella* are specialized arrangements of microtubules that extend from certain cells and are involved in cell motility. Prokaryotic flagella are structured very differently than eukaryotic flagella.

Microfilaments. Cell movement and support are maintained in part through the action of solid rods composed of actin subunits; these are termed *microfilaments*. Muscle contraction, for example, is based on the interaction of actin with myosin in muscle cells. Microfilaments move materials across the plasma membrane; they are active, for instance, in the contraction phase of cell division and in amoeboid movement.

Intermediate Fibers. These structures are a collection of fibers involved in the maintenance of cytoskeletal integrity. Their diameters fall between those of microtubules and microfilaments.

Membrane Transport Across the Plasma

It is crucial for a cell to control what enters and exits it. In order to preserve this control, cells have developed the mechanisms described in this section.

Permeability—Diffusion Through the Membrane

Traffic through the membrane is extensive, but the membrane is selectively permeable; substances do not cross its barrier indiscriminately. A cell is able to retain many small molecules and exclude others. The sum total of movement across the membrane is determined by *passive diffusion* of material directly through the membrane and selective transport processes through the membrane that require proteins.

Transport Proteins

Molecules that do not diffuse through the membrane can often get in or out of the cell with the aid of proteins in the membrane. There are three types of *transport proteins*: uniport, symport, and antiport. Uniport proteins carry a single solute across the membrane. Symport proteins translocate two different solutes simultaneously in the same direction; transport occurs only if both solutes bind to the proteins. Antiport proteins exchange two solutes by transporting one into the cell and the other out of the cell.

Diffusion/Passive Transport

Diffusion is the net movement of dissolved particles down their concentration gradients, from a region of higher concentration to a region of lower concentration. *Passive diffusion* does not require proteins since it occurs directly through the membrane. Since molecules are moving down a concentration gradient, no external energy is required.

Facilitated Diffusion

The net movement of dissolved particles down their concentration gradient—with the help of carrier proteins in the membrane—is known as *facilitated diffusion*. This process does not require external energy. Ion channels are one example of membrane proteins involved in facilitated diffusion, in which the channel creates a passage for ions to flow through the membrane down their concentration gradient. These ions will not flow through the membrane on their own. Some ion channels are always open for ions to flow through them, while other ion channels open only in response to some stimuli, such as a change in the voltage across the membrane or the presence of a molecule like a neurotransmitter that opens the channel.

Active Transport

Active transport is the net movement of dissolved particles against their concentration gradient with the help of transport proteins. This process requires external energy, and is necessary to

KAPLAN

maintain membrane potentials in specialized cells such as neurons. The most common forms of energy to drive active transport are ATP or a concentration gradient of another molecule. Active transport is used for uptake of nutrients against a gradient.

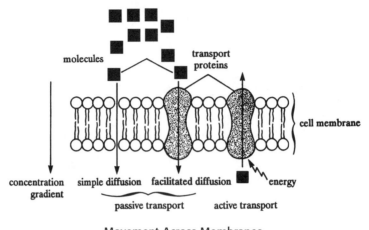

Movement Across Membranes

Osmosis

Osmosis is the simple diffusion of water from a region of lower solute concentration to a region of higher solute concentration. Water flows to equalize the solute concentrations. If a membrane is impermeable to a particular solute, then water will flow across the membrane until the differences in the solute concentration have been equilibrated. Differences in the concentration of substances to which the membrane is impermeable affect the direction of osmosis.

Endocytosis/Exocytosis

Endocytosis is a process in which the cell membrane forms a vesicle that contains extracellular material. Meanwhile, *pinocytosis* is the ingestion of liquids or small particles, while *phagocytosis* is the term assigned to the engulfing of large particles. In the latter, articles may first bind to receptors on the cell membrane before being engulfed. These processes differ from *exocytosis*, which occurs when a vesicle with the cell fuses with the cell membrane and releases its contents to the outside. This fusion of the vesicle with the cell membrane can play an important role in cell growth and intercellular signaling.

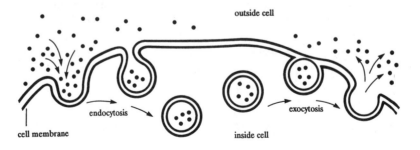

Endocytosis and Exocytosis

Viruses

Viruses are small packages of nucleic acid in a protein coat that replicate themselves in cells. Viruses are not cells, have no cytoplasm and carry out no biochemical activity of their own. They are completely dependent on living within a cell to carry out metabolic processes and replicate. For these reasons, viruses are not generally considered to be living organisms. Although they are not living, the mechanisms virus use to alter the cell cycle and other cellular processes have revealed a great deal about the mechanisms used by cells to perform the same functions.

There are a great variety of viruses. Some examples of the wide range of diseases caused by viruses are:

- Chicken pox (caused by varicella zoster)
- AIDS (HIV)
- Colds (rhinoviruses)
- Cold sores (herpes simplex virus I)

Viruses possess the characteristics of life only when they've infected a living host cell.

Organismal Biology

Living organisms must maintain constant interior conditions in a changing environment. The interior environment that cells must maintain includes water volume, salt concentration, and appropriate levels of oxygen, carbon dioxide, toxic metabolic waste products, and essential nutrients. Organisms must respond to their environment to avoid harm and seek out beneficial conditions, and must reproduce themselves. Single-cell organisms like prokaryotes or protists have relatively simple ways to meet these needs, while multicellular organisms have evolved more complex body plans that provide a variety of solutions to the common problems that all organisms face.

As multicellular organisms have evolved into larger and more complex forms over time, their cells have become more removed from the external environment and more specialized toward one specific function. These specialized cells form *tissues*, cells with a common function and often a similar form. Cells from different tissues come together to form *organs*, large anatomical structures made from several tissues working together toward a common goal. Organs in turn are part of organ systems, including systems for digestion, respiration, circulation, immune reactions, excretion, reproduction, the nervous system and the endocrine system.

Reproduction

One of the essential functions for all living things is the ability to reproduce, to produce offspring that continue a species. An individual organism can survive without reproduction but a species without reproduction will not survive past a single generation. Reproduction in eukaryotes can occur as either asexual or sexual reproduction. Prokaryotes have a different mechanism called *binary fission* for reproduction.

Mechanisms of Cell Division

One of the inherent features in reproduction is cell division. Prokaryotic cells divide, and reproduce themselves, through the relatively simple process of binary fission. Eukaryotic cells divide by one of two mechanisms: mitosis and meiosis. *Mitosis* is a process in which cells divide to produce two daughter cells with the same genomic complement as the parent cell; in the case of humans there are two copies of the genome in each cell. Mitotic cell division can be a means of asexual reproduction, and also is the mechanism for growth, development, and replacement of tissues. *Meiosis* is a specialized form of cell division involved in sexual reproduction that produces male and female gametes (sperm and ova, respectively). Meiotic cell division creates cells with a single copy of the genome in preparation for sexual reproduction in which gametes join to create a new organism with two copies of the genome, one from each parent.

Prokaryotic Cell Division and Reproduction

Prokaryotes are single-celled organisms and their mechanism for cell division, binary fission, is also their means of reproduction. As with all forms of cell division, one of the key steps is DNA replication. Prokaryotes have no organelles and only one chromosome in a single long circular DNA. The single prokaryotic chromosome is attached to the cell membrane, and replicated as the cell grows. With two copies of the genome attached to the membrane after DNA replication, the DNAs are drawn apart from each other as the cell grows in size and adds more membrane between the DNAs. When the cell is as big as two cells, the cell wall and membrane close off to create two independent cells. The simplicity of prokaryotic cells and the small size of their genome compared to eukaryotes may be a factor that assists in their rapid rate of reproduction, dividing as rapidly as once every thirty minutes under ideal conditions.

Bacteria and other prokaryotes do not reproduce sexually, but they do exchange genetic material with each other in some cases. *Conjugation* is one mechanism used by bacteria to move genes between cells by exchanging a circular extrachromosomal DNA with each other. In a process called *transduction*, viruses that infect bacteria can accidentally carry bacterial genes with them into a new cell that they infect. These processes can introduce new genes into bacteria, but do not involve the union of gametes from two parents that is involved in sexual reproduction.

Mitosis

Eukaryotic cells use mitosis to divide into two new daughter cells with the same genome as the parent cell. The growth and division of cells to make new cells occurs in what is known as the *cell cycle*. The cell cycle is a highly regulated process, linked to the growth and differentiation of tissues. Growth factors can stimulate cells to move through the cell cycle more rapidly, and other factors can induce cells to differentiate and stop moving forward through the cell cycle. Failure to control the cell cycle properly can result in uncontrolled progression through the cell cycle and cancer. Cancer cells contain mutations in genes that regulate the cell cycle.

The four stages of the cell cycle are designated as G_1, S, G_2, and M. The first three stages of this cell cycle are interphase stages—that is, they occur between cell divisions. The fourth stage, mitosis, includes the actual division of the cell.

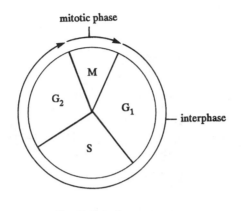

The Cell Cycle

Stage G$_1$. G$_1$ is characterized by intense biochemical and biosynthetic activity and growth. The cell doubles in size, and new organelles such as mitochondria, ribosomes, and centrioles are produced.

Stage S. This is the stage during which synthesis of DNA takes place (S is for synthesis). Each chromosome is replicated so that during division, a complete copy of the genome can be distributed to both daughter cells. After replication, the chromosomes each consist of two identical sister *chromatids* held together at a central region called the *centromere*. The ends of the chromosomes are called *telomeres*. Cells entering G$_2$ actually contain twice as much DNA as cells in G$_1$, since a single cell holds both copies of the replicated genome.

Stage G$_2$. The cell prepares for mitosis, making any of the components still needed to complete cell division.

Stage M (Mitosis and Cytokinesis). Mitosis, the stage in which the cell divides to create two similar but smaller daughter cells.

Asexual Reproduction

Asexual reproduction is any method of producing new organisms in which fusion of nuclei from two individuals (fertilization) does not take place. The fusion of nuclei from two parent individuals to create a new individual is *sexual reproduction*. In asexual reproduction, only one parent organism is involved. The new organisms produced through asexual reproduction form daughter cells through mitotic cell division and are genetically identical clones of their parents (save any mutations incurred during DNA replication). Asexual reproduction serves primarily as a mechanism for perpetuating primitive organisms and plants, especially in times of low population density. Asexual reproduction can allow more rapid population growth than sexual reproduction, but does not create the great genetic diversity that sexual reproduction does.

Binary fission occurs in prokaryotes, algae, and bacteria. In this process, a single DNA molecule attaches to a plasma membrane during replication and duplication, while the cell continues to grow in size. Hence each daughter cell receives a complete copy of the original parent cell's chromosomes.

KAPLAN

This type of reproduction occurs at a rapid pace. Undesirable, potentially harmful bacteria cells, for example, can reproduce every 20 minutes under optimal conditions.

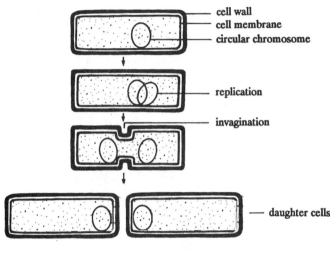

Binary Fission

Budding is a form of mitotic asexual reproduction that involves an unequal division of cytoplasm (*cytokinesis*) between the daughter cells and equal division of the nucleus (*karyokinesis*). The parent cell forms a smaller daughter cell that sprouts off with less cytoplasm than the parent. Eventually the daughter organism becomes independent and is released. Although budding is common in unicellular organisms like yeast, it also occurs in some multicellular organisms such as hydra, forming small identical copies of the parent.

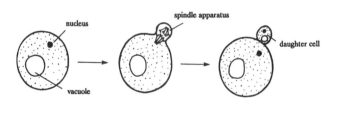

Budding

Asexual reproduction is not common in animals, although it does bring with it certain benefits. It is suitable for animal populations that are widely dispersed, as animals that practice asexual reproduction do not need to find another animal to fertilize them sexually. Asexual reproduction allows rapid growth of a population when conditions are suitable and has a much lower energetic cost than sexual reproduction. The two major types of asexual reproduction found in animals are *parthenogenesis* and *regeneration*.

When people think about asexual reproduction in animals, they usually have *parthenogenesis* in mind. During sexual reproduction, an ova does not develop without fertilization by a sperm, and the resulting zygote contains a diploid genome with one copy from each parent. In parthenogenesis, an egg develops in the absence of fertilization by sperm through mitotic cell division. This form of reproduction occurs naturally in bees: fertilized eggs develop into worker bees and queen bees, while unfertilized eggs become male drone bees. Artificial parthenogenesis can be performed in some animals. The eggs of rabbits and frogs, for example, can be stimulated to develop without fertilization, by giving them an electric shock or a pin prick.

Regeneration is the ability of certain animals to regrow a missing body part. Sometimes parts of an animal grow into a complete animal, resulting in reproduction. For example, the planaria (a flatworm), the earthworm, the lobster, and the sea star can all regenerate limbs or entire organisms. This process is similar in nature to vegetative propagation.

Sexual Reproduction

Most multicellular animals and plants reproduce sexually, as do as many protists and fungi. *Sexual reproduction* involves the union of a *haploid cell* from two different parents to produce diploid offspring. These haploid cells are the *gametes*, sex cells produced through meiosis in males and females. Gametes have a single copy of the genome (one of each chromosome), and diploid cells have two copies of the genome (two of each chromosome). In humans, all of the cells of the body are diploid, with the exception of the gametes. When the male gamete (the sperm) and the female gamete (the egg) join, a *zygote* is formed that develops into a new organism genetically distinct from both its parents. The zygote is the diploid single cell offspring formed from the union of gametes.

Sexual reproduction ensures genetic diversity and variability in offspring. Since sexual reproduction is more costly in energy than asexual reproduction, the reason for its overwhelming prevalence must be that genetic diversity is worth the effort. Sexual reproduction does not create new alleles (alternate forms of a given gene), though. Only mutation can do that. Sexual reproduction increases diversity in a population by creating new combinations of alleles in offspring and therefore new combinations of traits. Genetic diversity is not an advantage to an individual, but allows a population of organisms and its species to adapt and to survive in the face of a dynamic and unpredictable environment.

The diversity created by sexual reproduction occurs in part during meiotic gamete production and in part through the random matching of gametes to make unique individuals. The range of mechanisms involved in sexual reproduction in animals, including humans, is detailed below.

Gamete Formation

Specialized organs called *gonads* produce gametes through meiotic cell division. Male gonads, *testes*, produce male gametes, *spermatozoa*, while female gonads, *ovaries*, produce *ova*. A cell that is committed to the production of gametes, although it is not itself a gamete, is called a *germ cell*. The rest of the cells of the body are called *somatic cells*. Only the genome of germ cells contributes to gametes and offspring. A mutation in a somatic cell, for example, may be harmful to that cell or the organism if it leads to cancer, but a mutation in a somatic cell will not affect offspring since the mutation will not be found in germ cell genomes. Germ cells are themselves diploid and divide to create more germ cells by mitosis, but create the haploid gametes through meiosis.

The production of both male and female gametes involves meiotic cell division. Meiosis in both spermatogenesis and oogenesis involves two rounds of cell division, in which a single diploid cell first replicates its genome, then divides once into two cells each with two copies of the genome. Without replicating their DNA, these two cells divide again to produce four haploid gametes. Meiosis in both cases also involves recombination between the homologous copies of chromosomes during the first round of meiotic cell division. This recombination is one of the key sources of genetic diversity provided during sexual reproduction.

Human Male Reproductive System

The human male produces sperm in the *testes*, gonads located in the *scrotum*. The sperm develop in a series of small, coiled tubes within the testes called the *seminiferous tubules. Sertoli cells* in the seminiferous tubules support the sperm and *Leydig cells* make the *testosterone* that supports male secondary sex characteristics. The *vas deferens* carry sperm to the urethra that passes through the penis. During ejaculation, the *prostate gland* and *seminal vesicles* along the path add secretions to the sperm that carries and provides nutrients for the sperm as part of *semen.*

As gonads, the testes have a dual function; they produce both sperm and male hormones (such as testosterone). Leydig cells in the testis secrete testosterone beginning in puberty. *Testosterone* and other steroid hormones collectively called *androgens* induce secondary sexual characteristics of the male, such as facial and pubic hair, changes in body shape, and deepening voice changes.

Human Female Reproductive System

The key to understanding the human female reproductive system is to understand the menstrual cycle.

Ovaries are paired structures in the lower portion of the abdominal cavity. As part of the menstrual cycle, one ova develops each month within a follicle in an ovary. The follicle is a collection of cells around the ova that support its development and secrete hormones. Each ovary is accompanied by a *fallopian tube*, also called an *oviduct*, one on each side of the abdomen. During ovulation, an ovum leaves the ovary from the follicle and is ejected into the upper end of the oviduct.

The *menstrual cycle* is a repeating sequence of events in the tissues and hormones of the female body. At birth, all the eggs that a female will ovulate during her lifetime are already present in the ovaries, but these eggs develop and ovulate at a rate of one every 28 days (approximately), starting in puberty.

There are four stages in the menstrual cycle:
- The follicular stage
- Ovulation
- The corpus luteum (luteal) stage
- Menstruation

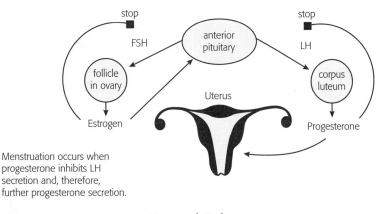

Menstruation occurs when progesterone inhibits LH secretion and, therefore, further progesterone secretion.

Menstrual Cycle

In the *follicular stage* of menstruation, FSH (follicle stimulating hormone) from the anterior pituitary gland stimulates a follicle to mature and produce estrogen. Estrogen promotes thickening of the uterine lining to support an embryo if fertilization occurs. This stage lasts approximately nine to ten days.

When the follicle is mature, a surge in LH secretion from the pituitary causes *ovulation*, the release of the ovum from an ovary through a fallopian tube. The ovaries also produce female sex hormones such as *estrogen*. Like male sex hormones, the female sex hormones regulate the secondary sexual characteristics of the female, including the development of the *mammary* (milk) *glands* and wider hip bones (pelvis). They also play an important role in the menstrual cycle, which involves the interaction of the pituitary gland, ovaries, and uterus. The *ovum* develops in a discontinuous process called *oogenesis* that is not completed in a single continuous process, unlike spermatogenesis. During development of female children ova progress to meiotic prophase I in the first round of meiotic cell division and then become arrested, stuck at this stage. These ova remain arrested in meiosis throughout the life of a woman, except for the ova that mature during each menstrual cycle and progress through this meiotic block. Women are born with all the *eggs* they will ever have, while males produce fresh sperm daily. This is the reason that genetic anomalies are more common in the eggs of older women; these anomalies have had years to accumulate in ova while sperm have a short life span. The LH surge is a key factor in ovulation and ovulation will not occur without it. Constant high levels of estrogen block the LH surge and block ovulation. This is the mechanism by which the birth control pill acts.

After ovulation, the remains of the follicle in the ovary create the *corpus luteum*. Lutenizing hormone from the pituitary stimulates the corpus luteum to produce progesterone and estrogen, which stimulates vascularization (growth of blood vessels) and lining formation of the uterus in preparation for implantation of the fertilized egg. This stage lasts 12 to 15 days. Then, if no fertilization or implantation has occurred, the increased estrogen and progesterone block LH production. Without LH, the corpus luteum atrophies and progesterone levels fall. Without progesterone, the thickened, spongy uterine wall that had been prepared for implantation breaks down. The degenerating tissue, blood, and unfertilized egg are passed out as *menstrual flow*. This stage lasts approximately four days, bringing the total to 28 days for the entire cycle.

KAPLAN

If fertilization occurs, the developing placenta produces HCG (*human chorionic gonadotrophic hormone*), which maintains the corpus luteum. The corpus luteum then continues to make progesterone and estrogen. Progesterone prevents menstruation and ensures that the uterine wall is thickened so that embryonic development can occur and pregnancy can continue. With time, the placenta develops and takes over the production of estrogen and progesterone for the duration of pregnancy.

Embryonic Development

The first step in development is *fertilization*. If sperm are present in the oviduct during ovulation, and a sperm succeeds in encountering the ovum, then fertilization can occur, forming a *zygote*, a single *diploid* cell. In fertilization, the egg nucleus (containing the *haploid number*, or *n* chromosomes) unites with the sperm nucleus (containing *n* chromosomes). This union produces a zygote of the original diploid or 2*n* chromosome number. In this way, the normal (2*n*) somatic number of chromosomes in a diploid cell is restored, and the cell has two homologous copies of each chromosome. Everything else in development up to adulthood consists of mitotic divisions.

If there are two or more eggs released by the ovaries, more than one can be fertilized. The result of multiple fertilizations will be fraternal (*dizygotic*) twins, which are produced when two separate sperm fertilize two eggs. Fraternal twins are related genetically in the same way that any two siblings are. Drugs to treat infertility often induce multiple ovulation and can lead to multiple birth pregnancies.

If there is only one fertilized egg, twins may still result through separation of identical cells during the early stages of cleavage (for example, the two-, four-, or eight-cell stage) into two or more independent embryos. These develop into identical (*monozygotic*) twins, triplets, and so forth, since they all came from the same fertilized egg and have essentially identical genomes. Identical twins are often used in human genetic studies to determine what traits are genetically inherited, since most differences between twins must be caused by their environment.

When the egg and the sperm join, they trigger a cascade of events that occur as the zygote begins to divide rapidly. These events, which are part of the process of fertilization, may occur either externally or internally.

External fertilization occurs in vertebrates that reproduce in water including most fish and amphibians. Eggs are laid in the water, and sperm are deposited near them in the water. The sperm have flagella, enabling them to swim through the water to the eggs. Since there is no direct passage of sperm from the male to the female, the sperm are likely to be diluted and the chances of fertilization for each ovum are reduced considerably. External fertilization also decreases the probability of survival of the young after fertilization since the developing animals are easy targets for predators. Internal fertilization is found in vertebrate land animals (like reptiles, birds, and mammals). The moist passageway of the female reproductive tract from the vagina through the oviducts provides a direct route to the egg for mobile sperm and increases the chance of fertilization.

The number of eggs produced depends upon a number of factors. One of these factors is the type of fertilization employed. Because very few sperm actually reach the egg during external fertilization, this process requires large quantities of eggs to ensure success. The type of development practiced by the organism is also significant. If development occurs outside the mother's body from the very beginning, many eggs are required to ensure survival of at least some of the offspring. Finally, the less care the parents provide, the more eggs are required to guarantee survival of enough offspring to continue the species.

Development of the Embryo. Cleavage of the embryo starts in the oviduct immediately after fertilization. The developing embryo travels down the oviduct, and, within five to ten days, implants itself in the uterine wall. Initially, the fertilized embryo divides into many undifferentiated cells. In the earliest stages, mitotic divisions result in one cell producing two cells, which produce four cells, which produce eight cells, and so on. This ultimately creates what is known as a *morula*, a solid ball of cells. Cells in the morula continue to rapidly divide mitotically to form the *blastula*, a hollow ball of cells (a single layer thick). The central cavity of the blastula is filled with fluid secreted by the cells, and is referred to as the *blastocoel*. More rapid division of cells at one end of the blastula causes an inpocketing or involution known as the two-layer *gastrula*. Two germ layers, the *ectoderm* and *endoderm*, are initially present, endoderm on the inside and ectoderm on the exterior. In a three-layer gastrula, *mesoderm* cells develop between the ectoderm and endoderm. This formation and rearrangement of the three germ layers is known as *gastrulation*.

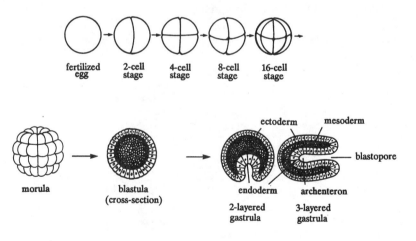

Cleavage of the Egg

Differentiation of Embryonic or Germ Layers. In the next stage of embryonic development, the cells of each germ layer begin to differentiate and specialize to form tissues, organs, and organ systems. Differentiation of cells occurs when the form and function of cells changes to reflect a distinct function or developmental fate. A cell is determined if its developmental fate is set in place even if it does not yet look differentiated. The ectoderm develops into the epidermis of skin, nervous system, and sweat glands. The endoderm becomes the lining of digestive and respiratory tracts, parts of the liver and the pancreas, and the bladder lining. Finally, the mesoderm develops into the muscles, skeleton, circulatory system, excretory system (except bladder lining), gonads, and the inner layer of skin (dermis).

KAPLAN

External Development of Embryo. External development occurs outside the female's body, in water or on land. The eggs of fish and amphibia, for example, are fertilized externally in water and develop in water inside the egg, feeding on the yolk. External development on land occurs in reptiles, birds, and a few mammals, such as the duck-billed platypus.

There are many adaptations for embryonic development within eggs and on land. One of these is a hard shell for protection, which is brittle in birds and leathery in reptiles. Embryonic membranes also help to provide a favorable environment for the developing embryo. Evolution of the egg was one of the adaptations that permitted terrestrial vertebrates to become more independent of water.

Types of embryonic membranes include the *chorion*, which lines the inside of the egg shell. This moist membrane permits gas exchange through the shell. The *allantois*, a saclike structure developed from the digestive tract, is another embryonic membrane. It carries out functions like respiration and excretion, particularly the exchange of gases with the external environment. The allantois layer has many blood vessels to take in O_2 and give off CO_2, water, salt, and nitrogenous wastes. A third embryonic membrane, the *amnion*, encloses the amniotic fluid. Amniotic fluid provides a watery environment for the embryo to develop in, and provides protection against shock. Finally, the *yolk sac* encloses the yolk. Blood vessels in the yolk sac transfer food to the developing embryo.

Internal Development. In animals that develop internally, fertilization and embryo development occur within the mother. This internal development can take a number of different forms, depending on whether or not a placenta is utilized in sustaining the embryo. The *placenta* includes tissues of both the embryo and the mother. It is the site at which exchange of food, oxygen, waste, and water can take place.

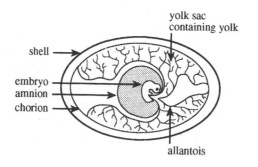

Egg

In some nonplacental animals, development occurs inside the mother, but the embryo lacks a placenta. Thus, there is no region of exchange of materials between the blood of the mother and the embryo. Eggs must therefore be relatively large, as their yolk must supply the developing embryo's needs. Tropical fish and opossums are examples of nonplacental animals. They develop inside the oviduct, obtaining food from the yolk of the egg, and are born alive after a relatively brief period of internal embryonic development.

In placental animals, there is no direct contact between the bloodstreams of the mother and the embryo. Transport is accomplished by diffusion and active transport between juxtaposed blood vessels of the mother and embryo in the placenta. The eggs of placental animals are very small, since the embryo is only briefly maintained until a placental connection is completed. Humans, for example, have no yolk, but they do have a yolk sac. The *umbilical cord* that attaches the embryo to the placenta is composed completely of tissues of embryonic, not maternal, origin. This cord contains the umbilical artery and vein. As in birds and reptiles, the amnion of placental mammals provides a watery environment to protect the embryo from shock.

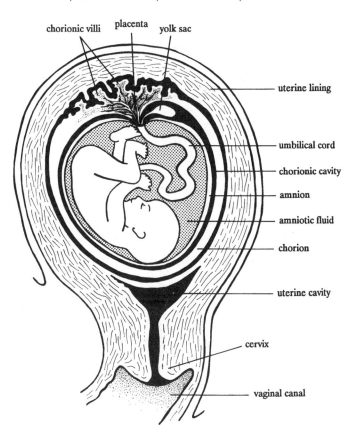

Human Embryo

Postembryonic Development. The development of the embryo to the adult is termed *maturation*. Maturation involves cell division, differentiation, increase in size, and development of a distinctive adult shape. Maturation can be interrupted, such as in the metamorphosis of arthropods, or uninterrupted, as in mammals. Differentiation of cells is complete when all organs reach adult form. Further cell division is needed only for repair and replacement of tissues. In humans, growth occurs rapidly in children, followed by sexual maturation during puberty.

KAPLAN)

Nutrition

Animals are multicellular heterotrophic organisms that must get their energy and raw material through the consumption of food. Food comes in large chunks of insoluble material mostly bound up in biological polymers that cells cannot access to use directly. Food must be digested to be absorbed and used by cells. Digestion involves *mechanical* breaking of food into small pieces, *chemical* breakdown of food into its molecular building blocks, followed by *absorption* of digested nutrients. Digestion can be intracellular, occurring through the action of intracellular enzymes, or extracellular, using enzymatic secretions in a gut cavity to break down nutrients into simpler compounds that are absorbed by cells lining the gut.

In many organisms, including humans, the mechanical breakdown of large fragments of food into small particles occurs through cutting and grinding in the mouth and churning in the digestive tract. The molecular composition of these food particles is unchanged by breaking food into smaller pieces, but making the pieces smaller gives enzymes greater access to the molecules in the food.

Ingestion and Digestion in Protozoa and Cnidarians

Protozoans utilize *intracellular digestion*. In amoebae, pseudopods surround and engulf food through *phagocytosis* and enclose it in food vacuoles. *Lysosomes* (containing digestive enzymes) fuse with the food vacuole and release their digestive enzymes, which break down macromolecules like proteins, nucleic acids, and carbohydrates into their building blocks. The resulting simpler molecules diffuse into the cytoplasm and unusable end products are eliminated from the vacuoles.

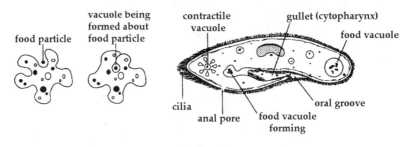

Protozoan Digestive System

In the *paramecium*, cilia sweep microscopic food such as yeast cells into the oral groove and cytopharynx. A food vacuole forms around food at the lower end of the cytopharynx. Eventually, the vacuole breaks off into the cytoplasm and progresses toward the anterior end of the cell. Enzymes are secreted into the vacuole and the products diffuse into the cytoplasm. Solid wastes are expelled at the anal pore.

Hydra (phylum *Coelenterata*, also called *Cnidarians*) employ both intracellular and *extracellular digestion*. Tentacles bring food to the mouth (ingestion) and release the particles into a cuplike sac. The endodermal cells lining this gastrovascular cavity secrete enzymes into the cavity. Thus, digestion principally occurs outside the cells (extracellularly). However, once the food is reduced to small fragments, the gastrodermal cells engulf the nutrients and digestion is completed intracellularly. Undigested food is expelled through the mouth. Every cell is exposed to the external environment, thereby facilitating intracellular digestion.

Ingestion and Digestion in Annelida

Since the earthworm's body is many cells thick, only the outside skin layer contacts the external environment. For this reason, this species requires a more advanced digestive system and circulatory system. Like higher animals, earthworms have a complete one-way, two-opening digestive tract. Their digestive tract is a tube that moves food through in one direction instead of a sac like in cnidarians. Having a tube is more efficient than a sac since food moves in one direction through the tube and digestion can become a stepwise process with specialization of parts of the tube for specific digestive. These parts of the digestive tube in annelids include the mouth, pharynx, esophagus, crop (to store the food), gizzard (to grind the food), intestine (which contains a large dorsal fold that provides increased surface area for digestion and absorption), and anus (where undigested food is released).

Ingestion and Digestion in Arthropoda

Insects have a similar digestive system as annelids, except that they utilize jaws for chewing and salivary glands for better digestion.

Ingestion and Digestion in Humans

The human digestive system consists of the *alimentary canal* and the associated glands that contribute secretions into this canal. The alimentary canal is the entire path of food through the body: the *oral cavity, pharynx, esophagus, stomach, small intestine, large intestine*, and *rectum*. Many glands line this canal, such as the gastric glands in the wall of the stomach and intestinal glands in the small intestine. Other glands, like the pancreas and liver, are outside the canal proper, and deliver their secretions into the canal via ducts.

Mechanical Digestion. Food is crushed and liquefied by the teeth, tongue, and peristaltic contractions of the stomach and small intestine, increasing the surface area for the digestive enzymes to work upon. *Peristalsis* is a wavelike muscular action conducted by smooth muscle that lines the gut in the esophagus, stomach, small intestine and large intestine. Rings of muscle circling the gut contract, and move a ring of contraction down the gut, moving the food within the gut as well.

Chemical Digestion. Several exocrine glands associated with the digestive system produce secretions involved in breaking food molecules into simple molecules that can be absorbed. Polysaccharides are broken down into glucose, triglycerides are hydrolyzed into fatty acids and glycerol, and proteins are broken down into amino acids.

Chemical digestion begins in the mouth. In the mouth, the *salivary glands* produce saliva that lubricates food and begins starch digestion. *Saliva* contains *salivary amylase* (ptyalin), an enzyme that breaks the complex starch polysaccharide into maltose (a disaccharide). As food leaves the mouth, the *esophagus* conducts it to the stomach by means of peristaltic waves of smooth muscle contraction.

KAPLAN

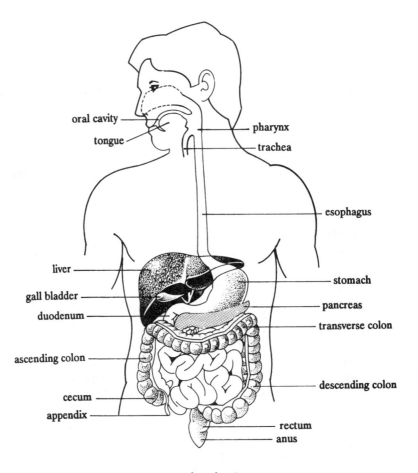

Human Digestive System

In the *stomach*, *gastric glands* produce *hydrochloric acid* and the enzyme *pepsin*. The acidity of the stomach provides the low pH environment necessary for the optimum enzymatic activity of pepsin. In addition, the acidity destroys ingested microorganisms. *Chyme* (partially digested food in the stomach) enters the *duodenum* through the *pyloric sphincter*.

The *liver* is also involved in digestion by producing *bile*, an important factor in fat digestion. Bile is stored in the *gall bladder* prior to its release into the small intestine. Bile salts are detergents that emulsify fats. *Pancreatic lipase* is produced and secreted by the *pancreas*, which is also responsible for manufacturing *amylase* (for starch digestion), *trypsin*, and *chymotrypsin* (for protein digestion).

As food enters the small intestine, digestion continues. Glands in the wall of the intestine produce aminopeptidases (for polypeptide digestion) and disaccharidases (for digestion of maltose, lactose, and sucrose). The pancreatic and intestinal enzymes in the small intestine are responsible for the bulk of digestion in the gastrointestinal tract. In addition, most of the absorption of the digested nutrients occurs here. The large intestine is devoted mainly to water and Vitamin K absorption, and the rectum acts as a transient storage place for feces prior to their elimination through the anus.

Circulation

Organisms make nutrients available to cells through a process called absorption. But these nutrients, along with gases and wastes, must also be transported throughout the body to be used. The system involved in transport of these materials to different parts of the body is called the *circulatory system*. Small animals have their cells either directly in contact with the environment or in close enough proximity that diffusion alone provides for the movement of gases, wastes and nutrients making a specialized system for circulation unnecessary. Larger, more complex organisms require circulatory systems to move material within the body.

Circulation in Protozoans and Cnidarians

Protozoans are single-celled organisms and cnidarians often have only two cell layers, with both layers in contact with the environment. Materials pass by simple diffusion across the plasma membrane between the cytoplasm and external environment, and streaming of cytoplasm within the cell (cyclosis). In hydra, for example, water circulates into and out of the body cavity, and all cells are in direct contact with the external environment.

Circulation in Annelida

Annelids are larger and more complex animals than cnidarians and most of their cells are not in direct contact with the external environment. A closed circulatory system indirectly moves food, water, and oxygen within the body, always within defined blood vessels. In annelids blood travels forward to the head (anterior) through dorsal blood vessels. Five aortic arches or "hearts" force blood down to the ventral vessel, which carries blood to the posterior and up to complete the circuit.

Annelids have no red blood cells, unlike vertebrates, but have hemoglobin-like pigment dissolved in their blood. Nourishment in the form of food and gases is diffused into the cells from the capillaries.

Circulation in Arthropoda

Arthropods (grasshoppers) utilize an open circulatory system. In an open circulatory system, blood flows within vessels some of the time but in some areas of the body it is not contained, flowing instead through open spaces called sinuses. Arthropods have a simple beating tube for a heart, which moves blood through a dorsal vessel and then out into sinuses. In these sinuses, blood is not enclosed in blood vessels but directly bathes cells, and exchange of food takes place (air exchange, meanwhile, is accomplished through a tracheal system of air tubes). Blood then reenters blood vessels. Mollusks also have an open circulatory system.

Circulation in Vertebrates

Vertebrates have closed circulatory systems, with a chambered heart that pumps blood through arteries into tiny capillaries in the tissues. Blood from capillaries passes into veins that return to the heart. The chambers of vertebrate hearts include atria and ventricles. *Atria* are chambers where blood from veins collects and is pumped into ventricles, while *ventricles* are larger, more muscular chambers that pump blood out to the body.

Fish have a two-chambered heart with one atria and one ventricle, in which the sole ventricle pumps blood into capillaries in the gills to collect oxygen. From the capillaries in the gills the blood is collected in arteries that move toward a second set of capillaries in the rest of the tissues of the body to deliver oxygen and nutrients. From there the blood passes back to the heart.

The problem with this set-up is that it takes a lot of pressure to pump blood through the first set of capillaries in the gills, and there is little pressure left afterward to pump the blood through the rest of the body. This set-up is not sufficient for the greater metabolic needs of terrestrial vertebrates. Amphibians have a three-chambered heart and birds and mammals have four-chambered hearts, with two atria and two ventricles. The right ventricle pumps deoxygenated blood to the lungs through the pulmonary artery. Oxygenated blood returns through the pulmonary vein to the left atrium. From there it passes to the left ventricle and is pumped through the aorta and arteries to the rest of the body. Valves in the chambers of the heart keep blood from moving backward. There are in effect two separate circulations, one for the lungs called the pulmonary circulation, and the systemic circulation for the rest of the body. Using a four-chambered heart to split the pumping of blood through the lungs from the pumping of the blood to the rest of the body allows much greater pressure in the systemic circulation than would be possible with a two-chambered heart.

The heartbeat a doctor hears through a stethoscope is the sound of the chambers of the heart contracting in a regular pattern called the *cardiac cycle*. The heart is composed of specialized muscle tissue called *cardiac muscle*. Cardiac muscle cells are connected together in an electrical network that transmits nervous impulses throughout the muscle to stimulate contraction. The transmission and spreading of the signal is highly controlled to coordinate the beating of the chambers. During each cardiac cycle, the signal to contract initiates on its own in a special part of the heart called the *sinoatrial node*, or the pacemaker region. Cells from this region fire impulses in regular intervals all on their own, without stimulation from the nervous system. Once the signals start, they spread through both atria, which then contract, forcing blood into the ventricles. The signal then passes into the ventricles and spreads throughout their walls, causing contraction of the ventricles and the movement of blood into the major arteries. The ventricular contraction occurs during the *systole* part of the cardiac cycle, and the atria contract as the ventricles relax, during the *diastole* part of the cardiac cycle.

The signal that causes the beating of the heart originates spontaneously within the heart without nervous stimulation, but the heart rate can be altered by nervous stimulation. The most important nervous stimulation of the heart is the vagus nerve of the parasympathetic system, which acts to slow the heart rate. The vagus nerve is more or less always stimulating the heart, and can increase the heart rate simply by stimulating the heart less than usual. The sympathetic nervous system and epinephrine increase the heart rate.

Arteries. The *arteries* carry blood from the heart to the tissue of the body. They repeatedly branch into smaller muscular arteries (arterioles) until they reach the capillaries, where exchange with tissues occurs. Arteries are thick-walled, muscular, and elastic, conduct blood at high pressure and have a pulse caused by periodic surges of blood from the heart. Arterial blood is oxygenated except for blood in the pulmonary artery, which carries deoxygenated blood from the heart to the lungs to renew the oxygen supply.

Veins. *Veins* carry blood back to the heart from the capillaries. Blood flows from capillaries to *venules* (small veins) to veins. Veins are relatively thin-walled, conduct at low pressure because they are at some distance from the pumping heart, and contain many valves to prevent backflow. Veins have no pulse; they usually carry dark red, deoxygenated blood (except for the pulmonary vein, which carries recently oxygenated blood from the lungs). The movement of blood through veins is assisted by the contraction of skeletal muscle around the veins, squeezing blood forward. Once it moves forward in this way, valves keep the blood from going back.

Capillaries. *Capillaries* are thin-walled vessels that are very small in diameter. Capillaries, not arteries or veins, permit exchange of materials between the blood and the body's cells. Their small size and thin walls assist in the diffusion of material through their walls. Also, some of the liquid component of blood seeps from capillaries to directly bathe cells with nutrients. Proteins and cells are too large to pass into the tissues and stay in the blood within the capillary walls. Some of the fluid that enters tissues passes directly back into the blood at the other end of the capillary, and the rest can circulate back in the lymphatic system. If the capillaries are too permeable or too much liquid stays in the tissues, swelling results.

Lymphatic System. *Lymph vessels* are a separate system independent of the blood system. This system carries extracellular fluid (at this stage known as lymph) at very low pressure, without cells. The *lymph nodes* are responsible for filtering lymph to rid it of foreign particles, they maintain the proper balance of fluids in the tissues of the body, and they are involved in the transport of chylomicrons as part of fat metabolism. The system ultimately returns lymph to the blood system via the largest lymph vessel, the thoracic duct, which empties lymph back into circulation shortly before it enters the heart.

The Blood. The fluid moved through the body by the circulatory system is the blood. The blood is composed of a liquid component, the plasma, and cells. The cells include red blood cells (*erythrocytes, platelets*), and white blood cells (*lymphocytes*). Each of these types of cells has specific functions.

The *plasma* is composed of water, salts, proteins, glucose, hormones, lipids and other soluble factors. The main salts in plasma are NaCl and KCl, in a composition that has been noted as similar to the composition of salt in sea water, our evolutionary origin. Calcium is another important salt in the extracellular fluid, including blood. The body regulates the blood volume and salt content through water intake and through excretion of urine. Oxygen is dissolved as a gas to a small extent in blood, although most oxygen is transported bound to hemoglobin in red blood cells. Carbon dioxide is converted to carbonic acid in the blood. Not only does this increase the solubility of carbon dioxide in the blood, but it creates a pH buffer that protects the body against large changes in the pH of blood. The glucose in blood is transported as a dissolved sugar for cells to uptake as needed. Hormones, both steroid hormones and peptide hormones, are transported in blood from one tissue where they are secreted to other tissues where they exert their actions. The protein component of plasma consists of antibodies for immune responses, fibrinogen for clotting, and serum albumin. The protein component of blood helps to draw water into the blood in the capillaries and prevent loss of fluid from the blood into the tissues, which would cause swelling.

Red blood cells are the most abundant cells in blood, and their primary function is to transport oxygen. The oxygen-carrying component of red blood cells is the protein *hemoglobin.* The hemoglobin molecule has evolved to deliver oxygen more efficiently in response to changes in the tissues. In periods of great metabolic activity in muscle, the pH of the blood can decrease and carbon dioxide increase, both of which tend to reduce the affinity of hemoglobin for oxygen and cause it to leave more oxygen in the tissue.

Blood Types. Red blood cells manufacture two prominent types of antigens, antigen A (associated with blood type A) and antigen B (blood type B). In any given individual, one, both, or neither antigen may be present. The same pattern appears in every red blood cell.

The plasma of every individual also contains antibodies for the antigens that are not present in the individual's red blood cells (if an individual were to produce antibodies against his or her own red cells, they would agglutinate and the blood would clump).

Immune System

The interior of the body is an ideal growth medium for some pathogenic organisms like disease-causing bacteria and viruses. To prevent this, the body has defenses that either prevent organisms from getting into the interior of the body or stop them from proliferating if they are within the body. The system that plays this protective role is called the *immune system.* The trick for the immune system is to be able to mount aggressive defenses, and, at the same time, to distinguish foreign bodies to avoid attacking one's own tissues and causing disease. This is exactly what happens in autoimmune disorders; the immune system attacks one's own tissues as if they were foreign invaders.

Passive immune defenses are barriers to entry. These include the skin, the lining of the lungs, the mouth and stomach. The skin is a very effective barrier to most potential pathogens, but if wounded, the barrier function of skin is lost. This is why burn patients are especially susceptible to infection. The lungs are a potential route of entry, but are patrolled by immune cells, and have mucus to trap invaders and cilia lining the respiratory tract to remove the trapped invaders. The spleen plays a role in the immune system in adults, and in embryos, plays a role in blood cell development.

Active immunity is conferred by the cellular part of the immune system. White blood cells are actually several different cell types that are involved in the defense of the body against foreign organisms in different ways. White blood cells include *phagocytes* that engulf bacteria with amoeboid motion, and various types of *lymphocytes,* B and T cells that are involved in the immune response. B cells produce *antibodies,* or *immunoglobins,* which are secreted proteins specific to foreign molecules such as viral or bacterial proteins. Helper T cells coordinate the immune response and killer T cells directly kill cells that are infected with intracellular pathogens like viruses or cells that are aberrant like malignant cells. A given B or T cell responds to a specific antigen. Since the body does not know what antigens or pathogens may attack it, the immune system creates a varied population of B and T cells in which each cell recognizes only one antigen, but the population of cells contains a huge range of specificities. If a B cell or T cell encounters an antigen that matches its specificity, then it is stimulated to proliferate and create more cells with the same specificity. This amplification of a clone of cells that respond to the invading antigen helps the body to respond and to remain immune to infection in the future by the same pathogen. When a B cell encounters an antigen that it recognizes, it proliferates to make more B cells that produce antibody. The stimulated B cells also produce memory cells that do not make antibody, but have the same specificity and will lie dormant for many years, ready to respond if the body is challenged again with the same antigen.

When you are vaccinated, you are injected with weakened or dead pathogens. Your body has a protective immune response to these pathogens stimulating B cells and T cells, so that when the real pathogen comes along, you're already protected!

Respiration

Cells performing aerobic respiration need oxygen and need to eliminate carbon dioxide. To do this, organisms must exchange gases with the environment. The respiratory system provides oxygen and removes CO_2. The oxygen is used to drive electron transport and ATP production and CO_2 is produced from burning glucose in the Krebs cycle. Even the most expert pearl divers cannot live without breathing for more than a few minutes. Gas exchange is accomplished via a variety of efficient ways, which range from simple diffusion to complex systems of respiration. We describe the adaptations employed by a range of organisms below.

Respiration in Protozoa and Cnidarians

Since every cell of these types of primitive organisms is in contact with the external environment (in this case, water), respiratory gases can be easily exchanged between the cell and the outside by direct diffusion of these gases through the cell membrane. Lipid bilayer membranes are fully permeable to oxygen and carbon dioxide.

Respiration in Annelida

Mucus secreted by cells at the external surface of the annelid's body provides a moist surface for gaseous exchange from the air to the blood through diffusion. The annelid's circulatory system then brings O_2 to the cells and waste products such as CO_2 back to the skin, excreting them into the outside environment.

Respiration in Arthropoda

The arthropod respiratory system consists of a series of respiratory tubules called *tracheae.* These tubules open to the outside in the form of pairs of openings called *spiracles.* Inside the body, the tracheae subdivide into smaller and smaller branches, enabling them to achieve close contact with most cells. In this way, this system permits the direct intake, distribution, and removal of respiratory gases between the air and the body cells. No oxygen carrier is needed and specialized cells for this purpose are not found. Since a blood system does not intervene in the transport of gases to the body's tissues, this system is very efficient and rapid, enabling most arthropods to produce large amounts of energy relative to their weights. The direct diffusion of air through trachea is one factor that limits body size in arthropods.

Respiration in Fish

Water entering a fish's mouth travels over numerous thin-walled, thread-like *gill* filaments that are well fed by capillaries. As water passes over these gill filaments, O_2 diffuses into the blood, while CO_2 leaves the blood to enter the water. Arteries then transport the oxygenated blood through the body. The blood in the gills and the water moving over the gills move in opposite directions, creating what is known as a countercurrent exchange mechanism for the exchange of gases between the blood and the environment, a very efficient mechanism for exchange. After passing over the gills, water passes out of the body through openings on either side of the head, taking the discarded carbon dioxide with it. Marine invertebrates also have gills to exchange gases with their water environment.

Respiration in Humans

Humans have developed a complex system of respiration to transport oxygen to their cells and to rid their bodies of waste products like carbon dioxide. First, the *lungs* are designed to move air between the exterior atmosphere and an interior air space that is in close contact with capillaries. Here, oxygen and carbon dioxide diffuse between the blood and air, blood circulates through the body to exchange gases with the tissues, and then returns to the lungs.

The lungs are found in a sealed cavity in the chest, bound by the ribs and chest wall and by the muscular *diaphragm* on the bottom. A membrane called a *pleura* surrounds the lungs and is held tightly against another membrane in the chest by a thin layer of liquid. The diaphragm is curved upward when released, and flattens when contracted, expanding the chest cavity. During inspiration, or inhalation, chest muscles move the ribs up and out as the diaphragm moves down; this creates both a larger chest cavity and a vacuum that draws air into the respiratory passages. The reverse process decreases the size of the chest cavity and forces air out of the lungs (exhalation). Exhalation is largely a passive process that does not require muscle contraction. During exhalation the elasticity of the lungs draws the chest and diaphragm inward when the muscles relax, decreasing the volume of the lungs and causing air to be forced out.

The breathing rate is controlled by a part of the brain, the *medulla oblongata,* that monitors carbon dioxide content in the blood. Excess CO_2 in the blood stimulates the medulla to send messages to the rib muscles and the diaphragm to increase the frequency of respiration.

The air passages involved in respiration consist of the *nose, pharynx, larynx, trachea, bronchi, bronchioles,* and the *alveoli.* The *nose* adds moisture and warmth to inhaled air, and helps to filter it, removing particulates and organisms. The *pharynx* is involved in diverting ingested material into the esophagus and away from the lungs to prevent choking. The *larynx* contains a membrane that vibrates in a controlled manner with the passage of air to create the voice. The *trachea* carries air through the vulnerable throat protected by flexible but strong rings of cartilage. At the end of the trachea the respiratory passage splits into the two lungs and into smaller and smaller passages that terminate in the tiny *alveoli,* tiny air sacs that are the site of gas exchange in the lungs.

The alveoli have thin, moist walls and are surrounded by thin-walled capillaries. Oxygen passes from the alveolar air into the blood by diffusion through the alveolar and capillary walls. CO_2 and H_2O pass out in the same manner. Note that all exchanges at the alveoli involve passive diffusion.

Since passive diffusion drives gas exchange, both in the lungs as well as the tissues, gases always diffuse from higher to lower concentration. In the tissues, O_2 diffuses into tissues and CO_2 leaves, while in the lungs this is reversed due to high oxygen pressure and low CO_2. CO_2 is carried in blood mainly as dissolved carbonate ions.

Thermoregulation and the Skin

The external temperature is part of the environment that life contends with and adapts to. Temperature affects organisms' rate of metabolic activity and rate of water loss. Extremes of temperature retard most life, although there are organisms that live only in boiling hot springs or at subfreezing temperatures.

Organisms must also develop ways to regulate heat. Cellular respiration transfers only some of the energy derived from the oxidation of carbohydrates, fats, and proteins into the high-energy bonds of ATP. Roughly 60 percent of the total energy is not captured; most of this is transformed to heat. The vast majority of animals are *cold-blooded*, or *ectothermic*—most of their heat energy escapes to the environment. Consequently, the body temperature of ectotherms, also known as *poikilotherms*, is very close to that of their surroundings. Since an organism's metabolism is closely tied to its body temperature, the activity of ectothermic animals such as snakes is radically affected by environmental temperature changes. As the temperature rises (within limits, since very high temperatures would be lethal), these organisms become more active; as temperatures fall, they become sluggish.

Some animals, notably mammals and birds, are endotherms; they are *warm-blooded*, or *homeothermic*. They have evolved physical mechanisms that allow them to make use of the heat produced as a consequence of respiration. Physical adaptations like fat, hair, and feathers actually retard heat loss. Homeotherms maintain constant body temperatures higher than the environment around them. Hence they are less dependent upon environmental temperature than poikilothermic animals, and are able to inhabit a comparatively greater range of variable conditions as a result.

In humans, the *skin* protects the body from microbial invasion and from environmental stresses like dry weather and wind. Specialized epidermal cells called *melanocytes* synthesize the pigment *melanin*, which protects the body from ultraviolet light. The skin is a receptor of stimuli, such as pressure and temperature, is an excretory organ (removing excess water and salts from the body) and also a thermoregulatory organ (helping control both the conservation and release of heat).

Sweat glands secrete a mixture of water, dissolved salts, and urea via sweat pores. As sweat evaporates, the skin is cooled. Thus, sweating has both an excretory and a thermoregulatory function. Sweating is under autonomic (involuntary) nervous control.

KAPLAN)

Subcutaneous fat in the *hypodermis* insulates the body. Hair entraps and retains warm air at the skin's surface. Hormones such as epinephrine can increase the metabolic rate, thereby increasing heat production. In addition, muscles can generate heat by contracting rapidly (shivering). Heat loss can be inhibited through the constriction of blood vessels (*vasoconstriction*) in the *dermis*, moving blood away from the cooling atmosphere. Likewise, dilation of these same blood vessels (*vasodilation*) dissipates heat.

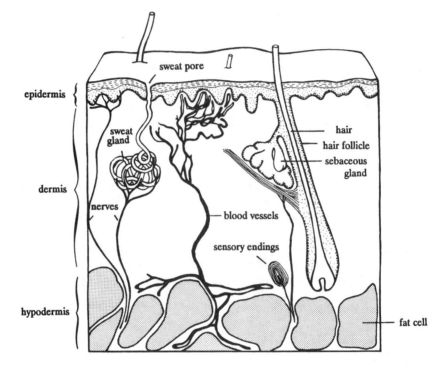

Human Skin

Alternate mechanisms are used by some mammals to regulate their body temperature. For example, *panting* is a cooling mechanism that evaporates water from the respiratory passages. Most mammals have a layer of fur that traps and conserves heat. Some mammals exhibit varying states of torpor in the winter months to conserve energy; their metabolism, heart rate, and respiration rate greatly decrease during these months. *Hibernation* is a type of intense or extreme torpor during which the animal remains dormant over a period of weeks or months with body temperature maintained below normal.

Excretion

Excretion is the term given to the removal of metabolic wastes produced in the body. (Note that it is to be distinguished from elimination, which is the removal of indigestible materials.) Sources of metabolic waste include:

Waste	Metabolic Activity Producing the Waste
Carbon dioxide	Aerobic respiration
Water	Aerobic respiration, dehydration synthesis
Nitrogenous wastes (urea, ammonia, uric acid)	Deamination of amino acids
Mineral salts	All metabolic processes

Excretion in Protozoa and Cnidarians

Remember that in these simple organisms, all cells are in contact with the external, aqueous environment. Water-soluble wastes such as the highly toxic ammonia produced by protein metabolism can therefore exit via simple diffusion through the cell membrane. Some freshwater protozoa, such as the paramecium, possess a contractile vacuole, an organelle specialized for water excretion by active transport. Excess water, which continually diffuses into the hyperosmotic cell from the hypo-osmotic environment (in this case, fresh water), is collected and periodically pumped out of the cell to maintain the cell's volume and pressure.

Excretion in Annelida

In annelids, two pairs of *nephridia* tubules in each body segment excrete water, mineral salts, and nitrogenous wastes in the form of *urea*. Fluid from the circulatory system is filtered out of the blood into fluid that fills the central body cavity. This fluid enters the nephridia tubules where some material is removed and other material is secreted into the urine before it is excreted from a pore with the nitrogenous wastes. Urine formation in this simple organism resembles to some extent the filtration and processing of urine that occurs in the mammalian kidney.

Excretion in Arthropods

Nitrogenous wastes are excreted in the form of solid uric acid crystals. The use of solid nitrogenous wastes is an adaptation that allows arthropods to conserve water. Mineral salts and uric acid accumulate in the *Malphigian tubules*; they are then transported to the intestine to be expelled along with solid wastes of digestion.

Osmoregulation

Osmoregulation may be defined as the ways in which organisms regulate the volume and salt content of their internal fluids. Saltwater fish, for example, live in a hyperosmotic environment that causes them to lose water and take in salt. In constant danger of dehydration, they must compensate by constantly drinking and actively excreting salt across their gills. Freshwater fish, in contrast, live in a hypo-osmotic environment that causes intake of excess water and excessive salt loss. These fish correct this condition by drinking infrequently, absorbing salts through the gills, and excreting dilute urine.

Human Excretory System

The principle organs of excretion in humans are the *kidneys*. The kidneys form urine to remove nitrogenous wastes in the form of urea as well as regulating the volume and salt content of the extracellular fluids. From the kidney the urine passes into an *ureter tube* that passes to the *urinary bladder* where urine is stored until urination occurs. During urination, the urine leaves the bladder through the *urethra*.

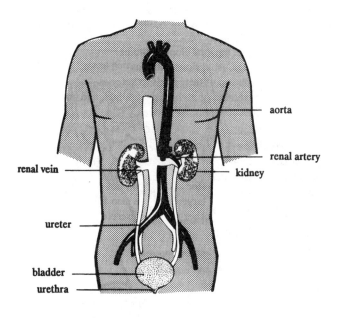

Human Excretory System

Endocrine System

The body has two communication systems to coordinate the activities of different tissues and organs, the nervous system and the *endocrine system*. The endocrine system is the network of glands and tissues that secrete *hormones*, chemical messengers produced in one tissue and carried by the blood to act on other parts of the body. Compared to the nervous system, the signals conveyed by the endocrine system take much more time to take effect. A nervous impulse is produced in a millisecond and travels anywhere in the body in less than a second. Hormones require time to be synthesized, can travel no more quickly than the blood can carry them, and often cause actions through inducing protein synthesis or transcription, activities that require time. However, hormone signals will tend to be more long-lasting than nerve impulses. When the nerve impulse ends, a target such as skeletal muscle usually returns quickly to its starting state. When a hormone induces protein synthesis, the proteins remain long after the hormone is gone.

Often the two systems work together. The *endocrine glands*, such as the pancreas or the adrenal cortex, can be the direct targets (effectors) of the autonomic nervous system. The hormone adrenaline acts in concert with the sympathetic nervous system to produce a set of results similar to those produced directly by sympathetic neurons.

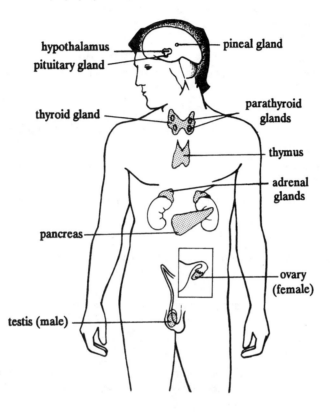

Human Endocrine System

Endocrine glands secrete hormones directly into the bloodstream. This is in contrast to *exocrine secretions* that do not contain hormones and are released through ducts into a body compartment. An example of exocrine secretion is the secretion by the pancreas of digestive enzymes into the small intestine through the pancreatic duct. Both endocrine and exocrine functions can be found in the same organ. The pancreas simultaneously produces exocrine secretions like digestive enzymes and endocrine secretions like insulin and glucagon that are released into the blood to exert their effects throughout the body.

Endocrine Glands

Hormones are secreted by a variety of glands, including the *hypothalamus, pituitary, thyroid, parathyroids, adrenals, pancreas, testes, ovaries, pineal, kidneys, heart,* and *thymus*. It is likely that additional tissues like skin and fat not traditionally considered glands also have endocrine functions. Some hormones regulate a single type of cell or organ, while others have more widespread actions. The specificity of hormonal action is determined by the presence of specific receptors on or in the target cells.

A common principle that regulates the production and secretion of many hormones is the *feed-back loop*. Often several hormones regulate each other in a chain.

Hypothalamus and Pituitary Gland. The *hypothalamus,* a section of the posterior forebrain, is located above the pituitary gland and is intimately associated with it via a portal circulation that carries blood directly from the hypothalamus to the pituitary.

The *pituitary gland* is a small gland with two lobes lying at the base of the brain. The two lobes, anterior and posterior, function as independent glands. The anterior pituitary secretes the following hormones:

- *Growth hormone* fosters growth in a variety of body tissues.
- *Thyroid stimulating hormone* (TSH) stimulates the thyroid gland to secrete its own hormone, thyroxine.
- *Adrenocorticotrophic hormone* (ACTH) stimulates the adrenal cortex to secrete its corticoids.
- *Prolactin* is responsible for milk production by the female mammary glands.
- *Follicle-stimulating hormone* (FSH) spurs maturation of seminiferous tubules in males and encourages maturation of follicles in the ovaries.
- Finally, *luteinizing hormone* (LH) induces interstitial cells of the testes to mature by beginning to secrete the male sex hormone testosterone. In females, a surge of LH stimulates ovulation of the primary oocyte from the follicle. LH then induces changes in the follicular cells and converts the old follicle into a yellowish mass of cells rich in blood vessels. This new structure is the corpus luteum, which subsequently secretes progesterone and estrogen.

The *posterior pituitary* is a direct extension of nervous tissue from the hypothalamus. Nerve signals cause direct hormone release. The two hormones secreted by the posterior pituitary are ADH and oxytocin.

- *ADH* (vasopressin) acts on the kidney to reduce water loss.
- *Oxytocin* acts on the uterus during birth to cause uterine contraction.

Thyroid Gland. The thyroid hormone, *thyroxine*, is a modified amino acid that contains four atoms of iodine. It accelerates oxidative metabolism throughout the body. An abnormal deficiency of thyroxine causes goiter, decreased heart rate, lethargy, obesity, and decreased mental alertness. In contrast, hyperthyroidism (too much thyroxine) is characterized by profuse perspiration, high body temperature, increased basal metabolic rate, high blood pressure, loss of weight, and irritability.

Parathyroid Glands. The parathyroid glands are small pealike organs located on the posterior surface of the thyroid. They secrete parathyroid hormone, which regulates the calcium and phosphate balance between the blood, bone, and other tissues.

Pancreas. The pancreas is a multifunctional organ. It secretes enzymes through ducts into the small intestine and secretes hormones directly into the bloodstream.

Adrenal Glands. The adrenal glands are situated on top of the kidneys and consist of the *adrenal cortex* and the *adrenal medulla.*

Adrenal cortex: In response to stress, the adrenal cortex synthesizes and secretes the steroid hormones collectively known as *corticosteroids.* The corticosteroids, derived from cholesterol, include glucocorticoids, mineralocorticoids, and cortical sex hormones.

Adrenal Medulla: The secretory cells of the adrenal medulla secrete hormones into the circulatory system. This organ produces *epinephrine* (adrenaline) and *norepinephrine* (noradrenaline).

Epinephrine increases the conversion of glycogen to glucose in liver and muscle tissue, causing a rise in blood glucose levels and an increase in the basal metabolic rate. Both epinephrine and norepinephrine increase the rate and strength of the heartbeat, and dilate and constrict blood vessels. These in turn increase the blood supply to skeletal muscle, the heart, and the brain, while decreasing the blood supply to the kidneys, skin, and digestive tract. These effects are known as the *"fight or flight response,"* and are elicited by sympathetic nervous stimulation in response to stress. Both of these hormones are also neurotransmitters.

Ovaries and Testes. The gonads are important endocrine glands, with testes producing testosterone in males and ovaries producing estrogen in females. See the section on reproduction earlier in this chapter for more details.

Nervous System

The nervous system enables organisms to receive and respond to stimuli from their external and internal environments. Your brain and spinal column regulate your breathing and your movement, and provide perception of sight, sound, touch, smell and taste. The nervous system allows organisms to not only perceive their environment but to respond to their experience, and to alter their behavior over time through learning.

To understand the nervous system, it is best to start with the basic functional unit of the nervous system—the *neuron*. The neuron is a specialized cell that is designed to transmit information via electrochemical signals. These signals are generated when the neuron alters the voltage found across its plasma membrane. The property that neurons have that allows them to carry an action potential is an excitable membrane.

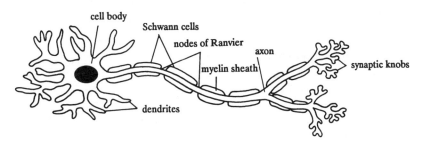

Neuron

The basic parts of the neuron's cell structure are the *cell body*, the *dendrites*, and the *axon*. The cell body contains the nucleus and most of the organelles and is the site of most protein synthesis and energy production in neurons. Dendrites receive chemical information from other neurons as changes in membrane potential and carry this information to the cell body. The axon is a very long, slender projection of the neuron that transmits signals from the cell body to the neuron's target.

Organization of the Nervous System

As organisms evolved and became more complex, their nervous systems underwent corresponding increases in complexity. Simple organisms can only respond to simple stimuli, while complex organisms like humans can discern subtle variations of a stimulus, such as a particular shade of color.

Invertebrates. Protozoa are single-celled and have no organized nervous system, although they do have receptors that respond to stimuli like heat, light, and chemicals. Cnidarians have a nervous system consisting of a network of cells, the nerve net, located between the inner and outer layers of the cells of its body. With a limited network, the responses of cnidarians to their environment are limited to simple actions like retracting tentacles and stimulating swimming. Annelids possess a primitive central nervous system consisting of a solid ventral nerve cord and an anterior "brain" of fused ganglia. These clusters of cells allow a richer network of neurons than a simple nerve net, and more sophisticated information processing that results in more complex behavior. Arthropods also have ganglia and a more complex nervous system than annelids with more specialized sense organs, including simple or complex eyes and a tympanum for detecting sound. The sensory input and information processing capability of arthropods allows for amazing rich and complex behavior like social behavior in these small organisms.

Vertebrate Nervous System

Vertebrates have a *brain* enclosed within the *cranium* and a *spinal cord* that together form the *central nervous system* (CNS) that processes, and stores information. Throughout the rest of the body is the *peripheral nervous system,* containing motor or efferent neurons that carry signals to effector organs like muscles or glands to take actions in response to nervous impulses. Sensory neurons in the peripheral nervous system convey information back to the CNS for processing and storage. Another division of the nervous system is into the autonomic and the voluntary components of the efferent pathways.

The Peripheral Nervous System. The peripheral nervous system carries nerves from the CNS to target tissues of the body and includes all neurons that are not part of the CNS. The peripheral nervous system consists of 12 pairs of cranial nerves, which primarily innervate the head and shoulders, and 31 pairs of spinal nerves, which innervate the rest of the body. Cranial nerves exit from the brainstem and spinal nerves exit from the spinal cord. The peripheral nervous system has two primary divisions, the somatic and the autonomic nervous systems.

The somatic motor nervous system. This system innervates skeletal muscle and is responsible for voluntary movement, generally subject to conscious control. Motor neurons release the neurotransmitter acetylcholine (ACh) onto ACh receptors located on skeletal muscle. This causes depolarization of the skeletal muscle, leading to muscle contraction. In addition to voluntary movement, the somatic nervous system is also important for reflex action.

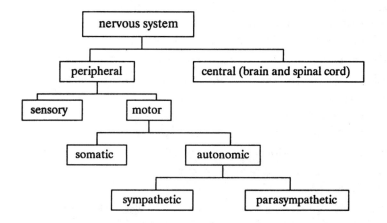

Organization of the Vertebrate Nervous System

The autonomic nervous system. The autonomic nervous system is neither structurally nor functionally isolated from the CNS or the peripheral system. Its function is to regulate the involuntary functions of the body including the heart and blood vessels, the gastrointestinal tract, urogenital organs, structures involved in respiration, and the intrinsic muscles of the eye. In general, the autonomic system innervates glands and smooth muscle, but not skeletal muscles. It is made up of the sympathetic nervous system and the parasympathetic nervous system.

- *The sympathetic nervous system.* This system utilizes norepinephrine as its primary neurotransmitter. It is responsible for activating the body for emergency situations and actions (the fight-or-flight response), including strengthening of heart contractions, increases in the heart rate, dilation of the pupils, bronchodilation, and vasoconstriction of vessels feeding the digestive tract. One tissue regulated by the sympathetic system is the adrenal gland, which produces adrenalin in response to stimulation. Adrenalin produces many of the same fight-or-flight responses as the sympathetic system alone.

- *The parasympathetic nervous system.* Here, acetylcholine serves as the primary neurotransmitter. One of this system's main functions is to deactivate or slow down the activities of muscles and glands (the rest-and-digest response). These activities include pupillary constriction, slowing down of the heart rate, bronchoconstriction, and vasodilation of vessels feeding the digestive tract. The principal nerve of the parasympathetic system is the vagus nerve. Most of the organs innervated by the autonomic system receive both sympathetic and parasympathetic fibers, the two systems being antagonistic to one another.

Human Brain

The human brain is divided into several anatomical regions with different functions including the following regions:

- **Cerebral cortex.** The cerebral cortex controls all voluntary motor activity by initiating the responses of motor neurons present within the spinal cord. It also controls higher functions, such as memory and creative thought. The cortex is divided into hemispheres, left and right, with some specialization of function between them ("left-brain, right-brain"). The cortex consists of an outer portion containing neuronal cell bodies (gray matter) and an inner portion containing axons (white matter).

- **Olfactory lobe.** This serves as the center for reception and integration of olfactory input.
- **Thalamus.** Nervous impulses and sensory information are relayed and integrated en route to and from the cerebral cortex by this region.
- **Hypothalamus.** Such visceral and homeostatic functions as hunger, thirst, pain, temperature regulation, and water balance are controlled by this center.
- **Cerebellum.** Muscle activity is coordinated and modulated here.
- **Pons.** This serves as the relay center for cerebral cortical fibers en route to the cerebellum.
- **Medulla oblongata.** This influential region controls vital functions like breathing, heart rate, and gastrointestinal activity. It has receptors for carbon dioxide; when carbon dioxide levels become too high, the medulla oblongata forces you to breathe. This is why when you hold your breath until carbon dioxide levels rise so high in your blood that you pass out, you will breathe involuntarily to bring an influx of oxygen into your body.
- **Reticular activating system.** This network of neurons in the brain stem is involved in processing signals from sensory inputs and in transmitting these to the cortex and other regions. This system is also involved in regulating the activity of other brain regions like the cortex to alter levels of alertness and attention.

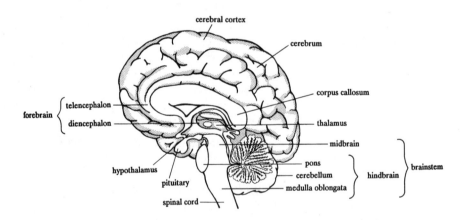

Human Brain

The *spinal cord* is also part of the CNS. The spinal cord acts as a route for axons to travel out of the brain. It also serves as a center for many reflex actions that do not involve the brain, such as the *knee-jerk reflex*. The spinal cord consists of two parts. The *dorsal horn* is the entrance point for sensory nerve fibers whose cell bodies are contained within the dorsal root ganglion. The *ventral horn*, on the other hand, contains the cell bodies of motor neurons. Fibers from the cerebral cortex synapse on the ventral horn motor neurons, thereby initiating muscular contractions.

Sensory Systems of the Nervous System

All complicated nervous systems are made more useful through input mechanisms that we know as our senses. Sight, hearing, balance, taste, smell, and touch provide an influx of data for the nervous system to assimilate.

Sight. The eye detects light energy and transmits information about intensity, color, and shape to the brain. The transparent *cornea* at the front of the eye bends and focuses light rays. These rays then travel through an opening called the *pupil,* whose diameter is controlled by the pigmented, muscular *iris.* The iris responds to the intensity of light in the surroundings (light makes the pupil constrict). The light continues through the *lens*, which is suspended behind the pupil. This lens focuses the image onto the *retina,* which contains photoreceptors that transduce light into action potentials. The image on the retina is actually upside down but revision in the cerebral cortex and interpretation result in the perception of the image right-side up. The image from both eyes is also integrated in the cortex to produce the binocular vision with depth perception that allows us to throw, catch and drive with improved ability. The shape of the lens is changed to focus images from nearby or far objects. To see nearby objects, the muscles attached to the lens are relaxed and the lens rounds up, focusing light more sharply. If the shape of the eye is either too short or too long, or if the lens becomes stiff with age, then the eye is unable to focus the image and corrective lenses may be required to bring images into focus.

Hearing and Balance. The ear transduces sound energy into impulses that are perceived by the brain as sound. Sound waves pass through three regions as they enter the ear. First, they enter the outer ear, which consists of the *auricle* (pinna) and the *auditory canal.* Located at the end of the auditory canal is the *tympanic membrane* (eardrum) of the middle ear, which vibrates at the same frequency as the incoming sound. Next, three bones, or *ossicles* (malleus, incus, and stapes), amplify the stimulus, and transmit it through the oval window, which leads to the fluid-filled inner ear.

This inner ear consists of the cochlea and semicircular canals. The *cochlea* contains the *organ of Corti,* which has specialized sensory cells called hair cells. Vibration of the ossicles vibrates the cochlea, causing specific regions within the cochlea to vibrate depending on the frequency of the tone. Louder sounds increase the strength of the vibration and the response. The stimulation of a specific set of hair cells triggers the hair cells to transduce the mechanical pressure into action potentials, which travel via the auditory nerve to the brain for processing.

The *semicircular canals* are used for balance. Each of the three semicircular canals in the inner ear is perpendicular to the other two and filled with a fluid called endolymph. At the base of each canal is a chamber with sensory hair cells; rotation of the head displaces endolymph in one of the canals, putting pressure on the hair cells in it. This changes the nature of the impulses sent by the vestibule nerve to the brain. The brain interprets this information to determine the position of the head.

Taste and Smell. *Taste buds* are chemical sensory cells located on the tongue, the soft palate, and the epiglottis. The outer surface of a taste bud contains a taste pore, from which microvilli, or taste hairs, protrude. Interwoven around the taste buds is a network of nerve fibers that are stimulated by the taste buds, and these neurons transmit impulses to the brainstem. There are four main kinds of taste sensations: sour, salty, sweet, and bitter. We lose taste buds as we age. This is why young children enjoy bland food such as macaroni and cheese, while adults tend to be more interested in spicier food.

Olfactory receptors are chemical sensors found in the olfactory membrane, which lies in the upper part of the nostrils. The receptors are specialized neurons from which olfactory hairs project. When odorous substances enter the nasal cavity, they bind to receptors in the cilia, depolarizing the olfactory receptors. Axons from the olfactory receptors join to form the olfactory nerves, which project direction to the olfactory bulbs in the base of the brain.

Motor Systems

One of the key systems of the body is the system of muscles that are effectors for the CNS. To exert an effect muscles also require something to act against, which is the skeletal system. Read on for explanations of the characteristic motor systems of members of the select group of organisms we have been returning to throughout this book.

Cilia and Flagella

Ciliates and *flagellates* are unicellular organisms that do not have discrete skeletal-muscular systems. Protozoans and primitive algae move by the beating of cilia or flagella. Amoebae, meanwhile, use cell extensions called *pseudopodia* for locomotion; the advancing cell membrane extends, and the cytoplasm liquifies and flows into the pseudopods.

Hydrostatic Skeletons

The muscles within the body wall of advanced flatworms such as planaria are arranged in two antagonistic layers, longitudinal and circular. As the muscles contract against the resistance of the incompressible fluid within the animal's tissues, this fluid functions as a hydrostatic skeleton. Contraction of the circular layer of muscles causes the incompressible interstitial fluid to flow longitudinally, lengthening the animal. Conversely, contraction of the longitudinal layer of muscles shortens the animal. This movement of muscle is similar to the peristaltic motion involved in the digestive system.

The same type of hydrostatic skeleton assists in the locomotion of annelids. Each segment of this animal can expand or contract independently. Annelids advance principally through the action of muscles on a hydrostatic skeleton, as well as through bristles in the lower part of each segment. These bristles, called *setae,* anchor the earthworm temporarily in earth while muscles push the earthworm ahead.

Exoskeleton

An *exoskeleton* is a hard external skeleton that covers all the muscles and organs of some invertebrates. Exoskeletons in arthropods are composed of chitin. In all cases, the exoskeleton is composed of noncellular material secreted by the epidermis. Although it serves the additional function of protection, an exoskeleton imposes limitations on growth. Periodic molting and deposition of a new skeleton are necessary to permit body growth. To cause movement, muscles attach to the interior of the exoskeleton. The giant insects in monster movies are not possible since the muscles in these monsters would not be strong enough to move the weight of the skeleton that would be required.

Endoskeleton

Vertebrates have an *endoskeleton* as a framework for the attachment of skeletal muscles, permitting movement when a muscle contracts by bringing two bones together. All voluntary movement involves muscle contraction bringing bones together. The endoskeleton also provides protection, since bones surround delicate vital organs. For example, the rib cage protects the thoracic organs (heart and lungs), while the skull and vertebral column protect the brain and spinal cord. The vertebrate skeleton contains *cartilage* and *bone,* both formed from connective tissue.

Cartilage, although firm, is also flexible and is not as hard or as brittle as bone. It makes up the skeletons of lower vertebrates, such as sharks and rays. In higher animals, cartilage is the principal component of embryonic skeletons, and is replaced during development by the aptly termed replacement bone. Because cartilage has no vessels or nerves, it takes longer to heal than bone.

Bone makes up most of the skeleton of mature higher vertebrates, including humans, and is made of calcium and phosphate salts and strands of the protein collagen. Bones are produced as a balance between deposition of new bone by osteoblasts, and reabsorption of old bone by osteoclasts that live in bone. *Osteoclasts* are cells that reabsorb bone and *osteoblasts* create new bone. Imbalance between these processes can lead to weakening of the bones such as in osteoporosis. During growth bone arises through the replacement of cartilage or through direct ossification. Bone produced through the latter process is called *dermal bone;* the bones of the skull are examples of this. In *replacement bone,* such as the long bones of the legs and arms, osteoblasts replace the cartilage that has already formed. A hollow cavity within each long bone is subsequently filled with *bone marrow,* the site of formation of blood cells. The long bones originate as cartilage, with ossification beginning in the middle, and the bones growing in the cartilaginous regions at the ends. As the bone grows, the region of ossification extends until growth ceases during adulthood and the bone become fully ossified.

While the division between dermal and replacement bone is based on embryologic origin, the division between spongy and compact bone is based on function and internal structure. *Spongy bone* is located in the central portions of bone, and consists of a network of hard spicules separated by marrow-filled spaces. The low density and the ability to withstand lateral stress are characteristics of bone that may be attributed to this type of spongy bone. *Compact bone,* located on the outer surfaces and articular surfaces, is responsible for the hardness of bone and its ability to withstand longitudinal stress. It consists of cylindrical units called *Haversian systems,* with these cells radiating around a central capillary within a Haversian canal.

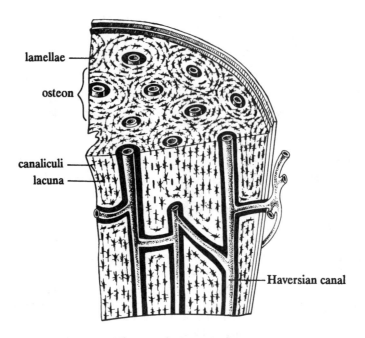

lamellae

osteon

canaliculi

lacuna

Haversian canal

Microscopic Bone Structure

Bones are connected at joints, either immovable joints as in the skull, or movable joints like the hip joint. In the latter type, ligaments serve as bone-to-bone connectors, while tendons attach skeletal muscle to bones and bend the skeleton at the movable joints. In the vertebrate skeleton, the *axial skeleton* is the midline basic framework of the body, consisting of the skull, vertebral column, and the rib cage. The *appendicular skeleton,* on the other hand, includes the bones of the appendages and the pectoral and pelvic girdles.

Muscle System

The muscle system serves as an effector of the nervous system. Muscles contract to implement actions after they receive nervous stimuli. For example, your arm muscles will automatically contract if you touch a hot stove. A skeletal muscle originates at a point of attachment to the stationary bone. The insertion of a muscle is the portion attached to the bone that moves during contraction. An *extensor* extends or straightens the bones at a joint—as in, for example, straightening out a limb. A *flexor* bends a joint to an acute angle, as in bending the elbow to bring the forearm and upper arm together. Bones and muscles work together like a lever system.

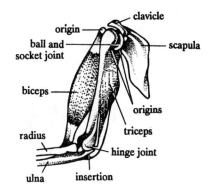

Muscle Movement

Types of Muscles. Vertebrates possess three different types of muscle tissues: *smooth*, *skeletal*, and *cardiac*. In all three types, muscles cause movement by contraction, and the contraction is caused by the sliding of actin and myosin filaments past each other within cells. The differences between the types of muscle include where they are located, what they do, and what the cells look like.

- *Smooth muscle,* or involuntary muscle, is generally found in visceral systems and is innervated by the autonomic nervous system. Each muscle fiber consists of a single cell with one centrally located nucleus. Smooth muscle is nonstriated, meaning it does not have clearly organized arrays of actin and myosin filaments. Smooth muscle is located in the walls of the arteries and veins, the walls of the digestive tract, the bladder, and the uterus. Smooth muscle contracts in response to action potentials, and the contraction is mediated by actin-myosin fibers like in other muscle, although the fibers do not have the clear organization they display in other muscle types. Smooth muscle cells in a tissue are connected to each other through junctions that allow electrical impulses to pass directly from one cell to the next without passing through chemical synapses.

nuclei

Smooth Muscle

- *Skeletal muscles,* or voluntary muscles, produce intentional physical movement. A skeletal muscle cell is a single large multinucleated fiber containing alternating light and dark bands called *striations,* caused by overlapping strands of thick myosin protein filaments that slide past thin actin protein filaments during muscle contraction. The actin and myosin filaments in skeletal muscle are organized into sections called *sarcomeres* that form contractile units within each muscle cell. The somatic nervous system innervates skeletal muscle. Each skeletal muscle fiber is stimulated by nerves through neuromuscular synapses. When a muscle cell is stimulated by a nerve, an action potential moves over the whole muscle fiber, releasing calcium in the cytoplasm of the cell. This calcium causes the actin and myosin to slide over each other, shortening the fibers and the cell. Many muscle cells are bundled together to create muscles.

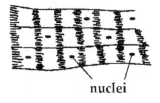

Skeletal Muscle

- *Cardiac muscle* is the tissue that makes up the heart. It has characteristics of both skeletal and smooth muscle. Cardiac muscle cells have single nuclei, like smooth muscle, and are striated like skeletal muscle. Cardiac muscle cells are connected by gap junctions like smooth muscle, so that cells can pass action potentials directly between cells throughout the heart and do not require chemical synapses. Cardiac muscle contraction is regulated by the autonomic nervous system, which increases the rate and strength of contractions through sympathetic stimulation and decreases their rate through the parasympathetic system. Cardiac muscle has an internal pacemaker responsible for the heartbeat that is modified by the nervous system but does not require the nervous system to maintain a regular heartbeat.

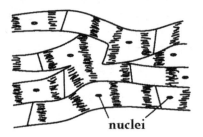

Cardiac Muscle

With that, we've covered the basics of the physiology you might be called upon to know on Test Day. The final topics associated with organismal biology that we need to discuss are those of animal behavior and plants.

Animal Behavior

Animals respond to their environment in a great variety of ways to increase their ability to survive and reproduce. As animals have evolved more complex nervous systems and motor systems, they have also evolved more complex behaviors. Some of these behaviors are inherited genetically while others are learned. Reflexes and fixed action patterns are examples of behaviors that are genetically determined, ingrained responses hardwired in the nervous system that do not require any learning. Many behaviors are a mixture of learned and instinctive actions. Through behavioral experiments and genetics scientists try to discern the role of "nature vs. nurture" in specific behaviors.

Patterns of Animal Behavior

Animal behavior is characterized by a number of different patterns. Simple organisms are capable only of simple, automatic responses to their environment, while more complex organisms are characterized by an increased reliance on mental processes like learning.

Reflexes are simple, automatic responses to simple stimuli. A simple reflex is controlled at the spinal cord level of a vertebrate, involving a direct pathway from the receptor to the motor nerve. The classic example is the knee-jerk reflex. When the tendon covering the patella (kneecap) is hit, stretch receptors sense this and action potentials are sent up the sensory neuron and into the spinal cord. The sensory neuron synapses with a motor neuron in the spinal cord, which, in turn, stimulates the quadriceps muscle to contract, causing the lower leg to kick forward. In polysynaptic reflexes, sensory neurons synapse with more than one neuron. A classic example of this is the withdrawal reflex. When a person steps on a nail, the injured leg withdraws in pain, while the other leg extends to retain balance.

Some behaviors such as avoiding predators are so important to survival that they cannot depend on learning. Learning is not possible in some circumstances where individuals grow without parents or adults and yet must immediately know how to eat, avoid predators and reproduce. *Fixed-action patterns* are used for behaviors that are important and cannot depend on learning. A fixed-action pattern is a complex, coordinated behavioral response triggered by specific stimulation from the environment. Fixed-action patterns are not learned and are not usually modified by learning. The particular stimuli that trigger a fixed-action pattern are more readily modified, provided certain cues or elements of the stimuli are maintained.

An example of a fixed-action pattern is the retrieval-and-maintenance response of many female birds to an egg of their species. Certain kinds of stimuli are more effective than others in triggering a fixed-action pattern. Hence an egg with the characteristics of that species will be more effective in triggering the response than one that only crudely resembles the natural egg. The characteristic movements made by animals that herd or flock together, such as the swimming actions of fish and the flying actions of locusts are fixed-action patterns, as is the spinning of webs by spiders.

Characteristics of the stimulus for the fixed-action pattern can be altered to determine what part of the stimulus is the most important factor. It can either be the size of eggs, their shape, their color, or the pattern of speckling that elicits care of a bird for eggs. The characteristic of the stimulus that triggers the response can be artificially manipulated to create a larger than normal response.

Other physical factors like hormones can exert important influences on behavior, particularly the influence of estrogen and testosterone on sex-specific behavior. Even if a behavior is learned, genetic biological components such as hormone expression and sexual maturation might be required for the behavior to be manifested. For example, hormones and sexual maturation play a key role in the ability of songbirds to perform their characteristic songs.

KAPLAN

Learning

Learned behavior involves a change in the way an animal behaves based on experience. Learning is a complex phenomenon that occurs, to some extent, in all animals. In lower animals, instinctual or innate behaviors are the predominant determinants of behavior patterns, and learning plays a relatively minor role in the modification of these predetermined behaviors. Higher animals, on the other hand, with their well-developed brains and neurological systems, learn the major share of their repertoire of responses to the environment.

There are limits, however, to what an organism is capable of learning. These limits can be either neurologic (the organism simply doesn't have the brain power) or chronologic (learning must occur during a narrow window during the organism's development in order to be successful).

These are specific time periods called *critical periods* during an animal's early development when it is physiologically capable of developing specific behavioral patterns. If the proper environmental pattern is not present during this critical period, the behavioral pattern will not develop correctly. In some animals there is also a visual critical period; if light is not present during this period, visual effectors will not develop properly later on, no matter how much stimulus is given.

Animal Interactions

Just as an organism communicates within itself via nervous and endocrine systems, it also requires methods to communicate with other members of its species. These methods include behavioral displays, pecking order, territoriality, and responses to chemicals. Pheromones can mark a territory or attract a mate, for example, creating a long-lasting message that can be detected over long distances in some cases. Visual communication between animals is quite common, since most animals have vision of some sort, and visual signals are a rapid way to communicate.

The olfactory sense is immensely important as a means of communication. Many animals secrete substances called pheromones that influence the behavior of other members of the same species. One type of pheromone, the releaser pheromone, triggers a reversible behavioral change in the recipient. For example, female silkworms secrete a very powerful attracting pheromone that will attract a male from a distance of two miles or more. In addition to their sex-attracting purposes, releaser pheromones are secreted as alarm and toxic defense substances.

Plants

Plants are so distinct in their body form and so important to life on earth that we present their physiology separately. Plants use the energy of the sun, carbon dioxide, water, and minerals to manufacture carbohydrates through photosynthesis. The chemical energy plants produce is used for respiration by the plants themselves and is the source of all chemical energy in most ecosystems.

Plant Organs

Although we may not usually think of plants having organs, their roots, stems, and leaves each have a defined function and are composed of tissues united around that function in the same manner as animal organs. Stems provide support against gravity and allow for the transport of fluid through vascular tissue. Water travels upward from the roots to the leaves and nutrients travel from the leaves down through the rest of the plant. The roots provide anchoring support, and remove water and essential minerals from the soil. In some plants the roots have a symbiotic relationship with bacteria that fix nitrogen from the atmosphere into a biologically available form that plants can use. The leaves are the primary photosynthetic tissue, generating glucose that can be used to drive all of the plant's biochemical energy needs.

One of the key plant tissues is the *xylem*, which contains cells that carry water and dissolved minerals upward from the roots to the rest of the plant. The xylem is structured differently in flowering and nonflowering plants. In nonflowering plants, or *gymnosperms*, cells called *tracheids* in the stem form a connected network. It is not the cells themselves that conduct water, however. When the cells die, they leave behind their cell walls connected together in one long channel for water transport. Flowering plants, or *angiosperms*, also conduct water through their xylem using the cell walls of dead cells, but in angiosperms the cell walls are more tubelike, making water transport more efficient. In trees, older xylem cells at the innermost layer die, forming the heartwood used for lumber. The outer layer of xylem is alive and is called the sapwood.

Transport in plants, as in animals, encompasses both absorption and circulation. In plants, circulation is called *translocation,* and mainly involves transporting water and carbohydrates. The rise of water up the xylem is caused by transpiration pull (as water evaporates from the leaves of plants, a vacuum is created), capillary action (the rise of any liquid in a thin tube because of the surface tension of the liquid), and root pressure exerted by water entering the root hairs.

Another important plant tissue is the *phloem.* The phloem transports nutrients from the leaves to the rest of the plant. This nutrient liquid is commonly called sap. In the phloem, cells are alive when they perform their transport function. The phloem cells are tube-shaped, moving the sap through the tube. Like terrestrial animals, plants need a protective coating provided by an external layer of epidermis cells. Another plant tissue is the *ground tissue,* involved in storage and support.

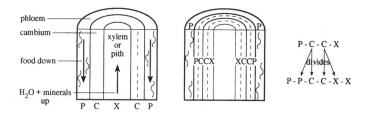

Parts of the Plant

Plant Cells

Plant cells have all of the same essential organelles as other eukaryotic cells, including the mitochondria, ER, Golgi, and nucleus. A major distinction of plant cells is the presence of the photosynthetic organelle, the *chloroplast* (see Cellular and Molecular Biology). Some plant cells contain large storage vacuoles not found in animal cells. Another distinct feature of plant cells is their cell wall. Each plant cell is surrounded outside of its plasma membrane by a stiff cell wall made of *cellulose*. The cellulose cell wall helps to provide structure and support for the plant. From grasses to trees, plants rely on cellulose from cell walls to help support the plant against gravity.

Plant Phyla

Within the plant kingdom there are several major phyla. One of the major distinctions for these plant groups is whether or not a plant has vascular tissue for the transport of fluids. Plants without vascular tissue are small simple plants called *nontracheophytes,* also known as bryophytes or non-vascular plants, and include mosses. The *tracheophytes* are the rest of the plants, including pines, ferns, and flowering plants. The evolution of vascular tissue was an important step in the colonization of land by plants, since it increases the support of plants against gravity, and increases their ability to survive dry conditions. Ferns, also known as *pterophytes,* are a phylum of tracheophytes that do not produce seeds, using spores instead for reproduction.

Gymnosperms

Gymnosperms represent the development of the seed, although they have no flowers, and the angiosperms are the flowering plants, the dominant plants in many ecosystems today. Each of these represented major evolutionary steps. *Gymnosperms* were the first plants to evolve the use of the seed in reproduction. Gymnosperms do not have flowers, and thus their name, which means "naked seed." Gingko trees are one example of gymnosperms, but by far the most common gymnosperms are the conifer trees such as pine, fir, and redwood. These trees have cones that are involved in reproduction, with one cone that produces male spores and separate cones that produce female spores. The female spores are enclosed in eggs that later develop into seeds after fertilization. Male spores are released as pollen that reaches female cones by wind dispersal usually. The seeds of gymnosperms, without a flower, also are not enclosed in a fruit and are quite small. When released by the female cone, the seeds may fall to the ground.

Angiosperms

Ferns were once dominant land plants and gymnosperms were dominant after that. Today the flowering plants, the angiosperms, are dominant. Most of the discussion of plant physiology will focus on the flowering plants due to their importance in ecosystems, and the great number of species they represent.

The stems of angiosperms are arranged with bundles of vascular tissues, separating the xylem and the phloem into organized layers. The *vascular bundles* in monocots are scattered through the stem cross section, while the vascular bundles in dicot stems are organized into a ring. Phloem cells are thin-walled and are found on the outside of the vascular bundle while xylem cells are found on the inside. Additional stem tissues are the *pith* involved in storage and the cortex to provide strength and structure. The *epidermis* on the outside of the stem protects tissues from the environment. Stems also have a layer of *cambium,* a tissue involved in growth. As cambium cells grow and divide, some of the cells differentiate to form xylem and others form phloem. This cambium contributes to growth of the plant, allowing stems to grow in thickness over time. Another layer of cambium lies beneath the bark of trees.

Like the stem, the root has an epidermis, cortex, phloem cells, xylem cells, and cambium cells. The epidermis contains the *root hair* cells. Root hairs are specialized cells of the root epidermis with thin-walled projections. They provide increased surface area for absorption of water and minerals from the soil through diffusion and active transport. The main functions of the root are absorption, which is accomplished through these root hairs, and anchorage of the plant in the ground. Some roots additionally function in the storage of food (such as the roots of turnips and carrots).

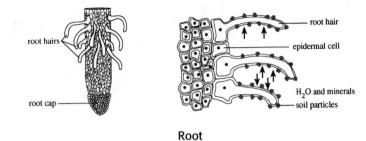

Root

Leaves are the other plant organ. To perform photosynthesis, leaves have adapted in various ways. First of all, the leaf has a waxy cuticle on top to conserve water. Its upper epidermis, the top layer of cells, has no openings, an adaptation which is also intended to inhibit water from being released. Another photosynthetic adaptation, the *palisade layer,* is the term given to elongated cells that are spread over a large surface area and contain chloroplasts. They are directly under the upper epidermis and are well exposed to light.

The leaf also possesses a *spongy layer,* where stomata open into air spaces that contact an internal moist surface of loosely packed spongy layer cells. Spongy cells contain chloroplasts. As in animals, this moist surface is necessary for diffusion of gases into and out of cells in both photosynthesis and respiration. Air spaces in leaves increase the surface area available for gas diffusion by the cells, allowing gaseous interchange of CO_2, H_2O, and O_2. The lower epidermis of the leaf is punctuated by *stomatal openings,* which further regulate the loss of water through transpiration and permit diffusion of carbon dioxide, water vapor, and oxygen between the leaf and the atmosphere. The size of these stomatal openings is controlled by guard cells. These cells open during the day to admit CO_2 for photosynthesis and close at night to limit loss of water vapor through transpiration.

One explanation for the mechanism by which the guard cells open and close is as follows: during the day, the guard cells, which contain chloroplasts, produce glucose. High glucose content in the cells causes them to swell up via osmosis. This condition is known as *turgor.* Because the inner wall of the guard cell is thickened, the swelling produces a curvature of the opening between the guard cells, and the stomatal opening increases. At night, photosynthesis ceases, cell turgor decreases, and the stomatal opening closes. During a drought, the stomata will also close during the day to prevent loss of water by transpiration. In this case, photosynthesis ceases because of a lack of CO_2.

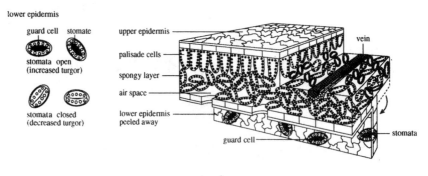

Leaf

Growth in Plants

Plant hormones, which are almost exclusively devoted to this function, are produced by actively growing parts of the plant, such as shoots and roots. They are also produced in young, growing leaves and developing seeds.

Auxins are an important class of plant hormone associated with several growth patterns, including *phototropism* (growth toward light) and *geotropism* (growth directed by gravity).

Auxins are responsible for phototropism, the tendency of the shoots of plants to bend toward light sources (particularly the sun). When light strikes the tip of a plant from one side, the auxin supply on that side is reduced. Thus the illuminated side of the plant grows more slowly than the shaded side. This asymmetrical growth in the cells of the stem causes the plant to bend toward the slower growing light side; thus the plant turns toward the light. Indoleacetic acid is one of the auxins associated with phototropism.

Geotropism is the term given to the growth of portions of plants towards or away from gravity. With negative geotropism, shoots tend to grow upward, away from the force of gravity. If the plant is turned on its side (horizontally), the shoots will eventually turn upward again. Gravity itself increases the concentration of auxin on the lower side of the horizontally placed plant, while the concentration on the upper side decreases. This unequal distribution of auxins stimulates cells on the lower side to elongate faster than cells on the upper side. Thus the shoots turn upward until they grow vertically once again.

With positive geotropism, roots, unlike shoots, grow toward the pull of gravity. In a horizontally placed stem, however, the effect on the root cells is the opposite. Those exposed to a higher concentration of auxin (the lower side) are inhibited from growing, while the cells on the upper side continue to grow. In consequence, the root turns downward.

Auxins produced in the terminal bud of a plant's growing tip move downward in the shoot and inhibit development of lateral buds. Auxins also initiate the formation of lateral roots, while they inhibit root elongation.

Other types of plant hormones include: gibberellins, which stimulate rapid stem elongation; cytokinins, which promote cell division; ethylene, which stimulates the ripening of fruit; and antiauxins, which regulate the activity of auxins.

Asexual Reproduction in Plants

Many plants utilize asexual reproduction, such as *vegetative propagation,* to increase their numbers. Natural forms of vegetative propagation include:

- **Bulbs.** These are parts of the root that split to form several new bulbs (an example is the tulip).

- **Tubers.** These modified underground stems have buds, such as the eye of a potato, which develop into new plants.

- **Runners.** Runners are plant stems that run above and along the ground, extending from the main stem. Near the main plant, new plants develop which produce new roots, as well as upright stems at intervals (as in lawn grasses).

- **Rhizomes.** *Stolons* is another term used for these woody, underground stems. They reproduce through new upright stems that appear at intervals, eventually growing into independent plants. The iris is a rhizome.

Meanwhile, artificial forms of vegetative propagation include:

- **Cutting.** When cut, a piece of stem of some plants will develop new roots in water or moist ground. Examples include the geranium and the willow. Plant growth hormones like auxins accelerate root formation in cuttings.

- **Layering.** The stems of certain plants, when bent into the ground and covered by soil, will take root. The connection between the main plant and this offshoot can then be cut, resulting in the establishment of a new plant. Blackberry and raspberry bushes reproduce in this manner.

- **Grafting.** Desirable types of plants can be developed and propagated using this method, in which the stem of one plant (*scion*) is attached to the rooted stem of another closely related plant (stock). One prerequisite for successful grafting is that the cambium (the tissue in stem that is not differentiated and allows stems to grow thicker) of the scion must be in contact with the cambium of the stock, since these two masses of undifferentiated cells must grow together to make one. Grafting does not allow for any mixing of hereditary characteristics, since the two parts of the grafted plant remain genetically distinct.

Sexual Reproduction in Plants

Most plants are able to reproduce both sexually and asexually; some do both in the course of their life cycles, while others do one or the other. In the life cycles of mosses, ferns, and other vascular plants, there are two kinds of individuals associated with different stages of the life cycles: the *diploid* and the *haploid.*

Diploid and Haploid Generations

In the diploid or *sporophyte* generation, the asexual stage of a plant's life cycle, diploid nuclei divide meiotically to form haploid spores (not gametes) and the spores germinate to produce the haploid or gametophyte generation.

The haploid or *gametophyte* generation is a separate haploid form of the plant concerned with the production of male and female gametes. Union of the gametes at fertilization restores the diploid sporophyte generation. Since there are two distinct generations, one haploid and the other diploid, this cycle is sometimes referred to as the *alternation of generations.* The relative lengths of the two stages vary with the plant type. In general, the evolutionary trend has been toward a reduction of the gametophyte generation, and increasing importance of the sporophyte generation.

How do these generations express themselves in common plants? In moss, the gametophyte is the green plant that you see growing on the north side of trees. The sporophyte variety is smaller, nongreen (nonphotosynthetic), and short-lived. It is attached to the top of the gametophyte, and is dependent upon it for its food supply. Spores from the sporophyte germinate directly into gametophytes.

In ferns, on the other hand, the reverse pattern may be observed, with the sporophyte of the species dominant. The gametophyte is a heart-shaped leaf the size of a dime. Fertilization produces a zygote from which the commonly seen green fern sporophyte develops. The sporophyte fern's leaves (the fronds) develop spores beneath the surface of the leaf. These spores germinate to form the next generation of gametophyte. In gymnosperms and angiosperms the haploid gametophyte is small and is not independent and is orders of magnitude smaller and more transient than the diploid plants, continuing the evolutionary trend over time for the sporophyte to increase in dominance of the cycle.

Sexual Reproduction in Flowering Plants

In flowering plants or angiosperms, the evolutionary trend mentioned above continues; the gametophyte consists of only a few cells and survives for a very short time. The woody plant that is seen (for example, a rose) is the sporophyte stage of the species.

The Flower. The flower is the organ for sexual reproduction of angiosperms and consists of male and female organs. The flower's male organ is known as the *stamen.* It consists of a thin, stalklike filament with a sac at the top. This structure is called the *anther,* and produces haploid spores. The haploid spores develop into pollen grains. The haploid nuclei within the spores will become the sperm nuclei, which fertilize the ovum.

Meanwhile, the flower's female organ is termed a *pistil.* It consists of three parts: the *stigma,* the *style,* and the *ovary.* The stigma is the sticky top part of the flower, protruding beyond the flower, which catches the pollen. The tubelike structure connecting the stigma to the ovary at the base of the pistil is known as the style; this organ permits the sperm to reach the ovules. And the ovary, the enlarged base of the pistil, contains one or more ovules. Each ovule contains the monoploid egg nucleus.

Petals are specialized leaves that surround and protect the pistil. They attract insects with their characteristic colors and odors. This attraction is essential for cross-pollination—that is, the transfer of pollen from the anther of one flower to the stigma of another (introducing genetic variability).

Note that some species of plants have flowers that contain only stamens ("male plants") and other flowers that contain only pistils ("female plants").

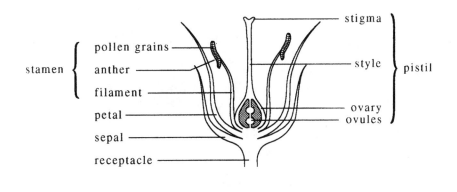

Parts of the Flower

The Male Gametophyte (Pollen Grain). The pollen grain develops from the spores made by the sporophyte (for example, a rose bush). Pollen grains are transferred from the anther to the stigma. Agents of cross-pollination include insects, wind, and water. The flower's reproductive organ is brightly colored and fragrant in order to attract insects and birds, which help to spread these male gametophytes. Carrying pollen directly from plant to plant is more efficient than relying on wind-born pollen and helps to prevent self-pollination, which does not create diversity. When the pollen grain reaches the stigma (pollination), it releases enzymes that enable it to absorb and utilize food and water from the stigma and to germinate a pollen tube. The pollen tube is the remains of the evolutionary gametophyte. The pollen's enzymes proceed to digest a path down the pistil to the ovary. Contained within the pollen tube are the tube nucleus and two sperm nuclei; all are haploid.

Female Gametophyte. The female gametophyte develops in the ovule from one of four spores. This embryo sac contains nuclei, including the two polar (*endosperm*) nuclei and an egg nucleus.

Fertilization. The gametes involved in this cycle of reproduction are nuclei, not complete cells. The sperm nuclei of the male gametophyte (pollen tube) enters the female gametophyte (embryo sac), and a double fertilization occurs. One sperm nucleus fuses with the egg nucleus to form the diploid zygote, which develops into the embryo. The other sperm nucleus fuses with the two polar bodies to form the endosperm. The endosperm provides food for the embryonic plant. In dicotyledonous plants, the endosperm is absorbed by the seed leaves.

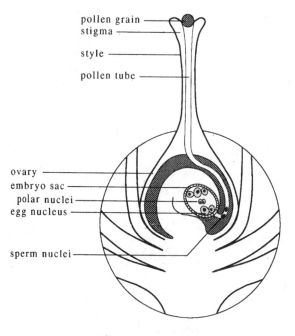

pollen grain
stigma
style
pollen tube
ovary
embryo sac
polar nuclei
egg nucleus
sperm nuclei

Fertilization in Angiosperms

Development of the Plant Embryo-Seed Formation. The zygote produced in the sequence above divides mitotically to form the cells of the embryo. This embryo consists of the following parts, each with its own function:

- The *epicotyl* develops into leaves and the upper part of the stem.

- The *cotyledons* or seed leaves store food for the developing embryo.

- The *hypocotyl* develops into the lower stem and root.

- The *endosperm* grows and feeds the embryo. In dicots, the cotyledon absorbs the endosperm.

- The *seed coat* develops from the outer covering of the ovule. The embryo and its seed coat together make up the seed. Thus, the seed is a ripened ovule.

Seed Dispersal and Development of Fruit. The fruit, in which most seeds develop, is formed from the ovary walls, the base of the flower, and other consolidated flower pistil components. Thus, the fruit represents the ripened ovary. The fruit may be fleshy (as in the tomato) or dry (as in a nut). It serves as a means of seed dispersal; it enables the seed to be carried more frequently or effectively by air, water, or animals (through ingestion and subsequent elimination). Eventually, the seed is released from the ovary, and will germinate under proper conditions of temperature, moisture, and oxygen.

Genetics

Classical genetics is the study of the patterns and mechanisms of the transmission of inherited traits from one generation to another. The foundations for this field were laid by the monk Gregor Mendel, who in the mid-19th century performed a series of experiments to determine the rules of inheritance in garden pea plants.

The study of classical genetics requires an understanding of *meiosis*, the mechanism of gamete formation. Mendel knew that alleles were inherited from each parent, and that these alleles were somehow linked to the various characteristics he studied in his peas, but it was not until meiosis was truly elucidated that the mechanisms behind heredity were understood.

Meiosis

In asexual reproduction, a single diploid cell (or cells) is used to create new identical copies of an organism. In sexual reproduction, two parents contribute to the genome of the offspring and the end result is genetically unique offspring. To do this requires that each parent contributes a cell with one copy of the genome. *Meiosis* is the process whereby these sex cells are produced.

As in mitosis, the gametocyte's chromosomes are replicated during the S phase of the cell cycle. The first round of division (*meiosis* I) produces two intermediate daughter cells. The second round of division (*meiosis* II) involves the separation of the sister chromatids, resulting in four genetically distinct haploid gametes. In this way, a diploid cell produces haploid daughter cells. Since meiosis reduces the number of chromosomes in each cell from $2n$ to $1n$, it is sometimes called *reductive division*.

Each meiotic division has the same four stages as mitosis, although it goes through each of them twice (except DNA replication, which only happens once). The stages of meiosis are detailed in the following paragraphs.

Interphase I: Gametocyte chromosomes are replicated during the S phase of the cell cycle, while the centrioles replicate at some point during interphase.

Prophase I: During this stage, chromatin condenses into chromosomes, the spindle apparatus forms, and the nucleoli and nuclear membrane disappear. Homologous chromosomes (matching chromosomes that code for the same traits, one inherited from each parent), come together and intertwine in a process called *synapsis*. Since at this stage each chromosome consists of two sister chromatids, each synaptic pair of homologous chromosomes contains four chromatids, and is therefore often called a *tetrad*.

Sometimes chromatids of homologous chromosomes break at corresponding points and exchange equivalent pieces of DNA; this process is called *crossing over* or *recombination*. Note that crossing over occurs between homologous chromosomes and not between sister chromatids of the same chromosomes. The chromatids involved are left with an altered but structurally complete set of genes.

The chromosomes remain joined at points called chiasmata where the crossing over occurred. Such genetic recombination can "unlink" linked genes, thereby increasing the variety of genetic combinations that can be produced via gametogenesis. Recombination among chromosomes results in increased genetic diversity within a species. Note that sister chromatids are no longer identical after recombination has occurred.

Metaphase I: Homologous pairs (tetrads) align at the equatorial plane of the dividing cells, and each pair attaches to a separate spindle fiber by its kinetochore.

Anaphase I: Homologous pairs separate and are pulled to opposite poles of the cell. This process is called *disjunction,* and it accounts for a fundamental Mendelian law. During disjunction, each chromosome of paternal origin separates (or disjoins) from its homologue of maternal origin, and either chromosome can end up in either daughter cell. Thus, the distribution of homologous chromosomes to the two intermediate daughter cells is random with respect to parental origin. Each daughter cell will have a unique pool of alleles provided by a random mixture of maternal and paternal origin. These genes may code for alternative forms of a given trait.

Telophase I and Cytokinesis: A nuclear membrane forms around each new nucleus. At this point, each chromosome still consists of sister chromatids joined at the centromere. Next, the cell divides through cytokinesis into two daughter cells, each of which receives a nucleus containing the haploid number of chromosomes. Between cell divisions there may be a short rest period, or interkinesis, during which the chromosomes partially uncoil.

Prophase II: The centrioles migrate to opposite poles and the spindle apparatus forms.

Metaphase II: The chromosomes line up along the equatorial plane once again. The centromeres divide, separating the chromosomes into pairs of sister chromatids.

Anaphase II: The sister chromatids are pulled to opposite poles by the spindle fibers.

Telophase II and Cytokinesis: Finally, a nuclear membrane forms around each new haploid nucleus. Cytokinesis follows and two daughter cells are formed. Thus, by the time meiosis is completed, four haploid daughter cells are produced per gametocyte. In females, only one of these becomes a functional gamete.

The following diagram summarizes the various stages of meiosis I and meiosis II. Notice that the random distribution of homologous chromosomes in meiosis, coupled with crossing over in prophase I, enables an individual to produce gametes with many different genetic combinations. Every gamete gets one copy of each chromosome, but the copy of each chromosome found in a gamete is random. For example, each gamete has a chromosome #9, but this chromosome can be either of the two copies of this chromosome. With 22 autosomal chromosomes, this factor alone allows for 2^{22} possible gametes, not including the additional genetic diversity created by recombination. This is why sexual reproduction produces genetic variability in offspring, as opposed to asexual reproduction, which produces identical offspring. The possibility of so many different genetic combinations is believed to increase the capability of a species to evolve and adapt to a changing environment.

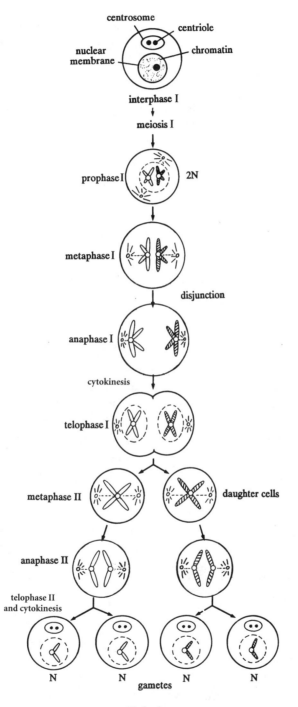

Meiosis

KAPLAN

Mendelian Genetics

Around 1865, based on his observations of seven characteristics of the garden pea, Gregor Mendel developed the basic principles of genetics—*dominance, segregation*, and *independent assortment*. Although Mendel formulated these principles, he was unable to propose any mechanism for hereditary patterns, since he knew nothing about chromosomes or genes. Hence his work was largely ignored until the early 1900s.

After Mendel's work was rediscovered, Thomas H. Morgan tied the principles of genetics to the chromosome theory. He linked specific traits to regions of specific chromosomes visible in the salivary glands of *Drosophila melanogaster*, the fruit fly. Morgan brought to light the giant chromosomes, at least 100 times the size of normal chromosomes, that are found in the fruit fly's salivary glands. These chromosomes are banded, and the bands coincide with gene locations, allowing geneticists to visibly follow major changes in the fly genome. Morgan also described sex-linked genes.

The fruit fly is a highly suitable organism for genetic research. With its short life cycle, it reproduces often and in large numbers, providing large sample sizes. It is easy to grow in the laboratory, but has a fairly complex body structure. Its chromosomes are large and easily recognizable in size and shape. They are also few in number (eight chromosomes/four pairs of chromosomes). Finally, mutations occur relatively frequently in this organism, allowing genes for the affected traits to be studied.

Some of the basic rules of gene transmission and expression are:

- *Genes* are elements of DNA that are responsible for observed traits.
- In eukaryotes, genes are found in large linear chromosomes, and each chromosome is a very long continuous DNA double-helix. Humans have twenty-three different chromosomes, with two copies of each chromosome in somatic cells.
- Each chromosome contains a specific sequence of genes arranged along its length.
- Each gene has a specific location on a chromosome.
- Diploid organisms have two copies of each chromosome and therefore two copies of each gene (except for the *X* and *Y* chromosomes in males).
- The two copies of each gene can have a different sequence in an organism and a gene can have several different sequences in a population. These different versions of a gene are called *alleles*.
- The type of alleles an organism has, its genetic composition, is called the *genotype*.
- The appearance and physical expression of genes in an organism is called the *phenotype*.
- Types of alleles include dominant and recessive alleles. A dominant allele is expressed in an organism regardless of the second allele in the organism. A recessive allele will not be expressed if the other allele for the gene an organism carries is a dominant one.
- A *homozygous* individual has two copies (two alleles) of a gene that are identical and a *heterozygous* individual has two different alleles for a gene.
- The phenotype of an individual is determined by the genotype.

Dominance of Phenotypic Traits

If two members of a pure-breeding strain are mated, their offspring will always have the same phenotype as the parents since they are all homozygous for the same allele. What happens if two different pure-breeding strains that are homozygous for two different alleles are crossed? In an example such as two different alleles for flower color, what often occurs is that all of the offspring of the cross match the phenotype of one parent and not the other. For example, if a pure-breeding red strain is crossed with a pure-breeding white one, perhaps all of the offspring are red. Where did the allele coding for the white trait go? Did it disappear from the offspring?

If it is true that both parents contribute one copy of a gene to each of their offspring, then the allele cannot disappear. The offspring must all contain both a white allele and a red allele. Despite having both alleles, however, they only express one—the red allele. Red is then a dominant allele and white a recessive allele, since it is not expressed in heterozygotes such as the offspring in this cross of two pure-breeding strains. Every human has two copies of each of their 23 chromosomes, with the exception of the X and Y chromosome in men.

Inheritance Patterns

Ethical restraints forbid geneticists to perform test crosses in human populations. Instead, they must rely on examining matings that have already occurred, using tools such as pedigrees. A *pedigree* is a family tree depicting the inheritance of a particular genetic trait over several generations. By convention, males are indicated by squares, and females by circles. Matings are indicated by horizontal lines, and descendants are listed below matings, connected by a vertical line. Individuals affected by the trait are generally shaded, while unaffected individuals are unshaded. When carriers of sex-linked traits have been identified (typically, female heterozygotes), they are usually half shaded in family traits.

The following pedigrees illustrate two types of heritable traits: recessive disorders and sex-linked disorders. When analyzing a pedigree, look for individuals with the recessive phenotype. Such individuals have only one possible genotype—homozygous recessive. Matings between them and the dominant phenotype behave as test crosses; the ratio of phenotypes among the offspring allows deduction of the dominant genotype. In any case in which only males are affected, sex-linkage should be suspected.

Recessive Disorders

Note how the trait skips a generation in the autonomal recessive disorder depicted in the following figure. Albinism is an example of this form of disorder.

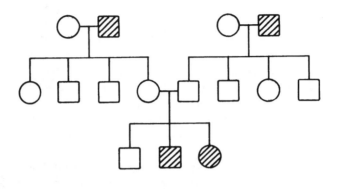

Recessive Disorder

Sex-Linked Disorders

Gender skewing is evident in this type of disorder, which includes traits such as hemophilia. Sex-linked recessive alleles are most often expressed only by males and transmitted from one generation to another by female carriers.

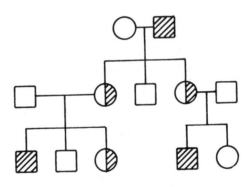

Sex-Linked Disorder

Non-Mendelian Inheritance Patterns

While Mendel's laws hold true in many cases, these laws cannot explain the results of certain crosses. Sometimes an allele is only incompletely dominant or, perhaps, codominant. The genetics that enable the human species to have two genders would also not be possible under Mendel's laws.

Incomplete Dominance

Incomplete dominance is a blending of the effects of contrasting alleles. Both alleles are expressed partially, neither dominating the other.

An example of incomplete dominance is found in the four-o'clock plant and in the snapdragon flower. When a red flower is crossed with a white flower, a pink blend is created. When two pink flowers are crossed, the yield is 25 percent red, 50 percent pink, and 25 percent white (phenotypic and genotypic ratio 1:2:1).

Codominance

In codominance, both alleles are fully expressed without one allele dominant over the other. An example is blood types. Blood type is determined by the expression of antigen proteins on the surface of red blood cells. The *A* allele and the *B* allele are codominant if both are present and combine to produce AB blood.

Sex Determination

Most organisms have two types of chromosomes: *autosomes*, which determine most of the organism's body characteristics, and *sex chromosomes*, which determine the sex of the organism. Humans have 22 pairs of autosomes and one pair of sex chromosomes. The sex chromosomes are known as *X* or *Y*. In humans, *XX* is present in females and *XY* in males. The *Y* chromosome carries very few genes. Sex is determined at the time of fertilization by the type of sperm fertilizing the egg, since all eggs contain *X* chromosomes only. If the sperm carries an *X* chromosome, the offspring will be female (*XX*); if the sperm carries a *Y* chromosome, the offspring will be male (*XY*).

Sex Linkage

Genes for certain traits, such as color blindness or hemophilia, are located on the *X* chromosomes. Hence these genes are linked with the genes controlling sex determination. These genes seem to have no corresponding allele on the *Y* chromosome, with the result that the *X* chromosome contributed by the mother is the sole determinant of these traits in males. Genes determining hemophilia and red-green color blindness are sex-linked (on the *X* chromosome). They are recessive, implying that they can be hidden by a dominant normal allele on the other *X*-chromosome in a female. For this reason, the female with two *X* chromosomes may carry, but will rarely exhibit, these afflictions. The male, on the other hand, with his *Y* chromosome, has no dominant allele to mask the recessive gene on his *X* chromosome. As a consequence of having a single copy of *X*-linked genes, males exhibit sex-linked traits much more frequently than females do.

Mutations

Mutations can create new alleles, the raw material that drive evolution via natural selection. Mutations are changes in the genes that are inherited. To be transmitted to the succeeding generation, mutations must occur in sex cells—eggs and sperm—rather than somatic cells (body cells). Mutations in nonsex cells are called somatic cell mutations and affect only the individual involved, not subsequent generations. A somatic mutation can cause cancer, but will have no affect on off-spring since it is not present in gametes. Most mutations are recessive. Because they are recessive, these mutations can be masked or hidden by the dominant normal genes.

Chromosomal Mutations

These mutations result in changes in chromosome structure or abnormal chromosome duplication. In crossing over, segments of chromosomes switch positions during meiotic synapsis. This process breaks linkage patterns normally observed when the genes are on the same chromosome. A translocation is an event in which a piece of a chromosome breaks off and rejoins a different chromosome.

Nondisjunction is the failure of some homologous pairs of chromosomes to separate following meiotic synapsis. The result is an extra chromosome or a missing chromosome for a given pair. For example, Down syndrome is due to an extra chromosome #21 (Trisomy 21). The number of chromosomes in a case of single nondisjunction is $2n + 1$ or $2n - 1$. In Trisomy 21, the individual has 47 chromosomes instead of the usual 46.

Polyploidy ($3n$ or $4n$) involves a failure of meiosis during the formation of the gametes. The resulting gametes are $2n$. Fertilization can then be either $n + 2n = 3n$ or $2n + 2n = 4n$. Polyploidy is always lethal in humans although it is often found in fish and plants. Finally, *chromosome breakage* might be induced by environmental factors or mutagenic drugs.

Gene Mutations

As discussed in the chapter on cellular and molecular biology, there might be changes in the base sequence of DNA that result in changes in single genes, changing one or more base pairs and the protein produced by reading the gene.

Mutagenic Agents

Mutagenic agents induce mutations including *uv* light, X-rays, radioactivity, and some chemicals that cause mutations by damaging DNA. Such agents are also typically carcinogenic, causing cancer.

This concludes our chapter on classical genetics. With the knowledge you have gained here, you should be able to look at your own family and study the heritability of certain traits. If you have blue eyes, a recessive trait, you must be homozygous for that trait; each of your parents gave you an allele for blue eyes. If one of your parents has brown eyes, he or she must be a heterozygote, possessing alleles for both blue and brown eyes.

Ecology

To understand how organisms live, biologists study molecules, cells, tissues and organs, breaking organisms down into their fundamental units. Organisms from bacteria to humans do not live on Earth in an isolated state, however. All organisms, including humans, live by interacting with other organisms and with the nonliving environment. Life on earth is a network of interacting organisms that depend on each other for survival. Ecology is the study of the interactions between organisms and their environment and how these shape both the organisms and the environments they live in.

Populations in the Environment

Since ecology seeks to understand life at a broader level than the organism, it is the population rather than the individual that is the basic unit of study in this discipline. A *population* is a group of members of the same species found in a given environment at a given time. They share the same gene pool. A *species* is a group of similar organisms that can produce viable, fertile offspring. Every environment will include many different interacting populations. These interacting populations are called a *community*. There are properties of populations that are not present in individuals, such as population growth and maximal population size. These distinct properties of populations are important for *ecosystems*. An ecosystem consists of a community and its abiotic environment.

One of the key characteristics of a population is its rate of population growth. At any given time a population can grow, stay the same, or shrink in size. The birth rate, the death rate, as well as immigration and emigration, and the population size determine the rate of growth, with the birth rate and death rate influenced by the environment. If the birth rate is high and the death rate is low, as in an environment where resources are unlimited, a population will grow rapidly. If a population of mice starts with a male and female mouse, breeds once every three months, producing six male and female offspring in each generation, the population will have over two million mice in two years. A single bacteria reproducing by binary fission every thirty minutes can produce 8 million bacteria in 12 hours. This form of population growth produces a curve with rapidly increasing slope or J-curve and is termed *exponential growth*, since every generation increases the population size in an exponential manner.

In nature, this rapid population growth may be observed when a population first encounters a favorable new environment, such as a rich growth medium inoculated with a small number of bacteria, or a fertile empty field invaded by a weed. Exponential growth cannot be maintained forever, though. A population of mice growing exponentially in a field of wheat will soon eat so much of the available food that starvation will occur; growth will slow and then halt. Bacteria reproducing without check would in a few days weigh more than the mass of the earth. Limitations of the environment prevent exponential growth from proceeding indefinitely. Reasons for a slowdown in the growth rate include a lack of food, competition for other resources, predation, disease, accumulation of waste, or lack of space, all acting more strongly to slow growth as the population becomes denser. Under these conditions, the growth curve may appear sigmoidal or logistic, producing an S-curve with rapid exponential growth at first, followed by a slowing and leveling off of growth. In this curve, the population size at the point where the growth curve is flat is the maximum sustainable number of individuals, called the *carrying capacity*, and is observed when the birth rate and death rate are equal (also known as zero growth).

In natural populations, the environment is constantly changing, and the carrying capacity varies with it. For example, the carrying capacity for rabbits in a grassy plain will be greater in a year of plentiful rain and lush vegetation growth than in a year of drought. Populations often have regular fluctuations in size, suggesting that the carrying capacity changes in a periodic manner. If a population of rabbits consumes all available vegetation, the carrying capacity will be reduced and the population size will fall until the vegetation regrows and the carrying capacity for rabbits is increased once again. An example that is often used is the size of hare and lynx populations in Canada. In this environment, the primary food of the lynx is the hare. The hare population size regularly cycles up and then crashes, perhaps due to the rapid spread of disease in crowded conditions. The lynx population size cycles along with that of the hare, crashing in size after the hare population crashes, then building in size once again after the hare population rebounds.

Different strategies of reproduction can produce different patterns of population growth. An example is the choice between sexual and asexual reproduction. Sexual reproduction occurs in most complex multicellular organisms, and helps to create and maintain diversity in the gene pool of a population. Asexual reproduction can allow a population to grow very rapidly, as occurs in some plant species that reproduce from shoots rather than seeds. The benefit of asexual reproduction is a reduced cost to produce new organisms. For example, it takes less energy for a plant to produce a shoot and reproduce asexually than for it to flower or to produce fruit and seeds. By reproducing through *parthenogenesis* (in which an egg divides in the absence of fertilization by a male), only female offspring are produced, all of which produce their own young, increasing by two-fold the rate of population growth. The cost of asexual reproduction is a reduction in genetic variability. Some species will reproduce asexually in times of abundant resources to maximize the opportunity for rapid growth, and reproduce sexually when resources are limited, perhaps generating the genetic diversity required to survive a changing environment.

Species also use two different strategies that affect the number of offspring produced in each generation and the amount of care they receive. In the first strategy, offspring reach sexual maturity very rapidly, and produce a large number of young in each generation that receive little or no parental care. Insects and plants often reproduce in this way, producing large numbers of eggs or seeds that are left in the environment to fend for themselves. In colonizing a new environment, a population with this reproduction pattern will grow exponentially to rapidly exploit this opportunity. The lack of parental care for a species with this strategy can cause a high death rate early in life when these species are in a competitive environment. For example, some marine species release their young as large number of eggs that develop without care. As a result, many are consumed early in life. The large number of young ensure survival despite the high mortality rate. Species with this reproductive strategy, known as r-selected species, are also prone to rapid crashes in population size as the environment rapidly becomes depleted of resources after a period of exponential growth.

The other reproductive strategy is to delay sexual maturity, have few young, and put a great deal of parental care into offspring. Large mammals often fall in this category. These species, known as k-selected species, have long life spans and are highly adapted to compete for resources in a competitive environment that is at, or near, the carrying capacity. Since these organisms invest so much into their young, they have a lower mortality rate. These species also have difficulty recovering from catastrophic decreases in their population size; examples include California condors or whooping cranes.

The Role of the Abiotic Environment in Population Growth

The size and growth of a population are affected both by the biotic (living) and abiotic (nonliving) portions of the environment. The abiotic portions include the air, water, soil, light and temperature that living organisms require. Not only are organisms dependent on the abiotic environment, but they in turn modify it. Plants create shade that alters the light environment for other plants, preserve water in the soil, consume carbon dioxide, and produce oxygen. The modifications of the environment by a population affect the types of species the population lives in.

Water is essential to all life and is a major component of all living things. Our bodies are made mostly of water. Animals must regulate their water content to ensure the proper volume and salt concentrations inside and outside of the cell.

Sunlight serves as the ultimate source of energy for almost all organisms. Green plants must compete for sunlight in forests. To this end, they develop adaptations to capture as much sunlight as possible (including broad leaves, branching, greater height, and vine growth). In water, the *photic zone*—the top layer through which light can penetrate—is where all photosynthetic activity takes place. In the *aphotic zone*, only animal life and other heterotrophic and chemoautotrophic life exist.

Oxygen supply poses no problem for terrestrial life, since air is composed of approximately 20 percent oxygen. Aquatic plants and animals utilize oxygen dissolved in water, where oxygen is present only in parts per million. Pollution can significantly lower oxygen content in water, threatening aquatic life. It can also benefit certain organisms at the expense of others.

Substratum determines the nature of plant and animal life in the soil. Some soil factors include:

- *Acidity (pH)*. Acid rain may make soil pH too low for most plant growth. Rhododendrons and pines, however, are more well suited to acidic soil.
- *Texture of soil and clay content.* These determine the quantity of water the soil can hold. Most plants grow well in loams that contain high percentages of each type of soil.
- *Minerals.* Nitrates, phosphates, and other minerals determine the type of vegetation soil will support.
- *Humus quantity.* This is determined by the amount of decaying plant and animal life in the soil.

Also included in the abiotic environment are inorganic chemicals required for life such as carbon and nitrogen. The movement of these essential elements between the biotic and abiotic environment form cycles that are central to all life on earth. Some organisms take the simple inorganic starting chemicals up from the soil and air and convert them into a biologically useful form. After material passes through the biological community, respiration and decay organisms return these chemicals to their inorganic state to begin the cycle again.

Populations in Communities and Ecosystems

The next level of biological organization beyond a population is a *community*, which is all the interacting populations living together in an environment. The populations within a community interact with each other in a variety of ways, including *predation*, *competition*, or *symbiosis*. These interactions affect the number of individuals in each population in the community and the number of different species in the community. The living community combined with the abiotic environment, the interactions between populations, and the flow of energy and molecules within the system define an *ecosystem*.

Predation is the consumption of one organism by another, most often resulting in the death of the organism that is eaten. Carnivores that consume meat, herbivores consuming plants only, and omnivores that consume both plants and animals are types of predators. Predation includes a zebra eating grass, a lion eating a zebra, a whale eating plankton, a paramecium eating yeast, or a Venus flytrap eating a housefly.

Predator and prey often coevolve, with the predator evolving to become more effective as the prey evolves to escape predation. Predator-prey relationships between populations in a community can influence the carrying capacity of prey populations involved and tend to achieve a balance such that the predator is effective enough to maintain its own population without decimating the prey it is dependent on. Predation can cause a community to maintain a greater diversity of species—without predation, one prey species will often predominate.

A competitive relationship between populations in a community exists when different populations in the same location use the same resource. *Competition* can be interspecific (between species) or intraspecific (between organisms of the same species). Integral in understanding interspecific competition is the idea of the ecological niche. If the habitat is the physical environment in which the population lives, the niche is the way it lives within the habitat, including what it eats, where it lives, how it reproduces, and all other aspects of the species that define the role it plays in the ecosystem. The niche occupied by each species is unique to that species and can in part define that species.

When two populations have overlap in their niches, such as by eating the same insects or occupying the same nesting sites, there is competition between the populations. Competition can drive the less efficient population out of the community, with the "winner" occupying the niche on its own. Another result of competition for a niche can be that evolution drives the two populations to occupy niches that overlap less, reducing the competition. For example, if two species of related birds compete for the same nesting site, then they may evolve to reduce competition by using different nesting sites. Even in an environment with several different herbivores, their niches are unique since they evolve to have different heights, different sizes, different teeth and digestive tracts to avoid competition for the same plants. Several closely related species of birds can live in the same tree and eat similar food, and yet occupy distinct niches by living in different part of the tree, with some near the crown, others in the middle, and still others close to the ground.

Symbionts live together in an intimate, often permanent association that may or may not be beneficial to them. Some symbiotic relationships are obligatory—that is, one or both organisms cannot survive without the other. Types of symbiotic relationships are generally classified according to the benefits the symbionts receive. Symbiotic relationships include commensalism, mutualism, and parasitism.

Commensalism. In this relationship, one organism is benefited by the association and the other is not affected. The host neither discourages nor fosters the relationship. The remora (sharksucker), for example, attaches itself to the underside of a shark. Through this association, the remora obtains the food the shark discards, wide geographic dispersal, and protection from enemies. The shark is totally indifferent to the association.

Mutualism. This is a symbiotic relationship from which both organisms derive some benefit. In the instance of the bird and rhinoceros, the rhinoceros aids the bird through the provision of food in the form of parasites on its skin. The bird in its turn aids the rhinoceros by removing the parasites and by warning the rhinoceros of danger when it suddenly flies away.

Parasitism. A parasite takes from the host but gives nothing in return; thus, the parasite benefits at the expense of the host. Examples of parasites include leeches, ticks, and sea lampreys. Parasitism exists when competition for food is most intense. Few photoautotrophs (green plants) exist as parasites.

Ectoparasites cling to the exterior surface of the host with suckers or clamps, bore through the skin, and suck out juices. Endoparasites, on the other hand, live within the host. In order to gain entry into the host, they must break down formidable defenses, including skin, digestive juices, antibodies, and white blood cells. Parasites possess special adaptations to overcome these defenses.

Parasitism is advantageous and efficient, since the parasite lives with a minimum expenditure of energy. Parasites may even be parasitic on other parasites. Thus, a mammal may have parasitic worms, which in turn are parasitized by bacteria, which in turn are victims of bacteriophages.

A prominent example of a parasitic relationship is that between the virus and its host cell. All viruses are parasites. They contain nucleic acids surrounded by a protein coat, and are nonfunctional outside their host cells. As viral nucleic acid enters the host, the virus takes over the host cell functions and redirects them into replication of the virus.

Competition is not restricted to interspecific interactions. Individuals belonging to the same species utilize the same resources; if a particular resource is limited, these organisms must compete with one another. Members of the same species compete, but they must also cooperate. Intraspecific cooperation may be extensive (as in the formation of societies in animal species) or may be nearly nonexistent. Hence, within a species, relationships between individuals are influenced by both disruptive and cohesive forces. Competition (for food or a mate, for example) is the chief disruptive force, while cohesive forces include reproduction, protection from predators, and destructive weather.

Community Structure

The populations within a community are organized in many different ways. Within the community, each population plays a different role depending on the source of energy for that population. Producers are organisms that get energy from the environment (the sun or inorganic molecules) and use this energy along with simple molecules (carbon dioxide, water and minerals) to drive the biosynthesis of their own proteins, carbohydrates, and lipids. Producers form the foundation of any community, passing on their energy to other organisms. In a terrestrial environment, green plants and photosynthetic bacteria are producers, using the energy of sunlight to produce biosynthetic energy through photosynthesis. In marine environments, kelp (algae), photosynthetic plankton (phytoplankton), and cyanobacteria are the main producers. There are even marine ecosystems at deep, dark ocean hydrothermal vents at which the entire community is based not on photosynthetic producers but on chemosynthetic bacteria that use the energy of inorganic molecules released from the volcanic vent to drive biosynthesis.

Consumers get the energy to drive their own biosynthesis and to maintain life by ingesting and oxidizing the complex molecules synthesized by other organisms. Herbivores (plant eaters), carnivores (meat eaters), and omnivores (eaters of both plants and animals) are all consumers. The adaptations of each consumer depend on the type of food it eats. Herbivores tend to have teeth for grinding and long digestive tracts that allow for the growth of symbiotic bacteria to digest cellulose found in plants. Carnivores are more likely to have pointed, fanglike teeth for catching and tearing prey and shorter digestive tracts than herbivores.

Decay organisms, also called decomposers, derive their energy from oxidizing complex biological molecules, but they do not consume living organisms. Decay organisms get energy from the biological organic molecules they encounter left as waste by producers and consumers, or the debris of dead organisms. They perform respiration to derive energy, and return carbon dioxide, nitrogen, phosphorous and other inorganic compounds to the environment to renew the cycles of these materials between the biotic and physical environments. Bacteria and fungi are the primary examples of decay organisms. Scavengers such as hyenas or vultures play a similar role, living on the stored chemical energy found in dead organisms.

The Food Chain and Food Web

The term *food chain* is often used to describe a community, depicting a simple linear relationship between a series of species, with one eating the other (see the figure below). A more realistic depiction of the relationships within the community is a *food web,* in which every population interacts not with one other population, but several other populations. An animal in an ecosystem is often preyed on by several different predators, and predators commonly have a diet of several different prey, not just one. The greater the number of potential interactions in a community food web, the more stable the system will be, and the better able it will be to withstand and rebound from external pressures such as disease or weather.

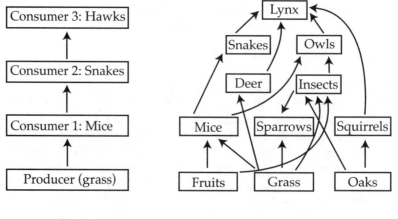

Food Chain   Food Web

Community Diversity

The number of species within a community is termed the community diversity. The types of interactions between populations within a community affect the number of species in the community, as well as the physical environment. Predation has been observed as one factor that increases the diversity of species in a community, and competition may do the same through selective pressure driving populations into distinct niches. Warm environments like the tropics with very high productivity have the greatest diversity, and colder environments have less community diversity. Topographic diversity increases community diversity, perhaps by creating a greater number of niches in the environment. Larger land masses or ecosystems also have a greater community diversity.

Changes in Community Over Time: Succession

Communities can change in composition over time, either as a result of a changing physical environment such as the climate or as the result of changes created by the populations that live in the community. When a population changes the environment it lives in, it may make the environment more favorable for some populations and less favorable for others, including itself. When a community changes as a result of organisms that live in the community, this is termed *succession*.

For example, a grassland may provide abundant sunlight and rich soil that lead to colonization by trees, followed by other trees that grow best in the shade of the pioneer trees. Successive communities are composed of populations best able to exist in each new set of conditions, both biotic and abiotic.

The community will continue to change until it arrives at combination of populations that do not change the environment any further, leaving the community the same over time in what is called the *climax community*. The climax community is stable over time, with each generation leaving the environment it resides in the same, and it will remain in place unless it is disturbed by climate change, fire, humans, or other catastrophes. If the climax community is disturbed, the series of community successions will begin again until a climax community is achieved once again. The type of climax community that is present in an environment depends on the abiotic factors of the ecosystem, including rainfall, temperature, soil, and sunlight.

Here's an example of the progression of a climax community in an aquatic environment. This community starts with a pond:

- *Step 1—pond.* This pond contains plants such as algae and pondweed and animals such as protozoa, water insects, and small fish.
- *Step 2—shallow water.* The pond begins to fill in with reeds, cattails, and water lilies.
- *Step 3—moist land.* The former pond area is now filled with grass, herbs, shrubs, willow trees, frogs, and snakes.
- *Step 4—woodland.* Pine or oak becomes the dominant tree of the climax community.

It is important to remember that the dominant species of the climax community is determined by such physical factors as temperature, nature of the soil, and rainfall. Thus the climax community at higher elevations in New York state is hemlock-beech-maple, while at lower elevations, it is more often oak-hickory. In cold Maine, the climax community is dominated by the pine; in the wet areas of Wisconsin, by cypress; in sandy New Jersey, by pine; in Georgia, by oak, hickory, and pine; and on a cold, windy mountain top, by scrub oak.

Biomes

The conditions in a particular terrestrial and climatic region select plants and animals possessing suitable adaptations for that particular region. Each geographic region is inhabited by a distinct community called a *biome*.

Terrestrial Biomes

Land biomes are characterized and named according to the climax vegetation of the region in which they are found. The climax vegetation is the vegetation that becomes dominant and stable after years of evolutionary development. Since plants are important as food producers, they determine the nature of the inhabiting animal population; hence the climax vegetation determines the climax animal population. There are eight types of terrestrial biomes that can be formed as a result of all these factors.

Tropical Forests

Tropical forests are characterized by high temperatures and, in tropical rain forests, by high levels of rainfall. The climax community includes a dense growth of vegetation that does not shed its leaves. Vegetation like vines and epiphytes (plants growing on the other plants) and animals like monkeys, lizards, snakes, and birds inhabit the typical tropical forest, or rain forest. Trees grow closely together in a dense canopy high above the ground; sunlight barely reaches the forest floor. The floor is inhabited by saprophytes living off dead organic matter. Tropical rain forests are found in central Africa, Central America, the Amazon basin, and southeast Asia, and are one of the most productive and diverse communities.

Savanna

The savanna (grassland) is characterized by low rainfall (usually 10–30 inches per year), although it gets considerably more rain than the desert biomes do. Grassland has few trees and provides little protection for herbivorous mammals (such as bison, antelopes, cattle, and zebras) from carnivorous predators. That is why animals that do inhabit the savanna have generally developed long legs and hoofs, enabling them to run fast. Examples of savanna include the prairies east of the Rockies, the Steppes of the Ukraine, and the Pampas of Argentina.

Desert

The desert receives less than ten inches of rain per year, and this rain is concentrated within a few heavy cloudbursts. The growing season in the desert is restricted to those days after rain falls. Generally, small plants and animals inhabit the desert. Most desert plants (for example, cactus, sagebrush, and mesquite) conserve water actively and animals avoid extreme heat, often by being nocturnal. Desert animals like the lizard, meanwhile, live in burrows. Birds and mammals found in the deserts also have developed adaptations for maintaining constant body temperatures. Examples of desert biomes include the Sahara in Africa, the Mojave in the United States, and the Gobi in Asia.

Temperate Deciduous Forest

Temperate deciduous or "broadleaf" forests have cold winters, warm summers, and a moderate rainfall. Trees such as beech, maple, oaks, and willows shed their leaves during the cold winter months. Animals found in temperate deciduous forests include the deer, fox, woodchuck, and squirrel. The forest floor is a rich soil of decaying matter, inhabited by worms and fungi. Temperate deciduous forests are located in the northeastern and central eastern United States and in central Europe.

Northern Coniferous Forest

Northern coniferous forests are cold, dry, and inhabited by fir, pine, and spruce trees. Much of the vegetation here has evolved adaptations for water conservation—that is, needle-shaped leaves. These forests are found in the extreme northern part of the United States and in Canada. The forest floor is dry and contains a layer of needles with fungi, moss, and lichens. Common animals include (in North America) moose, deer, black bears, hares, wolves, and porcupines.

Taiga

The taiga receives less rainfall than the temperate forests, has long, cold winters, and is inhabited by a single type of coniferous tree, the spruce. The forest floors in the taiga contain moss and lichens. Birds are the most common animal; however, the black bear, the wolf, and the moose are also found here. Taiga exists in the northern parts of Canada and Russia.

Tundra

Tundra is a treeless, frozen plain located between the taiga and the northern icesheets. Although the ground is always frozen (a condition called *permafrost*) the surface can melt during summer. It has a very short summer and a very short growing season, during which time the ground becomes wet and marshy. Lichens, moss, polar bears, musk oxen, and arctic hens make their homes here.

Polar Region

The polar region is a frozen area with very few types of vegetation or terrestrial animals. Animals that do inhabit polar regions, such as seals, walruses, and penguins, generally live near the polar oceans, surviving through preying on marine life.

Aquatic Biomes

In addition to the eight terrestrial biomes, there are aquatic biomes, each with its own characteristic plants and animals. More than 70 percent of the earth's surface is covered by water, and most of the earth's plant and animal life is found there. As much as 90 percent of the earth's food and oxygen production (photosynthesis) takes place in the water. Aquatic biomes are classified according to criteria quite different from the criteria used to classify terrestrial biomes. Plants have little controlling influence in communities of aquatic biomes, as compared to their role in terrestrial biomes.

Aquatic areas are also the most stable ecosystems on earth. The conditions affecting temperature, amount of available oxygen and carbon dioxide, and amount of suspended or dissolved materials are stable over very large areas, and show little tendency to change. For these reasons, aquatic food webs and aquatic communities tend to be balanced. There are two types of major aquatic biomes: marine and freshwater.

Marine Biomes

The oceans connect to form one continuous body of water that controls the earth's temperature by absorbing solar heat. Water has the distinctive ability to absorb large amounts of heat without undergoing a great temperature change. Marine biomes contain a relatively constant amount of nutrient materials and dissolved salts.

Freshwater Biomes

Rivers, lakes, ponds, and marshes—the links between the oceans and land—contain freshwater. Rivers are the routes by which ancient marine organisms reached land and evolved terrestrial adaptations. Others developed special adaptations suitable for both land and freshwater. As in marine biomes, factors affecting life in freshwater include temperature, transparency (illumination due to suspended mud particles), depth of water, available CO_2 and O_2, and most importantly, salt concentration.

Freshwater biomes differ from salt water biomes in two basic ways:

- Freshwater has a lower concentration of salt (greater concentration of water) than the cell, creating a diffusion gradient that results in the passage of water into the cell. Freshwater organisms have homeostatic mechanisms to maintain water balance by the regular removal of excess water, such as the contractile vacuole of protozoa and excretory systems of fish.
- Freshwater biomes (except for very large lakes) are affected by variations in climate and weather. They might freeze, dry up, or have mud from their floors stirred up by storms. Temperatures of freshwater bodies vary considerably.

Evolution and Diversity

Evolution provides a sweeping framework for the understanding of the diversity of life on earth. Living systems, from the cell to the organism to the ecosystem, arose through a long process through geologic time, selecting solutions out of diverse possibilities. What is the evidence that supports the evolutionary view of life? The evidence takes several forms.

The Fossil Record

Fossils are preserved impressions or remains in rocks of living organisms from the past. Fossils provide some of the most direct and compelling evidence of evolutionary change and are generally found in sedimentary rock. When animals settle in sediments after death, their remains can be embedded in the sediment. These sediments then might be covered over with additional layers of sediment that turn to rock through heat and pressure over many millions of years. The embedded remains turn to stone, replaced with minerals that preserve an impression of the form of the organism, often in a quite detailed state. Most fossils are of the hard bony parts of animals, since these are preserved the most easily. Fossils of soft body parts or of invertebrates are much more unusual, probably since these parts usually decay before fossil formation can occur. In some cases, however it appears that animals died in anaerobic sediments that resisted decay to provide soft-body fossils.

One of the questions about fossils when they are discovered is their age, to place the fossil in correctly in the timeline of life on earth. One way to place the date is to compare the location of the fossil sediment to other sedimentary rock formations in which the age is already known. Dating using *radioactive decay* is also very useful. Carbon dating is frequently used for material that is only a few thousand years old, but cannot be used for older material since the decay rate of carbon is too rapid.

Comparative Anatomy

One way to find the evolutionary relationship between organisms is by examining their external and internal anatomy. Animals that evolved from a common ancestor might be expected to have anatomical features in common that they share with their common ancestor. Alternatively, two organisms might share features that look the same but evolved from different ancestors and resulted in similar structures as a result of similar functions. When we compare the anatomies of two or more living organisms, we can not only form hypotheses about their common ancestors, but we can also glean clues that shed light upon the selective pressures that led to the development of certain adaptations, such as the ability to fly.

Comparative Embryology

Comparison of embryonic structures and routes of embryo development is another way to derive evolutionary relationships. The development of the human embryo is very similar to the development of other vertebrate embryos. Adult tunicates (sea squirts) and amphibians lack a notochord, one of the key traits of the chordate phylum, but their embryos both possess notochords during development, indicating these animals are in fact vertebrates with a common evolutionary ancestor even though the adults do not resemble each other. The earlier that embryonic development diverges, the more dissimilar the mature organisms are. Thus, it is difficult to differentiate between the embryo of a human and that of an ape until relatively late in the development of each embryo, while human and sea urchin embryos diverge much earlier.

Other embryonic evidence of evolution includes such characteristics as teeth in an avian embryo (recalling the reptile stage); the resemblance of the larvae of some mollusks (shellfish) to annelids (segmented worms), and the tail of the human embryo (indicating relationships to other mammals).

Molecular Evolution

If organisms are derived from a common ancestor, this should be evident not just at the anatomical level but also at the molecular level. The traits that distinguish one organism from another are ultimately derived from differences in genes. With the advent of molecular biology, the genes and proteins of organisms can be compared to determine their evolutionary relationship. The closer the genetic sequences of organisms are to each other, the more closely related they are in evolution and the more recently they diverged from a common ancestor.

Vestigial Structures

Vestigial structures are structures that appear to be useless in the context of a particular modern-day organism's behavior and environment. It is apparent, however, that these structures used to have some function in an earlier stage of a particular organism's evolution. They serve as evidence of an organism's evolution over time, and can help scientists to trace its evolutionary path.

There are many examples of vestigial structures in humans, other animals, and plants. The appendix—small and useless in humans—assists digestion of cellulose in herbivores, indicating humanity's vegetarian ancestry, while the animal-like tail in humans is reduced to a few useless bones (coccyx) at the base of the spine. The splints on the legs of a horse are vestigial remains of the two side toes of the eohippus.

The Population as the Basic Unit of Evolution

Evolution is the change in a population of a species over time. These changes are the result of changes in the gene pool of a population of organisms. Evolution does not happen in one individual, but in a population of a organisms. A *population* is a group of individuals of a species that interbreed. A *species* is a group of individuals capable of interbreeding to produce offspring that can reproduce. In classical genetics, it is observed that the genotype of organisms produces their phenotype, the physical expression of inherited traits. A population of organisms includes individuals with a range of phenotypes and genotypes. It is possible, however, to describe a population not by their individual characteristics, but by certain traits of the group as a whole, including the abundance of alleles within the whole population. The sum total of all alleles in a population is called the *gene pool* and the frequency of a specific allele in the gene pool is called the *allele frequency*. Each individual receives its specific set of alleles from the gene pool, and not every individual receives the same alleles, leading to individual variation in genotypes and phenotypes.

Hardy-Weinberg and Population Changes

The allele frequencies in the gene pool of a population determine how many individuals in a population get each allele and this in turn determines the phenotypes of individuals. If nothing changes the allele frequencies, then every generation will get the same alleles in the same proportions, and the population will not change over time. This idea is the foundation of population genetics and the central idea of *Hardy-Weinberg equilibrium* in population genetics.

According to the Hardy-Weinberg principle, allele frequencies in a population remain constant from generation to generation and a population is maintained in equilibrium as long as certain assumptions are met. If the assumptions are met, and the allele frequencies in the gene pool of a population are constant over time, the population does not change and evolution does not occur. If the assumptions are not true, then the allele frequencies of the population will change and the population will evolve.

The assumptions for Hardy-Weinberg equilibrium to be maintained are:

- Random mating (no isolation) must occur, so that no particular trait is favored. There can be no assortative mating (in other words, no organisms may select mating partners that resemble themselves).

- Immigration or emigration cannot take place.

- There must be no mutations.

- Large populations are required. As in all cases of probability, large samplings are needed to provide an accurate approximation of the expected occurence.

- Natural selection does not occur.

Under the above conditions, there is a free flow of alleles between members of the same species, while the total content of the gene pool is continually being shuffled. A constant gene pool is nevertheless maintained for the entire population. The constancy of the gene pool is always threatened by changes in the environment (which would favor certain genes), mutations, immigration and emigration (new genes introduced), or reproductive isolation (lack of random mating favors certain genes).

Disruption of Hardy-Weinberg Equilibrium in Evolution

The Hardy-Weinberg principle describes the stability of the gene pool. However, no population stays in Hardy-Weinberg equilibrium for very long, because the stable, ideal conditions needed to maintain it do not exist. The assumptions required for equilibrium cannot be met in the real world.

As conditions change, the gene pool changes and the population changes. Changes in the gene pool caused by breaking the assumptions are the basis of evolution.

Mutation

If the gene pool is not going to change, and there is no immigration or emigration, then there can be no new alleles that appear in the population. Mutations may be infrequent in a population as a result of the great accuracy of DNA replication, but DNA replication is never perfect and some mutations will occur at least infrequently. Radiation from the environment and environmental mutagens also contribute a low but inescapable level of mutation in any population. The mutations will not form a large part of allele frequency, but they do form an important component, as a source of variation in a population. Many mutations are harmful, but a small minority may confer a selective advantage in some way. Phenotypes are the material that evolution acts on in a population and mutations are the only source of truly new alleles that will result in truly new phenotypes.

Gene Flow

If two populations are separated from each other and do not interbreed, then the allele frequencies in their gene pools may be different from each other. If individuals move between the populations however, carrying their alleles with them, this creates gene flow, and will alter the frequency of alleles in both of the populations involved.

Population Size

One of the assumptions for the maintenance of Hardy-Weinberg equilibrium is that a population is large. Small populations are subject to random events that can statistically alter the gene pool. Changes in the gene pool caused by random events in a small population are called *genetic drift*. One example is a *population bottleneck*. If an event like a flood suddenly and dramatically reduces the size of a population, the allele frequencies of the survivors are not necessarily the same as the allele frequencies in the original population. When the population grows in size again, the allele frequencies in the new gene pool will represent the frequencies in the small bottleneck population, not the population before the reduction in size. A similar phenomena called the *founder effect* occurs in the colonization of a new habitat. When a new island forms, it might be colonized by a very small number of individuals from another population. Since the new population is founded by a small number of individuals, it is unlikely statistically that the island population will represent the same allele frequencies as the population they were derived from.

Nonrandom Mating

If a population is going to maintain constant allele frequencies, then alleles must be matched randomly in each new generation. This requires that individuals mate with each other without any preference for specific traits or individuals. If the phenotype of individuals influences mating, this will change allele frequencies and disrupt Hardy-Weinberg equilibrium. Most species are quite discerning in mate selection, however, blocking maintenance of Hardy-Weinberg equilibrium.

Natural Selection

Within a population of organisms, individuals are non-identical. Mutation is a source of new alleles, and sexual reproduction leads to constant shuffling of alleles in new genotypes. The variety of genotypes created in a population in this way creates a variety of phenotypes. If individuals have different phenotypes, then these individuals probably interact with their environment with differing degrees of success in escaping predators, finding food, avoiding disease, and reproducing. The differential survival and reproduction of individuals based on inherited traits is *natural selection* as described first by Charles Darwin.

Fitness is a quantitative measure of the ability to contribute alleles and traits to offspring and future generations. The key to fitness is reproduction and survival of offspring. Avoiding predators, finding food, resistance to disease and other factors that improve survival are likely to improve fitness but only to the extent that they lead to more offspring and more of the alleles involved in the future gene pool. Finding a mate, mating, successful fertilization, and caring for offspring are factors that can improve fitness as well. There are different strategies for improving fitness. For example, some animals have lots of offspring but provide little parental care, while other animals have few offspring but provide lots of care for each of them.

None of the other factors that alter Hardy-Weinberg equilibrium alter it in a directed fashion. Genetic drift, mutation, and migration are all random in their effects on the gene pool. Natural selection, however, increases the prevalence of alleles in a population that increase survival and reproduction. Alleles that increase fitness will over time increase in their allele frequency in the gene pool, and increase the abundance of the associated phenotype as well. This effect will change the population in a directed manner over many generations, creating a population that is better adapted to its environment.

Different types of natural selection can occur, including *stabilizing selection, disruptive selection* and *directional selection*. Traits in a population such as the height of humans are often distributed according to a bell-shaped curve. The type of selection that occurs can affect the average value for the trait or it can alter the shape of the curve around the average. *Stabilizing selection* does not change the average, but makes the curve around the average sharper, so that values in the population lie closer to the average. For example if both very small fish and very large fish tend to get eaten, then stabilizing selection may not alter the average fish size, but is likely to cause future generations to be closer to average.

Disruptive selection is the opposite, in which the peak value is selected against, selecting for either extreme in a trait, so that a single peak for a trait in a population tends to be split into two peaks. *Directional selection* alters the average value for a trait, such as selecting for dark wings in a population of moths in an industrial area.

Natural selection acts on an individual and its direct descendants. In some cases natural selection can also act on closely related organisms that share many of the same alleles. This type of natural selection, called *kin selection*, occurs in organisms that display social behavior. The key to fitness is that an organism's alleles are contributed to the next generation. Contribution of alleles can happen by an individual or by close relatives like siblings, aunts, uncles, etc., who share many of the same alleles. The evolution of social organisms is the result of the increased fitness that social behavior provides. Described cases of altruistic behavior in animals is probably the result of kin selection at work, in which an animal might sacrifice its own safety to allow relatives to survive, thereby increasing the fitness of itself and the whole social group it shares alleles with.

Speciation

As mentioned previously, a species is a group of organisms that is able to interbreed and produce viable, fertile offspring. The key to defining a species is not external appearance. Within a species, there can be great phenotypic variation, as in the domestic dog. What defines a species is reproductive isolation, an inability to interbreed and create fertile offspring. Actual interbreeding is not necessary to make organisms the same species. Two groups of animals may live in different locations and never contact each other to interbreed, but if a researcher transports some of the animals and they create fertile offspring, they are part of the same species. Horses and donkeys can interbreed and create offspring, the mule. The mule, however, is sterile, meaning the horses and donkeys are two different species.

Speciation, the creation of a new species, occurs when the gene pool for a group of organisms becomes reproductively isolated. At this point, evolution can act on that group that shares a gene pool separately from others. Two species can be derived from a single common ancestor species when two populations of a species are separated geographically or by a physical barrier.

Adaptive radiation is the production of a number of different species from a single ancestral species. Radiation refers to a branching out; adaptive refers to the hereditary change that allows a species to be more successful in its environment or to be successful in a new environment. Whenever two or more closely related populations occur together, natural selection favors evolution of different living habits. This results in the occupation of different niches by each population.

Lamarckian Evolution

Until it was supplanted by Darwin's ideas, the scientist Lamarck's theory was one of the more widely accepted explanations of the mechanisms of evolution. The cornerstone of Lamarck's hypothesis was the principle of use and disuse. He asserted that organisms developed new organs, or changed their existing ones, in order to meet their changing needs. The amount of change that occurred was thought to be based on how much or little the organ in question was actually used.

Unfortunately for Lamarck, this theory of use and disuse was based upon a fallacious understanding of genetics. Any useful characteristic acquired in one generation was thought to be transmitted to the next. An oft-cited example was that of early giraffes, which stretched their necks to reach for leaves on higher branches. The offspring were believed to inherit the valuable trait of longer necks as a result of their parents' excessive use of their necks. Modern genetics has disproved this concept of acquired characteristics.

It has now been established that changes in the DNA of sex cells are the only types of changes that can be inherited; because acquired changes are changes in the characteristics and organization of somatic cells, they cannot be inherited.

Classification and Taxonomy

The science of classifying living things and using a system of nomenclature to name them is called *taxonomy*. Carolus Linnaeus invented modern taxonomy in the 1700s, grouping organisms and naming them according to a hierarchical system.

Hence the order of classificatory divisions is as follows:

KINGDOM → PHYLUM → [SUBPHYLUM] → CLASS → ORDER → FAMILY → GENUS → SPECIES

The complete classification of humans is:

Kingdom:	Animalia
Phylum:	Chordata
[Subphylum:	Vertebrata]
Class:	Mammalia
Order:	Primates
Family:	Hominidae
Genus:	*Homo*
Species:	*sapiens*

Each *kingdom* has several major phyla. A *phylum* or division has several *classes*. Each class consists of many *orders*, and these orders are subdivided into *families*. Each family is made up of many *genera*. Finally, the *species* is the smallest subdivision.

All organisms are assigned a scientific name consisting of the genus and species names of that organism. Thus, humans are *Homo sapiens*, and the common housecat is *Felis domestica*.

The Protist Kingdom

The simplest eukaryotic organisms are the *protists*. Most, but not all, protists are unicellular eukaryotes. This group includes organisms that are eukaryotes but are not plants, animals, or fungi. The protists include heterotrophs like *amoeba* and *paramecium*, photosynthetic autotrophs like *euglena* and *algae*, and fungilike organisms like *slime molds*. Some protists are mobile through the use of flagella, cilia, or amoeboid motion. Protists use sexual reproduction in some cases and asexual reproduction in others.

The Fungi Kingdom

Fungi absorb nutrients from the environment. Fungi often feed off of dead material as their nutrition source, and are important along with bacteria in the decay of material in ecosystems. One of the distinguishing features of fungi is their cell wall made of chitin, unlike the cellulose found in plants. Fungi often form long slender filaments called hyphae. Mushrooms, molds and yeasts are all examples of fungi. Most fungi reproduce both sexually and asexually.

The Plant Kingdom

Plants are multicellular eukaryotes that produce energy through photosynthesis in chloroplasts, using the energy of the sun to drive the production of glucose. Plants are distinct from animals in that plants are usually nonmotile while animals move. Plant structure is adapted for maximum exposure to light, air, and soil by extensive branching; animals, on the other hand, are adapted usually in compact structures for minimum surface exposure and maximum motility. Animals have much more centralization in their physiology while plants often exhibit delocalized control of processes and growth.

The conifers are the most abundant gymnosperms today. About 200 million years ago gymnosperms replaced the nonseed vascular plants like ferns as the predominant plant forms on land. The angiosperms represent the flowering plants and are today the predominant plant group in many ecosystems. Like the gymnosperms, angiosperms produce seeds. The seeds of gymnosperms are "naked," growing without a large amount of nutritional material or protective tissues. Angiosperms produce flowers for fertilization and produce seeds that are surrounded by nutritional tissues. Angiosperm development involves a double fertilization: the fertilization of an egg by one sperm that grows into the embryo and the fertilization of two female nuclei by one sperm to form a triploid tissue that grows to form the nutritive component of the seed, the endosperm.

The Animal Kingdom

Animals are fairly easy to recognize: animals are all multicellular heterotrophs. The evolution of animals has included the evolution of a variety of body plans to solve problems like getting food, avoiding predators, and reproducing. Over time, animals have tended to become larger in size, and more complex, with greater specialization of tissues. Another trend in the animal kingdom has been the evolution of increasingly complex nervous systems to enable complex behaviors in response to the environment.

Different groups of animals have evolved different body shapes, reflecting their different life styles. Animals with *radial symmetry* are organized with their body in a circular shape radiating outward. The echinoderms like sea stars and the cnidarians like jellies are examples of animals with radial symmetry. Another common body plan is *bilateral symmetry*, in which the body has a left side and a right side that are mirror images of each other. Humans are a good example of bilateral symmetry, in which a plane drawn vertically through the body splits the body into left and right sides that look the same. The front of the body, where the head is located, is the anterior, and the rear of the animal is the posterior. The back of the animal, where the backbone is located in vertebrates, is the dorsal side (like the dorsal fin) and the front of the animal is the ventral side.

The method used to capture food is intimately tied to an animal's body shape. Animals with more active lifestyles have evolved increasingly complex nervous systems and motor systems to enable them to navigate their environment.

What follows are descriptions of the more abundant and important phyla in the animal kingdom.

Phylum Porifera (sponges). Animals probably evolved from simple colonial heterotrophic protists with groups of cells living together and starting to specialize for different functions. These simple animals, probably representing the first evolutionary step between protists and animals, are the *sponges, phylum porifera*. Sponges resemble a colonial organism, with only a small amount of specialization of cells within the animal, no organs, and distributed function. Sponges usually only have a few different types of cells, no nervous system, and if broken apart can reassemble into new sponges. With a saclike structure, sponges have flagellated cells that move water into the animal through pores into a central cavity and back out again. Cells lining the cavity capture food from water as it moves past.

Phylum Cnidaria (hydra, sea anemone, jellies). *Cnidarians*, also called coelenterates, have radial symmetry, with tentacles arranged around a simple gut opening. Their gut has only one opening to the environment through which food passes in and wastes pass out. They are aquatic animals and represent one of the earliest phyla of animals in evolution, with only two cell layers, the endoderm and ectoderm. With only two cell layers, cnidarians do not need circulatory or respiratory systems. These animals have a simple nerve net to respond to the environment, a decentralized system for simple responses to the environment such as retraction of tentacles or swimming motions with the body. The tentacles contain one of the trademarks of cnidarians, stinging cells called *nematocysts* that have a harpoon- like structure with toxins to capture prey. The life cycle of cnidarians can include a polyp stage and a medusa stage. The polyp is settled on a solid surface, with the mouth opening pointed upward while the medusa is a swimming form, with the mouth opening pointed downward. Polyps are asexual. Sea anemones on a rock in a cluster are often clones of each other that have reproduced by budding, competing for space with other clones. Sexual reproduction occurs in medusa, where sperm and eggs are produced and released into the environment for fertilization.

Phylum Platylhelminthes (flatworms). *Flatworms* are ribbonlike with bilateral symmetry. They possess three layers of cells, including a solid mesoderm but lack a circulatory system. Their nervous system consists of simple light detection organs, an anterior brain ganglion, and a pair of longitudinal nerve cords. Their digestive system is a cavity with a single opening, and they lack a coelom. These animals are not swift moving, using cilia to move over surfaces. A common flat-worm is the planaria, famous for its regeneration. The shape of the worm, elongated and without appendages, has evolved in many phyla, as a compact structure that is well designed for movement. Planaria are free-living but many flatworms are internal parasites, including flukes and tape-worms, deriving their nutrition by direct absorption into their cells from the host.

Phylum Nematoda (roundworms). *Nematodes* are roundworms, with three cell layers, including mesoderm, a complete digestive tract with two openings, a mouth and an anus, and a body cavity called a *pseudocoelom* around the gut. The pseudocoelom has muscle lining the interior body wall but not around the gut. This allows for very active movement but more of a wiggling motion than movement in a specific direction. Nematodes do not have respiratory or circulatory systems, exchanging gases directly with the environment. Roundworms are one of the most abundant animal groups, including huge numbers of free-living, scavenging species as well as parasites. The species *C. elegans* is a simple organism with only 950 cells, which has made it popular in modern biology for studies of cell differentiation and genetics.

Phylum Annelida (segmented worms). The earthworm and leeches are examples of annelid worms, commonly called *segmented worms*. The annelids are worms with segmented bodies and a coelom body cavity. The division of the body into segments and the presence of the coelom body cavity filled with water creates a hydrostatic skeleton that allows annelids complex, sophisticated movement, coordinated by a nervous system. Each segment has local control by a ganglion of nerves but these nerves are coordinated by a ventral nerve cord and a larger nerve collection that might be called a brain in the front of the worm. Annelids exchange gases directly with their environment through their skin, an important reason why they have moist skin and live in moist environments. Each segment has a twin set of excretory organs called *nephridia*. Annelids have a complete digestive tract with some specialization into organs along the tract and they also have a closed circulatory system with five pairs of hearts.

Phylum Arthropoda. Arthropods have jointed appendages, exoskeletons of chitin, and open circulatory systems. With an exoskeleton, the coelom of arthropods is reduced and less important in movement. The three most important classes of arthropods are insects, arachnids, and crustaceans. The exoskeleton of arthropods has muscles attached to its interior for movement. The exoskeleton provides protection, and has a variety of specialized appendages. The exoskeleton prevents gas exchange between the skin and exterior, however, as occurs in annelids, requiring the evolution of a respiratory system. Insects possess three pair of legs, spiracles, and tracheal tubes designed for breathing outside of an aquatic environment. Arachnids have four pair of legs and "book lungs"; examples include the scorpion and the spider. Most arthropods have complex sensory organs, including compound eyes, that provide information about the environment to their increasingly complex nervous systems. Crustaceans have segmented bodies with a variable number of appendages. Crustaceans like the lobster, crayfish, and shrimp possess gills for gas exchange. The exoskeleton of arthropods allowed them to colonize land and become the first winged organisms as well. Arthropods, particularly insects, remain one of the most abundant and varied groups of organisms on earth.

Phylum Mollusca. The *mollusks* include animals like clams, squid, and snails. In their body shape these animals do not resemble each other very much but they do share a few basic traits that lead biologists to classify them together as mollusks. These shared mollusk traits include a muscular foot, a mantle that secretes a shell, and a rasping tongue called the *radula*. Most mollusks are covered by a hard protective shell secreted by the mantle. Some mollusks like squid and octopi have a reduced, internal shell. Mollusks are mostly aquatic and use gills for respiration that are enclosed in a space created by the mantle, the mantle cavity. The gills are also involved in feeding, and move water over their surface with the beating of cilia.

Phylum Echinodermata. The *echinoderms*, which include sea stars and sea urchins, are spiny and have radial symmetry, contain a water-vascular system, and possess the capacity for regeneration. The echinoderms may not resemble the vertebrates but they share in common with chordates that they are deuterostomes. The water vascular system is a unique adaptation of the echinoderms, with a network of vessels that carry water to extensions called tube feet. The tube feet are the small suckerlike extensions in sea stars, sea urchins and sand dollars that allow the animals to adhere and to move. Echinoderms also have a hard internal skeleton formed from calcium deposits that assists in protection and locomotion.

Phylum Chordata. The chordates have a stiff, solid dorsal rod called the *notochord* at some stage of their embryologic development, as well as paired gill slits. Chordata have dorsal hollow nerve cords, tails extending beyond the anus at some point in their development, and a ventral heart. These adaptations may not sound impressive but they paved the way for the evolution of the vertebrates, a major subphylum of chordates.

The chordates probably originated from animals like tunicates, commonly called sea squirts. Adult tunicates are sessile filter feeders that do not resemble vertebrates at all. Tunicate larvae however are free-swimming, with a notochord and a dorsal nerve cord, and resemble tadpoles.

The *vertebrates* are a subphylum (smaller than a phylum, larger than a class) of the chordates that includes fish, amphibians, reptiles, birds and mammals. In vertebrates the notochord is present during embryogenesis but is replaced during development by a bony, segmented vertebral column that protects the dorsal spinal cord and provides anchorage for muscles. Vertebrates have bony or cartilaginous endoskeletons, chambered hearts for circulation, and increasingly complex nervous systems. The vertebrate internal organs are contained in a coelom body cavity.

The first vertebrates were probably filter-feeding organisms that evolved into swimming jawless fishes that were still filter feeders. Jawless fish such as lampreys and hagfish still exist today. The evolution of fish with jaws led to the development of the cartilaginous and bony fishes that are dominant today. These fish use gills for respiration, and move water over the gills through paired gill slits. The jaw allows fish to adopt new life styles other than filter feeding, grabbing food with their jaws. Cartilaginous fish (*class Chondrichthyes*) like sharks and rays have an endoskeleton that is made entirely of cartilage rather than hard, calcified bone. They have large, oil-producing livers for buoyancy regulation in water. Bony fishes (*class Osteichthyes*) have swim bladders for the regulation of buoyancy.

Two adaptations were important to set the stage for vertebrates to colonize the land. One was the presence of air-sacs that allowed some fish in shallow water to absorb oxygen from air for brief periods. The other adaptation was a change in the structure of fins to have lobes that allowed some degree of movement on land. Fish with these features evolved into the *amphibians* about 350 million years ago. Most amphibians like frogs and salamanders still live in close association with water and have only simple lungs or gills supplemented by oxygen absorbed through the skin. Another reason that amphibians are mostly associated with water is that amphibian eggs lack hard shells and will dry out on land. Amphibian larvae often live in water and then metamorphose into the adult form.

Reptiles became independent of water for reproduction through the evolution of hard-shelled eggs that do not dry out on land. The egg shell protects the developing embryo but still allows gas exchange with the environment. Reptiles also evolved more effective lungs and hearts and thicker dry skins to allow them a greater metabolic activity than amphibians and the ability to survive on land.

Birds evolved from reptilian relatives of dinosaurs with the development of wings, feathers, and light bones for flight. Birds also have four-chambered hearts and uniquely adapted lungs to supply the intense metabolic needs of flight. Birds have hard-shelled eggs and usually provide a great deal of parental care during embryonic development and maturation after hatching. A famous evolutionary intermediate from the fossil record is Archaeopteryx, which is dinosaurlike in some respects, but had feathers and wings.

Mammals are the remaining major class of vertebrates. Mammals have hair, sweat glands, mammary glands, and four-chambered hearts. The fossil record indicates that mammals evolved 200 million years ago and coexisted with the dinosaurs up until the major extinction 65 million years ago. At this time, mammals diversified to occupy many environmental niches and become the dominant terrestrial vertebrates in many ecosystems. Mammals are highly effective in regulation of their body temperature, and most mammals provide extensive care for their young. One small group of mammals, the *Monotremes* (for example, the duck-billed platypus), lay eggs. Other mammals gestate their embryos internally and give birth to young. Marsupial mammals give birth after a short time and complete development of young in an external pouch. *Placental* mammals gestate their young to a more mature state, providing nutrition to the embryo with the exchange of material in the placenta. *Marsupial* mammals were once widespread across the globe, but were replaced in most cases by placental mammals. Australia being isolated, it was a haven for marsupial mammals until the present day.

Among the mammals, the primates have opposable thumbs and stereoscopic vision for depth perception, adaptations for life in the trees and traits that have been important factors in the evolution of humans. Many primates have complex social structures. The ancestors of humans included *australopithecines*. Fossils indicate these ancestors were able to walk upright on two legs on the ground. Fossil remains of hominids such as *Homo habilus* from 2-3 million years ago display an increasing size of the cortex. *Homo habilus* probably used tools, setting the stage for modern humans, *Homo sapiens*.

KAPLAN

EARTH AND SPACE SCIENCE

Earth and space science includes the disciplines of astronomy, geology, meteorology, and ocean-ography. For more information on any of the topics presented here, enter any of the terms into a search engine and you should find a wealth of online resources.

Test Yourself

If Mercury's period of revolution is 88 days, Venus's is 225 days, Earth's is 365 days, and Mars's is 687 days, which planet takes the longest amount of time to revolve around the sun?

(A) Mercury

(B) Venus

(C) Earth

(D) Mars

The correct choice is **(D)**, Mars. The farther away from the Sun a planet is, the longer it takes to revolve around the Sun.

Astronomy

The solar system is made up of the sun, the eight planets, their moons, asteroids, and comets. The sun is so massive that its gravity causes the rest of the objects to follow paths around it. These paths are called *orbits*. The closer a planet is to the sun, the smaller the orbit it follows, so while the Earth takes about 365 days to complete an orbit, Neptune takes almost 165 years!

All of the planets' orbits lie in roughly the same plane. They also all travel around the sun in the same direction. The closest planet to the sun is Mercury, then Venus, Earth, Mars, Jupiter, Saturn, Uranus, and Neptune (a way to remember this order is the phrase "My Very Eager Mother Just Served Us Noodles").

The planets follow elliptical, not circular, orbits around the sun. This means each planet is some-times closer to the sun and sometimes farther away. The point at which a planet is closest to the sun is known as its perihelion, and the farthest point is called its aphelion.

Time Zones

Time zones were created to make the time of day when the sun is highest in the sky equal to noon all over the world. In order to do this, the earth is divided into 24 different time zones, all situated in reference to the *prime meridian*, the longitudinal line that runs through Greenwich, England (Greenwich Mean Time, or GMT). This spot was selected by astronomers in 1884 as having "universal time." The meridian on the opposite side of the Earth from the prime meridian is called the International Date Line.

The contiguous United States has four time zones: Eastern, Central, Mountain, and Pacific. Eastern Time is five hours behind GMT, Central is six, Mountain is seven, and Pacific is eight. Actual hours of daylight are not consistent throughout the year, so during World War I, many countries decided to conserve fuel and electrical power by adjusting their clocks to match the daylight hours. From spring to fall, clocks are set an hour ahead, and we are said to be on *Daylight Saving Time*. From fall to spring, the clocks are reset (set back an hour), and we are said to be on Standard Time. Some states, such as Arizona, ignore Daylight Saving Time and are on Standard Time throughout the year.

Rotation of the Earth

The Earth rotates along an axis that runs from the North Pole to the South Pole. It rotates at approximately 1000 miles per hour to make one full rotation every 24 hours (known as a *mean solar day*). To demonstrate the direction of spin, you would spin a typical classroom globe to the right. Looking up at the sky, this rotation gives the impression that the sun rises in the East and sets in the West. You can see this if you dim the lights and use a flashlight to watch how spinning the classroom globe causes different areas to be illuminated and then become dark again.

Seasonal Changes

The earth's axis of rotation is tilted 23 degrees from the plane of its orbit. Many classroom globes reflect this tilt. As the earth moves around the sun, the tilt causes some areas of the planet to face the sun more directly than other areas. This uneven exposure results in our experience of seasonal change.

Likewise, we observe the path of the Sun across the sky to change. In North America, that path is higher in the sky during the summer months and lower in the sky during the winter. The days are also longer in the summer than in the winter. The dates when the days are the longest or shortest are termed *solstices*. June 21 is the longest day of the year and is said to be the summer solstice. December 21 is the shortest day of the year and is called the winter solstice. Days when the day and night are the same length are called *equinoxes*. An equinox occurs between winter and spring (about March 21) and is called the vernal equinox. The other occurs between summer and fall (about September 21) and is referred to as the autumnal equinox.

Other Bodies in the Universe

In addition to our sun and the eight planets, other bodies in our solar system include moons, comets, asteroids, and dust clouds.

Moons, often referred to as satellites, are generally defined as bodies that orbit planets. They vary greatly in size. Several planets have more than one moon—Jupiter has at least 63, while Mercury and Venus have none. Our own moon is believed to have formed when a body about the size of Mars struck the Earth in its early existence. Most of the Earth's material was retained, but some of it clumped together to form the moon.

Asteroids are small rocky or metallic bodies that orbit the Sun. Although they are found throughout the solar system, most are located in a band between Mars and Jupiter known as the asteroid belt. All of the asteroids combined have a mass less than that of the Earth's moon.

KAPLAN

Other celestial bodies include exoplanets, centaurs, protostars, and dwarf planets such as Pluto and Ceres.

Comets are mixtures of ice and dust that have highly elliptical orbits (they pass closer to the sun and then travel much farther away before returning). When it is close to the sun, a comet is said to be active, and it ejects a long streamer of dust behind it. This streamer is illuminated by the sun and becomes the "tail" that can be visible from the Earth. This tail always points away from the sun. Halley's comet is one of the brightest and most widely known comets. Its orbit passes close enough to the sun for us to see it about once every 76 years (this last happened in 1986).

The other major bodies in the universe are stars, nebulae, and galaxies. *Stars* are large balls of superheated gas. They are so massive that the gravity they generate causes the gas at their cores to undergo *fusion*. This fusion emits enormous amounts of radiation in the form of heat and light. Stars are classified according to the wavelengths of light they emit (O, B, A, F, G, K, and M) and their luminosity (from brighter to dimmer: I, II, III, IV, and V). In addition, the numbers 1 through 10 describe the range between each wavelength, so our sun is a G2 V type star (G is a middle-of-the-road wavelength, not as hot as a blue star, not as cool as a red star; the 2 indicates that it is closer to a G type than a K type; and the V indicates that the sun is relatively dim).

Stars are created in huge clouds of superheated dust and gas called *nebulae*. A nebula is not uniformly dense—certain areas have more dust and gas than other areas. If an area becomes dense enough, the gravity it produces draws in surrounding gas and dust, and the gravitational pull becomes even stronger. Eventually, the gravity may compress the mixture so much that the resulting heat and pressure causes fusion, and a star is born.

Huge clusters of stars and nebulae are known as *galaxies*. Our own galaxy is known as the Milky Way, and it contains around 200 billion stars. It is a large spiral galaxy, and it has three parts: the disk, the bulge, and the halo. The disk is the flattened region with four "arms" containing relatively young stars (and us). The disk surrounds a bulge at the center of the galaxy that contains a high density of very old stars. The halo surrounds the disk and is a region of scattered older stars.

During the life cycle of a star, it is constantly trying to collapse inward due to its own gravity, and constantly being pushed outward by the pressure of its dense gas. This balance is preserved until the core uses up its available fuel, at which point the star may collapse upon itself. This collapse can trigger an enormous explosion, a supernova, during which time the dying star can outshine all of the other stars in a galaxy. An alternative is that the collapse may lead to a phenomenon known as a black hole. A black hole gets its name because the gravity it produces is so strong that nothing nearby can escape its pull—not even light. The Milky Way is believed to have an enormous black hole at its center.

Geology

The foundation of geology is the study of minerals, rocks, and landforms. *Minerals* are naturally occurring, inorganic, crystalline solids. They are referred to as inorganic because they are not formed by life processes. Minerals are composed of a latticework of crystals—small building blocks of repeating structures, called *unit cells*. Minerals are identified by their unique crystalline structure and composition. Over 5,000 different types of minerals have been identified, but only 200 are commonly found in nature.

Minerals are categorized by their chemical compositions and physical properties. Some of the basic groups based on chemical composition are the Native Elements (minerals formed from a single element), the Silicates (minerals containing both silicon and oxygen), and the Carbonates (minerals containing CO_3). Some physical properties used to distinguish mineral are hardness, luster, color, and cleavage.

- Hardness: the degree to which a mineral can be scratched. A mineral is rated on the Mohs hardness scale from softer (talc) to harder (diamond).

- Luster: how a mineral reflects light. A mineral's luster is determined to be metallic or non-metallic. Some further types of non-metallic lusters are glassy, dull, and adamantine (containing internal reflections).

- Color: the most common way to test color is by scratching the mineral on a porcelain plate and examining the resulting streak on the porcelain.

- Cleavage: the way a mineral breaks under pressure can reveal information about its crystalline structure. If a mineral breaks apart along straight lines, it exhibits a high degree of cleavage. If it shatters into differently shaped pieces, it has a low degree of cleavage.

Rocks are composed of mixtures of minerals. They are classified into the broad categories of igneous, sedimentary, and metamorphic based on how they were formed.

Igneous rocks are formed when liquefied materials, or melts, cool and crystallize. They can either be formed under the Earth's surface or above it. Those that form below the surface are called intrusive, and those that form above the surface are called extrusive. An example of an extrusive igneous rock would be obsidian—which forms from the outflow of a volcano.

Sedimentary rocks are formed from the dissolved or weathered remains of other rocks and minerals. They tend to have a diverse mixture of many different kinds of minerals. Most of the rocks found at the Earth's surface are formed through sedimentation.

Metamorphic rocks are formed when changes in pressure and temperature cause rocks to undergo changes in their basic chemical composition.

Soil and Rocks

After rocks are formed, they are exposed to both mechanical and chemical forces that act to break them down. This process is known as weathering.

Mechanical weathering causes a reduction in the size of rocks—breaking apart large rocks into smaller and smaller pieces (without actually changing their chemical composition). Common factors in mechanical weathering are water, wind, and ice. Rocks may be exposed to water through rainfall, through the crashing of waves, or by streams and rivers. The water may wash over the rocks and wear away small pieces, or the rocks may be tumbled along and gradually broken down by swiftly moving currents. Winds can also facilitate the weathering process by causing small particles to strike against rocks and thus chipping off other small particles. One of the most important aspects of mechanical weathering involves the repeated freezing and thawing of water and ice. If a rock becomes wet and then the temperature drops enough to freeze the water, the resulting expansion as the water turns into ice causes small cracks and fissures in the rock to expand. Over time, this greatly increases the surface area of the rock—exposing it even more to both mechanical and chemical weathering.

Chemical weathering differs from mechanical weathering in that it actually changes the chemical makeup of rocks. It occurs because certain minerals in rocks react to either the oxygen in the Earth's atmosphere or to acidic solutions found in water. *Oxidation* occurs because some minerals—such as iron (Fe)—can be stripped of electrons by exposure to oxygen. The opposite process can happen when some minerals—such as the carbonates—gain electrons through exposure to acidic rainwater. This loss or gain of electrons causes breakdowns in the crystalline structure of minerals. An example of the result is a cave—often formed when water dissolves carbonate rocks.

On the Earth's surface, weathered rock material mixes with organic matter to form soil. Soils vary according to the minerals found in regional rocks and also by the kinds of life present. Two broad classifications of soils are pedocals and pedalfers. Pedocals are soils found in dry regions where evaporation causes a general upward movement of water through the soil. Pedalfers are soils found in wet regions where water seeps downwards through the soil.

Layers of the Earth

Underneath its surface the Earth is not uniform. It is described as having four layers: the crust, the mantle, and the outer and inner core. The heaviest elements are in the core, and the lightest elements are found in the crust. Scientists have not been able to directly observe much of the interior of the Earth, but have instead drawn conclusions about its structure and composition from worldwide recording and analysis of seismic waves. These waves, generated by earthquakes, travel through the earth at different speeds depending on the materials they pass through, so scientists can infer from the results the location and composition of the different layers.

The outermost layer of the earth is called the *crust*. Although the crust is solid, it is broken into many pieces called plates. There are two kinds of plates: oceanic and continental. The oceanic plates are thinner (only 3–5 miles thick) compared to the continental plates (about 25 miles thick). Oceanic plates are also much denser.

The plates of the crust rest on top of a vast sea of semi-melted rock known as the *mantle*. The mantle is by far the largest layer of the Earth at 1,800 miles thick. The outer edge of the mantle is basically the region at which the temperatures (about 1,600 degrees Fahrenheit) are great enough to melt rock. At the bottom of the mantle temperatures reach upwards of 4,000 degrees Fahrenheit. The difference in temperature between the upper and lower mantle cause huge convection currents as warmer materials near the core rise towards the crust, cool, and sink to be heated again. It is these convection currents that are believed to cause the movements of the plates above.

While the crust and the mantle are composed primarily of solid or melted rock, the core contains the heaviest materials: the metals. Temperatures in the core range from 4,000 degrees Fahrenheit to 9,000 degrees Fahrenheit. The *outer core* is a region approximately 1,400 miles thick that is composed of the metals iron and nickel. The extreme heat in the outer core causes the metals to liquefy. The *inner core* is about 800 miles thick and is the hottest region of all, but here the pressures are so extreme that the metals are forced to remain in solid form. The molten iron in the outer core flowing around the stationary iron in the inner core is what generates the earth's magnetic field. This field serves to shield the Earth from deadly solar radiation—without it, life on Earth may never have been possible.

Plate Tectonics

It is important to understand that the tectonic plates include more than simply the Earth's crust. Both oceanic and continental plates are composed of the crust as well as a rigid layer of the upper mantle. Together, the crust and this layer are known as the *lithosphere*. Below the lithosphere lies the more fluid majority of the mantle—known as the *asthenosphere*. These plates cover the surface of the Earth, but there are geologically active regions at their boundaries where the plates interact with each other. There are four general types of such boundary regions: *convergent boundaries, divergent boundaries, transform boundaries*, and *plate-boundary zones*.

When plates move towards each other and collide they create a convergent boundary. Often, one of the plates will be pushed underneath the other—a process called *subduction*. Since there are two kinds of plates, there are three kinds of convergent boundaries.

Oceanic-oceanic: two colliding oceanic plates will cause one of the plates to be subducted under the other. A deep trench is formed along the subduction zone. As the subducted plate begins to melt, some of the resulting magma often rises to the surface to form volcanoes and/or volcanic islands.

Oceanic-continental: when an oceanic plate collides with a continental plate, the heavier oceanic plate is subducted. As when two oceanic plates collide, the subduction forms a deep trench along the boundary, and volcanoes may form in the leading edge of the continental plate. In addition, the lighter continental plate often buckles upwards. The Andes in South America are an example of such a convergent boundary.

Continental-continental: two colliding continental plates do not typically cause one of the plates to be subducted because the plates are much lighter than the layers underneath them. If you imagine two inflatable rafts being pushed together in a swimming pool, you can understand why continental plates are not subducted. Instead, they both buckle and are forced sideways and upwards. This process has led to the formation of the tallest mountain chain in the world, the Himalayas, along the boundary between the Eurasian Plate and the Indian Plate.

When underlying convection currents in the mantle act to pull plates away from each other, molten rock wells up from the mantle and creates new crust—adding on to each plate as they spread apart. The largest and most well known divergent boundary is the Mid-Atlantic ridge. It runs the length of the Atlantic from the tip of Africa northwards to the Arctic Ocean. Spreading at the rate of 2.5 cm per year, it is responsible for moving the Americas away from Europe and Africa over the last 100 to 200 million years. Not all such spreading occurs beneath the oceans— the Mid-Atlantic ridge crosses Iceland and creates both rifts (surface cracking) and volcanoes.

When two adjoining plates are passing by each other they create a transform boundary. In this case, neither plate is subducted, but as the two plates grind together they can create powerful earthquakes. One of the most well-known transform boundaries occurs between the North American continental plate and the Pacific oceanic plate. It is known as the San Andreas fault.

Sometimes the boundaries between plates are not as well defined. This can occur when smaller plates are caught between two larger plates, or when two larger plates have fractured near their boundaries to the degree that the boundary zones are now wide bands. In such cases, there are many various and complex interactions happening at once.

Mountains, Volcanoes, and Earthquakes

As discussed in the previous section on plate tectonics, tectonic activity is responsible for the formation of mountain chains, volcanoes, and the occurrence of earthquakes. This section describes these phenomena in more detail.

The processes of mountain formation are known as *orogenesis*. Mountains may be formed at convergent boundaries between large tectonic plates or through a process called accretion.

Just as there are three different types of convergent boundaries, there are three different types of mountain ranges formed along them.

Aleutian-type mountain building occurs at the subduction zone between two colliding oceanic plates. As one plate is subducted, molten rock wells upwards and can result in the formation of volcanic islands. If this process continues, mountains can form as more and more volcanic material is deposited.

Andean-type mountain building occurs at the subduction zone where a continental plate collides with a oceanic plate. There are two stages to this process.
1. passive margin phase—erosion and tidal action causes a buildup of sedimentation on the continent's edge (shelf).
2. active margin phase—the oceanic plate begins to subduct. The edge of the continental shelf buckles, and volcanoes may form.

Andean-type mountain building is characterized by the formation of two features: a volcanic mountain range, and an accretionary wedge formed when the sedimentation from the passive-margin phase crumples into a series of folds between the mountains and the ocean. A well-known example is the Sierra Nevada and the accompanying Coast Ranges in California.

Continental collisions can also build mountains. When two continental plates collide, since neither plate subducts they both are buckled upwards. The Himalayas were created in this manner.

An alternate form of mountain building occurs through a process known as continental accretion. This occurs when small fragments of crust collide with the edges of continental margins and are thrust upwards. Many small coastal mountains around the Pacific ocean were created through continental accretion.

Volcanoes occur when magma rises to the Earth's surface and escapes through weak points in the crust. Most volcanoes are found along the boundaries between tectonic plates, but they may also form in the interior of a plate.

Volcanoes have a definite life cycle of a period of intermittent eruptions during which they are said to be "active," the time in between eruptions when they are referred to as "dormant," and the time when eruptions have ceased and they are "extinct."

Volcano formation, or volcanism, occurs when a large chamber of magma builds below a central vent to the Earth's surface. Gas bubbles form in this chamber and build up the pressure that creates an *eruption*. Eruptions may be explosive or non-explosive. The products of an eruption can be lava flows (magma is called lava when aboveground), pyroclastic flows of superheated gases and ash, and ejected dust and rocks. *Pyroclastic flows* are the most deadly feature of volcanoes, as they may travel many miles across land or water at high speeds.

Three general categories of volcanic formation are spreading-center volcanism, subduction-zone volcanism, and intraplate volcanism. Those that occur at plate boundaries happen at convergent and divergent boundaries—not transform boundaries. Spreading center volcanism happens at divergent plate boundaries like the Mid-Atlantic ridge. Magma rises up through the rift created in the lithosphere and vents to the surface of the crust. As this surface is usually deep under the ocean, most volcanism of this type produces underwater lava fields—rarely forming a "typical" cone-shaped volcano. When subduction occurs at a convergent plate boundary, the subducted oceanic crust melts and produces a series of volcanoes along the edge of the other plate. If the non-subducting plate is also oceanic, the volcanoes form an *island arc*. If an oceanic plate subducts beneath a continental plate, a *volcanic arc* is formed on the edge of the continental plate.

Intraplate volcanism (also called "hot spot" volcanism) has a different mechanism and occurs independent of plate boundaries. Scientists believe it is due to a plume of unusually hot material that rises from near the bottom of the mantle. These plumes stay in one place as the plates move around above them, so when the magma breaks through the crust a chain of volcanoes can result—each one forming and then becoming less active as it moves away from the hot spot and the next one forms. This was the mechanism that formed the island chain of Hawaii, and it is the reason why only one of the islands (the "Big Island") still has an active volcano.

Volcanism has been determined to affect the earth's climate in several ways. Volcanic particles ejected into the atmosphere are known to have ozone-depleting effects. CO_2 emissions from the Earth's volcanoes total around 100 million tons per year and contribute to the greenhouse effect. Global warming due to the greenhouse effect is offset, however, by the cooling *"haze effect"* created when tiny droplets of sulfuric acid reflect solar radiation.

Earthquakes occur when kinetic energy released by geologic events causes vibrations in the Earth's crust. Earthquakes usually originate along the boundaries between tectonic plates. The movements of the plates cause the boundary zone to contain many *faults*—weakened narrow zones extending down into the Earth's crust. As the plates slowly move, pressure builds at the fault zones until the friction between the two sides of the fault is overcome. When this happens, they slip past each other suddenly and send seismic waves out through the surrounding crust. As plate boundaries generally contain many different faults, the energy released by one fault can cause others to slip as well—which is why aftershocks often follow large earthquakes.

Seismic waves are separated into *P waves* and *S waves* (short for "primary" and "secondary" waves). P waves are compression waves that cause back and forth movement along the direction the wave is traveling (imagine a line of balls attached to a long spring so that hitting one end causes a compression wave of three balls packed together to move along the spring). S waves cause movement perpendicular to the direction the wave is traveling (imagine shaking one end of a rope so that an "S"-shaped wave travels along the rope while actually moving the rope from side to side as the wave passes).

As seismic waves travel through the ground, scientists can record them using a machine called a *seismograph*. The resulting seismogram reveals the timing and intensity of the seismic waves. Using this data from seismographs all over the world, scientists can determine the strength of the earthquake and its origin, or *epicenter*.

Changes of the Earth over Time

Scientists look for evidence today that tells us what the Earth was like millions—even billions—of years ago. Earlier scientists had to rely on *relative dating*—the practice of deciding which fossils or rocks were older than others. This did allow for limited insight into the history of the Earth, but more accurate data was not available until the discovery of radioactivity led to radioactive dating techniques. These techniques allow for *absolute dating*—determining with varying degrees of accuracy the actual age of an object.

Historically there has been much debate about the age of the Earth. Religious interpretations yielded guesses of several thousand years. Early scientists, such as Lord Kelvin, argued that the Earth had been molten and would have taken approximately 100 million years to cool to its present temperature. Other scientists tried to determine how long it would have taken for the oceans to accumulate their salt content and arrived at a figure of 90 million years. Geoscientists today have used radiometric dating to determine that the oldest rocks found are around 4 billion years old. The general consensus is that the Earth's age is even older—approximately 4.6 billion years. This figure comes from dating of moon rocks, meteorites, and assumptions about the Earth's relationship to the moon and the formation of the solar system.

Although the history of the Earth has been characterized by continuous change, scientists have defined distinct periods of prehistoric time in order to facilitate research. Eons are the broadest divisions of time. There have been four eons: Hadean (earliest), Archaean, Proterozoic, and Phanerozoic. The Phanerozoic might generally be referred to as the "age of life" (although life actually began earlier). The Phanerozoic is further divided into eras, periods, and epochs. Together these divisions of time comprise the *Geologic Column*.

Hadean time *4.6–3.8 billion years ago*

This eon begins at the formation of the Earth and lasts until the planet cooled enough to form rocks. Therefore, it is not actually expressed in the geologic record. Most of the assumptions about this time comes from our study of the solar system, radioactive dating of meteorites and other materials, and our best theories about how and when the planets formed.

Archaean *3.8–2.5 billion years ago*

This eon marks the beginning of the geologic record and the formation of the oldest known rocks. Here we find evidence of the first life on Earth—bacteria microfossils approximately 3.5 billion years old. The atmosphere at the time would have been toxic to most modern life forms because it was probably composed mostly of methane and ammonia.

Proterozoic 2.5 billion–570 million years ago

This is a very long phase of Earth's history. During this time the first continents formed and oxygen began to build in the atmosphere. This time also marks the indication in the fossil record of the first eukaryotic cells. Fossils from the end of the Proterozoic show the emergence of the first true animals.

Paleozoic era 570–245 million years ago

The Paleozoic is the earliest era of the Phanerozoic eon. Fossils indicate an explosion in animal diversity at the beginning of the Paleozoic. Very rapidly, animals colonized most of the available habitats. Six major landmasses existed during this period. Although they did not resemble a modern map of the planet, those landmasses would eventually divide, combine, and migrate to their present locations and form the familiar continents. At the end of the Paleozoic, an enormous catastrophe wiped out as much as 99% of all planetary life. Scientists are still unsure of the causes of either the initial explosion of Paleozoic life or the eventual mass extinction. The end of the Paleozoic also witnessed the formation of the second supercontinent (Pangaea).

Mesozoic era 245–65 million years ago

The Mesozoic is the second era of the Phanerozoic eon. Great changes in the types of animal and plant life took place during the Mesozoic. Although the first mammals appeared early in the period, the Mesozoic was largely dominated by the dinosaurs (the reason why this era is commonly referred to as "the Age of the Reptiles"). Plant life in the early Mesozoic included a wide variety of exotic giant ferns and cycads. The middle of the Mesozoic saw the appearance of gymnosperms (such as modern pine trees), and by the late Mesozoic the familiar angiosperms had begun to diversify and dominate. Another mass extinction occurred at the end of the Mesozoic. It brought the reign of the dinosaurs to a close, and allowed the mammals to rise to a prominent position. South America separated from Africa near the end of the Mesozoic as Pangea started to break apart.

Cenozoic era 65 million years ago–present

The modern era within the Phanerozoic eon. The Cenozoic began with the extinction of the dinosaurs and still continues today. It is commonly referred to as "the Age of the Mammals." During the last 65 million years the Himalayas were formed, the Mediterranean Sea filled, and the continents took their familiar positions. The rise of the primates led eventually to *Homo sapiens*, or modern humans.

Plant and Animal Extinction

The evolution of life on Earth has been punctuated by several *mass extinctions*. The first occurred about 450 million years ago and wiped out much of the marine life that had developed. The largest mass extinction visible in the fossil record occurred around 250 million years ago and destroyed almost all life on the planet. Another marked the end of the age of the dinosaurs around 65 million years ago. Yet another mass extinction is occurring right now.

There is much speculation about the causes of the ancient catastrophes. Some appear to have been caused by climate changes such as Ice Ages, while others may have been caused by the blocking of sunlight due to widespread volcanic activity or even impacts from asteroids. The cause of the current mass extinction is undeniably human activity. Through predation, pollution,

KAPLAN

and other types of habitat destruction such as deforestation, humans are eliminating other life forms at rates estimated between 17,000 and 100,000 species per year. It is estimated that if this trend continues, humans will have accounted for the extinction of 50% of the planet's species by the year 2100.

Meteorology

Meteorology is the study of weather, and meteorologists are scientists who study and predict weather. To understand the creation and patterns of weather, you must begin with the study of the Earth's atmosphere.

The Earth's Atmosphere

The Earth's atmosphere is a mixture of gases (78% nitrogen, 21% oxygen, and 1% other gases) that protect us from the powerful rays of the Sun. The atmosphere is densest nearer to Earth and gradually thins out farther away from Earth. The two main layers of the atmosphere are the troposphere and the stratosphere.

The *troposphere* is closest to Earth. Its air is well mixed, and its temperature decreases with altitude, as air in the troposphere is heated from the ground up. Weather occurs in the troposphere. At any given moment, any part of the atmosphere can be stable or unstable. If it's unstable, then clouds can form, as pockets of air rise and cool. The less stable the atmosphere is, the more severe weather can be.

The atmospheric layer located above the troposphere is called the *stratosphere*. In this layer, temperature increases with altitude due to the absorption of ultraviolet light waves by the ozone molecules present here. Most ozone is concentrated around an altitude of 25 kilometers; this concentration of ozone is known as the *ozone layer*. Recently, scientists have conducted many studies on the ozone layer connected to the greenhouse effect. Scientists believe that the greenhouse effect is increasing the earth's temperature by trapping the sun's energy.

Weather

Weather occurs because our atmosphere is in constant motion. Changes in temperature, precipitation, fronts, clouds, and wind determine what kind of weather any given region experiences. Scientific explanations of weather phenomena primarily involve principles covered in earlier sections of this chapter: heat transfer (convection, conduction, and radiation), energy transformations (in thunder and lightning), and phase changes in the water cycle (precipitation, evaporation, and condensation).

As a result of these principles of interaction, hot, cold, warm, and cool air masses develop. They are usually very large (about the size of several states in the United States). There are four consistent air masses that affect the weather in the United States:

- continental polar air mass (over Northern Canada and Alaska)
- maritime polar air mass (over North Pacific Ocean)
- maritime tropical air mass (over the Gulf of Mexico and Caribbean)
- continental air mass (over the southwestern states and Mexico)

Air is composed of moving molecules of gas. These gas molecules are constantly moving and pushing on each other and on anything in their way; this movement is called *air pressure*. Air pressure can change depending on how many molecules are in a given space and how fast they are moving. When a high-pressure area collides with a low-pressure area, one of three possible air fronts can be formed: a warm front, a cold front, or a stationary front. In a *warm front*, warm air replaces cold air. The lighter warm air slips over the heavier cold air forming a gradual slope; clouds increase and become lower and steady precipitation results. In a *cold front*, the heavier cold air pushes the warm air up very fast, carrying moisture with it. Clouds form and violent storms develop between the two air masses. In a *stationary front*, neither the cold air nor the warm air advances and clouds form on both sides of the front.

Climate

The term *weather* is used to describe short-term changes in atmospheric conditions. The term that scientists use to explain long-term patterns of temperature, humidity and amount of sunshine is *climate*. There are several different types of climates in the world.

Equatorial	Near the equator; almost always sunny and warm; practically no seasons.
Tropical	Warm temperature, only two seasons: dry and wet.
Arid	Very low humidity and infrequent precipitation.
Temperate	Cool in the winter, warm in the summer; four distinct seasons; adequate humidity throughout the year.
Mediterranean	Hot and dry in the summer, cool in the winter; four distinct seasons; wet in autumn.
Cold	Very cold in the winter, cool in the summer.
Polar	Very cold in the winter, cold in the summer.
Mountainous	Temperatures change dramatically, generally cooler than the climate in which the mountain is situated.

The Water Cycle

In the *water cycle*, water from oceans, lakes, swamps, rivers, and plants can turn into water vapor. The water vapor then condenses into millions of tiny droplets that form clouds. Through precipitation, clouds lose their water, which is then absorbed into the ground or bodies of water. Water that was absorbed into the ground is absorbed by plants. Plants lose water (vapor) from their surfaces which then integrates back into the atmosphere. Water that runs off into rivers flows into ponds, lakes, or oceans where it evaporates back into the atmosphere.

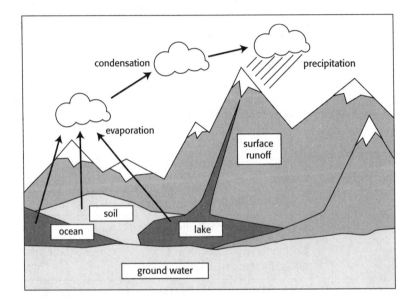

The Water Cycle

Wind

Wind is moving air. Wind is created when warm air rises and cool air rushes in to take its place. As air moves from high to low pressure in the northern hemisphere, it is deflected to the right by the *Coriolis force*. In the southern hemisphere, air moving from high to low pressure is deflected to the left by the Coriolis force.

The amount of deflection the air makes is directly related to both the speed at which the air is moving and its latitude. Therefore, slowly blowing winds will be deflected only a small amount, while stronger winds will be deflected more. Likewise, winds blowing closer to the poles will be deflected more than winds at the same speed closer to the equator. The Coriolis force is zero right at the equator.

Prevailing winds are a series of belts around the globe that produce steadily blowing winds near the surface. *Trade winds* are steady and flow toward the equator. Jet streams are narrow zones of very strong winds in the upper troposphere.

Winds move at different speeds and have different names based on the Beaufort Scale. This scale uses numbers from 0 to 12 and goes from calm air to breezes to strong winds or gales. Winds are also grouped by their direction. *Easterly* winds blow from east to west, while *Westerly* winds blow from west to east.

Seasons

The Sun is the center of the solar system. This fact, when discovered by Copernicus in the early sixteenth century, changed our understanding of the relationship between the Sun and Earth. We now know that Earth orbits the sun elliptically and, at the same time, spins on an axis that is tilted relative to its plane of orbit. This means that different hemispheres are exposed to different amounts of sunlight throughout the year. Because the sun is our source of light, energy and heat, the changing intensity and concentration of its rays give rise to the seasons of winter, spring, summer and fall.

The seasons are marked by solstices and equinoxes, which were discussed in the astronomy section of this chapter. Seasonal change affects the weather in the following ways. Around the time of the June solstice, the North Pole is tilted toward the sun and the Northern Hemisphere is starting to enjoy summer. The sun's rays are strong because they are directly overhead and are concentrated over a smaller surface area and traveling through a relatively small amount of energy-absorbing atmosphere before striking the earth.

While the Northern Hemisphere is entering summer, the South Pole is tilted away from the sun, and the Southern Hemisphere is starting to feel the cold of winter. The sun's rays are weak because they are spread over a greater surface area and must travel through more energy-absorbing atmosphere to before reaching the earth. The situations are reversed in December, when it's the Southern Hemisphere that basks in the most direct rays of the sun, while the Northern Hemisphere receives the weakest rays.

Water

The study of bodies of water and their characteristics is essential to understanding the world we live in. Scientists and oceanographers concentrate on the environments (biomes) that exist in various types of water, including ponds, lakes, rivers, oceans, and estuaries.

The Aquatic Biome

Water comprises the largest part of the biosphere, covering nearly 75% of the Earth's surface. Aquatic regions house numerous species of plants and animals. In fact, life began in water, billions of years ago when amino acids first started to mix. Without water, most life forms would be unable to sustain themselves and the Earth would be a barren place. Although water temperatures can vary widely, aquatic areas tend to be more humid and the air temperature cool. There are two basic types of aquatic biomes, freshwater (e.g., ponds and rivers) and marine (e.g., oceans and estuaries).

Tides and the Phases of the Moon

Tides are caused by the pull of the Moon and the Sun on the Earth's oceans. Their movement patterns are directly tied to the phases of the Moon. Let's go over these phases.

When, from Earth, the Moon appears smaller than a quarter full, it is called a *crescent moon*. When it appears larger than a quarter full, it is called a *gibbous moon*. When the moon appears to increase in size, it is going from the *new* phase to the *full* phase (*waxing*). When it appears to be getting smaller, it is *waning*.

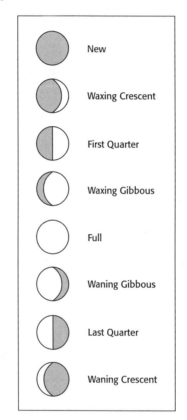

The Phases of the Moon

The moon moves through its phases on a daily schedule. If today the Moon were a waxing crescent, then tomorrow the crescent shape would appear larger, as the Moon approaches *first quarter*. After first quarter, the Moon is a *waxing gibbous*, and continues growing larger until it reaches *full moon*. The Moon would then appear to shrink, becoming first a *waning gibbous*, eventually reaching *third, or last, quarter*. Following last quarter it becomes a *waning crescent*, and continues to shrink until it becomes invisible at *new moon*.

The Earth and Moon pull on each other, creating tides. The Moon pulls more strongly on the side of Earth that faces the Moon than on the side that faces away from the Moon. Because the gravitational force on one side of the planet is different from that on the other side, it creates a *tidal force*. (Because of the Earth's tidal effect on the Moon, Earth-bound observers can only ever see one side of the Moon. It takes the Moon the same amount of time to rotate once as it does for the Moon to go around the Earth once. Tidal forces cause many of the moons of our solar system to have this type of orbit.)

When subjected to tidal forces, planets deform as if they are being pushed from the top and bottom. Two bulges appear on either side of the planet—*tides*. (Earth also bulges at the equator all the way around because it is spinning).

The moon pulls water toward it, which causes the bulge toward the moon. On the other side of the Earth, the Moon pulls the Earth away from the water. If you are on a coast and the moon is directly overhead, you witness a *high tide*. If the moon is directly overhead on the opposite side of the planet, you should also experience a high tide.

The Earth rotates 180 degrees in 12 hours. The Moon, meanwhile, rotates only 6 degrees around the earth in 12 hours. The twin bulges and the moon's rotation mean that any given coastal city experiences a high tide approximately every 12 hours and 25 minutes. Along the west coast of the United States, we experience four tides per day: two high tides and two low tides. When the Moon, the Earth, and the Sun are in a line, *spring tides* are formed, during which higher and lower than normal tides may occur. When the Moon, the Earth, and the Sun are at right angles to each other, *neap tides* are formed during which there is not a great deal of difference in the heights of the high and low tides.

SCIENTIFIC TOOLS AND METHODS

Test Yourself

A second grade science class is studying different types of soil. They have designed an experiment with settling jars to see which kind of soil has the most layers.

Each team of students examines three different types of soil: sand, clay, and loam. They look at each through a magnifying glass, touch it, and so on. Students then make a prediction as to which type of soil will have the most layers when it settles in a jar of water.

They notice that sand particles are slightly larger and more varied than the dusty clay particles. They also notice loam has the most sizes and types of particles, including some decaying vegetation and redwood bark.

Next, each team labels three different jars sand, clay, and loam and then places three tablespoons of each type of soil into the appropriately labeled jars. They add 2/3 cup of water to each jar, put the lids on, and shake each jar.

According to the students' observations, which type of soil is most likely to have the most layers when the soil settles?

(A) sand

(B) clay

(C) loam

(D) they will all have just one layer

The correct choice is **(C)**. The students noticed that loam has the most varied types and sizes of particles, which indicates that, when placed in a jar of water, it will most likely produce the most layers. Sand, **(A)**, has the next largest size and variety of particles, but the loam should produce more layers in water because it will also contain the floating particles from the decaying vegetation and bark, eliminating choice **(A)**. The fact that the decaying vegetation and bark floats ensures that the loam, at least, will have more than one layer, eliminating choice **(D)**. Clay, **(B)**, has fine, uniform particles which will create fewer layers than the loam, thus eliminating this choice.

The function of modern science is to test suspected explanations of *observations* about the natural world. An explanation for one or more observations is called a *hypothesis*, which, to be scientifically useful, should produce *testable predictions*. Scientific tests, or *experiments*, should be conducted under *controlled conditions* to produce the most reliable conclusions. Today, it is widely accepted that science follows certain rules and processes that make it a dependable source of information. But that was not always the case; the *scientific method* took years to develop. Early scientists conducted tests as they tried to prove or disprove theories. The birth of the scientific method as we know it today occurred in the late 1700s, through tests carried out by Italian naturalist Francisco Redi as he tried to disprove the concept of spontaneous generation.

In Redi's day, it was widely believed that living things could arise spontaneously from non-living, dead, or waste materials. To test this concept, Redi conducted a test. He placed decaying meat in two containers: one open, the other sealed. In time, maggots were observed in the meat in the open container, but none appeared in the closed container. Proponents of spontaneous generation insisted that spontaneous generation did not occur in the sealed container because no air was allowed in. But Redi conducted the test again, this time with one open container and one covered with cheesecloth, through which air could circulate (he suspected what we now know—that flies were the actual source of the maggots); and the cheesecloth-covered sample produced no maggots. Because of Redi's experimental design and use of *controls*, spontaneous generation was rejected as a scientific fact.

Controlled Experiments and the Scientific Method

It is difficult to achieve complete control over conditions in biological experiments, but scientists still strive to do so. *Controlled experiments* may be done in a laboratory environment with different *test groups,* similar to how Redi executed his experiment. One group, the *experimental group,* is specifically set up to test some critical aspect (the *variable)* of the hypothesis; another group, the *control group,* duplicates the experimental group but removes the variable (or, if that isn't possible, alters it in some significant way). In Redi's second test, the cloth-covered containers composed the experimental group (the cloth barrier was the variable), with the control group being the uncovered containers. Control tests may also be run to try to figure out how outside influences (*confounding factors*) may be affecting an experiment. *Results,* usually in some sort of number form (*quantitative data,* as oppose to non-number *qualitative data)* are collected from each group and compared. The comparison is a critical part of the process, as the scientific truth lies in the differences between collected data.

The scientific method is the most common method used today to test hypotheses; its steps are listed below:

1. Observe some aspect of the universe.
2. Invent a hypothesis consistent with observed phenomena.
3. Make predictions based on the hypothesis.
4. Test your predictions by experiments or further observations and modify your hypothesis based on the new results.
5. Repeat steps 3 and 4 until there are no discrepancies between hypothesis and experimental results.

When consistency is obtained, a hypothesis becomes a *theory*. A theory should provide a coherent set of propositions that explain phenomena, and a framework within which observations are explained and predictions are made.

The scientific method works so well because it is unprejudiced. If you are skeptical of a given researcher's findings, you can redo the experiment and determine whether his/her results are sound or baseless. A theory is only accepted when its results can be replicated by anyone.

KAPLAN

Glossary

Absorption: a process through which organisms make nutrients available to cells

Acceleration: the rate of change of an object's velocity

Acid: a solute that donates protons

Air pressure: the movement and collision of gas molecules in the atmosphere that can form into high- or low-pressure areas

Alleles: different versions of a gene in a population

Angiosperms: flowering plants

Auxins: an important class of plant hormones associated with growth patterns

Base: a solute that accepts protons

Binary fission: the reproductive mechanism of prokaryotes

Carbohydrates (saccharides): biological molecules that have important roles in energy metabolism and storage as well as the structure of cells and organisms

Central nervous system: a system comprised of the brain and spinal cord in vertebrates that processes and stores information

Charge: an excess or deficiency of electrons in a body

Circulatory system: a system for transporting nutrients and other essential materials throughout the body

Classical genetics: the study of the patterns and mechanisms of the transmission of inherited traits from one generation to another

Climate: long-term patterns of temperature, humidity and amount of sunshine

Condensation: the process by which gas reverts back into the liquid phase

Crust: the outermost layer of the earth

Deposition: the process by which a gas changes directly to the solid phase

DNA (deoxyribonucleic acid): the genetic material that contains genes responsible for the physical traits observed in all living organisms

Dynamics: the study of what causes motion

Ecosystem: a community and its abiotic environment

Electric current (direct, alternating): the flow of a charge

Endocrine system: the network of glands and tissues that secrete hormones

Endoskeleton: a framework for the attachment of skeletal muscles in vertebrates that also protects vital organs

Equinox: calendar dates when the day and night are the same length

Eukaryotic cells: multicellular organisms whose cells contain organelles

Evaporation (vaporization): the process by which liquid changes into the gas phase

Exoskeleton: a hard external skeleton that covers all the muscles and organs of some invertebrates

External fertilization: the process of fertilization in vertebrates that reproduce in water

Fault: weakened narrow zones in tectonic plates

Fertilization: the union of an egg nucleus with a sperm nucleus

Fitness: a quantitative measure of the ability to contribute alleles and traits to offspring

Fixed-action pattern: a complex, coordinated behavioral response triggered by specific stimulation from the environment

Food chain: a simple linear relationship between a series of species, with on eating the other

Food web: a depiction of the relationships within a community in which every population interacts with several other populations

Force: the push or pull on an object

Freezing (solidification, crystallization): the process by which a liquid changes into a solid

Galaxy: huge cluster or stars and nebulae

Gametes: sex cells produced through meiosis in males and females

Gene pool: the sum total of all alleles in a population

Genes: molecules that store and transfer genetic information

Genotype: an organism's genetic composition

Gravity: an attractive force felt by all forms of matter

Gymnosperms: nonflowering plants

Haploid cells: gametes that, when joined, produce diploid offspring

Hormones: chemical messengers produced in one tissue and carried by the blood to act on other parts of the body

Hypothesis: an explanation for one or more observations about the natural world

Immune system: the body's system of protection against invasion by unwanted organisms

Maturation: the development of an embryo to an adult

Meiosis: a specialized form of eukaryotic cell division involving male and female gametes

Melting (fusion): the process by which a solid changes into a liquid

Minerals: naturally occurring, inorganic, crystalline solids

Mitosis: an asexual reproductive process of eukaryotic cells in which cells divide to form two daughter cells with the same genetic makeup as the parent cell

Nucleic acids: essential informational molecules found in all living things

Organic compounds: chemicals that contain carbon; inorganic compounds do not contain carbon

Organs: large anatomical structures made from several tissues

Orogenesis: the processes of mountain formation

Osmosis: the simple diffusion of water from a region of lower solute concentration to a region of higher solute concentration

Ova: female gamete

Phenotype: the appearance and physical expression of genes in an organism

Photosynthesis: the foundation of all ecosystems wherein plants generate their own energy from the energy of the sun

Population: a group of members of the same species found in a given environment at a given time

Power: the rate at which work is done

Precipitation: part of the water cycle that produces hail, mist, rain, sleet, or snow

Predation: the consumption of one organism by another

Prokaryotic cells: unicellular organisms with a simple cell structure

Respiration: the bodily system used to transport oxygen to cells and rid the body of waste products like carbon dioxide

RNA (ribonucleic acid): a polymer of nucleotides associated with the control of cellular chemical activities

Scientific method: the accepted method for testing scientific hypotheses

Solstice: calendar dates when the days are longest or shortest

Solubility: the maximum amount of that substance that can be dissolved in a particular solvent at a particular temperature

Solvent: in a solution, the substance that does the dissolving; what is dissolved is known as the solute

Speciation: the creation of a new species

Species: a group of similar organisms that can produce viable offspring

Spermatozoa: male gamete

Static friction: the force that must be overcome to set an object in motion

Stratosphere: the layer of the atmosphere located above the troposphere in which most of the atmosphere's ozone is found

Sublimation: the process by which a solid changes directly to the gas phase

Symbiosis: a relationship between organisms in which they share an intimate, often permanent coexistence

Taxonomy: the science of classifying and naming living things

Tectonic plates: the thick slabs of rock that compose the outer portion of Earth

Theory: a tested hypothesis

Thermoregulation: the maintenance of a particular temperature of the living body

Tide: the alternate rising and falling of the surface of the ocean caused by the gravitational attraction of the Sun and Moon occurring unequally on different parts of the Earth

Tissues: specialized cells with a common function and similar form in multicellular organisms

Troposphere: the layer of the atmosphere located closest to the Earth's surface in which weather occurs

Vegetative propagation: asexual reproductive process of many plants, including bulbs and tubers

Zygote: the diploid single cell offspring formed from the union of gametes

KAPLAN

PRACTICE SET

1. Which of the following changes is not a physical change of matter?

    (A) evaporation
    (B) decomposition of old leaves
    (C) painting wood
    (D) cutting a copper wire

2. The modern periodic table is ordered on the basis of

    (A) atomic mass
    (B) atomic radius
    (C) atomic charge
    (D) atomic number

3. Inelastic collisions occur in

    I.   Real gases
    II. Ideal gases
    III. Fusion reactions

    (A) I and II
    (B) II and III
    (C) I and III
    (D) I only

4. What happens to the pH of a buffer system if one halves the concentration of both the acid and the salt?

    (A) Nothing
    (B) pH goes up because there is less total acid in the solution.
    (C) pH goes down because there is less conjugate base to mask the presence of the acid.
    (D) It depends upon the original concentration of acid and salt.

5. Solution X boils at 100.26°C and Solution Y boils at 101.04°C. Both solutions are at atmospheric pressure and contain the same solute concentration. Which of the following conclusions can be drawn?

    (A) The freezing point of Solution X is lower than that of Solution Y.
    (B) The vapor pressure of Solution X is higher than that of Solution Y at 100.26°C.
    (C) Solution X and Solution Y are immiscible.
    (D) The vapor pressure of Solution X is lower than that of Solution Y at 100.26°C.

6. The atomic theory could be used to analyze which of the following?

   (A) properties of hydrogen
   (B) the proliferation of bacteria
   (C) the AIDS epidemic
   (D) the motion of an object

7.

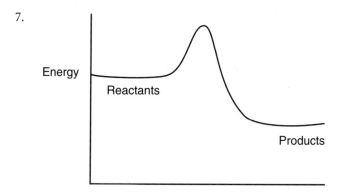

Reaction Pathway

The above graph depicts the energy associated with a specific reaction. In the overall reaction, is energy released into the environment or absorbed?

(A) Energy is released because the products are at a lower energy state.

(B) Energy is absorbed because the reactants are at a higher energy state.

(C) Energy is neither released nor absorbed.

(D) Energy is absorbed because the reactants are at a lower energy state.

8. A bear is chasing a woman through the forest. The enormous mass of the bear is extremely intimidating. If the woman runs through the woods in a zigzag pattern she will be able to use the large mass of the bear to her own advantage because

   (A) bears have poor peripheral vision, so the bear won't be able to keep the woman in its field of vision as she zigzags through the forest

   (B) the woman will be able to change her state of motion more easily than the bear because she has a smaller inertia

   (C) the bear cannot run fast because it is so heavy and will tire quickly

   (D) all of the above

KAPLAN

9. In an attempt to walk across a frozen lake, a skier tries to determine the best method for getting across the ice without cracking it. She takes into account pressure and force. Which of the following methods would most likely help the skier get across the lake without cracking the ice? (*Hint*: Pressure=Force/Area)

    (A) tip-toeing
    (B) walking upright
    (C) standing on one foot
    (D) crawling

10. A process in which food is broken down and energy is released is

    (A) diffusion
    (B) photosynthesis
    (C) respiration
    (D) mitosis

11. Vertebrates are members of the animal kingdom that have backbones. Which of these is NOT a vertebrate?

    (A) human
    (B) trout
    (C) alligator
    (D) earthworm

12. Which major body system protects the body's vital organs?

    (A) respiratory
    (B) circulatory
    (C) digestive
    (D) skeletal

13. Which of the following is a correct association?

    (A) mitochondria: transport of materials from the nucleus to the cytoplasm
    (B) Golgi apparatus: modification and glycosylation of proteins
    (C) endoplasmic reticulum: selective barrier for the cell
    (D) ribosomes: digestive enzymes most active at acidic pH

14. Which of the following are likely to negatively impact ecological systems?

    (A) the depletion of the ozone layer
    (B) the greenhouse effect
    (C) the extinction of certain species
    (D) all of the above

15. The rise in global temperature, by decreasing the desert water supply and thereby reducing the quantity of desert plant life, has affected a decrease in the population of small mammals in this climate. According to the food web below, which of the following statements describes accurately which group(s) would be most affected by the ecological changes to this climate?

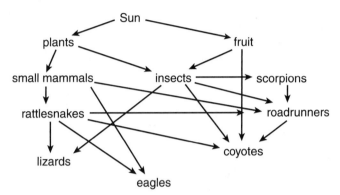

(A) All organisms in the food web would suffer sharp declines as their main food sources become increasingly scarce.

(B) The population of insects would increase because fewer small mammals would be eating them.

(C) The population of eagles would be adversely affected because one of their main food sources is becoming increasingly scarce.

(D) The population of rattlesnakes would increase since fewer small mammals would eat them.

16. Maple trees, apple trees, orchids, and palms are examples of

(A) gymnosperms

(B) bryophytes

(C) angiosperms

(D) chlorophytes

17. By 2050, the world population will reach 9 billion people. Which of the following environmental effects will likely accompany population growth?

   I. increased supply of groundwater
  II. consumption of natural resources
 III. destruction of habitats
 IV. decreased pollution

(A) I and II only

(B) II and III only

(C) I and III only

(D) II and IV only

KAPLAN

18. Sexually reproducing species can have a selective advantage over asexually reproducing species because sexual reproduction

    (A) is more energy efficient
    (B) allows for more genetic diversity
    (C) decreases the likelihood of mutations
    (D) always decreases an offspring's survival ability

19. During which phase of the Moon will the highest tides occur?

    (A) full moon
    (B) new moon
    (C) first quarter
    (D) new crescent

Use the diagram below to answer the question that follows.

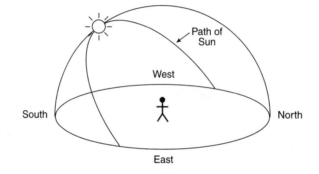

20. The above drawing shows the path of the Sun during a day. At what location and on which day would this path be observed?

    (A) Northern Hemisphere on a spring day
    (B) Northern Hemisphere on a winter day
    (C) Equator on a spring day
    (D) Southern Hemisphere on a winter day

21. It has been proven by accurate measurements that the Earth's circumference is larger around the equator than around the North and South poles. Which of the following best explains the reason for this phenomenon?

    (A) the Earth's rotation about its axis
    (B) the Moon's gravitational pull of the Earth
    (C) the Sun's gravitational pull of the Earth
    (D) the Earth's revolution around the Sun

22. Which of the following factors cannot be used to classify a newly discovered rock?

    (A) density
    (B) grain size
    (C) composition
    (D) age

23. Water is most dense during which of the following phases?

    (A) solid
    (B) liquid
    (C) gas
    (D) evaporation

24. It has been determined by scientists that the Himalayan mountain range is slowly growing taller. Which of the following phenomena could help explain this observation?

    (A) human activities around the mountain range
    (B) snowfall in the high altitude
    (C) the Indian subcontinent pushing against the Asian continent
    (D) gas emissions from the greenhouse effect

25. Which of the following mechanisms is NOT one that causes rocks to be broken down?

    (A) frost
    (B) abrasion
    (C) neutralization
    (D) oxidation

26.

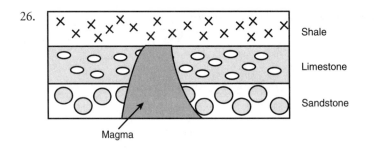

Magma

The diagram above represents a geological section of rock. List the following events in the correct order from oldest to most recent.

    I.   Deposition of limestone

    II.   Deposition of sandstone

    III.   Magma-producing volcanic eruption

    IV.   Deposition of shale

(A) I, II, III, IV

(B) II, I, III, IV

(C) IV, III, II, I

(D) III, I, IV, II

Constructed-Response Question 1

Complete the exercise that follows.

Heat is transferred from one material to another by conduction, convection and/or radiation. Insulators are devices used to minimize the transfer of heat energy. Using the example of a thermos bottle, explain how insulation works.

_____

_____

_____

_____

_____

_____

_____

_____

_____

_____

_____

_____

_____

_____

_____

_____

_____

_____

_____

_____

_____

_____

_____

Constructed-Response Question 2

Complete the exercise that follows.

Below is a diagram of Orographic Effect. Use the diagram and your Earth Science knowledge to answer the following question.

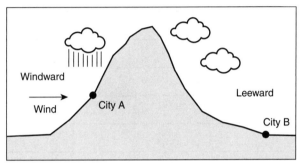

Discuss the climates of Cities A and B. What factors determine their climates?

_____

_____

_____

_____

_____

_____

_____

_____

_____

_____

_____

_____

_____

_____

_____

_____

_____

_____

ANSWER KEY

1 B	8. B	15. C	22. D
2. D	9. D	16. C	23. B
3. C	10. C	17. B	24. C
4. A	11. D	18. B	25. C
5. B	12 D	19. B	26. B
6. A	13. B	20. A	
7. A	14 D	21. A	

ANSWERS AND EXPLANATIONS

1.   B

A physical change is a change that does not result in the production of a new substance. Evaporation, **(A)**, the painting of wood, **(C)**, and the cutting of a copper wire, **(D)**, are all physical changes. Other examples of physical changes are: melting, freezing, condensing, bending, crushing, and breaking. The only change that is not a physical change of matter is **(B)**, the decomposition of old leaves, which is a chemical change (one that results in the production of another substance).

2.   D

When the Periodic Table was first being designed, it was thought that the periodicity of the elements could be explained on the basis of atomic mass. Mendeleev discovered that when the elements were arranged in order or increasing atomic mass, certain chemical properties were repeated at regular intervals. However, certain elements could not be fit into any group of a table based on increasing atomic mass. It was the discovery of the nucleus and its components that led scientists to order the elements by increasing atomic number, the number of protons.

3.   C

Ideal gases can be described by the Kinetic Molecular Theory of Gas. One part of this model is that collisions are elastic; there is no overall net gain or loss of energy. Inelastic collisions do occur in real gases. Also, a nuclear fusion reaction is a reaction in which two nuclei collide to form a new, heavier nucleus.

4.   A

A buffer solution is prepared from a weak acid and its conjugate base in near equal quantities. As long as these conditions are met, the pH should remain the same. A buffer solution with the concentrations of each of these components halved may have less ability to buffer, but the initial solution will have the same pH.

5.   B

This question deals with the colligative properties of solutions. It brings up several critical points about solutions. One is that the presence of a solute in a solution *always* raises the boiling point and lowers the freezing point, compared to those of the pure solvent. The more concentrated the solution, the higher the boiling point and lower the freezing point will be. Thus it is clear that choice **(A)** is incorrect; since Solution Y's boiling point is higher than Solution X's, its freezing point must be lower as well. Actually, you don't have enough information to say that this answer is right or wrong since you don't know the original freezing point or freezing point depression constant for either solution. There must be a better answer. The second important concept is that of vapor pressure, which is the topic of both choices **(B)** and **(D)**. A solution boils when its vapor pressure is equal to the atmospheric pressure. If a solution has a higher boiling point than another, it must have a lower vapor pressure. The vapor pressure of a solution increases as its temperature increases. Since it takes more heat to boil solution Y under the same atmospheric pressure, solution Y must have had a lower vapor pressure to begin with. Choice **(B)** is therefore correct, and **(D)** incorrect. Choice **(C)** concerns the solubility of the two solutions in each other. Again, we don't have enough information to say that this answer is correct. After all, we know nothing about the two solvents of solutions X and Y, only that they have the same concentration of solute in them and what the resultant boiling points are. That leaves **(B)** as the correct answer.

6. A

The atomic theory would be used to analyze the properties of hydrogen because it deals with the atomic level of matter. Choice **(B)** is a phenomenon that bacteriologists or microbiologists might study and would not be studied in relation to the atomic theory. Choice **(C)** is an example of an epidemiological study, while **(D)** is a concept studied in physics that might be analyzed by Newton's Laws.

7. A

As the graph depicts, the energy level of the reactants is greater than that of the products, illustrating that energy was lost during the reaction, thereby placing the products at a lower energy level. The only choice that corresponds to the graph is **(A)**. Choice **(B)** is incorrect because energy is not absorbed. If it were, the graph would show a higher peak on the products side. Choice **(D)** is incorrect because the reactants are at a higher energy state.

8. B

Inertia is every object's resistance to changing its speed and direction of travel. Things naturally want to keep going the way they were going. Furthermore, the more mass an object has, the more inertia it has, and the more it tends to resist changes in its state of motion. Therefore, because the bear has a larger inertia than the woman, the bear will have more difficulty changing direction rapidly, so **(B)** is correct. Choices **(A)**, **(C)**, and **(D)** are incorrect because the question is asking about using the mass of the bear to the woman's advantage, not about its vision or physical fitness.

9. D

Because P=Force/Area, the more surface area the skier covers, the lower the pressure exerted on the ice, thereby reducing the possibility of cracking the ice. Standing on one foot, **(C)**, creates the most pressure on the ice because this method provides the least amount of surface area. Tip-toeing, **(A)**, and walking upright, **(B)**, create more

surface area than standing on one foot, but crawling, **(D)**, provides the maximum amount of surface area of all the choices. Therefore, **(D)** is correct.

10. C

Respiration, **(C)**, is the process by which cells produce the energy they need to survive, turning food (fuel) and oxygen (air) into useable energy. Choice **(A)** is incorrect because *diffusion* is a process by which energy or matter flows from a higher concentration to a lower concentration and results in a homogeneous distribution. Choice **(B)** is incorrect because photosynthesis is the process by which green plants and certain other organisms use the energy of light to convert carbon dioxide and water into simple sugar glucose. *Photosynthesis* provides the basic energy source for virtually all organisms. Choice **(D)**, *mitosis*, is incorrect because mitosis is the process by which a cell's nucleus replicates and divides before the entire cell replicates.

11. D

An earthworm does not have a backbone. All of the other answer choices have backbones.

12. D

The skeletal system (the 206 bones in the human body) protects vital organs such as the brain, heart, and lungs. The respiratory system, **(A)**, supplies the blood with oxygen so that oxygen is delivered to all parts of the body. The heart, lungs, and blood vessels work together to pump blood through the circulatory system, **(B)**. The digestive system, **(C)**, breaks down food from larger molecules to smaller molecules so it may be used by the body.

13. B

The Golgi apparatus consists of a stack of membrane-enclosed sacs. The Golgi receives vesicles and their contents from the smooth ER, modifies them (as in glycosylation), repackages them into vesicles, and distributes them. In **(A)**, mitochondria are involved in cellular respiration, and in **(C)**, the ER transports polypeptides around the cell and to the Golgi apparatus for packaging. The ribosome **(D)** is the site of protein synthesis.

14. D

All of the choices negatively impact the ecosystem in different ways. The depletion of the ozone layer, **(A)**, and the greenhouse effect, **(B)**, change atmospheric conditions and microclimate conditions making it more difficult for organisms to adapt to their environment. The extinction of any species, **(C)**, has a major impact on the ecological system because the absence of a species significantly alters the food chain. Therefore, **(D)**, all of the above, is the correct choice.

15. C

According to the food web, eagles have only two food sources—small mammals and rattlesnakes. Due to the scarcity of one of their main food sources, their population would most likely decrease, so **(C)** is correct. Small mammals are the main food source for rattlesnakes, roadrunners, and eagles; however, the populations of plants, insects, scorpions, and fruit would barely be affected, making **(A)** incorrect. The population of insects would not likely be much affected by the decline in the small mammal population because small mammals do not generally eat insects. Therefore, choice **(B)** is incorrect. It is unlikely that the population of rattlesnakes would increase because one of their food sources decreases, making **(D)** incorrect.

16. C

Angiosperms are flowering plants that produce seeds enclosed in an ovary, e.g., the maple tree. Gymnosperms, on the other hand, do not have enclosed seeds; one example is the conifer.

17. B

As the world's population grows, crowding will likely generate more pollution, destroy natural habitats, and strain the water supply and other natural resources. Scientists believe that the size of the human population directly affects environmental problems including global warming, ozone depletion, and rain forest destruction. Statement I regarding an increased supply of groundwater is not related to population growth, making **(A)** and **(C)** incorrect. Since pollution will increase, not decrease as suggested in statement IV, **(D)** can be eliminated.

18. B

Asexual reproduction is more efficient than sexual reproduction in terms of the number of offspring produced per reproduction and the amount of energy invested. Overall, sexual reproduction is a much more time-consuming, energy-consuming process than its asexual counterpart. However, this method allows for more genetic diversity, making choice **(B)** correct.

19. B

Highest tide occurs when the gravitational forces on the Earth by the Moon and the Sun are greatest, i.e., when their positions are lined up, single file, in the order of Sun, Moon, and Earth. This positioning is observed during the new moon.

20. A

The path of Sun is located in the Southern sky, which eliminates the possibility of it being in the Southern Hemisphere; eliminating **(D)**. Choice **(C)** can also be eliminated since during a spring day on the equator, the path of Sun should be directly overhead. Choice **(A)** is the correct answer since during a spring day, Sun's path follows a higher arc as depicted in the drawing.

21. A

Earth's rotation about its axis causes the bulge around the equator. Gravity force due to either the Moon or the Sun may have some effect on the Earth, but not enough to cause the difference in circumference and thus **(B)** and **(C)** can be eliminated.

22. D

Density **(A)**, grain size **(B)**, and composition **(C)** are just some of the factors that scientists look at to classify rocks. The age of a rock does provide information but does not determine if a rock is sedimentary, igneous, or metamorphic.

23. B

Water is most dense during its liquid phase. This is why lakes freeze from top down—since ice is less dense than liquid, it floats on water. Water, when it freezes, forms a crystal structure that gives it less density than liquid.

24. C

The Indian subcontinent, which caused the formation of Himalayan mountain range, continues to push against the Asian continent, therefore causing the range's increase in height. Human activities **(A)** do contribute to our environment, but do not directly contribute to the growth of the mountain range. Snowfall **(B)** can make the mountains look taller, but the height of the mountains themselves is not affected by snow. The greenhouse effect **(D)** does not cause mountain growth.

25. C

Water, in a liquid state, seeps into cracks in rocks, and when it freezes (into frost, **(A)**), it expands, causing rocks to break. Rocks also can rub against one another causing one to break (abrasion, **(B)**). Oxidation **(D)** can make rocks weaker because oxygen in the atmosphere can combine with iron in rocks, causing breakage. Neutralization **(C)** occurs between acids and bases and would not contribute to rock breakage.

26. B

The deposition of sandstone is the oldest event, followed by the deposition of limestone. Then a volcanic eruption occurred, sending magma through the sandstone and limestone layers. The last event is the deposition of shale.

Constructed-Response Sample Essay 1

In some situations, it is desirable to keep heat from escaping a container or from entering an area. Insulation is a barrier that minimizes the transfer of heat energy from one material to another by reducing the conduction, convection, and/or radiation effects.

A good insulator is a poor conductor. Less dense materials are better insulators. The more dense the material, the closer together its atoms are. That means the transfer of energy of one atom to the next is more effective. Thus, gases insulate better than liquids, which in turn, insulate better than solids.

A thermos bottle not only has an evacuated lining to prevent heat transfer by conduction, but it also is made of shiny material to prevent radiation heat transfer. Radiation from warm food inside the thermos bottle is reflected back to itself. Radiation from warm outside material is reflected to prevent heating cold liquids inside the bottle.

Constructed-Response Sample Essay 2

The city situated on the windward side of a mountain, City A, receives a lot more rainfall than the city situated on the leeward side, City B. This is true because as wind carries air up the mountain on the windward side, the air cools. Moisture that was present in the air then changes into precipitation and, in turn, comes down as rain. Conversely, when the air reaches the other side of the mountain and warms up, it is dryer air, having lost moisture during the precipitation. Therefore, City B is very dry and rarely sees any rainfall.

Chapter Four: **Mathematics**

THE BIG PICTURE

The Mathematics section of the CSET focuses on content covered in the K–8, general education classroom in accordance with California's current math standards. When taking the CSET, you'll notice that much of the math section is derived from grades four through eight math standards.

The CSET assesses your knowledge of the fundamental principles of mathematics, your ability to communicate and show clear and effective understanding of the content, your utilization of various problem solving techniques, and your proficiency in logical reasoning. Advanced-level mathematics is not required for this exam.

Here are some common mathematical terms, used both in the classroom and on this test, that you must internalize: prime and composite numbers; prime factorization; rational and irrational numbers; proportional reasoning; perimeter; area; surface area; volume; acute, obtuse, and right angles; radius; diameter; and circumference. Please take note of any terminology you don't understand. It may be helpful to think of math as a second language; if you don't understand the terminology, you won't understand the math.

The multiple-choice math questions on the CSET are straightforward and focused on each of the mathematical domains. The questions are not meant to be tricky, but are meant to make you think critically about what is being asked. The test-taking strategies detailed in the next section will be helpful to you, both in preparation for the exam and on Test Day.

The key to scoring well on the math section of the CSET is to think about how you would explain the answers to these questions adequately and effectively to your students. Think about the examples, visuals, and strategies you might use to demonstrate the solution to a problem (e.g., make a table or a graph, write an equation or formula, find a pattern, work backwards, use logical reasoning, etc.). The constructed response sections will ask you to write an essay that should be completed in 10 to 15 minutes. Remember, the people scoring your constructed response short essay answers are teachers themselves, who have been in the classroom within the last five years, so they are in touch with current teaching practices.

THE KAPLAN METHOD

Multiple-Choice Questions

Step 1. Read the question carefully. As you read, underline or circle the key words and phrases that differentiate this particular question from all other possible questions.

Step 2. Rephrase the question to make sure you understand it. If possible, predict the correct answer.

Step 3. Read all the answer choices, eliminating (physically marking through) incorrect ones as you go.

Step 4. If two or more possible answer choices remain, go back to the question and search for matching/mirroring language or concepts that will point you toward the single correct answer.

Constructed-Response Questions

Step 1. Read each question carefully. As you read, underline or circle the key words and phrases that differentiate this particular question from all other possible questions.

Step 2. Note how many parts the question has. Be sure to include subparts in your count. Write this number in your test booklet, so you will be sure to answer each part of the question.

Step 3. Before you start writing, brainstorm for vocabulary words and relevant concepts. Make your notes in the margins of your answer sheet, so you will be sure to include them in your answer. If you don't have good command of the details for a particular question, be sure to include in your answer the big picture concepts, such as the reason for studying/teaching the subject.

Step 4. Organize your thoughts! Remember, you are being tested on your ability to clearly convey information.

NUMBER SENSE: NUMBERS, RELATIONSHIPS AMONG NUMBERS, AND NUMBER SYSTEMS

This section of the CSET surveys your knowledge of number systems, how numbers are built and can be taken apart, and the operations that can be performed with them. You'll begin to see patterns in the ways the base ten number system works and is organized. Numbers are arranged and are augmented in a logical hierarchy; they can be expanded and written in different notations; and their component parts (factors) can be revealed and classified. The manipulation of numbers (applying operations to them) also reveals predictable patterns to a number's increase or decrease. These patterns can be drawn, graphed, shown using numbers, and communicated in everyday situations. A thorough understanding of these concepts is absolutely critical to the next natural progression in mathematics—algebra. Please take note of any areas you need more work with, as the number sense section is aligned to the content domains of the CSET.

Test Yourself

The numbers {1, 2, 3, 4…} belong to what family of numbers?

(A) natural numbers

(B) irrational numbers

(C) rational numbers

(D) both (A) and (C)

When answering this question, your initial instinct might be to select **(A)**. This set of numbers is indeed part of the family of natural numbers, but remember that the family of natural numbers is also a subgroup in the family of rational numbers. Choice **(D)** is the correct answer.

Number Theory

Number theory is the study of numbers and their properties. It is the understanding of numbers (how they are made and can be dissected) and their relationships with other numbers. Number theory also examines the operations that can be performed among them.

The Arabic numerals, {0, 1, 2, 3, 4, 5, 6, 7, 8, and 9}, are used to create almost every numeral value we use today. In the base ten number system, a numeral's position in that system, or place value, determines the number's overall value. For example, in 1,234,567 the 3 represents $3 \times 10,000$, or 30,000. Also, in 0.01234567, the 5 represents $5 \times$ one millionth, or 0.000005 (5 millionths).

When examining the number systems we currently use, a logical classification can be seen.

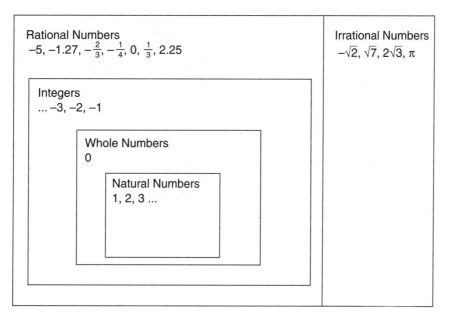

Ordering Real Numbers

Based on the structure of the real number system, numbers can be placed in order by their values. The CSET may ask you to order numbers in their various forms: as fractions and mixed numbers, decimals, and percentages. Utilizing proper conversion factors and your calculator will be invaluable as you work through the questions.

Test Yourself

Which of the following number sets is in order from least to greatest?

(A) $-0.6, -\frac{2}{3}, -\frac{1}{2}, 0$

(B) $0, -\frac{1}{2}, -0.6, -\frac{2}{3}$

(C) $-\frac{2}{3}, -0.6, -\frac{1}{2}, 0$

(D) $-\frac{1}{2}, -\frac{2}{3}, 0, -0.6$

To answer this question, one strategy would be to convert each number in the set to its decimal. form: $-0.6; -\frac{2}{3} \approx -.67; -\frac{1}{2} = -0.5; 0$. The question asks us which number set is ordered from least to greatest. The largest negative value (least) is $-0.67 \approx -\frac{2}{3}$. -0.6 is next, followed by -0.5, and finally 0. Choice **(C)** is correct.

Prime and Composite Numbers

As part of number theory, the CSET will require that you know what prime and composite numbers are and how to break down a larger number into factors of its primes, a.k.a. prime factorization. Common multiples between numbers will also be an area of importance. A prime number has exactly two positive integer factors: 1 and itself. Therefore, it makes sense that 1 cannot be a prime number since 1 and itself are the same number. As a result, 2 is the first prime number. For the CSET it is helpful to quickly recognize the first 10 to 15 prime numbers: 2, 3, 5, 7, 11, 13, 17, 19, 23, 29, 31, 37, 41, 43, 47, etc.

Composite numbers then are all other positive whole numbers: 4, 6, 8, 9, 10, 12, 14, 15, 16, 18, 20, etc. Composite numbers have more than two factors. Another way to understand prime and composite numbers is through visual arrangements called arrays. An array has the same number in each row and column, creating arrangements resembling rectangles and squares. Prime numbers can also be looked at as arrays with a unique set of factors making only one type of array.

5 is a prime number:

XXXXX (5 × 1) array

X
X
X
X
X

(1 × 5) array

7 is a prime number:

XXXXXXX (7 × 1) array

X
X
X
X
X
X
X

(1 × 7) array

Composite numbers have two or more sets of factors and make two or more distinctly different arrays.

4 is a composite number:

XXXX (4 × 1)

	X
XX	X
XX	X
(2 × 2) array	X
	(1 × 4) array

6 is a composite number:

XXXXXX (6 × 1) array

X	*XXX*
X	*XXX*
X	(3 × 2) array
X	
X	*XX*
X	*XX*
X	*XX*
(1 × 6) array	(2 × 3) array

Prime Factorization Using Factor Trees

All positive, whole numbers are made from a product of prime numbers. Thus, these numbers can be evaluated in terms of their prime factors. For example, you can find the prime factors for 112 using a factor tree.

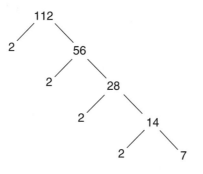

With this prime factor tree, you will see that $112 = 2 \times 2 \times 2 \times 2 \times 7$ or $2^4 \times 7$ are the prime factors of 112. Notice how the exponents are written in order from the greatest exponent to the least exponent.

Rules of Divisibility

The rules of divisibility given in the following chart may be helpful in finding divisors (or factors) of composite numbers.

Divisible by	Test	Example
2	The number is even.	934 is divisible by 2, since 934 is even.
3	The sum of the digits of the number is divisible by 3.	627 is divisible by 3, since the sum of the digits, $6 + 2 + 7 = 15$, and 15 is divisible by 3.
4	The number formed by the last two digits of the number is divisible by 4.	628 is divisible by 4, since the number formed by the last two numbers, 28, is divisible by 4.
5	The number ends in 0 or 5.	3,495 is divisible by 5, since the number ends in 5.
6	The number is divisible by both 2 and 3.	534 is divisible by 6, since it is divisible by both 2 (even number) and 3 (sum of the digits is 12, which is divisible by 3).
8	The number formed by the last three digits of the number is divisible by 8.	6,816 is divisible by 8, since the number formed by the last three digits, 816, is divisible by 8.
9	The sum of the digits of the number is divisible by 9.	6,381 is divisible by 9, since the sum of the digits of the number is 18, and 18 is divisible by 9.
10	The number ends in 0.	1,230 is divisible by 10, since the number ends in 0.

Common Multiples

The importance of common multiples in performing arithmetic operations cannot be overstated. When it comes to adding and subtracting fractions and mixed numbers, knowledge of common multiples is invaluable.

Steps to Finding the LCM (Least Common Multiple)

1. Find the prime factors that make up each number.
2. Multiply each prime factor the <u>greatest number of times</u> it occurs in <u>either number</u>.
3. The result is the LCM.

Example: Find the LCM of 15 and 125.

1. Prime factors of 15: 3, 5
2. Prime factors of 125: 5, 5, 5
3. Multiply each factor the greatest number of times it occurs in either number: 3 occurs once, 5 occurs three times.
4. $3 \times 5 \times 5 \times 5 = 375$
5. 375 is the LCM for 15 and 125.

It is important to note how this method for finding the LCM is clearer and more concise than listing the multiples of 15 and 125 until 375 is reached for both sets of numbers. This is an example of how number theory, the understanding of numbers and their properties, helps you on the CSET.

Scientific Notation

Test Yourself

Which expression below is INCORRECTLY written in scientific notation?

(A) 58×10^5
(B) 5.333×10^{-9}
(C) 1.8×10^{-6}
(D) 4.92×10^{10}

To answer this question, it is important to remember the steps to expressing numbers in scientific notation. Scientific notation is the product of a number between 1 and 10 multiplied by a power of 10. **(A)** should be 5.8×10^6 because 5.8 is a number between 1 and 10; 58 is not.

Sometimes numbers are too big or too small to write out in their entirety, as with the wavelength of a yellow photon (0.0000006 meter) or the average distance from the Earth to the Sun (93,000,000 miles). So mathematicians have come up with ways to express these very large and very small numbers using scientific notation. Scientific notation is the product of a number between 1 and 10 multiplied by a power of 10.

To write a number in scientific notation:

1. First move the decimal point to make a number between 1 and 10.

   35,000 becomes 3.5

   0.0005 becomes 5.0

2. Multiply by 10 raised to the power of the number of places you had to move the decimal point.

   35,000 into 3.5 × 4 places to the left = 3.5×10^4

   0.0005 into 5.0 × 4 places to the right = 5.0×10^{-4}

Therefore, the wavelength of a yellow photon is 6×10^{-7} meters and the average distance from the Earth to the Sun is 9.3×10^7 miles.

Exponential Notation

Notice that in order to write numbers in scientific notation, it's important to understand exponential notation. Exponential notation refers to the way exponents are expressed. The exponent of a base tells how many times the base is multiplied by itself.

Test Yourself

What is $(0.3)^3$ in exponential notation?

(A) 0.027

(B) 0.3×10^3

(C) 0.9

(D) $0.3 \times 0.3 \times 0.3$

Choice **(A)** is the answer in simplest form, while **(B)** and **(C)** are incorrect. Choice **(D)** correctly shows the answer in exponential notation.

Positive Exponents

Positive exponents are exponents expressed in positive terms.

Example: $2^4 = 1 \times 2 \times 2 \times 2 \times 2$ or $2 \times 2 \times 2 \times 2 = 16$ in simplest form.

$6^3 = 1 \times 6 \times 6 \times 6$ or $6 \times 6 \times 6 = 216$ in simplest form.

The Zero Rule

Any number to the zero power equals 1 and not zero. This is so because the base is multiplied the exponent number of times, so all you are left with is 1.

Example: $2^0 \neq 0$ equals 1.

The Rule of 1

Any base raised to the power of one is itself.

Example: $2^1 = 1 \times 2 = 2$ or just the base, 2.

$6^1 = 1 \times 6 = 6$ or just the base, 6.

Negative Exponents

When it comes to negative exponents, it is helpful to look at the inverse operation of multiplication, which is division.

Example: $2^{-4} = 1 \div (2 \times 2 \times 2 \times 2) = 1 \div 16 = \frac{1}{16}$ in simplest form.

$6^{-3} = 1 \div (6 \times 6 \times 6)$, or $1 \div 6^3 = 1 \div 216 = \frac{1}{216}$ in simplest form.

Product Rule for Exponents

When multiplying exponents with the same base, add the exponents and keep the same base.

Example: $2^4 \times 2^3 = 2^{4+3} = 128$

$6^3 \times 6^{-4} = 6^{3+(-4)} = 6^{-1} = \frac{1}{6}$

Quotient Rule for Exponents

When dividing exponents with the same base, subtract the exponents and keep the same base.

Example: $2^4 \div 2^3 = 2^{4-3} = 2^1$

$6^3 \div 6^{-4} = 6^{3-(-4)} = 6^7$

Power Rule for Exponents

When an exponent is raised to another power, multiply the exponents and keep the same base.

Example: $(2^4)^3 = 2^{4 \times 3} = 2^{12}$

$(6^3)^{-4} = 6^{3 \times (-4)} = 6^{-12}$

Computational Tools and Strategies

Test Yourself

Name the property illustrated below:

$$(4s - 25) \times 10s = 40s^2 - (10s \times 25)$$

(A) distributive property
(B) associative property
(C) commutative property
(D) multiplicative identity property

To answer this question, it is important to look at what is occurring on the left and right sides of the equation. On the left, $(4s - 25)$ is being multiplied by $10s$; on the right, $40s$ is being subtracted by $(10s \times 25)$. Two different operations are being performed, which makes all but one answer choice implausible–the distributive property. Choice **(A)** is correct.

An algorithm is a process used to solve a problem. Algorithms reveal relationships and patterns among numbers through the operations of addition, subtraction, multiplication, division, roots, and exponents. The following is a list of standard algorithms:

Multiplicative Identity is a process whereby a number multiplied by 1 equals itself.

Example: $365 \times 1 = 365$

Commutative Property is a process for addition and multiplication stating the order in which two numbers are added or multiplied does not change their sum or product.

Example:	$a + b = b + a$	$a \times b = b \times a$
	$44 + 55 = 55 + 44$	$25 \times 5 = 5 \times 25$

Associative Property is a process for addition and multiplication stating that the grouping of three numbers does not change their sum or product.

Example:	$(a + b) + c = a + (b + c)$	$(a \times b) \times c = a \times (b \times c)$
	$(15 + 5) + 20 = 15 + (5 + 20)$	$(5 \times 10) \times 15 = 5 \times (10 \times 15)$

Distributive Property is a process for addition and multiplication stating that when multiplying a number by a sum or difference, you may either add/subtract first and then multiply, or multiply first and then add/subtract.

Example:	$a \times (b + c) = a(b) + a(c)$	$a \times (b - c) = a(b) - a(c)$
	$5 \times (10 + 6) = 5(10) + 5(6)$	$5 \times (10 - 6) = 5(10) - 5(6)$
	$5 \times 16 = 50 + 30$	$5 \times 4 = 50 - 30$
	$80 = 80$	$20 = 20$

Operations with Whole Numbers and Fractions

The CSET will require you to perform operations with positive and negative exponents as they apply to whole numbers and fractions. The operations are adding, subtracting, multiplying, and dividing. When adding and subtracting fractions, it is crucial that you find the common denominators before performing an operation on the numerators. Finding common denominators is not necessary when multiplying and dividing fractions; multiplication works straight across and division with fractions involves multiplying by the reciprocal of the second term.

Test Yourself

Esther took a bag of cans that weighed $8\frac{2}{5}$ pounds to the

recycling center. Narisa took a bag of cans that weighed $3\frac{2}{3}$

pounds more than Esther's bag. How many pounds of cans

did Narisa take to the recycling center?

(A) $11\frac{4}{5}$ pounds

(B) $12\frac{1}{15}$ pounds

(C) $12\frac{4}{5}$ pounds

(D) $11\frac{4}{8}$ pounds

To answer this problem, you must first find the common denominator for fifths and thirds. Then add the fractions and whole number. In doing so, you'll find, the correct answer is $12\frac{1}{15}$ pounds of cans, **(B)**.

There is a set of prerequisite skills that is critical to making the math section of the CSET easy to pass. The skills are converting numbers to fractions, percents, and decimals and expressing a mixed number as a fraction.

To convert fractions to decimals, divide the numerator by the denominator. All fractions can be expressed as division problems. For example $\frac{4}{5}$ is $4 \div 5 = 0.8$.

A percent is a number divided by 100 (the word *percent* breaks down like this: *per* means *divided by* and *cent* means *100*; so *percent* means *divide by 100*). Therefore, 95% is 95 divided by 100 or 0.95 (pronounced "ninety-five hundredths," or "zero point nine five"). 250% means 250 divided by 100, or 2.5 ("two and five-tenths," or "two point five,") or $2\frac{1}{2}$ ("two and a half").

To express a mixed number as a fraction, here's an algorithm (a process) to remember: when converting a mixed number to a fraction, multiply the whole number by the denominator and then add the numerator. $2\frac{1}{2}$ becomes *two times two plus one*, which equals five-halves $\left(\frac{5}{2}\right)$. Similarly, $7\frac{3}{8}$ expressed as a fraction becomes $\frac{(7 \times 8) + 3}{8} = \frac{59}{8}$.

Adding Fractions and Mixed Numbers

1. Make sure there are common denominators.

2. Add the numerators, but remember the denominator doesn't change.

3. Express your answer in simplest form.

Sample Problem: $\frac{5}{8} + \frac{5}{12}$ (must find the Least Common Denominator or LCD before adding.)

Think of common multiples for 8 and 12:

   One way: List the multiples

   8, 16, 24, 32

   12, 24, 36

   Another way: Find their prime factors & multiply each prime factor by the greatest number of times it occurs in either number.

   8: $2 \times 2 \times 2$ ("2" occurs three times)

   12: $2 \times 2 \times 3$ ("2" occurs twice)

Least common multiple of 8 and 12: $2 \times 2 \times 2 \times 3 = 24$

Convert to common denominators: $\frac{5}{8} \times \frac{3}{3} = \frac{15}{24}$ and $\frac{5}{12} \times \frac{2}{2} = \frac{10}{24}$

Add the numerators: $\frac{15}{24} + \frac{10}{24} = \frac{25}{24}$

Write in simplest form: $\frac{25}{24} = 25 \div 24 = 1\frac{1}{24}$

Sample Problem: $2\frac{2}{3} + 3\frac{3}{8}$

Find the least common denominator:

   One way: 3, 6, 9, 12, 15, 18, 21, 24, 27

   8, 16, 24, 32

   Another way:

   8: $2 \times 2 \times 2$

   3: 3

Least Common Multiple for 3 and 8: $2 \times 2 \times 2 \times 3 = 24$

Convert to Least Common Denominators: $2\frac{2}{3} \times \frac{8}{8} = 2\frac{16}{24}$ and $3\frac{3}{8} \times \frac{3}{3} = 3\frac{9}{24}$

Add the whole numbers & fractions: $2\frac{16}{24} + 3\frac{9}{24} = 5\frac{25}{24}$

Write in simplest form: $5\frac{25}{24} = 6\frac{1}{24}$

Subtracting Fractions and Mixed Numbers

Subtraction of fractions is the same as the addition of fractions, except for the possibility of renaming the mixed number, in order to perform the operation.

Sample Problem: $3\frac{1}{4} - 1\frac{7}{8}$

Find the Least Common Denominator:

One way: List of multiples

4, 8, 12

8, 16, 24

Another way: Find their prime factors & multiply each prime factor by the greatest number of times it occurs in either number.

4: 2×2 ("2" occurs twice)

8: $2 \times 2 \times 2$ ("2" occurs three times)

Least Common Multiple of 4 and 8: $2 \times 2 \times 2 = 8$

Convert to the least common denominators: $3\frac{1}{4} \times \frac{2}{2} = 3\frac{2}{8}$

Rewrite the problem: $3\frac{2}{8} - 1\frac{7}{8}$

You must rename $3\frac{2}{8}$ to $2\frac{10}{8} - 1\frac{7}{8} = 1\frac{3}{8}$

Write answer in simplest form: $1\frac{3}{8}$

Multiplying Fractions and Mixed Numbers

(A helpful way to remember this algorithm is that multiplying fractions works straight across.)

When multiplying fractions, cross-canceling is another helpful way to get rid of potentially "messy" numbers.

KAPLAN

With the problem, $\frac{45}{52} \times \frac{13}{9}$, the answer would be $\frac{585}{468} = 1.25$ or $1\frac{1}{4}$. As long as you were careful when calculating the answer to this problem, things come out fine. But there's an easier way of doing things. Cross-canceling works by taking the numerator from one fraction and the denominator from the other and finding the Greatest Common Factor to factor out of both numbers. 52 and 13 have the greatest common factor of 13. Therefore, 13 can be factored out of both numbers, leaving 4 and 1 respectively. 45 and 9 have the Greatest Common Factor of 9. Therefore, 9 can be factored out of both numbers. The resulting expression has maintained the same proportional equivalence, therefore cross-canceling did not change anything in the process. It simply made the numbers easier to work with. Just make sure you do it correctly. And remember, it only works when multiplying fractions.

By using the cross-canceling method, $\frac{45}{52} \times \frac{13}{9}$ is equal to $\frac{5}{4} \times \frac{1}{1} = \frac{5}{4}$ or $1\frac{1}{4}$. Notice that this is a more efficient way to arrive at the answer.

Step One: Be sure each term is written in fraction form. (e.g., $2\frac{2}{5} = \frac{12}{5}$)

Step Two: Multiplication works straight across, so multiply numerators by each other and denominators by each other. (You can cross-cancel opposing numerators and denominators if needed.)

Step Three: Write your answer in simplest form.

Sample Problem: $\frac{5}{8} \times \frac{5}{12} = \frac{25}{96}$ (This answer is in simplest form since there are no common factors other than 1. Factors for 25: 1, 5, and 25. Factors for 96: 1, 2, 3, 4, 6, 8, 12, 16, 24, 32, 48, and 96.)

Sample Problem: $3\frac{1}{4} \times 1\frac{7}{8}$ (Change these mixed numbers into fractions before multiplying.)

To do this, think: Whole number "multiplied by" the denominator "plus" the numerator.

$3\frac{1}{4}$: think "3 multiplied by 4 plus 1" $= \frac{13}{4}$ and $1\frac{7}{8}$: think "1 multiplied by 8 plus 7" $= \frac{15}{8}$

Rewrite the problem as fractions: $\frac{13}{4} \times \frac{15}{8} = \frac{195}{32}$

Write in simplest form: $\frac{195}{32} = 195 \div 32 = 6\frac{3}{32}$

Dividing Fractions and Mixed Numbers

Dividing fractions is similar to multiplying fractions, with a few more steps. A helpful way to remember is that when dividing fractions, you multiply by the reciprocal of the second term.

A reciprocal is the inverse value of a number, like turning a number upside-down. For example, the reciprocal of 5 is $\frac{1}{5}$ and the reciprocal of $\frac{2}{3}$ is $\frac{3}{2}$. The reciprocal of $1\frac{2}{3}$ is found by expressing this as a fraction, $\frac{5}{3}$, then taking its reciprocal. $\frac{3}{5}$ is the reciprocal of $1\frac{2}{3}$. There is a mathematical property whereby a number multiplied by its reciprocal is equal to one. That's very important when you have the expression $\frac{2}{3}$ multiplied by x (written as $\frac{2}{3}x$), because to find the value of $1x$ (also known simply as "x"), you'd multiply that expression by the reciprocal of $\frac{2}{3}$, which is $\frac{3}{2}$, to get $1x$.

To divide a fraction:

1. Be sure each term is written in fraction form.
2. Multiply the first term by the reciprocal of the second term. (You can cross-cancel opposing numerators and denominators if needed.)
3. Write your answer in simplest form.

Example: $\frac{5}{8} \div \frac{5}{12}$

$\frac{5}{8} \times \frac{12}{5}$ (multiply by the reciprocal of the second term)

$\frac{60}{40} = \frac{3}{2} = 1\frac{1}{2}$ (simplest form)

Please note that it is also possible to cross-cancel during this operation. In doing so, the problem would look like $\frac{1}{2} \times \frac{3}{1} = \frac{3}{2}$. As you see, cross-canceling can bring the answer to simplest form more directly and is especially helpful when dealing with large numbers.

Sample Problem: $3\frac{1}{4} \div 1\frac{7}{8}$

Write each term as a fraction: $\frac{13}{4} \div \frac{15}{8}$

Multiply by the reciprocal of the second term: $\frac{13}{4} \times \frac{8}{15}$

Cross-cancel 4 in the denominator and 8 in the numerator to get: $\frac{13}{1} \times \frac{2}{15} = \frac{26}{15}$

Write in simplest form: $\frac{26}{15} = 1\frac{11}{15}$

Order of Operations

Test Yourself

Evaluate the following expression:

$5 \times (150 \div 5^2) + (41 + 3^2)$

(A) 280

(B) 200

(C) 80

(D) 61

To evaluate this expression correctly, the order of operations must be used. Working out the exponents within the parentheses, the expression can be simplified to $5 \times (150 \div 25) + (41 + 9)$, then to $(5 \times 6) + 50$, and finally this can be combined to the value of 80. Choice **(C)** is correct.

You may have heard of the mnemonic device for learning the order of operations in math: Please Excuse My Dear Aunt Sally (PEMDAS), but that's not the whole story. It misses a step… roots, which are the opposite of exponents. It should really be Parentheses, Exponents, Roots, Division, Multiplication, Addition, and Subtraction (PERDMAS) and should be done from left to right. In the order of operations, each operation has its opposite. Another way to look at this is:

Parentheses → Exponents or Roots → Multiplication or Division → Addition or Subtraction

Rounding, Estimating, and Placing Numbers Accurately on a Number Line

Test Yourself

Use the numbers below to answer the question that follows.

4,135

5,525

9,875

5,955

To estimate the sum of the given numbers, Cooper first rounds the numbers to the nearest hundred then adds the rounded values. What should his estimate be?

(A) 25,500

(B) 26,000

(C) 25,400

(D) 25,510

This question asks you to round each number to the nearest hundred before adding their sum. Choice **(B)** rounds to the nearest thousand, while **(D)** is rounded to the nearest ten. Choice **(A)** is rounded to the nearest 100 and is therefore the correct answer.

On the CSET, rounding and estimating will usually be found in word problems. You may be asked to compare an estimate to an exact answer. Rounding is the method used to estimate numbers. Numbers are rounded to specific place values, usually those that make it easiest to calculate the number mentally or with the least amount of work. Generally, closer estimates are achieved when rounding to a smaller place value, say the tens instead of hundreds or the hundredths instead of tenths.

Example:

	Rounded to the nearest ten	Rounded to the nearest hundred
6,125	6,130	6,100
5,427	5,430	5,400
4,339	4,340	4,300
7,895	7,900	7,900
	23,800	23,700

Exact Answer is <u>23,786</u>

Test Yourself

Where is *A* located?

(A) $\frac{1}{2}$

(B) $2\frac{1}{4}$

(C) $3\frac{2}{34}$

(D) $3\frac{2}{5}$

Notice that the distance between 2 and 3 is broken into fifths. Therefore the value of *A* is $3\frac{2}{5}$, choice **(D)**.

CSET questions related to placing numbers accurately on a number line will usually require you to convert number values among fractions, decimals, and/or percentages. Test-makers want to see if you can make sense out of numbers with the same values that are written differently or need to be in order to place them correctly. This assures them that you have a sense of the size or value of numbers relative to other numbers. When placing or assessing the value of numbers on a number line, it's important to look at what is given in the problem, as this will help in determining your strategy.

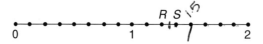

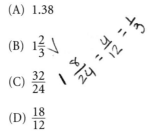

Which of the following points would fall between R and S?

(A) 1.38

(B) $1\frac{2}{3}$

(C) $\frac{32}{24}$

(D) $\frac{18}{12}$

Take a look at R and S on the number line. In order to figure out their value, you'd look at the interval dots between 0 and 1 and 1 and 2. Notice how the dots represent eighths, because they are broken up into eight parts per whole number. Therefore, R must be $1\frac{2}{8}$ (or $1\frac{1}{4}$ in simplest form) and S is $1\frac{3}{8}$. It's probably easiest to compare all of the numbers as decimals. That way you can clearly see which point's value would fall between R and S.

So, methodically, you want to start with changing R to its decimal value of 1.25 and S to 1.375 using division ($2 \div 8 = 0.25$, making 1.25; $3 \div 8 = 0.375$, making 1.375). Choice **(A)**, 1.38, is just slightly larger than S. Choice **(B)**, 1.666... (can be rounded to 1.67), is once again larger than S. Choice **(C)**, 1.333... (can be rounded to 1.33), falls in between R and S. Choice **(D)**, 1.5, is larger than R and S. Therefore, **(C)** is the correct answer.

ALGEBRA AND FUNCTIONS

Algebra is covered on the CSET in both multiple-choice and constructed-response sections. Being familiar with basic algebra will not only help you pass the test, but it will also make teaching mathematics to your students much easier, especially if you're teaching fourth, fifth, or sixth grade. Many problems in everyday life can be solved using arithmetic or trial and error, but using algebra allows you to solve everyday problems with greater ease and in a more organized fashion. The CSET will ask you to evaluate expressions; find solutions to equations; graph and interpret linear and/or quadratic equations onto a coordinate grid; translate information from word problems into equations or expressions; and use proportional reasoning to solve problems in arithmetic, algebra, and geometry.

Proportional Reasoning

Proportional reasoning is often seen on the CSET, as in the problem below, or in a word problem dealing with fractions or mixed numbers, such as in a cooking recipe. Setting up your proportion correctly is the key to success. Keep the same respective quantities on the left and right sides of the proportion, for example: sugar to flour = sugar to flour. From there, cross-multiply and then divide by the coefficient to get your answer in its single, positive form of the variable (i.e., $1x = 3$ or $1a = 7$, not $5x = 15$ or $2a = 14$).

Test Yourself

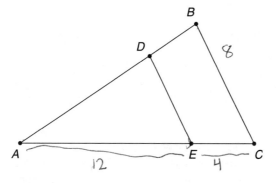

Given:

$\triangle ABC$ and $\triangle ADE$ are similar triangles

$\overline{AE} = 12$ $\overline{DE} = ?$

$\overline{EC} = 4$ $\overline{BC} = 8$

What is the length of $\overline{DE}$?

(A) 8

(B) 6

(C) 5

(D) 6.5

To complete this problem, proportional reasoning is a helpful strategy. Remember that a proportion is a comparison of two ratios. Proportional reasoning compares corresponding parts of both triangles to each other. See below:

$\left(\dfrac{AC}{BC}\right) = \left(\dfrac{AE}{DE}\right)$

$\left(\dfrac{16}{8}\right) = \left(\dfrac{12}{x}\right)$

$16x = 96$ (cross-multiply)

$x = 6$ (divide by the coefficient to find x)

Choice **(B)** is the correct answer.

Equivalent Expressions for Equalities and Inequalities and Representing Them on Graphs

Test Yourself

What is an equivalent expression for $-2x^2(4x + 5) + 12$?

(A) $-8x^3 - 10x^2 + 12$

(B) $8x^2 - 10x^2 + 12$

(C) $-6x^3 + 7x^2 + 12$

(D) $-8x^3 + 10x^2 + 12$

Remember that when distributing multiplication over addition, as in this problem, the $-2x^2$ is multiplied by both of the terms in parentheses. The $+12$ is not multiplied by $-2x^2$. It is simply added onto the end of the expression. $-2x^2(4x) = -8x^3$ and $-2x^2(5) = -10x^2$. Since adding a negative number is the same as subtracting its opposite, adding $-10x^2$ is the same as subtracting $10x^2$, this expression can be written as $-8x^3 - 10x^2 + 12$. Choice **(A)** is the correct answer.

The CSET will test your knowledge of how to evaluate expressions correctly. An expression in mathematics is made up of coefficients, variables, numbers, and operations. It expresses a value in mathematical form, but sometimes it is a bit messy and needs to be simplified (evaluated). The expression will probably have several terms to evaluate. Remember the hierarchy of the order of operations and evaluating from left to right. Let's also review the parts of an expression and the steps to simplifying it.

Example of a 4-term expression:

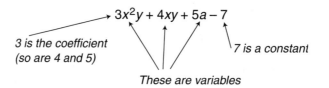

$3x^2y + 4xy + 5a - 7$

3 is the coefficient (so are 4 and 5)

7 is a constant

These are variables

Steps to simplifying an expression:

1. Perform all operations within parentheses.

2. Perform all exponential operations (includes roots).

3. Perform all multiplication and division operations from left to right.

4. Perform all addition and subtraction operations from left to right.

5. Combine like terms.

6. Reorder by placing terms with the largest exponents first.

Now let's try it!

$42 + 7y^2 - (2a^2 \times 4a^2) + 2(y^2 - 10)$ (Given expression)

$42 + 7y^2 - 8a^4 + 2y^2 - 20$ (Steps 1, 2, and 3)

$22 + 9y^2 - 8a^4$ (Step 5)

$-8a^4 + 9y^2 + 22$ (Step 6)

This evaluation of expressions can be of value when applied to both sides of an equation. An equation is a mathematical statement that compares two expressions and/or values to one another on each side of the equals sign (=). For example, $4x^2 - x + 6 = 2x^2 - 15x - 8$ is the same as $2x^2 + 14x = -14$. Here's how you know:

$4x^2 - x + 6 = 2x^2 - 15x - 8$

$-2x^2 \qquad\qquad -2x^2$ (move the variables to the left)

$2x^2 - x + 6 = -15x - 8$

$+15x \qquad\quad +15x$ (move the variables to the left)

$2x^2 + 14x + 6 = -8$

$\qquad\qquad\quad -6 \quad -6$ (move the constants to the left)

$2x^2 + 14x = -14$ (This is the given equation in its simplest form). That means it is equivalent to $4x^2 - x + 6 = 2x^2 - 15x - 8$.

When working with inequalities, it is important to remember when to flip the inequality sign. This occurs only when multiplying or dividing each side by a negative number. Addition or subtraction of terms from each side of an inequality does not change the direction of the inequality sign.

It is also important to remember that when solving for a variable, it should be expressed in its positive, singular form. So to solve for x in the equation $-3x + 3 \geq 12$, the answer would be $x \leq 3$. Here's how to solve for x:

$-3x + 3 \geq 12$

$\qquad -3 \quad -3$ (add -3 to both sides)

$-3x \geq 9$

After this, divide both sides of the inequality by -3 and also flip the inequality sign the other direction in order to express x in its single, positive form.

$x \leq -3$ is the value of x and is given in its simplest form. That means it is equivalent to $-3x + 3 \geq 12$.

Linear Equations and Their Properties

Test Yourself

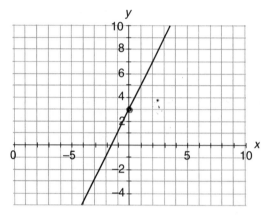

Find the linear equation shown on the coordinate graph above.

(A) $y = 2x + 3$

(B) $y = x + 3$

(C) $y = 2x - 1.5$

(D) $y = 2x - 3$

When looking for the linear equation shown here, remember the standard form for linear equations ($y = mx + b$) and pay close attention to where the line crosses the y-axis; it tells you the b term also known as the y-intercept. m is the slope, which in this case is positive, or sloping upward when moving along the x-axis from left to right. When examining the change from two points on the line, say $(-1,1)$ and $(0,3)$, there is a "rise" of two units along the y-axis, and a "run" of one unit along the x-axis. The slope formula could have also proved useful. It is a ratio that compares the change in y and the change in x from one set of coordinates to another. The formula is expressed as: rise over run $= y_2 - y_1$ over $x_2 - x_1$. The slope therefore is $\frac{2}{1}$ (rise over run) and the y-intercept (b) is 3, so the equation for this linear equation can be written as $y = 2x + 3$. Choice **(A)** is correct.

A basic understanding of linear equations and their properties is part of the CSET content domains. This content is seen in fifth-grade math textbooks that are aligned to California's current math standards. Let's first look at what the phrase "linear equation" means. "Linear" has to do with lines and "equation" has to do with comparing numbers (constants and/or variables) and operations via an "equals" sign. So, linear equations are equations that make lines when graphed onto a coordinate grid. By now, the steps to solving equations are probably already familiar to you. The trick is to understand how *solving* an equation can be translated to *graphing* the equation onto a coordinate grid. This translation takes place through an interpreter—charting points onto an *XY* table, when given the linear equation. It looks like this (notice how three points are chosen to substitute into the equation):

X	Y
1	
0	
−1	

The standard form for a linear equation is $y = mx + b$, where y is the variable representing the vertical axis, x is the horizontal axis, m is the slope (rise over run), and b is the y-intercept (or where the line meets the y-axis). When you think about it, a slope is just like the one many people ski on in the winter or hike up and down in the spring, summer, and fall. As you walk in the direction you're going, you are moving along an "x-axis" and since you are increasing or decreasing in altitude as you ascend or descend, you are moving along the "y-axis" too. This combination of horizontal and vertical movement up or down is known as *slope*. Slopes can be positive (ascending) or negative (descending). On a coordinate grid, a positive slope moves up and to the right, while a negative slope moves up and to the left.

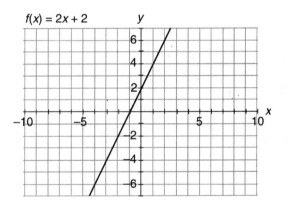

This is a linear equation representing a *positive slope*. The formula for this is shown at the top left. $f(x)$ means the function of x and often times is used in place of y. Recalling the standard form of linear equations, the equation $y = 2x + 2$, has a positive 2 as the m which means a positive 2 rise over positive 1 run (2 up and 1 to the right).

KAPLAN

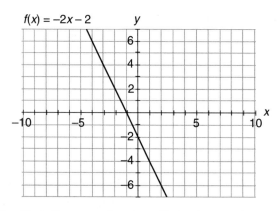

This is a linear equation illustrating a *negative slope*. Notice the equation $y = -2x - 2$. The m in $y = mx + b$ is -2 (a negative slope), which is equal to $-\frac{2}{1}$ or -2 rise over $+1$ run (meaning down "2" and to the right "1").

If an equation is not given in standard form, use algebraic rules to put it into that form. For example, $-3x = -y + 2$ would be equivalent to $y = 3x + 2$. That way, the slope and y-intercept can more clearly be seen.

Systems of Equations

Test Yourself

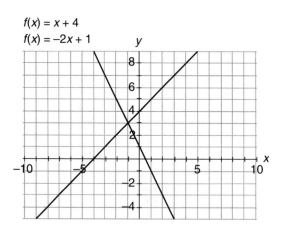

This system of equations is considered to be

(A) consistent

(B) inconsistent

(C) dependent

(D) independent

This question tests your knowledge of the math vocabulary used when describing systems of equations. A *consistent* system of equations has only one solution or one point where the two linear equations intersect. An *inconsistent* system shares no solution, meaning they never intersect. A *dependent* system shares an infinite number of solutions since they are equivalent equations and the same lines. An independent system of equations would be an invalid response. Choice **(A)** is the correct answer.

A system of equations is a comparison of two linear equations. Its purpose is to determine whether or not the two lines (linear equations graphed onto a coordinate grid) will meet. You can visualize this in three different ways: an intersection of two lines, a pair of parallel lines, or the same line that uses equivalent equations. When these lines intersect (and there is a common set of coordinates), this is called a *consistent system* of equations. An equation that exemplifies this is $y = x + 4$ and $y = 5x + 4$; notice, in this case, how they share the same y-intercept.

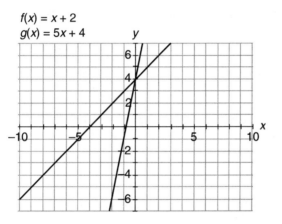

If the lines are parallel and there are no common coordinates, the system of equations is said to be *inconsistent*. An example of this is $y = 2x + 1$ and $y = 2x + 4$; they have the same slope, but different y-intercepts.

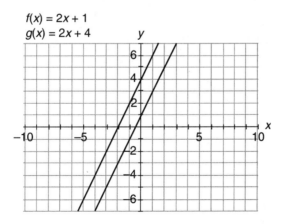

KAPLAN

A *dependent system* of equations exists when two equations have the exact same solution set every time, because they are equivalent. For example, you might think that $x - \frac{1}{2}y = 2$ is not the same as $y = 2x - 4$, but when you find the solutions for both x and y you will see that they are simply two different ways to say the same thing. It's like saying that $19 - (3 \times 5) = 4$ or $19 = (3 \times 5) + 4$; they're equivalent. In fact, you could prove that the two equations are equivalent and when graphed will be part of the same line. Since they are equivalent, their solutions are the same; and therefore, when the two equations are graphed, they make up the same line.

$$x - \frac{1}{2}y = 2$$

$$-x \quad -x \qquad\qquad\qquad \text{(subtract "}x\text{" from both sides)}$$

$$-\frac{1}{2}y = 2 - x$$

$$-2\left(-\frac{1}{2}y\right) = (2)(-2) - x(-2) \quad \text{(Multiply each term by "}-2\text{")}$$

$$y = 2x - 4 \qquad\qquad\qquad \text{(Put in the } y = mx + b \text{ form)}$$

Therefore, we've proved algebraically that $y = 2x - 4$ is equivalent to $x - \frac{1}{2}y = 2$

Since the two equations are equal and share the same solution set for x and y, they will make the same line when graphed.

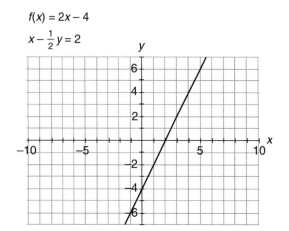

$f(x) = 2x - 4$

$x - \frac{1}{2}y = 2$

Multiplication, Division, and Factoring of Polynomials

The CSET may require you to perform operations on polynomials. *Polynomials* are algebraic expressions containing more than one term (hence the prefix "poly"). Multiplying polynomials is very similar to multiplying constants. For example, $x(x^2 + 3x - 2)$ is like multiplying $5(400 + 30 - 5)$. x is multiplied by each of the three terms in the trinomial, while 5 is multiplied by each of the three terms in parentheses. So, you get $x^3 + 3x^2 - 2x$ for the first expression and $2,000 + 150 - 25$ for the second expression. The first expression is written in simplest form—that's as far as you can go; but the second expression uses constants in all three terms, so they can be combined to get 2,125. When multiplying a trinomial and a binomial, the steps are slightly more complicated but are essentially the same.

Test Yourself

Evaluate the following expression:

$$\frac{x^5 - x^3}{x^2 - 3x + 2}$$

(A) $\dfrac{x^2(x + 1)}{x - 2}$

(B) $\dfrac{x^3(x + 1)}{x - 2}$

(C) $\dfrac{x^3(x^2 + 1)}{(x - 2)(x - 1)}$

(D) $\dfrac{x(x + 1)}{x - 2}$

Evaluating an expression means to simplify to lowest terms. To do this, be prepared to divide, multiply, and/or factor the expression in order to simplify it.

$\dfrac{x^5 - x^3}{x^2 - 3x + 2}$ — Rewrite the original problem.

$= \dfrac{x^3(x^2 - 1)}{(x - 2)(x - 1)}$ — The numerator term has x^3 factored out of both terms. The denominator term has been factored to its two binomials.

$= \dfrac{x^3(x + 1)(x - 1)}{(x - 2)(x - 1)}$ — The numerator term has been factored to its two binomials. The denominator term stays the same.

$= \dfrac{x^3(x + 1)}{(x - 2)}$ — Both $(x - 1)$ terms in the numerator and denominator simplify to 1 and need not remain in the expression. This is the same expression in simplest form.

Choice **(B)** is the correct answer.

Dividing polynomials works in a similar way. For example, let's compare $(4x^3 + 6x^2 - 2x \div 2x)$ and $(1{,}500 + 300 - 30) \div 30$. The first expression factors $2x$ from each term, and the second expression factors 30 from each term. Notice how factoring and dividing are the same, since multiplication and division are inverse operations. The first expression simplifies to $2x^2 + 3x - 1$, while the second expression simplifies to $50 + 10 - 1$. Again, in the second expression, like terms can be combined to equal 59.

Graphing and Solving Quadratic Equations

The standard form of a quadratic equation is $ax^2 + bx + c = 0$. Notice that the greatest exponent on x is 2 and the right side of the equation is equal to zero. When graphed, a quadratic equation will form a parabola that opens up or down, but never sideways.

To solve a quadratic equation, you can either factor the equation (using the FOIL method, to be explained shortly) or you can use the quadratic formula. Factoring doesn't work for all quadratic equations, but using the quadratic formula does. That's probably why we had to memorize it back when we took algebra in junior high or high school. In any case, these methods work to solve for the x term in the quadratic equation. This x value is where the parabola will cross the x-axis on a coordinate grid when it is graphed.

First, let's look at a few prerequisite skills used in factoring quadratic equations. A binomial is an expression that contains two terms (hence the prefix *bi*) in which each exponent that appears on a variable is a whole number.

Examples of binomials: $x + 2$, $2x + 5$, $x - 7$, or $3x - 4$.

FOIL stands for First, Outer, Inner, and Last terms in the multiplication of two binomials.

$$(a + b)(c + d) = \underset{\text{First}}{ac} + \underset{\text{Outer}}{ad} + \underset{\text{Inner}}{bc} + \underset{\text{Last}}{bd} \text{ is the common formula.}$$

Let's try it with constants and variables:

Example #1

$(x + 2)(x + 3) = x^2 + 3x + 2x + 6$ (then combine like terms)

$= x^2 + 5x + 6$ (a *trinomial*, an expression with three terms, is formed)

Example #2

$(2x + 4)(x + 2) = 2x^2 + 4x + 4x + 8$ (then combine like terms)

$= 2x^2 + 8x + 8$ (a trinomial is formed)

Example #3

$(x - 2)(x - 3) = x^2 + -3x + -2x + 6$ (then combine like terms)

$= x^2 - 5x + 6$ (a trinomial is formed)

Example #4

$(2x + 3)(3x - 4) = 6x^2 + -8x + 9x + -12$ (then combine like terms)

$= 6x^2 + x + -12$ or $6x^2 + x - 12$ (a trinomial is formed)

Now that you've seen what a binomial is and how to apply FOIL to make a trinomial, let's look back at the standard form of a quadratic equation: $ax^2 + bx + c = 0$

Notice that the expression on the left side of the equation is a trinomial. We've just created trinomials by multiplying binomials together using FOIL, so now we can factor trinomials to get two binomials. Since the product of two binomials is a trinomial, the binomials are the trinomial's factors. To factor an expression means to write the expression as the product of its factors. 6 is the product of 2×3, just as $6x^2 + x - 12$ is the product of $(2x + 3) \times (3x - 4)$. 2 and 3 are the factors of 6, just as $(2x + 3)$ and $(3x - 4)$ are the factors of $6x^2 + x - 12$.

Example #1:

$x^2 + 6x + 8 = ($ ___ $+$ ___ $)($ ___ $+$ ___ $)$

Think the inverse of FOIL. You might guess that the first terms in each binomials have to be x since $x^2 = x \times x$.

So we have: $(x +$ ___ $)(x +$ ___ $)$

To find the second terms of each binomial, let's look at the coefficient of the second term and the third term, 6 and 8 respectively. Think of two numbers whose product is 8 (the third term in the trinomial) and whose sum is 6 (the coefficient of the second term in the trinomial). To do this, let's list the factors of 8:

Factors of 8   Sum of Factors is 6

1 and 8 $1 + 8 = 9$

2 and 4 $2 + 4 = 6$ (This works!)

$x^2 + 6x + 8$ can be factored as $(x + 2)(x + 4)$.

KAPLAN

Example #2:

$x^2 - 2x - 8 = (x + \underline{})(x + \underline{})$

Think of two numbers whose product is 8 (the third term in the trinomial) and whose sum is -2 (the coefficient of the second term in the trinomial).

Factors of -8	Sum of Factors is -2
-1 and 8	$-1 + 8 = 7$
1 and -8	$1 + -8 = -7$
-2 and 4	$-2 + 4 = 2$
2 and -4	$2 + -4 = -2$ (That works!)

$x^2 - 2x - 8$ can be factored as $(x + 2)(x - 4)$.

Example #3:

$5x^2 + 12x + 4 = (5x + \underline{})\,(x + \underline{})$

Since the first terms are multiplied in the FOIL method to get the first term in the trinomial, we must look at the factors of 5: 1 and 5. Then we put them into the first terms of the binomials.

Now things change slightly. Look for the factors of the third term in the trinomial, 4. They are 1 and 4, -1 and -4, 2 and 2, and -2 and -2. Now write these into the table along with the first terms of the binomials, in this case $5x$ and x. Remember that the middle term of the trinomial is derived from adding the product of the outer and inner terms in the FOIL method.

Possible Factors	Sum of Products of Outer and Inner Terms is $12x$
$(5x + 1)(x + 4)$	$20x + 1x = 21x$
$(5x + -1)(x + -4)$	$-20x + -1x = -21x$
$(5x + 2)(x + 2)$	$10x + 2x = 12x$ (That works!)
$(5x + -2)(x + -2)$	$-10x - 2x = -12x$

$5x^2 + 12x + 4$ can be factored as $(5x + 2)(x + 2)$.

Example #4:

$6x^2 - 11x - 10 = (\_x + \_\_\_)(\_x + \_\_\_)$

The factors of positive 6 (in $6x^2$) are 1 and 6 or 2 and 3. When there is more than one set of factors for the first term of the binomials, use the medium-sized factors first. In this case, use 2 and 3. $(2x + \_\_\_)(3x + \_\_\_)$.

Now think of the factors of -10, since in the trinomial minus 10 is the same as adding negative 10. Then write them in a table, along with the first terms of the binomials.

Possible Factors	Sum of the Outer and Inner Terms is $-11x$
$(2x + 1)(3x + -10)$	$-20x + 3x = -17x$
$(2x + -1)(3x + 10)$	$20x + -3x = 17x$
$(2x + 10)(3x + -1)$	$-2x + 30x = 28x$
$(2x + -10)(3x + 1)$	$2x + -30x = -28x$
$(2x + 2)(3x + -5)$	$-10x + 6x = -4x$
$(2x + -2)(3x + 5)$	$10x + -6x = 4x$
$(2x + 5)(3x + -2)$	$-4x + 15x = 11x$
$(2x + -5)(3x + 2)$	$4x + -15x = -11x$ (That works!)

$6x^2 - 11x - 10$ can be factored as $(2x - 5)(3x + 2)$.

Okay, we're done with the prerequisite knowledge involved in factoring quadratic equations. Now, let's apply this to the actual work at hand. Remember that the standard form of a quadratic equation states that $ax^2 + bx + c = 0$. You've already learned how to identify the factors of a trinomial.

Here's where knowing how to factor trinomials helps us utilize the *Zero-Factor Property*. The Zero-Factor Property states that if the product of two factors is 0 (as is the case with the standard form of quadratic equations) then one (or both) of the factors must be equal to 0. It should be noted that, for the purposes of graphing the quadratic equations as parabolas, the Zero-Factor Property helps us determine where these parabolas will cross the *x*-axis. Now, back to the Zero-Factor Property. It states that if $a \times b = 0$, then it can be concluded that $a = 0$ or $b = 0$. To better understand this concept, let's try using constant numbers. If $a = 5$ and $b = 0$, then $(5) \times (0) = 0$. This is essentially what the Zero-Factor Property is stating. It's something we already understand when working with constants.

So, after factoring the trinomial into its two binomial factors we can set each of these binomial factors equal to zero.

Example #1:

$x^2 + 5x + 6 = 0$ is the same as $(x + 2)(x + 3) = 0$.

Using the zero-factor property, either $(x + 2)$ or $(x + 3)$ must equal 0 for the product to be equal to 0. Thus, we can write each individual factor as being equal to zero.

$$x + 2 = 0 \quad x + 3 = 0$$
$$x = -2 \quad x = -3$$

The solutions are -2 and -3.

We can check to make sure this works in the quadratic equation.

$$x = -2 \qquad\qquad x = -3$$
$$(x + 2)\,(x + 3) = 0 \qquad (x + 2)\,(x + 3) = 0$$
$$(-2 + 2)\,(-2 + 3) = 0 \quad (-3 + 2)\,(-3 + 3) = 0$$
$$(0)\,(1) = 0 \qquad\qquad (-1)\,(0) = 0$$

These solutions are proven to work for this quadratic equation.

Example #2:

$-2x^2 + 3x + 4 = 0$ cannot be factored, so we'll need to use the quadratic formula.

Steps to Solve a Quadratic Equation by Factoring

1. Make sure the quadratic equation is written in standard form: $ax^2 + bx + c = 0$.
2. Factor the trinomial.
3. Use the zero-factor property to solve the equation.

As you can see from Example #2, not all quadratic equations can be solved by the factoring method, so there is another viable option…the quadratic formula! The quadratic formula can be used to solve any quadratic equation. To use the quadratic formula, make sure the quadratic equation is written in standard form. Here's the formula:

Quadratic Formula

For a quadratic equation in standard form, $ax^2 + bx + c = 0$, where a is not equal to zero, the quadratic formula is:

$$x = \frac{-b \pm \sqrt{b^2 - 4ac}}{2a}$$

Let's solve the equation $x^2 + 5x + 6 = 0$ using the quadratic formula:

$$x = \frac{-b \pm \sqrt{b^2 - 4ac}}{2a}$$

$$x = \frac{-5 \pm \sqrt{5^2 - 4(1)(6)}}{2(1)}$$

$$x = \frac{-5 \pm \sqrt{25 - 24}}{2}$$

$$x = \frac{-5 \pm \sqrt{1}}{2}$$

$$x = \frac{-5 \pm 1}{2}$$

$$x = -\frac{4}{2} = -2 \text{ or } x = -\frac{6}{2} = -3$$

The solutions for x are -2 and -3.

Okay, now that we've gone over how to solve quadratic equations, it's time to graph them. Remember that, while linear equations make lines when graphed, quadratic equations make parabolas. These parabolas open either up or down. Just as the standard form of the linear equation, $y = mx + b$, revealed the slope and the y-intercept, the standard form of the quadratic equations reveals aspects of the parabola it graphs. By looking at the coefficient of the x^2 term (a in ax^2) you can determine whether the parabola will open upward or downward. It will open upward if the coefficient of the x^2 term is greater than 0 and it opens downward if that coefficient is less than 0.

Every parabola is symmetrical with respect to a vertical line that can be drawn through its vertex. This line of symmetry on the vertex of the parabola is called the axis of symmetry of the parabola. The x-coordinate (horizontal position on a coordinate grid) of the vertex can be found using this formula:

Formula for the Axis of Symmetry of a Parabola

$$x = \frac{-b}{2a}$$

Once the x-coordinate (horizontal position) of the vertex is found, you're half done. Now, you have to find the y-coordinate (vertical position of a coordinate grid). That's because to plot a point, like the vertex, you'll need an x and a y coordinate. To find the y-coordinate, substitute the value of the x-coordinate into the standard form of the quadratic equation.

Example #1

$$x^2 + 5x + 6 = 0$$

Formula for the Axis of Symmetry for a Parabola: $x = \frac{-b}{2a}$

$$x = \frac{-5}{2(1)}$$

$$x = \frac{-5}{2}$$

KAPLAN

Now let's find the y-coordinate by substituting the value of the x-coordinate in the quadratic equation.

$$y = x^2 + 5x + 6$$

$$y = \left(\frac{-5}{2}\right)^2 + 5\left(\frac{-5}{2}\right) + 6$$

$$y = \frac{25}{4} + \frac{-25}{2} + 6$$

$$y = \frac{25}{4} + \frac{-50}{4} + \frac{24}{4}$$

$$y = \frac{-1}{4}$$

The coordinates of the vertex of the parabola is $\left(\frac{-5}{2}, \frac{-1}{4}\right)$

Here are the steps to graphing a quadratic equation.

1. Determine whether the parabola opens upward or downward.
2. Use the Axis of Symmetry formula to find x.
3. Substitute the x-coordinate into the equation to find the y-coordinate, hence the vertex of the parabola.
4. Determine the y-intercept by substituting $x = 0$ into the standard form of the quadratic equation.
5. Determine the x-intercepts (if there are any) by substituting $y = 0$ into the standard form of the quadratic equation and solving for x.
6. Making use of the information from steps 1–5, draw the graph. Remember the parabola will be symmetric with respect to the vertical axis of symmetry.

Example #1

$$y = x^2 + 5x + 6$$

1. $a = 1$, which is greater than 0; so the parabola will open upwards.

2./3. We solved the axis of symmetry, using the formula $\frac{-b}{2a}$ above, and got the vertex coordinates of $\left(\frac{-5}{2}, \frac{-1}{4}\right)$.

4. To find the y-intercept, substitute $x = 0$ into the equation

$$y = (0)^2 + 5(0) + 6$$

$y = 6$, meaning the y intercept is 6; the coordinates are (0,6).

5. We've already found the x-intercept above, using the Zero Property, and got $x = -2$ and $x = -3$, thus the x-intercepts are at $(-2, 0)$ and $(-3, 0)$.

6. The graph for $x^2 + 5x + 6$ looks like this:

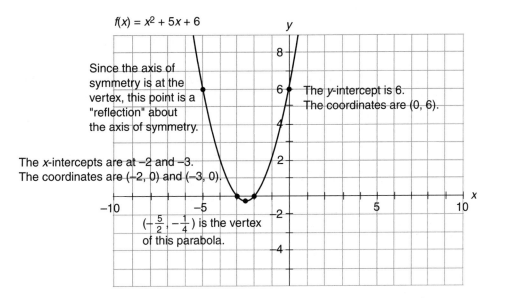

Since the axis of symmetry is at the vertex, this point is a "reflection" about the axis of symmetry.

$f(x) = x^2 + 5x + 6$

The y-intercept is 6. The coordinates are (0, 6).

The x-intercepts are at -2 and -3. The coordinates are $(-2, 0)$ and $(-3, 0)$.

$(-\frac{5}{2}, -\frac{1}{4})$ is the vertex of this parabola.

Example #2: $y = -2x^2 + 3x + 4$

1. $a = -2$, which is less than 0, so this parabola opens downward.

2./3. The axis of symmetry formula is $x = -\frac{b}{2a}$.

$$x = -\frac{3}{2(-2)}$$

$$x = -\frac{3}{-4}$$

$$x = \frac{3}{4}$$

Substitute in the equation to solve for the y-coordinate of the vertex:

$$y = -2x^2 + 3x + 4$$
$$y = -2\left(\frac{3}{4}\right)^2 + 3\left(\frac{3}{4}\right) + 4$$
$$y = -\frac{18}{16} + \frac{9}{4} + 4$$
$$y = 5\frac{1}{8}$$

The coordinates of the vertex are $\left(\frac{3}{4}, 5\frac{1}{8}\right)$.

4. To find the y-intercept, substitute $x = 0$ into the equation.

$y = -2(0)^2 + 3(0) + 4$

$y = 4$, meaning the y-intercept is 4; the coordinates are (0, 4)

5. To find the x-intercepts, use the Zero-Factor Property by the factoring method or quadratic formula. Since this equation cannot be factored, we'll use the quadratic formula.

$-2x^2 + 3x + 4$

$$x = \frac{-b \pm \sqrt{b^2 - 4ac}}{2a}$$

$$x = \frac{-3 \pm \sqrt{3^2 - 4(-2)(4)}}{2(-2)}$$

$$x = \frac{-3 \pm \sqrt{9 - (-32)}}{-4}$$

$$x = \frac{-3 \pm \sqrt{9 + 32}}{-4}$$

$$x = \frac{-3 \pm \sqrt{41}}{-4}$$

Since $\sqrt{41} \approx 6.4$,

$$x \approx \frac{-3 + 6.4}{-4} \approx \frac{3.4}{-4} \approx -0.85 \text{ or } x \approx \frac{-3 - 6.4}{-4} \approx \frac{-9.4}{-4} \approx 2.35$$

Therefore, the x-intercepts are -0.85 and 2.35, thus the x-intercepts are at $(-0.85, 0)$ and $(2.35, 0)$.

6. The graph for $-2x^2 + 3x + 4$ looks like this:

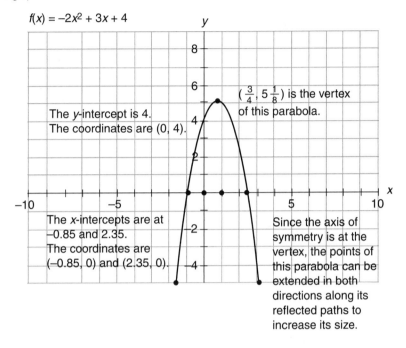

$f(x) = -2x^2 + 3x + 4$

The y-intercept is 4.
The coordinates are (0, 4).

$(\frac{3}{4}, 5\frac{1}{8})$ is the vertex of this parabola.

The x-intercepts are at −0.85 and 2.35.
The coordinates are (−0.85, 0) and (2.35, 0).

Since the axis of symmetry is at the vertex, the points of this parabola can be extended in both directions along its reflected paths to increase its size.

MEASUREMENT AND GEOMETRY

This section of the CSET tests your knowledge of upper elementary mathematics. The content coincides with the level of mathematics taught in the upper elementary and middle school grades. Showing proficiency with these skills is used as an indicator of your ability to teach measure and geometry concepts to your students. As you review the material in this section, take note of any areas needing further study. Upper grade (fourth through eighth grade) math texts and/or a math book geared for teaching elementary mathematics are recommended tools for further study, as are websites with practice problems in those areas.

Two- and Three-Dimensional Geometric Objects

Characteristics of Common Two- and Three-Dimensional Figures

Two-dimensional objects are flat and are also known as plane figures. Polygons (a variety of which are commonly used on the CSET) are two-dimensional, closed figures having three or more sides composed of only straight lines. They are named according to the number of sides they have. Examples of polygons include triangles, quadrilaterals, pentagons, and hexagons. Polygons can be regular or irregular. Regular polygons have equal sides, while irregular ones do not. Quadrilaterals include trapezoids, parallelograms, rhombi, rectangles, and squares. Other common two-dimensional figures include circles and parts of circles. Their areas and perimeters can be calculated by measuring their dimensions, and you must know the formulas for doing so.

Three-dimensional objects add the third dimension of depth or height to an object. With this, volume (the space that an object occupies) and surface area (the area of the object's faces) can also be calculated using formulas that you must be familiar with. Polyhedrons are also commonly found on the CSET. Polyhedrons are three-dimensional figures in which each face is a polygon, such as prisms and pyramids. Prisms have congruent and parallel bases. A pyramid has only one base, and its sides merge to a single point opposite the base. Both types of polyhedrons are named according to their bases. Other types of three-dimensional objects are cylinders, cones, and spheres.

Test Yourself

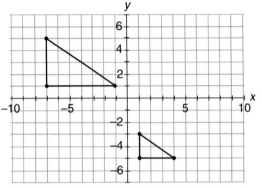

Which statement is true about these triangles?

(A) The two triangles are not proportionately similar.

(B) The two triangles are congruent.

(C) The two triangles are similar.

(D) The two triangles do not have the same proportionate area.

An understanding of the congruence and similarity of geometric figures is important to successfully answering this question. The two triangles are proportionately similar. The length of their sides are 4 : 6 and 2 : 3 (large triangle : small triangle). This makes the triangles similar to each other. They share the same angle measures because their corresponding sides are proportionate in length. To be congruent **(B)**, the triangles would have to be the same size, as well as have identical angle measures. Choice **(C)** is the correct answer.

Congruence, Similarity, or Lack Thereof

Test Yourself

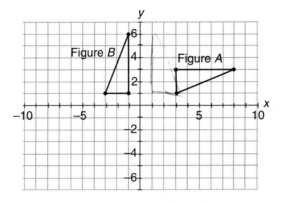

To go from Figure *A* to Figure *B*, what two movements occurred?

(A) a reflection and then a translation

(B) a translation and then a reflection

(C) a rotation, then a reflection

(D) a rotation and then a translation

To answer this question, the concepts of *translation* (sliding an object along an axis), *rotation* (turning an object about a point), and *reflection* (flipping an object about an axis) need to be understood. From Figure *A*, the triangle could have been rotated or turned 90-degrees counterclockwise, then reflected or flipped over the *y*-axis to be in the position of Figure *B*. See below.

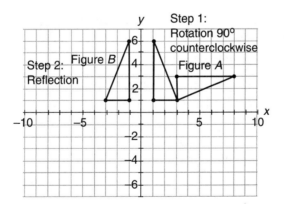

Choice **(C)** is the correct answer.

The term *congruence* refers to two figures having the same size and shape. Notice, on the following coordinate grid, the triangles' corresponding sides have equal lengths and thus their angles have equal measures. They share a 1 : 1 ratio of similarity.

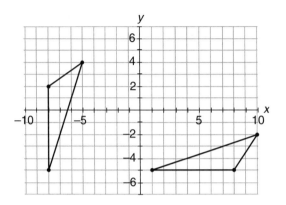

Similar figures share equal angle measures, but have sides of different lengths. Proportional reasoning is used to compare similar figures, such as similar triangles. Notice the lengths of each side in the two triangles below share a 2 : 1 ratio.

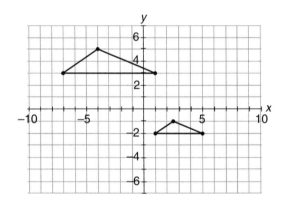

The triangles below do not share a proportional relationship in the length of their sides or in their angle measures. They are neither similar nor congruent, although they are both scalene triangles.

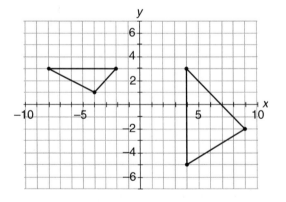

To prove the lack of congruency or similarity between two figures may require the use of proportional reasoning, understanding of the properties of parallel lines and corresponding angle measures, and/or knowledge of symmetry and how objects may appear to be different, but be congruent or similar. The following sections explain these aspects of geometry.

Identify Different Forms of Symmetry

The CSET deals with two forms of symmetry: line symmetry and rotational symmetry. *Line symmetry* is a property shown by a figure if, when reflected on line or folded, the two halves of that figure are congruent.

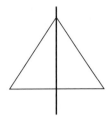

Line Symmetry

To understand line symmetry, you need to become familiar with three important concepts: translation, rotation, and reflection. Translating a figure is essentially sliding it. In fact, some math textbooks refer to this process as a *slide*. A rotation is turning a figure about a point and is commonly referred to as a *turn*. 90-degree turns clockwise and counterclockwise are common examples. A reflection is flipping a figure about an axis. It's akin to an "about face" direction given to a marching band or a group of soldiers.

Translation (Slide)

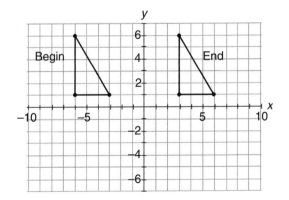

Rotation (Turn)

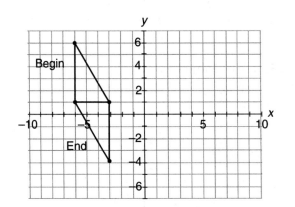

Reflection (Flip)

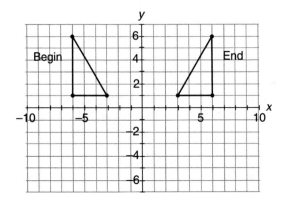

Rotational symmetry is a property possessed by a figure that, when it is pivoted less than 360° about a central point, still matches the original figure.

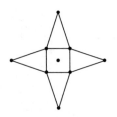

Rotational Symmetry

The Pythagorean Theorem and Its Converse

Test Yourself

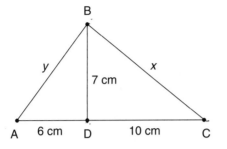

$\angle BDC$ and $\angle ADB$ are right angles. What are the lengths of x and y?

(A) $x = 12.2$ cm; $y = 9.2$ cm

(B) $x = 12$ cm; $y = 8$ cm

(C) $x = 11$ cm; $y = 8$ cm

(D) $x = 9.2$; $y = 12.2$ cm

To answer this problem, knowledge of the Pythagorean Theorem is crucial. This theorem states that $a^2 + b^2 = c^2$. Therefore substituting the values for a and b will yield the values of x and y.

To solve for x: $10^2 + 7^2 = x^2$

$$100 + 49 = x^2$$

$$149 = x^2 \text{ (to undo the exponent, take its root)}$$

$$12.206555 \text{ cm} = x$$

$$12.2 \text{ cm} \approx x$$

To solve for y: $6^2 + 7^2 = y^2$

$$36 + 49 = y^2$$

$$85 = y^2 \text{ (to undo the exponent, take its root)}$$

$$9.2195444 \text{ cm} = y$$

$$9.2 \text{ cm} \approx y$$

Choice **(A)** is the correct answer.

The *Pythagorean theorem* states that the sum of the squares of the lengths of the legs of a right triangle is equal to the square of the length of the hypotenuse. Symbolically, its formula is written $a^2 + b^2 = c^2$. Remember that this formula only applies to right triangles.

The converse of the Pythagorean theorem states that if $a^2 + b^2 = c^2$ and the angle opposite c is unknown, then that angle is a right angle; since the Pythagorean theorem only works for right triangles.

Properties of Parallel Lines

Test Yourself

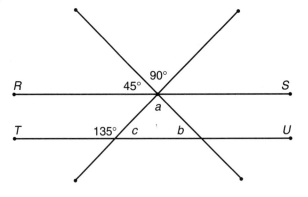

$\overline{RS}$ and $\overline{TU}$ are ‖ line segments.

Using what you know about the properties of parallel and intersecting lines, which statement is true?

(A) The measure of $\angle a$ is not 90°.

(B) $\angle b$ and $\angle a$ are supplementary angles.

(C) $\angle c$ and the adjacent, 135°-angle make complementary angles.

(D) $\angle b$ and $\angle c$ are congruent.

This question tests your knowledge of the property of parallel and intersecting lines and the angles measures they produce. $\angle a$ is in fact 90°, so **(A)** is incorrect. Supplementary angles are two angles equal to 180°, so **(B)** is also incorrect. Together, the adjacent angles mentioned in **(C)** are supplementary angles, not complementary ones, making **(C)** an incorrect choice. However, the measure of $\angle b$ and $\angle c$ is 45°; therefore they are congruent, making **(D)** the correct answer.

Parallel lines are lines that will never intersect. If another line crosses it, called a *transversal*, assumptions can be made regarding the measure of the angles created.

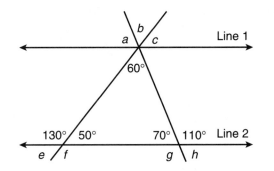

Since Line 1 and Line 2 are parallel, we can assume that

$\angle a + \angle b = 130°$

$\angle b + \angle c = 110°$

$\angle a = 70°$ and $\angle c = 50°$

Opposite angles are congruent: $\angle b = 60°$, $\angle e = 50°$, $\angle f = 130°$, $\angle g = 110°$, $\angle h = 70°$.

Congruent angles are angles having the same measure. $\angle e$ and the 50° angle are vertical angles. Therefore, they are congruent, meaning that both their angle measures are 50°.

The CSET test may include a diagram like the one above and ask you to infer the measurements of angles such as those found in said diagram. Therefore, it is important to draw upon what you know about transversals across parallel lines in order to perform well on the test.

Representational Systems, Including Concrete Models, Drawings, and Coordinate Geometry

Test Yourself

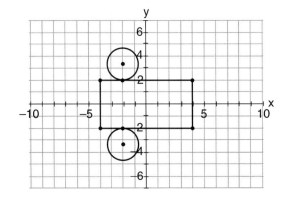

According to this coordinate grid, which statement is true?

(A) The cylinder, when formed, will stand parallel to the horizontal axis.

(B) The cylinder, when formed, will stand parallel to the vertical axis.

(C) A cylinder cannot be made from these two-dimensional shapes.

(D) None of the above

A cylinder can be made from this diagram. When the cylinder is formed, it will stand parallel to the vertical axis (the *y*-axis). Choice **(B)** is correct.

Concrete Representations of Geometric Objects

This section of the CSET asks you to be familiar with the construction of geometric objects and the various ways they may be represented. You should be familiar with drawings and diagrams, with or without using coordinate graphs, and you should be able to proficiently interpret them.

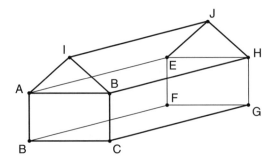

This diagram of a house is a pentagonal prism and is comprised of a rectangular prism and a triangular prism. Its volume can be calculated by dissecting it into the two types of prisms and then taking the area of the base in each prism and multiplying this value by the height (or in this case the length of the house). Parallel lines are seen on more than one plane. This figure has three planes total. In theory, a plane is a two-dimensional surface going off into two directions forever. It's like a table-top with no ends. Each end of this house can be seen as either a pentagon or a triangle and a rectangle. The vertices can be counted and angles can be measured, as can the lengths of the line segments. Mathematical attributes and calculations such as these are covered in this section of the CSET.

Representing Three-Dimensional Objects Through Two-Dimensional Drawings

Test Yourself

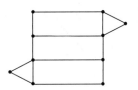

Name the three-dimensional object shown above.

(A) rectangular pyramid

(B) rectangular prism

(C) triangular pyramid

(D) triangular prism

This question tests your knowledge of the names of polyhedrons. Polyhedrons are three-dimensional shapes having only polygons for their faces. Because this shape has equal and opposite bases, it is classified as a prism. Prisms are named for their bases, so this is a triangular prism. Choice **(D)** is correct.

Visualizing three dimensions on paper requires seeing the flat, two-dimensional pattern that makes up an object. A cube, for example, is made from six squares; and a rectangular pyramid is made from a rectangle and four triangles. The CSET may ask you to identify the three-dimensional objects that a pattern makes, or it may ask you to determine which pattern will or will not make a three-dimensional object.

Two-dimensional pattern for a cube

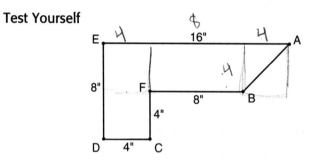

Two-dimensional pattern for
a rectangular pyramid

Test Yourself

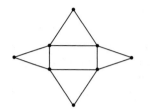

What is the area of the figure above?

(A) 72 in^2

(B) 56 in^2

(C) 128 in^2

(D) 64 in^2

To calculate the area of this figure, you must dissect it into smaller parts. One way this figure can be dissected is into a square, a rectangle, and a triangle.

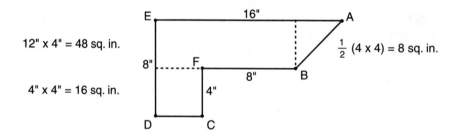

By adding these areas together, the total area of the figure can be calculated. It is 72 in². Therefore, **(A)** is correct.

Combining and Dissecting Two- and Three-Dimensional Figures into Familiar Shapes

The dissection of a parallelogram to rectangles of equal area is a prime example of this topic. Similarly, the area for a triangle and a parallelogram can be derived from the area of a rectangle.

It is understood that the area of a rectangle is found by multiplying the length and width.

Then, construct a parallelogram.

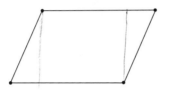

A triangular section is cut from the parallelogram and added to the other side.

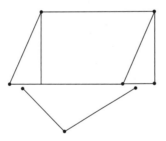

This, in turn, produces a rectangle with the same area as the parallelogram. Since the area is maintained, $A = b \times h$ for a parallelogram and $A = l \times w$ for a rectangle are proven to be the same.

Techniques, Tools, and Formulas for Determining Measurements

Test Yourself

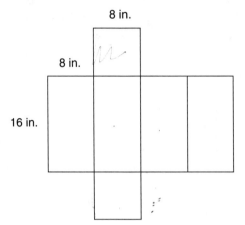

What is the surface area of the rectangular prism?

(A) 512 in^2

(B) 640 in^2

(C) 576 in^2

(D) 202 in^2

To find the surface area of a three-dimensional object, the area of each side must be determined. Notice how there are two sizes of sides in the four rectangles and two squares of the figure above. The rectangles' areas are 128 in^2 each and the squares' areas are 64 in^2 each.

128 in^2 × 4 sides = 512 in^2

64 in^2 × 2 sides = 128 in^2

Total surface area = 640 in^2

Choice **(B)** is correct.

Measuring Time, Length, Angles, Perimeter, Area, Surface Area, Volume, Weight/Mass, and Temperature Through Appropriate Units and Scales

Time

Time, as tested on the CSET, is often embedded in word problems requiring proportional reasoning.

Example:

If a machine makes 15 clicks per minute, how many clicks would you hear in 20 seconds?

To find the answer to this problem, you would first divide one minute into three 20-second intervals. Then you would divide the number of clicks per minute (15) by 3, which equals 5.

Some time problems require you to come up with appropriate algebraic equations.

Example:

Temperature in Fahrenheit = beeps per 15 seconds + 39.

1200 beeps per 30 minutes = what temperature?

To answer this question, convert 30 minutes to one-minute intervals, and then to 15-second intervals. Therefore, you divide by 30 to get one-minute intervals and divide by 4 to get 15-second intervals. So, 1,200 divided by 30 divided by 4 = 10. Add this to 39 and the temperature is 49 degrees Fahrenheit.

You may be asked to work with elapsed time.

Example:

It takes 25 minutes to bake a batch of biscuits. It is 1:30 P.M. If Janice has to leave for dance class at 4:45 P.M., how many batches of biscuits can she make?

First, determine the total amount of time allotted for baking: 3 hours 15 minutes, which is 195 minutes. 195 minutes divided by 25 minutes for each batch is 7.8 batches. Since only a whole number of batches can possibly be made, round down to 7 batches for your answer.

Time conversion problems may also be found on the CSET.

Example:

If Ray exercised for 2 hours, how many seconds did Ray exercise?

To compute this problem, convert hours to minutes, and then convert minutes to seconds. Mathematically, it would look like this:

2 hours × 60 minutes/hour × 60 seconds/minutes = 7,200 seconds. So 2 hours equals 7,200 seconds.

Length and Angle Measure

Problems involving length and angle measure require knowledge of geometry and algebra and the application of proportional reasoning. For example:

Example #1:

A right triangle has a hypotenuse of 20 cm and a base of 12 cm. What is its height?

Because this problem concerns a right triangle, use the Pythagorean Theorem ($a^2 + b^2 = c^2$) to find the solution. Substituting actual numbers, you have $12^2 + x^2 = 20^2$. The height of the right triangle is 16 cm.

Example #2:

Triangle *ABC* is an isosceles triangle. $\angle B$ has a measure of 110 degrees. What is the measure of $\angle A$?

To answer this problem, you'd have to recall that all triangles have a measure of 180 degrees, and isosceles triangles have two sides of the same length, meaning that their corresponding angles are congruent. (A quick sketch of this triangle may be helpful. Just be sure to make $\angle B$ about 110 degrees, an obtuse angle.) Subtracting 110 degrees from 180 degrees and dividing the difference by two will give you the measures of $\angle A$ and $\angle C$. Each angle is 35 degrees.

Perimeter, Area, and Volume

Perimeter, Area, and Volume calculations are applied to geometric figures.

Perimeter is measured in one dimension and is the one-dimensional or "linear" distance around a figure.

Area is measured in two dimensions with one dimension multiplied by another dimension to calculate the two-dimensional space taken up by the figure.

Volume is measured in three dimensions, each multiplied by the other, to calculate the three-dimensional space taken up by the object.

Here's a graphic organizer for conceptualizing perimeter, area, and volume:

	Dimensions	What it looks like
Perimeter	One dimension (linear units) units[1] just length	*(square diagram labeled "length")*
Area	Two dimensions (square units) units[2] length × width	*(square diagram labeled "width" and "length")*
Volume	Three dimensions (cubed units) units[3] length × width × height	*(cube diagram labeled "height", "width", and "length")*

Surface Area

Surface area is the two-dimensional measure of the faces of an object. A cube has six faces. To find its surface area, calculate the area of one of its faces and then multiply that number by 6.

Mass and Weight

Mass and weight are not the same. Mass is the amount of matter an object has, while weight is the measure of how much gravitational pull is acting on it. Even though mass and weight are not the same, they are proportionately related to each other on Earth. In other words, an object with greater weight also has a greater mass. Mass, in the metric system, is measured in grams, while, in our system of customary units, pounds are used. Weight and mass questions may require the use of proportional reasoning. The next example illustrates how weight can change depending on the pull of gravity.

Example:

The moon has $\frac{1}{6}$ the gravity of Earth. If you weigh 165 pounds on Earth, how much would you weigh on the moon?

To calculate this answer, set up a proportion:

$$\frac{x}{165} = \frac{1}{6}$$

$$6x = 165$$

x = 27.5 pounds on the moon

In the metric system, a connection can be made between mass and volume (capacity). A kilogram of water has a volume of exactly one liter, so 1 kg = 1 liter. (Capacity (volume) is measured in liters (metric units) or in ounces (customary units).)

Temperature

When converting units of temperature in Celsius and Fahrenheit, two formulas prove to be important: $C = \frac{5}{9}(F - 32)$ and $F = \frac{9}{5} \times C + 32$. In other words, to convert temperature in Fahrenheit to degrees Celsius, first subtract 32 then multiply by $\frac{5}{9}$. To convert temperature in Celsius to degrees Fahrenheit, multiply by $\frac{9}{5}$ then add 32.

212° F = 100° C　　　　　0° C = 32° F

Use the formula:　　　　Use the formula:

$C = \frac{5}{9}(F - 32)$　　　$F = \frac{9}{5}C + 32$

$C = \frac{5}{9}(212 - 32)$　　$F = \frac{9}{5}(0) + 32$

$C = \frac{5}{9}(180)$　　　　$F = 32°$

$C = \frac{5}{9} \times \frac{180}{1}$

$C = \frac{5}{1} \times \frac{20}{1}$

$C = \frac{100}{1} = 100°$

Metric and Customary Units

Test Yourself

3 millimeters are equivalent to

(A) $\dfrac{3}{1000}$ of a meter

(B) $\dfrac{3}{100}$ of a meter

(C) $\dfrac{3}{10}$ of a meter

(D) 3,000 meters

To answer this question, you'll have to recall what you know about the prefix values in the metric system. *Milli* is one-thousandth, so three millimeters are equivalent to three-thousandths of a meter. Choice **(A)** is correct.

It's good to commit to memory the common prefix values used in the metric system. Here's a helpful table:

Metric Prefix	Mathematical Value
Mega-	Million
Kilo-	Thousand
Hecto-	Hundred
Deka-	Ten
Deci-	One-tenth
Centi-	One-hundredth
Milli-	One-thousandth
Micro-	One-millionth

It's also useful to be able to convert metric to customary units. Here are some common conversions:

Length	Weight
1 inch (in) = 2.54 centimeters (cm)	1 ounce (oz.) = 28 grams (g)
1 foot (ft) = 30 centimeters (cm)	1 pound (lb.) = 0.45 kilograms (kg)
1 yard (yd.) = 0.9 meters (m)	1 ton (T) = 0.9 metric tonne (t)
1 mile (mi.) = 1.6 kilometers (km)	

Area	Volume
1 square inch (in²) = 6.5 square cm (cm²)	1 fluid ounce (fl oz.) = 30 milliliters (mL)
1 square foot (ft²) = 0.09 square m (m²)	1 quart (qt.) = 0.95 liters (L)
1 square mile (mi²) = 2.6 square km (km²)	1 gallon (gal.) = 3.8 liters (L)
	1 cubic foot (ft³) = 0.03 cubic meter (m³)
	1 cubic yard (yd³) = 0.76 cubic meter (m³)

Temperature
Celsius (Metric Units) and
Fahrenheit (Customary Units)
$C = \frac{5}{9}(F - 32)$
$F = \frac{9}{5}C + 32$

The CSET may ask you to convert within either metric or customary units. For example, you may be asked to convert from square yards to square feet or from cubic yards to cubic feet.

Example #1:

Convert 1 square yard to square feet.

To complete this task, recall that a square yard (yd²) is raised to the second power, and refers to two different dimensions: length and width multiplied together. One yard is equal to 3 feet and a square yard is equal to 3 feet in each dimension, length and width.

So, 1 yd² = (3 feet × 3 feet) = 9 ft².

It follows that 5 square yards is equal to 45 square feet, if 1 square yard is equal to 9 square feet (5 × 9 ft²).

Example #2:

Convert 1 cubic yard to cubic feet.

Remember that when something is cubed, it refers to the product of three dimensions: length, width and height. Since 1 yard is 3 feet in one dimension, then 1 cubic yard is 3 feet multiplied by three dimensions: 3 feet (length), 3 feet (width), and 3 feet (height). Thus, 1 yd³ = (3 ft × 3 ft × 3 ft) = 27 ft³. If you were thinking 9 ft³, you added instead of multiplied. Based on this conversion, 5 cubic yards is equal to 135 cubic feet (5 × 27 ft³).

Knowledge of conversions within both customary and metric units is important. Here's a helpful table.

Metric Units	Customary Units
Capacity (Volume)	**Capacity (Volume)**
1,000 milliliters (mL) = 1 liter (L)	8 fluid ounces (fl. oz.) = 1 cup (c.)
250 milliliters = 1 metric cup	2 cups = 1 pint (pt.)
4 metric cups = 1 liter	2 pints = 1 quart (qt.)
1,000 liters = 1 kiloliter (kL)	4 cups = 1 quart
	4 quarts = 1 gallon (gal.)
Mass	**Weight**
1,000 milligrams (mg) = 1 gram (g)	16 ounces (oz.) = 1 pound (lb.)
1,000 grams = 1 kilogram (kg)	2,000 pounds = 1 ton (T)
Linear Units	**Linear Units**
10 millimeters (mm) = 1 centimeter (cm)	12 inches (in) = 1 foot (ft)
100 centimeters = 1 meter (m)	3 feet = 1 yard (yd.)
1,000 meters = 1 kilometer (km)	5,280 feet = 1 mile (mi.)
	1,760 yards = 1 mile

Perimeters and Areas of Two-Dimensional Figures and Surface Areas and Volumes of Three-Dimensional Figures

The CSET will contain questions that require you to find the area, perimeter, volume, and surface area of two- and three-dimensional objects.

Test Yourself

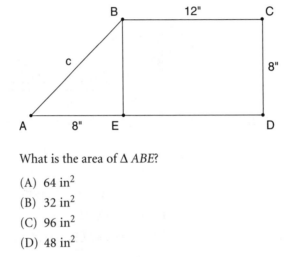

What is the area of $\triangle ABE$?

(A) 64 in^2

(B) 32 in^2

(C) 96 in^2

(D) 48 in^2

To answer this problem, you need to know the formula for finding the area of a triangle. Area is found by calculating half of the base multiplied by the height. The base is 8 and the height is 8. $\frac{1}{2}$ of (8 × 8) = 32 square inches. Choice **(B)** is correct.

Here's a helpful chart of common formulas for finding perimeter, area, surface area, and volume of various objects:

2-D Figure	Perimeter	Area
Triangle	$P = a + b + c$	$A = \frac{1}{2} \times b \times h$
Trapezoid	$P = s_1 + s_2 + b_1 + b_2$	$A = \frac{1}{2} h (b_1 + b_2)$
Parallelogram	$P = 2a + 2b$ or $P = 2 (a + b)$	$A = b \times h$
Rectangle	$P = 2l + 2w$ or $P = 2 (l + w)$	$A = l \times w$
Square	$P = 4s$	$A = s \times s$ or $A = s^2$
Circle	(Circumference) $C = \pi \times d$ Or $C = 2\pi r$	$A = \pi r^2$

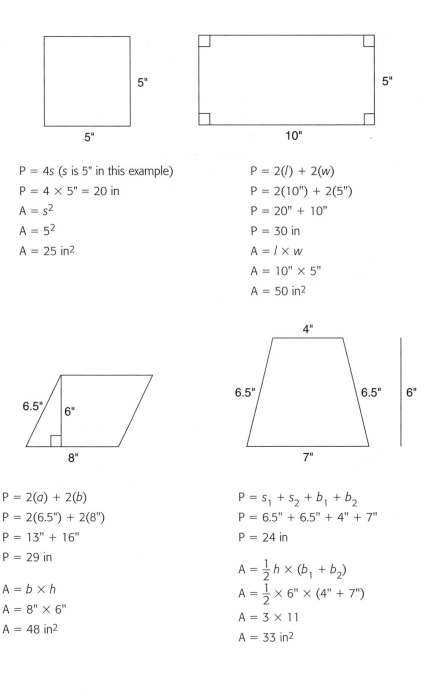

P = 4s (s is 5" in this example)
P = 4 × 5" = 20 in
A = s^2
A = 5^2
A = 25 in²

P = 2(l) + 2(w)
P = 2(10") + 2(5")
P = 20" + 10"
P = 30 in
A = l × w
A = 10" × 5"
A = 50 in²

P = 2(a) + 2(b)
P = 2(6.5") + 2(8")
P = 13" + 16"
P = 29 in

A = b × h
A = 8" × 6"
A = 48 in²

P = $s_1 + s_2 + b_1 + b_2$
P = 6.5" + 6.5" + 4" + 7"
P = 24 in

A = $\frac{1}{2}h \times (b_1 + b_2)$
A = $\frac{1}{2} \times 6" \times (4" + 7")$
A = 3 × 11
A = 33 in²

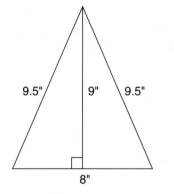

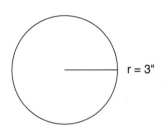

$P = a + b + c$

$P = 8" + 9.5" + 9.5"$

$P = 27$ in

$A = \frac{1}{2} b \times h$

$A = \frac{1}{2} \times 8" \times 9"$

$A = \frac{1}{2} \times 72"$

$A = 36$ in^2

$C = \pi \times 2r$

$C = 3.14 \times 2(3")$

$C = 3.14 \times 6"$

$C = 18.84$ in (approx.)

$A = \pi r^2$

$A = 3.14 \times 3^2$

$A = 3.14 \times 9"$

$A = 28.26$ in^2 (approx.)

3-D Figure	Surface Area	Volume
Prism	Add the areas of each face.	$V = Bh$ B is the area of the base and h is the height. (area of the base multiplied by its height)
Pyramid	Add the areas of the base and of each face	$V = \frac{1}{3}Bh$ B is the area of the base and h is its height. ($\frac{1}{3}$ the area of the base multiplied by its height)
Cylinder	1. Find the area of the two circular bases. 2. Find the area of the curved section by dissecting it into a rectangle. Use the circumference value as the length dimension and the height as the width dimension. 3. Then add these values together.	$V = \pi r^2 h$ (the area of the base multiplied by its height)
Cone	*Usually not asked on the CSET*	$V = \frac{1}{3}\pi r^2 h$ $\left(\frac{1}{3}\text{ the area of the base times its height}\right)$
Sphere	*Usually not asked on the CSET*	$\frac{4}{3}\pi r^3$

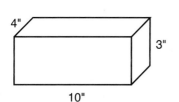 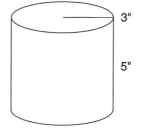

$V = l \times w \times h$

$V = 10" \times 3" \times 4"$

$V = 120 \text{ in}^3$

$C = \pi \times 2r$

$V = \text{Area of the base} \times \text{height}$

$V = \pi r^2 \times 5"$

$V = 3.14 \times 3^2 \times 5"$

$V = 3.14 \times 9" \times 5"$

$V = 141.3 \text{ in}^3 \text{ (approx.)}$

Surface Area: Add up the areas of each side

Two 10×3's $= 30 + 30 = 60 \text{ in}^2$

Two 10×4's $= 40 + 40 = 80 \text{ in}^2$

Two 3×4's $= 12 + 12 = 24 \text{ in}^2$

Surface of the rectangular prism $= 164 \text{ in}^2$

Surface area of the cylinder:

1. Dissect the curved section into a rectangle and find its area.

Cylinder's curved area is $30\pi \text{ inches}^2$.

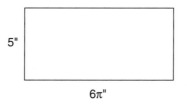

2. Find the area of the two circle bases.

   $A = \pi r^2$

   $A = \pi \times 3^2$

   $A = \pi \times 9$

   $A = 9\pi \text{ in}^2$ for one circle, 18π in for both circles

3. Add the area together to find the surface area of the cylinder:

   $30\pi \text{ in}^2 + 9\pi \text{ in}^2 + 9\pi \text{ in}^2 = 48\pi \text{ in}^2$ or $48 \times 3.14 = 150.72 \text{ in}^2 \text{ (approx.)}$

KAPLAN

Proportional Reasoning to the Construction of Scale Drawings or Models

Test Yourself

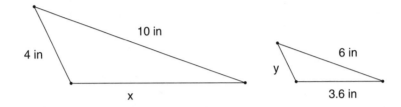

Use proportional reasoning to find the value of x and y.

(A) $x = 7; y = 2$

(B) $x = 7; y = 2.4$

(C) $x = 6; y = 2$

(D) $x = 6; y = 2.4$

To accurately solve this problem by using proportional reasoning, you must be sure to compare corresponding sides in the proportion.

To find x, the proportion would be:

$$\frac{10}{x} = \frac{6}{3.6}$$

$$36 = 6x$$

$$6 = x$$

To find y, the proportion would be:

$$\frac{10}{4} = \frac{6}{y}$$

$$10y = 24$$

$$y = 2.4$$

Choice (**D**) is the correct answer.

Problems like the one above requiring the application of proportional reasoning may be encountered on the CSET. It is important to remember that proportional reasoning is a comparison of two ratios. Whether that comparison involves corresponding sides of triangles or any other polygons makes no difference. The proportion must be set up properly in order to calculate the correct proportional answer. If it's not, you're not making a proportional comparison. Let's take a look at another problem.

The dimensions of a cube with sides equaling 2.5 cm in length are decreased to $\frac{1}{5}$ of its original scale. What are the lengths of the sides?

To solve this problem, use proportional reasoning.

$$\frac{2.5}{1} = \frac{x}{\frac{1}{5}}$$

$$x = 2.5 \times \frac{1}{5}$$

$$x = \frac{2.5}{5}$$

$$x = 0.5 \text{ cm}$$

Therefore, the sides of the cube would be 0.5 cm.

Using Measures to Analyze and Solve Problems

On the CSET, you may encounter problems requiring you to use measures such as miles per hour and other formulas to analyze and solve problems. It tests your sense of measurement in terms of time, length, area, volume, etc. Setting up algebraic equations makes for an organized way to solve a problem. The trick is to learn and remember equivalences from the preceding tables and the other formulas mentioned in this chapter.

Test Yourself

If a mountain biker rode 38 miles at an average speed of 8 mph, how long was the ride?

(A) 5 hours

(B) 4.5 hours

(C) 4.75 hours

(D) 5.5 hours

To answer this question, it is helpful to remember the formula:

distance = rate × time ($d = rt$)

By plugging in the actual numbers, you get 38 miles = 8 mph × time (in hours), or $38 = 8t$. Dividing by 8 on both sides gives you $t = 4.75$, making **(C)** the correct choice.

STATISTICS, DATA ANALYSIS, AND PROBABILITY

Questions pertaining to this section of the CSET will require you to be familiar with the basic terminology in statistics and data analysis, such as *mean, median, mode, range,* and *outlier.* You'll also view a variety of graphs and be asked to make inferences and answer questions based on the data provided. The content here is a close match to the math content taught in fourth- to sixth-grade classrooms.

Collection, Organization, and Representation of Data and Inferences, Predictions, and Arguments Based on Data

Test Yourself

Jordan has kept a log of his math test grades over the course of the semester. He needs to decide on the most appropriate graph to chart his data. Which graph should Jordan use?

(A) line graph

(B) circle graph

(C) bar graph

(D) tally table

To answer this question, it is important to recognize the purposes of different types of graphs. Line graphs are intended to show change over time, circle graphs show part-to-whole relationships, bar graphs compare amounts between groups, and tally tables record amounts in a generalized way. Since Jordan has kept a log of his grades over a period of time, a line graph **(A)** would be most appropriate graph to chart his data.

Representing and Interpreting a Collection of Data Through a Graph, Table, or Chart Representing a Data Set

A *survey* is a method of gathering data or information. This information is taken from a sample of the population. This sample can be biased or unbiased. In a *biased sample,* a group or groups within a population are not represented in the survey. In an unbiased sample, all groups within a population are represented. For example, a biased survey about public support for educational bond measures may exclude parents of private school students or elementary school teachers serving in high-performing schools, while an unbiased sample on this topic would include all groups within the population. To increase the validity of the survey, a random sample should be employed. In a *random sample,* every individual or group in the population has an equal chance of being chosen to take part in the survey.

Data collected from a survey can be displayed using various graphic formats. These graphs serve different purposes in mathematics, and the CSET aims to test your knowledge of them.

Line graphs are used to show change over time. The line graph below compares the science test scores of Rooms 11 and 13 over a six-week period.

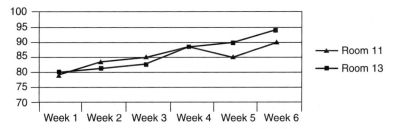

Circle graphs are used to show the part-to-whole relationships in a set of data. This circle graph shows the parts of a student's typical day during the school year.

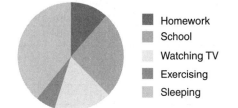

Bar graphs are used to compare data of different groups. The scores of three different little league basketball games are being compared in this bar graph:

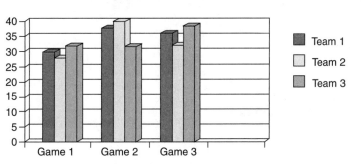

Tally tables and frequency tables are used to show amounts within categorical groups.

Favorite Color	Votes
Red	1111
Blue	11
Green	111

KAPLAN

Tally tables are useful when conducting surveys. The information from the tally table can be made into a *frequency table*.

Favorite Color	Votes
Red	4
Blue	2
Green	3

Cumulative Frequency Tables are the same as frequency tables, with the addition of a third column. This third column keeps track of cumulative amounts in the frequency table. See below.

School Book Fair

	Frequency (Number of Books Sold)	Cumulative Frequency (A Running Total of Frequencies)
Week 1	50	50
Week 2	72	122
Week 3	80	202
Week 4	100	302

Notice that the Cumulative Frequency column makes it easy to track total book sales at the end of each week.

Line plots are used to show the frequency of data on a number line. For example:

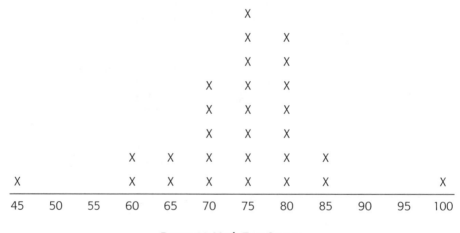

Room 12 Math Test Scores

From this line plot, statistical information can be extracted. Notice that the *mode* score on this test is 75. The *median* score is 72.5. The *average* is 74.11 (rounded to the nearest hundredth).

The *range* of the scores is 55. The *interval* used in this line plot is 5, and the *scale* of the line plot is 45 to 100. The *outlier* scores are 45 and 100, because they are separated from the rest of the data.

Stem-and-Leaf plots are used to display data in an organized way, according to place value. The *stem* represents the *tens* place value of the number being displayed. So, 1 is 1 ten, 2 is 2 tens or 20, and so forth. The *leaves* represent the *ones* place value of the number being displayed. So, in the first row of this Stem-and-Leaf plot, the numbers are 11, 13, 15, and 17. In the second row, they are 22, 24, 24, 28, and 28. This works the same with the rest of the rows.

Sit-Ups in 1 Minute

Stem	Leaves
1	1 3 5 7
2	2 4 4 8 8
3	1 5 5
4	2 2 2
5	9

This type of plot can be very informative. From this plot, there are 16 pieces of data. The *mode* number of sit-ups is 42. The *median* number of sit-ups is 28. The *mean* number of sit-ups is 29 and $\frac{1}{4}$. The *outlier* piece of data is 59, because it's separated from the rest of the data.

Box-and-Whisker plots show the distribution of a set of data on a number line. It allows for the range of the data to be seen. Box and Whisker plots show the median, the upper and lower quartiles, and the smallest and greatest values in the set of data, but do not show all of the scores. Suppose we take the following set of data to create a Box-and-Whisker plot: <u>10</u>, 17, 20, **50**, 60, 62, 70, **75**, 80, 84, 88, **90**, 92, 95, <u>100</u>.

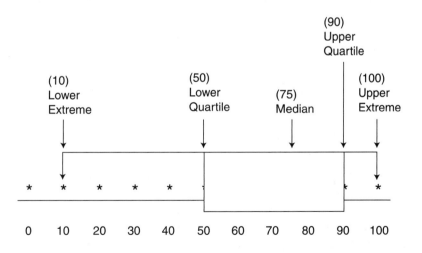

The *median* of the set of data is 75. The *lower quartile* is the median of the set of data to the left of 75. The *upper quartile* is the median of the set of data to the right of 75. It's like cutting a whole piece of paper in half, and then cutting each half into halves to make 4 quarters. Notice how not all 15 pieces of data are represented in this Box-and-Whisker plot.

Mean, Median, Mode, and Range of a Collection of Data

Test Yourself

Silverlake Charter School: Annual Teacher Salaries

$37,500	$32,000	$37,500	$29,500	$29,500
$44,000	$44,000	$42,000	$37,500	$55,000

What is the mean salary at Silverlake Charter School?

(A) $38,000

(B) $38,500

(C) $37,500

(D) $38,850

To find the mean, first find the sum of the data, and then divide by the number of pieces of data. Carefully calculate and double-check on your calculator. The mean comes to $38,850, **(D)**.

An *average* is a value that is representative of a collection of data. *Mean, median,* and *mode* are three common, but different averages. Each is calculated differently and may yield different results for the same set of data. The CSET usually includes questions in this area because this content is commonly taught in fourth-, fifth-, and sixth-grade classrooms throughout California. We'll use this set of data for an example:

Colin's Science Test Grades: 49, 75, 50, 78, 78, and 90.
(Note that there are six pieces of data.)

To find the *mean*:

1. Find the sum of the data.

49 + 75 + 50 + 78 + 78 + 90 = 420

2. Divide by the number of pieces of data.

420 ÷ 6 = 70

The mean value is 70.

To find the *median*:

1. Order the pieces of data from least to greatest.

49 50 75 78 78 90

2. Find the piece of data in the middle. If there are two pieces of data in the middle, then find their sum and divide by 2.

Since both 75 and 78 are the pieces of data in the "middle," their sum is 153 and when divided by 2, the answer is 76.5.

The median value is 76.5.

To find the *mode*:

Find the piece of data that occurs most often. (Note that sometimes there may be no mode in a set of data.)

78 occurs twice in the set of data while the other numbers occur only once.

The mode value is 78.

To summarize, you can see how, for the same set of data, we came up with different numerical values for the mean (70), median (76.5), and mode (78). You might be wondering how the mean, median, and mode can all be considered the "average" in a set of data. To answer this, it's helpful to look at the normal distribution of data—the Gaussian distribution (named after Carl Friedrich Gauss).

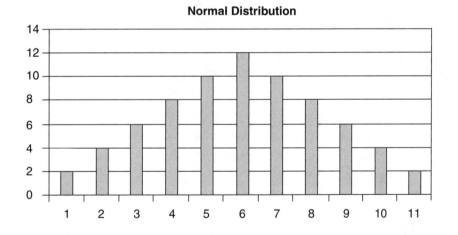

Normal Distribution

In a normal distribution, the mean, median, and mode all have the same value. The normal distribution is associated with the commonly known bell-shaped curve. The range of a set of data is the difference between the largest and smallest values in the set. The range of Colin's Science Test scores is 90 − 49 = 41.

Basic Notions of Chance and Probability

Some CSET math questions are designed to test your understanding of simple probabilities and the variety of ways they can be expressed. Using your knowledge of fractions and performing the operation of multiplication are key elements to successfully answering these questions. It may also be important to know the difference between the *odds* of an event and the *probability* of an event. Probability test questions will be similar to those given to 4th- to 8th-grade math students.

Test Yourself

Using a standard 52-card deck, a card is selected at random. What is the probability of a selecting a jack, queen, or king?

(A) 23%

(B) 6%

(C) 3%

(D) 12%

To answer this problem, we need to figure out how many of these "face" cards there are in the 52 card standard deck. Since there are four suits in a standard deck and three face cards per suit, 4 suits × 3 face cards = 12 face cards out of 52 total cards. By changing the fraction, 12/52 to a decimal, and then to a percentage, we see that there is a 23% probability of selecting a jack, queen, or king. Choice **(A)** is correct.

Probability, as seen on the CSET, mirrors the types of probability problems and data analysis you'd teach in a fourth- to sixth-grade elementary classroom. The *probability* of an event is the same as how likely the event is to happen, and this likelihood can be calculated using simple math. It can be looked at in terms of likely outcomes divided by total possible outcomes. See below:

$$\text{Probability of an Event} = \frac{\text{likely outcomes}}{\text{total possible outcomes}}$$

Written in this form, as part-to-whole ratio, the numerical value of any probable event will be a value between 0 and 1. Algebraically it is expressed as $0 \leq P(E) \leq 1$, where $P(E)$ stands for the Probability of an Event. Here are a few other facts about probabilities to consider:

1. The probability of an event that cannot occur is 0.
2. The probability of an event that must occur is 1.
3. The sum of the probabilities of all possible outcomes of an experiment is 1.

Let's take a look at some examples to illustrate the three points listed above. We'll use a standard 52-card deck and calculate the probability of randomly selecting one card that is:

1. A heart and a spade
2. A red or a black suit
3. A diamond or any other card

1. Notice the word *and* in this example. This means that *both* events must occur to satisfy this condition. Since it is not possible to select one card that is both a heart and a spade, the probability is 0. (This is also known as a mutually exclusive event.)

2. There are four suits in a deck of cards: hearts, diamonds, spades, and clubs. Hearts and diamonds are red suits, while spades and clubs are black suits. Since all of the suits are red or black, the probability of choosing a card that is a red or black suit is 100% or 1.

3. There are 13 diamonds in a 52-card deck. That means that 13 out of 52 cards are diamonds. This can be simplified to 1 out of 4 or $\frac{1}{4}$. When we add this to the other $\frac{39}{52}$ or $\frac{3}{4}$ of the remaining deck, we get $\frac{52}{52}$, $\frac{4}{4}$, or $\frac{1}{1}$. These equivalent fractions all equal 1, illustrating that the sum of all possible outcomes is 1.

Now that you are familiar with some of the background knowledge regarding probability, let's turn our attention to a sample space of equally likely outcomes. Suppose that you wanted to calculate all of the possible outcomes when a spinner cut into two sections is spun and a die is rolled. The spinner has two possible outcomes, red or blue, and the die has six possible outcomes, 1, 2, 3, 4, 5, or 6. The possibilities could be listed using a tree diagram, in which case we are creating a sample space of equally likely outcomes. See below:

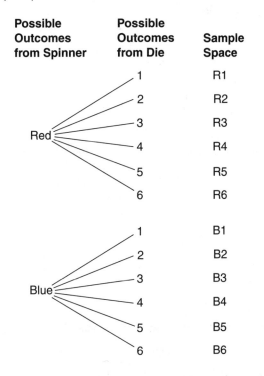

Another important area of probabilities deals with compounded probabilities, which involve multiplication. For example, to figure out the probability of flipping heads with a coin three consecutive times, we need to look at the probability of flipping heads each of the three times. Then we

KAPLAN

multiply these probabilities together. The probability of heads is 1 out of 2 or $\frac{1}{2}$. The probability of flipping heads three consecutive times is $\frac{1}{2} \times \frac{1}{2} \times \frac{1}{2} = \frac{1}{8}$. There is a 1 out of 8 probability of flipping heads on a coin three consecutive times. The same could be done with a die, say rolling a five three consecutive times. The probability of rolling a five is 1 out of 6 or $\frac{1}{6}$, so rolling a five three consecutive times is $\frac{1}{6} \times \frac{1}{6} \times \frac{1}{6} = \frac{1}{216}$. That's a probability of 1 time out of 216 times. In other words, it's not very likely, but it's certainly not impossible.

Complementary, Mutually Exclusive, Dependent, and Independent Events

Test Yourself

One of the numbers in the diagram below is chosen at random.

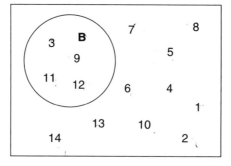

What is the probability that the number chosen is in Set B?

(A) $\frac{10}{14}$

(B) $\frac{4}{10}$

(C) $\frac{2}{5}$

(D) $\frac{2}{7}$

To answer this question, count the total number of numerals in the diagram to determine the denominator of the probability. The numerator will be the number of numerals in Set B. $\frac{4}{14}$ is the probability. Reduce to $\frac{2}{7}$ and you have the correct answer, **(D)**.

Complementary probability is defined as having only two possible outcomes. For example, if the probability of Chris winning a bike race is $\frac{5}{8}$, then the probability of him losing the bike race is $\frac{3}{8}$.

Notice how the only possible outcomes are winning or losing the race. Also, if there is a 0.1 chance that you'll be late for school, then there is a 0.9 chance that you'll be on time.

When probabilities are mutually exclusive, it is impossible for two events to occur simultaneously. For example, it is not possible to pick both an ace and a king when choosing one card from a deck of cards. Since this type of question is so obvious and takes little, if any, effort to work out, it is usually not tested. It is more important to know the concept because it's part of the content domain on the CSET.

Probabilities are dependent or independent if they occur without replacement or with replacement, respectively. Events are independent when the outcome of one event has no effect on the outcome of the other event. For example, chances of selecting the same two cards from a deck of cards with replacement are considered to be independent. Both probabilities are 4 out of 52 (or 1 out of 13) and are independent of one another, since the cards are replaced each time.

So the probability of choosing two aces in a row, with replacement, is $\frac{1}{13} \times \frac{1}{13} = \frac{1}{169}$.

Events that are dependent depend on the outcome of the previous events. If a queen is randomly chosen from a deck of cards without replacement, the probability of choosing a second queen is dependent upon the outcome of the previous event. The probability of the first event is 4 out of 52, while the probability of the second is 3 out of 51, since one of the four queens in the deck was chosen the first time, leaving only 3 in the deck. So the probability of choosing two consecutive queens without replacement, when a queen is chosen on the first draw, is

$$\frac{4}{52} \times \frac{3}{51} = \frac{12}{2,652} = \frac{1}{221}.$$

Expressing Probabilities in a Variety of Ways

Test Yourself

Two percent of the U.S. population is born gifted (I.Q. of 130 or above). What is another way to express this probability?

(A) The odds of being born gifted are 1 to 49.

(B) The probability of being born gifted is 2 in 10.

(C) The probability of not being born gifted is 4 in 5.

(D) The probability of being born gifted is 1 in 49.

Odds and probabilities are sometimes stated incorrectly. Odds are given using the word "to" and are a ratio of the *odds in favor* to the *odds against* the occurrence. If there is a 2% chance of being born gifted, that is 2 out of 100 or 1 out of 50. If the probability is 1 in 50 (not 1 in 49, as in **(D)**), the odds are 1 for being born gifted to 49 against being born gifted. Thus, the odds of being born gifted are 1:49. Choice **(A)** is correct.

KAPLAN

It is important that you are aware of the many ways probabilities can be expressed. You can use fractions, percents, decimals, numbers, and words or symbols. If there is a 3 out of 5 probability of rain tomorrow that is equal to a

$\frac{3}{5}$ chance of rain

60% chance of rain

0.6 chance of rain

6 in 10 chance of rain

Notice how each of these probabilities is expressed as a *parts of a whole* relationship. What would happen if you were to express things as a *part to part* relationship? This would be a ratio between parts, and you would now be talking about *odds*. Odds and probability statements are sometimes stated incorrectly. Odds are expressed as ratios. That is why the word *to* is used to express them. Odds are either given *in favor* or *against* a particular event. When this occurs, it is possible to determine the probability of an event. For example, if the odds against Alex getting into M.I.T. are 11:1 (11 to 1), then the probability of Alex not getting into to M.I.T. are 11 in 12. The probability of him getting accepted to M.I.T. is 1 in 12. Notice that the ratio, 11 to 1 represents 12 parts total, with 11 parts against and 1 part for the outcome to occur.

TIPS FOR CONSTRUCTED-RESPONSE QUESTIONS IN MATHEMATICS

In the CSET constructed-response questions on mathematics, you will be asked to demonstrate your understanding of the four mathematics content domains (number sense; algebra and functions; geometry; and probability, statistics, and data analysis) by completing two short constructed-response items. It is important to use accurate and correct vocabulary and examples when responding to the questions. Thoughtful and deliberate planning is highly recommended, since the answer document allows only about $\frac{2}{3}$ of a standard letter-size page to write your answer. Here are the competencies you may be asked to demonstrate, taken from the content standards for mathematics:

- identify and prioritize relevant and missing information in mathematical problems
- analyze complex problems to identify similar simple problems that might suggest solution strategies
- represent a problem in alternate ways, such as words, symbols, concrete models, and diagrams, to gain greater insight
- consider examples and patterns as means to formulating a conjecture
- apply logical reasoning and techniques from arithmetic, algebra, geometry, and probability/statistics to solve mathematical problems
- analyze problems to identify alternative solution strategies
- evaluate the truth of mathematical statements (e.g., whether a given statement is always, sometimes, or never true)
- apply different solution strategies (e.g., estimation) to check the reasonableness of a solution
- demonstrate that a solution is correct

- explain mathematical reasoning through a variety of methods, such as words, numbers, symbols, charts, graphs, tables, diagrams, and concrete models
- use appropriate mathematical notation with clear and accurate language
- explain how to derive a result based on previously developed ideas, and explain how a result is related to other ideas

Here are four examples of the type of constructed-response questions you might encounter on the CSET:

Question 1

1. The relationship of a cube's side to its volume can be shown in several different ways. Using what you know about algebra and geometry,

    a) Identify and explain the significance of the volume formula for a cube.

    b) Create a table for this relationship and graph it onto a coordinate grid. Use side measures of 1, 2, 3, and 4.

    Be sure to clearly and thoroughly show your work.

Sample Response 1

a) The volume formula of a cube is $V = s^3$. This formula takes into account the fact that the faces of a cube are squares, and squares have equal sides represented with the symbol s. Volume is a measure of three separate dimensions: length, width, and height. In this case, these dimensions are equal and are represented by s.

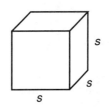

b) Here's the table and graph of the relationship between the side length of a cube and its volume.

Cube's Side (s)	Volume (s^3)
1	$1^3 = 1 \times 1 \times 1 = 1$
2	$2^3 = 2 \times 2 \times 2 = 8$
3	$3^3 = 3 \times 3 \times 3 = 27$
4	$4^3 = 4 \times 4 \times 4 = 64$

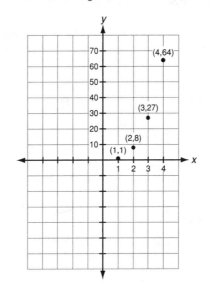

Question 2

2. This data represents 12 scores on a math test:

   7, 22, 8, 9, 7, 18, 15, 10, 20, 21, 20, 83

   Using your knowledge of statistics and data analysis,

   a) Find the mean, median, and mode, and indicate which measure of central tendency would best represent the typical math test score.

   b) Demonstrate how to create a box-and-whisker plot and explain its significance in representing this set of data.

Sample Response 2

a) The mean is found by adding up all of the pieces of data and then dividing by the number of pieces of data. The sum of the data is 240. 240 ÷ 12 pieces of data = 20. The mean is 20.

The median is found by finding the middle term in an ordered set of data. If there is an even number of data, there will be two middle terms. To resolve this, find the mean of the two middle terms.

   7, 7, 8, 9, 10, **15**, **18**, 20, 20, 21, 22, 83

   15 + 18 = 33; 33 ÷ 2 = 16.5

The median is 16.5.

The mode is the most frequently occurring piece of data. Sometimes, a set of data contains two modes. This is, in fact, the case with this set of data. There are two 7s and two 20s. This data is bimodal.

The measure most representative of the typical score would have to be the median score of 16.5. The mean score is skewed, due to the one very high math score of 83. This would be considered an outlier score since it is located far away from the rest of the data if put onto a line plot.

b) Box-and-whisker plots show the distribution in a set of data on a number line. It allows the range of the data to be seen. Box-and-whisker plots show the median, the upper and lower quartiles, and the smallest and greatest values in the set of data, but do not show all of the data.

The set of data must first be ordered to determine the median.

   7, 7, 8, 9, 10, 15, 18, 20, 20, 21, 22, 83

16.5 is the median of the two middle scores of 15 and 18. The lower quartile score is found by finding the median of the set of data to the left of the median: 7, 7, 8, 9, 10. The lower quartile is 8. The upper quartile is found the same way, but uses the data to the right of the median: 20, 20, 21, 22, 83. The upper quartile is 21. The extreme high score is 83 and the extreme low score is 7.

Finally, these scores are formatted onto a box-and-whisker plot:

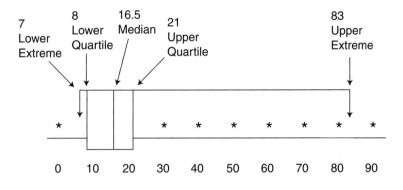

Question 3

3. Using your knowledge of number sense and probability,

    a) Represent all possible outcomes of simultaneously flipping one coin and rolling one six-sided die.

    b) What is the probability of each outcome? Express your answer both as a fraction and as a decimal rounded to the nearest thousandth.

Be sure to clearly and thoroughly show your work.

Sample Response 3

a) To answer this part of the question, we need to consider the possible outcomes of both the coin (heads or tails) and the die (1, 2, 3, 4, 5, or 6). A table or a tree diagram would represent two viable ways to clearly show these possible outcomes.

Table:

Coin	Die	Coin	Die
H	1	T	1
H	2	T	2
H	3	T	3
H	4	T	4
H	5	T	5
H	6	T	6

Tree Diagram:

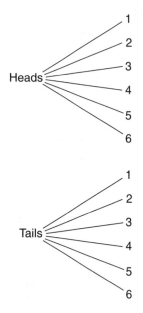

b) The probability of either outcome of the coin toss is $\frac{1}{2}$, and the probability of rolling any particular number on the die is $\frac{1}{6}$. These events are independent of each other. The probability of any particular outcome can be found by multiplying $\frac{1}{2}$ by $\frac{1}{6}$. This will give a probability of $\frac{1}{12}$. To express $\frac{1}{12}$ as a decimal rounded to the nearest thousandths, divide the numerator by the denominator. $1 \div 12 = 0.083$.

Question 4

4. There are 120 lockers in a school hallway, and each locker is numbered from 1–120. Lucy puts blue stickers on every odd numbered locker. Starting at the fifth locker, she puts a green sticker on every fifth locker. Finally, Lucy starts at the sixth locker and puts a yellow sticker on every sixth locker.

    a) What is the probability of a locker having both a blue and a green sticker?

    b) What is the probability of a locker having both a green and a yellow sticker?

    c) How many lockers have two stickers? Show your work.

    Clearly indicate how you arrived at your answer. You will be graded on the correctness of your methods, as well as the accuracy of your answer.

Sample Response 4

This following table may prove helpful in figuring out the location of each color sticker:

Blue	Odd	$120 \div 2 = 60$ $\frac{60}{120} = \frac{1}{2}$
Green	Every 5th	$120 \div 5 = 24$ $\frac{24}{120} = \frac{1}{5}$
Yellow	Every 6th	$120 \div 6 = 20$ $\frac{20}{120} = \frac{1}{6}$

a) There are 12 lockers with both a blue and a green sticker. Lockers with blue stickers are odd, and every fifth locker has a green sticker. Multiples of five end in 0 or 5, so these multiples alternate even/odd. There are 24 stickers that are multiples of five, so half of them are odd fifths. The probability is $\frac{12}{120} = \frac{1}{10}$.

b) There are 4 lockers with both a green and a yellow sticker. The common multiple of 5 and 6 is 30. By dividing 120 by 30 to get 4, there are 4 multiples of 30 from 1–120. (They are 30, 60, 90, and 120). The probability is $\frac{4}{120} = \frac{1}{30}$.

c) There are two two-sticker combinations: since multiples of 6 aren't odd, there cannot be any lockers with both blue and yellow stickers. There are 12 lockers with both blue and green stickers, and there are 4 lockers with both a green and a yellow sticker. In all there are 16 two-sticker combinations out of 120 lockers.

GLOSSARY

Algebraic expression: a collection of variables, numbers, parentheses, and operation symbols

Algorithm: a general procedure for accomplishing a task

Angle: a geometric figure formed when two rays share a common endpoint, named with the vertex as the middle letter (e.g., ∠ABC or ∠CBA)

Area: the number of square units needed to cover a surface

Binomial: an expression containing two terms in which each exponent that appears on a variable is a whole number

Chord: a line segment with endpoints on a circle

Circumference: distance around a circle

Compass: a tool used to draw a circle

Composite number: any natural number that is divisible by any number other than 1 and itself

Cone: a solid figure that has one flat circular base and one curved surface

Congruent: figures that have exactly the same size and shape

Constant: a symbol that represents a specific quantity

Cylinder: a solid figure with two flat circular bases and one curved surface

Domain: the set of x values in a function

Diameter: a chord passing through the center of a circle (a radius is half of a diameter)

Equally likely outcomes: any outcome has the same chance of occurring as any other outcome

Equation: two algebraic expressions joined by an equal sign

Evaluate: to find the value of the expression for a given value of the variable

FOIL Method (First, Outer, Inner, and Last terms of two binomials): used to multiply two binomials

Formula: a set of symbols used to express a mathematical rule

Function: a special type of relation where each value of the independent variable (x) corresponds to the unique value of the dependent variable (y)

Function table: a table that matches each input value with an output value; the values of the output are determined by the function; for example, for the function $y = 2x + 2$:

$y = 2x + 2$	
Input (x)	Output (y)
−2	−2
−1	0
0	2
1	4
2	6

Greatest Common Divisor (GCD): the largest number that divides without remainder, instrumental when reducing fractions

Integers: whole numbers and negative whole numbers: …−3, −2, −1, 0, 1, 2, 3…

Intersecting lines: lines that cross at one point

Interval: the difference between two numbers on a scale, such as intervals of 2 or 5

Irrational numbers: real numbers that can be expressed as non-repeating, non-terminating decimals: $-\sqrt{11}$, $\sqrt{2}$, $2\sqrt{3}$, π (pi, commonly approximated to 3.14 or $\frac{22}{7}$)

Least Common Multiple (LCM): the smallest number that can be divided into two or more numbers without remainder, useful when finding common denominators

Line: an endless straight path passing through two points

Line segment: part of a line between two endpoints

Linear function: equations in the form of $y = mx + b$; every graph of a linear function is a straight line

Mean: also known as the arithmetic mean, and commonly called the average, it is the sum of the data divided by the number of pieces of data

Median: the value in the middle of a ranked set of data

Mode: the piece of data that occurs most often

Natural numbers: counting numbers: 1,2,3…

Odds in favor (of an event): with respect to theoretical probability, a ratio comparing the probability of likely outcomes to the number of unlikely outcomes; odds against an event are the reverse ratio

Outlier: a piece of data that is located away from the rest of the data

Parallel lines: lines that never intersect

Parallelogram: a quadrilateral having two pairs of congruent sides and two pairs of parallel sides

Perimeter: distance around a figure

Perpendicular lines: lines that intersect at 90° angles

Plane: an endless, two-dimensional, flat surface

Point: a point that marks an exact location in space, such as on a number line or on a coordinate grid

Polygon: a two-dimensional closed plane figure composed of three or more line segments named according to the number of sides they have (e.g., triangle, quadrilateral, pentagon, hexagon, octagon, decagon, etc.)

Polyhedron: a solid figure with polygons for faces (solid figures are three-dimensional figures)

Prime factorization: the process of breaking a number down into a product of prime numbers

Prime number: any natural number greater than 1 that has exactly two factors (or divisors): 1 and itself

Prism: a polyhedron that has two congruent bases, in which all other faces are rectangles; named by the polygons that form their bases (e.g., triangular prism, rectangular prism, pentagonal prism, hexagonal prism, etc.)

Probability: with respect to theoretical probability, a ratio comparing the number of favorable outcomes of an event divided by the total number of outcomes of an event

Protractor: a tool used to measure angles

Pyramid: a polyhedron with only one base with all other faces being triangles that meet at the same vertex (triangular pyramid, square pyramid, pentagonal pyramid, hexagonal pyramid)

Quadratic function: equations in the form of $y = ax^2 + bx + c$; every graph of a quadratic function is a parabola that opens up or down

Random sample: a sample drawn in such a way that each time an item is selected, each item in the population has an equal chance of being chosen

KAPLAN

Range: the set of *y* values in a function; in probability, the difference between the highest and lowest values in a set of data

Rational number: any number that can be expressed as a quotient of two integers and can be expressed as a terminating or repeating decimal: $-5, -1.27, -\frac{2}{3}, -\frac{1}{4}, 0, \frac{1}{3}, 2.25$

Ray: a part of a line that begins at an end point, goes through another point, and then goes on forever in one direction

Real numbers: both rational and irrational numbers

Rectangle: a quadrilateral having two pairs of congruent sides and four right angles

Rhombus: a quadrilateral having four congruent sides and two pairs of congruent angles

Scale: a series of numbers placed at fixed distances; the scale of a graph should be larger than the largest piece of data being graphed, such as a scale of 0 to 100

Similar: figures that have the same shape and proportional size

Similar polygons: polygons having congruent corresponding angles and proportional corresponding sides

Solution: the number or numbers that replace the variable to make the equation a true statement

Solve an equation: to find the value or values for the variable that make(s) the equation true

Sphere: a solid figure that has no base and one curved surface

Square: a quadrilateral having four pairs of congruent sides and four right angles

Three-dimensional: a measure in three distinct dimensions, such as length, width, and height

Trapezoid: a quadrilateral having only one pair of parallel sides

Trend: when examining a graph, it is where data increase, decrease, or remain the same over time

Trinomial: an expression containing three terms in which each exponent that appears on a variable is a whole number

Two-dimensional: a measure in two distinct directions, such as length and width

Unbiased sample: a sample that is representative of the entire population with regard to income, education, sex, race, religion, age, political affiliation, etc. (a biased sample is its opposite)

Variable: a value that can change or vary, usually represented with the letters of the alphabet

Vertex: the point where two of the sides meet on a polygon

Vertical line test: used to determine if a graph is a function; if a vertical line can be drawn so that it intersects the graph at more than one point then each *x* does not have a unique *y*, and therefore the graph is not a function

Whole numbers: natural numbers and zero: 0,1,2,3...

X-axis: the horizontal line on a coordinate grid

Y-axis: the vertical line on a coordinate grid

PRACTICE SET

1. A DVD player regularly sells for $130.00. It is on sale for 25% off. What is the price of the DVD player?

    (A) $32.50
    (B) $97.50
    (C) $87.50
    (D) $162.50

2. Twenty-seven pounds of meat will be divided into $\frac{1}{3}$ pound portions. Then they will be put into four-portion packages. How many packages can be made?

    (A) 81 packages
    (B) 36 packages
    (C) 21 packages
    (D) 20 packages

3. Four basketball players took part in a free-throw shooting contest. They each shot 8 free throws. Jasmine made 5 of her shots, Juniper made just over 87% of her shots, Marcia made 50% fewer shots than Juniper, and Reece made a quarter of her shots. What is the correct order of participants from the player that made the least number of shots to the player that made the most?

    (A) Jasmine, Marcia, Juniper, Reece
    (B) Reece, Marcia, Juniper, Jasmine
    (C) Reece, Jasmine, Marcia, Juniper
    (D) Reece, Marcia, Jasmine, Juniper

4. The approximate age of the Earth is thought to be 4,550 million years. What is the number in scientific notation?

    (A) 4.555×10^9
    (B) 4.55×10^9
    (C) 4.55×10^{-9}
    (D) 45.5×10^8

5. Max had $180.00 to spend on video game equipment. After he did his shopping, he had $45.00 left. By what percent did his spending money decrease?

    (A) 75%
    (B) 25%
    (C) 33%
    (D) None of the above

6. Evaluate the following expression.

$$\frac{8(12 - 3^2)}{12}$$

(A) -72

(B) -7 and $\frac{2}{3}$

(C) 3

(D) 2

Use the numbers below to answer question 7.

1,279

1,523

1,210

1,748

1,595

1,871

1,786

7. To estimate the sum of the numbers given above, Brittney first rounds each number to the nearest ten and then adds the rounded values. By how much will Brittney's answer differ from the actual sum?

(A) 10

(B) 8

(C) 12

(D) 20

Use the chart below to answer question 8.

Velo Cycling U.S.A.

# of bike racks (R)	Total # of bikes in stock (T)
0	5
1	8
2	11
3	14

*The data above can be graphed as a linear equation.

8. All of the following statements about the data above are true except

(A) The equation can be written $T = (3)R + 5$.

(B) The slope of this linear equation is 3.

(C) The T-intercept is at 5 on the T-axis.

(D) This slope of this equation is negative, going down and to the right.

9. A car rental company charges a $20 fee plus 35 cents per each three miles driven. What is the cost of the rental if you drive 465 miles?

   (A) $54.25

   (B) $74.25

   (C) $162.75

   (D) $155.00

10. Use the graph below. What is the linear equation written in standard form?

    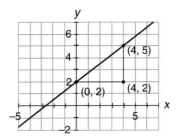

    (A) $y = -\frac{3}{4}x - 2$

    (B) $y = \frac{3}{4}x + 2$

    (C) $y = -\frac{4}{3}x - 2$

    (D) $y = \frac{4}{3}x + 2$

11. Solve for x.

    $-8(x + 1) + 3(2x - 2) \geq 44$

    (A) $x \geq 29$

    (B) $x \geq -29$

    (C) $x \leq 29$

    (D) $x \leq -29$

Use the information below to answer question 12.

Pennel's CDs 4 Less Superstore sells CDs for $5.75 each.

Number Purchased	Cost ($)
0	0
1	5.75
2	11.50
3	17.25
4	23.00
5	28.75

12. Which of the following is a portion of the graph of the data in the table?

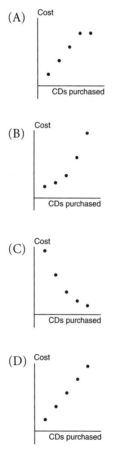

(A) Cost

CDs purchased

(B) Cost

CDs purchased

(C) Cost

CDs purchased

(D) Cost

CDs purchased

13. Forty-nine hours of overtime must be split among three workers. The second worker will be assigned twice as many hours as the first. The third worker will be assigned seven less than twice as many hours as the second. What equation matches this scenario?

    (A) $x + 2x + (2x - 7) = 49$

    (B) $x + 2x + 2 + (2x - 7) = 49$

    (C) $x + 2x + 2 - (2x - 7) = 49$

    (D) $x + 2x + (4x - 7) = 49$

14. All statements regarding the parabola created by the quadratic equation $-2x^2 - 7x + 4$ are true except

    (A) The parabola opens downward.

    (B) The vertex of this parabola is at $(-1, 10)$.

    (C) The solutions for x are $\frac{1}{2}$ and -4.

    (D) The y-intercept is 4.

    Use the information below to answer question 15.

    Trapezoids A and B are similar. The dimensions of Trapezoid A are twice that of Trapezoid B.

    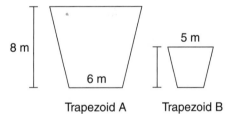

    Trapezoid A   Trapezoid B

15. What is the area of Trapezoid B?

    (A) 64 m^2

    (B) 128 m^2

    (C) 32 m^2

    (D) 16 m^2

KAPLAN

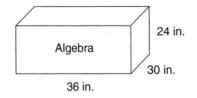

24 in.

Algebra

30 in.

36 in.

16. What is the surface area of the algebra box above?

(A) 5,328 in²

(B) 5,760 in²

(C) 2,664 in²

(D) 4,896 in²

ICE CREAM

The diameter of the base is 14 inches.

The height of the ice cream container is 30 inches.

17. When the above ice cream container is filled to capacity, what is its volume in cubic inches?

(A) 659.4 in³

(B) 4,615.8 in³

(C) 1,318.8 in³

(D) 4,410.0 in³

Use the information below to answer question 18.

The diagram below shows a sidewalk around a circular garden.

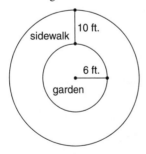

sidewalk 10 ft.

6 ft.

garden

18. What is the area of the sidewalk?

(A) 220π ft²

(B) 64π ft²

(C) 72π ft²

(D) 224π ft²

19. Samantha drove at 35 miles per hour for 30 minutes and at 60 miles per hour for 45 minutes. How far did she travel?

    (A) 58 miles

    (B) 55.5 miles

    (C) 63 miles

    (D) 62.5 miles

20. Albert took a super shuttle from City X to City Y during peak, rush-hour traffic. The trip is a distance of 175 miles. The bus took 180 minutes to get there. What was the average speed of the bus expressed in miles per hour?

    (A) 97.2 mph

    (B) 58.3 mph

    (C) 102.8 mph

    (D) 60 mph

Use the information below to answer question 21.

Below are the science test scores for twelve students in Mr. Lee's class:

50	75	80	90
50	72	75	72
72	98	85	75

21. Each statement regarding the data above is true except

    (A) The mean is 74.5.

    (B) The range is 48.

    (C) The mode is 50.

    (D) The median is 75.

22. **Number of Sit-Ups in 1 Minute**

Stem	Leaves
1	3
2	3 4 4
3	2 9
4	1 6
5	5 7 7
6	1 4

Each statement regarding the data above is true except

(A) The median is 41.

(B) This plot is organized according to place value.

(C) The range is 51.

(D) The outlier is 61.

23. Below is a chart showing the ratio of eggs to cups of blueberries in a muffin recipe.

Eggs (x)	4	6	8	e	24
Cups of Blueberries (y)	6	b	12	30	36

What inferences can be made from the data above?

(A) the ratio of eggs to cups of blueberries is 2:3

(B) $b = 8$ and e $= 10$

(C) if this were graphed on a coordinate grid, the slope would be $\frac{3}{2}$

(D) both (A) and (C)

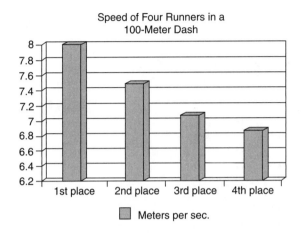

Speed of Four Runners in a
100-Meter Dash

☐ Meters per sec.

24. Based on the bar graph shown above, which of the following conclusions is true?

(A) Everyone ran faster than 7 meters per second.

(B) The best possible rate for the 100-meter dash is 7.9 meters per second.

(C) The second place runner was twice as fast as the third place runner.

(D) The third and fourth place runners were closest in time to one another.

25. Pretend you are using two six-sided, standard dice labeled #1–6 and roll them one at a time. Then, you spin a spinner divided into quarters labeled #1–4. What is the probability of rolling two even numbers and spinning a 2?

(A) $\frac{1}{16}$

(B) $\frac{1}{8}$

(C) $\frac{5}{8}$

(D) $\frac{9}{16}$

26. A bag is filled with 15 candies. There are five red candies, four blue, three brown, two yellow, and one green. Byron removes a candy from the bag. Without replacing the first candy, he takes a second. What is the probability both candies are brown?

(A) 1 out of 35

(B) 2 out of 7

(C) 1 out of 7

(D) 2 out of 29

KAPLAN

Constructed-Response Question 1

Complete the exercise that follows.

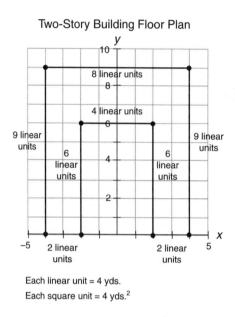

Two-Story Building Floor Plan

Each linear unit = 4 yds.
Each square unit = 4 yds.²

The graph above shows a plain view of a two-story building. The perimeter of the building has been labeled. Each unit on the *x*- and *y*-axes represents a distance of 4 yards. Using your knowledge of geometry and algebra:

a) What is the square yardage of the two-story building?

b) What is the square footage of the two-story building?

Be sure to thoroughly explain how you arrived at the answer.

_____

_____

_____

_____

_____

_____

_____

_____

_____

_____

Constructed-response Question 2

Complete the exercise that follows.

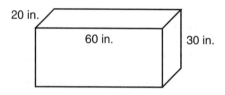

Christopher is planning to fill the above container with cubes. The entire volume of the container must be occupied with these cubes, and all the cube tiles must be the same size. Their dimensions must be whole numbers, so Christopher must make his calculations carefully. After pondering the situation, he enlists the help of his teacher.

Using your knowledge of number theory and geometry:

a) Identify three different sizes of cubes that could be used to completely fill the container with cubes.

b) Determine the smallest number of cubes that could be used to fill the entire container.

Show all of your work carefully and thoroughly.

_____

_____

_____

_____

_____

_____

_____

_____

_____

_____

_____

_____

_____

_____

_____

_____

_____

KAPLAN

ANSWER KEY

1. B	8. D	15. D	22. D
2. D	9. B	16. A	23. D
3. D	10. B	17. B	24. D
4. B	11. D	18. A	25. A
5. A	12. D	19. D	26. A
6. D	13. D	20. B	
7. B	14. B	21. C	

ANSWERS AND EXPLANATIONS

1. B

If a DVD player is 25% off, you're paying 75% of the actual price. 0.75 × $130.00 is $97.50. If you'd rather calculate 25% of $130.00 instead, be sure to subtract this amount from $130.00 to get the price of the DVD player.

2. D

This is a multi-step problem requiring the use of division. When calculating 27 lbs of meat divided into $\frac{1}{3}$ pound portions, be sure to take the reciprocal of the second term, $\frac{1}{3}$. This comes out to 27 × 3 = 81 portions.

Then 81 portions are divided into groups of 4 yielding 20 packages and 1 portion left over. The remainder, in this case, is dropped since it is three portions short of being a complete package.

3. D

This problem requires converting numbers to percents. Jasmine's 5 out of 8 is equivalent to 62.5%, Juniper made over 87%, Marcia made about 43.5% (roughly half of Juniper's shots), and Reece made 25% of her shots. From here, the order from least to greatest becomes clear.

4. B

It's important not to be fooled by 4,550 million, since a thousand million is a billion. Scientific notation is written as a number between 1 and 10 multiplied by a power of 10. A million is equivalent to 10^6 and a thousand is 10^3, yielding 10^9. 4.55×10^9 is the same as 4.55 billion or 4,550 million.

5. A

Proportional reasoning is a good strategy to use for this problem. Remember that percent means "over 100" or "divided by 100" and a percent decrease is the amount decreased over 100. To find the percent decrease, set the money spent over the total and compare that to the percent. It looks like this:

$$\frac{\$135 \text{ spent}}{\$180 \text{ total}} = \frac{x}{100}$$ (this is the percent decrease, since $135 was spent out of $180.)

$$180x = 13,500 \text{ (Cross products)}$$

$$x = 75 \text{ (divide both sides by 180)}$$

$\frac{75}{100}$ is 75%, the decrease in spending money.

6. D

Knowledge of the order of operations is helpful here: Parentheses, Exponent, Roots, Divide, Multiply, Add, and Subtract from left to right.

$\frac{8(12 - 3^2)}{12}$ Do the exponents in the parentheses first.

$= \frac{8(12 - 9)}{12}$ Combine like terms in the parentheses.

$= \frac{8(3)}{12}$ Multiply the numerators.

$= \frac{24}{12}$ Simplify the fraction via division: 24 ÷ 12 = 2.

$= 2$ Final answer.

7. B

Rounding to the nearest ten for each number and comparing this to the actual answer reveals a difference of 8. Use of the provided calculator may save time on this type of problem.

8. D

Questions pertaining to linear equations should be expected. When reading this table, a comparison to the x-axis and y-axis should be drawn. The zero value for R reveals the y intercept of 5. The equation is similar to $y = 3x + 5$, R being x and T being y. The slope on this graph is positive as witnessed from the coefficient of 3 and seeing the increase of 3 bikes per each 1 rack.

9. B

Proportional reasoning, again, becomes important to solving this multi-step problem. Notice that the cost is 35 cents per "three miles" when setting up the proportion.

$$\frac{\$0.35}{3 \text{ miles}} = \frac{x}{465} \text{ miles}$$

$$3x = 162.75 \text{ (Cross products)}$$

$$x = 54.25 \text{ (divide both sides by 3)}$$

Add the $20.00 fee to the mileage cost and the total becomes $74.25.

10. B

Understanding and knowing the standard form of linear equations becomes imperative when deciphering a line's equation on a coordinate grid. Notice where the line crosses the y-axis: at 2. The slope of the line or "rise over run" can be found by starting at a point on the line that exactly crosses an x and y interval, say (0,2) for example. From (0,2), rise three units upward along the y-axis and run to the right 4 units along the x-axis. Notice that you arrive at a point exactly on the line, (4,5). These (x,y) coordinates represent answers that satisfy the equation $y = \frac{3}{4}x + 2$.

11. D

When solving inequalities, remember that whenever you divide or multiply by a negative number to both sides of an equation, the sign flips in the opposite direction. The order of operations must also be followed to avoid mistakes.

$-8(x + 1) + 3(2x - 2) \geq 44$ (apply the distributive property to both terms)

$-8x - 8 + 6x - 6 \geq 44$ (combine like terms)

$-2x - 14 \geq 44$ (add the opposite of -14 to both sides)

$-2x \geq 58$ (divide both sides by -2)

$x \leq -29$

12. D

In the table for Pennel's CDs 4 Less Superstore, each CD costs $5.75 regardless of the quantity purchased. When graphed, the cost will increase relative to the number purchased in a consistent manner, meaning the line representing this change will always be straight. It will move upward and to the right, so **(D)** is the only graphic representation of this data.

13. D

Translating words into algebraic equations is the skill required here. A total of 49 hours is divided among 3 workers. Let x be the first worker; $2x$ is the second worker with twice as many hours as the first. $4x - 7$ is the third worker, who has seven less than twice the second.

14. B

Understanding and being able to apply the standard form of quadratic equations, the zero property, the axis of symmetry formula, and the factorization of polynomials are imperative to answer this question successfully. The standard form of a quadratic equation is $ax^2 + bx + c$. When a is greater than 0 the parabola opens up. This a term is -2 so the parabola opens downward. The axis of symmetry formula used to find the x-coordinate of the vertex is $-\frac{b}{2a}$. To find the y-coordinate, the x-coordinate value needs to be substituted into the standard form of the quadratic

equation. The coordinates, $(-1, 10)$ are incorrect. They should be $(-1$ and $\frac{3}{4}$, 10 and $\frac{1}{8})$. Applying the zero property via factoring the polynomial yields the values of $\frac{1}{2}$ and -4 for x. These are where the arms of the parabola cross the x-axis. The y intercept is 4 via setting the equation to y and substituting 0 for x:
$y = -2(0)^2 - 7(0) + 4$.

15. D

The formula for the area of a trapezoid is $\frac{1}{2}h(b_1 + b_2)$. Since the two trapezoids are in proportion by a 2 : 1 ratio, the values of their heights and bases can be found. Applying the formula, $\frac{1}{2}(4) \times (5 + 3) = 16$ m².

16. A

The surface area of a rectangular prism is the sum of the area of its six faces. There are three pairs of congruent faces. There are:

two 30" × 24" = 720 × 2 = 1,440

two 36" × 24" = 864 × 2 = 1,728

two 36" × 30" = 1080 × 2 = 2,160

Total surface area is 5,328 in.²

17. B

The volume of a cylinder is the area of the base (written as A) multiplied by its height. $V = A \times h$. Pi (π) multiplied by the radius squared is the formula for finding the area of a circle, the base of the cylinder. The radius is 7 in. if the diameter is 14 in. Its height is 30 in. 3.14×7 in.² × 30 in. = 3.14×49 in. × 30 in. = 4,615.8 in³.

18. A

To find the area of the sidewalk, the area of the smaller, inner circle needs to be subtracted from the area of the larger outer circle. Pi (π) multiplied by the radius squared is the formula for the area of a circle. The radius of the smaller, inner circle is 6 ft., while the larger outer circle's radius is 16 ft.

Bigger circle: $\pi \times (16\ ft)^2 = 256\pi$ ft²

Smaller circle: $\pi \times (6\ ft)^2 = 36\pi$ ft²

The difference is 220π ft².

19. D

To solve this problem, calculate the miles driven for each of the two legs of the journey. 35 miles per hour × $\frac{1}{2}$ an hour is the same as dividing 35 by 2 to get 17.5 miles. Then 60 miles per hour × $\frac{3}{4}$ of an hour is $\frac{180}{4} =$ 45 miles. The sum is 62.5 miles driven.

20. B

The question asks for the answer to be expressed in miles per hour. The problem gives us 175 miles in 3 hours (180 minutes = 3 hours). 175 miles ÷ 3 hours will yield miles per hour. The quotient is $58\frac{1}{3}$ miles per hour.

21. C

Knowledge of the basic concepts of data analysis is tested here. The mean is 74.5. The range of the data, the difference between the greatest and least piece of data, is 48. This set of data is bimodal beccause there are three 72s and 75s.

22. D

The stem-and-leaf plot is useful when plotting many pieces of data onto a graph. The median, or middle term in an ordered set of data, is 41. All stem and leaf plots are organized according to place value. The range of the data is 51, since $64 - 13 = 51$. But the outlier, the piece of data away from the rest of the data, is not 61. It's 13, since 13 is 10 sit-ups away from the next smallest piece of data, 23.

23. D

Being able to interpret tables of data into linear equations is the step just beyond being able spot patterns or "rules" controlling the way a set of data functions. Hence, the name *function tables*. The ratio of cups of blueberries to eggs is a 3 : 2 ratio. By using this ratio, the solution for *b* is 9 and *e* is 20. Notice the *x* and *y* next to Eggs and Cups of Blueberries. The ratio 3 : 2 also refers to the slope of the line this linear function (a.k.a. linear equation) creates. The equation in standard form would be $y = \frac{3}{2}x + 0$.

24. D

By looking carefully at the data on this bar graph, it is clear that the third and fourth place racers have the closest split times. The fourth place runner ran slower than 7 meters per second. The first place winner ran 8 meters per second and the second place finisher certainly did not run twice the speed of the third place finisher.

25. A

The probability of rolling an even number with two dice, one at a time, is $\frac{1}{2} \times \frac{1}{2} = $ a $\frac{1}{4}$ probability. Landing on a 2 with a spinner divided into quarters, #1–4, has a 1 out of 4 probability. When calculating compound probabilities, multiplication is the operation used, so $\frac{1}{4} \times \frac{1}{4}$ is $\frac{1}{16}$. Therefore, there is a $\frac{1}{16}$ probability of rolling two even numbers and having that spinner land on a 2.

26. A

This is a dependent probability problem, since it occurs without replacement. The key words here are *second consecutive*. The probability of choosing a second consecutive brown candy is a compound probability problem that takes into account the first outcome. It can be worked out like this:

Probability of the first brown candy is $\frac{3}{15} = \frac{1}{5}$.

Probability of the second consecutive brown candy, after the first brown one was chosen, is $\frac{2}{14}$ or $\frac{1}{7}$.

These compound events are multiplied and yield $\frac{1}{35}$. Therefore, there is a $\frac{1}{35}$ chance of choosing two brown candies.

Constructed-response Sample Essay 1

This assignment asks us for two things, the square yardage and square footage of the two-story building. We also must give a rationale for the steps that were used.

a) What is the square yardage of the building?

1. When working with an irregular polygon, it is helpful to divide it into smaller polygons. I have divided this floor plan into three rectangles, two of which are congruent. Their dimensions are:

One 8 unit by 3 unit rectangle.   *Conversion factor: 1 unit = 4 yards

Convert the 8 unit by 3 unit rectangle to a 32 yard by 12 yard rectangle.

$A = l \times w$

$32 \times 12 = 384 \text{ yds}^2$

Two 2-unit by 6-unit rectangles.   *Conversion factor: 1 unit = 4 yards

Convert the 2-unit by 6-unit rectangle to an 8 yard by 24 yard rectangle.

$A = l \times w$

$8 \times 24 = 192 \text{ yds}^2$ times two rectangles*

384 yds^2 for both rectangles.

2. To calculate the square yardage of one floor, add the sum of the three smaller rectangles:

$384 \text{ yds}^2 + 384 \text{ yds}^2 = 768 \text{ yds}^2$

3. To calculate the square yardage of both floors, multiply this amount by two:

$768 \text{ yds}^2 \times 2 = 1{,}536 \text{ yds}^2$

The area in square yards is $1{,}536 \text{ yds}^2$.

b) What is the square footage of the two-story building?

1. Conversion factor: 1 yard = 3 feet

1 square yard = 1 yard $\times$ 1 yard

Therefore, $1 \text{ yd}^2 = 3 \text{ feet} \times 3 \text{ feet} = 9 \text{ ft}^2$.

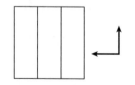

2. Convert square yards to square feet using the conversion factor. This will yield the square footage of both floors.

$$1{,}536 \text{ yds}^2 \times 9\text{ft}^2/1 \text{ yd}^2 = 13{,}824 \text{ ft}^2$$

The area in square feet is 13,824 ft^2.

Constructed-response Sample Essay 2

a) In order to find the possible size of the cubes used to fill the container (which is a rectangular prism), a closer look at the dimensions of the container is needed. The length is 60 in, the width is 20 in, and the height is 30 in. The common factors found in each of these numbers will help determine the compatible size of the cubes. We'll also need to use the formula for volume of a rectangular prism. Volume = length $\times$ width $\times$ height or the volume equals the area of the base times its height.

List of common factors:

　　60: 1, 2, 2, 3, and 5

　　20: 1, 2, 2, and 5

　　30: 1, 2, 3, and 5

These are the common factors:

　　$1 \times 1 \times 1$

　　$2 \times 2 \times 2$

　　$5 \times 5 \times 5$

　　$10 \times 10 \times 10$ (Combining both the factors 2 and 5)

That means that cubes of these sizes will fill the entire container.

Now it's time to divide the dimensions of the cubes into the dimensions of the container.

This will give us the number of cubes that will fit into the length, width, and height of the rectangular prism. By substituting these values into the volume formula, $V = l \times w \times h$, the total number of cubes can be calculated.

For the:
1" $\times$ 1" $\times$ 1" cube:

　　length-wise (60) width-wise (20) height-wise (30)

Therefore, there are $60 \times 20 \times 30$ cubes of this size. That's 36,000 of them.

2" $\times$ 2" $\times$ 2" cube:

　　length-wise (60 ÷ 2 = 30) width-wise (20 ÷ 2 = 10) height-wise (30 ÷ 2 = 15)

Therefore, there are $30 \times 10 \times 15$ cubes of this size. That's 4,500 of them.

KAPLAN

5" × 5" × 5" cube:

length-wise (60 ÷ 5 = 12) width-wise (20 ÷ 5 = 4) height-wise (30 ÷ 5 = 6)

Therefore, there are 12 × 4 × 6 cubes of this size. That's 288 of them.

10" × 10" × 10" cube:

length-wise: (60 ÷ 10 = 6) width-wise: (20 ÷ 10 = 2) height-wise: (30 ÷ 10 = 3)

Therefore, there are 6 × 2 × 3 cubes of this size. That's 36 of them.

b) In order to find the smallest number of cubes used to fill the container, we'll use the calculation for the biggest sized cube, the 10" by 10" by 10" cube.

The smallest number of cubes is 36 ten-cubic-inch cubes.

PART THREE

Subtest 3

ABOUT SUBTEST 3

Subtest 3 of the CSET Multiple Subjects Exam has the reputation of being the easiest of the three sections to pass. For one thing, it is the shortest of the three. There are 39 multiple-choice questions, rather than the 52 questions found on each of the other two subtests. Instead of four constructed-response questions, Subtest 3 has three.

The three content domains covered by Subtest 3 are physical education, human development, and the visual and performing arts. There will be 13 multiple-choice questions in each of the three areas and one constructed-response in each area.

One good thing about Subtest 3 is that the fields of human development and physical education overlap a great deal in terms of the big picture. If you have a solid grounding in the developmental process and needs of children, you can apply much of that knowledge in developing an understanding of the special considerations of physical education.

Many of the questions require you to take basic information and apply it to a particular context. Others probe your comprehension of the underlying reasons for a particular kind of educational strategy. So as you read the information, don't just sit back and let it wash over you. Actively engage yourself with the material. Think about children you have known and situations you have encountered. Try to apply the information to the classroom. That will prepare you for the variety of questions you will encounter on the CSET.

The visual and performing arts questions may pose more of a challenge unless you have already developed and pursued an interest for the arts. The arts covered in Subtest 3 are visual art, music, dance, and theater. Successful candidates are expected to possess knowledge sufficient to teach students the basic principles of creating and appreciating works of art in these four areas.

There is a fair amount of technical vocabulary you must master for the four arts areas. Additionally, you are expected to be familiar with the fundamental histories of these arts, as well as their varying expressions in different cultural traditions. Fortunately, the mastery of art fundamentals enriches your life immeasurably and, in turn, the lives of your students. You will always be glad that you understand the work of artists and performers in a deeper, richer way.

Chapter 5: **Physical Education**

THE BIG PICTURE

The primary thing to keep in mind as you prepare for this portion of Subtest 3 is the *goal* of Physical Education for elementary– and middle-school-aged children. What is the purpose of Physical Education? In a nutshell, the answer is this: Physical Education should promote lifelong participation in physical activity. Physical Education programs and classes must be structured and conducted to promote physical activity outside of and beyond school.

The state framework for Physical Education (cde.ca.gov/ci/pe/cf) sets forth a progression of activities and approaches that is designed to engender enthusiasm for physical activity. Enthusiasm for activity is the goal of Physical Education classes for children. Therefore, it is important for you to keep in mind the kinds of things that will promote enthusiasm for physical activity: successful attempts at learning (regardless of such factors as gender, body types, and abilities of individuals); developmental appropriateness of activities and teaching styles; and the fostering of cooperation over competition, particularly during the primary grades. This portion of the exam tests your ability to teach Physical Education in such a way that your students will enjoy the activities as well as acquire the necessary skills.

Constructed-response questions in this subject area require you to keep in mind the overall goal of Physical Education as well as such sound teaching principles as scaffolding and step-by-step instruction. You may be asked questions that require you to structure a lesson plan to teach any one of a variety of activities to any specified age group from kindergarten through eighth grade (though past tests have focused on the elementary grades). A well-structured lesson in Physical Education will include the basic components of warm-up, instruction, activity, and feedback.

Many of the questions on this section of the CSET are presented in the form of a scenario. You are asked to evaluate the scenario based on your knowledge of developmental appropriateness with respect to Physical Education. Our discussion of the content specifications will present information broken down by grade level so you can think about what skills and challenges are appropriate to those grade levels.

As you study, it may be useful to make a guide for yourself by grade level. Each content domain has information specific to the various developmental levels; but if you put, for example, all kindergarten developmental information in one place, it may help you get a clearer picture of the developmental needs of kindergartners across the content domains.

Use Your Past Experiences

If you are an athlete yourself, you're in luck on this part of the test. You can use your memories of teachers and coaches whose positive attitudes and step-by-step instructional skills encouraged your participation and enriched your life.

On the other hand, maybe you avoid physical activity because of your unfortunate experiences in or out of school—maybe you were always picked last for team sports, or classmates laughed at your attempts to learn, or...well, unfortunately, that list is a long one. If that is the case, you can also draw on your life experiences—for what *not* to do, or what *not* to allow in your Physical Education classes.

Use Your Outside Knowledge

Physical Education as a discipline draws on other subjects for much of the information you need. Specifically, many of the concepts you need to know come from physical science (action-reaction, friction), biology (biomechanics, health benefits of fitness), human development (positive self-image, developmental appropriateness), and even history and the arts (cultural and historical aspects of dance and other movement forms). Your knowledge of these subject areas will serve you well as you tackle the specific demands of Physical Education subject matter and questions.

In particular, it is very important to thoroughly understand the physical, mental, emotional, and social stages of human development. Many CSET questions about Physical Education require you to apply your knowledge of these stages to questions about specific situations. Questions will include a reference to a specific age or grade level, and you will be required to consider developmental appropriateness in your answer, in addition to applying your knowledge of biomechanical principles, fitness concepts, or other content domains.

THE KAPLAN METHOD

Multiple-Choice Questions

1. Read the question carefully. As you read, underline or circle the key words and phrases that differentiate this particular question from all other possible questions.
2. Rephrase the question to make sure you understand it. If possible, predict the correct answer.
3. Read all the answer choices, eliminating (physically marking through) incorrect ones as you go.
4. If two or more possible answer choices remain, go back to the question and search for matching/mirroring language or concepts that will point you toward the single correct answer.

Constructed-Response Questions

1. Read each question carefully. As you read, underline or circle the key words and phrases that differentiate this particular question from all other possible questions.

2. Note how many parts the question has. Be sure to include subparts in your count. Write this number in your test booklet, so you will be sure to answer each part of the question.

3. Before you start writing, brainstorm for vocabulary words and relevant concepts. Make your notes in the margins of your answer sheet, so you will be sure to include them in your answer. If you don't have a good command of details for a particular question, be sure to include in your answer the big picture concepts, such as the reason for studying/ teaching the subject.

4. Organize your thoughts! Remember, you are being tested on your ability to clearly convey information.

MOVEMENT SKILLS AND KNOWLEDGE

There are three main areas of knowledge related to movement on this section of the CSET. They are: basic movement skills, exercise physiology, and movement forms. We will discuss them in terms of development and expectation by grade level. The CSET focuses on the elementary grades, but a question may arise that requires you to know guidelines for grades six through eight; therefore those are included here.

It is important to remember that these are expectations and guidelines. Any given child or group of children may exceed these expectations or be unable to meet them. You need to know these expectations, but you must remain aware that part of your challenge as a teacher is to create lessons that enable children at all levels of ability to experience success in Physical Education.

Test Yourself

Which of the following activities can be used to practice locomotor skills?

(A) skipping to music

(B) absorbing the force of a thrown ball

(C) balancing on a see-saw

(D) performing hamstring stretches

The correct answer is **(A)**, skipping to music. Locomotor skills are movements requiring location change. Absorbing the force of a thrown ball **(B)**, balancing **(C)**, and stretching **(D)** do not require location changes.

Basic Movement Skills

Primary Grades (K–2)

At this age, children are learning how to control their bodies, particularly acquiring and refining their gross motor skills. They enjoy extending their bodies' capabilities. Teachers can enhance this by providing opportunities to have fun in their individual spaces, as the children's ability to cooperate with each other is limited.

In the primary grades, children are introduced to *biomechanical principles* such as center of gravity and application of force. They begin to combine these principles with their developing understanding of time and space in relation to their bodies and activities.

In kindergarten, children work on balancing, as they practice *nonlocomotor skills,* such as bending, stretching, and twisting. They also practice balancing as they walk in groups without bumping each other.

Kindergartners are learning such *locomotor skills* as running, jumping, skipping, and galloping. They may enjoy a simple obstacle course that allows them to practice these movement skills.

Kindergarten children can be encouraged to strike a ball, using any part of the body except the head. They can throw and kick, though many will not be skilled at catching.

First-graders are improving in their catching abilities as well as throwing and kicking. They are improving in their spatial awareness, and can engage in movement exploration by responding to such directions as *faster, slower, over, under, behind,* and *through.* Activities, such as an obstacle course, may be structured around these concepts.

By second grade, most children will be able to change direction quickly and safely. They can move backwards without falling, and are skilled at jumping, including jumping rope. They have mastered all the basic locomotor skills.

Second-graders are adept at throwing a ball overhand, with a side orientation. They understand and demonstrate the principle of *opposition* when throwing.

Middle Grades (3–5)

As children move into the middle grades, they have mastered the basic locomotor and nonlocomotor movement skills. Their fine motor skills are improving dramatically, as evidenced by their handwriting. They understand the underlying principles of biomechanics and how to apply them to skill improvement (for example, by following through when throwing, kicking, or striking a ball).

Third-graders can dribble a ball with hands or feet. They can begin to combine locomotor and nonlocomotor movements in relation to music (dancing). They use their understanding of body positions (low, middle, high levels) to learn stretching exercises.

In fourth grade, children can leap off of either foot. They can safely challenge themselves by jumping for height or distance. They can also dribble a ball, with hands or feet, while moving within a group, as required in basketball or soccer.

Fifth-grade children have mastered most of the basic movement skills required for organized play. Now they are ready to start applying these basic skills to the specific movements necessary for team and individual sports.

Upper Grades (6–8)

In middle school children focus on individual and team activities they enjoy. Having mastered the basic movement skills, they learn the specific skill sets needed to participate in their favorite activities. They also understand biomechanical principles such as action/reaction and the causes and effects of spin and torque.

Middle schoolers can throw a variety of objects (flying discs, footballs, etc.) for distance and accuracy. They are able to learn and perform dances and other movement routines, and investigate outdoor activities such as hiking and rope courses.

In all their activities, adolescents use mature motor patterns, which they improve by the conscious application of biomechanical principles. They improve and maintain muscle strength, enhance cardiovascular function, and learn and practice advanced stretching/flexibility routines.

Exercise Physiology: Health and Physical Fitness

As one means of encouraging lifelong participation in physical activity, teachers are expected to know and to convey to their students the benefits of health and fitness and the risks of inactivity. This knowledge includes understanding the components of physical fitness, such as flexibility, strength, and cardiovascular endurance. It also includes knowing about medical factors such as asthma and diabetes and how these factors affect children's participation in physical activities, as well as the possible cause and effect relationship of obesity and diabetes. Of course, children are introduced to this information gradually, in keeping with their developmental stages.

Primary Grades (K–2)

In kindergarten, children are introduced to the main parts of the body, both internal (heart, lungs, stomach) and external (hands, feet, arms, legs). They learn that they breathe more quickly and their heart beats faster when they exercise, and that this helps the lungs and heart to develop.

First-graders learn about food and proper eating as a part of their well-being. They begin to understand how bodies change as they grow in height and weight.

By second grade, children can count their pulse rate after exercise and at rest. They are becoming more aware of their bodies' needs for healthy food and exercise, as well as their individual medical conditions (e.g., asthma, diabetes).

Middle Grades (3–5)

In third grade, children can understand the purpose of warm-up activities such as stretching. These activities are designed to minimize the chance of injuries during exercise. In a warm-up activity, muscles and joints receive added oxygen-carrying blood and are loosened up in preparation for use.

KAPLAN

Fourth-graders should be able to describe the health benefits of regular exercise. Exercise strengthens the immune system, enhancing disease resistance (fewer colds). It also helps prevent adult diseases such as heart disease and high blood pressure. Exercise helps academic performance, enhances confidence, and reduces stress. It is also a good way to form and enhance friendships.

By the end of fifth grade, children have been introduced to the components of fitness. These are flexibility (e.g., stretching), muscular strength and endurance (e.g., chin-ups), cardio-respiratory endurance (e.g., jogging), and body composition. Students understand that these fitness components are the elements of a personal fitness plan.

Upper Grades (6–8)

In sixth grade, students consolidate their knowledge of the components of fitness. They understand that these components are interrelated, with an emphasis on the health benefits of flexibility and endurance. They know which kinds of activities contribute to the development of each fitness component, and are beginning to participate in physical activities that interest them outside of school.

Sixth grade is also a good time to emphasize the role of heredity and hormones/gender differences on body type as well as the relative strengths of each body type, in order to minimize the psychological impact of having bodies that don't fit the societal ideal.

Seventh-graders are learning to measure themselves against standards in terms of technique, accuracy, distance, and speed. They are taking more responsibility for their own fitness programs. This is a good time to introduce the concept of FIT, which stands for Frequency, Intensity, and Time. These are factors that improve fitness when applied as part of an exercise regimen. Conditioning is also influenced by the principles of overload, progression, and specificity; these principles can be introduced as students begin to set their own fitness goals. Teachers should be familiar with and able to discuss these principles and concepts.

In eighth grade students analyze their cardio-respiratory endurance, muscular strength and endurance, flexibility, and body composition in order to set goals. Using the concepts of FIT and the principles of overload, progression, and specificity, they devise their own plans for reaching their goals.

Movement Forms: Content Areas

Because you never know which activities and grade levels you may be asked about on the CSET, the best strategy is to learn the history, rules, strategy, and social etiquette for a number of common sports and activities. Among the sports that may be covered are softball, volleyball, soccer, basketball, handball (the playground variety), and badminton. Know how many players are on each team and the basic rules, mode, and etiquette of play.

Dance is also a thread that runs through the guidelines. Dance is versatile, adaptable to different skill and age levels, and easily integrated into an arts unit. It is important to remember to integrate Physical Education with academic subjects such as math (batting averages, graphs of progress), science (biology, physical science), and the arts (dance, music).

Another type of physical activity that is easily adapted for all ages and ability levels is gymnastics, beginning with balancing skills in kindergarten and progressing through simple tumbling in the middle grades to more advanced skills in the upper grades. Study the state guidelines for what skills are age-appropriate.

PHYSICAL GROWTH, PERSONAL DEVELOPMENT, AND SELF IMAGE

No matter what kind of multiple-choice or constructed-response question you face on the Physical Education section of the CSET, you must always consider the implications of children's personal development and self-image when choosing the correct answer. Remember, the goal of Physical Education is to promote lifelong participation in physical activity. A child who feels inadequate in Physical Education is not going to continue with physical activity any longer than is required.

Test Yourself

Which of the following is the most important consideration in making physical education activities suitable for children with asthma?

(A) excuse the children from all activities involving aerobic stress

(B) instruct children to breathe through their mouths whenever possible

(C) insist the children have inhalers with them at all times

(D) allow children to participate at their own pace during aerobic activities

The correct answer is **(D)**. Aerobic exercise develops much-needed cardiovascular strength in children with asthma, but it is important to allow them to pace themselves, resting whenever they need to. The other choices are incorrect. Mouth breathing **(B)** is sometimes necessary, though not particularly desirable. Not all children with asthma have inhalers **(C)**, and over-dependence on inhalers can be a problem. Many children with asthma develop the self-image of being inadequate when it comes to physical activities. It is important to help them recognize that they can participate, and even excel, in physical activities; not treat them "differently" by excusing them from physical education class **(A)**.

Physical Growth and Personal Development

There are two dimensions of physical growth that are relevant to this content domain: the development of fine and gross motor skills, and the influence of growth spurts on movement and coordination. Cognitive development also plays a part in the progressive mastery of skills and strategies. Physical growth proceeds at an uneven pace for most children; periods of apparent lack of progression are followed by dramatic spurts of development, and vice versa.

As was mentioned in the section on movement skills and knowledge, gross motor skills develop before fine motor skills. Gross motor skills involve the arms and legs; kindergartners are engaged in learning to coordinate these movements and to maintain their balance. By third grade, students have mastered the basic gross motor skills and are gaining the muscle mass and strength to apply these skills.

As they master gross motor skills, children are also starting to improve their fine motor skills. For example, first-graders will be able to throw a ball, but without much accuracy or refinement. Each year, students will gain in the ability to quickly hit a target, until eighth grade, when they learn how and when to apply spin to the ball.

Usually about first or second grade, children become aware of differences in individual growth rates. That is the time to begin discussing growth with them. Typically, individuals vary in the timing and extent of their growth spurts, but they steadily gain in size and strength until puberty. From third grade through fifth grade, there is a gradual but dramatic gain in size, muscle mass, and strength. At this age, girls tend to outpace boys in refining their fine motor skills, while boys already have the edge in muscle mass and strength.

Girls begin to reach puberty in fifth or sixth grade, boys not until seventh or eighth grade. This is the time of dramatic growth and development. Until this time, girls and boys are roughly equal in size and strength. The fact that girls, on average, reach puberty sooner than boys means that seventh- and eighth-grade girls are often taller than the boys in their classes. Because girls, after puberty, develop a higher ratio of fat to lean tissue, boys are stronger than even similar-sized girls after puberty. During major growth spurts, students may seem clumsy. At the end of such spurts, however, they are better able to coordinate their movements and perform motor tasks. This information can be reassuring to children in the midst of growth spurts.

About the same time girls start reaching puberty, around fifth grade, students grow increasingly aware of different body types, in terms of both appearance and performance. They begin to grasp the implications of possessing ectomorphic (thin), endomorphic (fat), or mesomorphic (muscular) body types. For example, a thin, long-legged child may be a faster runner than most but may not excel at strength activities, whereas a large, muscular child may be a slower runner but can throw a ball farther. It is vital at this stage to continue working with children to help them accept individual differences and their own body types.

Teachers must also provide instruction in the impact of factors such as exercise, relaxation, good (or inadequate) nutrition, stress, and substance abuse on well-being. Exercise and relaxation complement each other; exercise aids relaxation, and relaxation is necessary after exercise to allow muscles to recuperate and grow.

Good nutrition sets the stage for health and success. Proper diet provides the energy necessary to perform, physically and mentally. Fruits and vegetables, meat or other protein sources, complex carbohydrates, even fats all play a necessary role in good nutrition. Fiber is also important to a well-rounded diet, although it provides no calories (fuel for energy).

Stress is most often thought of as negative, but everyone experiences stress; it's how you deal with stress that makes the difference. Exercise is an excellent way to rid the body of stress-related hormones and to clear the mind. In a positive sense, muscle stress induced by exercise is the way in which muscles grow stronger, provided the exercise is followed by relaxation and that the body has sufficient nutrients available to form new muscle tissue.

Substance abuse is a serious threat to health. Alcohol abuse is the single most deadly form of substance abuse among adolescents and adults, and it also produces the most common adverse effects on babies born to substance abusing mothers (e.g., fetal alcohol syndrome). Students should be encouraged to seek help if they identify substance abuse in themselves, or in one of their friends or family members.

Self Image

All children, of all ages, are strengthened physically, mentally, and emotionally by participation in Physical Education and physical activity. With appropriate guidance, they become comfortable with their bodies and competent in physical skills. Constructive attitudes and physical competencies will encourage their lifelong participation in physical activity, which will make them healthier and happier.

It is important to find a way to include all students in play, regardless of their gender, race, culture, abilities, disabilities, or religion. It is also important to avoid situations in which any child feels hopelessly inadequate or shunned. Do not select captains to pick the teams one by one, as this leaves less able children waiting until everyone else has been picked. Competition is less important than cooperation at all ages, but particularly in the primary grades. The goal is for every child to feel like a winner. Remember this goal if you are asked to write a constructed response about any sport or game.

On the other hand, some students who do not excel in the classroom will experience a rare feeling of accomplishment on the playing field. The teacher must strike a balance between encouraging athletic excellence in capable students and contributing to low self-esteem in less able students. For example, avoid always asking the same few students to demonstrate new skills. (You can apply this in the classroom as well.)

It is also important to keep in mind the developmental capabilities of children of various ages. In the primary grades, children are not ready for structured competitive activities; they create their own competition during normal play. In the middle grades, children can develop healthy attitudes toward victory and defeat as they learn to participate in organized sports. Upper-grade children should be ready to set their own goals, secure in the realistic assessment of their strengths and needs for improvement. Goal setting is the best way to encourage fitness improvement in older children and adults. Implementing developmentally appropriate physical activities builds positive self images in your students, a primary goal of Physical Education.

SOCIAL DEVELOPMENT

In today's rapidly changing, increasingly diverse world, it is vital to teach children to accept and value differences. Physical Education class is an excellent place for this instruction. The teacher's charge and challenge is to find ways to promote fitness and health among all children, regardless of gender, race, culture, ability, or disability.

Test Yourself

Which of the following is of most importance in designing a physical education activity for an elementary school class?

(A) include practice of both locomotor and nonlocomotor skills

(B) ensure that children play cooperatively in small groups

(C) structure the activity so that all the children can enjoy participating and enhance their movement skills

(D) relate the activity to at least one academic discipline

The correct answer is **(C)**. The main goal of physical education is to encourage lifelong participation in physical activity. The other choices also are desirable in most contexts, but not as important as **(C)**.

Social Aspects of Physical Education

Learning to accept and respect the differences of others is a desirable life skill. Respect learned in Physical Education class becomes respect practiced in the classroom and on the playground. Respect leads to cooperation.

One reason competition is discouraged until the middle grades is that cooperation and respect lead to responsible social behavior. In the primary grades, it is much more appropriate for children to learn to work together than to learn to compete with each other.

In kindergarten, children are very egocentric; they find it difficult to understand viewpoints different from their own. Even when they are placed in groups, they work primarily as individuals and learn to cooperate only with practice. Competition works against this important developmental task.

Primary-aged children have a very limited understanding of and memory for rules. When rules must be followed, it is necessary to give clear, simple instructions and then supervise them closely. Most of the time, it is best to let these children play creatively on their own. Second graders can work with partners, learning to give and receive encouragement and to practice fair play.

By third grade, children can begin working in groups toward a common goal. In the middle grades, children work well in small groups of no more than five members. This allows each child to practice leading and following. In these groups, children can learn to work out problems on their own. They begin to formulate their own solutions to conflicts that may arise. It is now time for them to learn wholesome attitudes toward competition as well as toward success or failure.

They begin to understand that cheating undermines fairness and fun, and they also begin displaying increased awareness of social etiquette.

In sixth through eighth grades students are increasingly able to participate as team members rather than as individuals who happen to be on a team. They understand that following the rules promotes fairness and that there's more to the game, whatever it may be, than just winning or losing. Social skills and confidence have increased, and students are now fully responsible for their social behavior.

Cultural and Historical Aspects of Movement Forms

In geographical regions where there has been much immigration, there is wide variation in the forms and styles of physical activities. Teachers must take cultural differences into account when setting expectations and teaching rules. One of the best ways to teach respect for diversity is to model it.

Teaching dances from various regions of the world is a good way to encourage appreciation of cultural diversity. Even children in the primary grades can enjoy basic dance movement. Folk dances from all over the world can supplement and cement the information learned in the middle and upper grades' social science and history classes. Enjoyable dances include the Hora from Israel, the Pata Pata from South Africa, and of course, the Electric Slide from the good old USA.

Physical Education was emphasized in the ancient Greek culture, and it has gone in and out of favor ever since. Despite budget difficulties, it has become apparent that there is a need for increased physical activity in today's sedentary world. Since there are fewer active jobs, adults have to seek out physical activity or risk loss of health due to inactivity. That is the reason for the renewed emphasis on Physical Education classes and for the goal of encouraging lifelong participation in physical activity.

Glossary

Abduction: moving a part of the body away from the axis or middle of the body

Adduction: moving a part of the body toward the axis or middle of the body

Asthma: a controllable, chronic disorder, characterized by sudden attacks of coughing and difficulty breathing

Biomechanical principles: the forces governing the interaction of the body with the natural universe (see Chapter 3 for discussion of action/reaction, gravity, friction, etc.). These include the ball handling-related concepts of force projection and force absorption.

Body composition: the ratio of fat tissue to muscle and other lean tissues in the body

Cardio-respiratory endurance: the ability of the circulatory and respiratory systems to continue supplying oxygen to the body during prolonged exercise

Diabetes: a controllable, chronic disorder, requiring insulin treatment and dietary monitoring to maintain stable blood sugar levels

Fine motor skills: movements using small muscle groups (writing, grasping, finger snapping, etc.)

Flexibility: the ability of a joint to move in a range of motion (usually the wider the range, the better)

Frequency: in relation to exercise, how often an exercise is performed (every day, every other day, etc.)

Gross motor skills: movements using large muscle groups (running, throwing, catching, etc.)

Intensity: in relation to exercise, how difficult an exercise session is (lifting with one pound weights vs. two pound weights)

Locomotor movement: movement that results in location change (hopping, skipping, galloping, etc.)

Muscular endurance: the ability of a muscle to perform repetitions of a task

Muscular strength: the ability of a muscle to exert force on an object

Nonlocomotor movement: movement that does not result in location change (bending, twisting, stretching, etc.)

Opposition: when throwing a ball, the foot opposite the throwing hand steps forward

Overload: in relation to fitness, the concept that the only way to progress is to increase the level of difficulty

Progression: in relation to fitness, the concept that level of difficulty should be gradually increased, beginning at a difficulty level corresponding to the initial fitness level

Specificity: in relation to fitness, the concept that specific types of exercise are appropriate to increase specific types of fitness (jogging for cardiovascular fitness, crunches for abdominal muscles)

Time: in relation to exercise, for how long an exercise is performed in a single session

PRACTICE SET

1. Repeatedly hitting a tennis ball against a wall best illustrates which principle of biomechanics?

   (A) force absorption
   (B) friction
   (C) body awareness
   (D) action/reaction

2. Dionte is a typical kindergartner. Which of the following would be *most* difficult for Dionte?

   (A) listening to instructions from the teacher
   (B) recognizing other students' points of view
   (C) playing with a group of fellow students
   (D) trusting an adult's directions

3. A second-grader progresses from catching a bean bag to catching a basketball. This learning concept is an example of

   (A) transfer and feedback
   (B) understanding force, time, space, and flow
   (C) development of gross motor skills
   (D) unilateral activity

4. Which statement best describes why a physical education teacher should *not* use the expression "Kick 'em while they're down!" during her sixth graders' soccer game?

   (A) Violent children usually become violent adults.
   (B) Strenuous exercise is not an important element of a healthy lifestyle.
   (C) Children will often repeat what they have heard to their parents.
   (D) Healthy competition includes responsible social behavior.

5. Which of the following is an example of a nontraditional individual sport in the United States?

   (A) water polo
   (B) fencing
   (C) wrestling
   (D) track

6. Concerning students' physical development, when does the most noticeable gain in coordination and muscle strength occur?

    (A) grades K–2
    (B) grades 3–5
    (C) grades 6–8
    (D) during puberty

7. Which line in the table below accurately matches an activity with a type of skill required to successfully perform that activity?

Line	Activity	Type of Skill Required
1	Jumping jacks	Hand-eye coordination
2	Finger snapping	Gross motor skills
3	Swaying to music	Nonlocomotor skills
4	Throwing a basketball	Fine motor skills

    (A) Line 1
    (B) Line 2
    (C) Line 3
    (D) Line 4

8. Nita is a middle-school student whose parents divorced shortly before the death of her favorite aunt. Nita's friend Ned says that Nita has started abusing sleeping pills and diet pills. Which of the following statements is *most* useful in helping Nita's substance abuse?

    (A) Substance abuse can be an attempt to cope with depression or stress-related problems.
    (B) Substance abuse impacts the physical and emotional well-being of youth.
    (C) Athletic performance can be adversely affected by substance abuse.
    (D) Middle-school students are often influenced by peers to experiment.

9. At which of the following grade levels can students appreciate the reasons for rules in competitive games and be fully responsible for their actions in competitive play?

    (A) grade 2
    (B) grade 4
    (C) grade 6
    (D) grade 8

10. Which of the following is an example of dynamic balance?

    (A) skipping across a balance beam

    (B) posing in fifth position in ballet

    (C) performing a head stand

    (D) standing on one leg

    Use the description below of a second grade activity to answer question 11.

Human Pyramid
1. Ten players (who are willing to be climbed on) volunteer, as do two good spotters.
2. On the mat, the four largest players form the bottom row, on their hands and knees, shoulder-to-shoulder.
3. With the help of the spotters, the next three largest players carefully climb onto the bottom row, forming a second row on their hands and knees.
4. Players and spotters should watch that hands and knees are *not* pressing on spines or necks.
5. Is the pyramid steady? With the help of the spotters, two players climb up to form the third row.
6. With the help of the spotters, the lightest player forms the pyramid point!

11. This activity primarily promotes which responsible social behavior among elementary-age students?

    (A) setting goals and achieving them

    (B) using specific safety practices related to supporting the body weight of other children

    (C) encouraging extensive physical contact and activity among many children

    (D) promoting appreciation of personal differences and rights of others

12. Drew is a fifth grader with a mesomorph body type. With which of the following physical activities will Drew most likely require assistance?

    (A) throwing a football

    (B) twisting through an obstacle course apparatus

    (C) hitting a baseball a good distance

    (D) arm wrestling

13. In primary-grade physical education, which of the following will best help develop a positive self-concept?

(A) defining winners and losers

(B) teaching goal setting

(C) ensuring equal participation and achievement

(D) directing students to rate each other's accomplishments

Constructed-Response Question

Complete the exercise that follows.

Using your knowledge of the components of physical fitness and age-appropriate
activities, discuss how to design activities that enhance development of the following
in your class of third graders:

Flexibility

Muscle strength

Muscle endurance

Cardio-respiratory endurance

_____

_____

_____

_____

_____

_____

_____

_____

_____

_____

_____

_____

_____

_____

_____

_____

_____

_____

_____

_____

_____

ANSWER KEY

1. D	5. B	9. D	13. C
2. B	6. B	10. A	
3. A	7. C	11. B	
4. D	8. A	12. B	

ANSWERS AND EXPLANATIONS

1. D

Action/reaction is the P.E. term that is based on Newton's 3rd Law: "Every action has an opposite and equal reaction." A bouncing ball is a clear example of this law: a ball that is bounced, thrown, or hit will return with the same force, if no other force interferes with it. Although force absorption **(A)** and friction **(B)** are principles of biomechanics, hitting a tennis ball against a wall does not illustrate them. It is virtually impossible to make a connection between a bouncing tennis ball and the concept of body awareness **(C)**.

2. B

While children of kindergarten age often participate in activities as a group, they are generally focused on themselves, each as an individual. Kindergartners are egocentric; therefore, they posses a minimal idea of other people's viewpoints **(B)**. Listening to a teacher **(A)**, playing with a group **(C)**, or trusting an adult **(D)** may be problematic for some kindergarteners, but not the *most* problematic.

3. A

Transfer and feedback is the ability to transfer previous learning of a movement or technique (such as catching a bean bag), while making adjustments to perform a new skill (such as catching a basketball). Understanding force, time, space, and flow **(B)** is not necessary to be able to catch a basketball. Gross motor skills **(C)** are not a learning concept; neither is unilateral activity **(D)**.

4. D

Students need to understand and learn the necessity of responsible social behaviors, such as civility and good sportsmanship—even during competitive sports. P.E. teachers need to recognize the developmental appropriateness of cooperation, competition, and responsible social behaviors for youth of different ages. Encouraging students to shout negative "cheers" (promoting unhealthy competition) would be counterproductive to this goal. Choices **(A)** and **(C)** are outside the scope of the responsibility of a P.E. teacher. The statement in **(B)** does not relate to the influence of a teacher's cheers on students.

5. B

Fencing is the only nontraditional individual sport listed among these choices. Water polo **(A)** is considered a nontraditional team sport (not an individual one); soccer is a traditional team sport. Wrestling **(C)** dates back to the ancient Greeks and has enjoyed a long tradition in this country as well. Track **(D)** does include both individual and team events, but it is considered a traditional sport in American schools.

6. B

Even considering the unpredictability of growth in height, the physical development of third–, fourth–, and fifth-graders includes the most noticeable gain in coordination and muscle strength.

7. C

Jumping in place does not require hand-eye coordination, so **(A)** is incorrect. Gross motor skills should be matched with throwing a basketball and fine motor skills should be matched with finger snapping, eliminating **(B)** and **(D)**. Swaying is an example of a nonlocomotor skill—a movement that is performed in a fixed place, including turning/twisting; stretching/bending, and static balancing, making **(C)** the correct choice.

8. A

While all of the statements are accurate, only choice **(A)** speaks to the likely underlying cause of Nita's substance abuse—the recent stresses in her life. It is important that teachers understand the dangers, causes, and impact of alcohol, tobacco, and drug abuse. All teachers are charged with protecting the physical and emotional well-being of their students; a physical education teacher, however, is in a special position to address wellness issues. She or he might, for example, suggest exercise and relaxation techniques as safe alternatives to pills. Additionally, listening to Nita or directing her to a counselor could help her get through this rough period.

9. D

Children often participate in organized sports before reaching the eighth grade. At this level, the emphasis of organized sports is on lead-up games, physical fitness, personal growth, and healthy lifestyle choices. By eighth grade, however, students can appreciate the necessity and desirability of rules in competitive games. They are also fully accountable for their actions at this age.

10. A

Dynamic balance describes the stability achieved when a person is in motion, such as skipping across a balance beam **(A)** or riding a bicycle. The other three choices—posing in a ballet position **(B)**, doing a headstand **(C)**, and standing on one leg **(D)**—are examples of static balance, which is achieved when a person is balanced while holding a pose, being close to motionless.

11. B

While all of the choices concern responsible social behaviors, **(B)** is most relevant to this activity, which cautions safety ("carefully," "with the help of spotters," "players and spotters should watch that hands and knees are *not* pressing on spines or necks."). Children will need to exercise safety practices while cooperating to build a human pyramid. Additionally, practicing and alternating spotters builds safety skills for tumbling and gymnastics.

12. B

A student's body type (endomorph, mesomorph, or ectomorph) usually begins to affect his or her athletic performance around fifth grade. From the primary grades on, however, a P.E. teacher must teach students that physical capabilities and limitations can be a function of body type. The mesomorph student will most likely excel in activities that include the application of force, such as throwing a football **(A)**, hitting a baseball **(C)**, and arm wrestling **(D)**, but may be less coordinated with motor skills requiring agility or mobility, such as twisting through an obstacle course apparatus **(B)**.

13. C

Particularly in the primary grades, a child feels a great sense of accomplishment and self-worth when she or he has mastered an activity or a physical education concept. Students take pride in themselves when they are encouraged to participate and achieve at a level that fits them. P.E. lesson plans for the primary grades should take into account student differences in height, weight, and body type—helping to ensure equal participation and achievement **(C)**. Primary-grade students are not yet ready to practice goal setting in physical education **(B)**. Defining winners and losers **(A)** or directing students to rate each other **(D)** could contribute to feelings of inflated self-worth on the part of the "rater" or winner or feelings of diminished self-worth on the part of the student being rated or loser, making these choices incorrect.

Constructed-Response Sample Essay

The four components of physical fitness often form various combinations during games and sports. For example, I might enhance flexibility (range of motion at the joints) by having my third graders devise floor routines with stretching, swaying, and tumbling on mats in time to rhythms. My students could combine nonlocomotor and locomotor movements to build flexibility and grace by trying various travel patterns in relation to music. This assignment might include basic flips, cartwheels, and handstands—building muscular strength, which is developed thorough stress and tension applied during repetition.

A par-course or obstacle course that includes chin-ups, leg lifts, jumping, and skipping will improve muscle strength as well as muscle endurance—the ability of muscles to continue performing without fatigue. My students might dribble a ball continuously, using the hands and feet to control it, building both endurance and flexibility. Maintaining aerobic activity for a specified time is important for developing cardio-respiratory endurance, which refers to the circulatory and respiratory systems' ability to deliver oxygen to the body during exercise. My third graders might increase their endurance by running longer and longer relays, which might also involve passing a baton to a teammate for coordination and teamwork skills.

Chapter 6: **Human Development from Birth through Adolescence**

THE BIG PICTURE

As teachers deal with whole individuals and groups, the CSET tests their mastery of concepts related to social and physical development as well as cognitive development. They are expected to understand and apply ideas about genetic (internal) influences on development as well as social (external) influences. They must demonstrate an ability to identify similarities and differences among children and—most importantly—understand a variety of strategies for maximizing individual potential, including that in children with special needs.

In overall terms, teachers must understand multiple perspectives on human development, including the concept of multiple intelligences, characteristics and benefits of creative play, and the impact of various physical and social factors on an individual's development. On the CSET, they must demonstrate their understanding of these concepts by correctly identifying successful strategies for maximizing individual and group learning and for minimizing the negative impact of unfavorable external influences on children's development.

As you read this discussion of cognitive, social, and physical development and their influences on overall development, take the time to carefully consider their implications on the classroom. You might want to keep a running commentary, filled with examples of the concepts presented, drawn from children you have known or read about. This will help you practice transforming abstract theory into concrete application. Many Human Development questions on the CSET will provide you with a scenario, to which you will have to apply sound theory and practice. Your notes, drawn from your experience, will prepare you for success.

THE KAPLAN METHOD

Multiple-Choice Questions

1. Read the question carefully. As you read, underline or circle the key words and phrases that differentiate this particular question from all other possible questions.

2. Rephrase the question to make sure you understand it. If possible, predict the correct answer.

3. Read all the answer choices, eliminating (physically marking through) incorrect ones as you go.

4. If two or more possible answer choices remain, go back to the question and search for matching/mirroring language or concepts that will point you toward the single correct answer.

Constructed-Response Questions

1. Read each question carefully. As you read, underline or circle the key words and phrases that differentiate this particular question from all other possible questions.

2. Note how many parts the question has. Be sure to include subparts in your count. Write this number in your test booklet, so you will be sure to answer each part of the question.

3. Before you start writing, brainstorm for vocabulary words and relevant concepts. Make your notes in the margins of your answer sheet, so you will be sure to include them in your answer. If you don't have a good command of details for a particular question, be sure to include in your answer the big picture concepts, such as the reason for studying/teaching the subject.

4. Organize your thoughts! Remember, you are being tested on your ability to clearly convey information.

COGNITIVE DEVELOPMENT

Test Yourself

According to Piaget's breakdown of developmental milestones, a child of which of the following ages would be most likely to understand the law of conservation?

(A) four

(B) six

(C) nine

(D) fourteen

The correct answer is **(C)**. Children from ages seven to eleven fully grasp the law of conservation (that a tall, thin glass holds the same amount of liquid as a short, stout glass does).

Stages of Cognitive Development

Although there are numerous theorists with varying perspectives on cognitive development, it is generally accepted that there are sequential stages all children proceed through as they develop. Both the *cognitive constructionists* (e.g., Piaget) and the *social constructivists* (e.g., Vygotsky) agree on that point, though there are some differences in their approaches. The good news is that, so far, the CSET has not asked test-takers to know these theorists or their theories by name. The bad news—not so bad, really—is that you will be asked to understand the implications of the theories and to apply them in hypothetical situations.

Jean Piaget is probably regarded as the most influential child development theorist in education today. His work with children began with his fatherly interest in his own children's development. He was trained as a biologist and he applied his observational techniques to his children, learning that even the brightest children had difficulty mastering certain concepts before attaining sufficient age and experience.

Piaget realized that children (and adults) interpret a new experience in terms of their previous understandings. He called this *assimilation. Accommodation* is the process by which the child incorporates new experience into previous understandings, and modifies those existing concepts to include the new information. Piaget is called a cognitive constructivist because he wrote about the way children construct their own knowledge of the world.

Piaget is perhaps best known for his theories about the developmental stages all children pass through, in a specific order. That is not to say that you should think of Piaget's developmental schema as rigid and absolute. Rather, think of it as a guideline to what you might expect from children at various ages.

In Piaget's breakdown of developmental milestones, the first eighteen months to two years are spent in the *sensori-motor stage.* The child's task during this time is twofold: first, using her senses, she must learn to differentiate between herself and the external world. She learns that objects are distinct from her. Second, she achieves *object permanence*, i.e., realizes that a seen object still exists after being hidden from sight.

After mastering the sensori-motor stage, the child enters the *pre-operational stage.* This stage lasts from roughly two years to seven years of age. During this stage, the child still has difficulty entering into the viewpoints of others; she is trapped in an egocentric perspective. Increasingly, she is learning to use words for the purpose of labeling and ordering the world. She begins the process of symbol manipulation by using words for objects that are not present.

From ages seven to eleven (the stage focused on in the CSET), the child is in the *concrete operational stage.* She can reason with concrete objects in concrete situations. She realizes that a tall, thin glass, for example, holds the same amount of water as a short, fat glass or that a pile of pennies can contain the same number as a spread-out display of pennies. This is the *law of conservation.* She understands that objects can change form (solid to liquid and back) and remain the same object. This is known as *reversibility.* She also begins to understand the viewpoints of others, or at least to recognize that others' viewpoints are different from her own.

Also in the concrete operational stage (the stage of most elementary school children) the child learns deductive logic, which involves the consideration of two concepts or relationships at the same time. Piaget calls this ability *transitivity*. *Seriation* (from the same root as the word *serial*), or the act of putting things in order, is made possible by the child's mastery of transitivity. The pre-operational child will have difficulty with sorting objects by, say, size. The concrete operational child has no problem sorting by size or color or other characteristics. This lays the groundwork for mastering arithmetic and science.

At around eleven years of age, children enter into the world of abstract thought. They can grasp the hypotheses of science experiments, or algebraic equations, or philosophy. This is the stage of *formal operations.* Some children enter this stage later than eleven, some continue to struggle with abstractions into adulthood. According to Piaget, the most important factor in learning to perform formal operations is the influence of opportunities to practice. The implication for teachers, especially in the middle and upper grades, is to create and provide a wealth of opportunities for children to practice abstract reasoning, including during creative play.

If you want more information about Piaget, there are numerous books and articles on his theories available. You could try researching them on the Internet by, for example, typing *Piaget + Education* into a search engine. As you read, think about children you have known and try to identify characteristics of each stage in their actions.

Stages of Moral Development

A theorist who expanded on Piaget's thinking about moral development is Lawrence Kohlberg. Kohlberg identifies three main levels of moral reasoning, each level with two stages, though he maintains that some people don't progress beyond the first two levels (or even the first level).

Young children are at the *pre-conventional level* of moral development. In the first stage, they avoid wrongdoing, as they understand it, in order to avoid punishment. This is a reflection of their egocentrism, a main characteristic of young children. In the second stage, they focus on fairness (stealing is wrong because it's unfair) and understand that each person acts in his or her own best interests (if I hit you, you'll hit me back).

The *conventional level* of moral development focuses on what one is supposed to do. In stage three, children want to do what is defined as right by those around them—mother, father, teacher. They seek approval from authority figures. In stage four, awareness expands to society and its laws. Children understand that social order, the fabric of society, depends on voluntary cooperation of its citizens (what if everybody stole?). Respect for authority is at its height.

In Kohlberg's third level of morality, individuals think about the principles underlying society's laws and norms. Their adherence is to those principles, such as inalienable rights, not to the specific laws themselves (fifth stage). Those in the sixth stage are willing to disobey, or even fight against, laws or societal norms they believe subvert the universal moral principles.

Kohlberg's approach requires teachers to provide opportunities for children to practice making decisions. The democratic process can be an instrument of learning. One implication of Piaget's and Kohlberg's theories is that children naturally seek out situations in which to develop their potentials. This means that enabling creative play is an excellent way to foster cognitive and moral development. As with cognitive development, moral development depends on opportunities for practice.

Stages of Language Development

As was discussed in Chapter 1, language and thought are intimately bound together in humans. Our very capacity for thought develops through our mastery of language. If we learn a second language, we develop new ways to think about the world.

Children spend their pre-school years mastering language fundamentals. When they enter school, their ability to express themselves is still limited. Because of their stage of cognitive development, their thoughts are expressed in language that reflects their egocentrism ("I want...", "give me..."). There is little ability to reflect on their thoughts before speaking; whatever comes out of a six-year-old's mouth is exactly what that child is thinking, as best she can express it.

Between the ages of six and twelve, children's vocabularies grow tremendously. Their facility with conversation grows as well, and they begin to be able to think before they speak. This ability is a double-edged sword, as it enables children to say something other than what they are really thinking and often results in an experimentation with telling the truth (or not). Increased vocabulary and experience using language also enable abstract thought (formal operations).

Play and Cognitive Development

In the primary grades, as was discussed in Chapter 5, children start by playing side-by-side and gradually move into partnered play and small group play. A favorite activity is anything involving fantasy or make-believe. In this make-believe mode, children are actively problem solving and developing their cognitive abilities.

Another major cognitive task for children in the primary grades is learning to control their bodies. Although there are structured activities that aid in this task (see Chapter 5), children naturally pursue it with great enthusiasm of their own accord. As they make use of playground equipment they are exploring the interaction of their bodies with the world thus pursuing this crucial developmental task.

By the middle grades, children are beginning to gravitate toward team play and to develop the necessary cooperation and interaction with peers. Along with this increasing ability to cooperate with others comes the ability to work together to define and resolve conflict. Play is an important means of developing problem-solving skills. Fantasy play has become more complex, drawing on their expanded experiences and understanding of the world.

In the upper grades (middle school), children are beginning to master formal operations. As they do so, they start to create and utilize strategies that require them to anticipate situations in such sports as basketball. Sports strategies, such as pre-determined plays, aid in memory development as well. Creative play tends to be more structured, within the bounds of recognized art forms.

Memory Development

Teachers can help children develop their memories by teaching them *meta-cognition.* Meta-cognition is simply thinking about thinking. In other words, children can learn to consciously think about how they learn. An example of a strategy for meta-cognition is the memory-building strategy of *rehearsal.*

Even a kindergartner can learn rehearsal as a memory strategy. For instance, when teaching the colors of the rainbow, a teacher can prompt the children to repeat the colors frequently until they can easily remember them. Children under the age of nine or ten, however, cannot be expected to apply this strategy without being prompted.

After age ten or so, children who have been taught the rehearsal strategy can apply it spontaneously in a variety of situations. For example, to remember the name of a new acquaintance, a child may repeat it to himself several times.

Intelligence

For most of the twentieth century, a heated debate raged about intelligence. Much of the argument centered on the relative importance of nature (heredity) vs. nurture (environmental influences). At times it seemed that those arguing one side wanted to deny that the other had any influence whatsoever. Debate has settled down a bit now, and it is generally agreed that both heredity and environment influence the development of intelligence in individuals. Everyone is born with genetically determined potentials, but how those potentials develop depends to a large extent on what opportunities and encouragement a person encounters, particularly in the formative years.

While debating intelligence, scientists, psychologists, and others still seemed to agree about what constituted intelligence. They created tests to quantify it, and the results were often used to justify racist and other biased views. A breakthrough came in 1983 when Howard Gardner published a book claiming to have identified seven distinct types of intelligence—not just one. Gardner has now added an eighth to his list of *multiple intelligences.* The eight are: linguistic, spatial, logical-mathematical, musical, intra-personal (e.g., introspection), interpersonal (social), bodily-kinesthetic, and naturalist. Everyone possesses these intelligences in varying degrees.

What does the idea of multiple intelligences mean for teachers? For one thing, it means that most standard IQ tests haven't caught up with what we now know about intelligence. And it means that teachers have an improved framework to use in being sensitive to individual differences in learning styles and interests. You can help students develop their unique talents and abilities and teach them that everyone is differently-abled. For example, if a student is suffering because he's not talented in logical-mathematical thinking, you can help him appreciate and develop his interpersonal strengths (or another type of intelligence) and then learn to apply them to help his math performance. A student who feels successful is then more motivated to work hard in areas that may be more challenging.

It is also important for teachers to inform themselves about factors that make it difficult for students to experience success in the classroom. External influences will be discussed in a subsequent section of this chapter, but just as every student has different abilities, every student has challenges to overcome. One type of challenge that can be difficult to spot is actually a range of conditions known as *learning disabilities.* Learning disabilities are often related to the way individual brains process information, including visual stimuli. Dyslexia, a developmental reading disorder, and dyscalculia, which involves difficulty with math, are types of learning disorders. Attention Deficit Disorder (ADD), in which students have trouble focusing attention, and ADHD, which includes a hyperactivity component, are related disorders that make classroom success difficult. If a student seems to be a bright "underachiever", you should suspect a learning disability. A discrepancy between ability and achievement is one of the main signs of such a condition.

SOCIAL AND PHYSICAL DEVELOPMENT

Test Yourself

A child that has formed secure attachments prior to entering school will demonstrate all of the following characteristics EXCEPT

(A) forms friendships easily

(B) aggression toward other students

(C) self-confidence in relation to her physical environment

(D) feelings of competency

The correct answer is **(B)**. Children with secure attachments demonstrate all of the other characteristics listed, and are therefore successful in the school environment.

Attachment Theory

A baby is born completely dependent on one or more caregivers. The baby's experience of the trustworthiness of her caregivers (when I'm hungry, am I fed? when I'm lonely, am I picked up?) has an enormous impact on her later ability to form trusting, loving relationships with others. A child who is incompetently or inconsistently cared for does not feel worthy of care—she feels unlovable and has difficulty forming attachments to others. She may be timid or aggressive and will be hesitant and uncertain in new situations. A child who has formed secure attachments, on the other hand, has a sense of competency, forms friendships easily, and is confident exploring her physical environment. She trusts others and herself. This is the premise of *attachment theory,* an idea that has strong implications for teachers in the classroom.

Self-Concept

The child who seems hostile to you and other children or who resists new situations feels, at the deepest level, unlovable. He has a negative self-concept (how he thinks about himself) and low self-esteem (his feelings about himself). While it may not be within your power to completely convince him otherwise, knowing attachment theory can help you develop empathy and understanding for his plight. Human development specialists also agree that children with attachment difficulties can be helped by exposure to adults who consistently demonstrate trustworthiness and caring attitudes. Negative self-concepts can also be improved by the act of experiencing success. Sound educational methods (pedagogy) lead to increased experiences of success, so that when you help your students academically, you are supporting their positive self-concepts as well.

Autonomy

Humans have an innate drive toward independence. We achieve independence by mastering skills, whether physical (toilet training), mental, or emotional. We accept responsibility for our own behavior. Psychologists and human development specialists know this as *autonomy*. In educational terms, autonomy is the individual's acceptance of responsibility for her own learning.

A student cannot accept responsibility for his own learning unless he knows why he is learning and how to go about it. To explain this concept is part of a teacher's responsibility. As a student progresses, he must be explicitly taught the concepts and skills that will enable him to become an autonomous learner. This is another form of meta-cognition, which was discussed earlier in relation to memory development.

Identity

Prior to adolescence, children identify with others—originally with family then, during the early academic years, with authority figures. Coinciding with the middle school years, however, children start trying to answer the question, *Who am I?* They start looking to those more like themselves to help answer this question. In other words, peer relationships are an important means of determining the answer to the *who am I* question.

It is vital for teachers and other adults to give adolescents guidance in their search for self-definition, to help them make good choices and decisions, and to aid their explorations of their values and attitudes. It is important to give them increasing responsibility for their own actions. Finding one's own identity isn't easy, and there are many cultural and societal influences that can lead adolescents astray as they search for themselves. Increased responsibilities point them in the direction of adulthood. They come to see themselves as responsible adults, which must be part of the answer to their question.

Social Development of Children and Young Adolescents

Social development in the individual is the process of organizing energy and activity at progressively higher levels in order to increase the utilization of human potential. In other words, we are social creatures who achieve more as we become better able to use our abilities to further our advancement rather than wasting our energies in destructive behaviors. There are many facets to social development and numerous theorists have written on the topic. For information on the theories of Jean Piaget (mentioned previously in this chapter), Lev Vygotsky (see discussion of the Zone of Proximal Development in Chapter 1), or Erik Erikson, to name three of the most influential, you can use the Internet or go to any library.

Some of the ways in which the theorists agree point toward the implications of social development theory for educators. They agree, for example, that children learn through complex interactions with their physical and social world. An environment rich in opportunities for new encounters provides opportunities for children to encounter new information that causes them to challenge their previous assumptions and then incorporate the new knowledge into a higher level of understanding. In a social sense, children learn from teachers, from peer interactions, and on their own.

Behavioral Expectations by Grade Level

Primary Grades (K–2)

Even children entering kindergarten can understand simple, concrete rules. They can learn to wait their turn, to sit at a table, and to refrain from hitting their neighbors. However, they will have to be constantly reminded of the rules, as they really do not understand the reasons behind the rules. Their memories are not well-developed, nor is their moral reasoning. They follow rules to avoid punishment. As kindergarteners become first-graders, then second-graders, their memories gradually develop, and they start to become aware that there are reasons for the rules.

Middle Grades (3–5)

Children in third through fifth grades are learning about fairness, and they start to understand why there must be rules. They are in the conventional stage of moral development. At this age, they begin to cooperate with one another and can even work in small groups to create rules that they will follow. They can practice simple conflict resolution skills and are becoming increasingly accountable for their own behavior.

Upper Grades (6–8)

Middle school students are fully responsible for their own behavior. They understand, and can remember and follow the rules, and are mastering the subtleties of social etiquette.

Children with Special Needs

There are many different kinds of special needs in children. They may be related to sensory and physical development, to cognition and learning, or to their behavioral and emotional development. Any of these needs may result in difficulty communicating and interacting with others and so affect their social development. Sometimes these needs are recognized at birth or in the preschool years. Often, however, the needs will not be identified until the child enters the classroom.

It is an important part of their social development for children to learn to appreciate diversity of ability. Inclusion of children with special needs in all activities, as much as possible, is beneficial to all parties concerned. However, these children can also present special challenges for teachers and classmates. As the teacher, it is vital that you form a partnership to work with the child's parents and other members of the educational team in formulating an Individual Education Plan (IEP) that will enable the child to progress socially and academically.

Physical Development

For a more thorough discussion of physical development, see Chapter 5, Physical Education. Remember that children develop at varying rates, and when a child is experiencing a growth spurt, he may be awkward and clumsy. It is important to design physical activities so that all children, including those with special needs, can take part, even if in limited ways. In that context, remember that there are both gross motor (arm, leg) skills and fine motor (finger, manipulative) skills. Gross motor skills develop before fine motor skills, and all children develop at different rates.

INFLUENCES ON DEVELOPMENT

Some developmental differences in children are caused by physical or organic causes such as genetic predispositions or differences of physical or mental ability in children with special needs. Others are caused by the complex interactions of individuals with their environment.

The biggest influence on a child's social development is the parent/child interaction. Socioeconomic status (family income) plays a part in academic achievement, but a parent/child interaction that stresses the importance of academics can overcome socioeconomic handicaps. As was discussed in the earlier section on attachment, a healthy parent/child relationship gives the child the security needed to venture out into the world with confidence.

In addition to socioeconomic status, there are sociocultural factors playing a role in a child's development. These include racial and cultural perspectives, which can affect a child's development in the educational arena. Part of your job as a teacher is to identify and become familiar with the sociocultural perspectives of the children in your classroom, so that you can be sensitive to them.

There has been much research that demonstrates the power of preconceptions and biases on achievement. If the teacher believes a child will not do well, that child tends to not do well, and vice versa. Be aware of this power you have and educate yourself about gender, racial, cultural, and other biases so that you avoid unintentionally inhibiting the development of any child in your classroom.

There are also many influences on students' development that are outside of your control. These include abuse within the family, whether physical or emotional, and neglect. Signs of abuse or neglect in your students include hostility and aggression (often linked to abuse), or apathy and depression (in the case of neglect). Upper grade students may also engage in substance abuse as a means of attempting to escape their problems. In these cases, information is your best weapon and hope. If possible, find out what is going on. More serious cases may warrant intervention, but consult first with your principal and/or school counselor.

Glossary

Accomodation: the process by which a child incorporates new experience into previous understandings, and modifies those existing concepts to include the new information

Assimilation: the process by which a child interprets a new experience in terms of his previous understandings

Attachment theory: states that a child that has formed secure attachments to others is confident in exploring her physical environment, forms friendships easily, and possesses a sense of competency; while the opposite is true of a child that has not formed secure attachments to others

Autonomy: acceptance of responsibility of one's behavior

Concrete operational stage: a stage of cognitive development during which a child acquires reasoning skills and is able to differentiate between her viewpoints and others'

Conventional level: a level of moral development during which a child focuses on what one is supposed to do and begins to understand social order

Formal operational stage: a stage of cognitive development during which a child enters into the world of abstract thought

Learning disabilities: treatable conditions suffered by many students

Meta-cognition: thinking about thinking

Multiple intelligences: one of eight distinct types of intelligence developed by Howard Gardner

Object permanence: the concept that a seen object still exists after being hidden from sight

Pre-conventional level: a level of moral development during which a child avoids wrongdoing only to evade punishment

Pre-operational stage: a stage of cognitive development during which a child is trapped in an egocentric perspective, but is also mastering language skills

Self-concept: how a child thinks about himself

Self-esteem: a child's feelings about himself

Sensori-motor stage: a stage of cognitive development during which a child learns to differentiate between herself and the external world

PRACTICE SET

1. Evan, a nine-year-old of average development, is learning to play backgammon. During this concrete operational stage of development, Evan would *not* be able to

    (A) choose an appropriate move in reaction to his opponent's move

    (B) understand and follow the basic rules of the game

    (C) think three moves ahead to imagine his opponent's potential combinations

    (D) complete a game by moving all his backgammon pieces around and off the board

2. Teachers have great influence as sociocultural mediators in reducing cultural prejudice in their classrooms. For example, if a teacher asks "How would it feel if you had to eat alone at a separate lunchroom table just because you have blue eyes?" this would encourage students to think critically and promote

    (A) interpersonal intelligence

    (B) anger management

    (C) cultural segregation

    (D) academic achievement

3. Two-year-old Sally calls a horse a "kitty" because she only knows one kind of four-legged animal. According to Piaget's work on cognitive development, this is an example of

    (A) accommodation

    (B) animism

    (C) circular reaction

    (D) assimilation

4. Which of the following best describes how developmentally-appropriate play affects cognitive development in the typical seventh-grader?

    (A) The child explores movement, which involves testing, observing, and organizing information during play.

    (B) The child is more aware of others and the idea of teams, which fosters conflict resolution and peer interaction.

    (C) The child is able to run set plays in sports like basketball, which affects memory development.

    (D) The child has a tendency toward fantasy, which fosters creative thinking skills.

5. Which of the following statements best reflects the causal reasoning of most children aged 11 years and older?

   (A) "When I dance outside, the rain comes down."

   (B) "Superman makes the rain."

   (C) "A big wind makes the rain."

   (D) "Condensation of millions of cloud droplets makes the rain."

6. What is the biggest influence on a student's academic achievement aside from his or her teachers?

   (A) the family's socioeconomic status

   (B) interaction between parent(s) and child

   (C) the educational level of the parent(s)

   (D) access to a public library

7. Children with learning disabilities can typically be characterized as having

   (A) below-average test scores

   (B) an inability to perform abstract thought

   (C) discrepancies between abilities and academic performance

   (D) short-term memory deficits

8. As defined by Piaget, in which of the following situations does 14-year-old Ariana exhibit formal operations?

   (A) Ariana conducts an experiment in reversibility, changing ice to water then back to ice.

   (B) Ariana computes the value of y in $3y = 15$.

   (C) Ariana cannot understand how Theo can enjoy science fiction magazines.

   (D) Ariana sculpts and paints a clay bowl.

9. What would be the best way for a teacher to influence a typical 13-year-old to stop smoking?

   (A) Tell her she will eventually be caught and have to serve detention.

   (B) Remind her it is against the law.

   (C) Ask her concerned friends to tell her they honestly think smoking is a disgusting and uncool habit.

   (D) Tell her that she will cause future heart and lung damage to herself.

10. Of the following, which is the most logical implication of Howard Gardner's theory of multiple intelligences?

    (A) Children with special needs will exhibit intellectual maladaptive behaviors.

    (B) Most intelligence testing should emphasize math and linguistics.

    (C) All children are strong in naturalist intelligence, the ability to observe patterns in nature.

    (D) Teachers should appeal to a balanced combination of all intelligences.

11. When Casey teaches her little brother Robbie that two different-sized glasses are holding the same amount of milk, although one *looks* like it holds more, she is demonstrating her understanding of

    (A) conservation

    (B) animism

    (C) meta-cognition

    (D) transitive inference

12. At the hands-on science museum, a group of young children have just constructed vehicles out of building blocks. Karen holds up her truck and proudly says, "This truck was made by me." Frankie shouts "I built my car," while Natasha says "My blocks!" Jimmy shows off his car: "I make it!" Based on language and syntax development, which child most closely demonstrates the speech patterns of a seven-year-old?

    (A) Karen

    (B) Frankie

    (C) Natasha

    (D) Jimmy

13. Best friends Connor and Erika are both eight years old. Which of the following gross motor skills is Erika most likely to perform better than Connor at this age?

    (A) throwing a ball

    (B) running

    (C) broad-jumping

    (D) balancing

Constructed-Response Question

Complete the exercise that follows.

Erin is an average girl who is trying but having difficulty organizing a series of blocks from smallest to largest. Discuss these questions:

What is Erin's stage of cognitive development?

What is most likely Erin's age range?

What is an example of a related skill in cognitive development that Erin might not yet possess?

_____

_____

_____

_____

_____

_____

_____

_____

_____

_____

_____

_____

_____

_____

_____

_____

_____

_____

_____

ANSWER KEY

1. C	5. D	9. C	13. D
2. A	6. B	10. D	
3. D	7. C	11. A	
4. C	8. B	12. A	

ANSWERS AND EXPLANATIONS

1. C

During the period Piaget describes as concrete operations (7–11 years old), logical operations can be applied to concrete problems, e.g., making an appropriate move in response to an opponent's move **(A)**. This means the rules to games can be learned and applied by an average child **(B)** and **(D)**. However, complex deductions and abstract thinking—such as thinking three moves ahead to imagine an opponent's potential combinations **(C)**—are not possible until a child enters the period of formal operations (more than 11 years old).

2. A

Cultural prejudice is a limited (and limiting) view of a targeted group. Teachers should emphasize critical thinking skills, learning about cultural differences, and tolerance of diversity to minimize cultural prejudice in their classrooms. Promoting interpersonal intelligence **(A)** is the best answer to the question because this kind of intelligence includes a range of skills that lead to a broader understanding of the world, such as being a good listener, cooperating and compromising, and considering another's perspective. Anger management **(B)** and academic achievement **(D)** are not being tested by the question. Cultural segregation would NOT be promoted by posing the question, therefore **(C)** is an incorrect choice.

3. D

Piaget teaches that children fit new information into existing schemes. *Assimilation* refers to the way children incorporate this new information ("horse") with existing schemes ("a four-legged animal is a kitty") in order to form a new cognitive structure ("that four-legged animal must be a kitty"). *Accommodation* **(A)**, involves the same skills as assimilation, with the addition of modification of existing concepts to include new information. *Animism* **(B)**

describes a stage of religious development not covered on the CSET. *Circular reaction* **(C)**, is a subset of Piaget's sensorimotor stage, occurring primarily before the age of two, making it incorrect.

4. C

At about grades 6–8, adolescents begin to create and master offensive and defensive strategies in games and sports—such as chess and checkers strategies and running set plays. Students of this age have already passed through the stages mentioned in **(A)**, **(B)**, and **(D)**, and continue to hone these skills. These children are becoming better at evaluating choices, reasoning in the abstract, and anticipating conflicts and resolutions.

5. D

The statements in **(A)**, **(B)**, and **(C)** describe reasoning a child might possess at developmental stages earlier than that of an 11-year-old, making them incorrect choices. In preschool, children cannot yet think logically about causality, cause and effect. They usually believe their thoughts cause actions ("When I dance outside, the rain comes down.") or that reality is defined by appearance ("A big wind makes the rain."). Later, they attribute causality to an all-powerful force ("Superman makes the rain.") or other elements in nature ("A big wind makes the rain."). At about age 11 and older, a child approaches an adult explanation ("Condensation of millions of cloud droplets makes the rain."), making **(D)** the correct choice.

6. B

While all of the responses contribute to a child's academic success, the biggest influence, aside from a teacher, is parent/child interaction. A teacher can encourage a parent to help with reading, homework, research, and classroom projects; to attend school events, field trips, and parent/teacher meetings; to take the child to the library and museums; and to read aloud together.

7. C

Typically, children with learning disabilities (LD) are of normal or above-average intelligence. They have emotional and/or physical disorders (visual, auditory, language learning, perceptual-motor, attention deficit, or hyperactive) that interfere with their academic performance **(C)**. Children without LD earn below-average test scores, so **(A)** can be eliminated. Some children and (even some adults) have difficulty performing abstract thought regardless of whether or not they have a learning disability, making **(B)** an incorrect choice. Short-term memory deficiency is not considered an indicator of LD, so you can eliminate **(D)**.

8. B

Formal operations constitute reasoning that is abstract or hypothetical—such as philosophy, science hypotheses, or algebraic equations (the concept behind a variable in "the value of y in $3y = 15$"). Choices **(A)** and **(D)** are concrete operational situations—working with concrete objects in concrete situations. Choice **(C)** is a preoperational situation (difficulty seeing others' points of view).

9. C

An average 13-year-old, according to Kohlberg's Theory of Moral Development, will not care as much about punishment **(A)**, society's laws **(B)**, or abstract ideas about the future **(D)**, as she will care about peer pressure and the opinions of her friends **(C)**.

10. D

Since children have different combinations of intelligences with multiple dimensions—linguistic, logical-mathematical, spatial, bodily-kinesthetic, musical, interpersonal, intra-personal, and naturalist, appealing to a combination of intelligences in the classroom is the most stimulating and successful approach. The other choices are incorrect: Gardner's theory does not include implications for children with special needs **(A)**; if test content were to reflect his theory, it should include equal parts of each defined intelligence, not an emphasis on math and linguistics **(B)**; and the statement in **(C)** is false because not every child is strong in naturalist intelligence.

11. A

Conservation is the concept that if you alter the appearance or shape of an object, its basic properties do not change. Choice **(B)**, *animism*, describes a stage of religious development not covered on the CSET and is therefore incorrect. *Meta-cognition* means thinking about thinking and is not illustrated by the example in the question; **(C)** is incorrect. *Transitive inference* **(D)** refers to the ability of a child to make connections between related concepts and does not describe the example in the question.

12. A

Karen's statement, "This truck was made by me," **(A)** uses the most sophisticated syntax and vocabulary in this group, one that is normal for a child of seven. The other children's statements **(B)**, **(C)**, and **(D)**, use syntax and vocabulary found more often in children of younger age groups.

13. D

At the age of eight, most girls are better at balancing and coordinated hand-manipulation skills than boys of the same age. Furthermore, most boys at this age are taller and weigh more than girls. Boys will generally have greater arm and leg muscle coordination at this stage of physical development—making them stronger runners **(B)**, jumpers **(C)**, throwers **(A)**, kickers, and hitters.

KAPLAN

Constructed-Response Sample Essay

The ability to arrange objects in logical progression—such as from smallest to largest, or from shortest to longest—is called seriation. According to Jean Piaget's four Stages of Cognitive Development, seriation is not mastered until about 7 years old, at the beginning of Stage 3. Stage 3 is the concrete operations period of middle childhood (about 7–11 years old). Therefore, Erin is still in Stage 2 of cognitive development, what Piaget calls the pre-operational stage of early childhood, which encompasses ages 2 through 7. Since she is trying to accomplish seriation, she is probably around 5–7 years old, since an infant or toddler can only perform simple tasks (Stage 1, the sensorimotor stage in Piaget's system). On the other end of the spectrum, adolescents can begin to perform difficult reasoning and abstract thinking (Stage 4, called the formal operations stage includes ages 12 years through adulthood).

A related concrete operational skill that Erin will soon possess (but has yet to master) is transitivity, the ability to draw conclusions about a relationship between two things based on a relationship to a third. For example, the blue block is larger than the red block, and the red block is larger than the yellow block. Using transitivity leads to the logical conclusion is that the blue block is larger than the yellow block. During Stage 3, Erin will master both transitivity and seriation (a type of transitivity), as well as other problem-solving skills.

Chapter 7: **Visual and Performing Arts**

THE BIG PICTURE

The state of California considers the visual and performing arts to be an integral part of education in all grades. A fundamental goal of arts education is to expose each child to each artistic discipline at each grade level. Direct personal involvement is required in order to foster understanding of these disciplines. Process (creation), as well as product, is emphasized. In a time when schools are squeezed for money and teachers are pressed for time, you might wonder why the arts are still relevant. The answer to that question lies in the nature and purpose of education itself.

The arts are unsurpassed in their ability to help children develop self-confidence, creativity, understanding, and problem solving skills. They also promote cooperative approaches, reasoning abilities, responsibility, and persistence. The arts incorporate elements of all other disciplines and they speak to all parts of a person, uniting mind and body, and developing multiple intelligences. The qualities the arts help develop are the qualities that make successful citizens and leaders. Most of all, the arts help students make sense of their own lives by validating or challenging their perceptions. Through the arts, children come to understand the lives and perspectives of other humans from other times, places, and circumstances. Those are just some of the reasons arts education is vital to a curriculum.

Three Modes of Instruction

The state framework (cde.ca.gov/ci/vp) covers four arts disciplines. They are: dance, music, theater, and visual arts. Teachers are expected to employ three modes of instruction in each of the four areas.

Subject-centered instruction develops knowledge in all components of the discipline. This instruction covers the basic knowledge, skills, and vocabulary of each discipline that is necessary for competence in the arts. It promotes the intrinsic value of the arts—the creativity, thinking skills, and sheer joy they engender. Artistic perception is at the heart of this instruction.

Instruction connecting the arts disciplines to each other helps students see the connections among the arts. For example, a musical theater production incorporates skills and knowledge from theater, dance, music, and visual arts (through sets and costume design).

KAPLAN

Instruction connecting the arts and other core subjects helps students connect the critical thinking skills and information they learn in the arts to such subjects as literature, science, and especially history and social science. This is one of the instrumental values of the arts. Students learn to use symbolic forms to recover and recreate meaning; and students with different kinds of intelligence can be reached more easily (see the concept of multiple intelligences in Chapter 6). The arts also help students make sense of their own lives, by learning to see connections, relationships, and applications across the arbitrary boundaries and dividing lines so frequently constructed between people or ideas.

Four Components of Instruction

Each of the four arts disciplines taught in elementary school has four instructional components. They are described below:

Artistic perception is basic artistic literacy. Students learn to use elements unique to the arts to help them process sensory information, engage in reflection, analysis, and synthesis, and learn to understand and create meaning.

Creative expression is practice creating or performing works of art.

Historical and cultural context involves instruction in understanding the time, place, and context of artworks. Art is created by people that live in a specific set of circumstances, which must be understood to fully appreciate the work. Artworks are living records of the people who created them. They are an excellent way to stimulate student interest in history and geography.

Aesthetic valuing is the act of assessing and pursuing the meaning of artworks. It is the process of making informed judgments. Developing critical thinking skills is one of the primary benefits of arts education.

Assessment

Assessment in arts instruction is best accomplished by open-ended means, such as portfolios and performances. Curriculum-embedded assessments, such as group projects and journals, are excellent tools. Student compositions in the various art areas are enjoyable for the students and also accomplish the goal of direct personal involvement. Additionally, composition requires students to utilize all four components of instruction (see previous section).

Special Needs

Students with special needs can be included in arts education with some adaptation. There is theater for the deaf; there is wheelchair dance; and there is music by touch, to name but a few creative solutions to the challenges. Students with limited English proficiency (LEP) often experience their greatest success in art classes, as they use their senses to process information.

THE KAPLAN METHOD

Multiple-Choice Questions

1. Read the question carefully. As you read, underline or circle the key words and phrases that differentiate this particular question from all other possible questions.

2. Rephrase the question to make sure you understand it. If possible, predict the correct answer.

3. Read all the answer choices, eliminating (physically marking through) incorrect ones as you go.

4. If two or more possible answer choices remain, go back to the question and search for matching/mirroring language or concepts that will point you toward the single correct answer.

Constructed-Response Questions

1. Read each question carefully. As you read, underline or circle the key words and phrases that differentiate this particular question from all other possible questions.

2. Note how many parts the question has. Be sure to include subparts in your count. Write this number in your test booklet, so you will be sure to answer each part of the question.

3. Before you start writing, brainstorm for vocabulary words and relevant concepts. Make your notes in the margins of your answer sheet, so you will be sure to include them in your answer. If you don't have a good command of details for a particular question, be sure to include in your answer the big picture concepts, such as the reason for studying/ teaching the subject.

4. Organize your thoughts! Remember, you are being tested on your ability to clearly convey information.

DANCE

Though perhaps the most obvious connection of dance is with physical education, dance actually promotes development of the whole human being. It connects mind and body, integrating children's mental and physical processes, and enhancing their verbal skills as well as their appreciation for diversity. Dance particularly enhances the kinesthetic, spatial, musical, logical-mathematical, and interpersonal forms of intelligence.

In order to teach dance to students, you must be familiar with the elements of dance: *space, time, levels,* and *force/energy.* You may be asked to write a constructed response that, for example, requires you to incorporate these four elements into a proposed lesson plan for creating dance/movement with a group of children of a specified age. You may also be asked to demonstrate a knowledge of various styles of dance from a range of times, places, and cultures. If this is outside your area of expertise, you might want to research folk dances from different parts of the world, ballroom dances (e.g., waltz, tango, cha cha, samba), and formal dance traditions (e.g., ballet and modern dance). In the past, the CSET has included multiple-choice questions asking you to match a particular dance style with its country of origin (e.g., flamenco from Spain, tarantella from Italy).

Test Yourself

As part of an instructional unit in dance, a teacher has a group of second-grade students compose a dance in which they use their bodies to illustrate addition and subtraction problems. This teacher is using dance to

(A) assess student comprehension of math
(B) help children connect with math using their kinesthetic intelligence
(C) satisfy a cross-curricular instructional requirement
(D) teach aesthetic valuing to the students

The correct answer is **(B)**. Dance appeals to kinesthetic and spatial intelligences, among others. Students who are strong in these areas but not in logical-mathematical intelligence may find this a particularly useful type of activity.

Social Dance

Throughout human history, dance has frequently served social purposes. Dance has enjoyed popularity as a means of individual expression, but it has most often taken forms that are strongly influenced by social pressures. Most traditional and contemporary cultures hold dances that facilitate courtship and showcase individual charms as well as promote group harmony and enjoyment. Often, one gender at a time took the dance floor/performance space. Couples dancing, such as ballroom dance, is a relatively new development.

In Europe, beginning in the seventeenth century, nobility adapted peasant dances to perform in royal courts so they could display their finery. Early dances, such as the allemande and the minuet (named for its tiny steps), evolved into the eighteenth century dance in 3/4 time known as the waltz. The waltz was originally banned in respectable society because the partners, a couple, actually touched! By the nineteenth century, the waltz had swept the continent and spread to the Americas. The polka originated in Eastern Europe in the 1800s and spread to America, though it never became fashionable in European courts.

The flamenco originated in Spain among gypsy dancers, though some of its influences date back to India (as do the gypsies themselves). Square dancing, still popular in America, traces its roots to European folk dancing.

In the twentieth century, social dancing performed as a couple enjoyed an explosion of popularity. These dances are known collectively as ballroom dancing. Many of the styles originated in the Caribbean islands and are fusions of African dance and European styles, as is the music to which they are performed. These dances include the mambo, samba, meringue, and rumba. Salsa is related to these Latin and Afro-Caribbean dances. The tango became popular in Argentina and spread to North America and Europe. The foxtrot, Charleston, swing dance, twist, and western dances (such as line dancing or the Texas Two-Step) all developed in the United States in the twentieth century.

Performance Dance

Asian countries have strong classical performance dance traditions. Chinese Opera (also known as Peking or Beijing Opera) evolved over two hundred years ago from folk traditions that were then combined with opera, ballet, acrobatics, and other elements to form a dramatically rich and exacting artistic form. The classical dances of India are primarily Hindu religious expressions, performed by female dancers, and centuries old, often portraying mythologies in dramatic dance form.

The preeminent European form of performance dance is ballet, which has its roots in court performances given during the Italian Renaissance. It is generally considered to have developed in seventeenth and eighteenth century France, however. In the nineteenth and twentieth centuries, Russia boasted many of the world's foremost ballet dancers and dance companies. Ballet utilizes elaborate costumes and scenery. Its movements are highly stylized and technical in nature. The choreography is precise and must be followed exactly, as it usually tells a story in movement form.

In the early twentieth century, American dancers such as Isadora Duncan rebelled against the constricting requirements of classical ballet. They shed their shoes and adopted free-flowing costumes in order to better express their ideas and feelings. They called their new dance style modern dance. Martha Graham is often called the mother of modern dance. She taught a generation that included the African American dancer/choreographer Alvin Ailey, who since founded a well-known company. Katherine Dunham incorporated Afro-Caribbean movement styles into modern dance and ballet techniques. Twyla Tharp is a modern dance artist working today to extend the boundaries of performance dance in new directions.

The Elements of Dance

Space, in dance, is the immediate spherical area surrounding a dancer's body. It extends in all directions. Dancers shape their space as they move, change direction or path or level, and extend their range. Space can also refer to dancers' performance location.

Time, in dance, can be formally measured in meter (as in music) or, less formally, in terms of body rhythms, such as heartbeat, breath, or even human emotions. Considerations of time are: duration (how long it lasts), rhythm (regular or irregular), tempo (how fast or slow), phrasing (the arrangement of units into patterns), and accent (emphasis).

Levels refers to the series of horizontal planes rising, one above the other, from the performance surface, through which dancers move. Ballet is an example of a dance form that makes extensive use of levels, as dancers leap into the air and perform lifts.

Force/energy is the dancers' transformation and release of potential energy into kinetic energy. This is how dancers move. These movements reveal the effects of gravity on body mass. They also project relationships (emotional and physical/spatial) and intentions. Some types of dance movements are: sustained, collapsing, suspended, swinging, and percussive. Each type of movement has its own set of related emotions and time characteristics.

Artistic Perception

Artistic perception in dance includes mastery of dance vocabulary, kinesthetic awareness, and appreciation for one's own and others' unique ways of moving. Students physically experience dance techniques and improvisation as they learn movement communication skills and motor efficiency.

In kindergarten, artistic perception includes learning to respond to simple oral instructions (e.g., reach, turn, walk) and the vocabulary of opposites (e.g., wiggle/freeze, high/low). Fourth-graders are expected to be able to use dance vocabulary to describe movements (e.g., unity, variety, force) and to physically connect movement phrases (units) with smooth transitions. Eighth-graders should be able to use dance vocabulary fluently to describe and analyze the elements and components of dance. Their range of movements is expanding in scope and in size of movements; and they understand artistic intent, whether theirs or others'.

Creative Expression

Through the creative medium of dance, students learn to use intuition as a source of movement inspiration. They also acquire the ability to recreate structured movement forms. They develop respect and appreciation for their own creative movement expressions as well as those of others.

In the primary grades, children begin expressing emotions through movement. They learn to use improvisation to respond to various kinds of music and oral prompts. Younger children dance alone; second graders are learning to work with partners. By third grade, students begin to apply choreographic principles, processes, and skills to create and communicate meaning. They can work in small groups on dance compositions. Middle school students can create, memorize, and perform a variety of simple dance forms (e.g., ABA, rondo). They are fluent improvisers and are able to work cooperatively in groups to create dance.

Historical and Cultural Context

Understanding dance history helps children develop an understanding of the cultural contributions of all human groups, past and present. They learn to see the influences of one cultural group on another and develop an appreciation of diverse historical and cultural perspectives.

Kindergartners start learning about simple folk dances from around the world, including their functions (religious, social, ceremonial) and development. By second grade, students can name and perform rhythms from various dance traditions. Fifth-graders learn about dances specific to eighteenth and nineteenth century America. They understand that there are differences between participatory and performed dances, and that men and women may have differing roles in dance. Eighth-graders can describe the functions of dance in traditional societies (e.g., courtship, ritual, entertainment) and compare and contrast different forms of dance.

Aesthetic Valuing

As students acquire knowledge of dance composition and performance, criteria for making informed judgments about composition and performance emerge. Out of discussions with teachers and classmates, students learn to present reasoned descriptions of their aesthetic choices and the standards they have developed through learning and experience.

In kindergarten children learn how to distinguish one dance from another, based on such basic features as music, setting, costume, and speed. By third grade, students can explain and demonstrate how to be good audience members for performances. They can express evaluations of dance performances in terms of focus, strength, coordination, and communication of emotion and ideas. In middle school, students can critically evaluate dance in terms of the elements of dance, the craft of choreography, and the impact of music, performance space, costumes, and other considerations.

MUSIC

Music is as old and as widespread as humanity. All cultures at all times participate in the musical expression of emotions. Perhaps the oldest instrument is the human voice, but percussive rhythm is as natural and as old as tapping your foot or clapping your hands.

Music is made up of tonal-rhythmic patterns; music education teaches the mental processes that allow us to appreciate, perform, and even create those patterns. In elementary school, effective musical instruction includes the four components common to all arts instruction: artistic perception, creative expression, historical and cultural context, and aesthetic valuing. The instruction should be progressive, from kindergarten through successive grades, and one of the main goals is to help children develop a lifelong appreciation for and involvement with the music of many cultures and time periods, not just the popular music of the moment.

Music is one of the subjects that has a lot of vocabulary to master. It is impossible to present the concepts of music theory without using this vocabulary; so if you've never studied music, it's time to get out those index cards. Your reward will be threefold: a passing score on the CSET, an enriched ability to be an effective teacher, and an increased personal appreciation of music. Additional music vocabulary can be found in the curriculum framework for music at www.cde.ca.gov/be/st/ss/mumain.asp

Test Yourself

The word *music* derives from which of the following sources?

(A) the German word for amusing

(B) the old English tradition of thinking, or musing, about compositions

(C) the tendency of musicians to imbibe fermented Muscat grapes

(D) the mythological Greek sisters known as the Muses

The answer is **(D)**. The Muses were nine goddesses who ruled over the arts and sciences. Both the word *amusing* and *musing,* a synonym for *thinking,* are derived from the same source.

The Elements of Music

All music is made of common elements. They are: *rhythm, tempo, melody, harmony, dynamics, timbre,* and *form.* These elements can be combined and utilized in countless ways. Students learn to appreciate a diverse range of music and progress to being able to create music, using appropriate vocabulary and musical notation to describe pitch, rhythm, dynamics, tempo, articulation, and expression.

Rhythm

The rhythm of a piece of music is what keeps it moving. Rhythm consists of a pattern of long and short sounds (beats), in combinations of stressed and unstressed beats. When the pattern of stressed, or accented, sounds is uneven, the resulting type of rhythm is called *syncopation.*

Tempo

The tempo of music is the rate at which it moves, the speed at which the beats follow one another. Music with a rapid tempo is sometimes called *upbeat* music, although the term *upbeat* can also refer to unaccented beats. (Think of a symphony conductor: when her arms go down, that's an accented beat, the *downbeat;* when her arms go up, that's an unaccented beat, the *upbeat.*)

Melody

The melody of music is what is commonly referred to as the *tune.* It is a succession of musical *tones,* or notes, based on mathematical progressions of a scale, that resonate at different *pitches* (wavelengths, or *frequencies* of sound). This relationship of music to math is one reason studies have shown that children who study music improve their math scores.

Harmony

A note of a different pitch on the scale that sounds good (harmonious) when played simultaneously with the melody is said to be played in *harmony.* Again, harmonies are based on mathematical progressions. When three or more harmonious notes are played together, they are known as a *chord.* Any instrument with multiple strings (piano, guitar) can play chords; instruments such as the trumpet and the clarinet play only single tones, not chords. Much of the art of the composer/arranger is in putting together different instruments playing different, yet harmonious, combinations of sound. Some musical forms, such as modern classical music and some popular forms (punk, some jazz) use unharmonious sounds, called *dissonance,* to produce an unsettling effect.

Dynamics

Within a single piece of music, there may be louder and softer sections. This variation constitutes the *dynamics* of the piece. Very dynamic music has a lot of variation in the volume at which it is played.

Timbre

Each musical instrument, including each human voice, has a distinctive quality to the sound. This distinctiveness is the *timbre* of the instrument. A flute, for example, has a bright, pure, sweet quality; a bassoon has a dark, ominous quality. Listen to Tchaikovsky's *Peter and the Wolf* for a brilliant—and suitable for children—demonstration of how composers use the timbres of various instruments to create mood.

Timbre relates to size and shape, in other words, to the physical properties of instruments (physics). A baritone saxophone, for instance, has a long and wide, curved body; a soprano saxophone is short, straight, and thin. Naturally, the timbre of the soprano sax is much thinner and higher.

Form

In music, *form*—as the word implies—is the shape, structure, or organization of a piece. The composer uses unity and repetition, as well as contrast and variety, to give form to her work. For example, the classical sonata is a standard form consisting of three sections (in this case, an ABA form). The first section presents a theme; the second section presents a secondary theme; and the final section restates the original theme. A song with several verses, each followed by a chorus (refrain), is another example of a standard form.

Musical Notation

Teachers are expected to know the basics of musical notation. You've probably seen sheet music, even if you don't know how to read it. It may look strange to you, but compared to learning to read words, it's a breeze.

Musical notes are written on a group of lines and spaces known as a musical *staff.* The staff has five lines and four spaces (the spaces between the lines). Each line or space corresponds to a specific note, or musical tone. The note correspondences you need to know for the CSET are those for the *treble clef,* or the notes that are played by the right hand on the piano. The symbol at the beginning of the line tells you what clef you're looking at. A bass clef, played with the left hand on a piano, and so having a deeper sound, looks like this (but don't worry about reading music in the bass clef for the CSET):

Here's what a treble clef looks like on a staff:

In the treble clef, starting from the bottom, any note that appears on the first line is the note *E.* The next line up is *G,* the middle line is *B,* then comes *D,* and the top line is *F.* (You can remember this order by using the mnemonic device *Every Good Boy Does Fine.*) The spaces, from bottom to top, are *F, A, C,* and *E.* (What does that spell?) This begins to make sense when you notice that if you put the lines and spaces in order, from bottom to top, they run in alphabetical order: *E, F, G,* (then, starting with *A*) *A, B, C, D, E,* and *F.* When a composer wants to use notes that are outside the range of the staff, he just pretends there are more lines and spaces. That is why you may see notes above or below the staff. In determining what notes those are, simply determine what letter(s) comes before (or after, if you're going up the scale) the bottom (or top) line of the staff. For example, the space below the bottom line of the staff is *D,* the line below that is *C* (its special name is *middle C*), and so on. To help you count, middle *C* actually has a little line drawn through the note, as though it were another line of the staff.

There are eight notes in a octave, and their names are *A, B, C, D, E, F,* and *G.* (What letter comes next? *A,* then *B,* then *C*…) You may notice that only seven letters of the alphabet are used. That's because no matter which letter you start with, you always end an octave by playing the same note you started with, only an octave higher. This concept may make more sense when you think of the system of naming notes called *solfege.* Solfege is the group of familiar syllables used to designate the notes of an octave: do, re, mi, fa, so, la, ti, do. Sing them to yourself, and notice how the first note and the last note are an octave apart.

In western music, most scales are composed of one octave, or eight notes. The distance between each note is known as an *interval,* though in standard scales not all intervals are equal; some are whole intervals (steps) and some are half-intervals (half-steps). The particular note on which a scale starts (and ends) is determined by its *key.* The scale of C major, for example, begins and ends on C. It is beyond the scope of this review to list all possible keys and show you how to identify each one; but if you are asked to name the key of a particular line of music you are shown, just look at the first note of the piece and choose that note as the key.

If you see one or more symbols at the beginning of a line of music that look like the following figures, those symbols signify that all notes on the line or space on which the symbol appears are played either one half-step above (*sharp*) or one half-step below (*flat*) the note, every time you see it in the piece, unless you see a *natural* symbol immediately preceding the note. If the sharp symbol appears on the third space up, for example, it means that every C in the piece is a C sharp, unless it is immediately preceded by the natural symbol.

C natural

The numbers that appear at the beginning of the line of notation are the *time signature* of the piece. 4/4 time (say "four, four time") is the most common time signature for children's music. In 4/4 time, there are four beats to the *measure* (measures, or *bars* are delineated by the vertical lines on the staff), and a quarter note gets one beat. Here are the time values of some common notes, the whole note, the half note, the quarter note, and the eighth note:

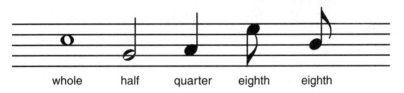

whole   half   quarter   eighth   eighth

If the quarter note gets one beat, as in 4/4 time, the eighth note gets a half beat, the half note gets two beats, and the whole note gets four beats. Notice that this aspect of music, too, is based on mathematics. The number of beats per bar is the number at the top of the time signature, and the type of note that gets a beat is on the bottom. So, in 2/4 time, there are two beats per bar (measure), and a quarter note gets one beat. In 2/2 time, there are two beats per measure (bar), and a half note gets one beat (meaning a quarter note gets a half beat, a whole note gets two beats, etc.). Finally, if any note has a dot that looks like a period following it, its time value is increased by half. Thus, in 4/4 time, a dotted half note has a time value of three beats instead of two.

If there is to be a pause, with no music for a fraction of a beat or more, the composer puts a *rest* in place of a note. This is a good time to take a breath, if you're singing. This figure shows rests with various time values:

eighth   quarter   half   whole

If all this seems confusing to you, find someone who has a keyboard and knows the basics of reading music. It's not as complex as it seems at first. In a half hour, you will probably feel comfortable reading (even playing) simple melodies.

Music History

In order to help children appreciate a variety of musical forms, it is necessary for a teacher to have a basic knowledge of the history and development of those forms. Music can helpfully be classified in two main ways: classical vs. popular traditions and western vs. non-western music.

Classical Music

Classical music in the west has its roots in the chants of medieval European monks. Their use of *polyphonic* (consisting of many tones or voices) harmonies and development of musical notation laid the groundwork for Italian composers in the sixteenth century to write operas in the developing *baroque* style (characterized by extravagance and complexity). Bach and Handel composed instrumental music in the early eighteenth century, and Mozart dominated the late part of the century. Beethoven reached his height in the early nineteenth century and pioneered the Romantic style. Stravinsky, Cage, and Glass are three of the most well-known composers of the twentieth century.

Previous CSET questions have focused on the instrumental composition of symphony orchestras and other classical groups, such as the chamber orchestra. You are also expected to know the families of musical instruments (strings, brass, woodwinds, and percussion), and to know what instruments are in each family. Resources on these topics are readily available in libraries and on the Internet.

The eastern hemisphere has its own classical traditions, though Asians have traditionally not thought of music as an art separate from dance, theater, and visual components. Indian music is intertwined with religious expressions and features sophisticated vocal styles as well as such instruments as the multi-stringed sitar (an instrument popularized in western music by the Beatles). Chinese music, in its classical form, is associated with Chinese philosophy and its forms have been relatively stable, at least since the second century B.C.E. The musical instruments are divided into eight categories, depending on the material from which they are made. These eight categories produce eight kinds of tones, which have correspondences in Chinese cosmology. The scale is *pentatonic*, corresponding roughly to the notes made by the black keys on a piano, so the sound produced is very different from western music. Japanese music took the form of either religious chanting or of productions for a court setting. The latter form was traditionally bound up with other art forms, as in the Kabuki tradition, which incorporates music, dance, and theater in stylized performances. The koto is a Japanese stringed instrument, related to a zither; taiko is a type of percussive music performed by drum ensembles.

Popular Music

As was stated earlier, people have always and everywhere made music. In the absence of a long, formal tradition, most music is considered to be popular music. All folk music is popular music, and each culture has its favorite forms. The CSET is most likely to ask about distinctively American forms of popular music.

As communication and interaction among cultural groups has accelerated in the past century or so, new forms of music have evolved in America. The primary traditions that have influenced each other come from Africa and Europe. African slaves brought to America their traditional music, which was much more rhythmically rich than European music—either popular or classical. As slaves were exposed to Christian hymns, their songs evolved into gospel music. Freed African Americans heard European folk music and classical music, and began playing the blues and later, jazz. Jazz, in particular, is a distinctively American musical form, influenced by the rhythmical complexities of Africa and the melodic intricacies of Europe.

Teaching Music

The most natural way to begin musical education is by having children listen to simple songs and then repeat them. The most important consideration in selecting songs for children to sing is to keep it simple and within their vocal range. (The *range* of a song is the distance between its lowest note and its highest note.) As with any other subject, make sure the students can experience success, so that they are enthusiastic about pursuing music further.

Simple rhythms also promote success in music education. One way to enhance rhythmical awareness is to clap out a simple beat for the class and have them repeat it back to you. Through this exercise, they learn to listen and become aware of both tempo and beat.

Another way to keep introductory music simple is to pick songs with simple phrasing. A *phrase* in music is similar in concept to a phrase in language: it expresses an idea. Often, a phrase is how long you sing before taking a breath. In fact, you might find a rest sign at the end of a phrase.

THEATER

Theater is, above all, a collaborative medium. Usually, a playwright works alone to write a play; but after that, a multitude of collaborators is required in order to produce it. As a result, theater is unsurpassed in the arts as a way of teaching and practicing communication skills. Dramatization is also an excellent way to develop empathy for members, as well as the arts, of other cultures.

Test Yourself

Over the course of a semester, a sixth-grade class researches, writes, and performs a play about Confucius. Which of the following intelligences does this activity exercise?

(A) naturalist and intra-personal

(B) spatial and logical-mathematical

(C) linguistic and interpersonal

(D) bodily-kinesthetic and musical

The correct answer is **(C)**. Theater offers opportunities to cultivate each of Howard Gardner's multiple intelligences, but it particularly exercises the linguistic and interpersonal intelligences, emphasizing as it does the collaborative process and the creative use of language.

KAPLAN

The Process

Typically, a *producer* (traditionally, the person who acquires the necessary funds and acts as administrator of the production) will discover, or have recommended to him, a play that suits his needs. In the case of elementary school productions, that producer will typically be the teacher. The producer chooses a *director* (the person who oversees the actual staging of the production) and *casting* begins. Casting typically consists of having actors audition for the roles; though in elementary school, this process is often either skipped altogether, or consists of informal sessions of *improvisation*. Improvisation is the process of using spontaneous movement and speech to create a character, mood, or situation. Children love improvisation once they understand there are no right or wrong ways to, for example, portray bacon frying in a pan. Improvisation allows children to tap their creative potential for expressing emotions, and the practice of improvisational exercises lead to the ability to create and portray characters on the stage.

Once a play is cast, there may be a *cold reading* of the script. A cold reading is a reading by actors who have never before spoken the *dialogue* lines of the play. This is the beginning of the rehearsal process. Later in the rehearsal process, the director will call the actors' attention to such elements of speaking the lines as *diction*, the pronunciation of the words and the way in which they are spoken, and *projection*, the volume and clarity of speaking required for an actor to be heard by an audience.

Equally important to casting the actors is the recruitment of a *stage crew*. These are the people responsible for all the technical aspects of a show. The crew will include a *stage manager*, who runs the performance from backstage and supervises the other crew members, as well as the set designer(s), makeup artist(s), costumer(s), lighting crew, sound crew, and *prop* supervisor. Prop stands for properties; these are the small objects actors handle onstage. The smaller the production, and the budget, of course, the smaller the crew typically is, with one person handling multiple jobs.

Rehearsals continue with the actors gradually learning their lines, until eventually they are *off-script*. The director/teacher explains concepts of staging, such as *blocking* (deciding where and when actors will move on stage), *actor's position* (the orientation of actor to audience, e.g., profile, front, back), and the areas of a stage. The areas of a stage can be confusing at first. *Stage left* is the left side of the stage, *from the perspective of an actor facing the audience*. *Stage right* is the right side of the stage, *from the perspective of an actor facing the audience*. *Upstage* is the part of the stage farthest from the audience; *downstage* is the part of the stage closest to the audience. You can remember upstage and downstage if you know that when the terminology originated, stages were actually tilted (rather than seats rising in tiers) so that audiences could see the back of the stage (upstage) as well as the front (downstage).

Actors learn vocabulary such as *monologue*, a long speech without interruption performed by a single actor, and *motivation*, a character's immediate reason for acting the way she does or saying what she says. A character's *objective* is that character's overall goal within the play. The director is responsible for the *pacing* of the production (the speed at which the play moves along, and its dynamic flow).

As the *ensemble* (the group collaborating on the play) becomes a cohesive group, the actors and technical crew learn how to recognize their *cues*. A cue is an individual's signal (physical or verbal) that a response is required. For example, an actor's cue to enter, to speak, or to exit, may be a line of dialogue. A crew member working the spotlight may also be cued by that same line, for example, to "pick up and follow" (with the spotlight) the entering actor.

Finally, as the performance date draws near, the cast and crew are ready for a *run-through* (a rehearsal that goes from the beginning of the play to the end, without stopping). The director *gives notes* (suggestions and corrections), and then it is time for the *dress rehearsal(s)*. A dress rehearsal is the final step before the production. All crew members are involved, to make sure the technical elements are ready; and actors wear full costume and makeup. After that, it's show time!

Other Theater Skills

Not all dramatizations have to be such big productions, of course. *Informal theater,* which is typically not intended for public viewing, can take place right in the classroom, with any level of preparation by the participants. Informal theater would, of course, have very low *production values* (the technical components, including acting and directing, of a production).

Another dramatic activity that is enjoyable and educational is *pantomime,* which is using movement, gesture, and facial expression to convey ideas and emotions without the use of words. Students can also engage in the practice of *tableaux* (singular form, tableau), the silent depiction of a static scene, often the reproduction of a painting or other picture. Several tableaux, succeeding one another on a stage, constitute a *pageant.* There is also a variety of *theatrical games* designed to develop acting skills. Viola Spolin wrote several books on the subject, including activities appropriate for children. These activities can, among other things, help promote *sense memory* (sight, sound, taste, touch, smell), which is used by actors to deepen their character development. Even storytelling and puppetry are creative forms that teach basic dramatic skills to budding *thespians* (actors). It is important to remember that experimentation is an important part of the dramatic process. Creative play encourages dramatic skills, and is a valuable end in itself. Theater is about process as much as product.

History of Theater

Western theater derives from the Greek theatrical tradition that originated around 500 B.C.E. Theater in ancient Greece evolved from religious rites honoring the god Dionysus. Some Greek playwrights, such as Aeschylus, Sophocles, and Euripides, are still considered some of the world's greatest. Originally, the plays were performed in competition; actors wore masks with exaggerated expressions instead of makeup; and the chorus, which carried on a running commentary about the action, was the focus of attention. Later, the characters became more important and plays featured a hero, or *protagonist,* who had a fatal flaw that brought about his downfall. There was also an *antagonist* (a villain), against whom the protagonist was pitted. The audience became caught up in the fate of the protagonist, and his inevitable downfall brought about a group release of emotions (a *catharsis*) that cleansed the collective psyche. At this time, the genre of a play was inevitably tragedy, as opposed to comedy.

When Christianity became the official religion of Rome, theater was forbidden by the church and declined in popularity. In the Middle Ages, drama was invariably religious in nature. Inspired by the sacrifice of Christ, medieval dramatists mounted numerous *mystery* plays. Other plays took the form of morality tales, featuring an Everyman (i.e., you and me) in a right-vs.-wrong scenario, or of dramatized Bible stories.

It wasn't until the Renaissance that true theater enjoyed a rebirth. In the sixteenth century in Italy, *commedia dell'arte* developed as a system of loud, colorful improvisations using *stock* (standard) characters. Later in that century, Queen Elizabeth of England presided over a flourishing theater scene. The best-known playwrights of the period were William Shakespeare and Christopher Marlowe. At that time, women were forbidden to appear on the stage; so women's parts were played by boys.

Since the Renaissance, the theater has flourished in Europe and in America. One of the best-known genres to develop in the twentieth century was *Theater of the Absurd*, which portrayed life as an unfathomable mystery, at best, and often as a ridiculous and pointless endeavor.

Asian theatrical traditions, as was discussed in the music and dance sections, are not easily classifiable according to our arts categories. *Kabuki* and *Noh* are two Japanese arts forms that may appear on the CSET. Noh is the more serious of the two forms, using only male actors to tell highly stylized stories through dance and poetry. Kabuki, meaning song or dance, is a traditional form of Japanese theater founded in 1603 in Kyoto. One of the most visually striking aspects of kabuki is the exaggerated makeup worn by the actors, especially those playing the most dramatic roles. Ornate costumes designate the class, traits, or age of a character by color, contour, and textile. Elaborate wigs are worn for men, women, and demons. Beautifully painted fans are a vital prop in kabuki: they are used to imply or mime a wide range of text-related meanings, ranging from swords or spears to running water and mountain ranges. Floral arrangements may be present, but are part of the larger complex set design. Some other important characteristics of Kabuki theater include the *mie,* where the actor holds a picturesque pose to establish his character or a theme, and the *hanamichi*, an entry path on which the actor becomes the character.

Performance Spaces

The most common type of performance space for theater today is the *proscenium.* This is the type of stage you see in most auditoriums. It is named after the proscenium arch that frames the actors, as you look at the stage. This is the type of stage space that is described with the terms *upstage* and *downstage*. The most extreme downstage area, closest to the audience, is called the *apron* of the stage. As a teacher/director, you want to avoid placing actors (*blocking*) in this area, so that no child falls off the stage in the excitement of performance.

Another type of stage is the *arena* stage, meant to be viewed from all sides. It is also called *theater in the round.* Circuses use arena stages, as did the Roman Coliseum. In Elizabethan times, the *thrust stage* was common. This kind of stage juts out into the audience, so it is viewed from three sides. An example of a modern thrust stage is the fashion runway.

Performers, however, don't require a stage at all. *Street theater* has always been popular, and the classroom or playground is a perfectly appropriate space for informal performance.

Educational Implications

If you are asked to write a constructed response about dramatic process, be sure to note the age of the children in the question, and then apply the information in this section, keeping in mind developmental appropriateness of activities. In general, the younger the children, the more informal and basic the lessons. As you write, keep in mind the four components of arts education: artistic perception, creative expression, historical and cultural context, and aesthetic valuing. Be sure your answer takes into consideration all four components.

VISUAL ARTS

When a child becomes able to grasp a crayon, she starts making marks in an attempt to express herself. Self-expression is a universal human urge. Unfortunately, many children become discouraged in the early years of school as their peers (and sometimes teachers) urge them not to color outside the lines or tell them that their attempt to draw a dog looks like a cow. Art is a way of perceiving the world and expressing those perceptions. There is no single right way to perceive or to express oneself. Art education encourages children to learn the vocabulary, skills, and concepts of visual art so that they can more effectively express themselves, whatever their perceptions and artistic ideas may be.

The visual arts include painting, drawing, printmaking, photography, sculpture, assemblage arts, electronic arts such as film and video, architecture, ceramics, textile arts, and commercial design. As you assimilate the information that follows, think about what kinds of activities are appropriate for elementary and middle school visual arts classes. As with all the arts areas, think also about how to effectively incorporate technology, such as computers and the Internet, into visual arts education, for example, by using videotape in the process of feedback and assessment of student work. Consistent with the other arts as well, elementary visual arts education approaches the subject through four main avenues or concepts: artistic perception, creative expression, historical and cultural context, and aesthetic valuing. More information, including a breakdown of goals and activities by grade level, can be found in the state frameworks for arts education at www.cde.ca.gov/be/st/ss/vamain.asp.

Test Yourself

The earliest known human visual art is found where?

(A) in Paris' Louvre Museum

(B) inside the pyramids in Egypt

(C) on shell fragments in Mesopotamia and northern Africa

(D) on scratched and painted cave walls in Europe and Australia

The answer is **(D)**. The early human communication form we call *cave art* has been discovered in Europe (dating from more than 30,000 years ago), Australia (up to 60,000 years ago), and all over the world. Visual art is a very old form of human expression.

The Elements of Art

The elements of art are the ingredients the artist has to work with. They are: *color*, *form*, *line*, *shape*, *space*, and *texture*. Each element is present to some degree in every work of visual art.

Color

Color is what we see as a result of the reflection or absorption of light off any surface. The three characteristics of color are: hue, intensity, and value. *Hue* is the characteristic we think of as color. In the spectrum, there are six hues: red, orange, yellow, blue, green, and violet. *Intensity* is the brightness of color, its vividness. *Value* refers to the gradations of light and darkness on the surface of an artwork or to the darkness or lightness of an individual hue or neutral color.

Form

Form refers to the way an artwork's elements are put together, as opposed to its content or subject matter. In a two-dimensional artwork, form is the illusion of three-dimensionality. In a three-dimensional artwork, form refers to the mass and volume of the work.

Line

A *line* is the movement of a point through space. When you speak of line in drawing or painting, for example, you can describe its characteristics in terms of width, length, direction, and curvature or flow.

Space

Space is the absence of shape or form; it is the emptiness that defines shape and form. Conversely, space is defined by the shapes and forms around and within it.

Shape

Shape is the two-dimensional equivalent of form. Shape (and form) can be man-made or *organic* (occurring in nature). It can be open or closed, structured (geometric) or free-form.

Texture

Texture is the tactile quality of a work of art. It can be an actual, touchable element, as in sculpture; or it can be an implied tactile quality, as in a painting.

The Principles of Art

The *principles of art* are the concepts used to organize the *elements of art*. They are: *balance*, *contrast*, *dominance*, *emphasis*, *movement*, *repetition*, *rhythm*, *theme*, and *unity*. You must be able to fluently use the language and concepts of art in both multiple-choice and constructed-response questions. For example, you may be presented with a reproduction of a painting and asked to discuss it in terms of the elements and principles of art. You may want to practice this before the exam. Sit down with a painting (a black and white reproduction is best, for purposes of the exam) and go through the principles and elements, seeing what you can say about each one in terms of that particular painting. It's important to keep in mind that there is no one right thing to say about a work of art. Your opinion, your reactions to the art, are just as valid as anyone else's. The crucial thing is to be able to use the right vocabulary in appropriate ways.

Balance

Balance in a work of art is how the artist's arrangement of the elements achieves equilibrium. There are three types of balance in art: *symmetry, asymmetry,* and *radial balance.* If a painting has symmetrical balance, for example, the two sides created by drawing an imaginary line down the middle, from top to bottom, will be mirror images of each other. An asymmetrical painting or drawing is not exactly the same on both sides, but it has unequal elements which, taken together, create a feeling of equal visual weight. Radial balance is achieved by having a center from which elements, such as line and color, radiate outward towards the edges. These concepts are presented here in terms of *two dimensions.* Some artworks, such as sculpture, however, are *three-dimensional.*

Contrast

Contrast, as the word implies, is the juxtaposition of opposites (black and white, light and dark, rough and smooth, etc.) within an artwork. You can often most easily find the contrast, or degree of difference, between light areas of a painting and dark areas. Another kind of contrast to take notice of is the difference between *negative space* and *positive space.* Notice that objects are surrounded by more or less empty space, which serves to define the objects.

Dominance

Sometimes when you look at an artwork, one element or aspect immediately calls your attention. That one aspect is said to be *dominant.* The artist has chosen to emphasize one subject or part of the design above all others. The question to ask yourself is *why this, and not something else?* Your answer to that question will help you ascertain the artist's reason for creating that artwork. In other words, what idea, mood, or emotion does the artist want to convey; what is the *theme* of the work? An element or aspect that is of lesser importance, or dominance, is said to be *subordinate.*

Emphasis

When an artist chooses to stress one element over another (for example, a strongly geometric design stresses line and shape), that element is *emphasized.* It stands out more than the other elements do.

Movement

Movement can be spoken of in two ways with relation to a work of art. There is the sense of movement, or action, within the artwork itself; and there is the movement of the observer's eyes across and within the work. Often there will be a *focal point* in an artwork, one point or small area which first draws the eye. Artists design a work so that the eye then moves in a particular direction or directions to absorb the rest of the piece. When you first look at an artwork, notice how your eye moves as you take in the details (this is easier with larger works or reproductions).

Repetition

Often an artist will repeat elements (colors, shapes, lines) several times within a single artwork. This pattern of *repetition* can serve any of a number of purposes. It can enhance dominance, serve the theme, help achieve balance, and so forth. Look for repetition within an artwork and try to understand its purpose. Remember, an artist makes a conscious choice to include something in her work; ask yourself *why the repetition,* and it will help you understand the work of art.

Rhythm

A regular repetition of shape or line creates a sense of *rhythm*. The rhythm is often meant to evoke movement, as in the case of an artist's rendition of waves.

Theme

The *theme* of a work of art is essentially the reason the work was created. Usually, by the time you finish considering all the elements and principles, you can come up with an answer to the question *why did the artist decide to create this particular work* or *what does the artist want me to get out of viewing this art?* There may be *variations* on the theme, the dominant idea or feature, within the artwork. An example would be a painting of a row of people, sitting and staring vacantly at a television. The theme might be *how television keeps you from thinking,* and each individual person would be a variation on that theme.

Unity

Good artworks have an overall sense of *unity,* a sense that all the elements are related, that they fit together and form a coherent whole. The unity is most often *harmonious,* but it may also be *disharmonious,* if different elements seem to be working against each other or clashing.

Visual Arts Media

In visual art, the term *media* (singular form, *medium*) refers to the materials or methods that may be used to create art. Some common media are paint (oil, watercolor, acrylic) and canvas, paper, cloth, charcoal, pen or pencil, crayon or marker, wood, clay, metal, film, and tape. Actually, almost any material can become a medium for creative visual expression.

Collage and assemblage are less common media that may be appropriate for use in the classroom. *Collage* is a method in which one or more various materials (e.g., paper or cloth) are glued or otherwise attached to a background surface. It is an artistic activity that is appropriate even for very young children. *Assemblage* is the same idea carried out in three dimensions, so that you end up with a sculptural piece, which is composed of a collection of similar or dissimilar objects, including, possibly, found objects. *Mixed media* is the general term applied to any work of visual art that is created from two or more media, usually those that are not commonly used together.

Art History

Although the cave art of Europe and Australia is the oldest visual representation considered art that we currently know about, there is every reason to believe that we may discover even older art records. Africa, commonly believed to be the area from which early humans migrated to the rest of the world, is still yielding its secrets to archeologists. Within the past few years, incised ocher (an iron oxide material) has been discovered and dated to almost 100,000 years ago. That means the proto-humans (ancestors of our species, *homo sapiens*) alive at that time were using some sort of stylus (sharp, pointed instrument) to make marks on the medium of ocher. Humans have a universal urge to create art, to express ourselves, in artistic media. Every culture, at every period of history, has created art. As you learn about other cultures, past and present, be sure to learn about their art and artists.

Our western art traditions—as with so much of our culture—can be traced back to the Greeks and Romans. During the Medieval Period, most art was created for churches and so had a religious theme. In the Renaissance, art flowered, fueled partly by renewed knowledge of classical Greek and Roman art. Artists depended on wealthy patrons for support, however; as a result, the patrons generally chose the subject matter. One important development in the Renaissance was the first use of the concept of *perspective* to create the illusion of three dimensions on a two-dimensional surface. For a description of the visual techniques used to create the illusion of perspective, try this website: mathforum.org/sum95/math_and/perspective/perspect.html.

For several centuries, art flourished in Europe. Artists were generally considered good only if their work presented images in a realistic fashion. This trend was at its height in France in the nineteenth century when Claude Monet and some like-minded artist friends rebelled and started painting in the Impressionist style. This school of art was designed to capture and portray scenes the way the human eye sees them, with movement and changing light, not as a static scene. The Impressionists changed the way people thought about art. Within forty years, by 1908, Pablo Picasso and another group of artists were inspired by African sculptures to start painting in a completely different way. They learned to see objects and scenes in terms of their component geometric shapes (circles, triangles, and so forth). Then they separated the components and rearranged them so that a triangle representing the nose might appear to be located on top of the oval representing the head. They called this style of art *cubism.* Though the cubist style did not last more than about twelve years, it again changed the basic premises of the art world. The twentieth century saw the evolution of *abstract art,* or artwork in which there is little or no effort to represent an object or scene in realistic terms. Art might represent abstract ideas, or it might present concrete objects with no apparent reference to the physicality of the object represented.

Other areas of the world have their own art traditions and histories. For an excellent overview of world art history, complete with reproductions of artworks, go to the Metropolitan Museum of Art website at metmuseum.org/toah/splash.htm, or search the Internet for other websites. Art, like all the other subjects covered in the CSET, enriches your life as you learn about it. It is a joy and a privilege to spend your life learning about the world and sharing your knowledge and enthusiasm with your students.

Glossary

Antagonist: in theater, a villain against whom the protagonist is pitted

Bass clef: musical notes played with the left hand on a piano, having a deeper sound than those in the treble clef

Blocking: where and when actors move on stage during a theatrical production

Chord: three or more harmonious notes played together; instruments with multiple strings (piano, guitar) can play chords

Collage: an artwork composed of various materials

Color: what we see as a result of the reflection or absorption of light off any surface, its main characteristics being hue, intensity, and value

Dialogue: exchange of lines between actors in a theatrical production

Dynamics: in a piece of music, the variation between louder and softer sections

Force/energy: a dancer's transformation and release of potential energy into kinetic energy; how dancers move

Form: in music, the shape, structure, or organization of a piece

Form: in visual art, the way an artwork's elements are put together, as opposed to its content or subject matter

Harmony: when a note of a different pitch on a musical scale sounds good when played simultaneously with a piece's melody

Improvisation: the use of spontaneous movement and speech to create a character, mood, or situation

Interval: the distance between notes on a musical scale

Levels: the series of horizontal planes rising, one above the other, from the performance surface, through which dancers move

Line: in visual art, the movement of a point through space, described in terms of width, length, direction, and curvature or flow

Measure (or bar): a grouping of a specified number of musical beats located between two consecutive vertical lines on a staff

Melody: the tune of a piece of music

Monologue: a dramatic speech performed by one actor

Pageant: a series of tableaux performed on stage

Phrasing: how long the melody of a piece of music is performed, defined by when a breath is taken

Pitch: wavelengths or frequencies of sound

Proscenium: the most common type of performance space, named for the proscenium arch that frames the actors

Protagonist: the hero of a theatrical piece

Rhythm: in music, the pattern of stressed and unstressed beats

Shape: in visual art, the two-dimensional equivalent of form

Space: in dance, the immediate spherical area surrounding a dancer's body, extending in all directions

Space: in visual art, the absence of shape or form

Staff: a group of lines and spaces upon which musical notes are written

Symmetry: in art, a type of visual balance, where, if an imaginary line is drawn down the middle, each side mirrors the other

Syncopation: in music, an uneven pattern of stressed beats

Tableau: in theater, the silent depiction of a static scene

Tempo: the rate at which musical beats follow one another

Texture: the tactile quality of a work of art

Theme: the reason a work of art was created

Timbre: the distinctive quality of a particular sound

Time: in dance, formally measured meter or, more informally, the rhythms of a dancer's body movements

Time signature: musical notation indicating the number of beats per bar and the type of note that gets a beat

Treble clef: musical notes played with the right hand on a piano, having a higher sound than those in the bass clef

PRACTICE SET

1. The type of dance that is developed through the traditions of a culture and passed down from generation to generation is

    (A) ballroom dance
    (B) folk dance
    (C) modern dance
    (D) ballet

2. "Resistance" by sculptor Cindy Jackson is a study in bronze. Among the following questions a teacher might ask his eighth-grade class, which pertains *least* to this sculpture?

    (A) How does the artist use line and form to show strength and balance?
    (B) Why is the title "Resistance" amusing?
    (C) Why do you think this is a powerful relief sculpture?
    (D) How does Jackson make a static work embody movement?

3. Which of the following is *not* an American form of popular music?

    (A) blues
    (B) baroque
    (C) country
    (D) jazz

4. Traditional Kabuki theater, originating in seventeenth-century Japan, continues to be performed in modern-day Japan. What aspects of the visual arts are essential elements of a kabuki production?

    (A) masks, costumes, and sets
    (B) masks, wigs, costumes, and sets
    (C) makeup, wigs, costumes, and floral arrangements
    (D) makeup, wigs, fans, costumes, and sets

Use the following figure to answer question 5.

5. In music notation, ledger lines are lines added above or below the staff. The notes on the ledger lines in the figure above are both

(A) A

(B) B flat

(C) middle C

(D) C sharp

6. Tragedy is a form of drama that can be traced as far back as Greek theater. The hallmarks of a tragedy are all of the following *except*

(A) The hero's pain appears to the audience to be just and fair.

(B) The hero's pain is to some extent redemptive.

(C) The play's denouement is catastrophic.

(D) The play's denouement is inevitable.

7. A stately court dance in triple time, which originated as a rustic French dance and was introduced to the court in the seventeenth century, is the

(A) waltz

(B) minuet

(C) scherzo

(D) paso doble

8. On a musical staff, the length (in time) that a note lasts is indicated by

(A) its size

(B) its shape

(C) its pitch

(D) its position

9. In the production of an upper-grade school play, the student producer would most likely be in charge of

   (A) casting the play

   (B) overseeing lighting and sound for the production

   (C) giving notes to the actors

   (D) overseeing the budget and the box office

10. Which of the following types of artwork would be most suitably executed by first graders?

    (A) assemblage

    (B) still-life oil painting

    (C) collage

    (D) maquette

11. A proscenium stage has the configuration of

    (A) a square or rectangular stage that can be viewed from all four sides

    (B) a stage with an arch that frames the actors as they are viewed from the front

    (C) a stage that juts out into the audience and can be viewed from three sides

    (D) a round stage with an audience circling it

12. Which of the following sections includes the smallest number of instruments in a traditional orchestra?

    (A) string

    (B) woodwind

    (C) percussion

    (D) brass

13. In dance, the qualities of movement are called sustained, percussive, suspended, swinging, and collapsing. What is the term for the release of potential energy into movement (also called the dynamics of dance)?

    (A) force

    (B) gesture

    (C) space

    (D) phrasing

Constructed-Response Question

Use the song "So Long, I'll See You, Hasta la Vista" below to complete the exercise that follows.

So long I'll See You, Hasta la vista

Melody originally from an old Jewish closing hymn

© D. Saphra 1998

Using your knowledge of vocal music, prepare a response in which you:

Describe the melody, rhythm, and form of this song; and

Discuss one reason why this song would be appropriate for elementary school students to sing.

_____

_____

_____

_____

_____

_____

_____

ANSWER KEY

1. B	5. C	9. D	13. A
2. C	6. A	10. C	
3. B	7. B	11. B	
4. D	8. B	12. C	

ANSWERS AND EXPLANATIONS

1. B

Folk dance is also called ethnic dance, traditional dance, or country dance and derives from the traditions, music, and costumes of a specific culture. For example, a dance included in all Russian folk dance repertoires is the "troika" (meaning three-horse team), where dancers in teams of three imitate the prancing of horses pulling a sled or a carriage. Ballroom dance (A) is a form of dance involving specific patterns performed by a pair of dancers and was developed in the European courts of the seventeenth century. Modern dance (C) was developed in twentieth century America as an offshoot of ballet (D), which originated in seventeenth and eighteenth century France.

2. C

All of the questions (A), (B), and (D) are valid to ask a class of eighth-graders, who are able to discuss abstract ideas and exchange insights. Choice (C) wouldn't be appropriate to Jackson's work because the sculpture is free-standing, whereas a *relief* is sculpted figures projecting from a background. An example of a relief is Saint-Gaudens' famous memorial to Colonel Shaw and the first African-American infantry unit, located in Boston (which took Gaudens 14 years to finish).

3. B

Blues (A), country (C), and jazz (D) are American-born forms of popular music, as are musicals and folk music. Blues originated with the call-and-response songs of southern slaves. Jazz has its roots in European classical and African/Caribbean music. Choice (B), baroque, is not a form of American popular music, but is classical music of the Baroque period in Europe (1600–1750). The most famous baroque music was written by German composers Bach, Telemann, and Handel. During this fertile period, both operas and our modern scale system were developed.

4. D

There are no masks in kabuki, so choices (A) and (B) are incorrect. Floral arrangements are a nonessential element of kabuki, making (C) incorrect and (D) the best choice. The essential visual arts ingredients of kabuki are makeup, wigs, fans, costumes, and sets.

5. C

On both staffs, the note is a middle C. Notice there are no flat or sharp symbols next to the note or next to the clef, which would indicate that the note is either flat or sharp.

6. A

Elements of a classic tragedy include: the play's denouement is inevitable (D) and catastrophic (C); the hero's suffering is disproportionate to his guilt; the hero's anguish appears to the audience as unjust and unfair (the opposite of (A), making it the correct choice); the hero's pain appears to be beyond human endurance; the hero's pain is to some extent redemptive (B).

7. B

The minuet—a dance so called because of its small, dainty steps (*menu* = small)—was popular in seventeenth-century European royal courts. The minuet was adapted as a musical form by such composers as Lully, Mozart, and Haydn. The waltz was introduced to the royal courts in the eighteenth century, so (A) is incorrect. A scherzo (C) developed from the minuet and shares its 3/4 time signature, but it is a musical device found in symphonies, string quartets, sonatas and similar works, not a dance. The paso doble (D) is a Spanish style of dance, which was developed in France.

8. B

The shape of a note determines its length in time. Whole notes have an open oval shape and are held for a count of four beats; half notes have an open oval shape with a stem (count of two beats); quarter notes have a solid oval shape and a stem (1 beat); and eighth notes have a solid oval shape, with a flagged stem (1/2 beat). The size **(A)**, pitch **(C)**, and position **(D)** of a note on a musical staff do not indicate length.

9. D

While the student producer might have say in casting **(A)** the play and/or adding notes for the cast **(C)**, he or she would oversee (or assist the teacher in overseeing) the financial end of the production—such as the box office and the budget for costumes, makeup, sets, rentals, publicity, and printing **(D)**. The student director helps the teacher run the auditions and the rehearsals. The stage manager and/or the tech director oversee the props, makeup, costumes, set design, curtains, sound, and lighting **(B)**. Other students may take roles as set designer, construction manager, prop manager, wardrobe mistress/master, makeup director, lighting and sound designers, publicity director, box office manager, and so on.

10. C

An assemblage **(A)** is a three-dimensional work where a collection of objects is unified in a sculptural work. A still-life oil painting **(B)** illustrates an arrangement of inanimate objects in oils—a medium that is too advanced for young children. A maquette **(D)** is a small, preliminary model of a larger sculpture or building. Collage (a composition of various materials), is the perfect art form for young students, since they are at the collecting/categorizing stage of learning. The children can play with the concepts of texture, color, and shape as they glue wrapping paper, buttons, ribbon, cloth, macaroni, stickers, leaves, and glitter onto construction paper or a butcher-paper mural.

11. B

Proscenium stages are the most common stage configuration for auditoriums. The audience out front becomes "the fourth wall." The proscenium comprises an arch, usually with a curtain or scrim hanging within the arch and an "apron" in front of the curtain. Choice **(C)** describes a thrust stage, which was popular in Shakespeare's era. Choices **(A)** and **(D)** describe arena stages, which can be square, rectangular, oval, or round, and are surrounded by the audience. The stage in a circus, for example, is an unraised arena stage.

12. C

The string section of a traditional orchestra **(A)** has a minimum of ten first violins, eight second violins, six violas, four cellos, and two basses. The woodwind section **(B)** usually has two flutes/piccolos, two clarinets, two oboes, and two bassoons. The brass section **(D)** is usually two trumpets, four French horns, three trombones, and one tuba. The smallest section is the percussion, with timpani (kettle drums), and two or three other percussion instruments, such as chimes or xylophone.

13. A

Force is the term for releasing potential energy into movement; gesture **(B)** is all expressive movements of the body not supporting weight; space **(C)** refers to the location of a performed dance or the immediate spherical space surrounding the body; phrasing **(D)** is the way in which the parts of a dance are organized.

Constructed-Response Sample Essay

This is a bilingual goodbye song for young children to sing and move to. The song is in the key of D major with a seven-note range. It derives from an old Jewish closing hymn. Rhythmically it is a simple melody, using only quarter and eighth notes. "So Long, I'll See You, Hasta la Vista" is a 12-bar song written in 4/4 time, to be sung "andante" at a moderately slow tempo, a walking pace. The children could weave in lines in and out to say goodbye to each other or form two concentric circles moving in opposite directions.

This song would be appropriate to teach to young elementary students to unite and calm them down when they say goodbye at the end of the day. The simple and repetitive lyrics are soothing. Its range and simplicity are suitable for beginning singers. Both the melody and the lyrics of "So Long, I'll See You, Hasta la Vista" can be easily taught by rote. Students who are just beginning to read words and/or musical notes can hold the sheet music to learn or to practice the song. For children unfamiliar with Spanish, this song could introduce them to the phrases "hasta la vista" and "adios amigos," which could easily lead to our sharing other Spanish songs and dances ("La Cucaracha," for example) and learning more Spanish together. Children who speak Spanish could peer-teach the pronunciation of the Spanish phrases.

PART FOUR

Test-Taking Skills

Chapter 8: **Meeting the Test**

The CSET is a test in more ways than one. On a literal level, it's an examination that tests your knowledge of seven distinct subject areas. In a figurative sense, the CSET is a test of your will to become a fully credentialed teacher. You have the brainpower to successfully meet this challenge. The question is, do you have the willpower? The answer to that question must be *yes*.

You may be feeling overwhelmed by the magnitude of this test, but even the most monumental task is manageable when you break it down into small pieces. That's where your study plan comes in.

YOUR STUDY PLAN

Maybe you started with the Introduction and worked your way straight through this book. If so, you now have a pretty good idea of your strengths and weaknesses. You have taken the practice tests, marked up the book with your highlighting pen, and checked out some additional resources to enhance your knowledge. Now all you need to do is find the time to do your final preparations. Congratulations to you on your hard work. Keep it up, and the prize you're after—a clear credential—will be yours.

If you're reading these words before completing the book and taking the practice exams, doing those things will be your next step. Find out what areas you need more work on, so that you can schedule your exam dates in the proper order.

Set Goals

Make your goals as concrete as possible. Instead of, for example, *learn more science* as a goal, try making a list of the specific things you need to learn, such as *learn to diagram animal life cycles,* or *learn about geologic processes.* When you've mastered something, mark it off your list, and reward yourself with a small treat—you've earned it.

KAPLAN

Schedule Your Study Time

The CSET is regularly administered on Saturdays (unless you have a religious conflict, in which case you will take the specially-administered Sunday exam). As you search your schedule for blocks of time you can devote to studying, see if Saturday morning is open. Don't groan—there's a reason for studying on Saturday mornings. If you are used to sleeping late on Saturday morning, when the exam date rolls around, your body and mind are going to resent being deprived of their leisure routine; and you can't expect them to fully cooperate! Schedule practice tests or make up your own questions to write constructed responses for, and do those on Saturday mornings while you train for this exam that will get you the job you want.

Attitude Matters

As a teacher, you need to be a coach as well as an instructor. Practice on yourself. Tell yourself what a good job you're doing. Pat yourself on the back when you master new material. Praise yourself for sticking to your schedule, and gently remind yourself of your goals when you suffer a lapse of self-discipline.

Affirmations can work wonders. When you check the mirror in the morning, take an extra moment to tell yourself that your hard work is going to pay off. Say out loud, "I am going to pass the CSET." If you don't believe yourself, say it again, with conviction. Expectations tend to be fulfilled.

Prepare

Your motivational skills really come into play as test day nears. Many of us are not confident of our test-taking abilities. You may have had the experience in the past of thinking you were prepared for an exam, only to blank when faced with the test questions. Maybe that's never happened, but you're thinking that it could. If you find yourself thinking thoughts like that, just put a stop to it, immediately.

If you must dwell on something in the middle of the night, dwell on an image of yourself calmly remembering what you've learned on test day. Imagine feeling good when you walk out of the test room. Think about the timeline you're creating, or just get out of bed and run through a few flash cards. You are preparing for this exam, and that means you will pass.

Stay Positive

In the exam room it's even more critical to monitor your thoughts, so that you think only positive things. Negative thoughts during the exam lead to panic. Panic leads to the inability to think clearly. If you start worrying during the exam, just stop for a few moments and focus on your breathing. Breathe in for a count of eight, then out for a count of eight, making sure to exhale completely. Keep it slow and steady. Deep, regular breathing heads off the fight-or-flight response, that adrenaline-fueled rush of blood to the arms and legs (where you don't need it), and away from the brain (where you do need it).

If you can train yourself to think of the exam as an interesting challenge, you are much less likely to experience fearful thoughts during the test. Mental discipline will serve you well on the CSET, but don't forget to also prepare your body by getting some exercise and plenty of rest.

THE WEEK OF THE EXAM

The Saturday before you take any part of the CSET, wake up early and take a final practice test. Notice your improvement from the very first practice exam you took. Then start going back over your notes. Try to condense a page of notes into a single paragraph and that paragraph into a single sentence. Take those sentences and see how much you can say about each one.

Be Concise

Here's an example of the art of being concise. This is the essence of what you need to know about each of the seven subjects, condensed into seven sentences:

- **Reading, Language, and Literature**—Whether it's a word, a text, or a process, break it down into component parts, then reassemble it.
- **History**—One thing leads to another in surprisingly predictable ways, as the cycle of history repeats itself.
- **Science**—Every portion and every process, no matter how large or how small, fits perfectly into its part in the functioning of a larger whole.
- **Math**—There's never just one right way to solve a problem, but a good estimate is always a great way to check your solution.
- **Physical Education**—If it doesn't make you want to stay active, it's not the right kind of physical education for you.
- **Human Development**—Practice applying the theories to situations and people you know, so you will really understand them.
- **Visual and Performing Arts**—Just enjoy the arts, and don't forget your flashcards!

Tomorrow's the Day

The day before the exam, close the books and put away your notes. Studying today will just make you more anxious. Instead of obsessing over what you still don't know, remind yourself of how much you've learned and how well you've prepared.

Check for your admission ticket and put it with your required identification, your number two pencils, and a jacket or sweater in case the room is cold. Pack yourself a light snack to take with you to the exam. You are not generally allowed to eat in the exam room, but you can always get permission to leave the room. You can stretch your legs, clear your mind, and eat your snack if you are hungry. A snack with some protein is best. Nuts are a good source of protein, as are hard-boiled eggs and cheese. Whatever you do, stay away from sugary snacks; those will boost your energy briefly, but that boost is followed by a terrible crash—not what you need in the middle of writing a constructed response. Also, pack a generous-sized water bottle, so you don't get thirsty during the exam.

Spend the evening doing something relaxing, and go to bed early. If you feel compelled to do something productive, find a movie that is set in a time period and place you'd like to learn more about. Have a good dinner, watch the movie, and get a good night's sleep. Set your alarm early enough that you don't have to rush to get to the test site. Stay relaxed.

Test Day

On the day of the exam, get up in plenty of time and have a leisurely breakfast. Don't eat a big breakfast, though, unless that is what you usually do. Something with protein will stay with you longer than a piece of toast will, but don't force yourself to eat anything too out of the ordinary.

Check one more time for your admission ticket, identification, pencils, and jacket. Make sure you have directions to the test site and gas in the car, or that you know the public transportation route. Leave in plenty of time to get to the test site, just in case traffic is unexpectedly bad.

As you wait for the exam to begin, monitor your thoughts. If you feel anxious, do your deep breathing or tense and relax your muscles. Look around the room and smile when someone meets your eyes. Thousands of people just like you have already passed the CSET. You have worked hard, and you are prepared. Good luck!

PART FIVE

CSET Practice Test

Chapter 9: **Subtest 1 Practice Test**

TEST DIRECTIONS

This practice test contains two sections, a multiple-choice section (52 questions) and a constructed-response section (4 assignments). You may work on the sections in any order you wish.

In the multiple-choice section, read each question carefully and choose the one best answer. Directions for the constructed-response sections appear immediately before those assignments.

When taking the actual CSET, you will have one five-hour test session in which to complete the subtest(s) for which you registered.

SCORING

Remember, if you do not pass one or more subtests, you may reregister and retake those subtests. There is no limit to the number of times you may take any subtest that you have not passed. This helps takes the pressure off you, the test-taker, and gives you more choice.

Following the actual CSET, your responses to the multiple-choice questions will be scored electronically. Scores are based on the number of questions answered correctly, so there is no penalty for guessing.

Your responses to the constructed-response questions are scored by qualified California educators using focused holistic scoring. With this method, scorers judge the overall effectiveness of each response, while focusing on a set of performance characteristics that have been identified as important. For more details on how the CSET is scored, visit cset.nesinc.com.

Ready, set…

Good luck!

Subtest 1 Answer Sheet

Remove (or photocopy) this answer sheet and use it to complete the practice test.

1. Ⓐ Ⓑ Ⓒ Ⓓ Ⓔ   14. Ⓐ Ⓑ Ⓒ Ⓓ Ⓔ   27. Ⓐ Ⓑ Ⓒ Ⓓ Ⓔ   40. Ⓐ Ⓑ Ⓒ Ⓓ Ⓔ

2. Ⓐ Ⓑ Ⓒ Ⓓ Ⓔ   15. Ⓐ Ⓑ Ⓒ Ⓓ Ⓔ   28. Ⓐ Ⓑ Ⓒ Ⓓ Ⓔ   41. Ⓐ Ⓑ Ⓒ Ⓓ Ⓔ

3. Ⓐ Ⓑ Ⓒ Ⓓ Ⓔ   16. Ⓐ Ⓑ Ⓒ Ⓓ Ⓔ   29. Ⓐ Ⓑ Ⓒ Ⓓ Ⓔ   42. Ⓐ Ⓑ Ⓒ Ⓓ Ⓔ

4. Ⓐ Ⓑ Ⓒ Ⓓ Ⓔ   17. Ⓐ Ⓑ Ⓒ Ⓓ Ⓔ   30. Ⓐ Ⓑ Ⓒ Ⓓ Ⓔ   43. Ⓐ Ⓑ Ⓒ Ⓓ Ⓔ

5. Ⓐ Ⓑ Ⓒ Ⓓ Ⓔ   18. Ⓐ Ⓑ Ⓒ Ⓓ Ⓔ   31. Ⓐ Ⓑ Ⓒ Ⓓ Ⓔ   44. Ⓐ Ⓑ Ⓒ Ⓓ Ⓔ

6. Ⓐ Ⓑ Ⓒ Ⓓ Ⓔ   19. Ⓐ Ⓑ Ⓒ Ⓓ Ⓔ   32. Ⓐ Ⓑ Ⓒ Ⓓ Ⓔ   45. Ⓐ Ⓑ Ⓒ Ⓓ Ⓔ

7. Ⓐ Ⓑ Ⓒ Ⓓ Ⓔ   20. Ⓐ Ⓑ Ⓒ Ⓓ Ⓔ   33. Ⓐ Ⓑ Ⓒ Ⓓ Ⓔ   46. Ⓐ Ⓑ Ⓒ Ⓓ Ⓔ

8. Ⓐ Ⓑ Ⓒ Ⓓ Ⓔ   21. Ⓐ Ⓑ Ⓒ Ⓓ Ⓔ   34. Ⓐ Ⓑ Ⓒ Ⓓ Ⓔ   47. Ⓐ Ⓑ Ⓒ Ⓓ Ⓔ

9. Ⓐ Ⓑ Ⓒ Ⓓ Ⓔ   22. Ⓐ Ⓑ Ⓒ Ⓓ Ⓔ   35. Ⓐ Ⓑ Ⓒ Ⓓ Ⓔ   48. Ⓐ Ⓑ Ⓒ Ⓓ Ⓔ

10. Ⓐ Ⓑ Ⓒ Ⓓ Ⓔ   23. Ⓐ Ⓑ Ⓒ Ⓓ Ⓔ   36. Ⓐ Ⓑ Ⓒ Ⓓ Ⓔ   49. Ⓐ Ⓑ Ⓒ Ⓓ Ⓔ

11. Ⓐ Ⓑ Ⓒ Ⓓ Ⓔ   24. Ⓐ Ⓑ Ⓒ Ⓓ Ⓔ   37. Ⓐ Ⓑ Ⓒ Ⓓ Ⓔ   50. Ⓐ Ⓑ Ⓒ Ⓓ Ⓔ

12. Ⓐ Ⓑ Ⓒ Ⓓ Ⓔ   25. Ⓐ Ⓑ Ⓒ Ⓓ Ⓔ   38. Ⓐ Ⓑ Ⓒ Ⓓ Ⓔ   51. Ⓐ Ⓑ Ⓒ Ⓓ Ⓔ

13. Ⓐ Ⓑ Ⓒ Ⓓ Ⓔ   26. Ⓐ Ⓑ Ⓒ Ⓓ Ⓔ   39. Ⓐ Ⓑ Ⓒ Ⓓ Ⓔ   52. Ⓐ Ⓑ Ⓒ Ⓓ Ⓔ

1. Which of the following reflects the order of study, from the smallest units of a language to the larger meaning of a language?

    (A) semantics, syntax, morphemes, phonemes

    (B) morphemes, phonemes, syntax, semantics

    (C) phonemes, morphemes, syntax, semantics

    (D) phonemes, morphemes, semantics, syntax

2. Why is it important for children to link phonemes to the graphic letters and letter combinations that signify those sounds?

    (A) English has the most examples of phonemic variety, such as the sounds of the letter *g* in *girl, gentle,* and *cough.*

    (B) Phonemic awareness is a precondition for learning to read, although it is not a consequence of reading.

    (C) Children who learn strategies for linking phonemes to graphic representations become better readers and better spellers.

    (D) The state of California requires that children be tested in phonemic awareness.

3. In which of the following sentences is the italicized word used correctly?

    (A) The weather has no *affect* on my habits.

    (B) How does flying *effect* your stomach?

    (C) With rewards, we can *affect* a change in his behavior.

    (D) My performance evaluation *affects* my salary.

4. Deficiencies in English language usage by young children can most often be attributed to the fact that

    (A) the same letter always has the same sound in English

    (B) young children are still learning arbitrary phonemes and morphemes

    (C) different languages have different phonemes

    (D) children have poorly developed oral language abilities

5. Emergent speech, along with a "grammar explosion," typically occur at what age?

    (A) birth to one year

    (B) two to five years

    (C) six to eight years

    (D) eight years to adult

6. Teaching metacognitive skills to your students is important because

    (A) students learn better when they understand how they learn

    (B) students will then understand the etymology of words

    (C) students will conclude that learning is totally subconscious

    (D) students will be able to compete among themselves

7. Which of the following is an example of *scaffolding* to help a first-grader with language acquisition?

    (A) Let the student sound out words on her own.

    (B) Give the child cards with the letter *b* on them to tape onto classroom items they identify with an initial *b* sound, such as *ball* or *book*.

    (C) Have the student read new words silently while you observe.

    (D) Meet with the child's parents to discuss reading games that they might play with her.

8. What is the most likely reason that Mindy, a first-grader, cannot read the word *plow*?

    (A) The word is too long.

    (B) The word is not a cognate.

    (C) The word is not in her oral vocabulary.

    (D) The word cannot be sounded out.

GO ON TO THE NEXT PAGE

9. A seventh-grade student is writing a composition explaining how the Mars rovers, Spirit and Opportunity, were built and launched. Which one of the following writing genres would most appeal to the reader's senses?

   (A) descriptive

   (B) narrative

   (C) expository

   (D) persuasive

10. Which of the following sentences contains a dependent clause?

    (A) Crystal likes animals more than people, so she volunteers at the animal shelter.

    (B) After 11:30 in the morning, the Come Back Inn serves only lunch and dinner.

    (C) Daniel, my lab partner, has the annoying habit of chewing with his mouth open.

    (D) As she curtsied, the lady blushed.

Read the excerpt from "The Eternal Quest" by Debra Blank below; then answer question 11.

The first is the wear-and-tear hypothesis that suggests the body eventually succumbs to the environmental insults of life. The second is the notion that we have an internal clock which is genetically programmed to run down. Supporters of the wear-and-tear theory maintain that the very practice of breathing causes us to age because inhaled oxygen produces toxic by-products. Advocates of the internal clock theory believe that individual cells are told to stop dividing and thus eventually to die by, for example, hormones produced by the brain or by their own genes.

[from *HyperGrammar*, produced by the Writing Centre at the University of Ottawa.]

11. Which of the following would be a restatement of the topic of this paragraph?

    (A) There are two broad theories concerning what triggers a human's inevitable decline to death.

    (B) Some scientists believe that humans contain an "internal clock" which forces them eventually to die.

    (C) The wear-and-tear theory has more followers than the internal clock theory.

    (D) We all must die some day.

12. Which of the following sentences is not punctuated correctly?

    (A) "I will be president one day," Amanda declared. "I will be the first female president."

    (B) "I will be president one day," declared Amanda. "I will be the first female president."

    (C) "I will be president one day. I will be the first female president." Amanda declared.

    (D) "I will be president one day. I will be the first female president," declared Amanda.

GO ON TO THE NEXT PAGE

Read the excerpt below; then answer questions 13–14.

[1]E. B. White wrote books, including *Stuart Little* and *Charlotte's Web,* for both children and adults. [2]He also wrote essays and humorous sketches for *The New Yorker* magazine. [3]Funnily enough for such a famous writer, he always said that he found writing difficult and bad for one's disposition, but still he kept at it! [4]White once revealed, "All that I ever hope to say in books is that I love the world. [5]I guess you can find that in there, if you dig around. [6]Animals are part of my world and I try to report them faithfully and with respect."

13. Where would be the best place to insert the sentence "What, then, did E. B. White have to say in his writing?"

    (A) after Sentence 1
    (B) after Sentence 2
    (C) after Sentence 3
    (D) after Sentence 4

14. White was known for his self-deprecating humor. Which sentences give the reader hints of this?

    (A) Sentences 3 and 5
    (B) Sentences 3 and 6
    (C) Sentences 1 and 3
    (D) Sentences 2 and 4

15. Which of the following would be most important to include in the middle section of a persuasive essay?

    (A) a summary of the logical steps in the essay's argument
    (B) an explanation of why the issue addressed by the essay is important
    (C) a rebuttal of alternative points of view
    (D) a description of why the author chose that topic

16. Which is the correct order of the writing process?

    (A) drafting, prewriting, revising, editing
    (B) prewriting, editing, drafting, revising
    (C) webbing, drafting, proofreading, editing
    (D) prewriting, drafting, revising, editing

17. Fluency in which of the following languages would be *least* helpful in learning English as a second language?

    (A) Latin
    (B) Danish
    (C) French
    (D) German

18. In a dramatic soliloquy, the speaker is usually

    (A) speaking to a group of people
    (B) speaking to a second person who replies
    (C) speaking to a second person who does not reply
    (D) alone

19. The major source of story conflict in Greek and Roman mythology is

    (A) Man versus Nature
    (B) Man versus the Gods
    (C) Man versus other Man/Men
    (D) Man versus Himself

20. Lucy is a third-grader who skips over eight or more words per page because she doesn't recognize them. Which of the following would be the *best* action that Lucy's teacher could take to help Lucy improve her vocabulary?

    (A) present new words to the class before he instructs the children to start reading
    (B) encourage Lucy to try strategies to decipher new words, such as using context clues
    (C) select easier texts for Lucy
    (D) assign Lucy a reading peer who knows more than Lucy does

GO ON TO THE NEXT PAGE

21. Which part of the word *infallibility* means "not"?

    (A) *in*

    (B) *fal*

    (C) *libil*

    (D) *ity*

22. All of the following transition phrases express cause and effect *except*

    (A) as a result

    (B) even though

    (C) consequently

    (D) therefore

23. Which of the following terms refers to the set of linguistic practices belonging to one person, as opposed to the linguistics of an entire group?

    (A) idiom

    (B) accent

    (C) dialect

    (D) idiolect

24. Which of the following terms applies to where a story takes place, including the physical surroundings, time period, and social environment?

    (A) theme

    (B) point of view

    (C) plot

    (D) setting

Read the poem "I Dream'd in a Dream" by Walt Whitman below; then answer questions 25–26.

I DREAM'D IN A DREAM

I dream'd in a dream I saw a city invincible to the attacks of the

whole of the rest of the earth,

I dream'd that was the new city of Friends,

Nothing was greater there than the quality of robust love, it led the rest,

It was seen every hour in the actions of the men of that city,

And in all their looks and words.

25. The passage above is an example of

    (A) prose

    (B) haiku

    (C) free verse

    (D) metered poetry

26. Which of the following words best describes the tone of the poem?

    (A) angry

    (B) hopeful

    (C) weepy

    (D) disillusioned

GO ON TO THE NEXT PAGE

Use the map below to answer question 27.

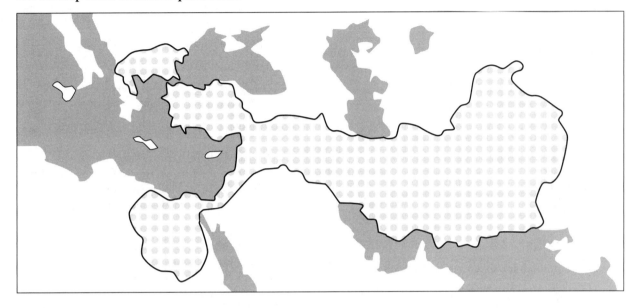

27. The patterned land area on the map above shows the extent of the empire associated with which of the following conquerors?

    (A) Julius Caesar

    (B) Alexander the Great

    (C) Charlemagne

    (D) Hernan Cortes

28. Which of the following best describes mechanisms by which Islam has spread throughout its history?

    (A) military conquest and trade incentives

    (B) enslavement and domination

    (C) missionaries and enticement

    (D) economic welfare and religious sacrifice

29. Which of the following is the period of European history that produced advances in science that revolutionized our conception of Earth's place within the universe?

    (A) Medieval

    (B) Renaissance

    (C) the Romantic Era

    (D) Enlightenment

30. Which of the following names the Chinese philosophical system that emphasizes living in balance with the natural world?

    (A) Confucianism

    (B) Buddhism

    (C) Taoism

    (D) Hinduism

31. Which of the following social sciences is based on the seminal concept of the law of supply and demand?

    (A) economics

    (B) sociology

    (C) anthropology

    (D) history

GO ON TO THE NEXT PAGE

32. In medieval Europe which of the following was most directly influenced by the Roman Catholic church?

    (A) the signing in 1215 of the Magna Carta

    (B) the emergence of trade guilds

    (C) the growth of trade with Russia

    (D) the founding of universities

33. Which of the following was the initial driving force behind European exploration of the Americas?

    (A) the need to locate new land for an expanding population

    (B) the desire to export Christianity to the native peoples

    (C) the search for a sea route to Asia

    (D) the search for new staple crops to feed the European population

34. Which of the following is the system of state regulation and economic control practiced by European nations prior to the emergence of capitalism?

    (A) mercantilism

    (B) communism

    (C) socialism

    (D) barter

35. Which of the following inventions launched the Industrial Age?

    (A) the cloth sail

    (B) the wheel

    (C) the printing press

    (D) the steam engine

36. Which of the following is considered the first declaration of self-government in the New World?

    (A) the Mayflower Compact

    (B) the Magna Carta

    (C) the Articles of Confederation

    (D) the Declaration of Independence

37. Today's residents of Washington, DC share a complaint about the government with the pre-Revolutionary War American colonists. Which of the following best states that complaint?

    (A) "Women are citizens too!"

    (B) "No taxation without representation!"

    (C) "One person, one vote!"

    (D) "Don't tread on me!"

The excerpt below, from *Objections to the Proposed Constitution*, was written by one of the nation's founders, George Mason. Read the excerpt and then answer question 38.

The President of the United States has no constitutional council (a thing unknown in any safe and regular Government) he will therefore be unsupported by proper information and advice; and will generally be directed by minions and favorites—or he will become a tool to the Senate—or a council of state will grow out of the principal officers of the great departments; the worst and most dangerous of all ingredients for such a council, in a free country; for they may be induced to join in any dangerous or oppressive measures, to shelter themselves, and prevent an inquiry into their own misconduct in office.

38. George Mason, in these objections to the Constitution that was soon to be adopted, represented the concerns of which of the following groups?

    (A) the Masons

    (B) the Federalists

    (C) the Democratic-Republicans

    (D) the Abolitionists

39. The Missouri Compromise of 1820 was designed to resolve conflict in which of the following areas?

    (A) slavery

    (B) warfare

    (C) elections

    (D) taxation

GO ON TO THE NEXT PAGE ⟩

KAPLAN

40. One advantage the Union possessed over the Confederacy in the Civil War was an existing naval force. It used this navy in several ways, but its most effective use was

    (A) as floating hospitals, a medical use
    (B) to bombard southern port cities, a show of military force
    (C) to move Union forces quickly, a transport use
    (D) to blockade southern ports, an economic use

41. After the Civil War, Reconstruction was a difficult phase in the nation's history. Reconstruction ended in 1877 as a direct result of which of the following events?

    (A) the passage of the Fourteenth Amendment
    (B) the close presidential election of 1876
    (C) the creation of the Ku Klux Klan
    (D) the impeachment of President Andrew Johnson

42. The Homestead Act of 1862 led to a major displacement of which of the following groups of people?

    (A) African-Americans
    (B) Amerindians
    (C) Irish-Americans
    (D) Chinese-Americans

43. The Sherman Antitrust Act of 1890 was the most significant act in U.S. history designed to restrict the growth of

    (A) federal government
    (B) state governments
    (C) income taxes
    (D) corporations

44. Which of the following had the greatest effect on the growing political, economic, and social cohesion of the United States in the last half of the nineteenth century?

    (A) the end of Reconstruction
    (B) the Homestead Act
    (C) advances in transportation and communication
    (D) realization of Manifest Destiny

45. Which of the following skills was shared by geographically-separated native California peoples in pre-Columbian times?

    (A) bowl and basket weaving
    (B) sculpting copper figures
    (C) irrigation of arid land
    (D) superior horsemanship

46. Which of the following names the environmentally-destructive mining process that came into use as the Gold Rush wound down in 1853?

    (A) panning
    (B) tunneling
    (C) strip mining
    (D) hydraulic mining

47. Many Chinese and other Asians came to California when they heard about the discovery of gold. During the Gold Rush, they faced discrimination and denial of their rights. Which of the following opportunities attracted the largest number of Chinese immigrants to California after the Gold Rush ended?

    (A) establishment of Chinese eateries
    (B) work on the transcontinental railroad
    (C) proximity to Hawaii
    (D) pursuit of higher education

GO ON TO THE NEXT PAGE ⟩

48. In 1911 California adopted a new state constitution, inspired by the national progressive movement. Which of the following names the principle underlying the goals of these progressive reformers?

    (A) initiative

    (B) immigration reform

    (C) popular sovereignty

    (D) referendum

49. Ellis Island, in New York City harbor, was the entry point for many European immigrants to the United States. Its counterpart, outside of San Francisco, was which of the following?

    (A) Angel Island

    (B) Alcatraz Island

    (C) Golden Gate Island

    (D) Half Moon Bay

50. Which of the following led to a wave of migration into California in the 1930s?

    (A) the growth of the aerospace industry

    (B) the Dust Bowl

    (C) the National Highway System

    (D) the Mexican Workers' Act

51. Much of California's twentieth century history revolves around the story of water rights. Which of the following bodies of water was inadvertently created by a water project gone awry?

    (A) Lake Shasta

    (B) the Salton Sea

    (C) Mono Lake

    (D) Lake Arrowhead

52. The Central Valley Project was a large-scale reclamation project that irrigated large portions of the Central Valley at the expense of wetlands to the north. This project was one of many projects that were a U.S. government response to which of the following events?

    (A) World War I

    (B) World War II

    (C) the Great Depression

    (D) the Roaring Twenties

GO ON TO THE NEXT PAGE

KAPLAN

CONSTRUCTED-RESPONSE DIRECTIONS

Prepare a written response for each assignment. Read each assignment carefully and think about how you will organize your response before you begin to write.

The assignments are intended to assess subject matter knowledge, not writing ability. However, your responses must be presented clearly in order to be fairly evaluated by your audience, educators in the field.

—————————————————

Constructed-Response Assignment 1

Complete the exercise that follows.

Describe the different kinds of third-person points of view used in writing. Be sure to provide examples.

_____

_____

_____

_____

_____

_____

_____

_____

_____

_____

_____

_____

_____

_____

_____

_____

_____

_____

_____

Constructed-Response Assignment 2

Complete the exercise that follows.

In learning about Standard American English, we discover that it is a dynamic language that is always growing and changing. Discuss the following:

- three reasons why the English language is dynamic
- examples of changes in the language

_____

_____

_____

_____

_____

_____

_____

_____

_____

_____

_____

_____

_____

_____

_____

_____

_____

_____

_____

_____

_____

_____

Constructed-Response Assignment 3

Complete the exercise that follows.

There have been many crucial inventions that have had lasting impacts on world, national, or regional history.
- Pick one such invention.
- Discuss how this invention affected the course of history.
- Include specific examples in your discussion.

_____

_____

_____

_____

_____

_____

_____

_____

_____

_____

_____

_____

_____

_____

_____

_____

_____

_____

_____

_____

Constructed-Response Assignment 4

Complete the exercise that follows.

The framers of the Constitution faced several challenges in the form of conflicting philosophies and interests among various groups within the new republic. Using your knowledge of the Constitution, prepare a response in which you:

- identify two areas of conflict the framers tried to resolve
- explain how the framers resolved, or attempted to resolve, the conflicts

_____

_____

_____

_____

_____

_____

_____

_____

_____

_____

_____

_____

_____

_____

_____

_____

_____

_____

_____

_____

_____

KAPLAN)

STOP

Chapter 10: Subtest 1 Answers and Explanations

ANSWER KEY

1. C	14. A	27. B	40. D
2. C	15. C	28. A	41. B
3. D	16. D	29. B	42. B
4. B	17. B	30. C	43. D
5. B	18. D	31. A	44. C
6. A	19. B	32. D	45. A
7. B	20. B	33. C	46. D
8. C	21. A	34. A	47. B
9. A	22. B	35. D	48. C
10. D	23. D	36. A	49. A
11. A	24. D	37. B	50. B
12. C	25. C	38. C	51. B
13. C	26. B	39. A	52. C

1. C

The correct order moves from phonemes (the basic building blocks of sounds) to morphemes (sounds or sound combinations that create meaning and words) to syntax (the structure of sentences) to semantics (the structure, meaning, and context of a language). Choices **(A)**, **(B)**, and **(D)** do not reflect the correct order.

2. C

Research has shown that children who learn conscious strategies for linking phonemes to their graphic representations become both better readers and better spellers. There are other languages with variation in pronunciation of the same phoneme **(A)**. Choice **(B)** is only half right: phonemic awareness is a precondition for learning to read *and* it is a consequence of reading. Choice **(D)**, that the state of California requires that children be tested in phonemic awareness, is false—although, in general terms, all reading and spelling tests measure phonemic awareness to some degree.

3. D

The homonyms *affect* and *effect* are often confused. Choice **(A)** would be correct if it read *The weather has no effect on my habits* (*effect* meaning "influence"). Choice **(B)** would be correct if written *How does flying affect your stomach?* (*affect* being a verb here that means "influence"). Choice **(C)** would be correct if it read *With rewards, we can effect a change in his behavior.* (*Effect* is rarely seen as a verb, but when it is, it means "to bring about" and is usually teamed with *a change*.)

4. B

Choice **(B)** is correct because young children have not yet absorbed or memorized all the arbitrary phonemes and morphemes of our language (e.g., *desk* is the morpheme that represents the actual thing that is a desk, but there is no reason why this is so). Choice **(A)** is untrue; **(C)** is true but does not address why children would have trouble in English. Choice **(D)** is a generalization that may or may not be true.

5. B

While children progress at different rates in language learning, it is typical for two- to five-year-olds **(B)** to experience both emergent speech and a grammar explosion. Children

of this age experiment with rules of pronunciation, spelling, grammar, and sentence structure. Choices **(A)**, **(C)**, and **(D)** reflect the wrong age groups. Teachers should understand milestones in language acquisition and definable stages of development: birth to one year: cooing, then babbling; one to two years: holophrastic speech; eighteen months to thirty months: telegraphic speech; two to five years: emergent speech/grammar explosion; five to seven years, intermediate language fluency; seven years to adult, increased fluency.

6. A

Metacognition is the process of thinking about thinking. For example, a student is using metacognitive skills if she notices that she is having more trouble learning comma rules than capitalization rules or if it strikes her that she should double-check the spelling of a word before accepting it as fact. Metacognition explains why children of different ages deal with learning tasks in different ways: they have developed new strategies for thinking. Research studies confirm this conclusion; as children get older they demonstrate more awareness of their thinking processes. Teaching metacognitive skills to your students will help them get a handle on *how* they learn **(A)**, leading them to understand and better employ learning strategies that relate to their own weaknesses and strengths. The remaining choices, **(B)**, **(C)**, and **(D)**, are unrelated to metacognitive skills.

7. B

Scaffolding is the support a teacher gives a student to help him or her move up to the next learning plateau. Only **(B)** expresses a scaffolding technique with direct interaction between the teacher and the student. Choice **(A)** and **(C)** have the child doing her own work alone, while being observed. Choice **(D)** may well be a good technique to help the *parents* get to the next level of helping their child acquire language skills and for them to be the scaffold for their child at home.

8. C

Recall that a child's speaking ability is an important factor in learning to read. Even when first-grader Mindy might try to sound out *plow*, she is unable to comprehend a word that is not in her speaking or listening vocabulary **(C)**. Choices, **(A)**, **(B)**, and **(D)**, do not explain this phenomenon.

9. A

Both **(B)**, narrative and **(C)**, expository, could possibly be appropriate rhetorical approaches for a composition on how the Mars rovers, Spirit and Opportunity, were built and launched. However, the clue in this question is "appeal to the reader's *senses*." Descriptive writing **(A)** by definition paints a picture while appealing to the senses. Since the question did not mention a controversy or an opinion, persuasive writing **(D)** would be incorrect.

10. D

Recall that a *clause* is a group of words consisting of a subject and a predicate, the two main types being *independent* and *dependent*. An independent clause can stand alone as a viable simple sentence. A dependant clause cannot stand alone as a sentence—it "depends" on an independent clause. In correct choice **(D)**, "As she curtsied, the lady blushed," *As she curtsied,* while a short clause, is nevertheless a dependent clause (*she* is the subject, *curtsied* the verb form). The clause *the lady blushed* is the independent clause—it can stand on its own. Choice **(A)** is a compound sentence; **(B)** is a simple sentence with a long introductory prepositional phrase. Choice **(C)** is a simple sentence with an appositive (*my lab partner*) and two prepositional phrases (*of chewing, with his mouth open*).

11. A

This paragraph is a straightforward description of two possibilities, neither of which is preferred over the other **(C)**. It would be wrong to mention only one of the possibilities (the "internal clock" in **(B)**) or to describe the paragraph as a philosophical discussion of death itself, as in **(D)**, ("We all must die some day").

12. C

When a quotation begins a sentence, use a comma before the attributive phrase, which in this case is *Amanda declared.* Remember, a comma is not necessary if an exclamation point or a question mark is inside the quotation marks (e.g., "I will be president one day!" Amanda shouted. or "Will I be president one day?" Amanda asked.) Choices **(A)**, **(B)**, and **(D)** are correctly punctuated.

13. C

The best place to insert the sentence "What, then, did E. B. White have to say in his writing?" would be after Sentence 3 and before Sentence 4 **(C)**. The question logically follows up on the idea presented in Sentence 3: White found writing difficult, yet he stuck with it. The questions falls naturally before he "reveals" what he feels he is saying in his works, simply that he loves the world. The other three choices, **(A)**, **(B)**, and **(D)** do not work for the placement of this question.

14. A

Clues to E. B. White's self-deprecating humor appear in Sentences 3 ("he found writing . . . bad for one's disposition") and 5 ("I guess you can find that in there, if you dig around."). The words *bad for one's disposition* in Sentence 3 sound like the author of this passage is quoting something White has said about himself (or certainly thought); its implication is that White felt he got cranky when he wrote. In Sentence 5, White's choice of the clauses *I guess* and *if you dig around* display a modest character.

15. C

The middle section of a persuasive essay contains the pros and cons of alternative points of view. A summary of the logical steps in the essay's argument **(A)** would come at the end of the essay. An explanation of why the issue addressed by the essay is important **(B)** and/or a description of why the author chose this topic **(D)** would come in the introduction section.

16. D

The order of the writing process is prewriting (brainstorming, webbing, outlining, clustering), drafting (the initial writing), revising (rewriting, adding, or subtracting), editing (adjusting grammar and syntax), and proofreading (checking for errors in punctuation and spelling). The other three possibilities, **(A)**, **(B)**, and **(C)** are incorrectly ordered.

17. B

English has many root words and cognates derived from Latin **(A)**, French **(C)**, and German **(D)**. Of the four choices, Danish **(B)** is the least related to English and, consequently, would be the least helpful.

KAPLAN

18. D

Frequently used in plays and prose, the speaker of a soliloquy (*solus* = alone) is alone **(D)**, eliminating all other choices. Hamlet's "To be or not to be" speech in Shakespeare's *Hamlet* is a famous soliloquy. Both choices **(A)** and **(C)** could describe a dramatic monologue, in which the speaker (*mono* = one) addresses one or more people, who do not speak. An example of a dramatic monologue can be found in Shakespeare's *Henry V*, when the title character delivers his St. Crispen's Day speech, rallying his men for war. Choice **(B)** describes a dialogue (*dia* = two), a conversation between two people or among three or more people. In fact, Shakespeare uses all of these speech forms in all of his plays.

19. B

The word *Man* in this question is not meant to be sexist; it refers to (all of) Mankind. Greek and Roman mythology tell stories explaining how elements of nature and of human nature came to be (sun, moon, fire, curiosity, vanity), but the overarching story conflict in the majority of the Greek and Roman myths arises from "Man versus the Gods." Man versus Nature **(A)**, Man versus other Man/Men **(C)** and Man versus Himself **(D)** are conflicts that appear in a few myths, but most often as sub-plots.

20. B

While **(A)** may sound good at first, many students cannot remember the spellings or meanings of vocabulary words given in advance; they need to read/hear/see the words in context in order to decipher meaning. Selecting an easier text **(C)** is not a good solution if Lucy is only missing eight or so words per page of a third-grade-level book (she is not so far behind that she should drop a level). Assigning a reading pal usually only works if the mentor is two or more grades beyond the reader, which sets up a mentoring relationship that is beneficial to both reading pals. Assigning a peer "who knows more than Lucy does" **(D)** would most likely be damaging to Lucy's self-esteem and confidence.

21. A

Prefixes beginning with the letter "i" often mean "not," for example, in-, il-, im-, and ir-, as in *infallibility, illegal, impossible*, and *irresponsible*. Other prefixes that can mean "not" are *a-* as in *amoral* and un- as in *unconstitutional*.

Playing games with prefixes, suffixes, root words, and cognates pulls students in a fun way to learn morphemes, the building blocks of language. Even with a couple dozen morphemes, children can play detective to find the meanings of hundreds of English words.

22. B

Transition words and phrases that express cause and effect include *as a result* **(A)**, *because, consequently* **(C)**, *for this purpose, so, then, therefore* **(D)**, and *to this end*. The phrase *even though* **(B)** belongs to the group of transition phrases that express contrast, such as *although, but, despite, however, in contrast, instead, on the contrary*, and *on the one hand, on the other hand*.

23. D

Here is an example of a question where you can probably use the process of elimination if you don't know the word *idiolect*. You probably know the other three terms: *idiom, accent*, and *dialect*. *Idiom* **(A)** is the usage or vocabulary that is characteristic of a specific group of people. *Accent* **(B)** is a distinctive manner of oral expression, as a Cockney accent or Southern drawl, and can apply to an individual or a community. It is one aspect of linguistic practice, not a set of practices. *Dialect* **(C)** is the usage or vocabulary that is characteristic of a specific group of people. Therefore, *idiolect* **(D)** refers to a linguistic system used by an individual.

24. D

Even though a story's theme (the central or unifying concept) may pertain to time period and social environment, it does not have anything to do with locale, making **(A)** incorrect. Point of view **(B)** is the story's perspective and may be first person ("Call me Ishmael"), second person ("If you're looking for trouble, you've found it in this story"), or third person ("Dorothy thought the twister was going to carry Toto away"). Plot **(C)** is what happens in the story, usually a struggle of some sort.

25. C

The Whitman poem "I Dream'd in a Dream" is an example of free verse (unrhymed verse without a consistent metrical pattern). Although these lines lack regular meter, they are more rhythmic than normal prose. If the passage were prose **(A)**, it would have neither lines that divide as they do, nor capital letters for *Nothing, It,* and *And,* which do not begin new sentences. Choice **(B)**, a haiku, is a Japanese verse form with three short lines of 5, 7, and 5 syllables, respectively. Metered poetry **(D)** is usually rhymed and has a consistent metrical pattern.

26. B

The tone of this poem is hopeful, even defiantly purposeful, as if Whitman is saying "this was a dream, but it *can* happen!" The poem's yearning for peace, friendship, and love brings to mind John Lennon's song "Imagine." Further, "I Dream'd in a Dream" is a strong-sounding phrase, rhythmically, and includes three strong consonant "d" sounds. Whitman's choice of words also sets a hopeful tone: "invincible to the attacks of the/whole rest of the earth," "new city of Friends" (capitalized for emphasis on the possibility of such as place), "greater," "robust love…/It was seen every hour…in all their looks and words." There is no proof through either sentiment or word choice of the presence of the tones listed in **(A)**, **(C)**, and **(D)** (angry, weepy, or disillusioned).

27. B

From the age of 20, when he inherited the throne of Macedonia, until he died at age 33, Alexander the Great seemed invincible. His first conquest was Greece, and from there he went on to conquer most of his known world. The body of water at the left of the map is the Mediterranean Sea. Notice the "boot" of Italy sticking down into the water, about to kick the island of Sicily; it is a good reference point. Alexander's empire did not include present-day Italy, home of the Roman Empire. You might also want to look up maps of the Ottoman Empire and early Islamic conquests for comparison, as maps of empires often show up on the CSET.

28. A

Islam spread rapidly during the prophet Muhammad's lifetime and in the centuries after his death. The prime mechanisms of this spread were the same as those for most religious or philosophical systems: military conquest and trade incentives. While both missionaries **(C)** and domination of conquered people **(B)** play a role in the spread of religion, most conquered people will eventually convert to the religion of their conquerors because it is in their economic self-interest.

29. B

Renaissance is a French word that means *rebirth.* The Renaissance started in northern Italy in the thirteenth century and spread northward through Europe over about three hundred years. Many people think of the Renaissance in terms of magnificent art; but in the fifteenth and early sixteenth centuries, the Italian scientists Copernicus and Galileo challenged Church orthodoxy when their research suggested that the Earth and its creatures were not at the center of the universe. This created many problems for the scientists with the Church, which criticized and tried to silence them, but eventually was forced to acknowledge their correctness. The Medieval period **(A)** came before the Renaissance, while the Romantic Era and Enlightenment came after. A timeline will help you keep these periods straight.

30. C

The essence of Taoism is balance; one must strive to live in accordance with the order and harmony of all existence. Everything has its place within the polarities of *yin* and *yang*, which must remain balanced to maintain harmony. Both Buddhism **(B)** and Confucianism **(A)** are also practiced in China; but Buddhism emphasizes mindfulness of every moment, while Confucianism emphasizes respect in an orderly society. Hinduism **(D)** is practiced primarily in India and very little in China.

31. A

Economics is the social science that deals with the production, distribution, and consumption of goods and services. People make economic choices based on cost-benefit analyses and their perception of the existence of scarcity. One of the most basic principles of economics is the law of supply and demand, which governs the price people are willing to pay for a given product or service (less if it's plentiful; more if it's scarce). Both sociology **(B)** and anthropology **(C)** are social sciences that study groups of people and human systems, and history **(D)** is the social science that umbrellas all the other topics in this chapter.

32. D

In medieval Europe the Catholic church controlled access to books and to education. Church officials started many schools, most of them associated with a particular monastery, where boys could be educated. Upon finishing school, many of these boys then became priests. Some of these schools later grew into universities. King John signed the Magna Carta **(A)** at the insistence of his lords. Trade guilds **(B)** emerged on their own, as serfs left the manors to settle in the towns that sprang up during this period. Trade with Russia **(C)** was limited during the medieval period.

33. C

During the Crusades, Europeans had developed a taste for Asian spices; so Asian trade had become a lucrative business. Each of the seafaring European nations wanted to be first to locate a shorter, more profitable route to India in order to establish dominance in the spice trade. Spreading Christianity **(B)** and locating new land on which to live **(A)** were not factors in the initial drive for exploration, and staple crops such as corn and potatoes **(D)** were a welcome result of exploration but not the cause.

34. A

Mercantilism **(A)** was practiced by European nations in an effort to assure prosperity by regulating and coordinating the production of goods while protecting domestic economies from foreign competition. It was a precursor to the 20th century "command economies" of the Soviet Union and China. Capitalism, which evolved from mercantilism, concentrates wealth in the hands of private individuals with limited government interference—*laissez faire*. Socialism **(C)** is an economic philosophy espoused by Karl Marx that distributes wealth to the workers who produce it. Communism **(B)** extends socialistic redistribution of wealth by the state to include government control in social and political arenas as well. Barter **(D)** is an informal system of the exchange of goods or services among individuals.

35. D

Prior to James Watt's invention of the steam engine, there was no effective way to power the machinery that made the Industrial Age possible. Not only did the steam engine originally power industrial machinery, it also powered the steamships and locomotives that transported raw materials

and manufactured goods from place to place. The cloth sail **(A)**, the printing press **(C)**, and the wheel **(B)** were all discovered long before the Industrial Age, and therefore could not have launched it.

36. A

On November 11, 1620, the men aboard the Mayflower signed an agreement. They knew they had sailed off course and were concerned about the stability of their colony in an unknown area. That agreement was called the Mayflower Compact, and their signatures were their consent to be bound by this document of self-government. The Magna Carta **(B)** was signed in England in 1215, and both the Articles of Confederation **(C)** and the Declaration of Independence **(D)** were signed in America after the Mayflower Compact.

37. B

Although the residents of Washington, DC pay federal income taxes, their representative in Congress has no vote. This fact makes many Washington, DC residents unhappy, much as the colonists were. In the years before the American Revolution, Britain levied a number of taxes on the colonies; when the colonists protested, the Crown hiked taxes. That led to the rallying slogan, "No taxation without representation!" Today, women enjoy full citizenship in Washington, DC; though equal rights for women were not given much thought in pre-Revolutionary America, when the slogan "Women are citizens too!" **(A)** might have been used. The concept of one person, one vote in early U.S. history was actually more like, "One free man, one vote!"**(B)**, and does not relate to today's voting situation in which all citizens may vote. "Don't tread on me!" **(D)** is a motto found on some early U.S. flags.

38. C

The Democratic-Republicans were concerned during the Constitutional Convention of 1787 that too much power was being concentrated in the hands of the federal government. They preferred to have more power in the hands of the states, as individuals could have more influence over state governments. This disagreement about the locus of power continues to this day, with the struggle between states/individuals and a powerful federal government. The Masons **(A)** is a private organization, to which many founders belonged. The Federalists **(B)** favored a strong central government, and they prevailed in writing the Constitution. The Abolitionists **(D)** gained power in the next century, as they worked to abolish slavery.

39. A

The Missouri Compromise was one of a series of measures aimed at preventing serious conflict over slavery **(A)** as new territories entered the Union. As a result of this compromise, Missouri was admitted as a slave state, Maine entered as a free state and slavery was prohibited north of the 36°30′ Line that came to separate free and slave states in the Louisiana Purchase territory. Neither this, nor any other, compromise was successful indefinitely; and the conflict over the slavery issue culminated in the Civil War.

40. D

The use of the Union navy to blockade southern ports was a brilliant tactic that cut off the Confederacy's lucrative cotton trade and limited the South to the supplies it had on hand. Since the Confederacy had no manufacturing to speak of, it slowly ran out of such vital supplies as munitions and was forced to surrender. None of the other choices accurately reflects a major use of the Union naval forces in the Civil War.

41. B

In the election of 1876, Republican Rutherford B. Hayes and Democrat Samuel Tilden vied for the Presidency. Amid disputed returns and allegations of voter fraud on both sides, no clear winner could be determined in several states. An electoral commission was assembled, with an equal number of Republicans and Democrats and five members of the U.S. Supreme Court. After a vote strictly along party lines, Hayes was declared the winner. Democrats threatened to boycott the electoral college (if you don't understand how the electoral college works, look it up; you may well find questions on this topic on the CSET) and were finally persuaded to accept the results after cutting a deal to end Reconstruction. Federal troops were withdrawn from the remaining three states they occupied, and the stage was set for almost another century of blatant discrimination against blacks in the South. Keep in mind that from its creation as an abolitionist party shortly before the Civil War until the 1970s, the Republican party was despised in the white South as the

party of Lincoln; and the South always voted solidly for the Democratic candidate in presidential elections.

42. B

The Homestead Act was designed to populate the Great Plains states west of the Mississippi River after the Civil War. Any individual over 21 who would promise to live on the land and cultivate it for a period of five years could claim 160 acres, on a first-come-first-served basis. Of course, often the 160 acres had inconvenient prior inhabitants who had to be dealt with. Sometimes the native peoples were placed on tiny reservations in undesirable locales; other times they tried to defend their land and were overwhelmed by superior military forces (during the Indian Wars).

43. D

The Sherman Antitrust Act placed limits on the extent to which firms or corporations **(D)** could consolidate, or form a trust, as a means of reducing their competition and controlling prices within a particular industry. Since then, there have been additional laws designed to regulate and prevent anti-competitive business practices. One of the most recent uses of these laws was a suit filed against Microsoft, which was accused of practices that prevented other companies from effectively competing for customers in certain areas of the software giant's business.

44. C

The growth of a national network of railroads in the last half of the nineteenth century helped create a nationwide market for goods. Improved transportation and communication advances such as the telegraph, and later the telephone, made it possible to have a national discourse as well as facilitating increased travel across the continent. Prior to these advances, regionalism was dominant in the United States; but following these and subsequent advances such as radio, television, and the Internet, the United States has grown ever more cohesive as a cultural and political entity.

45. A

Using the native materials at hand, California Indians wove tight, aesthetically pleasing baskets for practical and ceremonial use. The various kinds of baskets were highly prized and frequent items of trade, along with shells, foods, and other craft items. The tribes along the Colorado River in the arid eastern part of the state had learned to irrigate their crops **(C)**, but they were the only tribes to practice agriculture. The tribes along the central coast did not work in copper, although they were adept at carving in soapstone **(B)**. No tribe had access to horses prior to the arrival of the Spanish **(D)**.

46. D

In the process of hydraulic mining, powerful hoses shot water at the hillsides in order to wash away the soil and possibly discover gold. There were two problems with this technique: it washed the hillsides into the creeks, killing the fish; and it forced miners to become laborers working for the large companies that could afford the equipment. Neither panning **(A)** nor tunneling **(B)** is as destructive to the environment, though both were used during the Gold Rush. Strip mining **(C)** is environmentally destructive but was not practiced in gold mining during the Gold Rush.

47. B

Along with Irish immigrants, Chinese laborers made up most of the workforce that endured dangerous conditions and low pay to build the railroads across the country. Many members of the first wave of Chinese immigrants moved to San Francisco, where they lived in a community that became North America's oldest Chinatown. Some started restaurants **(A)**, but not as many as worked on the railroad. Higher education **(D)** was beyond their reach in the beginning, as they faced continued discrimination. There were far more Japanese immigrants than Chinese in Hawaii **(C)**, so proximity to that area wouldn't have affected Chinese immigration.

48. C

Popular sovereignty can be defined as *the rule of the people*. Progressives are interested in giving power as directly as possible to the people. Mechanisms that reflect this principle include the initiative **(A)**, the referendum **(D)**, and the recall, which was exercised in 2003 to recall the governor. The exercise of popular sovereignty is more difficult in practice than it seems in theory, and California's system has many critics.

49. A

Although Angel Island was billed as the "Ellis Island of the West," its primary function was to control the flow of Chinese and other Asians into the country. The Chinese Exclusion Act of 1882 had made the Chinese officially unwelcome, and Angel Island became more of a detention facility than a point of entry.

50. B

During the Great Depression of the 1930s, the Great Plains states experienced a severe drought that turned the region into a "dust bowl." Many small farmers had to leave the area, and many of them moved to California. They came to be known as "Okies," because many of them came from Oklahoma. A number of them first became migrant workers, and they went on to become a culturally conservative force that still exerts strong influence in the Central Valley and other areas of inland California. The aerospace industry **(A)** didn't take off in California until World War II. The National Highway System **(C)** was largely built in the 1950s and 60s after the arrival of the Okies, though improved roads certainly made travel easier for those who arrived in automobiles.

51. B

In 1900 construction began on an aqueduct to bring water from the Colorado River to the arid Colorado desert seventy miles away. The newly renamed Imperial Valley thrived with its new water supply. Several years later the aqueduct's new owners tried to increase the water flow, and the result was a flood that created the Salton Sea. Lake Shasta **(A)** and Lake Arrowhead **(D)** are manmade lakes, created purposely by dams. Mono Lake **(C)** is a natural lake that has been threatened by the water needs of the Los Angeles area.

52. C

The Works Projects Administration (WPA) was a federal government response to the Great Depression, with its overwhelming unemployment and need for public works. Many dams and other large-scale projects were undertaken by the WPA. As part of the Central Valley Project, the Shasta Dam was constructed. It is the second largest dam in the U.S., after Hoover Dam, also a WPA project.

Constructed-Response Sample Essay 1

Third-person point of view can be recognized by the author's use of the pronouns *he, she, it* or *they*. There are three types of third-person point of view: third-person objective, third-person limited, and third-person omniscient.

In *third-person objective*, the narrator presents observable details and does not have access to the internal thoughts of characters or background information about the setting or situation. A character's thoughts, for example, are inferred only by what is expressed openly, in actions or in words. ("Nick, turning red, looked frustrated after he hit his thumb with the hammer.") This point of view is also known as third-person dramatic because it is generally the way drama is developed.

In *third-person limited*, sometimes called third-person sympathetic, the narrative voice relates what is in the mind of one point-of-view character (sometimes of a select few characters). ("When he felt her eyes on his swollen thumb, Nick hated himself for being so clumsy.")

In *third-person omniscient*, the narrative voice may convey information from anywhere, including the thoughts and feelings of any of the characters. This all-knowing perspective allows the narrator to roam freely in the story's setting and even beyond. ("Little did Nick or the other villagers suspect that his swollen thumb would lead to a strange development the very next day.") This approach is used sparingly in literature because all of the tricks are given away, so there may be little guesswork.

Constructed-Response Sample Essay 2

Three of the reasons that Standard American English is a flexible, evolving language are

- the addition of new pop culture terms and phrases
- the constant presence of technology in our lives
- the influence of global communication

English is a living, "breathing," language that evolves with the times. Words and phrases are accepted into our language because of pop culture, technology, and international influences.

It used to take many years for the major dictionaries—Webster's and the Oxford English Dictionary (OED)—to add a new term to their reference books, such as *Catch-22* from the Joseph Heller novel. Now hip-hop-turned-mainstream terms like *jiggy* and *bling-bling* are added to the dictionary after they have been circulating for only a few years. For example, the term *bling-bling*, which describes the showy hip-hop style of diamonds and gold jewelry, was coined by the New Orleans rap family Cash Money Millionaires in the late '90s. The term gained national awareness (at least among youth) with the song "Bling Bling." The term has been added to the OED already!

KAPLAN

It seems that the infusion of high tech in our lives is changing our language almost daily. As we invent or discover new items and processes, our high tech vocabulary evolves. Some examples are Mars rovers, e-mail, DVDs, modem, download, website, pixels, upgrade, TiVo, cell (phone), Googling, and dotcoms.

Finally, the influence of global communication—which we experience daily through foreign films, CNN, online newspapers, and international foods—gives us words such as animé (Japanese animation), jihad (Arabic for struggle), sushi (Japanese food), détente and ballet (French), and bistro (Russian for café).

Constructed-Response Sample Essay 3

One of the most important inventions of all time was the printing press, invented during the European Renaissance by Johannes Gutenberg. An immediate effect of this invention was the Protestant Reformation, started by Martin Luther as a protest against practices of the Roman Catholic Church that he found offensive. Luther was able to get the word out about his protest because he printed numerous copies of his Theses and distributed them.

Another example of an effect of the printing press was the spread of learning during the Renaissance. Before its invention, books had to be copied by hand, which took a long time. Books were so rare that most people didn't have any reason to learn to read. The Church controlled most libraries and most access to schooling. Once books were available, people learned to read, which made the demand for books (and then newspapers, pamphlets, etc.) grow. More reading material was printed, and then more people learned to read. They no longer depended on the Church to teach them everything.

This growth in learning led to the Enlightenment, in which science and philosophy and literature flowered. The Enlightenment led to the American Revolution (and then the French Revolution, and others) and the establishment of our democratic government—another example of the effects of Gutenberg's invention. Our public education system is yet another effect. It grew directly out of the thirst for learning that resulted from the invention of the printing press.

Constructed-Response Sample Essay 4

One of the disagreements in the early republic was over which should have more power, the federal government or the states. A second disagreement among the framers was between the small states and the large states over whether all states should have equally powerful roles in the federal government or whether larger, more populous states should have more power. That debate was resolved by establishing two houses of Congress. In the House of Representatives, each state is represented according to its population (favoring large states); in the Senate, each state has two senators, no matter how small it is. The Electoral College also favors less populous states over larger ones.

The disagreement over the proper role of the federal government was a serious one, and it continues to this day. The framers of the Constitution addressed this issue by embracing federalism—the concept that power should be balanced between the federal government and the state governments.

On one side of the debate, the Federalists, led by James Madison, John Adams and Alexander Hamilton, believed that a strong federal government could be trusted to do the right thing more often than the states could. The Anti-Federalists believed in protecting individual rights and granting more power to the states.

The Constitution was written to favor a strong federal government (perhaps a reaction to the too-weak Articles of Confederation), but then the first ten amendments to the Constitution were adopted within a few years to appease the Anti-Federalists. Known collectively as the Bill of Rights, these amendments guarantee individual protection against civil rights violations by the government.

Chapter 11: **Subtest 2 Practice Test**

TEST DIRECTIONS

This practice test contains two sections, a multiple-choice section (52 questions) and a constructed-response section (4 assignments). You may work on the sections in any order you wish.

In the multiple-choice section, read each question carefully and choose the one best answer. Directions for the constructed-response sections appear immediately before those assignments.

When taking the actual CSET, you will have one five-hour test session in which to complete the subtest(s) for which you registered.

SCORING

Remember, if you do not pass one or more subtests, you may reregister and retake those subtests. There is no limit to the number of times you may take any subtest that you have not passed. This helps takes the pressure off you, the test-taker, and gives you more choice.

Following the actual CSET, your responses to the multiple-choice questions will be scored electronically. Scores are based on the number of questions answered correctly, so there is no penalty for guessing.

Your responses to the constructed-response questions are scored by qualified California educators using focused holistic scoring. With this method, scorers judge the overall effectiveness of each response, while focusing on a set of performance characteristics that have been identified as important. For more details on how the CSET is scored, visit cset.nesinc.com.

Ready, set…

Good luck!

Subtest 2 Answer Sheet

Remove (or photocopy) this answer sheet and use it to complete the practice test.

1. Ⓐ Ⓑ Ⓒ Ⓓ Ⓔ   14. Ⓐ Ⓑ Ⓒ Ⓓ Ⓔ   27. Ⓐ Ⓑ Ⓒ Ⓓ Ⓔ   40. Ⓐ Ⓑ Ⓒ Ⓓ Ⓔ

2. Ⓐ Ⓑ Ⓒ Ⓓ Ⓔ   15. Ⓐ Ⓑ Ⓒ Ⓓ Ⓔ   28. Ⓐ Ⓑ Ⓒ Ⓓ Ⓔ   41. Ⓐ Ⓑ Ⓒ Ⓓ Ⓔ

3. Ⓐ Ⓑ Ⓒ Ⓓ Ⓔ   16. Ⓐ Ⓑ Ⓒ Ⓓ Ⓔ   29. Ⓐ Ⓑ Ⓒ Ⓓ Ⓔ   42. Ⓐ Ⓑ Ⓒ Ⓓ Ⓔ

4. Ⓐ Ⓑ Ⓒ Ⓓ Ⓔ   17. Ⓐ Ⓑ Ⓒ Ⓓ Ⓔ   30. Ⓐ Ⓑ Ⓒ Ⓓ Ⓔ   43. Ⓐ Ⓑ Ⓒ Ⓓ Ⓔ

5. Ⓐ Ⓑ Ⓒ Ⓓ Ⓔ   18. Ⓐ Ⓑ Ⓒ Ⓓ Ⓔ   31. Ⓐ Ⓑ Ⓒ Ⓓ Ⓔ   44. Ⓐ Ⓑ Ⓒ Ⓓ Ⓔ

6. Ⓐ Ⓑ Ⓒ Ⓓ Ⓔ   19. Ⓐ Ⓑ Ⓒ Ⓓ Ⓔ   32. Ⓐ Ⓑ Ⓒ Ⓓ Ⓔ   45. Ⓐ Ⓑ Ⓒ Ⓓ Ⓔ

7. Ⓐ Ⓑ Ⓒ Ⓓ Ⓔ   20. Ⓐ Ⓑ Ⓒ Ⓓ Ⓔ   33. Ⓐ Ⓑ Ⓒ Ⓓ Ⓔ   46. Ⓐ Ⓑ Ⓒ Ⓓ Ⓔ

8. Ⓐ Ⓑ Ⓒ Ⓓ Ⓔ   21. Ⓐ Ⓑ Ⓒ Ⓓ Ⓔ   34. Ⓐ Ⓑ Ⓒ Ⓓ Ⓔ   47. Ⓐ Ⓑ Ⓒ Ⓓ Ⓔ

9. Ⓐ Ⓑ Ⓒ Ⓓ Ⓔ   22. Ⓐ Ⓑ Ⓒ Ⓓ Ⓔ   35. Ⓐ Ⓑ Ⓒ Ⓓ Ⓔ   48. Ⓐ Ⓑ Ⓒ Ⓓ Ⓔ

10. Ⓐ Ⓑ Ⓒ Ⓓ Ⓔ   23. Ⓐ Ⓑ Ⓒ Ⓓ Ⓔ   36. Ⓐ Ⓑ Ⓒ Ⓓ Ⓔ   49. Ⓐ Ⓑ Ⓒ Ⓓ Ⓔ

11. Ⓐ Ⓑ Ⓒ Ⓓ Ⓔ   24. Ⓐ Ⓑ Ⓒ Ⓓ Ⓔ   37. Ⓐ Ⓑ Ⓒ Ⓓ Ⓔ   50. Ⓐ Ⓑ Ⓒ Ⓓ Ⓔ

12. Ⓐ Ⓑ Ⓒ Ⓓ Ⓔ   25. Ⓐ Ⓑ Ⓒ Ⓓ Ⓔ   38. Ⓐ Ⓑ Ⓒ Ⓓ Ⓔ   51. Ⓐ Ⓑ Ⓒ Ⓓ Ⓔ

13. Ⓐ Ⓑ Ⓒ Ⓓ Ⓔ   26. Ⓐ Ⓑ Ⓒ Ⓓ Ⓔ   39. Ⓐ Ⓑ Ⓒ Ⓓ Ⓔ   52. Ⓐ Ⓑ Ⓒ Ⓓ Ⓔ

1. The properties of light can best be explained by assuming that light is composed of:

    I. Particles
   II. Waves
  III. Atoms

(A) I only

(B) II only

(C) I and II

(D) II and III

2. Which of the following generalizations *cannot* be made about the phase change of a pure substance from solid to liquid?

(A) It involves a change in potential energy.

(B) It involves no change in temperature.

(C) It involves a change in kinetic energy.

(D) It involves a change in entropy.

3. The product formed when oxygen and hydrogen are mixed in a test tube at room temperature is

(A) hydrogen peroxide

(B) water

(C) a base

(D) no reaction takes place

4. Which of the following will favor the melting of ice in a closed container if all other parameters are kept constant?

(A) adding water with a temperature of 0°C

(B) lowering the temperature below 0°C

(C) lowering the pressure

(D) raising the pressure

5. Roller coasters follow certain rules related to energy. Which of the following statements concerning roller coasters is true?

(A) Roller coasters have the lowest speed at the highest point of the ride.

(B) Roller coasters have the highest speed at the highest point of the ride.

(C) Roller coasters have the lowest speed at the lowest point on the ride.

(D) None of the above.

6. Which of the following would most likely change the sound of a radio?

(A) vibrations

(B) sunlight

(C) X-rays

(D) pitch

7. A roller coaster car is at the top of a hill. At this point in the ride it is at its maximum

(A) potential energy

(B) kinetic energy

(C) potential and kinetic energy

(D) speed

8. An electron travels in the plane of the page from left to right, perpendicular to a magnetic field that points into the page. The direction of the resulting magnetic force on the electron will be in the plane of the page and

(A) upwards

(B) downwards

(C) to the left

(D) to the right

GO ON TO THE NEXT PAGE

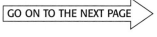

9. In order for photosynthesis to occur in plants, which of the following elements is required?

   (A) oxygen

   (B) carbon dioxide

   (C) iron

   (D) all of the above

10. Blood pressure is the pressure that the blood exerts on the walls of the arteries. If pressure is indirectly proportional to volume, which of the following pharmacological agents would you recommend to effectively treat high blood pressure?

    (A) an agent that reduces the volume of blood

    (B) an agent that increases the pressure against the walls of the arteries

    (C) an agent that increases volume of the arteries through dilation

    (D) an agent that decreases the volume of the arteries through constriction

11. Which one of the following processes includes all others in the list?

    (A) diffusion

    (B) osmosis

    (C) passive transport

    (D) facilitated transport

12. Which of the following is most closely related to the process of dialysis?

    (A) osmosis

    (B) radioactivity

    (C) heat

    (D) acidity

13. A mathematician sets out to measure humidity levels in different regions. In which of the following regions would she find the lowest relative humidity?

    (A) the Sahara desert

    (B) a busy city

    (C) the Amazon rain forest

    (D) a grass plains region

14. Damsel flies and dragonflies can live in the same ecosystem because

    (A) they occupy different niches

    (B) they are both insects

    (C) dragonflies have stronger wing muscles than damsel flies

    (D) they mate at different times of the year

15. A grass species on the island is homozygous at 40 different loci that are heterozygous on the mainland. These loci affect leaf shape, stem height, the opening and closing of stomata, and root length, among other traits. Which of the following is true?

    (A) The plant reproduces only in an asexual manner.

    (B) The plant is less able to evolve to fit a new environment in the event of a climate change.

    (C) Migration of seeds from the mainland eliminates genetic diversity in the gene pool of the plant.

    (D) The grass species requires pollination by birds.

GO ON TO THE NEXT PAGE

KAPLAN)

16. Which one of the following scientific theories could be used to explain the homologous structural changes that have occurred in specific organisms in the past 10,000 years?

    (A) atomic theory

    (B) theory of relativity

    (C) theory of evolution

    (D) law of conservation of energy

17. Years ago, the most common color for a certain type of moth was light gray; dark gray moths existed, but were rare. The light gray color camouflaged the moths from predatory birds. Then, an industrial plant moved into the area, spewing soot and other industrial waste into the air. Now, the most common color for this type of moth is dark gray. Light gray moths are rare because darker moths are better camouflaged given the introduction of pollution to the environment.

    The name for this process is

    (A) distribution

    (B) stabilization

    (C) selection

    (D) continuation

    Use the diagram below to answer the question that follows.

    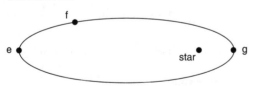

18. A newly discovered planet's path around its star is represented in the above diagram. When is the planet moving the fastest?

    (A) point e

    (B) point f

    (C) point g

    (D) The planet is moving at same speed at each point on its orbit.

19. What causes the Moon to have different phases as seen from Earth?

    (A) the Moon's rotation

    (B) the Earth's rotation

    (C) the Moon's revolution around the Earth

    (D) the Earth's revolution around the Sun

20. It's Tuesday at 5 AM at the Prime Meridian. If you ignore Daylight Savings Time, what day and time is it at the International Date Line?

    (A) Monday at 5 PM

    (B) Tuesday at 5 PM

    (C) Wednesday at 5 AM

    (D) Wednesday at 5 PM

21. The Sun provides energy for all the plants on Earth. What is the source of Sun's energy?

    (A) fusion of hydrogen atoms

    (B) fission of hydrogen atoms

    (C) fusion of helium atoms

    (D) fission of helium atoms

22. Which of the following provides the strongest evidence that the Ice Age existed in the Earth's past?

    (A) the Farmer's Almanac

    (B) plant and animal fossil records

    (C) radioactive dating to determine the age of rocks

    (D) an historical diary from the 1500s

GO ON TO THE NEXT PAGE

23. The distance from an earthquake's site to a seismographer can be determined by the arrival time of the earthquake's P waves and S waves. Why do P waves and S waves arrive at a seismograph station at different times?

    (A) P waves are transverse waves that travel faster than S waves.

    (B) P waves are longitudinal waves that travel faster than S waves.

    (C) The speed of P and S waves increases in denser materials.

    (D) S waves are transverse waves that travel faster than P waves.

24. In New York City, summer days are warmer than winter days because

    (A) due to Earth's tilt about its rotational axis, in the summer, New York City is closer to the Sun and has longer days than it does during the winter

    (B) during the summer, the ocean's currents bring warmer water to New York City

    (C) during the winter, colder air moves down from Canada to New York City

    (D) during the summer, the Earth is at its farthest point from the Sun

25. Which of the following positions would produce a lunar eclipse?

    (A) the Moon's path is in the Sun's shadow

    (B) the Moon's path in the Earth's shadow

    (C) the Moon's path is between the Earth and the Sun

    (D) the Earth's path is in the Sun's shadow

26. A sixth-grade class is conducting an experiment on temperature and the rate of development of tadpoles. Twenty tadpoles are divided into two groups, and their temperatures are kept constant by two water heaters set to different temperatures. The tadpoles are from the same spawn (egg mass).

To ensure the validity of this experiment, which of the following elements of experimental design must be considered?

    I. The size of the group is large enough to account for individual variances.

    II. A control group should be set up to correspond to each group

    III. Except for the variation in temperature, all conditions of the experiment are identical.

    IV. The tadpoles are randomly distributed among the test groups.

    (A) I only

    (B) II and III only

    (C) I, III, and IV

    (D) all of the above

27. Which of the following illustrates the operation, $1\frac{7}{8} \times 4\frac{2}{3}$?

    (A) Colin ran $4\frac{2}{3}$ miles on Saturday. He plans to run $1\frac{7}{8}$ as far tomorrow.

    (B) The length of a rectangular air field is $1\frac{7}{8}$ miles and its area $4\frac{2}{3}$ miles.

    (C) Victoria's cookie recipe requires $1\frac{7}{8}$ pounds of sugar for every $4\frac{2}{3}$ pounds of flour.

    (D) Normally, Bridgett's commute to work takes a mere $4\frac{2}{3}$ minutes. Last Monday, it took her $1\frac{7}{8}$ minutes longer.

GO ON TO THE NEXT PAGE

KAPLAN

28. In a town with a population of 7200 people, 12% percent of the population is evenly distributed in grades 7 through 12. How many students are in grade 7?

    (A) 173

    (B) 144

    (C) 172

    (D) 123

29. The diagram below shows a mathematical operation.

    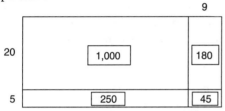

    Which statement best describes the diagram above?

    (A) The expression $1,000 + 250 + 180 + 45$ is represented.

    (B) The multiplication algorithm for 59×25 is illustrated using an area model.

    (C) The partial products add up to 1,475.

    (D) Multiplication is the same as addition, only faster.

30. A light year is the distance light travels in one year in a vacuum. It is equivalent to 5,900,000,000,000 miles. What is this number in scientific notation?

    (A) 5.9×10^{-13}

    (B) 5.9×10^{13}

    (C) 5.9×10^{12}

    (D) 59×10^{11}

31. The problem below shows the steps in finding the product of two numbers using the standard multiplication algorithm. The missing digits in the problem are represented by the symbol $\square$.

    What is the hundreds digit in the product of the two numbers?

    ```
          4 □ 7
       ×     5 6
       ─────────
        2 □ 6 □
    + 2 □ 3 □ □
    ─────────────
    □ □ □ □ □
    ```

    (A) 4

    (B) 3

    (C) 5

    (D) 9

GO ON TO THE NEXT PAGE

Use the table below to answer the question that follows.

Diameter	Circumference
0.0	0
1.0	3.14
2.0	6.28
3.0	9.42
4.0	12.56

32. The table above gives the circumference of several circles of different diameters. Which of the following graphs best represents the data in the table?

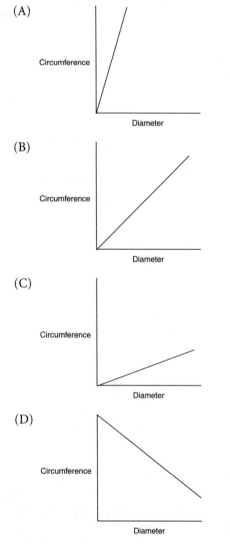

(A)

(B)

(C)

(D)

Use the graph below to answer the question that follows.

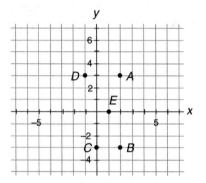

33. Point E is on a line with a slope of -3 in the x-y plane. Which of the following points is also on the line?
    (A) Point A
    (B) Point B
    (C) Point C
    (D) Point D

34. Simplify.

    $(x^2 - 5x + 1) - (x^2 + 4x + 7)$

    (A) $x - 6$
    (B) $-9x - 6$
    (C) $-x + 8$
    (D) $2x^2 - x + 8$

35. Divide a number by two and add four times the same number and two. The answer is 38.

    Which of the following equations matches these statements?

    (A) $2n + \frac{4}{n} + 2 = 38$

    (B) $\frac{n}{2} - 4n + 2 = 38$

    (C) $2n + 4n + 2 = 38$

    (D) $\frac{n}{2} + 4n + 2 = 38$

GO ON TO THE NEXT PAGE

36. A computer technician charges a $50 service call plus a $25 hourly rate. If this equation was graphed onto a coordinate grid, which of the following assumptions can be made?

(A) the y-intercept would be 50

(B) the slope would be 25

(C) it has no y-intercept

(D) both (A) and (B)

Use the figure below to answer the question that follows.

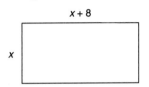

37. The length of the rectangle above is 8 units longer than its width. Which expression could be used to represent the area of the rectangle?

(A) $x^2 + 8x$

(B) $x^2 - 64$

(C) $x^2 + 8x + 8$

(D) $x^2 + 16x + 64$

38. Oranges in a grocery store display are stacked in the shape of a pyramid. Each of the 6 layers of the stack is a triangle. There are 56 oranges altogether. The top layer has one orange, the second layer has 3 oranges, the third has 6 oranges, and the fourth layer has 10 oranges. How many oranges are in the 5th and 6th layer?

(A) The fifth layer has 20 oranges and the sixth layer has 46 oranges.

(B) The fifth layer has 16 oranges and the sixth layer has 20 oranges.

(C) The fifth layer has 14 oranges and the sixth layer has 22 oranges.

(D) The fifth layer has 15 oranges and the sixth layer has 21 oranges.

Use the diagram below to answer the question that follows.

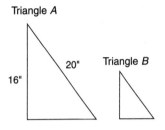

39. Triangle A and Triangle B are similar right triangles. The proportional relationship of their size is 2 to 1. Using what you know about the similarity of two figures, what is the area of Triangle B?

(A) 28 in.^{2}

(B) 24 in.^{2}

(C) 48 in.^{2}

(D) 96 in.^{2}

40. Which of the following statements about a rectangular pyramid are true?

(A) It consists of a rectangle and four congruent triangles.

(B) It consists of a rectangle and two pairs of congruent triangles.

(C) It consists of a rectangle and four right triangles.

(D) It consists of two rectangles and two pairs of congruent triangles.

GO ON TO THE NEXT PAGE

KAPLAN

41. The triangle below has sides of lengths 4, 8, and $\sqrt{80}$.

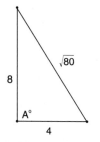

Which statement below can be used to find the measure of $\angle A$?

(A) $\angle A$ looks to be in proportion to a 90° angle.

(B) Since $4^2 + 8^2 = (\sqrt{80})^2$, by the converse of the Pythagorean Theorem, $\angle A$ is 90°.

(C) Since $4 + 8 = \sqrt{80}$, $\angle A$ is 90°.

(D) The Pythagorean Theorem cannot be used here to determine the measure of $\angle A$, but one can see that $\angle A$ looks to be 90°.

42. This diagram shows a science classroom's counter-top with an area cut out for a sink.

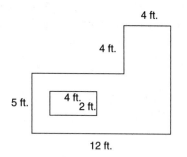

What is the area of the countertop?

(A) 68 ft^2

(B) 76 ft^2

(C) 81 ft^2

(D) 72 ft^2

43. An assembly line's conveyer belt moves at a rate of 10 miles in 5 hours. How many feet per minute does the belt move? (1 mile = 5,280 ft.)

(A) 5,280 ft./min.

(B) 176 ft./min.

(C) 10,560 ft./hr.

(D) None of the above.

44. 4 cubic yards is how many cubic feet?

(A) 108 ft^3

(B) 324 ft^3

(C) 432 ft^3

(D) 1,728 ft^3

45. A machine produces pencils at a rate of 520 per hour. A newer model produces pencils at a rate of 25 per minute. At the end of 2 hours, how many pencils are produced if they both work together?

(A) 1,040 pencils

(B) 3,000 pencils

(C) 4,040 pencils

(D) 1,960 pencils

46. What is the area of the figure below?

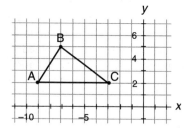

(A) 18 units^2

(B) 9 units^2

(C) 10 units^2

(D) 12 units^2

GO ON TO THE NEXT PAGE

47. A right triangle is removed from a rectangle as shown in the figure below. Find the area of the remaining part of the rectangle.

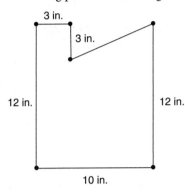

3 in.

3 in.

12 in.   12 in.

10 in.

(A) 109.5 in.^{2}

(B) 120 in.^{2}

(C) 99 in.^{2}

(D) 110 in.^{2}

48. A teacher has 35 students in her math class. She wants to display their math test scores on the board. What is the most appropriate graph to for her to use?

(A) line graph

(B) circle graph

(C) box-and-whisker plot

(D) stem-and-leaf plot

49. The annual incomes for employees at Unfair Corp. are $20,000, $30,000, $40,000, $47,000, $52,000, $57,000, and $2,250,000. Which measure of central tendency would best characterize the income of a typical employee at Unfair Corp.?

(A) mean income

(B) median income

(C) mode income

(D) midrange income

50. Four-fifths of the 65 members of a club attended a meeting. Twenty-seven of those attending the meeting were male. Which one of the following questions can be answered with the given information?

(A) How many females are in the club?

(B) How many males are in the club?

(C) How many female members of the club attended the meeting?

(D) How many male members of the club did not attend the meeting?

51. Each of the numbers 5 to 34 inclusive is written on a separate piece of paper and placed in a bag. If one of these pieces is randomly selected from the bag, what is the probability that the number on it will be a prime number?

(A) 0.31

(B) 0.71

(C) 0.30

(D) 1.0

52. A woman decides she wants to have eight children, all girls. How might she figure out the probability of having a girl eight times in a row?

(A) She should add the chances of having a girl for each child to get a 1/16 probability.

(B) She should divide her chances of having a girl for each child to get a 64 probability.

(C) She should subtract her chances of having a girl and get a –3 probability.

(D) She should multiply her chances of having a girl for each child and get a 1/256 probability.

GO ON TO THE NEXT PAGE

KAPLAN

CONSTRUCTED-RESPONSE DIRECTIONS

Prepare a written response for each assignment. Read each assignment carefully before you begin to write. Think about how you will organize your response before you begin to write.

The assignments are intended to assess subject matter knowledge, not writing ability. However, your responses must be presented clearly in order to be fairly evaluated by your audience, educators in the field.

_____

Constructed-Response Assignment 1

Complete the exercise that follows.

What happens when the temperature of any type of molecule changes? How is the physical object comprised of those molecules affected by temperature change? Use examples to explain your answer.

_____

_____

_____

_____

_____

_____

_____

_____

_____

_____

_____

_____

_____

_____

_____

_____

_____

_____

Constructed-Response Assignment 2

Complete the exercise that follows.

Cell membranes will allow small molecules such as oxygen, water, carbon dioxide, ammonia, glucose, etc. to pass through. But they will not allow larger molecules such as sucrose, starch, protein, etc. to pass through. If an animal or plant cell is placed into a liquid containing water, one of three things will happen. What are they?

_____

_____

_____

_____

_____

_____

_____

_____

_____

_____

_____

_____

_____

_____

_____

_____

_____

_____

_____

Constructed-Response Assignment 3

Complete the exercise that follows.

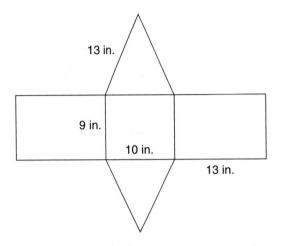

The diagram above is a triangular prism. The triangular faces are 10" at their base and have sides of 13". Of the three rectangles, two are congruent and have dimensions of 9" by 13", while the incongruent rectangle has a dimension of 9" by 10".

Using your knowledge of algebra and geometry, calculate the volume and surface area of this polyhedron.

Thoroughly explain how you arrived at your answer.

_____

_____

_____

_____

_____

_____

_____

_____

_____

_____

_____

_____

Constructed-Response Assignment 4

Complete the exercise that follows.

At local pizza shop, the price for a medium cheese pizza is $6.50, and the price for a large cheese pizza is $14.00. The diameters of the large and medium pizzas are 18 inches and 12 inches, respectively. Both pizzas are the same thickness. Using your knowledge of geometry and number sense,

a) Determine which size is the better buy.

b) Calculate the area of each size per dollar.

Thoroughly explain how you arrived at your answer.

_____

_____

_____

_____

_____

_____

_____

_____

_____

_____

_____

_____

_____

_____

_____

_____

_____

_____

_____

_____

STOP

KAPLAN

Chapter 12: **Subtest 2 Answers and Explanations**

ANSWER KEY

1. C	14. A	27. A	40. B
2. C	15. B	28. B	41. B
3. D	16. C	29. B	42. A
4. D	17. C	30. C	43. B
5. A	18. C	31. D	44. A
6. A	19. C	32. A	45. C
7. A	20. B	33. B	46. B
8. B	21. A	34. B	47. A
9. B	22. B	35. D	48. D
10. C	23. B	36. D	49. B
11. A	24. A	37. A	50. C
12. A	25. B	38. D	51. C
13. A	26. C	39. B	52. D

1. C

Light is considered in a class by itself but the different behaviors of light can be explained by thinking of it as either a particle or a wave. The ability of light to show interference is a wave property, while the photoelectric effect is a property best described through a particle model.

2. C

When a phase change occurs, the internal energy of the system—that is, the total energy contained in the system—will change. The potential energy of the system during the phase change is the same as the internal energy. Therefore, when a solid melts into a liquid, the potential energy of the substance will change. Solids have a defined temperature, known as the melting point, at which they change to liquid. At this temperature, any energy added to the solid will go toward changing the phase, not changing the temperature, until all the solid has changed to liquid. We have already shown that the phase change occurs at a constant temperature, and because a change in kinetic energy is associated with a temperature change, the kinetic energy in the solid to liquid transition will remain the same.

3. D

No reaction takes place. In order for a reaction to take place to produce H_2O, energy must be added to the system (typically in the form of heat).

4. D

This question asks you which of the choices will increase the rate at which ice melts in a closed container. If you lower the temperature, you are tipping the equilibrium toward the ice, so **(B)** is wrong. To deal with pressure changes, we must apply Le Chatelier's principle, which says that a system in equilibrium that is subject to stress will shift its equilibrium so as to relieve the stress. If the pressure is lowered, as in **(C)**, the system will counteract the change in pressure by shifting its equilibrium toward the phase that is less dense. In the case of water, that is the ice. Remember that water has a strange property in that the solid form, ice, at zero degrees Celsius is less dense than the liquid phase, water, at that temperature. Since the reduction of pressure drives the systems to produce ice, **(C)** is incorrect. However, **(D)**, an increase in pressure, will have the opposite effect and the water will be

produced preferentially, meaning that the ice is melting faster. **(A)** favors ice formation.

5. A

This question tests the concept of conservation of energy. As a roller coaster moves downwards, its speed increases. The highest point of the ride will be the point where all of the kinetic energy has transferred to potential energy, making the speed equal to zero at that instant. Therefore, **(A)** is correct.

6. A

The sound of a radio is produced through vibrating electrical charges that produce different sounds. Sunlight **(B)** produces energy in the form of light and heat. X-rays **(C)** produce radioactivity and pitch **(D)** is a property of sound itself.

7. A

The law of conservation says that energy cannot be created or destroyed, but it can be converted from one form to another; therefore, in an idealized world without friction, the sum of potential and kinetic energies would remain constant. Potential energy means stored energy. Therefore, at the top of a hill, the roller coaster car has its maximum potential energy because it will speed up going down the hill, and a minimum kinetic energy, or energy of motion, because it is moving slowly. As it gains speed moving down the hill it gains kinetic energy, but loses potential energy. Therefore, **(B)**, **(C)**, and **(D)** are incorrect.

8. B

To answer this question, we simply apply the right-hand rule. Since the particle is an electron, the direction of qv is opposite to that of v or from right to left. When you point your thumb in this direction and your fingers into the page along the direction of the magnetic field, the palm of your right hand points in the direction of the force that is downwards.

9. B

Photosynthesis is the process by which green plants create their own food using energy from the sun, carbon dioxide from the air, and water to create oxygen and glucose. Carbon dioxide, **(B)**, is the only element listed which is required for photosynthesis to occur. Oxygen, **(A)**, is released into the air as a product of photosynthesis, but is

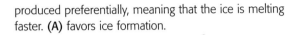

not required for it to occur. Iron, **(C)**, is an element contained in some plants, but also not required for photosynthesis.

10. C

The question states that blood pressure is an exertion on the walls of the arteries. Therefore, **(A)** can be eliminated since it considers blood volume not arterial volume. Constriction of the arteries would cause a reduction in volume and therefore an increase in pressure, so **(D)** is incorrect. Choice **(C)** is correct because by increasing volume through dilation of arterial surface area, pressure is decreased.

11. A

Diffusion is the transport of substances without using an outside source of energy. Osmosis, **(B)**, includes only the transport of water, and can therefore be eliminated. Choices **(C)** and **(D)**, passive and facilitated transport, refer to the transport of substances either down a concentration gradient or using a molecule, respectively.

12. A

Osmosis is the passive transport of water based on cell membrane selectivity. Dialysis is most similar to osmosis because it uses what is called a dialyzing membrane to permit small molecules and ions to pass through, but larger molecules are retained, thereby filtering out certain toxic material from the blood.

13. A

Humidity depends on the amount of plant life available in each region. The Sahara desert, having the least plant life, is the least humid of the choices. Cities **(B)**, rain forests **(C)**, and grassy regions **(D)** all have a higher relative humidity than desert areas because they contain more plant life.

14. A

In the same ecosystem, there can never be two species in the same niche; if two species are found together here, they *must* occupy different niches.

15. B

The plant species has much less genetic variability in its gene pool than the same species on the mainland. Natural selection requires genetic variability in a population. If all of the individuals are the same, then they will all have the same fitness and there can be no selection. The grass species will not be able to evolve in the presence of climate change or other situations.

16. C

Atomic theory, **(A)**, refers to matter at the particulate level. The theory of relativity, **(B)**, and the law of conservation of energy, **(D)**, discuss the force, energy, and motion associated with matter. The remaining choice, **(C)**, the theory of evolution, examines (among other things) the homologous structure of organisms as evidence for structural changes in organisms, and is therefore the correct choice.

17. C

Selection, **(C)**, is the process by which species can inherit certain characteristics that make them more likely to survive. Choice **(A)**, *distribution*, is incorrect because it means the natural geographic range of an organism. Choice **(B)**, *stabilization*, is incorrect because it means the act of being stable and unchanging. *Continuation*, **(D)**, is incorrect because it means the act of continuing or staying the same.

18. C

According to Kepler's laws, the planet is moving the fastest when it is closest to its star, which, in the diagram, is at point g, **(C)**. Choice **(D)** can be eliminated because a planet's speed is not constant as it travels through its orbit.

19. C

The Moon's revolution around the Earth causes the Moon to be in various positions in respect to the Earth and the Sun, which causes the phase changes that are observable from Earth. The Earth and Moon's rotations do not contribute to phase change, so **(A)** and **(B)** can be eliminated. The Earth's revolution around the Sun is responsible for seasons, not phases of the Moon, making **(D)** incorrect.

20. B

The International Date Line is located exactly 180 degrees from the Prime Meridian. Around the Earth, every 15 degrees equals a one-hour time change. $\frac{180}{15} = 12$, therefore, the time at the International Date Line should be 12 hours ahead of the time at the Prime Meridian. The time is ahead instead of behind, because the International Date Line is where the day first changes of all the places on Earth.

21. A

The fusion of hydrogen atoms **(A)** to form helium atoms provides the Sun's energy. Fission is how we get energy from our nuclear power plants.

22. B

Since the Ice Age existed over 10,000 years ago, you can eliminate **(A)** and **(D)**. Plant and animal fossil records best indicate the weather conditions that existed in Earth's past. Radioactive dating **(C)** employs various methods that differ in accuracy, cost and applicable time scale, making it a weaker source of evidence than fossil records.

23. B

Although the speed of P and S waves does increase in denser materials **(C)**, this fact does not answer the question of why P and S waves travel at different speeds. P waves are longitudinal waves and S waves are transverse waves. Longitudinal waves travel faster than transverse waves, making **(D)** incorrect. Choice **(A)** is wrong because P waves are not transverse waves.

24. A

New York City is located in the Northern Hemisphere. During summer months, the Earth's tilt brings the Northern Hemisphere closer to the Sun, which causes the days to be longer (and therefore warmer). The Earth is farthest from the Sun during the winter months, not the summer months, making **(D)** incorrect. Choices **(B)** and **(C)** are results of the seasons, not causes of them.

25. B

A lunar eclipse occurs when the Moon's revolution is in the Earth's shadow **(B)**. A solar eclipse occurs when Moon's path is between the Earth and the Sun **(C)**.

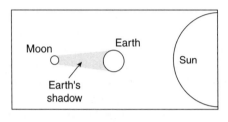

Lunar Eclipse

26. C

It is important to account for the size of the group because all species have some natural variation (statement I). It is also important to keep all conditions of the experiment identical so that other variables are not introduced that may affect the outcome (statement III). Finally, it is important to randomly distribute the tadpoles so that individual characteristics other than temperature do not affect the tadpoles (statement IV). Therefore, **(C)** is the correct choice because it includes all of the statements that must be considered. Having a control group to correspond to each group (statement II) isn't necessary; therefore **(B)** is incorrect.

27. A

When Colin runs $4\frac{2}{3}$ miles on Saturday and plans to run $1\frac{7}{8}$ of that distance tomorrow, he's taking a fraction of something. To take an amount of something implies multiplication. Choice **(B)** implies division, **(C)** gives a ratio, and **(D)** implies the operation of addition.

28. B

This is a multi-step problem requiring the operation of multiplication and division. First, 7,200 people should be multiplied by 12% or 0.12 to get 864. Then, divide 864 by the 6 grade levels (7 thru 12). This equals 144 students per class, since the number in each grade is distributed evenly.

29. B

This diagram exemplifies the array model of multiplication. Applying F.O.I.L. to binomials to yield polynomials is related to this common algorithm. Choices **(A)** and **(C)** are not incorrect, but they're not the one best answer.

30. C

Scientific notation is expressed as a number between 1 and 10 multiplied by a power of 10. 5.9 trillion miles can be written in scientific notation as 5.9×10^{12}, since a trillion is followed by 12 place values.

31. D

To complete this problem, start with the ones digit in the multiplier and carry out the algorithm as usual. Once the 2 in "42" is written in the first partial product, the tens place value in the multiplicand will be clear. It must be 2, so the problem reads 427×56, which equals 23,912. The hundreds digit is 9.

32. A

When comparing the circumference values to its diameter, there is a consistent unit of increase in circumference with each unit of increase in diameter: pi (approximately 3.14). Since the growth is consistent, the graph that it makes is also consistent; it's a straight line. Graph A illustrates this growth in proportion with the data in the table. Graph B does not match the data accurately and neither does graph C. Graph D does not have any relation to the given data.

33. B

The slope of a line is defined as its rise over run (rise divided by its run). The rise is measured along the y-axis of a coordinate grid, and the run is measured along the x-axis. If Point E is on a line with a slope of negative three, it has a negative rise (down 3 units vertically from point E) and a positive run (across 1 unit to the right). By doing this, you'll land on point B, which is part of the line crossing Point E.

34. B

The expression here cannot be factored into binomials, so it can therefore be simplified using the order of operations. $x^2 - x^2$ combine to get 0; $-5x$ and $-4x$ combine to get $-9x$; and $1 - 7 = -6$. The answer is $-9x - 6$.

35. D

Translating word problems into algebraic is a skill that strengthens with practice, for both you and your students. Dividing numbers are the same as expressing them as fractions. A number divided by 2 is the same as n/2. "And" refers to the operation of addition; four times a number implies multiplication. The word "is" means "equals."

36. D

Knowledge and familiarity with converting word problems expressing a function come up often on the CSET, as they do in this question. The $50.00 service call charge is the y-intercept or "b" term because it is a fee in addition to the hourly rate. The hourly fee is the slope or the "m" term in the standard equation, $y = mx + b$. The slope is a positive one, moving up and to the right because the each hour worked incurs a positive fee going to the technician.

37. A

Using the well known formula for the area of a rectangle, $A = l \times w$, substitute l with "$x + 8$" and w with "x" and simplify. $(x + 8)$ multiplied by $x = x^2 + 8x$.

38. D

A useful strategy for solving this problem is to literally draw out the triangular layers of each stack of oranges, using dots. In doing so, you'll notice a pattern for these so called "triangle numbers." It starts with 1, then 3, then 6, then 10, then 15, and finally 21. What you notice is a function relating the layer number to the number in each descending layer: you added 2, then added 3, then added 4, then added 5, then 6. It works much like a cumulative frequency table.

39. B

This is a two-step process to solve for the area of Triangle *B*. Since the size ratio is 2:1, the two corresponding sides are 10 and 8. These triangles are right triangles, so the Pythagorean theorem becomes immediately useful. The formula, $a^2 + b^2 = c^2$ is substituted by the values of 10 an 8, accordingly. 10 is the hypotenuse, since it is the side opposite the 90° angle and 8 corresponds to the "*b*" term.

$a^2 + 64 = 100$ (add the opposite of 64 to both sides)

$a^2 = 36$ (take the square root of both sides to get the value of "*a*")

$a = 6$

Now it's time to apply the formula for the area of a triangle.

$\frac{1}{2}(b \times h)$ (*b* here means base)

$\frac{1}{2}(6 \times 8)$

$\frac{1}{2}(48) = 24$

The area of Triangle *B* is 24 in.^{2}

40. B

Pyramids are polyhedrons with only one base. Their sides are made of triangles. The base of a rectangular pyramid will have two pairs of congruent sides corresponding to its pairs of longer and shorter sides. Therefore it makes sense that it will have one rectangle and two pairs of congruent triangles. Choice **(A)** refers to a square pyramid, **(C)** does not exist as a polyhedron, and **(D)** refers to a rectangular prism.

41. B

The converse of the Pythagorean Theorem states that if $a^2 + b^2 = c^2$ is true, the angle opposite *c* is a right angle. The square of 4(16) plus the square of 8(64) do equal 80(16 + 64 = 80), which is $(\sqrt{80})^2$.

42. A

To calculate the area of this polygon, it needs to be broken down into simpler polygons, say 2 rectangles, with dimensions of 9 ft. by 4 ft. and 8 ft. by 5 ft. The sum of these areas (36 + 40), 76 ft^2, then has the area of the sink (2 ft. by 4 ft.) or 8 ft.^{2} subtracted from it. The remaining area is 68 ft^2.

43. B

This problem requires the conversion of two types of units. First 10 miles per 5 hours is proportionally equivalent to 2 miles per hour. $\left(\frac{10}{5} = \frac{2}{1}\right)$. Next, there are 5,280 feet in each mile. If there are two miles, that's 10,560 feet. Two miles per hour is the same as 10,560 feet per hour. The question asks us for feet per minute, so we can convert hours to minutes by dividing by 60 (60 minutes per hour). After dividing, the quotient is 176 ft./min.

44. A

1 yard = 3 feet and 1 cubic yard means 1 yard × 1 yard × 1 yard. Since each yard is equal to 3 feet, this measure can be substituted in place of 1 yard. Therefore, 1 cubic yard = 3 feet × 3 feet × 3 feet = 27 cubic feet. That means there are 27 cubic feet in one cubic yard. Multiply this by 4 to get the total: 27 cubic feet × 4 = 108 cubic feet. (Remember: 4 cubic yards is 4 yd. × 1 yd. × 1 yd., *not* 4 yd. × 4 yd. × 4 yd. The latter is actually 64 cubic yards.)

45. C

To answer this problem successfully, separate calculations need to be done for each machine and then added together. Let's calculate the pencils produced by the old machine: 520 per hour for two hours. This is the same as 520/hour × 2 hours of work. This machine will produce 1,040 pencils in two hours. The newer machine produces at a rate of 25 per minute. This rate needs to be multiplied by 60 minutes in an hour to get the rate of pencils per hour: 25 per min. × 60 min. per hour = 1,500 per hour. This value is multiplied by 2 hours of work and produces 3,000 pencils in two hours. The sum of the two values is 4,040 pencils in two hours if the two machines work together.

46. B

The formula for the area of a triangle is $\frac{1}{2}(b \times h)$. The base is 6 units and the height is 3. By substituting those values into the area formula, the answer is 9 units^2.

$$\frac{1}{2}(6 \times 3) = \frac{1}{2}(18) = 9$$

47. A

To solve this problem, the simplest way would be to calculate the area of the rectangle, and then subtract the area of the missing triangle. The height of the triangle can be found by subtracting 3 from 10 to get 7, the length of the missing piece. The rectangle's area is $10 \times 12 = 120$ in.^{2}. The triangle's area is $\frac{1}{2}(3 \times 7) = \frac{1}{2}$ of $21 = 10.5$. The difference comes to 109.5 in.^{2}.

48. D

The purpose of a stem-and-leaf plot is to display many pieces of data. A box-and-whisker plot would only show the highest and lowest scores, the median, and the two quartile scores. It would not show all 35 scores. The circle and line graphs are simply the wrong ones to use, as they would not display these individual scores correctly or feasibly.

49. B

Since there is one employee at Unfair Corp. who makes much more than the others ($2,250,000), both the mean and midrange values would be greatly skewed. The midrange is taking the difference between the highest and lowest and dividing by 2. There is no mode in this set of data. Based on the data, the median will be the most indicative of the typical employee salary.

50. C

For this problem, it helps to work out some of the values from the given information. This helps make more tangible the abstract concepts being addressed here. By calculating the $\frac{4}{5}$ of the 65 people who attended the meeting $\left(\frac{4}{5} \times 65 = 52\right)$, it becomes clear that the number of men (27) and women $(52 - 27 = 25)$ who attended the meeting are known. What is not known is the number of each gender in the entire club. A careful reading of the answer choices reveals that **(A)**, **(B)**, and **(D)** cannot be known with the information given so far.

51. C

The common error in this type of problem is to simply subtract 5 from 34 and forget to count both ends of the number range. $34 - 5$ is 29, but by counting the number at both ends, it becomes clear that there are 30 numbers being considered, not 29. Some may prefer to write the numbers out, which will help in identifying the prime numbers. There are 9 prime numbers (5, 7, 11, 13, 17, 19, 23, 29, and 31) from 5 to 34 inclusive. 9/30 simplifies to $\frac{3}{10}$, which is equivalent to 0.30.

52. D

This compound probability is highly unlikely, but not impossible. Compound probability problems utilize the operation of multiplication. The probability of each individual outcome is compounded together via multiplication before arriving at an answer. There is 1 out of 2 chance of having a girl for each child. $\frac{1}{2}$ to the eighth power is 1 out of 256. Probabilities will always be expressed as a number no larger than 1 and no smaller than 0.

Constructed-Response Sample Essay 1

Temperature changes greatly affect all types of molecules. When the temperature increases, most materials expand, especially gases. For example, as you heat a balloon, the gas inside will expand, making the balloon larger. If you were to heat a tennis ball, the gas inside will expand, such that it will bounce better when hot than when cold.

But you have to be careful about materials changing their state or characteristics with temperature, just as water changes to ice. The rubber in a tennis ball will get very hard in the freezer, and it could melt when in the oven.

Constructed-Response Sample Essay 2

1. If the medium surrounding the cell has a higher water concentration than the cell (a very dilute solution), the cell will gain water by osmosis. Water molecules are free to pass across the cell membrane in both directions, but more water will come into the cell than will leave. The cell is likely to increase in size.

2. If the medium is exactly the same water concentration as the cell, there will be no movement of water across the cell membrane. Water crosses the cell membrane in both directions, but the amount going in is the same as the amount going out, so there is no overall movement of water. The cell will stay the same size.

3. If the medium has a lower concentration of water than the cell (a very concentrated solution), the cell will lose water by osmosis. Again, water crosses the cell membrane in both directions, but this time more water leaves the cell than enters it. Therefore the cell will shrink.

Constructed-Response Sample Essay 3

a) To find the volume of the triangular prism, we'll use the formula Area of the base multiplied by its height. To find the area of the base, find the height of the triangle. A vertical line of symmetry can help us do just that. Two right triangles, one on each side of the line of symmetry will be created. From here, we can use the Pythagorean Theorem to calculate the height of the triangle. $a^2 + b^2 = c^2$

$$5^2 + b^2 = 132$$

$$2^5 + b^2 = 169$$

$$b^2 = 144$$

$$b = 12$$

Now we can calculate the area of the base as $\frac{1}{2}(10 \times 12) = \frac{1}{2}$ of $120 = 60$ in.^{2}

The height of the rectangular prism is 9". Therefore, 60 in.^{2} × 9 in. = 540 in.^{3} The volume of this triangular prism is 540 in^3.

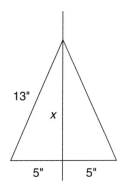

b) To calculate the surface area, we need to find the area of each of the five faces that make up this rectangular prism.

The two congruent triangular bases are 60 in.^{2} each.

The two congruent rectangles, 9" by 13", are 117 in.^{2} each.

The rectangle attached to the two triangular bases, 9" by 10" is 90 in.^{2}

The sum of the areas is 120 in.^{2} + 234 in.^{2} + 90 in.^{2} = 444 in.^{2}

The surface area is 444 in.^{2}

KAPLAN

Constructed-Response Sample Essay 4

a) In order to determine which size is a better buy, the area of each size, a large and medium, needs to be determined.

Area of a large pizza with a diameter of 18 inches (a radius of 9 inches)

$A = \pi r^2$

$A = 3.14 \times 9^2$

$A = 3.14 \times 81$

$A = 254.34$ in.^{2}

Area of a medium pizza with a diameter of 12 inches (a radius of 6 inches)

$A = \pi r^2$

$A = 3.14 \times 6^2$

$A = 3.14 \times 36$

$A = 113.04$ in.^{2}

Next, let's compare the respective areas of each size to their price by dividing the area by the price. This will give us the area of pizza per dollar.

A large cheese pizza:

254.34 in.^{2} for $14.00

$254.34 \div \$14.00 = 18.167142 \approx 18.17$ in.^{2} per dollar

A medium cheese pizza:

113.04 in.^{2} for $6.50

$113.04 \div \$6.50 = 17.390769 \approx 17.39$ in.^{2} per dollar

The large size gives you slightly more pizza per dollar, so it's the better buy.

b) We've already calculated the area of each size per dollar in the work shown above. Based on the prices at the local pizza shop, the large pizza gives you approximately 18.17 in.^{2} per dollar, and with the medium, you get approximately 17.39 in.^{2} per dollar.

Chapter 13: **Subtest 3 Practice Test**

TEST DIRECTIONS

This practice test contains two sections, a multiple-choice section (39 questions) and a constructed-response section (3 assignments). You may work on the sections in any order you wish.

In the multiple-choice section, read each question carefully and choose the one best answer. Directions for the constructed-response sections appear immediately before those assignments.

When taking the actual CSET, you will have one five-hour test session in which to complete the subtest(s) for which you registered.

SCORING

Remember, if you do not pass one or more subtests, you may reregister and retake those subtests. There is no limit to the number of times you may take any subtest that you have not passed. This helps takes the pressure off you, the test-taker, and gives you more choice.

Following the actual CSET, your responses to the multiple-choice questions will be scored electronically. Scores are based on the number of questions answered correctly, so there is no penalty for guessing.

Your responses to the constructed-response questions are scored by qualified California educators using focused holistic scoring. With this method, scorers judge the overall effectiveness of each response, while focusing on a set of performance characteristics that have been identified as important. For more details on how the CSET is scored, visit cset.nesinc.com.

Ready, set…

Good luck!

Subtest 3 Answer Sheet

Remove (or photocopy) this answer sheet and use it to complete the practice test.

1. Ⓐ Ⓑ Ⓒ Ⓓ Ⓔ   14. Ⓐ Ⓑ Ⓒ Ⓓ Ⓔ   27. Ⓐ Ⓑ Ⓒ Ⓓ Ⓔ
2. Ⓐ Ⓑ Ⓒ Ⓓ Ⓔ   15. Ⓐ Ⓑ Ⓒ Ⓓ Ⓔ   28. Ⓐ Ⓑ Ⓒ Ⓓ Ⓔ
3. Ⓐ Ⓑ Ⓒ Ⓓ Ⓔ   16. Ⓐ Ⓑ Ⓒ Ⓓ Ⓔ   29. Ⓐ Ⓑ Ⓒ Ⓓ Ⓔ
4. Ⓐ Ⓑ Ⓒ Ⓓ Ⓔ   17. Ⓐ Ⓑ Ⓒ Ⓓ Ⓔ   30. Ⓐ Ⓑ Ⓒ Ⓓ Ⓔ
5. Ⓐ Ⓑ Ⓒ Ⓓ Ⓔ   18. Ⓐ Ⓑ Ⓒ Ⓓ Ⓔ   31. Ⓐ Ⓑ Ⓒ Ⓓ Ⓔ
6. Ⓐ Ⓑ Ⓒ Ⓓ Ⓔ   19. Ⓐ Ⓑ Ⓒ Ⓓ Ⓔ   32. Ⓐ Ⓑ Ⓒ Ⓓ Ⓔ
7. Ⓐ Ⓑ Ⓒ Ⓓ Ⓔ   20. Ⓐ Ⓑ Ⓒ Ⓓ Ⓔ   33. Ⓐ Ⓑ Ⓒ Ⓓ Ⓔ
8. Ⓐ Ⓑ Ⓒ Ⓓ Ⓔ   21. Ⓐ Ⓑ Ⓒ Ⓓ Ⓔ   34. Ⓐ Ⓑ Ⓒ Ⓓ Ⓔ
9. Ⓐ Ⓑ Ⓒ Ⓓ Ⓔ   22. Ⓐ Ⓑ Ⓒ Ⓓ Ⓔ   35. Ⓐ Ⓑ Ⓒ Ⓓ Ⓔ
10. Ⓐ Ⓑ Ⓒ Ⓓ Ⓔ   23. Ⓐ Ⓑ Ⓒ Ⓓ Ⓔ   36. Ⓐ Ⓑ Ⓒ Ⓓ Ⓔ
11. Ⓐ Ⓑ Ⓒ Ⓓ Ⓔ   24. Ⓐ Ⓑ Ⓒ Ⓓ Ⓔ   37. Ⓐ Ⓑ Ⓒ Ⓓ Ⓔ
12. Ⓐ Ⓑ Ⓒ Ⓓ Ⓔ   25. Ⓐ Ⓑ Ⓒ Ⓓ Ⓔ   38. Ⓐ Ⓑ Ⓒ Ⓓ Ⓔ
13. Ⓐ Ⓑ Ⓒ Ⓓ Ⓔ   26. Ⓐ Ⓑ Ⓒ Ⓓ Ⓔ   39. Ⓐ Ⓑ Ⓒ Ⓓ Ⓔ

1. Increased awareness of health and fitness issues across the United States has led to which of the following trends in physical education at the K–8 level?

    (A) An increase in the use of standardized testing to evaluate students' understanding of health and fitness issues.

    (B) A decrease in the amount of time dedicated to physical fitness, along with an increase in time dedicated to health education.

    (C) A greater emphasis on programs designed to promote lifelong participation in physical activity and healthful choices.

    (D) A return to traditional physical conditioning methods such as calisthenics and circuit training.

2. A fourth-grader named Hector is overweight. Hector will be considered mildly obese when the percentage of his body fat exceeds

    (A) 5%

    (B) 10%

    (C) 25%

    (D) 40%

3. The following lines identify basic nonlocomotor, locomotor, and manipulative motor skills. Which line does NOT correctly match a skill with its appropriate category?

Line	Nonlocomotor	Locomotor	Manipulative
1	bending	leaping	catching
2	twisting	skipping	kicking
3	stretching	galloping	throwing
4	rocking	swaying	grasping

    (A) Line 1

    (B) Line 2

    (C) Line 3

    (D) Line 4

4. The family fitness program for seventh-grader Tomoyuki includes swimming laps. To start, Tomoyuki and his mother agree to swim laps three times a week for 15 minutes each session. According to the FIT criteria for fitness training—frequency, intensity, and time—which of the following is an accurate application of the principle of *time* to this program?

    (A) increasing the number of sessions each week from three to four

    (B) to increase upper body strength, doing the crawl without kicking for every other lap

    (C) alternating the number of sessions each week: first three, then four, then three

    (D) gradually lengthening the duration of each session from 15 to 40 minutes

5. One goal of upper elementary P.E. programs is to establish esteem-building competition during structured group sports and games. To that end, which of the following tactics is likely to be most effective in forming equitable teams?

    (A) Teams are chosen by the P.E. teacher, based on a child's skill level.

    (B) The two best players become team captains and alternately select team members.

    (C) Teams are chosen by alternating last names alphabetically.

    (D) The teams are chosen based on alternating boys and girls.

6. When should P.E. students become fully accountable for understanding rules, for their behavior, and for social etiquette, such as taking turns and fair play?

    (A) grades K–2

    (B) grades 3–5

    (C) grades 6–8

    (D) not until high school

GO ON TO THE NEXT PAGE

7. Which choice among the following is *not* one of the three components of food from which the body produces energy?

   (A) carbohydrates

   (B) proteins

   (C) fiber

   (D) fats

8. Which of the following activities is most age-appropriate in encouraging problem-solving among middle school P.E. students?

   (A) demonstrating both accuracy and distance in throwing a Frisbee

   (B) participating in vigorous calisthenics for a designated time

   (C) deciding to whom to throw a bean bag in order to escape a tag

   (D) participating in small-group design of a game, such as keeping a flag away from opponents while moving through an obstacle course

9. Which of the following lines represents the correct order—from simplest to most advanced—in a second-grade tumbling program?

1	Animal movements	Balance stunts	Inverted balance	Individual stunts
2	Inverted balance	Individual stunts	Animal movements	Balance stunts
3	Individual stunts	Animal movements	Individual stunts	Balance stunts
4	Balance stunts	Animal movements	Inverted balance	Individual stunts

   (A) Line 1

   (B) Line 2

   (C) Line 3

   (D) Line 4

10. Teaching ball-throwing to third graders would include all of the following movement techniques except

    (A) arm swings back in preparation for throw

    (B) elbow moves forward

    (C) trunk rotates away from throwing side of body before throw

    (D) weight of foot shifted to non-throwing side during follow-through

11. Hiking is a sport that, in its casual form, primarily involves

    (A) movement skills

    (B) muscle strength

    (C) hand-eye coordination

    (D) team competition

12. In third and fourth grades, P.E. groups should not number more than five because

    (A) students cannot work towards a common goal with more than five to a group

    (B) students of this age can express appreciation for cooperation only among five or fewer teammates

    (C) children in these grades are very egocentric and self-involved

    (D) smaller groups provide everyone with several turns, allowing experimentation with leading and following

13. A proper warm-up in an individual fitness program, lasting approximately 10 to 15 minutes, might include all of the following except

    (A) bending

    (B) push-ups

    (C) abduction

    (D) stretching

GO ON TO THE NEXT PAGE

14. In her eighth-grade classroom, Ms. Healy facilitates group discussions about the books her students have read. She encourages students to explore themes, character development, plot lines, and symbolism. According to Piaget's four stages of cognitive development, which kind of learning is going on here?

    (A) preoperational

    (B) concrete operational

    (C) formal operational

    (D) post-conventional

15. Which of the following statements concerning language acquisition and thought is *not* valid?

    (A) Young children use private speech (self-talk) to avoid learning formalized speech.

    (B) Language is not just an expression of knowledge; it is also a powerful tool in shaping thought.

    (C) A student learning English as a second language must be competent in his primary native language before he can understand new concepts in English.

    (D) Intelligent expression such as speaking and writing cannot take place until knowledge exists.

16. A group of children are asked, "Why is it wrong to lie?" Which of the following answers represents the *least* advanced stage of moral development?

    (A) "Because it is not fair to the person you lied to."

    (B) "Because people should tell the truth."

    (C) "Because you might get a time out."

    (D) "Because what if everybody lied all the time?"

17. Which of the following best describes how developmentally appropriate play affects cognitive development in the typical seventh-grader?

    (A) The child explores movement, which involves testing, observing, and organizing information during play.

    (B) The child is more aware of others and the idea of teams, which fosters conflict resolution and peer interaction.

    (C) The child is able to run set plays in sports like basketball, which affects memory development.

    (D) The child has a tendency toward fantasy, which fosters creative thinking skills.

18. Which of the following statements does *not* describe the impact of health issues on learning?

    (A) Lack of sleep affects attentiveness and ability to perform in the classroom.

    (B) Alcohol and drug abuse can cause abnormal physical and emotional development.

    (C) Peer group pressure and approval affect student behavior.

    (D) Inadequate or poor nutrition may lead to drowsiness, hyperactivity, or inattentiveness.

19. At one preschool, the students are allowed to draw on the playground walkway with large colored chalk sticks. When Berta tries to draw on the walls, her teacher directs her instead to a pad on an easel, where Berta can practice applying chalk to paper. This process of taking existing cognitive knowledge and modifying it to fit a new experience is called

    (A) equilibrium

    (B) accommodation

    (C) animism

    (D) centration

GO ON TO THE NEXT PAGE

KAPLAN

20. Valya, a kindergartner, separates from her mother easily and ignores her when she comes to pick Valya up from school. Valya is from a Russian immigrant family. All but which of the following would be reasonable educational implications of this situation?

    (A) It would be wise for the teacher to observe Valya's interactions with her classmates to see how she relates to others.

    (B) Cultural differences may be in play here, as they can be a variable in types of attachments children display and are comfortable with.

    (C) It is better that Valya ignores her mother rather than clinging to her.

    (D) Valya may in fact have secure relationships with others, since infant attachment is not the only path to social competence in children.

21. "A T-rex eats a T-bone!" is an associative rehearsal strategy Sierra made up to remember that the dinosaur Tyrannosaurus rex is a meat-eater. At what age would Sierra be able to spontaneously develop and apply this rehearsal strategy?

    (A) three years old

    (B) five years old

    (C) seven years old

    (D) ten years old

22. Twelve-year-old Lisa brags at her lunchroom table that her aim is so good, she once killed a bird with a slingshot. The kids laugh. However, Lisa's classmate Ricky says, "I think that's awful. Killing any creature for sport is wrong. Don't you think that bird had a soul?" Which of the following choices represents the clearest educational implication of this moral discussion?

    (A) There is a sequential foundation upon which higher moral principles develop and grow.

    (B) Children respond differently to various moral dilemmas depending on age, maturity, education, and socioeconomic influences.

    (C) A child's mind seeks a state of equilibrium.

    (D) Teachers should avoid presenting materials in the classroom that are beyond a child's moral development.

23. According to Erikson's Stages of Social Development, which of the following would most likely be within the capacity of nine-year-old Rebecca?

    (A) feeling good about writing and directing a funny skit for school assembly

    (B) being concerned about today's peacekeeping efforts will affect future generations

    (C) wondering whether she will get married

    (D) sensing that her life has been meaningful

24. Measurements of a child's vocabulary, word usage, and ability to express thoughts are the basis for determining the child's

    (A) socialization

    (B) language development

    (C) private speech

    (D) rehearsal strategies

GO ON TO THE NEXT PAGE

25. Tyrone is a good student who can be annoying because he is always moving around the classroom to his own "beat." Tyrone is very able in P. E. activities. He actually concentrates best in class when his fingers and feet are tapping, and he hums while reading. According to Gardner's Multiple Intelligences, Tyrone's major learning styles appear to be

    (A) spatial and bodily-kinesthetic

    (B) musical and intrapersonal

    (C) linguistic-verbal and musical

    (D) bodily-kinesthetic and musical

26. Which of the following is *not* a cause of mental retardation?

    (A) trauma to the fetus during childbirth

    (B) the mother's use of drugs or alcohol during pregnancy

    (C) attention deficit disorder (ADD)

    (D) certain genetic abnormalities

27. Which of the following is an incorrect association?

    (A) the samba : Brazil

    (B) the Charleston : United States

    (C) the cha-cha : West Indies

    (D) the flamenco : Mexico

28. Which of the following is *not* a characteristic of abstract art?

    (A) the foreshortening of objects or figures

    (B) nonrepresentational use of line, form, and color

    (C) objects are often distorted

    (D) the subject matter is stated in a simplified or abbreviated manner

29. The first known Western classical music, called Gregorian chants, came from which period in European musical history?

    (A) the Renaissance

    (B) the Baroque Period

    (C) the Middle Ages

    (D) the Romantic Period

30. In theater, the portion of the play's action that immediately follows the climax of the play, where conflicts are resolved and the plot is concluded, is called

    (A) flashback

    (B) denouement

    (C) exposition

    (D) vomitoria

31. An artist's use of *value* in a painting or drawing contributes to all but which of the following?

    (A) linear perspective

    (B) the enhancement of shape and form on a flat surface

    (C) the mood of the piece

    (D) contrast among figures and objects

GO ON TO THE NEXT PAGE

Use the excerpt below to answer the question that follows.

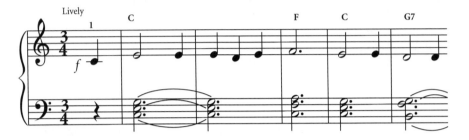

32. The melody shown above represents the opening bars of which of the following songs?

    (A) "Row, Row, Row Your Boat"
    (B) "When the Saints Go Marching In"
    (C) "Three Blind Mice"
    (D) "For He's a Jolly Good Fellow"

33. The first known theaters in Europe appeared between 600 and 200 B.C.E. in which country?

    (A) England
    (B) Greece
    (C) France
    (D) Italy

34. All of the following are examples of axial movement except

    (A) arabesque
    (B) stretching
    (C) grand jeté
    (D) bending

35. The instruments within the woodwind family that do *not* have reeds are

    (A) piccolo and flute
    (B) piccolo, flute, and oboe
    (C) flute and bassoon
    (D) piccolo, flute, and trumpet

Use the drawing below to answer the question that follows.

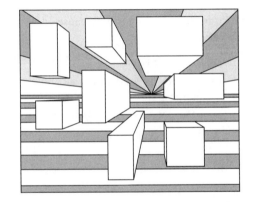

36. The boxes in the drawing above are floating

    (A) above the horizon line
    (B) below the horizon line
    (C) level to the horizon line
    (D) near the vanishing point

37. As a theater exercise, a third-grade teacher asks each student to mime an object in motion—such as a piece of frying bacon, a swaying palm tree, or a melting ice cube. This exercise is likely to encourage students to think about all of the following *except*

    (A) how to translate the characteristics of an object into a pantomime
    (B) the frustration of nonverbal communication
    (C) how movement can communicate ideas
    (D) the similarities among all types of people

GO ON TO THE NEXT PAGE

38. *Tone* in music is defined as

    (A) the organized sequence of single notes

    (B) the location of a note related to its highness or lowness

    (C) the smallest unit of a musical sound

    (D) the loudness or softness of a musical note

39. All of the following statements communicate a reason to include dance in grade K–8 curricula except:

    (A) Dance offers an alternative mode of expression that contributes to students' sense of self.

    (B) Dance encourages competition in the early primary grades.

    (C) Dance aids in the understanding of one's own culture and other cultures.

    (D) Dance implements good health by encouraging physical fitness.

GO ON TO THE NEXT PAGE

CONSTRUCTED-RESPONSE DIRECTIONS

Prepare a written response for each assignment. Read each assignment carefully before you begin to write. Think about how you will organize your response before you begin to write.

The assignments are intended to assess subject matter knowledge, not writing ability. However, your responses must be presented clearly in order to be fairly evaluated by your audience, educators in the field.

Constructed-Response Assignment 1

Complete the exercise that follows.

You are teaching physical education to grades 3–5 in a multi-ethnic school. How might you best accomplish multiple-subject integration within your physical education classes?

_____

_____

_____

_____

_____

_____

_____

_____

_____

_____

_____

_____

_____

_____

_____

_____

_____

Constructed-Response Assignment 2

Complete the exercise that follows.

Discuss what is meant by the concept of multiple intelligences. Give three examples of how this concept can be used in the development of strategies for teaching students with learning disabilities (LD).

_____

_____

_____

_____

_____

_____

_____

_____

_____

_____

_____

_____

_____

_____

_____

_____

_____

_____

_____

_____

_____

_____

_____

_____

Constructed-Response Assignment 3

Complete the exercise that follows.

Complete the exercise that follows.

Francisco de Goya (1746–1828) was a Spanish painter and muralist who produced a varied body of work—from royal portraits to religious paintings to cartoons, including paintings depicting what he called "the innumerable foibles and follies to be found in any civilized society."

Based on "Fight with Cudgels" (1820–23) above and your knowledge of art history, discuss why you think Goya is often called "the first of the moderns."

_____

_____

_____

_____

_____

_____

_____

_____

_____

_____

_____

_____

STOP

Chapter 14: **Subtest 3 Answers and Explanations**

ANSWER KEY

1. C	11. A	21. D	31. A
2. C	12. D	22. B	32. D
3. D	13. B	23. A	33. B
4. D	14. C	24. B	34. C
5. A	15. A	25. D	35. A
6. C	16. C	26. C	36. C
7. C	17. C	27. D	37. D
8. D	18. C	28. A	38. C
9. A	19. B	29. C	39. B
10. C	20. C	30. B	

1. C

Choice **(A)**, an increase in standardized testing, may be occurring in other subjects, but not in Physical Education. While health education is a vital part of P.E. **(B)**, it is not leading to a decrease in the amount of time for physical fitness. Current trends are exploring dance and stress-reducing exercises, not returning to calisthenics and circuit training **(D)**. The correct choice, **(C)**, reflects that reduced physical activity among young people in recent decades has led to a movement among physical educators to promote lifelong physical activity in its many possible forms. The astonishing increase in the number of youth who are overweight or physically unfit has further led to increased awareness of (and education in) aerobics, diet, health, and substance abuse issues.

2. C

If an individual's body-fat index (percentage of body fat) exceeds 25%, the person is considered mildly obese. Choices **(A)** and **(B)** reflect incorrect percentages. At 40% **(D)**, the person is considered to be moderately obese. Physical educators can teach that risk factors associated with obesity include heartburn, high cholesterol levels, high blood pressure, and increased likelihood of diabetes and heart disease.

3. D

Choices **(A)**, **(B)**, and **(C)** are correct; only swaying, in Line 4 **(D)**, is in the wrong column. Swaying is a nonlocomotor skill, which means it is a movement that is performed in a stationary position—in place. Locomotor skills, such as running, leaping, and skipping are movements that change location. Manipulative skills involve handling or moving an object, such as catching or kicking a ball.

4. D

FIT is the acronym for frequency, intensity, and time. These are factors that improve fitness when applied as part of an exercise regimen. Careful manipulation of any one or more of the criteria during either a single exercise routine or an ongoing fitness program will improve results. Choices **(A)** and **(C)** refer to the FIT criteria of *frequency*, how often and at what intervals the exercise is performed. Choice **(B)** refers to *intensity*, increasing the difficulty of a task. Only **(D)** refers to *time*, the duration for which an exercise is performed in a single session.

5. A

The best esteem-building strategy for forming equitable teams is for the P.E. instructor to choose teams based on his or her knowledge of student abilities—both strengths and weaknesses **(A)**. When the two best players choose teams **(B)**, they will likely select all the best players first, which diminishes the self-esteem of less-skilled players. Forming teams alphabetically **(C)** may or may not produce inequitable teams; choosing on the basis of gender **(D)** means the best players are still chosen first and/or a boys-vs.-girls battle may ensue.

6. C

Middle school students should be expected to understand social etiquette and fair play within the context of sports and games, **(C)**. Most younger students in grades K–5, **(A)** and **(B)** would be accumulating knowledge of the history, rules, and etiquette of games and sports. Sixth through eighth graders are emotionally and intellectually ready to know why rules are necessary, how to follow them, and how to interact with their peers appropriately. This knowledge should be absorbed well before the high school years **(D)**.

7. C

Choice **(C)**, fiber, is the roughage that we need to keep our digestive systems healthy. Carbohydrates **(A)** are sugars and starches that our bodies use as the first source of energy; fats **(D)** are usually the back-up source of energy when carbohydrates have been depleted; the body's last resort for energy is protein **(B)**—its main function being to build muscle tissue.

8. D

The last two activities, **(C)** and **(D)**, involve the most problem-solving, but **(C)** is age-appropriate for the lower elementary grades, and **(D)** is age-appropriate for the middle school grades. Designing any game requires problem-solving (devising rules, strategies, and consequences). Designing a game with fellow students also requires cooperation and the ability to reach a consensus. Choices **(A)**—Frisbee throwing—and **(B)**—calisthenics—do not require many problem-solving skills.

9. A

Of the four activities mentioned, the simplest, or least complex, would be animal movements, which might include swaying, dragging feet, squatting, and jumping. Then balancing—first upright and then inverted—comes next in difficulty; finally, individual stunts, such as cartwheels, splits, and flips, are most complex among these four activities. The other lines, then, **(B)**, **(C)**, and **(D)**, do not represent the correct order, from simplest to most advanced.

10. C

Choices **(A)**, **(B)**, and **(D)** would be included in teaching ball-throwing. Teaching throwing includes demonstrating the mechanical principle of opposition: the thrower's trunk rotates *towards* the throwing side of the body, not *away* from it **(C)**, before the throw. The ball is thrown, followed by the throwing arm crossing over the body, with the weight shifted to the non-throwing side during follow-through.

11. A

One clue in this question is the word *primarily.* Hiking primarily requires movement skills such as walking and climbing, along with endurance. Muscle strength **(B)** becomes most important in long-distance hiking or in mountain climbing. Hand-eye coordination **(C)** is not of primary importance because a hiker is generally not manipulating anything (except tying items onto a backpack). Hiking is considered an individual or group activity, but not a team sport **(D)**.

12. D

Third and fourth graders can handle larger groups, but they tend to thrive in groups of three to five children, where everyone can have several turns and natural leaders and followers emerge. This age group is not as egocentric as the K–2 students **(C)**, and, in fact, they are generally ready to explore relationships. They might be able to work toward a common goal with more than five to a group **(A)**, but not until about seventh grade do students express an appreciation for cooperation **(B)**.

13. B

Push-ups are an anaerobic calisthenics used to build muscles and flexibility, not to loosen and warm up the body in preparation for exercise or sport. Warm-up movements include choices **(A)**, **(C)**, and **(D)**: bending, stretching, rotating, abduction (moving a part of the body away from the axis or middle of the body), and adduction (moving a part of the body toward the axis or middle of the body).

14. C

According to Jean Piaget, students learning at the formal operational stage (about 11 years old and up) are capable of abstract thinking, complex deductions, and problem-solving—all of which are necessary for analyzing literature in Ms. Healy's classroom. Choices **(A)** and **(B)** refer to earlier stages of less sophisticated cognitive processes. Choice **(D)**, post-conventional, refers to the advanced level of morality described by Lawrence Kohlberg, where ethical choices rise above the laws of society.

15. A

Choices **(B)**, **(C)**, and **(D)** are valid statements. Choice **(A)** is invalid, since young children use self-talk to enter into formalized speech. The work of both Chomsky and Vygotsky supports the theory that some time in early childhood (around age three to four), children start private speech or self-talk ("Now I feed this dolly...") to organize and self-regulate their own behavior. Vygotsky believes that private speech is responsible for all higher levels of speech.

16. C

At the earliest stage of moral development, a child's moral judgments and decisions are based on a perceived need to follow the rules, coupled with a desire to avoid punishment **(C)**. Children's ideas on morality increasingly reflect other factors as they grow older—such as the reactions and feelings of others **(A)**, the need to maintain social order **(D)**, motivations underlying an act, and what makes for a good society **(B)**.

17. C

At about grades six to eight, adolescents begin to create and master offensive and defensive strategies in games and sports—such as chess and checkers strategies and running set plays. Students of this age have already passed through the stages mentioned in **(A)**, **(B)**, and **(D)**, and continue to hone these skills. These children are becoming better at evaluating choices, reasoning in the abstract, and anticipating conflicts and resolutions.

18. C

While it is true that peer group pressure and approval affect student behavior—especially among adolescent students—**(C)** is not as directly related to learning or health issues, as **(A)**—lack of sleep, **(B)**—alcohol and drug abuse, and **(D)**—inadequate and poor nutrition are.

19. B

According to Piaget's theories, *accommodation* **(B)** is a form of adaptation, where a child takes an existing scheme and adjusts it to fit a new experience. In this case, Berta is adjusting from drawing on the ground to drawing upright and from drawing on cement to drawing on paper. A teacher may guide students in these adjustments, giving less and less help as their students mature and learn to make accommodations more smoothly. *Equilibrium* **(A)** is a child's search for a balance in adapting to new things. *Animism* **(C)** is endowing inanimate objects with life-like qualities, such as a child's saying, "that umbrella is crying!" *Centration* **(D)** is focusing on one piece of information at a time, while disregarding others.

20. C

There is no evidence that anxious-avoidant attachment (ignoring her mother) is better (or worse) than anxious-resistant attachment (clinging to her mother). They are both merely observable patterns of attachment between caregiver or parent and child. The other three statements— **(A)**, **(B)**, and **(D)**—are logical educational implications of Valya's behavior.

21. D

Age three **(A)** is too young to develop such a strategy. When a child is around five to seven years old, **(B)** and **(C)**, rehearsal strategies (repetition and association) can be introduced by parents and teachers, but the child cannot yet invent or apply them spontaneously. Young children need constant reminders and guidance with rehearsal strategies. At about nine or ten years old **(D)**, children are able to independently develop and apply rehearsal strategies such as "A T-rex eats a T-bone!"

22. B

Choices **(A)** and **(C)** are valid, but neither is the "clearest educational implication" in this situation. Choice **(D)** could be debated. Choice **(B)** is the best answer because these two children, while the same age, respond in different ways to an ethical issue. Lisa is looking for peer approval ("Lisa brags at their lunchroom table"), which is a common trait of middle childhood (Kohlberg's conventional level of morality). While Ricky is the same chronological age as Lisa, he seems more morally mature ("Don't you think that bird had a soul?") and is willing to risk being unpopular by offering an opinion that his peers may not support (Kohlberg's post-conventional level of morality).

23. A

Erikson describes the major conflict for children aged 6–12 years as "industry vs. inferiority." Rebecca's self-esteem is tied to her success with writing and directing a skit; what follows is her successful resolution of the "industry vs. inferiority" struggle. Choice **(B)** is for adults of 40–65 years, who are concerned with "generativity vs. stagnation." Choice **(C)** is most often a concern of the 19–40-year age group ("intimacy vs. isolation."), while **(D)** is a reflection that comes late in life, at 65 years and above ("ego integrity vs. despair").

24. B

Vocabulary, syntax, word usage, and the ability to understand and express thoughts are all components of language development. Private speech **(C)** is self-talk that may be words, phrases, or nonsense repeated to oneself. Rehearsal strategies **(D)** are memory tricks like repetition and association that contribute to cognitive development. Choice **(A)**, socialization, entails much more than vocabulary, word usage, and ability to express thoughts.

25. D

Choices **(A)**, **(B)**, and **(C)** do not fit Tyrone's profile of learning styles, while **(D)** does. Tyrone uses his body to help him learn (Bodily-Kinesthetic Intelligence). Movement seems to be an integral part of his ability to think. He probably will be an active athlete and dancer. His teacher might exploit this ability, for example, by having Tyrone move around the room and touch each item while giving its name in Spanish. Further, Tyrone loves rhythms and music (Musical Intelligence), and these traits may actually help him concentrate or absorb information. In science class, Tyrone and other musical/rhythmic learners might memorize the Periodic Table of Elements with a rap or a song. Gardner says we all have a mixture of intelligences and abilities.

26. C

Children who are mentally retarded (also called *educationally delayed*) are defined as having an IQ level of 70 or below. Children within the range of mild to severe retardation nevertheless show significant improvement with early diagnosis and loving guidance from teachers. Choices **(A)**, **(B)**, and **(D)** are causes of mental retardation. ADD, **(C)**, is a separate learning disability where a child may have a normal or high IQ but has difficulty focusing attention.

27. D

Each answer pair represents a dance and its country of origin. The samba is a lively, hip-swaying ballroom dance based on Afro-Brazilian folk dancing to music in 2/4 time, also called "samba." The Charleston (named after Charleston, South Carolina) was popular in the 1920s and is danced in 8-count—solo, with a partner, or in groups (usually facing lines). The cha-cha is a ballroom dance originating in the West Indies, where couples take two slow steps followed by three quick small steps, with swaying movements of the hips. The flamenco originated with Andalusian gypsies of southern Spain, later spreading to other Latin countries. Flamenco is performed by one or two dancers and is characterized by a fast-paced, vigorous and rhythmic acoustic guitar and castanet-clicking dancers who clap and stamp their feet.

28. A

While the foreshortening of objects or figures using the laws of perspective may be a design element of a specific abstract work, it is not a characteristic of abstract art. In the abstract genre of art, artistic content depends on internal rather than pictorial representation; therefore, objects are nonrepresentational, simplified, and often distorted.

29. C

In the Middle Ages, Gregorian chants—also known as plainsong—were a musical form of the Catholic Church of the 6th century on, where male voices (monks) sing one part in unison. The lyrics are passages from the Bible. The music has no feeling of tempo, and most of the motion of the notes is step-wise. This is meditative music, meant to remind the listener of God. If it had a beat, one would want to dance or move around, which would draw the focus away from God. Gregorian chant was systemized by Pope Gregory the Great.

30. B

The correct answer is the element of traditional dramatic theory called *denouement*, **(B)**. Choice **(A)**, *flashback*, is a time-manipulation device, whereby a scene from earlier in the story is shown. Choice **(C)**, *exposition*, is the information necessary to tell the audience, such as what occurred before the action in the play started or what off-stage events happened during the action of the play. Choice **(D)**, *vomitoria*, derived from Roman theater, are the tunnels that allow actors to reach portions of a stage, or to exit and enter the stage.

31. A

Value is defined as the lightness or darkness of a color or hue or the amount of light and dark areas in a composition, ranging from black to white, shadows to light. Value affects form/shape **(B)**, contrast **(D)**, and mood **(C)**—for example, dark areas can suggest unease, secrecy, or melancholy; light areas can suggest happiness or enlightenment. Linear perspective **(A)** is a different element of art, one that creates depth by using parallel lines converging on a vanishing point.

32. D

The English song "For He's a Jolly Good Fellow" is a simple, lively tune with a time signature of 3/4. It is based on a rousing cheer and is considered to be one of the three most sung songs in the English language (with "Happy Birthday to You" and "Auld Lang Syne").

33. B

Western theater was born in ancient Greece, beginning as early as 1200 B.C.E. as religious rites, evolving into performing competitions, and then full dramas. The performances took place in the daytime on hillsides, which later transformed into outdoor amphitheaters. Annual drama competitions would last all day for several days.

34. C

Axial movement is motion anchored to one spot, usually a foot or feet. Movement is organized around the axis of the body and is not designed for travel from one location to another. Arabesque is a ballet pose which has the dancer standing on one leg, with the other leg stretched out to the back (at a 45-, 90-, or 135-degree angle) and one arm usually stretched out to the front. Stretching and bending both involve pulling away from the body's axis, while the body remains stationary. The correct choice is grand jeté, a long horizontal ballet jump starting from one leg and landing on the other. In the middle of the jump, the dancer may be doing a split in midair.

35. A

Both the oboe and the bassoon are instruments in the woodwind family, but they use reed mouthpieces. For this reason, **(B)** and **(C)** are incorrect. Choice **(D)** includes the trumpet, which is in the brass family, and is played by air blown from the mouth, with lips pressed against a metal mouthpiece that is not a reed.

36. C

The artist determines the viewer's eye level by choosing the position of the horizon line, controlling whether the viewer feels above, below, or at eye level with the boxes in the drawing. If the boxes were floating above the horizon **(A)**, the horizon line would be drawn near the bottom of the page, and the viewer would feel like he's lying on the ground. If the boxes were floating below the horizon **(B)**, the horizon line would be drawn near the top of the page, and the viewer would feel like he had a bird's-eye view. Choice **(D)** is incorrect because the boxes are not near the vanishing point, which is in the far distance. (Note that lines that are parallel or perpendicular to the horizon line don't appear to go back in space, such as the top, bottom, and side edges of the floating boxes.) Choice **(C)** is correct because the viewer is at eye level with the horizon. Another way to determine this is to observe that the angular lines of objects at your eye level, touching the horizon line, converge both downward and upward [e.g., the lines of objects above your eye level (above the horizon line) converge downward, and the lines of objects below your eye level (below the horizon line) converge upward.]

37. D

Since the theater students were asked to impersonate objects, not people, **(D)** would not apply here. However, the third graders would likely develop **(A)** an understanding of the characteristics of an object (e.g., bending into the shape of a cube, then having body parts slowly spread out on the floor, as if parts of the cube were melting), **(B)** how frustrating it can be to mime something, with no verbal communication, and **(C)** how movement can communicate ideas (e.g., lying on the floor and jumping around, changing shape, like bacon in a skillet).

38. C

A tone—also called a note—is the smallest unit of a musical sound. Choice **(A)** is the definition of melody; **(B)** is the definition of pitch. Choice **(D)** is describing dynamics, the varying degrees of volume in music.

39. B

All of the choices are correct except for **(B)**. The current philosophy of California educators is to encourage cooperation, not competition, in the early grades.

Constructed-Response Sample Essay 1

Physical education teachers—and all teachers—have the responsibility of adapting lesson plans that explore multiple intelligences (from Howard Gardner's theories); that address multiple abilities/disabilities; and that enjoy multi-cultural games, sports, and dances. All three of these goals can be accomplished within a multiple-subject orientation as well, by integrating physical education with math, science, English and other languages, history and social science, the visual and performing arts, and even home economics. After all, no one subject can be separated from others and stand alone.

Some ideas on activities that would stimulate multiple-subject integration appropriate to my third–, fourth–, and fifth– graders follow. (The subjects will overlap, of course.)

Students learn to score a baseball game; make charts of students' fitness scores; calculate percentages of body fat; discuss averages and probabilities. (Math)

Students learn about anatomy, the laws of motion, friction, and gravity and play movement games to illustrate; reports on the body's systems: for example, fifth-grader Tim gives a short report on the lungs. (Biology, Physics)

Students practice communicating while playing in groups; we sing in other languages while learning dances from other cultures; we perform marches and creative dance; students use drums for movement and discussing tempo and rhythm. (English; other languages; Music; Dance)

Students learn where multicultural games, dances, and sports originate; the history of each sport we play in the U.S. (History; Social Science)

Students discuss the importance of good nutrition, food groups; how we grow health issues. (Home Ec; Health)

Constructed-Response Sample Essay 2

Because children with learning disabilities (LD) have difficulty processing information, teachers should try various activities that communicate to all of the child's senses. Gardner's multiple intelligences system encourages variety and creativity, since he claims that every learner responds to different learning modes. Gardner defined eight learning styles; for example, linguistic-verbal, spatial, and logical-mathematical. He claims we all have one or two dominant styles and possess the others to varying degrees.

Teachers of LD students need to be flexible and imaginative. The teacher of an LD student with a musical learning style might have the student write a poem and then compose a melody for it. To reduce stress—which exacerbates certain learning disabilities—a teacher could allow students to take untimed tests and/or oral tests (especially good for verbal learners). A teacher might encourage hands-on instruction and active experimentation, to reach those students with strong spatial or bodily/kinesthetic or naturalist abilities.

KAPLAN

Constructed-Response Sample Essay 3

The moderns believed that an artist's vision was more important than tradition. They supported bold technique, personal themes, and free, new forms of expression. Moderns often used everyday people as subjects. Goya's "Fight with Cudgels" is modernist, far from the classical and rococo painting styles of his time. He paints a passionate fight in the Romantic style of the later 1800s. Romanticism was a rejection of the themes of order, calm, harmony, idealization, and rationality. This painting rejects those themes with its ugly, edgy, raw quality. Goya seems to be asking the viewer "Isn't this battle pointless?"

There is a lot of movement on the canvas, suggested with thick, dark, bold strokes. Also, the figures are off-center as if they were in motion when the painter captured them, as if they will be moving right off the canvas! Notice the many diagonal lines in the painting, which suggest movement: the boys' arms, the cudgels, even the bodies—nothing is drawn on a horizontal or vertical axis. The diagonal lines and the anti-violence themes of Goya influenced fellow-Spaniard Pablo Picasso, especially in his anti-war mural *Guernica*.

Bright clouds behind the right-hand figure bring attention to his swinging; our eyes are drawn to him. Since his body has the longest diagonal and his opponent has blood dripping from his ear, face, and neck, he will probably be the victor. Goya's emphasis on the foreground with a blurry and faded background predates the French modernist Edouard Manet, who was also influenced by Goya. The nightmarish quality of the painting supports Goya's personal opinion about violence; in expressing his thoughts and feelings frankly, he announces a modern view.

Getting Started: **Advice for New Teachers**

So you've passed the CSET with flying colors and fulfilled all the requirements for becoming a teacher in California. Now it's time to put all your learning into practice!

FINDING THE RIGHT POSITION

It is common knowledge that more good teachers are needed across the country. "In the next four years, as many as one third of America's 3.2 million teachers could retire. The U.S. Department of Education projects that by 2014 … our nation's schools will hire as many as 1 million new teachers." (Source: *U.S. News & World Report*, October 15, 2009). But finding the right job for you can be a daunting process.

1. Do Your Research

First, determine the grade levels and/or subjects you are most interested in teaching. Make sure you have fulfilled all the qualifications for teaching in California. The basic credential requirements for a five-year preliminary credential are as follows:

- Bachelor's degree or higher from an accredited university
- Teacher preparation program
- Passing score on the CBEST
- "Developing English Language Skills"—a reading instruction course
- U.S. Constitution course
- Demonstration of subject competency through a subject matter exam (CSET) and/or subject matter program
- Computer technology course

To teach elementary school, you need the Multiple Subject Teaching Credential, which will allow you to teach preschool, kindergarten, Grades 1–12, and adult education. In addition to the requirements above, you must take:

- The Reading Instruction Competence Assessment (RICA)
- The CSET

To teach middle or secondary school, you need a Single Subject Teaching Credential, which will allow you to teach specific subjects in a departmentalized classroom. You may be authorized for preschool, kindergarten, Grades 1–5, and adult classes. For your preliminary credential, you must meet the basic requirements above, along with demonstrating subject matter competency by:

- passing the appropriate CSET exams
- completing an approved single subject program

For all of the above, you will receive a Professional Clear Credential after fulfilling the basic requirements and the five-year preliminary credential by completing one of two options:

- Professional Teacher Induction Program
  OR
- National Board Certification

> Requirements for teaching special education or vocational education are more complicated. Information on these credentials, along with all the basics, can be found at *www.teachcalifornia.org*. You may also visit the California Commission on Teacher Credentialing at *www.ctc.ca.gov*.

2. Identify Where You Would Like to Work

Next, make a list of the districts and/or schools where you would most like to work. Many school districts have websites on which they post job openings. In addition, you should call the district office to find out if there are any positions open and what their application procedures are. The California Department of Education website has a directory of school districts at *http://www.cde.ca.gov/re/sd/*. An Academic Performance Index for California schools can be found at *http://api.cde.ca.gov/*. Go to *www.teachcalifornia.org* for a general overview of teaching in California and choosing a school district.

Use the Internet as a resource. In addition to the many general websites for job hunters, there are websites devoted solely to teaching jobs. A few websites will ask you for a subscription fee, but there are many others with free listings. A list of some of these sites, including those specific to California, can be found at the end of this chapter.

3. Attend Job Fairs

Job fairs are a good way to learn about openings and to network with other education professionals. Many schools within the California State University and University of California host teaching job fairs. In addition, use resources such as the California Association for Employment in Education, *http://www.caeelink.org/fairs.htm* to find a job fair near you. Several of the websites for job-seekers listed at the end of this chapter also have job fair listings by state.

Remember that you are assessing potential employers as much as they are assessing you. Consider asking the following:

- What is the first professional development opportunity offered to new teachers?
- What additional duties outside the classroom are expected of teachers?
- When can I expect to meet my mentor?
- What is the top school-wide priority this year?
- What kinds of materials or resources will be available in my classroom? (if applicable)
- What is your policy on lesson planning?
- What are my team members like?

You may also want to ask about the demographics of the student population and what kinds of unique challenges they present. If you feel comfortable, you might also want to ask to see the classroom you would be using.

4. Sign Up for Substitute Teaching

Substitute teaching can be another good strategy for getting your foot in the door in a particular school or district, even if there are no permanent jobs available. Think of this as an opportunity to impress principals and to learn from other teachers about possible openings. You can even submit your resume to the principals in the schools where you are substitute teaching and give them the chance to observe you in the classroom.

STARTING IN THE CLASSROOM

Don't get disillusioned if you're not immediately comfortable in your role as a teacher. Give yourself time to adjust, and don't hesitate to ask for advice from others. Be persistent about finding a mentor who can provide support during your first year and beyond. Try to find one in your subject area and determine how much experience you would like that person to have. For the sake of convenience, it's a good idea to find someone who has a similar class schedule or daily routine.

Teach Rules and Respect

With students, be friendly but firm. Establish clear routines and consistent disciplinary measures early on. This way, the students have a firm understanding of what is expected of them and when certain behaviors are appropriate. Have the principal review your disciplinary plan to make certain that he or she will support it and that there aren't any potential legal issues. Be aware of how cliques and social hierarchies impact classroom dynamics, and don't underestimate the power of your own advice.

Although disciplinary issues vary according to grade level, there are some general tips you may find helpful in setting rules in the classroom:

- Often, troublesome students misbehave merely to get your attention. Reduce this negative behavior by paying the least amount of attention when a student is acting out and giving that child your full attention when he or she is behaving.
- When it comes to establishing classroom rules, allow your students to have some input. This will increase their sense of empowerment and respect for the rules.
- Convince all of your students that they are worthwhile and capable. It is easy to assume that struggling students are lazy or beyond help–do not allow yourself to fall into this trap.
- When disciplining students, absolutely avoid embarrassing them in any way, shape, or form, especially in front of their peers.
- Double standards and favoritism will lose you the respect of all your students–always be firm, fair, and consistent. Never talk down to your students.
- Avoid becoming too chummy with your students. Young teachers often feel that they must make "friends" with students, particularly in the older grades. However, it's important to maintain some professional distance and to establish yourself as an authority figure.
- Admit your mistakes. If you wrongly accuse a student of doing something she did not do, make an inappropriate joke, or reprimand a student more harshly than necessary, be sure to apologize and explain. If a parent or administrator criticizes you for your mistake, calmly explain how you felt at that moment and why. Also, explain how you plan on handling that kind of situation in the future.

Do Your Homework

Any veteran teacher will tell you that you will spend almost as many hours working outside the classroom as you do with your students. Preparing lessons and grading homework and tests can take an enormous amount of time, so it's a good idea to be as organized as possible. You should also take some time to think about what your expectations will be: will you grade every homework assignment or just some of them? Will you give students an opportunity to earn extra credit? What kind of system will you use for grading tests? Obviously these requirements will vary according to grade level, but there are some general suggestions that you may find helpful in preparing assignments.

Finally, you should always give yourself time to wind down and distance yourself from the classroom. This is essential to prevent burnout or resentment over a lack of free time, and will allow you to pursue other interests and personal relationships.

Design Lesson Plans Early

Before you start planning, be aware of holidays off, assemblies, and similar interruptions. Design your lessons accordingly. Similarly, be sure you know your content, your state's standards, your school's expectations, and the ins and outs of child development. Be prepared with multiple learning styles and differentiated teaching strategies.

Try to develop time-saving strategies. Saving your lesson plan outline as a template on the computer can be very helpful–instead of rewriting the whole plan every day, you can just fill in the blanks.

Establish Rules for Grading Homework

Along with establishing a consistent disciplinary policy early on, it's important to develop grading guidelines. Some teachers set the bar high at the beginning of the year by grading a little tougher than they normally would. Just as many students will underachieve if they think you are a soft grader, they will work hard to meet your expectations if your standards are high. However, it's important to assess your students' abilities and set realistic standards.

Grading every single assignment can get overwhelming; sometimes verbally assessing comprehension is enough. Rubrics are another useful tool for outlining expectations and scoring, as well as making sure you cater to the needs of all your students. They are also effective when students grade each other.

Returning graded assignments as soon as possible sets a good example, keeps your workload manageable, and prevents students' interest from waning. However, you should never use a student's work as an example of what not to do.

Consider sending grades home on a regular basis and getting them signed by a parent in order to keep everyone aware of students' progress. This prevents students and parents from being blindsided by poor grades.

Don't confuse quietness for comprehension. Check in with all students because some may be afraid to admit that they don't understand what's going on. If you feel there is a problem, don't wait to address a student's needs. If you believe that a student may have an undiagnosed disability, let your principal know and follow your school's procedure.

Finding tangible rewards for students' achievements is a great way to keep them motivated, particularly if you focus their efforts around gradually earning the rewards. These types of incentive systems work particularly well in the elementary grades.

Deal with Parents Early On

Establish a relationship with parents from the beginning–frequent, positive communication is essential to helping the children attain the best education possible. Here are a few tips for keeping in touch with parents:

- Make phone calls, even if you're just going to leave a message. Doing so will allow you to share good news and help guardians become more familiar with you.
- Give students homework folders that frequently travel between school and home.
- Be ready to deal with breakdowns in communication: it may be necessary to send multiple messages home.
- Send home a short newsletter of things to come.

Set Up Parent-Teacher Conferences

Meeting with parents can often be intimidating for new teachers, particularly if a student is not performing well. It's a good idea to seek guidance from experienced teachers, and communicate with administrators if you encounter problems. In addition, try to follow these general guidelines when talking with parents:

- Remain professional. Don't take heated words personally, have good things to say about the student, choose your words carefully, keep examples of the student's work on hand, and document what is said during the meeting.
- Allow parents to ask the first question. This will help you understand their tone and their concerns.
- Be as thick skinned as possible when dealing with problems: some parents want to vent a little before getting to the crux of the issue. Let them vent, try to put them at ease, and then look for a solution or compromise.
- If a parent becomes excessively confrontational, inform an administrator.
- Be confident. Listen to what the parents suggest, but also stand up for what you believe is the best course of action.

Build Relationships with Colleagues

Meet as many teachers in the building as you can: not only will you gain valuable insights about the inner workings of the school, but you'll also make new friends. Don't be afraid to step up and ask questions when information isn't offered. Veteran teachers are a tremendous resource for all kinds of information, ranging from labor contracts to strategies for staying sane under pressure. Also, get to know the other new teachers. These people will be valuable sounding boards and will help you feel less alone.

Earn the respect of your colleagues by stepping up to committee work, and by proving yourself to be a reliable, competent teacher. You should also be polite and friendly with the staff and custodians: you'll need their help for all sorts of reasons.

Finally, be professional, timely, and unafraid to calmly share your opinions or disagree with administrators. Your professionalism and enthusiasm will earn you their respect and ensure that your needs are met.

Dealing with Paperwork

Be aware of what kinds of paperwork you need to fill out and file, including the school Improvement Plan, special education forms relating to Individualized Education Plans, budget requests, reading and math benchmarks, and permanent record cards. Try to sit with fellow teachers when filling out forms. Their companionship will make these tedious tasks more fun.

Understanding Unions

Depending on your school district, you may be part of a teacher's union. It is important to gain a clear understanding of union requirements. Know:

- how much money will be deducted from your paycheck for union dues
- how you can obtain a copy of the most recent union contract

For more information about teachers' unions in California, visit *cta.org*, the California Teacher's Association, or *cft.org*, the California Federation of Teachers.

ADDITIONAL RESOURCES

Books

Capel, Susan, Marilyn Leask, and Terry Turner, *Learning to Teach in the Secondary School: A Companion to School Experience*. Taylor & Francis, 2005.

Dillon, Justin. *Becoming a Teacher.* McGraw-Hill, Open University Press, 2001.

Goodnough, Abby. *Ms. Moffett's First Year: Becoming a Teacher in America.* Public Affairs, 2004.

Howe, Randy. *First-Year Teacher: What I Wish I Had Known My First 100 Days on the Job: Wisdom, Tips, and Warnings from Experienced Teachers.* Kaplan, 2007.

Maloy, Robert W., and Irving Seidman. *The Essential Career Guide to Becoming a Middle and High School Teacher*. Bergin & Garvey, 1999.

Parkay, Forrest W., and Beverly Hardcastle Stanford. *Becoming a Teacher, 6th Edition.* Allyn & Bacon; 6th edition, 2003.

Shalaway, Linda, and Linda Beech (Editor). *Learning to Teach…Not Just For Beginners* (Grades K–8). Scholastic, 1999.

Starkey, Lauren. *Change Your Career: Teaching as Your New Profession.* Kaplan, 2007.

Staff of *U.S. News and World Report. U.S. News Ultimate Guide to Becoming a Teacher.* Sourcebooks, 2004.

Wiggins, Grant, and Jay McTighe. *Understanding by Design*. Prentice Hall, 2001.

Wong, Harry K., and Rosemary T. Wong. *The First Days of School: How to Be an Effective Teacher.* Harry K. Wong Publications, 2001.

Magazines and Journals

American Educator

Harvard Educational Review

The New York Times "Education Life"

The *Phi Delta Kappan*

Internet Resources

cset.nesinc.com/CS_viewPT_PDF_opener.asp
An additional full practice CSET

teachernet.com/htm/becomingateacher.htm
Community for K–8 educators

pbs.org/firstyear/beaTeacher/
PBS: How to become a teacher

newsweekshowcase.com/teacher-training/Newsweek
Teacher education and recruitment. Teaching as a second career

eric.ed.gov/
Education Resources Information Center–large teaching and education database

aft.com
American Federation of Teachers

proudtoserveagain.com/pages/808014/index.htm
Troops to Teachers program–gives former members of the U.S. military the opportunity to become public school teachers–can help with certification, job searching, etc.

ed.gov
U.S. Department of Education

theteachersguide.com

behavioradvisor.com

teach-nology.com
Free and easy-to-use resources for teachers

kidsource.com

Sites with Tips from Teachers

intel.com/education/tools/index.htm
Teachers' input on teaching and learning how to teach, with tools and resources

teachingtips.com
Tips from an experienced teacher

atozteacherstuff.com
A teacher-created site listing online resources and tips

Lesson Plan Sites

Brainpop.com
Hundreds of videos & games in all school subjects

education-world.com

theteacherscorner.net

lessonplansearch.com

www.lessonplanspage.com

teachnet.com

General Teaching Job Sites

schoolspring.com

teachers-teachers.com

job-hunt.com/academia.shtml

educationjobs.com

abcteachingjobs.com

k12jobs.com

jobs2teach.doded.mil/Jobs2Teach/J2TDefault.asp
Part of the Troops to Teachers website

wanttoteach.com/newsite/jobfairs.html
National teaching job fair website

www.udel.edu/csc/teachers.html
MBNA Career Services Center: A list of resources for teachers

California Resources

cde.ca.gov
California Department of Education

teachcalifornia.org
Info for teachers and those considering it. This site gives you an opportunity to "try being a teacher" by doing sample teacher's work online. Also lists median salaries.

teachcalifornia.org/job/index.html
Job listings

cta.org/CTA.htm
California Teachers Association. Includes news, workshops, teaching tips, and information on grants and awards. Also explains the benefits of membership in the CTA, including insurance.

ctc.ca.gov
California Commission on Teacher Credentialing

california.teachers.net/
Includes jobs and chat boards for teachers

edjoin.org
Over 10,000 California job postings for grades K–12

caeelink.org
California Association for Employment in Education

cta.org/CTA.htm
California Teacher's Association

cft.org
California Federation of Teachers